THE TRIUMPH OF NANCY REAGAN

KAREN TUMULTY

SIMON & SCHUSTER
New York London Toronto Sydney New Delhi

Simon & Schuster
1230 Avenue of the Americas
New York, NY 10020

First Simon & Schuster hardcover edition April 2021

Interior design by Kyle Kabel

Manufactured in the United States of America

1 3 5 7 9 10 8 6 4 2

Library of Congress Cataloging-in-Publication Data

Names: Tumulty, Karen, 1955– author.
Title: The Triumph of Nancy Reagan / Karen Tumulty.
Description: New York : Simon & Schuster, [2021] | Includes bibliographical references and index. | Summary: "The definitive biography of the fiercely vigilant and politically astute First Lady who shaped one of the most consequential presidencies of the 20th century: Nancy Reagan"—Provided by publisher.
Identifiers: LCCN 2020031177 | ISBN 9781501165191 (hardcover) | ISBN 9781501165214 (ebook)
Subjects: LCSH: Reagan, Nancy, 1921-2016. | Reagan, Nancy, 1921-2016—Family. | Presidents' spouses—United States—Biography. | Reagan, Ronald. | Regan family. | United States—Politics and government—1981-1989. | Washington (D.C.)—Biography. | California—Biography.
Classification: LCC E878.R43 T86 2021 | DDC 973.927092 [B]—dc23
LC record available at https://lccn.loc.gov/2020031177

ISBN 978-1-5011-6519-1
ISBN 978-1-5011-6521-4 (ebook)

To my husband, Paul,
and our sons, Nick and Jack

CONTENTS

Introduction 1

Chapter One 9

Chapter Two 27

Chapter Three 53

Chapter Four 75

Chapter Five 105

Chapter Six 129

Chapter Seven 143

Chapter Eight 171

Chapter Nine 199

Chapter Ten 221

Chapter Eleven 239

Chapter Twelve 267

Chapter Thirteen 289

CONTENTS

Chapter Fourteen 315

Chapter Fifteen 341

Chapter Sixteen 355

Chapter Seventeen. 375

Chapter Eighteen 387

Chapter Nineteen 411

Chapter Twenty 433

Chapter Twenty-One 463

Chapter Twenty-Two. 495

Chapter Twenty-Three. 515

Chapter Twenty-Four 531

Chapter Twenty-Five 565

Acknowledgments 579

Bibliography 585

Notes 589

Index 633

INTRODUCTION

> Reagan knew where he wanted to go, but she had a better sense of what he needed to do to get there.
>
> —Lou Cannon, *President Reagan: The Role of a Lifetime*

The second weekend of February 1983 found much of the Eastern Seaboard trapped by one of the biggest snowfalls of the century. Dubbed the Megalopolitan Blizzard, it caught forecasters off guard. The nation's capital, notoriously ill-equipped for extreme weather, was paralyzed under a frozen blanket seventeen inches deep. In suburban areas, the snow was twice as heavy, hitting new records. All of this meant the president and first lady had to cancel their plans to go to Camp David on Friday afternoon as they customarily did. But even though they were stuck in the White House for the duration, there were delights to be had as the most self-important city in the world bent to the will of Mother Nature. When the blinding storm yielded to brilliant sunshine, Washington took on the feel of an Alpine village. Beyond the edge of the South Lawn, hundreds of people in parkas and wool caps were getting around on cross-country skis.

George P. Shultz, only seven months into his tenure as secretary of state, had just returned the previous Thursday from a long trip to Asia, which included a stop in China. Coming back, he had barely beaten the storm. The first flakes were falling as his government plane touched down at Andrews Air Force Base. On Saturday afternoon, as Washington began digging out, Shultz got a call from Nancy Reagan. "Why don't you and your wife come over and have supper with us?" she asked. There would be just the four of them, upstairs in the White House family quarters.

"So, we go over, and we're having a nice time, and then all of a sudden the president and Nancy—both of them—are asking me about the Chinese leaders: What are they like as people? Do they have a sense of humor? Can you find their bottom line? Do they really *have* a bottom line?" Shultz recalled. From there, the conversation moved on to the Soviet Union, and the president began to talk about his own ideas for engaging America's superpower enemy. Shultz was struck by how much Ronald Reagan had thought about this; how self-confident he sounded about his abilities as a negotiator. And then suddenly the new secretary of state realized that the purpose of the evening was not entirely social. Nancy had planned it so that Shultz would begin to understand something important about her husband—something that had the potential to change history.

"I'm sitting there, and it's dawning on me: this man has never had a real conversation with a big-time Communist leader and is dying to have one. Nancy was dying for him to have one," Shultz told me, still marveling at the moment more than thirty years later. Until that dinner, he had not really been sure that such a dialogue was possible. This, after all, was a president who had branded the Soviet Union as ruthless and immoral, and who was presiding over the biggest peacetime military buildup in US history. The Reagan administration, except for a few figures like Shultz, was populated by hard-liners who believed there could never be any such thing as a working relationship with Moscow. Did Ronald Reagan really see himself as the unlikely peacemaker who could lift the shadow of potential nuclear annihilation under which the entire planet had lived for nearly four decades? As Nancy Reagan would later put it: "For years, it had troubled me that my husband was always being portrayed by his opponents as a warmonger, simply because he believed, quite properly, in strengthening our defenses. . . . The world had become too small for the two superpowers not to be on speaking terms, and unless that old perception about Ronnie could be revised, nothing positive was likely to happen."

Shultz began to understand something else that night: he had found an invaluable ally in a first lady who understood her husband as no one else did—who was, in fact, the only person in the world to whom the president was truly close. In the years that followed, he would grow to appreciate more the unseen role that she played in protecting and shaping the Reagan presidency. Nancy rarely set foot in the West Wing, but her presence was felt by everyone who worked there. When she was displeased about something, they all knew it, and those who were not in her good graces tended not to last for long.

"She watched the people around, both in the White House and around in the Cabinet. She had a pretty good idea who was really serving himself or herself and who was working for the president," Shultz said. "I always thought anybody with any brains would make a friend of the first lady."

Ronald Reagan was endowed with enormous gifts: vision, ambition, optimism, and an ability to make the country believe in itself. He also enjoyed the benefit of being perpetually underestimated. But it was Nancy, wary by nature, who was the shrewder judge of people. Their son, Ron Reagan, described his mother as the skeptic—and the enforcer—that his ingenuous father needed to succeed in a business as cynical and opportunistic as politics. "My father was as good a man as you'll find in politics, or life for that matter. Very easygoing, very easy with people, very trusting of people. He was almost entirely guileless. There was no cynicism in him whatsoever. He tended to assume that other people—certainly people who were working for him and professed similar sensibilities—were like that too," Ron said. "My mother, on the other hand, understood that people had hidden agendas and that not everybody who talked a good game would back that up. She was unforgiving when she thought somebody had betrayed my father. When somebody needed to go, she was the one to know it first and, often as not, to make that happen."

Stu Spencer, who served as Ronnie's chief political strategist from the dawn of his career in California, described the Reagans as "an inseparable team politically and personally. He would never have been governor without her. He would never have been president without her." Nor without her might he have survived in the Oval Office, much less departed with a renown that would continue to shape politics for more than a generation after he left. That she would be capable of filling this role was far from obvious in her early naive days as California first lady, but over the years, Nancy grew to understand her power and to use it with great effect. When Ronnie's presidency was on the brink of collapsing under scandal during his second term, it was Nancy who remained clear-eyed enough to put together the rescue effort. She was relentless and ruthless in engineering the firing of Donald T. Regan, his autocratic White House chief of staff. "Her particular quality was she was street smart," Reagan biographer Edmund Morris said. "She was aggressive and a street fighter, which Reagan was not. She handled all the nasty business."

Nancy exercised an influence unlike any first lady before or since. She was not the conscience of her husband's presidency, as Eleanor Roosevelt had been to FDR. She claimed no policy portfolio, as Hillary Clinton did—disastrously, on health care—during Bill Clinton's first term in the Oval Office. Nor was Nancy secretly running the government in her husband's stead, though some critics compared her with Edith Wilson, who essentially assumed President Woodrow Wilson's duties for the last year and a half of his second term after he suffered a near-fatal stroke in 1919.

Hers was the power that comes with intimacy. The first lady was the essential disinterested observer of the ideological battles and power struggles that went on in the White House, because she had but one preoccupation: Ronald Reagan's well-being and success. She knew what he needed—rest, time to himself, encouragement—to be able to perform at his best, and she made sure he got it. Nancy also recognized that, unless he had the right set of people advising him, he could be led astray by his trusting nature and tendency to delegate. Her instincts, time would show, were usually right. "She was the guardian," said James A. Baker III, who was the president's first chief of staff and later his Treasury secretary. "She had a terrific political antenna, much better than his, in my view."

And yet, though she was hypervigilant in tending to her husband's image, Nancy was confoundingly clueless about managing her own. He was called the Teflon President because nothing bad ever seemed to stick to him. If that was the case, she was the Velcro First Lady. She made many missteps, and the damage from them adhered. Terrified for Ronnie's safety after he was nearly killed by a would-be assassin just two months after he took office, she turned to an astrologer to determine when and how he should travel and make public appearances. Her purchase of more than $200,000 worth of White House china created a headache for her husband amid a recession during which the Reagan administration was cutting poverty programs. She "borrowed" designer clothes and did not give them back.

Feminists held a particular kind of scorn for a first lady who gazed at her husband as if in rapture and who proclaimed over and over again that her life did not begin until she met Ronnie. Betty Friedan, a mother of the modern women's equality movement, had been a year ahead of Nancy at Smith College. Friedan declared the first lady to be "an anachronism" who would deny "the reality of American women today—what they want to be and what they need to be." Just a few of the names that Nancy was called: The Iron Butterfly. The Belle of Rodeo Drive. Fancy Nancy. The Cutout Doll. The Evita of Bel-Air. Mommie Dearest. The Hairdo with Anxiety. The Ice Queen. Attila the Hen.

Nancy was complicated, and just about everyone who dealt with her found her difficult at times. But while she had the image of a haughty socialite, the first lady in person could be charming and, truth be told, more engaging company than her husband. Nancy was worldly, an excellent listener, an eager gossip. She had at the ready a deep, disarming laugh. It was the opposite with Ronnie. For all his affability, there was a remoteness to his nature. He was at heart a loner who liked people but didn't need them.

"He doesn't let anybody get too close," Nancy acknowledged. "There's a wall around him. He lets me come closer than anyone else, but there are times when even I feel that barrier." She understood that Ronnie's penchant for self-isolation developed as a survival skill. He was the child of an alcoholic father who led his family from one uncertain situation into another. The collapse of Ronnie's first marriage devastated him. Nancy learned to grapple with and ultimately overcome his emotional inaccessibility during their frustrating, on-again-off-again courtship. "You can get just so far to Ronnie, and then something happens," she reflected. "It took him a long time, I think, to feel that he could really trust me."

Nancy too had a precarious early life. She was the product of a broken marriage, estranged from her birth father and left for a time with relatives by her mother. The trauma left her forever insecure and anxious, but also fearless when she discerned threats to the happiness and wholeness that she and Ronnie finally realized in each other. "Every marriage finds its own balance," she wrote. "It's part of Ronnie's character not to confront certain problems, so I'm usually the one who brings up the tough subjects—which often makes me seem like the bad guy." The couple filled in the voids of each other's personalities so completely that there wasn't much room left for anyone else—including their four children, two from his first marriage and two they had together. A dysfunctional family was the collateral heartbreak that accompanied the Reagans' epic love.

The final, sad chapter of the Reagans' lives together would bring another reassessment of Nancy. Even her harshest critics were moved by the stoicism and devotion she showed during the last decade of her husband's life, as he descended deeper and deeper into Alzheimer's disease. For the acclaim and sympathy that finally came her way, Nancy paid the highest price imaginable. Theirs had been a monumental story, and she was left to write the ending alone. "Not being able to share memories is an awful thing," she said.

If there were ever to be an epitaph that finally solved the riddle that was Nancy Reagan, it might be the words with which she once admonished a biographer, Bob Colacello: "Don't say I was tough. I was *strong.* I had to be, because Ronnie liked everybody and sometimes didn't see or refused to see what the people around him were really up to. But everything I did, I did for Ronnie. I did for love. Remember, Bob, the most important word is *love.*"

CHAPTER ONE

"I've always wanted to belong to somebody and to love someone who belonged to me," Nancy Reagan once wrote. "I always wanted someone to take care of me, someone I could take care of."

That yearning took root early in a bewildered, sensitive, and deeply insecure child. She was born Anne Frances Robbins in New York City, on July 6, 1921—though for decades, she would say it was two years later. Nicknamed Nancy from the start, this baby was the product of a bad match between an ambitious actress and an aimless car salesman. The couple would soon go their separate ways.

Nancy's mother, Edith Luckett, was known to her friends as Edie or DeeDee or Lucky. That last nickname may have been the one that fit best. It was by a stroke of luck that Edith had made her debut on the stage, shortly before the turn of the twentieth century. A winsome, golden-haired girl, she could often be found hanging around the Columbia Theater in downtown Washington, DC, where her older brother Joe managed the front office. One night, a boy who had been cast as Little Willie in the popular Victorian Era melodrama *East Lynne* suddenly took sick just as the curtain was about to rise on his death scene. Edith, who had just turned eleven, was shoved into his nightie and told to play it big. "So impressive was her work that one woman in the balcony became hysterical, her cries and groans being heard in every corner," the *Washington Times* wrote later of the "infant phenom." As the curtain fell, Edith stood up and waved to the audience.

Thus began a lifetime of grabbing opportunity when it presented itself and creating it when it didn't. Edie quit school before she was sixteen and found her way to New York, where she made the most of her brother's theater connections. Networking, as things turned out, was a talent that would serve her longer and more usefully than anything she would ever do on the stage.

She was outspoken and socially liberal. In 1913 the *Philadelphia Inquirer* wrote of the young actress: "Edith Luckett is an earnest suffragist. . . . She believes that a radical change would be effected . . . were women permitted to vote against the present system." This was nearly seven years before that would happen, with the ratification of the Nineteenth Amendment to the US Constitution.

Edie played small parts on Broadway, and bigger ones with regional theater companies, which were thriving across the country in the early twentieth century. She toured with some of the biggest names of the era, including legendary musical showman George M. Cohan and Irish tenor Chauncey Olcott. While she was doing summer stock at the Colonial Theater in Pittsfield, Massachusetts, she fell in love with a handsome twenty-three-year-old insurance agent named Kenneth Robbins. In late June 1916, after a two-month courtship, the couple drove across the state line in his Cadillac roadster to be married in Vermont.

Kenneth came from faded New England gentility. Whatever money his family might have had was long gone. He was an only child, and "kind of a momma's boy," according to one relative. His parents, with whom he lived, were not thrilled by the match between their son and an older actress. A newspaper account in the July 21 *Washington Evening Star* hinted of a hush around the wedding:

"Miss Edith Luckett, one of Washington's prominent actresses, who played stock and amateur theatricals in this city before she became associated with Broadway stars, was secretly married June 27 to Kenneth S. Robbins of Pittsfield, Mass. The ceremony was performed by Rev. George S. Mills of the Congregational Church of Bennington,

Vt.," the story said. "The news of the marriage became known by the returning of the marriage license to Pittsfield, where Mr. Robbins resides with his father and mother, Mr. and Mrs. John N. Robbins." The newspaper also noted that the bride "does not intend to give up the stage for the present, at least, and has agreed to appear in a new New York production which will have its initial performance shortly."

So, their union was strained from the start. Edie was not cut out for life in a Berkshires farmhouse and insisted upon moving to New York. The couple rented a house in Flushing, a working-class neighborhood of Queens. Ken tried his hand as a theatrical booking agent, one of many endeavors at which he would fail. The only clients he could get, he would joke later, were "a one-legged tap dancer and a cross-eyed knife thrower." A few months after the United States entered World War I in 1917, Ken enlisted in the army, where he served for a little more than a year. Soon after his return, Edie became pregnant. She refused her husband's pleas that they move back to Pittsfield to raise their child near his family.

The marriage was effectively over by the time Nancy was born. Her father, by then selling cars in New Jersey, was not present at Sloane Hospital for her arrival. The delivery, by forceps, was botched, leaving the infant's right eye shut. If it stayed that way for two weeks, a doctor warned Edie, Nancy might be partially blind. The new mother was furious and accused the physician of rushing the birth so that he could make the golf date she had heard him discussing just before they put her under. "If my little girl's eye doesn't open, so help me God, I'm going to kill you," Edie told him. Nancy's eye turned out to be fine, but the forceps left a small scar on the right side of her face that was visible for the rest of her life.

Motherhood did not slow down Edie or cramp her style. She asked her most famous friend, the great silent-movie star Alla Nazimova, to be the baby's godmother. Though Nazimova is all but forgotten today, she was at one point the highest-paid actress in the world. She and Edie had been close from the time Nancy's mother had played a small part as an unmarried pregnant passenger aboard a yacht in Nazimova's 1917 Broadway play *'Ception Shoals*.

The Crimea-born Nazimova—whom Nancy called "Zim"—had a wildly unconventional lifestyle. Nazimova made little secret of her sexual relationships with women, and was considered a founding mother of early Hollywood's underground network of lesbian and bisexual actresses. Among its other members, it was said, were screen sirens such as Greta Garbo and Marlene Dietrich. Those who knew what was going on in their closet called them "the sewing circle."

There is no evidence that Nazimova and Edie were anything more than friends and confidants. But it is easy to see why the two of them got along. "Edith was a New Woman, a suffragist and careerist who refused to grow up female in the accepted sense," Nazimova biographer Gavin Lambert wrote. "Although she chose acting as a means of self-advancement, her real talent was in the theatre of life."

Edie ran with a crowd that included promising young actors Spencer Tracy and Walter Huston. She entertained at parties with tales of her life and pedigree, saying she had been raised on a Virginia plantation and attended an exclusive private school. None of that was true. Edie's parents had moved to Washington from Virginia in 1872, before the first of their five children were born. Her father, Charles, was a shipping agent for the Adams Express Company on F Street, where he spent fifty-two years handling batches of money for the US Treasury and local banks. Edie, the baby of the family, attended the city's public schools. Nonetheless, Nancy's mother spoke with what Lambert described as "an almost absurdly refined Southern accent. She dropped her guard but not her accent to use four-letter words and tell breathtakingly dirty jokes."

After she and her husband split, Edie had the additional imperative of earning a living for herself and her daughter. Nancy claimed she spent the first two years of her life as a "backstage baby," being carted by her plucky, penniless mother to the theater and post-curtain-call parties. An often-repeated story of Nancy's early years was how the famous actress Colleen Moore first spotted Edie at a fancy party on Long Island. "She was a beautiful blonde, and she had the biggest blue eyes you ever saw. And she was carrying a tiny baby in her arms,"

Moore recalled. When Moore asked her host who this woman was and whether she always hauled that baby around, he told her: "She has no choice. She just got divorced, and she doesn't have a penny." Moore decided she must get to know this determined mother. They became friends for life.

The full truth, it would appear, made for less of a tender story. The arrival of an inconveniently timed baby did not fit with Edie's plans. Her child took second place to pursuing her acting career and her busy social life. In 1982 Nancy received a letter and a set of photos from a woman named Katherine Carmichael, who wrote that she had been the future first lady's live-in nanny. The letter suggests that Edie was not as financially strapped as her daughter said she was—and perhaps as Nancy had been led to believe. From the start, Edie left Nancy for extended periods in the care of others. "Your mother travelled at times in her work as an actress; I was in full charge of you when your mother was not there. I would wheel you to Central Park every day weather permitting, I would guess for over a year, and I loved it, you were a darling," Carmichael recalled in the letter, which is among Nancy's papers at the Ronald Reagan Presidential Library & Museum. "I remember your mother was either going abroad or in a show touring this country, and you were being sent to Virginia with relatives. All these years I would often wonder about you, and finally came across a clipping in our Portland Maine newspaper and recognized your father and mother names. I was so glad to know how well you are doing."

Though the accompanying photos are not in the file, it would appear from her response that Nancy recognized herself as the baby in the old images. She replied: "How nice of you to write and send the snapshots. I can't say I remember you—being a little young at the time!—but I do remember how I looked forward to being with mother.

"Thank you for looking after me so well," she added. "I'm glad I wasn't too much trouble."

Carmichael's memory was off, but only by a bit. Once Nancy was out of diapers, Edie did indeed put her in the care of an aunt and uncle. The aunt—not the place where Nancy landed—was named Virginia.

C. Audley and Virginia Galbraith lived in a modest Dutch colonial in the Battery Park neighborhood of Bethesda, Maryland, on the outskirts of Washington, DC. They converted their sunroom so that the child could have a place to sleep. Virginia was the opposite of her sister, Edie, in almost every way—so proper that she referred to her husband as "Mr. Galbraith" and went into the bathroom to undress at night. The Galbraiths were kind to Nancy; their outgoing daughter Charlotte, later a talented artist and Olympic-caliber diver, became almost a sister to the younger girl. Nancy would be a bridesmaid in her cousin Charlotte's 1942 wedding, and Charlotte would name a daughter after Nancy.

But the next six years cast a permanent shadow on Nancy's spirit, leaving her with an insecurity and wariness that lasted. "It was a crucial moment in my mother's life, and one that she never really got over," said Nancy's son, Ron Reagan. "I'm not a psychologist, but I think she suffered from a kind of separation anxiety ever since and was very concerned about being left—being abandoned—her whole life."

Her daughter, Patti, also discerned that something rooted in childhood trauma haunted her mother: "She always harbored a need to be noticed. I suspect she grew up clamoring for control, because the world was unpredictable, because people left her and hurt her."

From the time Nancy was two years old until she was eight, her mother was an occasional and fleeting presence. Nancy would later come to understand that the emptiness of those early years without Edie left an imprint that subsequently affected her ability to deal with her own rebellious children. "Maybe our six-year separation is one reason I appreciated her so much, and why we never went through a period of estrangement," she wrote. "It may also explain why, years later, during the 1960s, I couldn't really understand how children—including my own—could turn against their parents. I always wanted to say, 'You don't know how *lucky* you are that we had all those years together.' "

In September 1925 four-year-old Anne Frances Robbins was enrolled in Washington's prestigious Sidwell Friends School, where many of the city's most prominent families sent their children. The

Galbraiths paid her tuition at first. A registration form identified her mother as Mrs. K. S. Robbins, though it appears to have been signed in Edie's absence by Virginia. Chubby, wide-eyed Nancy began kindergarten at Sidwell's Suburban School, a structure newly built from timbers reputed to have been first used for Woodrow Wilson's inaugural viewing stand. On her report cards, Nancy was described as smart, engaging, and eager to please. One teacher's note from June 1927 reads: "A very bright child, very popular with the children, and a blessing to the teacher. Nancy does everything well."

She held tea parties for her dolls by the Galbraiths' front steps, less than ten miles from the presidential mansion where one day she would throw fifty-five glittering state dinners. A little boyfriend would cart her around the neighborhood in his red wagon. Nancy made her first trip to the White House when Calvin Coolidge lived there. Her aunt and uncle took her for the annual Easter Egg Roll for children on the South Lawn, where first lady Grace Coolidge was known to appear with a pet raccoon named Rebecca that she kept on a leash.

The brightest moments of Nancy's life were Edie's visits, which to her daughter felt "as if Auntie Mame herself had come to town." The worldly actress taught Nancy and the Galbraiths the latest dances, like the Charleston. She brought gifts that included a wig of long, blonde ringlets, just like those of Mary Pickford, the silent-screen actress known as "America's sweetheart." Nancy, whose own hair was bobbed, wore it constantly. Occasionally, Nancy's aunt took her to New York to see Edie perform, and the child fell in love with the musty backstage smells that she came to associate with her mother. One Christmas, the stagehands built Nancy a dollhouse.

Yet there are spans during this unsettled period in which there is no record of where Nancy was or who she was with. In February 1926, not five months after she arrived at Sidwell, its files show the four-year-old was withdrawn for the remainder of the term. "Left the city," read a notation in the school's files. She returned for the 1926–27 academic year but was absent from kindergarten twenty-five days of the third marking period. The explanation: "Went to Trenton, N.J." Nancy may have been temporarily reunited with Edie, who in March 1926 was starring in Plainfield, New Jersey, in a play titled, ironically enough, *Dancing Mothers*. Or she might have been with her father, who also lived in New Jersey. Perhaps another relative took her in, or she was ill. What Nancy remembered from around that time was a bout with what she understood to be "double ammonia," during which the little girl cried for the absent Edie and thought to herself: "If I had a child, and she got sick, I'd be with her."

Sidwell's records also include a 1928 anthology of compositions by its students. Where other first graders wrote chirpy little essays about their pets, Nancy offered a fantasy of an intact, perfect family and an image that evoked her own lonely reality: "The little girl was walking with her mother and father. They were looking for flowers, and there was not a flower in the garden."

As an adult, Nancy bristled when it was suggested that her mother had abandoned her. But a complex set of emotional forces were set in motion by Edie's absence. One speech she gave as first lady stands out for its raw honesty about how that time in her life left its mark. Nancy was being honored in 1986 at Boys Town, the famous orphanage in Omaha founded by Father Edward J. Flanagan. The purpose of the event was to give recognition to her antidrug advocacy. But she had another message she wanted to deliver to the 430 children in the audience: "The reason I'm here today is not because of the award, but because of you. There was a time when I didn't quite know where I belonged, either.

"What I wished for more than anything else in the world was a normal family," Nancy said, her voice cracking and her eyes welling up. "Do you know what happens when you hurt inside? You usually start closing your heart to people. Because that's how you got hurt in the first place—you opened your heart. Another thing that happens is that you stop trusting people, because somewhere along the way, they probably didn't live up to your trust.

"And there's another thing that happens when you've been hurt. You start to think you're not worth much. You think to yourself, 'Well, how can I be worth anything, if someone would treat me in this terrible way?' So I understand why you feel beaten down by it all."

Speechwriter Landon Parvin, who drafted that address and many others for the first lady, recalled a line that Nancy quoted often in her public appearances. It was from the William Inge play *The Dark at the Top of the Stairs*, in which a mother says of her children: "I always thought I could give them life like a present, all wrapped in white with every promise of success."

"For some reason, she couldn't deliver this line without getting tears in her eyes," Parvin told me. "I always tried to figure, was she talking about her mother, or her children? What was it that always brought tears to her eyes?"

Nancy's biological father aroused no such misty sentimentality. "Since Kenneth Robbins was such a small part of my life, it is impossible for me to think of him as my father," she wrote in *Nancy*, her sanitized 1980 autobiography coauthored with Bill Libby. Kenneth and Edie divorced, quietly and amicably, in late 1927. He remarried in August 1928. Edie remained on good terms with her ex-husband and occasionally helped him out financially.

Their daughter gave various and conflicting accounts of how much contact she had with her father as she was growing up. The evidence suggests he was a bigger part of her life than she acknowledged. In the 1980 memoir, she wrote she had visited Kenneth only "a few times when I was young" and that "there had never been any relationship of any kind." Her 1989 autobiography, *My Turn*, indicated she last saw him when she was an adolescent. But there is at least one photo of Nancy with him, both of them looking relaxed and happy, that was taken in Massachusetts in 1941, when she was around twenty and in college. Other relatives recall him going to see her frequently in her early years in Bethesda and later in Chicago.

Nancy claimed that there was a traumatic moment, one that brought an irreparable rupture. It came, in her telling, while she was staying at his apartment. He said something insulting about her mother. Nancy announced angrily that she wanted to go home, and he locked her in a bathroom. That was the end of her contact with her biological dad, she said, adding that it left her with a lifelong fear of being in locked rooms. Nancy never specified when, exactly, this event happened. Her father's relatives were skeptical that it did, at least not in the way she told it. They said in various news articles over the years that it would have been unlike Robbins, a sweet if aimless man, to have behaved so brutally.

Her stepbrother, Richard Davis, was also doubtful of Nancy's account, which he did not recall her telling in the years when they were growing up. He had his own theory: Robbins was part of a chapter of her life that she simply wanted to forget; one that she preferred to pretend had never happened. "Ken Robbins was a rather decent chap, actually," Dick said. "I think once Nancy got away from her situation with Edith's sister and Charlotte, she probably felt pretty superior."

Kenneth mourned this lost connection to his only child. When he died in 1972, relatives found in his wallet an old photo of him with Nancy. His mother, Anne, known as Nanee, continued to visit her sole grandchild even after Nancy moved to Los Angeles to become an actress in the 1940s.

Files at the Reagan Library include a 1982 letter to the first lady from a Vermont man named Peter Harrison. He wrote that he spent a few years of his childhood in Verona, New Jersey, near Kenneth, his second wife, Patsy, and his mother, Anne. In later years, Harrison wrote, "I remember Ken telling us his daughter Nancy was getting married to the movie star Ronald Reagan. How proud he would be to know that you are now the First Lady. He mentioned you often." He also noted that Nancy's grandmother had given him a bloodstone ring, which Harrison's wife wore every day.

Nancy's reply conspicuously makes no mention of her father, who had died a decade earlier: "I received your letter and was happy to learn of your friendship with the Robbins family. Grandmother Robbins was very special to me, and I am glad to know that you have taken such good care of her ring and that your wife is enjoying it."

Kenneth Robbins's finances deteriorated with a series of bad investments after World War II. A second cousin, Kathleen Young, told the

Los Angeles Times's Beverly Beyette that she phoned the California governor's mansion several times in 1970. She wanted to alert Nancy that her biological father, whose second wife had recently died, was ill and needed money. Young said her calls were never returned. "Maybe the right word didn't get to the right place," she said.

Though a *Look* magazine profile of the California first lady written around then mentioned her biological father, that detail in the magazine article "was never picked up by the press, for which I was grateful," Nancy said. (Ironically, it would be Kenneth Robbins's bloodline that in 1985 qualified the nation's first lady for acceptance into membership in the Daughters of the American Revolution.) His obituary, published in the *New Jersey Herald* on February 4, 1972, included no reference to his famous daughter. It noted only: "He is survived by several nieces and nephews."

As an adult, Nancy rarely reminisced about her early years. Her own children have only a vague sense of them. When I asked her son, Ron, about her whereabouts during the months where there are gaps in her school records, he told me that "details of this period were scarce. Your guess is as good as mine." Stu Spencer, Ronnie's earliest and closest political strategist, said Nancy's reticence contrasted with the nostalgic bent of her husband, who often told stories of the early hardships that had formed his character: "Reagan talked about his childhood, but I never heard her talk about hers. She'd never talk about it."

Douglas Wick, an Academy Award–winning movie producer whose parents were close to the Reagans, knew Nancy from the time he was in grade school. A close friend and admirer of hers through the end of her life, Wick came to believe that the pain of Nancy's early childhood helped explain the keen radar she developed about other people and made her wary of letting them know too much about her. Both were a means of protecting herself.

"She had so much fear, from the instability of her own upbringing and whatever demons she had from that; in her background, where she was embarrassed, so embarrassed, not to have a mother—a regular mother—so embarrassed not to have a regular father," Wick explained.

"I always thought shame and embarrassment were what she most feared. Hence, she was very good at going stealth, not revealing her true self, except when she felt comfortable."

*

Nancy's official biography as California first lady wipes her story entirely clean of its complicated beginnings. That document, which is in the records of the Reagan Library, begins with two lies: "Nancy Davis Reagan was born in Chicago, the only daughter of Dr. and Mrs. Loyal Davis." But maybe that was simply how she saw it. Seven-year-old Nancy got a new beginning in the spring of 1929, when Edie arrived in Bethesda to deliver a big announcement. She sat on her daughter's bed and told her she was getting married. They were moving to Chicago. Together.

So entered the second most important man in Nancy's life, and the only one she would ever again think of as her father. Edie met Loyal Davis, a thirty-one-year-old associate professor of surgery at Northwestern University, on a ship to England in July 1927. With her daughter in Maryland, Edie was headed for a European vacation with two friends from the theater. Most accounts say she had an acting gig there; her diary suggests it was primarily a pleasure trip. Loyal was on his way to deliver a presentation in London on neurosurgery, his specialty, which was then in its infancy.

At the time he met Edie, Loyal's own personal life was in turmoil. His eight-year marriage to a former nurse named Pearl McElroy was collapsing. Pearl had declined his entreaties to leave their two-year-old son, Richard, in the care of her mother in Chicago and join Loyal on the voyage to England. "Perhaps I did not insist strongly enough," he conceded later. So Loyal shared a cabin with another doctor.

In her diary, Edie recorded her impressions of that journey aboard Hamburg-American's SS *New York,* a state-of-the-art luxury liner launched just the year before. The journal is a tan leather volume, with the initials *E.L.* embossed in gold. Friends had given it to her so that she could compile a keepsake of the trip. One entry notes that on the evening of July 15, her first full day at sea, Edie "went to the movie—met Doctor Davis—he joined me for liquer [*sic*] after the movies—we all walked on deck." Edie also asked her fellow passengers to write inscriptions in her journal. One is an awkwardly affectionate note from Loyal Davis, who wrote that he found Edie "most charming."

As was usually the case, Edie drew attention and admirers wherever she went. Her diary suggests that she was juggling several suitors on the voyage, including one young man she deemed "a pest. He is a very intellectual cultured boy but he follows me around from noon till nite & it's a nuisance." The captain threw a surprise dinner party for her birthday on July 16. At a masquerade ball a week into the voyage, Edie wrote that she "dressed up like a colored 'mammy.' [An] old woman came up to me & said, 'Hey, you, stop flirting with my husband. I've watched you since you got on board & I'll get you good before you get off the boat.'" Edie's friends, including her new acquaintance Loyal Davis, intervened with the woman and "took her in the hall & told her they would have the capt. put her in chains if she annoyed me again."

Amid the gaiety, Edie wrote often how much she missed her little girl. "I do nothing but talk about my baby to everyone," says one entry dated July 21. And from Paris the following week: "Sunday spent the day at Fontainebleau. Would have been heavenly if my baby had been with us." A poem written in the diary by her friend and traveling companion Jack Alicoate, a Broadway writer and producer, also hinted at signs of stress and longing beneath Edie's happy-go-lucky exterior:

> Remember they're calling you Lucky
> And the kid that's dependent on you
> So up with that chin and keep plucky
> The world will belong to you too.

Edie was closing in on forty, though she still claimed she was nearly a decade younger. That meant she was reaching an age, whether she acknowledged the number or not, when her stage career would not go on much longer. Meanwhile, she would soon have another concern: Nancy's aunt and uncle were being transferred to Atlanta by the Southern Railroad, leaving her with nowhere to put the child.

Edie needed some new options. She needed them fast. And as it happened, both professional and personal opportunities were opening for her in Chicago. She got a part at the city's Blackstone Theatre playing opposite Spencer Tracy in George M. Cohan's farce *The Baby Cyclone*. Then followed another one there in *Elmer the Great*, a Ring Lardner baseball comedy starring her old friend Walter Huston, who by then had become a big name.

All of which gave her a chance to resume the romance that had begun as a shipboard fling with Loyal Davis. He was back in Chicago, living miserably and alone in a hotel. Not long after Loyal returned from the European trip on which he had met Edie, his wife, Pearl, went to visit friends in Los Angeles. "It was but a week or so later that she informed me that she was going to Reno, Nevada, to seek a divorce," he recalled.

Pearl had been resentful of the expectations that came with being a proper doctor's wife and had little interest in Loyal's surgical and academic endeavors. She and her rigidly demanding husband fought over her sloppy housekeeping and her indifferent approach to caring for their son. Word went round that Pearl was also having an affair with another physician, one of Loyal's best friends. Loyal was devastated and worried what the stigma of a failed marriage might do to his career.

One day Dr. Allen B. Kanavel, who had established the Department of Neurological Surgery at Northwestern University Medical School, took Loyal aside in an empty room at Wesley Memorial Hospital. His mentor told the young doctor that he knew about his personal situation and offered some advice: "Never hug a bad bargain to your breast." Loyal decided not to contest the divorce.

*

Loyal and Edie were not an obvious match, either in demeanor or background. As Nancy put it: "My father was tall and dark; my mother was short and blonde. He was a Republican; she was a Democrat. He was often severe; she was always laughing. He was an only child; she came from a large family. He was reserved; she knew everybody."

But Edie's arrival in his life brought air and light to Loyal's constricted, work-centered existence. She introduced him to the glamorous and colorful characters she had cultivated in the theater. She charmed his colleagues. "My professional and personal life became calm and happy," Loyal wrote. "She taught me to change my asocial tendencies and habits, to develop a sense of humor, to retain my desire and energy to succeed but to relax and enjoy the association of friends."

Still, after the disgrace of a divorce, Loyal was not sure whether an actress—in this case, a foulmouthed one with a blemished marital history of her own—would be suitable as a doctor's partner for life. So once again, he looked to Kanavel for guidance. "Dr. Kanavel invited himself to her apartment for her to cook dinner to make certain, he told her, whether it was right for us to be married," Loyal said.

Kanavel approved, and even served as best man for Loyal and Edie's wedding at Chicago's Fourth Presbyterian Church during an early heat wave on May 21, 1929. Their other attendant was eight-year-old Nancy, who wore a blue pleated dress and carried flowers. "I was happy for Mother, but I can remember, even then, feeling twinges of jealousy—a feeling I was to experience years later, from the other side, after I married a man with children," Nancy recalled. "Dr. Davis was taking part of her away from me, and after being separated from Mother for so long, I wanted her all to myself."

The story of that 1929 wedding is one that Nancy repeated many times. In her personal documents at the Reagan Library is a certificate from the ceremony, signed by the church's pastor, Harrison Ray Anderson. But New York City records show that Edie and Loyal actually were married the previous year in a wedding they apparently kept a secret. It happened on October 20, 1928, at St. Luke's, a Lutheran church on West Forty-Sixth Street, just a couple of blocks from the Lyceum Theatre, where Edie was performing during the brief Broadway run of *Elmer the Great.* That was a Saturday, so they presumably had to squeeze in their vows around a two thirty matinee and an eight thirty evening show. The witnesses were Walter Huston and his costar in the play, Nan Sunderland, who became his wife a few years later. Clergyman William Koepchen did the officiating.

The certificate they all signed identifies Edie under her married name of Edith Robbins. It also lists her age as thirty-two, the same as Loyal's, and her birthplace as Petersburg, Virginia. (District of Columbia birth records indicate she was born in that city, six years earlier than she claimed on the New York marriage registry.)

All of this furtiveness surrounding the wedding raises questions: Why the rush to get married, less than a year after they had met? Why wait to tell Nancy of the existence of a stepfather until the following year? And why go through the charade of an engagement and a second ceremony in Chicago?

One possibility is that there was a pregnancy scare or other imperative to legalize their union before they acknowledged it publicly. Perhaps their passion was so great that they simply could not wait any longer to live together. Whatever the reason for the urgency, this marriage turned out to be a long and happy one. Edie and Loyal remained delighted with and devoted to each other for more than five decades.

Nancy's mother had charted a new direction for both her own life and that of her little girl. "She saw Loyal as her lifeline and grabbed on without letting go," Edie's pal Lester Weinrott, a Chicago radio producer and director, later told author Kitty Kelley. "She wanted to legitimize herself and give her daughter a break."

Loyal provided a safe landing and also a launch pad. The son of a poorly educated railroad man, he had the drive it took to become recognized as one of the country's most brilliant men of medicine. "The pair of sculptured hands cast in bronze that serve as book-ends at the apartment of Dr. and Mrs. Loyal Davis at 215 Lake Shore Drive are Dr. Davis' own hands," the *Chicago Tribune* noted in 1935. "Mrs. Davis had Sculptor Bernard Frazier do the hands of Dr. Davis, famous brain surgeon."

His professional accomplishments notwithstanding, it was Edie's spark, her savvy, her genius for knowing who to know that propelled the Davises into Chicago's elite. "Over the years, she transformed herself and this dour little man from the wrong side of the tracks in Galesburg, Illinois, into something that Chicago society had to pay attention to," Weinrott said. "It was the greatest performance she ever gave, and I salute her for it."

Loyal recognized that as well. "She works in mysterious ways," he once said of his wife. "She's better known in Chicago than I am, and there is no question of that."

Forged together by an unconditional faith in what they could do as a couple, Edie and Loyal both complemented each other's strengths and compensated for the weaknesses in the other. The parallels to the Reagans are impossible to miss. Dick Davis, Loyal's son from his first marriage, moved in with the family in 1939, when he was twelve years old. As he told me the first time we talked: "Nancy's marriage to the president mimicked her mother."

So whatever scars Edie's early absence and neglect left on Nancy, she had bequeathed to her daughter two priceless gifts: the security Nancy craved and a prototype for the kind of love partnership that would provide it. Edie's lesson to Nancy was that one plus one could be ever so much more than two. The right kind of union could be both a refuge and a ride on a comet. "If you want to understand Nancy Reagan, look at her mother," said Robert Higdon, an aide and longtime friend to the first lady.

Edie died from Alzheimer's disease in 1987. As Nancy sorted and packed her mother's belongings, she came across a small gold ring engraved with both of their initials: *E-N*. The nation's first lady slipped it on her own finger. "No one," she said, "will ever know the debt I owed my mother."

CHAPTER TWO

The headline over a full-page *Chicago Tribune* story on Sunday, January 7, 1940, declared: "Society Bids Farewell to the 1930s and Greets '40s."

> *"Good-by to the Dirty Thirties—*
> *Life Begins in Forty."*

That was how a society columnist who went by the pen name "Cousin Eve" began a breathless roundup of the holiday-season events that ushered in a new decade for the city's advantaged class. One of the celebrations mentioned in her column that Sunday was a coming-out party that had taken place ten days earlier at Chicago's most exclusive club, the Casino. "Seldom has this beautiful private club looked as chic. Dr. and Mrs. Davis received in the loggia with their bud, among bouquets and baskets of winter roses," the columnist gushed. "The debutante was fresh as a rose herself in white gauze frosted in silver."

Nancy, then in her freshman year at Smith College, in Massachusetts, had fretted over every detail of the late-afternoon tea dance at which she made her formal debut into society. She and Loyal had an argument—the only one her stepbrother, Richard, remembered between them—over the surgeon's stern decree that there would be no alcohol. "I think he was very disgusted by people who drank," Dick said. "He simply did not want to see these teenagers intoxicated, and put his foot down, very hard. This upset her because all of her girlfriends were having these debut parties and served liquor. She didn't want to be different in that sense."

Nancy should not have feared the party would be a dud—not so long as the arrangements were in the hands of her mother. Edie had timed it to coincide with the arrival in Chicago of Princeton University's Triangle Club theater troupe. Edie invited them all, ensuring that Nancy's tea dance would be teeming with eligible young men. In her *Chicago Tribune* column, "Cousin Eve" took note of how the oval ballroom's soft lights caught the gleam of red cellophane bows and illuminated the party's whimsical decorations, which included sparkly top hats with criss-crossed walking sticks. A ten-man orchestra was "beating so lustily the tom-toms that one heard their throb in the street. So young was this party and so carefree the dancers that my neighbor, a lovely in middle thirties, sighed deeply, and yearned to begin life all over again."

The grandiloquent prose aside, it was understandable that Americans in all walks of life were looking for a fresh beginning at the dawn of the 1940s. The nation was struggling to climb out of a catastrophic economic collapse, and, across the ocean, forces of extremism were building for another world war, which had already begun in Europe. No one knew then that they were just a few years away from the biggest bloodbath in human history.

Chicago had seen more than its share of suffering during the Great Depression, particularly in its early years. Even before the 1929 stock market crash, its municipal government had become virtually insolvent, and by early 1932, the city's emergency relief funds were depleted. Chicago's unemployment rate at one point reached 50 percent. Breadlines and soup kitchens were common; one of the biggest was run by the gangster Al Capone on South State Street. In the heart of the city near Grant Park, destitute men built a huge shantytown of discarded bricks, wood, and sheet metal. They facetiously called it Hooverville, after the highly unpopular president they blamed for their troubles. The name quickly caught on, and Hoovervilles sprang up across the country.

But all of this misery was a world away from Nancy's privileged existence as a young woman coming of age along the eastward-bending shoulder of elegant and fashionable Lake Shore Drive, which was among the city's fanciest addresses. "When my mother met Loyal Davis and brought me to Chicago, it was like the happy ending to a fairy tale," Nancy said. The Davises lived in several apartments as they moved upward onto Chicago's famed Gold Coast. By the time Nancy was in her teens, they had settled onto the fourteenth floor of a classically styled lakefront building near the Drake Hotel. The hotel was where heads of state and European royalty stayed when they were in the Windy City. Nancy cut through the Drake lobby on her daily walk to school and breathed in the ambience.

Summers for young Nancy meant eight weeks at Camp Kechuwa on the upper peninsula of Michigan, where the Lake Michigamme water was so clean that the girls brushed their teeth with it. "Will you please tell Mother that I wove a rug for the guest bathroom. How do you like my book plates I made? I hope you like them," Nancy wrote in one undated letter to Loyal. "I passed a safety test for canoeing so I can go out in a canoe alone."

Among Nancy's other childhood pleasures were trips to visit Loyal's parents in Galesburg. It is a town forty-five miles northwest of Peoria, one of seven spots where Abraham Lincoln and Stephen Douglas debated during their storied 1858 race for the US Senate, which former congressman Lincoln lost to the incumbent but emerged from as a nationally prominent figure. Galesburg is also where a little boy nicknamed Dutch Reagan had once lived briefly.

Loyal's father, Al Davis, built Nancy and Dick a playhouse in the backyard of the family home at 219 Walnut Avenue. The first lady reminisced in a March 1981 letter that it was a place "which I adored and spent many make-believe hours in. Little did I dream at that time that my playhouse would someday be the White House." Nancy did, however, have aspirations. Once, the neighborhood children put on a show in the Davis yard, to an audience seated on chairs that Al borrowed from a local mortuary. Nancy sang "The Sidewalks of New York" and announced at the end of her performance that the next time anyone in the town saw her, it would be on a movie screen.

For the first two years after her 1929 move to Chicago, Nancy attended University School for Girls. In 1931, still known as Nancy Robbins, she was enrolled in the more prestigious Chicago Latin School for Girls, then located in a four-story brick building at 59 East Scott Street, a half mile from the Davises' apartment. Tuition by the time she graduated from high school, in a class of fourteen young women, was $650 a year, which for nearly half the Depression-era families in Chicago represented more than six months of income.

Girls Latin followed a progressive educational approach known as the Quincy Method, which had begun catching on across the country in the late eighteen hundreds. Its students were expected to take woodshop and spend at least twenty minutes each day in outdoor recess, a rare requirement among elite female schools at the time. But other parts of its curriculum were far more structured and conventional. One dreaded ritual was the annual posture walk, where girls would parade and be judged on how they carried themselves. The winner was awarded a letter, as if standing up properly were a varsity sport. They all wore blue skirts with white blouses, except on Fridays, when the uniform was a navy silk dress with white collar and cuffs. Makeup, nail polish, and jewelry—beyond a watch and one ring—were banned. Students were expected to stand when a parent or faculty member entered the classroom and remain on their feet until a teacher signaled them to be seated.

Nancy's nickname was "Pinky," a playful reference to the color of the cotton underwear she wore in sixth grade; her good friend Jean Wescott was called "Whitey" for hers. Nancy "was not particularly a good student and not a good athlete," her stepbrother, Dick, told me. But she was popular—"the personification of a southern belle," according to Girls Latin's 1937 yearbook. Nancy played forward on the field hockey team and was president of both the Athletic Association and the sophomore class. The seniors a year ahead of her jokingly bequeathed Nancy a scrapbook to hold all her pictures of screen idol Tyrone Power. Wescott, who would later be her roommate at Smith, recalled: "We bought every movie magazine. She liked Bing Crosby. I liked Ronald Reagan. She said, 'I don't know what you see in Ronald Reagan.'"

In one area, Nancy outshone everyone else. "Nancy's social perfection is a constant source of amazement," her 1939 yearbook marveled. "She is invariably becomingly and suitably dressed. She can talk and even better listen intelligently, to anyone from her little kindergarten partner at the Halloween party, to the grandmother of one of her friends. Even in the seventh grade, when we first began to mingle with the male of the species, Nancy was completely poised. While the rest of us huddled self-consciously on one side of the room, casting surreptitious glances at the men, aged thirteen, opposite us, Nancy actually crossed the yawning emptiness separating the two groups and serenely began a conversation—with a boy."

She already styled herself an actress in training and starred in the senior play—presciently, one called *First Lady*—as a character named Lucy Chase Wayne, the scheming wife of a presidential candidate. "Nancy knows not only her own lines but everyone else's," the yearbook noted. "She picks up the cue her terrified classmates forget to give, improvises speeches for all and sundry. Just a part of the game for Nancy."

In her senior year, Nancy was also selected to be student judge, a position that involved meting out punishments to girls who had committed infractions such as coming back from lunch wearing a smidge of lipstick, or failing to pass the daily noon inspection of their desks for neatness. She did not cut any slack. "Nancy had a very effective approach to a culprit, looking straight at her and asking, 'Why did you do that?'" one retired teacher wrote.

Her grades were mediocre, which teachers attributed not to lack of effort or intelligence but anxiety. "She works very faithfully and does well from day to day. In spite of much experience, she is nervous about examinations and never does herself justice on them," read one note in her record. "Fine cooperation and attention. Accurate, does not guess. Extremely good visual memory and observation which might be used pedagogically," another noted. "Her daily work is better than her tests."

*

The Latin School files also hint at an early disquietude that accompanied the "fairy-tale" turn Nancy's life had taken. "When she entered the school, her mother had just remarried, and Nancy had an adjustment to make to her stepfather, Dr. Loyal Davis, a brain specialist of whom she stood in awe," one teacher wrote.

It is not surprising that she might have been intimidated by her new stepfather at first. Loyal ("a terrible name, and quite a handicap," he said) was the proud, stern son of a locomotive engineer. Growing up in Galesburg, he lived with his parents on a street known as Scab Alley, in a set of row houses that had been built by the railroad during an 1888 strike. His father never made it as far as high school, having been forced to go to work at the age of seven. But Al Davis was determined that his only child would earn a living with his head, not his back. On nights when Al was not away on runs to Chicago for the Burlington Railroad, he monitored his son's schoolwork at the kitchen table. "My father knew nothing about my studies and couldn't aid me, but he sat next to me as though his presence would help," Loyal wrote later.

Fueled by those expectations and his own inner drive, Loyal was an unbending perfectionist, obdurate and disciplined from an early age. One year when he was in grade school, Loyal compiled a perfect Sunday school attendance record at Galesburg's Grace Episcopal Church, his sights set on a prayer book that was to be awarded to a boy and a girl. Loyal donned a black cassock and white surplice to lend his quavery voice to the choir and carried the cross at the head of the procession into services. He even pumped the organ.

But at the end of the year, the prize went to a boy whose father owned the town's largest department store. "I was the only boy to have such a record, and I knew that," Loyal wrote in his 1973 memoir, still burning at the injustice of it. "I was angered and crushed in spirit. When I got home, I announced I would never go back to the church again."

From then on, Loyal proclaimed himself a nonbeliever: "I have never been able to subscribe to the divinity of Jesus Christ nor to his virgin birth. I don't believe in his resurrection, or a heaven or hell as places. If we are remembered and discussed with pleasure and happiness after death, this is our heavenly reward and mortality for having led a good life."

He graduated from high school at sixteen as his class valedictorian, attended nearby Knox College for two years on scholarship, and then headed to Chicago and Northwestern University Medical School, from which he received his degree in 1918 at the age of twenty-two. After an internship at Cook County Hospital, he joined a general-medicine practice back in Galesburg.

This was right around the time he married nurse Pearl McElroy. "She was beautifully impressive in her black velvet dress with her black hair and brown eyes, the first time we met as the result of a date arranged by telephone by a mutual friend," Loyal recalled. "Our courtship was short, and there was no chance to learn about each other's idiosyncrasies."

Those became apparent soon enough. "I was unable to accept her dislike and ineptitude for housekeeping. She had left a small town for the attractions in Chicago; she was not prepared to settle down to life in Galesburg," Loyal said. There were also financial problems, as his practice was not earning much, and Loyal had to borrow to furnish their apartment and pay for a Velie coupe automobile.

So, in search of "security as against an uncertain future," he headed back to Northwestern to train as a neurosurgeon. In 1923 and 1924, Loyal did a stint in Boston working under Dr. Harvey Cushing, considered among the most renowned surgeons in history. (As first lady, Nancy would get the postal service to issue a stamp in Cushing's honor in 1988.) Afterward, Loyal returned to Northwestern and joined the faculty as an associate professor.

Loyal inspired more fear than affection in those he taught. He could call the roll in class by memory and demanded silence in the operating room. On Saturday mornings he held clinics where he drilled first-year medical students on how to take a patient's history and make a diagnosis. For those aspiring physicians, these sessions felt "like sitting on a powder keg waiting for someone to light a match," recalled Harold L. Method, a one-time All-America football player who went on to be a prominent surgeon himself. "Woe to the student who was not properly attired—clean shaven, clean shirt, tie, and jacket." Indeed, Loyal, who sported a stylish wardrobe at a time when most doctors on the hospital staff wore white shirts and gray suits, was known to expel from class students whose grooming and clothes did not meet his standards. "If you are to become a doctor," he decreed, "you must look like one."

But there was another, softer side to Loyal Davis. Frank Stinchfield, a student of his in 1932, was too poor to replace his tattered overcoat. One day he found an expensive new Burberry in his locker, with a note that said only: "For Frank." Not for months would Stinchfield, later a pioneer in hip replacements, discover the identity of his mysterious benefactor. As he recounted the story at a 1982 memorial service for his old professor: "It wasn't until spring cleaning that I discovered a sales slip from Abercrombie & Fitch in an inside pocket, which read: 'Sold to Dr. Loyal Davis.'"

One of the harshest stories about Loyal—difficult to nail down but told often—came to light in *Ronnie and Jesse*, a 1969 book by journalist and biographer Lou Cannon about the political rivalry between the conservative California governor and assembly speaker Jesse Unruh, a fearsome liberal. The detail about Loyal comes as an aside to the book's main narrative.

"A California physician who interned under Dr. Davis remembers that his fellow interns chafed under his strictness. In those days the interns were frequently called to deliver babies in the city's Negro districts, and they would, on occasion, be asked by the mother to suggest a name for the child they had helped bring into the world. The interns invariably suggested the name Loyal Davis, a practice that was brought to the attention of the esteemed surgeon and finally prompted a bulletin board edict that interns were in no case to assist in naming an infant."

In her scorching 1991 biography of Nancy, Kitty Kelley wrote that the interns did this "out of spite" and revulsion to what she claimed was their professor's "virulent racism." Others have denied that bigotry was among Loyal's faults. His longtime medical partner Daniel Ruge, who was also the first Reagan White House physician, told author Bob Colacello in 1981: "I had a patient one time whose name was Loyal Davis Washington. I think it was done more as a joke, but you can't tell. It's true, a lot of people didn't like him. He was a strong personality."

Kelley also wrote that Edie was a racist who once berated actress Carol Channing for bringing the singer Eartha Kitt, an African American, to a party at the Davis apartment. In a letter to Nancy after the book was published, Channing accused Kelley of having "fabricated a malicious story" and offered a vastly different one: "Your mom was a dear friend. When Eartha Kitt called while I was playing in Chicago in 'Wonderful Town' "—which would have been around 1954—"I took her to see your mother, and being the lady that she was, she secured a hotel for Eartha," Channing wrote. "All we theater folk depended on your mother to supply those necessities like schools for our children, doctors, playgrounds—the essentials of life."

Granted, Edie was a product of a different time. She told racist jokes and was known to have used the word *nigger*. But other accounts attest to her empathy with the plight of African Americans in the era before the civil rights movement. In a 1985 interview for the Black Women Oral History Project at Harvard University, Etta Moten Barnett, a contralto and actress who played Bess in George Gershwin's 1942 Broadway revival of *Porgy and Bess*, talked of her own friendship with Nancy's mother. The two of them had gotten to know each other while working in radio in Chicago.

The African American star noted that it was Edith, not she, who voiced characters who spoke in black dialect on the radio programs on which they performed. That was the kind of practice that would make modern audiences cringe. Still, Barnett insisted, Edith "just could not stand discrimination. Any time she thought that I might be going into a situation where I might be discriminated against, she wanted me to let her know. You talk about Miss Lillian—what's his name's mother? You know, Carter's mother." (President Jimmy Carter's mother was known for her kindness to blacks, including receiving them in her parlor in Plains, Georgia, when that was not generally done by whites in the Deep South.) "She could not hold a light to Edith Davis if she got started, because she just couldn't stand it. She just was very much against discrimination, and she let it be known in very good, strong language."

Barnett recalled telling Edie that she planned to bring her granddaughter up to Chicago from Memphis and hoped to enroll her in Girls Latin. According to Barnett's account, Edie replied: "When Nancy went to Latin School, they didn't have any Negroes there. Now, if you have any trouble, you let me know. I don't want no foolishness from those damn people."

There was another thing that Barnett said she noticed when she became friends with Edie: a tension between mother and daughter, who at times seemed like they were almost in a competition for the affection of a man who did not offer it easily. As Barnett put it: "Nancy made on over her father—*step*father —who adopted her, more than she did her mother, like she was probably prouder of him or something."

Or perhaps it was a craving for validation and acceptance. When Loyal arrived in Nancy's life, she became part of a new family, but in at least one important sense, she was still an outsider in her own home. That she did not carry the name of the man she so adored was a source of awkwardness and shame. So it was a momentous day when Nancy Robbins arrived at school with an announcement: "You can call me Nancy Davis from now on."

From the moment she was legally adopted, Nancy would recognize no other identity. She once held up her hands during an interview with Reagan biographer Edmund Morris and declared: "I have his hands—surgeon's hands."

"You mean your real father, not your stepfather's?" Morris asked, perplexed.

Nancy replied, this time more firmly: "I have *my father's* hands."

In the files of the Reagan Library is an essay that Nancy wrote in October 1938, when she was a senior in high school. The composition is titled "Surgeon Extraordinary." For most of it, Nancy described herself in the third person, as the daughter of a most impressive man. Her version of events indicates that she had asked Loyal to adopt her the previous year—in 1937—as a way of "telling him that she was grateful and that as far as she was concerned, he would always be tops." When she made the request to become his daughter, Nancy wrote, "he understood, because by that time, they had reached the place where no words were necessary."

But that is not exactly how it happened. Nancy had engineered her adoption herself, with a preternatural determination for a girl her age. She sought out Orville Taylor, a neighbor who was a lawyer, and asked him how to go about it. On a trip to New York, she met with Kenneth Robbins near Grand Central Station and presented him, apparently by surprise, with papers to sign relinquishing his rights as her biological father. Her account of that meeting is still more evidence that Robbins felt deeply attached to his only child and was not the uncaring figure she later portrayed him to be. He was wounded by her request, as was Nanee Robbins, his mother. "He came with my grandmother to meet me under the clock at the Biltmore Hotel," Nancy recalled. "I explained what I wanted to do, and they agreed, reluctantly. I'm sure it hurt my grandmother terribly."

Then she sent a wire to Loyal in Chicago. Her message contained only two words: "Hi Dad."

Loyal had taken no role in making it happen. As Nancy's son, Ron, put it: "The way she [told] it was that he was happy to adopt her, but that she would need to ask to be adopted. That had to be her desire, her choice, and she needed to make the request. I'm not sure exactly how that went, but that seems a little bit cold to me." Loyal's hesitation stemmed not from a lack of affection but rather from his sense of propriety. He wrote later that adopting Nancy was something he had wished for "very much but was somewhat hesitant to institute the proceeding because her father and paternal grandmother were alive."

The timing of all of this, and precisely how it unfolded, remain vague. Her brother, Dick, told me she was adopted when she was sixteen, which suggests it was around the latter half of 1937 or the first half of 1938. In Girls Latin yearbooks, her name changed from Nancy Robbins to Nancy Davis between her freshman and sophomore years. That puts it at an earlier point, somewhere around 1936. Her adoption petition was not filed in Cook County until later, on April 19, 1938, according to Kitty Kelley's book.

So, her adoption does not appear to have happened as quickly or cleanly as she later claimed it did. What is clear is how badly she yearned for her bond with Loyal to be legally recognized and how slow he was in embracing the idea. She had been living under his roof for at least six years, and possibly close to nine, before her stepfather granted what Nancy wanted more than anything else and claimed her as his daughter. Her attachment to Loyal, her need for the security that came with belonging to him, foreshadowed the intensity of what Nancy would one day feel for Ronnie, though the two most important men in her life were different in nearly every way. The stepfather she held in awe was a prickly figure—a man of high professional standards and inflexible personal ones. Once, over dinner, she asked him what he thought happiness was. Loyal told her: "Nancy, the answer to happiness is almost twenty-five hundred years old, and it's basically what the Greeks said. It's the pursuit of excellence in all aspects of one's life."

From the beginning of their life together, Nancy had spent as much time as she could at Loyal's side. She accompanied him on visits with patients in Joliet and other towns near Chicago. When she was in her teens, Loyal permitted her to watch from a glassed-in balcony as he performed brain surgery. "My father seemed to perform miracles," she said.

Her stepbrother, Dick, was a frequent visitor during Nancy's early years in Chicago and moved in permanently when his mother, Loyal's first wife, Pearl, died of tuberculosis in 1939. As Nancy had, Dick saw his new blended family as the storybook ending to a sad, unsettled chapter of his childhood. "I hate to say it, but I didn't care for my biological mother at all. I really didn't have a mother. She drank a lot," he told me. Dick ran away from home several times.

When he first met his stepsister, the forlorn little boy looked with envy on the life that Nancy was living in Chicago and the affection that his father showered on her. "My first memory of Nancy was probably when she was in the third or fourth grade," Dick recalled. "In those days, she wore a school uniform: tunic, knee socks, and a beret. At the beginning of the school year, my father and I would walk her to the corner of the drive and get her off to school. She had a bouncy gait, was very vivacious, and was a happy child. She would speak to everyone on the way.

"With each step, the tunic, which was too short, would sort of pop up in the air, and we'd see her bloomers. Father would say, 'Richard, Nancy has on those dreadful navy-blue bloomers, doesn't she?' and I would dutifully agree. And then he'd say, with a big, broad smile, 'Isn't she just the most wonderful child?'"

Nancy and Loyal often spoke to each other in pig Latin, treating the made-up language as their secret code. When she was fifteen years old, her brother recalled, Nancy still sat on Loyal's lap. She nestled there as the family listened to the 1936 radio broadcast in which King Edward VIII of Great Britain abdicated his throne to marry the woman he loved, twice-divorced Wallis Simpson, a commoner from America.

Nancy "was a flirt, no doubt about that," Nancy's mother told author Anne Edwards. "Aren't all little girls? She always tried to get Loyal's attention, and he responded. Why wouldn't he?"

There was another reason Loyal and Nancy were so close. In temperament, she was more like her straitlaced adoptive father than like her effervescent biological mother. Her sense of propriety matched his, and she worked hard to win his approval. "He wanted me to earn his love," she once told her daughter, Patti, as though the parental bond were subject to some sort of initiation rite. "He wanted to be sure that I was serious about it. So I did everything he wanted. I never disobeyed him."

Among Nancy's personal papers at the Reagan Library is an undated, typewritten note from Loyal about some unmentioned infraction she had committed. He apparently slipped the missive into her room after she had gone to sleep. "Nancy dear," he began, "I am sorry too that you had a little lapse of memory. We won't do that again, will we? You must always be the ladylike Nancy that you really are, regardless of what other little girls with whom you play do or say.

"Night big boy. Sleep tight. I'll wake you in the morning when I leave."

He signed it "Doctor Loyal," which was the name that Nancy continued to call him after he adopted her. "I knew he would have loved it if I had called him Dad, and in retrospect I wish I had," Nancy said. "But at the time, I just couldn't."

Even after Nancy left for college, her father remained her center of gravity, her primary source of the reassurance she craved. The Reagan Library files contain another letter from Loyal, postmarked December 6, 1939. That was surely a time of both excitement and stress for Nancy. She was adjusting to her first semester at Smith while preparing to make her debut in Chicago a few weeks later. In it, Loyal seems to be trying to soothe some angst on her part:

> Nance dearest,
>
> We've both left unsaid a number of things that each of us knew to be true and fully understood. I'm sure you know I love you, but I'm afraid I haven't told you so enough.
>
> I'm repaid more than enough by your love and respect which you've given me and by knowing you are honest, frank, direct and dependable. These are things which many of us have to acquire in later years, but you have them already. There has never been, and will not be ever, any question in my mind that you are trying to do a good job.
>
> Lots and lots of love dearest
>
> "Poppy"

Nancy's attachment to and reverence for Loyal would beget one of the enduring myths about Ronald Reagan. It would often be said, mostly by Ronnie's friends from Hollywood, that Nancy and her father influenced the future president's conversion from Franklin D. Roosevelt–worshiping union leader to a hard-Right, anti-Communist, antitax crusader. There is no real evidence that was true. Ronnie "was already moving to the right before he met her. He was sitting at the Brown Derby complaining how it made no sense to make more than one or two movies a year because of the ninety percent marginal tax rate," said columnist George Will, who became a confidant of Nancy's. "The idea that she turned Ronald Reagan, that's just one of the myriad ways people had of saying Reagan was a cardboard figure, whereas the more you learn about Ronald Reagan from his diaries and all the rest, the more you realize he was very much his own man and a tough politician."

Though Loyal was rock-hard in his conservatism, and always voted the Republican ticket, he rarely got involved in electoral politics. One exception was in 1940, when he served on the National Committee of Physicians for Wendell W. Willkie for President. The ostensibly nonpartisan organization supported the GOP nominee against Roosevelt, whom it accused of trying to engineer a government takeover of medicine. On the other hand, both Loyal and Edie were close friends with the Democratic politicians who ran Chicago. And Loyal accepted with good humor the fact that his own vote was always canceled out by that of his ardently Democratic wife. "If he had any real interest in politics, I wasn't aware of it. And I know that he didn't influence Ronnie's views," Nancy insisted. "In fact, when Ronnie first decided to go into politics, my father cringed at the prospect of his beloved son-in-law stepping into what he called 'a sea of sharks.'"

What fascinated Ronnie most about his father-in-law was Loyal's deep knowledge of medicine. "A friend would mention a disease, and Reagan could recall word for word what Loyal Davis said would be the progression of it," recalled Michael Deaver, the aide who was personally closest to both of the Reagans. The only major policy question on which

Ronnie is believed to have consulted Loyal was whether to legalize abortion. The issue came up early in his governorship, in 1967, when the legislature presented him with a bill that would give California the most liberal state abortion law in the nation. Loyal helped convince his son-in-law to sign the measure, according to Reagan biographer Cannon.

Loyal did speak up publicly—and showed courage—on other salient, politically charged issues, but they generally had to do with controversies that were roiling his own profession. As early as 1953, more than a decade before a landmark surgeon general's report identified cigarette smoking as a cause of cancer, he was among a group of prominent physicians calling for the tobacco industry to finance extensive research into whether its product was a carcinogen. In 1954 he wrote a provocative novel about a small-town doctor agonizing over euthanasia as he watches the love of his life struggle with hopeless, intolerably painful stomach cancer. Where Loyal waged his most heated public battle was over "fee-splitting": a once-common, unethical practice in which doctors made payments to each other in exchange for referrals. Some in the Chicago Medical Society circulated petitions in the early 1950s calling for him to be expelled, a drastic punishment for challenging the way other physicians made money. The society conducted an investigation. It decided in March 1953 to drop the matter and let him remain in the professional association.

That was not the only area in which Loyal was a thorn in the medical establishment and its way of doing business. He publicly declared that health insurance was no more than a license for doctors to overcharge. Fees, he believed, should be based, as his were, on patients' ability to pay, with factors such as their income, other financial responsibilities, and number of children taken into consideration. When Nancy was first lady of California and later of the nation, she would from time to time get letters from people grateful for the life-saving treatment Loyal had provided them and their loved ones decades before. Often they mentioned how little he had charged them.

Nor did Loyal become any more popular among his fellow surgeons when he declared, at a November 1960 medical meeting in Montreal, that half the operations in the United States were performed by doctors not adequately trained in surgery. "How much of this type surgery is bungled no one knows, and not all of it results in disaster," Loyal said. "Surgeons properly qualified by training and education encounter difficulties in performing operations, but the difference between the qualified and unqualified man is that the former is able to correct the error." Loyal regularly referred to state licensing systems as "legalized mayhem."

Time did not soften Loyal's reputation for arrogance among his professional colleagues and the resentments he fostered in the interns he had traumatized. In 1975, more than a decade after Loyal had retired, a senior medical student named Cory Franklin found himself flustered and struggling through his final oral exam in surgery at Northwestern Medical School. He was sure he would fail. And then came a bewildering final question from the professor who was administering the test: "Who is Loyal Davis?"

Franklin confessed he had no clue.

"That's the right answer!" the professor declared jubilantly. "That SOB thought everyone would remember him forever. I just love to hear students say they don't know who he is."

*

In the years when Loyal was rising professionally, medicine was a prestigious field. But it was no way to get rich—at least, not wealthy enough to afford a Lake Shore Drive standard of living, which for the Davises included having a live-in maid and cook. Loyal charged $500 for a brain operation, and less, if he thought a patient could not afford his standard fee. (Translated into 2020 dollars, $500 in the mid-1930s would have been somewhere in the neighborhood of $10,000.) He got no compensation at all for his position as chairman of the Department of Surgery at Northwestern University's medical school. Things for the Davises tightened financially when World War II began. Loyal was told that his skills were needed in the hospitals that the army was building in the European theater, and he shipped off as a lieutenant colonel consulting on neurological surgery. During the war, he developed a helmet that protected pilots from shrapnel wounds and advanced the treatment of high-altitude frostbite. He would be discharged from the army after a year, when he suffered a bout of amoebic dysentery and then developed a kidney stone.

Though Edie had given up the stage, she had continued—by necessity—to earn money. This had been the case from the beginning of the Davises' marriage. Radio, which in the early 1930s was entering its heyday, offered the aging actress an opportunity to make a new turn. One of her lucrative gigs was on a popular national soap opera, *Betty and Bob.* Edie played two roles on the melodrama, switching back and forth between society matron May Drake, the mother of the main character, Bob, and Gardenia, his black maid. ("Sho is good tuh have you back, Mr. Bob.")

Each workday, Edie would tuck her graying curls under a smart Bes-Ben hat, slip on white kid gloves, and head for the Wrigley Building studio, with a stop at a Merchandise Mart florist for a fresh corsage. She made it her business to have a word with everyone she regularly saw along the way, swapping stories and jokes with the Drake Hotel doorman and with the policeman directing traffic. "She knew them all, and they all knew her," recalled Les Weinrott, who started writing for *Betty and Bob* in the summer of 1936. "It was not uncommon to be walking down Michigan Avenue with Edie and have a cabbie shout, 'Hi, Miz Davis!' "

Edie was working at the CBS station WBBM in the 1940s when she met a twenty-four-year-old announcer named Mike Wallace, later famous for his penetrating interviews on *60 Minutes*. Though she was old enough to be his mother, Edie and the new kid became buddies. "Edie was gregarious and high spirited and, at the time, the bawdiest woman I had ever met," Wallace remembered. "I frequently ran into her in the station's green room, where we all gravitated for coffee and gossip, and invariably, she would greet me with some choice obscenity and then proceed to relate, with lip-smacking glee, the latest dirty joke she had heard." Wallace recalled Edie's daughter, Nancy, as "a prim and proper young lady who often wore white gloves and Peter Pan collars. Although I didn't know her well in those days, she struck me as being shy and reserved—almost the opposite of her exuberant mother."

Exuberance alone, however, was not going to win Edie acceptance into Chicago's elite circles. During the early years after she married Loyal, she had not fit in well with the stuffy doctors' wives at Northwestern University's Passavant Memorial Hospital, where wealthy Chicagoans went for their medical care. The city's social order was not as airtight as that of New York or Boston, but being an actress still carried a whiff of disrepute. Nancy once came upon her mother sobbing in a bedroom after Edie had overheard another woman making a catty remark about her.

Edie found her opening by becoming an organizer and indefatigable fund-raiser for charity. The society pages carried regular tidbits about Edie's work as president of the Women's Faculty Club, where she held card parties for the Northwestern medical school's free clinic, and her role in a $100,000 campaign for Herbert Hoover's Finnish relief effort. During World War II, she put out a public appeal for donations of chocolate cake, chewing gum, and cigarettes for the soldiers coming through the Red Cross Canteen that she helped run. In 1946 Edie led a force of twenty thousand doorbell-ringing women raising money for the Chicago Community Fund. Two years later, she chaired the women's division of the local American Brotherhood campaign, a drive by the National Conference of Christians and Jews "to further interracial and interfaith amity." She also became a regular on the city's best-dressed lists and in 1952 was proclaimed Chicago's "Sweetest Woman of the Year."

Some early accounts of Edie's endeavors included mentions of her young daughter. A photo of fourteen-year-old Nancy appeared in the November 10, 1935, edition of the *Chicago Tribune,* with the caption "Miss Nancy Davis is the daughter of Mrs. Loyal Davis, who is interested in the success of the ball the alumni of Northwestern University will give Friday at the Drake hotel in celebration of the university's 80th anniversary. Miss Davis will attend the ball."

Through all of this, Edie showed her characteristic knack for ingratiating herself with the right people. "I think if you wanted to put it in cruel terms, she was a social climber," her stepson, Dick, told me. "My father was not part of the Chicago establishment, but Edith made it a point to cultivate a friendship of—for instance, Narcissa Thorne. She was Montgomery Ward, very respected, an old Chicago dame. Edith cultivated all of these important women in Chicago and got them on the board of the hospital. My father would object to Edith having dinner parties. She had to force him to have dinner parties and entertain these 'important people.'"

Among Edie's closest confidants was Colleen Moore, the woman she had met at that long-ago party in New York where Edie was carting around her baby. Moore had been among the most famous actresses of the silent-movie era. Her bobbed hair and short skirts helped launch the flapper craze; as the writer F. Scott Fitzgerald once put it, Moore was the torch that lit the "flaming youth" of the 1920s. In 1932 Moore married her third husband, Chicago stockbroker Homer Hargrave Sr., and moved to the Gold Coast, where she and Edie renewed their friendship. Moore and Edie talked nearly every day; Nancy would later name Colleen the godmother of her first child, Patti. Moore was both wealthy and whimsical. At the depths of the Depression, she spent nearly a half million dollars to build an eight-square-foot dollhouse, known as the Fairy Castle. Exquisitely detailed, it stood almost six feet tall. Moore employed nearly a hundred people to construct it.

While Edie was forging a new life in Chicago, she kept up her old connections as well. Her friends from the theater were constantly coming through town. In those days, show people regularly crossed the country by rail between Hollywood and New York, with a stop in Chicago. Many rode in on the luxurious Santa Fe Super Chief, which was known as "the train of the stars." Nancy's godmother, Nazimova, was one such visitor in transit. After a railroad breakdown forced the fading silent-screen star to spend twenty-four hours with the Davises in Chicago in 1940, Nazimova wrote to her longtime lover, actress Glesca Marshall, that eighteen-year-old Nancy was "extraordinarily beautiful, Doodie, and the face which has every right to be bold and assertive has instead a soft dreamy quality. And add to this a figure of 'oomph!' You'd go crazy about the child."

Boldface names were a regular sight at the Davis apartment. "When I came home from school in the afternoon, it wasn't unusual to find Mary Martin in the living room, or Spencer Tracy reading the newspaper, or the breathtaking Lillian Gish curled up on the sofa, talking with Mother," Nancy said. "Spencer Tracy stayed with us so often that he became practically a member of the family."

Indeed, it said something of Edie's diplomatic skills that she managed to maintain a friendship with Tracy's wife, Louise, while also cultivating his costar and paramour Katharine Hepburn, with whom the actor began a celebrated quarter-century-long affair in 1941. Nancy's scrapbook includes news clippings of her mother out and about with both women at various times in Chicago. One item notes: "Spencer Tracy's daughter Susie had her first date here in Chicago last week. Mrs. Loyal Davis, the Tracys' hostess, asked Carl G. Leigh Jr. to arrange a date for just-16 Susie. . . . Miss T, as Mrs. Davis has nicknamed her, wore a small blue and white checked suit and navy blue and white spectator shoes. Her brown hair is cut short. She cut the bangs in front herself."

There was a darker side to those frequent visits by Tracy. He was among the most beloved movie idols of his day, the Oscar-winning star of *Boys Town* and *Captains Courageous*. What his legions of fans did not know was that Tracy was a violent alcoholic who occasionally needed a discreet place to recover from his benders. It was Loyal and Edie to whom he sometimes turned. Loyal, chief of surgery at Passavant Hospital, was able to arrange for Tracy to stay at the hospital on a private floor, where he would be out of the reach of prying gossip columnists. Nancy's stepbrother recalls Tracy—who would later help set up Nancy's screen test at Metro-Goldwyn-Mayer—drying out three or four times at Passavant. "There were, maybe, five or six beds. It was sort of the VIP floor. All hospitals used to have that, until Medicare,"

Dick Davis said. "He was a terribly nice man, just marvelous. I never saw him intoxicated. After he got through this alcoholic withdrawal, he would stay in our apartment for several days and then go on about his business."

Among the Davises' closest friends were Walter Huston and his actress wife Nan Sunderland, who had been the witnesses to Edie and Loyal's secret wedding in 1928. Huston, a one-time vaudevillian, was among the greatest character actors of the era and the patriarch of four generations of performers, including his granddaughter Anjelica Huston. The year Nancy arrived in Hollywood, the man she grew up calling "Uncle Walter" won a 1949 Academy Award for his portrayal of a talkative old prospector in *The Treasure of the Sierra Madre.* His son, John, won the Best Director Oscar for that same movie. (Ronald Reagan, to his everlasting regret, turned down a part in that picture because he was already committed to another one, a modestly successful romantic comedy called *The Voice of the Turtle.*)

Loyal became Huston's doctor and his friend. Nancy's father would jokingly admit to being perplexed that the actor could get $75,000 for doing a movie, while he earned only $500 for a life-saving operation, "and all my care was exceptional." During a couple of summers, the Davises vacationed at Huston's getaway in Running Springs near Lake Arrowhead, California. The actor had a magnificent three-story lodge on the edge of a mountain overlooking the San Bernardino National Forest. After dinner, everyone would sit on a couch that went around the fireplace and listen to him read. Among those who dropped by were the director Joshua Logan and a boyish actor named James Stewart, who played his accordion and sang to Nancy under the stars. She was thrilled when Jimmy Stewart invited her to come dancing with him at the Palladium in Hollywood. Loyal said no.

Nancy was captivated by these earthbound gods and goddesses, who possessed a magical ability to transport the masses into their world of make-believe. As she wrote in her memoir: "One summer we wrote and produced our own little home movie. There I was, *acting*—and with real professionals like Mother, Uncle Walter, and Nan (who had played Desdemona to Uncle Walter's Othello on Broadway). My brother, Dick, was behind the camera, and Uncle Walter and I were the stars."

Huston saw that Nancy had show business ambitions and gently advised Edie to discourage them. While the girl was attractive, her looks—that "soft, dreamy quality" that so captivated Nazimova—were not going to stand out among the busty, blonde sweater girls and dark, smoky beauties who were in favor in Hollywood at the time. "She has a little talent, but she's demure," Huston told Edie, according to Nancy's brother. Dick's own assessment of his stepsister concurred with Huston's: "Socially, she was outgoing, but not in front of an audience. She liked to sing, but did not have a good voice." Katharine Hepburn also told Nancy not to set her heart on making it as an entertainer. "She sent me a long letter warning that acting was a very difficult profession and that I had seen only the glamorous parts," Nancy said. "Mother's friends were stars, she reminded me, but most would-be actresses ended up as waitresses and receptionists. It was sobering advice, but I wasn't put off."

*

Politics was another world to which Edie introduced her daughter during those formative years in Chicago. Urban political machines, such as the one that ran Nancy's hometown, were practical, businesslike endeavors: knowing how to get things done was more important than party labels or ideological purity. The Davises were close friends with legendary—and legendarily corrupt—Democratic mayor Edward J. Kelly and his wife, Margaret, who were their neighbors on East Lake Shore Drive.

Loyal and Edie sat in Margaret Kelly's box at the 1944 Democratic convention in Chicago, where Franklin D. Roosevelt was nominated for an unprecedented fourth term in the White House, despite the open secret among party insiders that the president's health was in serious decline. Mayor Kelly's maneuvering during that convention was instrumental in securing the second spot on the ticket for Missouri senator Harry Truman over sitting vice president Henry A. Wallace, whom Kelly and his allies regarded as too progressive. It would turn out to be a move of historic significance when Roosevelt died less than three months after his 1945 inauguration.

Edie's political connection to the mayor had also put her in a less welcome spotlight. This was back on June 4, 1943, when a headline on the second page of the *Chicago Tribune* blared: "Mystery Veils Identity of a Policewoman." Below it in smaller type was a subhead: "Mrs. Loyal Davis Denies Pay Roll Name Is Hers." The sardonically written story told of an intrigue that arose when city records revealed that a woman by the name of Mrs. Edith Davis, who lived at 199 Lake Shore Drive, was working as a temporary policewoman on the municipal payroll. This Edith Davis—whom city records indicated had the same birthdate and birthplace as Edie claimed—was getting a city salary of $2,141 a year, or northward of $30,000 in today's dollars. The newspaper then hilariously described Edie's reaction when a reporter confronted her:

"Mrs. Loyal Davis, whose first name coincidentally is Edith and who lives at 199 Lake Shore Drive, last evening raised her eyebrows at this bit of news and vehemently denied that she was, or ever has been, a policewoman. Mrs. Loyal Davis is the wife of a prominent neurologist and surgeon serving in the army medical corps overseas as a lieutenant colonel.

"Early in the evening, Mrs. Davis—Mrs. Loyal Davis—was reported by her maid to be at a dinner party, but shortly afterwards she answered her own door with pin curls in her hair and two newspapers under her arm. She denied emphatically that she is or was a policewoman."

Edie, whose newspaper photo caught her without her false teeth in, deflected the embarrassment with her typical flair. At lunch the next day at the Casino Club, she greeted the other society matrons: "Bang, bang! Stick 'em up! I'm Dick Tracy!"

So, what was really going on? The payments to Edie had started the previous August. That was right around the time of Loyal's military enlistment and two years after the cancelation of *Betty and Bob*, when things had become more stressful financially for the Davises. Nancy later offered an elaborate—and unconvincing—explanation for how her mother ended up on the city payroll. While Loyal was overseas, Edie had helped start a Chicago Service Men's Center near the navy yard. Her daughter claimed that when she discovered "some of these young kids were being picked up by prostitutes and infected with venereal diseases, she had herself sworn in as a policewoman so she could go out on the streets of Chicago and protect those boys."

Perhaps Edie was involved in some sort of undercover operation. It is more likely, however, that the mayor was looking for a backdoor way to pay her for political work she was doing on his behalf. That included helping to write, direct, and produce his weekly radio speeches. Kelly, who came from a working-class background, certainly needed the professional assistance. He was famous for his malapropisms, which included pronouncing vitamins as "vitamums," and once introducing Admiral William Halsey, the acclaimed World War II commander, as "Alderman Halsey."

Just twelve weeks before the story of her supposed secret life as a policewoman broke, Edie—a Democrat—gave a radio testimonial in favor of Kelly's reelection titled: "A Republican Woman's Appraisal of Mayor Kelly." She declared, without irony, that "Mayor Kelly has proved his right to be called the best mayor Chicago ever had. There has never been a single scandal connected with his administration which involved either himself of any member of his Cabinet."

One night, when Edie was throwing yet another of her dinners, Loyal was startled to see both Kelly and Republican governor Dwight Green arrive. Surely, he thought, his wife had made some horrible error. The two men had run a bitter campaign against each other in 1939 for Chicago mayor. So Loyal was astonished by what actually happened when they encountered each other in his apartment. Not only did the opposing party bosses greet each other warmly, but after dinner, they huddled in private conversation. The governor then asked to use the phone and, when he returned, assured the mayor that he had "taken care of" whatever it was they had been discussing. "Until then," Loyal marveled, "I thought political rivals must be dyed-in-the-wool enemies but soon learned that this is more apparent in campaigns than it is in the day-to-day administration of government."

Reagan biographer Bob Colacello put it this way: "What Edith understood and Loyal would learn was that power transcends political affiliation, and ideology need not get in the way of social success. In other words, whom you know is more important than what you believe." Those pragmatic lessons about cultivating influence and turning adversaries into allies would not be lost on Edie's daughter.

CHAPTER THREE

When Nancy filled out a questionnaire for the twenty-fifth reunion of her Smith classmates in 1968, the first lady of California listed this as her occupation: "Politics! And wife and mother."

Smith College was, as Girls Latin had been, a rigorous academic environment that catered to daughters of wealth and privilege. Tuition at the time was $600 a year, plus $500 for room and board, which was more than it cost to go to Yale University. "I always had it in my mind that I wanted to go to Smith," Nancy told Judy Woodruff in an interview for a Public Broadcasting System documentary broadcast in 2011. But not many young women came to the Northampton, Massachusetts, campus in 1939 with an eye toward making a professional mark of their own. Fulfilling their dreams meant finding the right mate, raising his perfect children, and keeping dinner warm when he stayed late at his office.

Bettye Naomi Goldstein, a brainy girl from Peoria, was a year ahead of Nancy at Smith. She recalled: "You had no women role models, virtually none, that combined serious work with motherhood [and] marriage, which had become almost exaggerated values for women." Bettye dropped the coquettish *e* from the end of her first name and took her husband's surname when she got married. At her fifteenth reunion in the late 1950s, Betty Friedan did a survey of her Smith classmates and was struck by how unhappy they seemed in their confining lives as highly educated suburban housewives. The former Bettye Goldstein realized she was one of them herself, left with a "nameless, aching dissatisfaction" because she had never pursued a career in psychology after doing graduate work in the field. Friedan's book about what she called "the problem that has no name" was published in 1963. *The Feminine Mystique* became the manifesto that sparked the feminist movement. Those rigid, midcentury values that Friedan rejected were the very ones Nancy Reagan would one day come to represent for scornful feminists. "She has not advanced the cause of women at all," Friedan told *Time* magazine in 1985. "She is like Madame Chiang Kai-shek, doing it the old way, through the man."

At Smith, Nancy was not a particularly serious student. She would later joke that she majored in "English and drama—and boys." When she first stepped onto the ivy-strewn campus, pampered young women still had the luxury of dealing with nothing more nettlesome than finding ways to get around their weekend curfews. But when Nancy was a junior in 1941, everything changed with the bombing of Pearl Harbor and the start of a war that would inflict a crushing toll on her generation. For a perpetually insecure and anxious girl on the cusp of adulthood, those years would be yet another lesson that she could never take security or stability for granted. As Nancy put it later, the most important education she got in college was "that life is not always easy, and romances do not always have romantic endings. I went through difficult changes and emotional experiences, and I learned that you have to take life as it comes and be prepared for sudden twists of fate."

Nancy's initial plan had been to spend a year or two at Smith and then head toward the allure and excitement of the theater. Unless and until the right man came along. But Loyal, whose own education had changed his destiny, insisted she stay and earn her degree. She did what she was told, but not with much enthusiasm or aptitude for academics. "She'd come back from Smith at Christmas, and she was not a good student at all," recalled her stepbrother, Dick. "As a senior at Smith—and I being a senior at the Latin School—I'd do her physics problems for her, which amused everybody." In her 1980 autobiography,

Nancy acknowledged, "I had a terrible time with science and math. My mind just did not seem to function correctly for these subjects."

Her roommate during the first two years was Jean Wescott, her good friend from Girls Latin. They lived steps from the center of campus, on the first floor of Talbot House, which had a cozy living room and a big front porch. Nancy studied on the banks of picturesque Paradise Pond and "gorged myself with the blueberry muffins at Wiggins Tavern." At night, when peanut butter and jelly sandwiches were set out at the dorm, Nancy took three. Her weight shot up to 143 pounds, adding to her already plump five-foot-four-inch frame and prompting Loyal to insist that she watch her diet—which she did, strenuously, for the rest of her life. Her weight and eating habits would become a visible barometer of her anxiety level, dropping sharply if she was feeling under stress. As first lady, Nancy claimed to be a reasonably healthy 106 pounds, but there were persistent rumors that she was anorexic, as well as a legend that she chewed each bite thirty-two times. (Reporters who watched her at meals were known to count under their breaths.) Nancy was also self-conscious about her thick legs—she would later be devastated by a catty journalist who referred to them as "piano legs"—and exercised regularly to trim them.

Even for the sheltered women of Smith, the horrors that were taking place across the ocean were impossible to ignore. Just three weeks before Nancy's first day of classes her freshman year, Adolf Hitler invaded Poland on September 1, 1939. Poland's allies England and France declared war on Germany two days later. Then Hitler took Denmark and Norway in the spring of 1940. Belgium, the Netherlands, and Luxembourg fell shortly after that, and by June 1940, France was occupied by the Germans.

When Nancy returned to Northampton for her sophomore year, the United States was torn over whether to join the allied forces in the cause of stopping the German military. According to a recollection in the Smith College yearbook, "This was the year we sold carnations for Britain one day and gardenias for Peace Day the next. Fortunately, this detachment kept the war from our well-ordered lives." But by the spring semester of 1941, with England bravely carrying on the fight but teetering on the brink of defeat, "the question of our responsibility intruded itself more and more. Drinking champagne at the Tavern was uncomfortably reminiscent of the luxurious appointments of the Maginot Line," the lavish fortifications that had given France a false sense of security.

With all the darkness in the news, there were still diversions. One afternoon Nancy and her friends cut class to watch a murder trial that was going on at the Hampshire County Courthouse. The defendant was a man who had caught his wife with a lover and killed him. "We were all terribly excited about it," Nancy told a reporter forty years later. "I imagined that the wife was going to look like Carole Lombard and the husband would resemble Clark Gable. But when this fat, unattractive couple walked in, it sort of lost its excitement."

The Smith yearbooks from those years carry no mention of Nancy receiving academic distinctions or honors. Nor are there indications that she was a leader in campus activities. But she kept a busy social life. "She was very pretty and popular and always had men come calling," recalled Frances Hawley Greene, Nancy's roommate her junior and senior years. "She had boyfriends at Amherst, Yale, Princeton, and Dartmouth, and she used to go away quite often at weekends."

Her calendar was just as full during breaks from school, some of which were spent in sunny Phoenix, where Loyal and Edie started going to escape the midwestern winters. A *Chicago Tribune* photo from March 1940 shows Nancy in a sarong with a flower in her hair, fixing what would later become famous as "the gaze" on an heir to the Wrigley chewing gum fortune. "Miss Nancy Davis and Wrigley Offield were two young Chicagoans at the South Seas party given recently by Mr. Offield's brother-in-law and sister, Mr. and Mrs. Denis E. Sullivan, Jr., at the Arizona Biltmore in Phoenix," the caption said. "Miss Nancy is spending her spring vacation from Smith with her parents, Dr. and Mrs. Loyal Davis, at the desert hotel."

Her most serious beau was a Princeton student named Frank Birney, the rich, handsome son of a Chicago banker. They had met at Nancy's debutante party, where Birney had been the first member of the Triangle Club to show up. He had sensed her nervousness about her big event and put her at ease by going through the receiving line over and over, making her laugh each time by assuming a different voice and pretending to be an additional guest. When Nancy returned to Smith, she and Frank became an item, seeing each other on weekends. She went to Princeton for football games and dances; Frank came to Smith for parties. Occasionally, they rendezvoused in New York. They began talking, though not all that seriously, about marriage.

Eight days after the December 1941 bombing of Pearl Harbor by the Japanese, Nancy and Frank's courtship came to an abrupt and tragic end. "Frank was planning to go to New York. He must have been late, because he ran across the tracks to catch his train, not realizing how fast the train was moving," Nancy wrote in her 1989 memoir. "The engineer pulled so hard on the emergency brake that he broke it, but he couldn't stop the train, and Frank was killed instantly."

What surely made twenty-year-old Frank Birney's death even harder to accept was the fact that it was not the accident that Nancy and his family claimed it was. He had killed himself. State police concluded he had jumped from behind a pole in front of an eastbound Pennsylvania Railroad express train. The locomotive was going seventy miles per hour when the engineer spotted him and blew the whistle. Frank's mangled body was dragged more than a hundred feet before the train finally came to a stop. He had been carrying no identification or money, which was peculiar for someone supposedly headed to New York. According to a local newspaper account, his classmates told investigators that the Princeton senior "had been in a despondent state lately because his grades had not come up to his own expectations." Frank's mother gave Nancy a silver cigarette case with his name engraved on it, which was a present Nancy had bought for him the previous Christmas. She held on to that keepsake for the rest of her life. "It was the first time that anybody I was close to had died, and it was a tremendous shock," Nancy recalled. "My roommate forced me to go out and take long, brisk walks."

By Nancy's senior year at Smith, the war abroad defined almost everything about life at home. Existence was regimented by Meatless Mondays, gasoline rationing, air-raid drills, blood drives. Women of Smith shoveled their own snow and did without their customary maid service. They looked askance at those who left coffee in their cups or precious butter on their plates. Some of Nancy's classmates helped out local farmers, who were hard pressed by labor shortages. Smith women picked their asparagus and weeded their onions.

There were fewer beaus at the ready to take them out on Saturday nights. In their stead came letters from overseas, which arrived with a censor's stamp. Campus housing and classrooms were bursting at the seams, owing to the fact that much of Smith had been turned over to the first classes of officers for the US Naval Reserve's women's branch, better known as WAVES, an acronym for Women Accepted for Volunteer Emergency Service. A new class of five hundred female midshipmen arrived every month for sixty to ninety days of strenuous training. As the WAVES marched by silently in their uniforms to classes and meals, Smithies noticed themselves standing a little straighter.

Another of Smith's contributions to the war effort—one in which Nancy participated—was the Factory Follies. This was a thirty-three-woman morale-boosting musical troupe that entertained at lunch and break time in more than a dozen war plants across the Connecticut River Valley. Their revue, which toured in the spring of 1943, opened with a chorus marching across the stage, singing:

> Make with the maximum, give with the brawn.
> Make with the maximum, smother that yawn.
> Tell the boys we'll stand behind 'em till the lights come on.
> And we'll make with the maximum.
>
> Make with the maximum, give with the brain.
> Make with the maximum, gonna raise Cain.
> Tell the boys in boats and tanks, tell the guy who flies a plane.
> That we'll make with the maximum.

Switch on, contact, turn on the juice,
Double the output, and here's my excuse:
Life can be pretty when you're being of use.
Hey! Fellas! We've gotta produce.

Nancy played the sophisticated "Glamour Gal," a shirker on the production line. Glamour Gal lamented that she missed her prewar life of luxury:

Maybe you're right
But the yacht was fun,
Cocktails at five and
Dinner at the Stork,
Long drives in the country,
To get away from New York.

Nancy also acted in a few plays on campus, including a musical comedy called *Ladies on the Loose*. At one of the college's annual Rally Day shows, she and her classmates tap-danced in Morse code, and sang: "Dit-dit-dit-dah! We'll win this wah." But Smith was not known as a training ground for serious actresses. She was one of only three theater majors in 1943. The college did not even have a full-fledged theater department until her senior year. The closest thing Nancy got to actual professional experience was on summer breaks, when she apprenticed on "the straw-hat circuit" doing summer stock in Wisconsin and New England. She cleaned dressing rooms, painted scenery, sold tickets, and tacked up flyers around town. Only rarely did she get to act. In her three years of summer stock, Nancy delivered a total of one line—"Madam, dinner is served"—when she played a maid in a production starring Diana Barrymore, a lesser member of the famous theater family.

In 1941 Nancy worked at the Bass Rocks Theater in Gloucester, Massachusetts, where she developed what she remembered as a "big crush" on one of its visiting stars, Buddy Ebsen. He would become most famous for his starring role as Jed Clampett in the 1960s TV sitcom

The Beverly Hillbillies, but at the time, Ebsen was known for movies that put his dancing talent to use. Backstage, Nancy was so entranced by one of his performances that she forgot her own task, which was to turn on the musical sound effect when his character pretended to play a Victrola. Nancy realized her mistake, fumbled, and started the tune late, then rushed out of the theater in tears. Ebsen "followed me outside and told me it was all right, not to worry, and the world was brighter again," she said. As starstruck as she obviously was, Nancy in later life downplayed the idea that she'd ever harbored serious ambition: "When I graduated, I went on to become an actress, not really because I wanted a career. I was never really a career woman, but only because I hadn't found the man I wanted to marry. I couldn't sit around and do nothing, so I became an actress."

May commencement ceremonies for the 408 women of the Smith College class of 1943 were somber and spare. Bowing to shortages and to the national mood, the college dispensed with the gayest of its traditions. There was no parade of colorfully dressed alumnae waving placards with witty slogans, no procession of juniors with a train of ivy on their shoulders, no roses carried by the seniors. Attendance was limited to parents and families of the graduates, who had to stay in the dorms because there was nowhere else to house them. Loyal, still stationed in Europe, did not make it back for the ceremony; nor, apparently, could Edie, because of wartime travel restrictions that gave priority on trains to military personnel. The college did broadcast a special program from Smith president Herbert Davis's house. "The class of 1943 did not go, as commencement orators used to be fond of saying, out into the world. For four years, they have participated, as students, in a world at war," the announcer said. "They are not leaving the little world for the great world; they have lived in the great world all along."

On graduation day, about twenty-five members of Nancy's class were already married, and a greater number were engaged to be. She herself was dating a wealthy Amherst College boy off and on. Just over a year later, in June 1944, Nancy announced her plans to marry

James Platt White Jr., who by then was stationed on an aircraft carrier in the Pacific. "The young couple met during their college days and renewed their friendship when Navy orders took Lieutenant White to Chicago," the city's *Daily News* noted. "Both brunette, they made an attractive couple at parties and benefits during the year in which he was stationed in Chicago on the aircraft carrier *Sable*." When her godmother Nazimova was introduced to Nancy's fiancé over dinner, he made a strong impression. Nazimova wrote in her diary: "I think I met one of our great future statesmen, perhaps even a president."

Their intention was to be married when the war ended, but Nancy abruptly canceled the engagement shortly after it was announced. "It was a heady, exhilarating time, and I was swept up in the glamour of the war, wartime engagements, and waiting for the boys who were away. I realized I had made a mistake. It would have been unfair to him and to me. It wasn't easy to break off the engagement, but it was the best thing for us both. We were not meant to be married, but we remain friends," she wrote in her 1980 memoir.

Her brother has a different explanation: when White came home on leave, Nancy discovered he was homosexual. White "was extremely handsome and was a naval aviator, and they had, sort of, a rendezvous or a pre-engagement party in California, when she found out he was gay," Dick Davis told me. This discovery was not something Nancy ever discussed with her stepbrother. "Edith told me, actually. Edith would know things like that, you know, about everybody," he said.

After Nancy became a nationally known political figure, her past romantic life was a sensitive subject. Dick said she "went to great trouble when she got to the White House" to make sure that no one ever learned the truth about the breakup of her first engagement. White, who became a partner in a New York City importing firm, was discreetly silent about their long-ago betrothal. "All I can tell you, all I will tell you, is that Nancy was a lovely, lovely girl. It was just one of those wartime things," he told *Parade* magazine in one rare interview. When White became seriously ill, he got in touch with the nation's first lady indirectly through her friend Jerry Zipkin, a fixture on the New

York City social scene who was also gay. It was through Zipkin that Nancy learned White had died.

From the time she was a young woman, many of Nancy's closest friends were gay. "Nancy's affinity for homosexual men has been frequently remarked upon, but it would hardly have been so noteworthy if she had stayed in show business instead of marrying an actor who went into politics. She was close to a number of lesbian and bisexual women over the years, starting with her godmother and her circle of friends, but this, too, is not unusual in the entertainment world," biographer Colacello noted. "If gay men were attracted to the young Nancy Davis, it was probably for the same reasons that straight men were: she was pretty, lively, well dressed, a good dancer, a great listener, and, like her mother, a natural-born coquette. She knew how to flirt with a man in a way that was flattering and unthreatening, which may explain why gay men felt especially comfortable with her. And when she was out with a man, she gave him her full attention."

*

Having broken her engagement in the summer of 1944, Nancy once again found herself confronting an uncertain, unmoored future. She had returned to Chicago after her graduation to be with her mother while Loyal remained overseas. Edie had temporarily sublet the Lake Shore Drive apartment and moved into the Drake Hotel, no doubt to lift some of the strain on their finances. Nancy looked for ways to fill her days. She joined the Chicago Junior League and volunteered twice a week at the Service Men's Center, the military social club that her mother had helped set up. She also worked as a salesgirl at Marshall Field's, Chicago's flagship department store. It was an experience memorable mostly for the time she chased down a female shoplifter she had spotted slipping a piece of jewelry into her purse. Nancy also trained as a nurse's aide at Cook County Hospital. Her first patient died as she was giving him a bed bath, something Nancy didn't realize until she asked a medical resident why the sick man's skin had gotten so oddly cold on a hot day.

Nancy was growing restless and bored. Her salvation came when she received a call from her mother's famous friend ZaSu Pitts, a comedienne with doleful eyes and a warbly voice, who was known for playing ditzy characters. Pitts was taking her Broadway play *Ramshackle Inn* on the road and offered Nancy a tiny part. It did not take much acting skill. She played a girl who was kept in the attic, except for one scene in which she burst onto the stage and said three lines. Though a small start, Nancy was grateful and recognized her good fortune was not of her own doing. "This wouldn't be the last time I benefited from Mother's network of friends in show business," she wrote. "I don't think I would have had much work as a stage actress if it hadn't been for Mother. There was just too much competition, and I didn't have the drive that Mother had."

She joined the cast in Detroit. Reviews of the production were brutal, but audiences turned up anyway to see Pitts. It "played eight months in New York and two years on the road despite the disdain of most critics," a Boston newspaper noted. As *Ramshackle Inn* made its way across the country, Nancy and Pitts became close. The star shared her hotel rooms and dressing rooms with the young actress, who became her protégée. They eventually ended up back in New York, and the play closed in the summer of 1946.

Nancy decided to stay in New York and try her luck there. For a twentysomething just after the end of World War II, there could hardly have been a more exciting place to live than Manhattan. With other world capitals in ruins, Gotham took on a swagger. Scarcity and sacrifice were suddenly things of the past. An unprecedented building boom was under way. The nightclubs and theaters were packed. Broadway was at the dawn of a golden era. But finding her own way to the footlights was a challenge and an ordeal. Nancy modeled a bit, took acting and voice classes. She forced herself to show up for auditions that she found "frightening and embarrassing" but did not land many parts. She was fired from one she did get, on the third day of rehearsal. The director told her, "It's just not working."

The only Broadway role she ever snagged was playing a lady-in-waiting named Si-Tchun in the 1946 musical *Lute Song*. That production would be remembered as the first big break for a young Russian-born actor named Yul Brynner. Nancy was not among his fans. "All the girls were so crazy about Yul. One young girl I remember committed suicide over him," Nancy told interviewer Judy Woodruff of PBS. "I wasn't too impressed, really. Every time he'd tell a story about his background, it always changed."

Nancy had read for the part in producer Michael Myerberg's office. "After all of the tryouts, readings, refusals, and waiting for refusals by telephone, it was unbelievable how swift and easy it was when I heard the magic words, 'You've got the part,'" she recalled. But she was puzzled when the producer added: "You look like you could be Chinese." The real story was that the show's leading lady—Mary Martin, another of Edie's friends—had demanded Nancy be given the job. Martin intervened again when the director John Houseman tried to get rid of Nancy during the early weeks of rehearsals. She had dyed her hair black but was unconvincing as a Chinese handmaiden. "John," his star told him, "I have a very bad back, and Nancy's father Loyal Davis is the greatest [neurosurgeon] in the USA. We are not letting Nancy go." Only later, in Houseman's memoirs, did Nancy learn that her first big break was not due to her talent. Houseman wrote that he had offered her the role through "the usual nepotistic casting. . . . At Mary's behest, to play the princess's flower maiden, we engaged a pink-cheeked amateurish virgin by the name of Nancy Davis."

When *Lute Song* closed after only four months, ZaSu Pitts came through with parts for Nancy in two more plays, one of which was a touring revival of a comedy called *The Late Christopher Bean.* An August 1947 review of an early performance at the Saratoga Spa Playhouse in upstate New York takes note near the end of "a Miss Nancy Davis, who looks wholesome as a ripe red apple, even though little is required of her except to be the decent one of the two Haggett daughters." Nancy pasted her reviews, even tepid ones, into her scrapbook, along with congratulatory cards and telegrams. Many were from famous names such as the Tracys and the Hustons. Others were not so well known, but meaningful. One note, delivered with flowers for the Chicago opening of *Christopher Bean,* was from the lawyer and Lake Shore Drive neighbor who had helped arrange Nancy's adoption by Loyal. It said: "To my adorable Nancy from your general counsel and greatest admirer, Orville Taylor."

Her life in a fourth-floor walkup at 409 East Fifty-First Street had its frustrations, but it was not exactly one of hardship. Nancy got around on the crosstown bus and felt safe walking home through Midtown Manhattan late at night. Loyal and Edie kept her afloat financially. Though she was a young, single woman, Nancy was drawn to her parents' mature circle of friends, who helped keep her occupied. "Fortunately, I wasn't entirely alone in the big city. When I was living on East Fifty-First Street, the Hustons had an apartment around the corner. Lillian Gish, another family friend, had one nearby. They often took me out to eat or to a show, or had me over to little parties," she recalled. "I used to go watch Spence rehearse for a play he was opening in, *The Rugged Path.* He was very nervous about returning to the stage, but he was very good, as he always was." Tracy's mistress Katharine Hepburn, who lived on East Forty-Ninth Street, had an aversion to going out and often invited Nancy over to keep her company.

Nancy also dated, though no one exclusively. Her social life intertwined with her professional ambition. Nancy kept company with Max Allentuck, a prominent theater manager who worked with some of the biggest producers of the era; they remained friendly enough that in 1981, when one of his plays came to Washington, she invited him to lunch and to tea at the White House. Her most frequent companion was Kenneth Giniger, the publicity director at publisher Prentice Hall. This friendship was another of Edie's arrangements. Giniger sometimes booked his authors for interviews on a midmorning radio show that Edie hosted in Chicago. When Edie suggested he look up her daughter in New York, he did. Giniger took Nancy to see-and-be-seen nightspots such as the Stork Club and El Morocco, and made sure her name popped up occasionally in the newspaper columns.

One day in the fall of 1948, Edie called her daughter to let her know that if she heard from someone who said he was Clark Gable, she should not assume it was a prank. The movie star known as the "King of Hollywood" was coming to New York, and Spencer Tracy had given him Nancy's number. Sure enough, Gable called, and the two of them went out every day for a week, usually ending up at the Stork Club. Gable charmed Nancy; he sent flowers, and they held hands. "He had a quality that good courtesans also have—when he was with you, he was really *with* you," Nancy recalled later.

This was never a serious romance, however. The *Gone With the Wind* star was twenty years older than Nancy and in a rocky phase of his life. Gable was drinking too much, was having a string of affairs, and had never truly gotten over the death of his third wife and soulmate, actress Carole Lombard, in a 1942 plane crash.

Still, being seen with him created a brief and welcome stir around Nancy. The movie magazines and gossip columns buzzed with speculation about the famous star and the unknown actress. Those clippings, too, made it into Nancy's scrapbook. Typical was one that said: "At the party in New York that Tommy Joyce gave in honor of Clark Gable and Walter Pidgeon, Clark arrived with Nancy Davis on his arm. Nancy, according to my informant, is a beautiful little brunette. Clark gave her the typical Gable treatment, devoting himself to her—so much so that some of the people present said, 'This is it!'" Another, apparently from a Chicago newspaper, reported: "A twosome that has New York agog is our Nancy Davis and the great Clark Gable who are seen together hitting the night spots every evening. Nancy is the beautiful and talented daughter of Dr. and Mrs. Loyal Davis." Probably closest to the truth was what Dorothy Kilgallen wrote in her syndicated column, The Voice of Broadway: "Nancy Davis, the lass who dated Clark Gable so often on his last visit here, wasn't unhappy about the resulting publicity. She has theatrical ambitions."

Nancy was realistic enough to recognize that, as she once put it, "I wasn't setting show business on fire." In the six years after she graduated from Smith, she performed in only four plays—three of them thanks to the beneficence of her mother's friend ZaSu Pitts. She also knew that as she moved into her late twenties, casting directors would no longer be looking at her for ingenue roles on the stage. There was no true love in sight to carry her away from all of it—and a real danger of developing a reputation as a girl whose phone number gets passed around a lot.

So, Nancy decided to try something different, making a professional move that more established stage actors of the day would have considered to be beneath them. She began taking roles in the new medium of television, some of it in low-budget, live dramas on *Kraft Television Theatre*. "Enthusiastic about television, Nancy looks forward to the day when video will have its own stars, would like a dramatic show of her own," *Mademoiselle* magazine wrote in November 1948. That sounded far-fetched at the time. Four major networks were broadcasting prime-time schedules seven nights a week, but fewer than 6 percent of Americans had television sets in their homes, and just 44 percent told a Gallup opinion poll they had ever even seen a program.

Edie might have influenced her daughter's openness to television, as Nancy's mother had been an early enthusiast. She launched Chicago's 1946 Community Fund Drive with a Monday-night broadcast from the studios of WBKB, which had just that year received its license to become the first commercial TV station outside the eastern time zone. Two screens were set up in the window of the Fair Store on State Street—a giant department store where Ronald Reagan's father had once worked as a clerk—so that the curious could get what the *Chicago Tribune* called "their first helping of television." It caused a sensation. "A vacationing Iowan postponed his shopping to take in the entire show," the *Tribune* wrote. The newspaper raised the possibility that someday "it will be as much fun to sit in your favorite armchair and view famous entertainers as it will be to observe the efforts of athletes. More, maybe."

Early black-and-white technology was crude, requiring actors to slather on greenish pancake makeup and black lipstick. Performers farsighted enough—or desperate enough—to venture into television did not exactly get star treatment. "Television, by the way, is difficult work for an actress," Nancy told columnist Inez Wallace a few years later.

"There is no pay for rehearsals, as there is in radio or stage work. And the worst of that is that television requires more rehearsals than either of the other two vehicles. And the makeup on television is ghastly. It makes a young girl of sixteen look like an old hag." Still, it was work. In early 1949 Nancy's agent phoned. Someone at Metro-Goldwyn-Mayer had seen her in a TV production of an obscure comedy called *Broken Dishes.* They wanted to bring her out to California for a screen test. "This was one opportunity that none of my family friends had anything to do with," she marveled. This bolt from the blue is her version of events. Later, it would be said that, once again, others had a hand in arranging Nancy's move to Hollywood.

She started packing as soon as she hung up the phone. Her next call was to her mother. Edie swung into action, getting in touch with her old friend Spencer Tracy, who, as it happened, was one of the studio's most bankable stars. He was happy to assist. Not only was he close to the Davises, but he owed them for helping him through the darkest hours of his battles with alcohol. And he was grateful to Nancy personally for the kindnesses she had shown to his deaf son, John, who stayed with her when he was visiting New York.

Tracy made sure that Nancy's would be no pro forma screen test conducted by the usual technicians the studio assigned to unknowns. He arranged for it to be directed by the celebrated "woman's director" George Cukor, who had a gift for drawing out magical performances from actresses such as Katharine Hepburn in *The Philadelphia Story,* Greta Garbo in *Camille,* and a female ensemble cast that included Joan Crawford, Norma Shearer, and Rosalind Russell in *The Women.* Reading lines with Nancy was the promising actor Howard Keel, newly signed by MGM. Camera work was done by George Folsey, who over his career was nominated thirteen times for cinematography Oscars. MGM gave her weeks of coaching in advance.

Cukor privately deemed her to have no talent. But in his hands, Nancy did well enough. In early 1949 she signed a seven-year, $250-a-week contract, with an option for the studio to terminate. Many years later, Nancy would learn to her great amusement that MGM's commitment to her was one reason the studio took a pass on a promising young bit actress named Marilyn Monroe.

The studio system that ran Hollywood was nearing the end of its heyday, but the fantasy factories still controlled the destinies of actors and actresses. And none of the Big Five studios was so powerful or prestigious as Metro-Goldwyn-Mayer. It was run by Ukrainian immigrant Louis B. Mayer, a junk dealer's son who had moved west from Massachusetts. The tyrannical Mayer had built a star-making machine like nothing ever seen before. Movies, he said, were "the business of making idols for the public to love and worship and identify with. Everything else was secondary." Or as Elizabeth Taylor, one of his biggest successes, once put it: "L. B. Mayer and MGM created stars out of tinsel, cellophane, and newspapers."

To Nancy, joining Metro felt like "walking into a dream world." The opportunities for an actress under contract were endless: she could study French, or take lessons in singing and horseback riding. She could go on the sets and learn by seeing how the greatest actors and actresses did it. "Everything was a big step up for me when I signed with Metro, everything," she remembered later.

There have been more than a few theories as to how and why someone of Nancy's modest accomplishments got such special consideration and treatment from the powerhouse of Hollywood studios. Her arrival generated no small amount of jealousy and sniping on the MGM lot. Many years later, after she had become a household name, salacious tales would circulate in Hollywood about the extent and nature of Nancy's sexual activity in her days as a young actress. Some of this should be treated skeptically. Nancy was far from the first woman to become famous and then find that men who knew her in her early days were boasting about her supposed availability. If a few of these stories were true, it would hardly have been unusual for a thirtyish single woman to have a healthy interest in sex. And no daughter of Edie's would have been naive about how things worked.

What appears to have been the case is that several forces beyond Tracy's influence were at work on her behalf. One of them was the fact that she had drawn the interest of Benjamin Thau, MGM's vice president of talent. "I always recommended Nancy for parts. She was sweet and appealing—one of the most popular girls on the lot," he said later. Thau, a middle-aged and unprepossessing bachelor, was known for demanding sexual favors from actresses. His "casting couch" was said to be the busiest in Hollywood. Nancy was widely presumed, both at the time and since, to have been his girlfriend. In his book *Make-Believe: The Story of Nancy & Ronald Reagan,* author Laurence Leamer wrote that Nancy regularly spent Saturday mornings closeted with Thau in his office suite.

It would be nearly seventy years before women in Hollywood would stand up against harassment and join with other feminist voices to launch the #MeToo movement. Back in the 1940s, sexual favors were seen as part of the bargain for actresses seeking good roles. When he was an old man, Thau claimed to Leamer that even Nancy's screen test had been his idea. He, like Gable, had been given her number as someone to call when he was in New York—from a friend who told him she was "a nice girl who likes company." While they were at dinner in Manhattan in early 1949, he recalled suggesting, "Nancy, why don't you come out and make a screen test?"

Some details of his story do not add up. For instance, as biographer Colacello noted later, Thau claimed he and Nancy had gone to see Spencer Tracy onstage—which was impossible, because Tracy's final play had closed two years before Thau's date with Nancy supposedly took place. However, Nancy's own scrapbook indicates that she and Thau did have some kind of relationship after she arrived in Hollywood. He appears in a newspaper photo with Loyal and Edie. The clipping does not have a date, but clues suggest Thau and Nancy's parents were together in Arizona just a few weeks after Nancy signed with MGM. They are shown chatting during the intermission of a production of *Born Yesterday* at Phoenix's recently opened Sombrero Playhouse. The show started its run at the end of March 1949. Nancy is not in that picture with Thau and her parents, but she and he are together in one from July 1950, which was more than a year later. They are seated at a table celebrating Nancy's twenty-ninth birthday at the Cocoanut Grove, a leading night spot in Los Angeles. The other couple in the photo are MGM chief Louis B. Mayer and his wife, Lorena. Nancy is the only one of the four wearing a smile.

For her part, Nancy insisted to Colacello that there had been no blind date with Thau in New York and that the two of them had never been an item. "When I came out to Los Angeles to do the test and stayed—yes, then I saw him, had dinner with him, and so on," she said. "I was *not* his girlfriend. He took a liking to me, that's true . . . and I liked him as a friend."

But as Colacello pressed her—asking, for instance, whether Thau grew jealous when she began going on dates with other men, including Ronnie—Nancy became blunter and more candid in her answers. "I don't know. I was not *his*," she insisted. "He would have liked to have married me. I did not want to marry him. . . . He was a strange little man, really. He gambled a lot. I think he gambled all his money away. I finally got through to him that the answer was no. And that was it."

What may also have ended things was the fact that Loyal had taken a strong dislike to Thau and told his daughter so. Fortunately for Nancy, the vice president of talent was not her only important ally in the studio's executive offices. Her well-bred manner made a good impression on Dore Schary, MGM's cerebral, socially conscious head of production. Where studio chief Mayer had built his reputation on splashy star-making extravaganzas, Schary was interested in producing quieter "message pictures" that had a story to tell and a lesson to teach. (This clash of philosophies would help bring about Mayer's ouster in 1951, with Schary replacing him as MGM president.) Schary took a shine to the surgeon's daughter partly on Tracy's recommendation. "The girl knows how to look like she's really thinking when she's onstage," Tracy told him.

Nancy was getting a late start by Hollywood standards, so one of the first things she and the studio did was shave two years off her age, declaring her to be twenty-five years old instead of the twenty-seven she actually was. On the publicity questionnaire she filled out shortly after signing her contract, Nancy listed as her phobias "superficiality, vulgarity, esp. in women, untidiness of mind and person—and cigars!" Asked for the rules by which she governed her life, Nancy offered an answer that might in later years have a familiar ring to those among her husband's advisers who crossed her: "Do unto others as you would have them do unto you. I believe strongly in the law of retribution—you get back what you give." Most telling of all was what she stated as her greatest ambition: "to have a successful, happy marriage."

Judging by the volume of clippings in her scrapbooks, MGM made sure Nancy got some buzz, no small share of it along story lines the studio PR men manufactured. There was a four-page photo spread in *Movie Stars Parade* magazine of a young Peter Lawford going on a date with "city slicker Nancy Davis" and teaching her how to ride a horse. Another, in *Movie Life,* shows fellow contract players, supposedly her pals, helping her move into a new apartment. In some columns, Nancy offered beauty tips. One of the more puzzling was a recommended nightly moisturizing ritual, as reported in *McCall's,* that was capped off by Nancy's advice to "take a wooden picnic fork and slide gently over and over your face until all cream has disappeared." For publicity shoots, Nancy wore clothes loaned from Amelia Gray's high-priced boutique in Beverly Hills. The practice of borrowing or accepting free designer styles was standard in Hollywood but would get her in trouble when she got to the White House.

MGM's publicity machine recycled and inflated the intrigue around Nancy's handful of dates with Gable, turning it into a supposed rivalry with actress Ann Sheridan, known from her World War II pinups as the "Oomph Girl." A June 1949 feature in *Modern Screen* was headlined, "Which Girl Has the Gable?" The magazine noted archly how Nancy had come out of nowhere to land an MGM contract and offered a preposterous theory that Gable had engineered it all: "In the movie business, made-to-order success like this doesn't come very often—and that's just the thing. The path to fame she is walking seems to be so expertly paved, so conveniently shortened and cleared of all the usual difficulties, that there's a touch of magic about it. And when you look around for whomever may be waving the potent wand that's accomplishing all this for her—darned if an awful lot of things don't point to the Great Gable himself." As for which girl would get the Gable, the star himself answered the question six months later, when he married Lady Sylvia Ashley, a British model, actress, and socialite. He was back on the market three years later, however.

Though the Hollywood columnists were being told by their MGM whisperers to keep an eye on Nancy as "a comer," she did not strike some as obvious movie star material. Columnist Inez Wallace wrote: "When Nancy Davis was pointed out to me on the MGM lot, I couldn't believe they intended to build her up. She looks more like a character actress than a leading lady, although she is really a cross between Kathryn Grayson and Claudette Colbert."

Wallace was assured that Nancy was still a work in progress. "'Wait until a year from now, when Nancy has had the glamour treatment,' I was told, 'and you'll never recognize the girl you see now. They all look like that when they first come out here. But after our makeup men and hairdressers get through with them, they seem to have a new face and a new personality,'" the columnist informed her readers.

Nancy's yellowed trove of breathless press clippings notwithstanding, she would never get the "glamour treatment," at least not on the screen. She nearly always played pre-matronly types, the competent secretary, the perfect wife, but without the breezy edge someone like Myrna Loy brought to that kind of part. The columnist Walter Winchell noted in 1951: "Nancy Davis has the unique distinction of being pregnant in all but one of her movies."

Most of the eleven pictures she did, Nancy herself acknowledged, "are best forgotten." Some were simply dreck. Her lack of success surely did not calm her insecurities in an environment where, as she noted, she might spot Lana Turner in the commissary at lunch or be seated in a makeup chair next to Ava Gardner. Still, Nancy was a more talented and supple actress than she is usually given credit for being. Cary Grant, who once did a screen test with her, said afterward, "She did something many actors didn't know how to do. She listened to the other actor." Her acuity about the people around her, which she had honed from childhood as a survival skill, came through in her performances. As Reagan biographer Edmund Morris once described it, "her gift was to vibrate like a membrane to the sonority of other speakers."

Today her acting abilities tend to be judged by the worst of her pictures, which still show up on cable television now and then. These are usually ones from the latter, leaner years of her film career. One of the most dreadful of these low-budget projects was 1957's *Hellcats of the Navy*, costarring her and Ronnie, as both of their film careers hit bottom. "That picture ended movies for me," Ronnie later said. A better gauge of Nancy's talents was her first starring role, in Schary's *The Next Voice You Hear*. The movie was not a hit and did not age well, but Nancy's reviews were solid. The *New York Times* described her as "delightful as [the] gentle, plain, and understanding wife."

*

Her personal life was a relatively quiet one by Hollywood standards. Nancy lived in an apartment in the comfortable Westwood section of Los Angeles's west side and hired a woman to come in three days a week to clean and cook. She went to dinner parties and on dates that were often arranged by the studio. "I had always heard stories about the wild side of Hollywood, but I never saw much evidence of it—the heavy drinking, the drugs, promiscuity, and all the rest," she wrote later. "I'm not so naive as to think that such things never went on; they do in every town. But it wasn't part of my life. I wasn't a starlet either on or off the screen."

In September 1950 Louella Parsons, one of the reigning queens of the gossip columns, asked Nancy if there was a special man in her life. "Not yet," she replied. "I won't be trite and say I am married to my career, but that's pretty much the truth." Except that it wasn't the truth. In fact, Nancy already had fixed her sights on the man she was convinced was The One. The question was how to pin him down—and how to convince him that she was the woman who could mend his broken heart.

CHAPTER FOUR

"You know," Ronald Reagan once mused, "if Nancy Davis hadn't come along when she did, I would have lost my soul."

The once-upon-a-time version of how the two of them met went like this: one evening in late October 1949, as Nancy was reading the *Hollywood Reporter*, a leading entertainment industry trade daily, she spotted her own name on a list of 208 supposed Communist sympathizers. It was alarming to see "Nancy Davis" among them. Suddenly the young contract player understood why she had been getting mail from left-wing organizations.

With the Red Scare enveloping and dividing Hollywood, there was plenty of reason to be worried about being tagged as a Communist, especially if you were an actress who had just arrived. At the time, Nancy was making a movie called *East Side, West Side* and went to its renowned director, Mervyn LeRoy, for advice on how to straighten out this error. The studio arranged for friendly columnists to write items pointing out that the person mentioned on the list was *another* actress named Nancy Davis. Two of those stories, dated November 1 and November 7, are pasted in Nancy's scrapbook. One noted: "When a young actress, who happens to be 100 percent American, comes face-to-face with the fact that another woman whose name is identical is active in 'extra liberal activities'—that calls for a double dose of aspirin."

Nancy wasn't satisfied, so she asked LeRoy to get in touch with Ronald Reagan, the president of the Screen Actors Guild. (Ronnie said later that he was disappointed when he realized the famous director wasn't calling to offer him a part.) LeRoy reported back to Nancy that SAG would stand behind her. By then, however, she had decided nothing short of a face-to-face with the union president would settle her nerves. At least, that's what she told LeRoy. In truth, "I had seen some of his pictures, and, on-screen, at least, he seemed nice and good-looking—someone I wanted to meet," Nancy would admit later.

Ronnie called and suggested dinner that night. It would have to be a quick one. He claimed to have an early call at the studio the next morning. Nancy recognized that as a standard white lie employed by Hollywood people. It was a bail-out option against the possibility that a blind date would turn out to be a dud. So, her pride a little bruised, Nancy fibbed that she had an early call too.

She opened the door of her apartment two hours later to a man who in the flesh was every bit as handsome as she had seen on-screen—even though he was leaning on two canes. During a charity baseball game, Ronnie had broken his right thighbone in a half dozen places. He had just been released from the hospital after having spent nearly two months in traction. For his part, Ronnie had expected a typically flashy MGM starlet. He saw instead "a small, slender young lady with dark hair and a wide-spaced pair of hazel eyes that looked right at you and made you look back."

They headed to trendy LaRue's on the Sunset Strip. Ronnie told Nancy there was a simple solution to her problem. "Have the studio change your name," he said. "You would hardly be the first." Naturally, he couldn't have known how much it meant to her to be called Nancy Davis, or the years she had waited, or the effort she had put into earning the validation that came with that identity. There could be only one reason she would ever change it—and it wasn't her career. She replied firmly: "Nancy Davis is my name."

Before long, the pretexts of having to be home early for sunrise calls were forgotten. Nancy was entranced by Ronnie's lack of movie-star ego and his seemingly bottomless inventory of amusing stories. As for him: "I had discovered her laugh and spent most of my time trying to say something funny. A lot of George Burns and Georgie Jessel material got an airing that night, and not always with credit given." He was fascinated to learn that she was the daughter of a brilliant surgeon and had grown up in a household where movie legends like Spencer Tracy and Walter Huston were practically family. Ronnie also discovered she had never seen the ribald entertainer Sophie Tucker, known as the "Last of the Red Hot Mamas," who was opening at Ciro's nightclub a block away. They went for the first show and stayed for the second one. Despite his bum leg, Ronnie gamely tried some steps on the dance floor with Nancy. They had a late snack afterward with Tucker herself, and it was three thirty before they called it a night. "I don't know if it was love at first sight, but it was something close to it," Nancy recalled.

So goes the opening scene of the script for their love story. It appeared that fate's hand was at work, bringing together by seeming happenstance two people who were perfect for each other. But, in fact, Nancy had been looking for a way to catch Ronnie's eye, though he apparently was oblivious. Jill Schary Robinson, the daughter of MGM production head Dore Schary, claims that her mother had invited both Nancy and Ronnie to a dinner party some weeks before their supposedly blind date. Jill was only a teenager, but she knew that something was up with Nancy, relating to me, "Even I could see she was dazzled by Mr. Reagan." Her mother, Miriam Schary, told author Anne Edwards she had arranged the evening specifically because Nancy wanted an opportunity to meet Ronnie. He, alas, "was obviously preoccupied and there were ten for dinner that night. I don't recall his saying much to Nancy."

Lynne Wasserman, daughter of Ronnie's agent Lew Wasserman, told me that she has seen a photo of the future first couple at an even earlier social gathering held right after Nancy arrived in Los Angeles in 1949. It was a big celebration that the elder Wasserman and Anita May, whose husband's family owned a leading department store chain, held every year on March 15 to celebrate their birthdays. Lynne Wasserman says she is sure of her facts on this one: "Ronnie and Nancy met at Tom and Anita May's." Nancy was also looking for other avenues that might bring the two of them together. How else to explain the fact that an actress newly arrived in Hollywood had already put in an application to run for a seat on the Screen Actors Guild board?

However their paths finally crossed, it seems safe to stipulate that Nancy set her sights on Ronnie early and that she was not going to let him slip past her. Nancy, after all, had declared upon her arrival at MGM that her major goal in life was to find a husband. She even showed friends at the studio a list she had compiled of Hollywood's most "eligible bachelors." Ronnie's name was at the top. "Subtlety has never been Nancy's forte," biographer Edmund Morris wrote, "but the fact remains that when Dutch rang the bell of her apartment that November night, leaning heavily on two canes, the door opened on a future beyond their combined powers of belief."

*

After their first date, Nancy and Ronnie had dinner again the next night, and the night after that, and the one after that. "For the first month or so we must have gone to every restaurant and nightclub in Los Angeles," Nancy wrote. But the rush of early romance stalled and sputtered, in no small part because Ronnie wasn't ready to settle down with anyone. He was newly divorced from his first wife, Academy Award–winning actress Jane Wyman, and still in shock over the fact that she had gotten bored with him and walked out.

Ronnie was carrying a torch for Wyman that shone like a klieg light and had not yet given up on the possibility of a reconciliation. In the meantime, he had discovered that a suddenly single movie actor—even one whose career was on the downward slide—did not lack for available female companionship. His business manager gave him a stern lecture after discovering that Ronnie was spending $750 a month in nightclubs. In his biography of Ronnie, Edmund Morris made a tally of the women that he went out with in the two years after his first date with Nancy. Morris came up with "at least sixteen different young and beautiful actresses, from Doris Day and Rhonda Fleming to the peachy and not-yet-legal Piper Laurie. God knows how many more there were or how many came back to spend the night with him in his hillside apartment, with its celestial view of the sparkling city. He was always shy about speaking of such matters when I interviewed him as an old man, and, to tell the truth, I didn't think it was my biographical business." Ronnie did admit to sleeping with so many women that he once woke up with one of them and realized he did not know who she was.

All this sexual hyperkinesia aside, Ronnie would later acknowledge that when he met Nancy, he was broken inside. His heart, as he put it, was in a "deep freeze." And as a result, he almost blew his chance for happiness with her. "This story, I know, will be a disappointment to those who want romance neatly packaged. The truth is, I did everything wrong, dating her off and on, continuing to volunteer for every Guild trip to New York—in short, doing everything which could have lost her if Someone up there hadn't been looking after me," he wrote. "In spite of my determination to remain foot-loose, in spite of my belief that the pattern of my life was all set and would continue without change, nature was trying to tell me something very important."

It would take a long time before he understood what that was. In later years, he would often quote Clark Gable: "There's nothing more important than approaching your own doorstep and knowing that someone is on the other side of the door, listening for the sound of your footsteps." Ronnie in particular had an emotional need for such a woman. In his life, he had known three of them. One was his devoted and protective mother; the second, his grounded, tough-willed high school sweetheart; and finally, his restless and ambitious first wife. The trio had little in common except strength and determination. But all of them had connected with something inside him, something that he kept the rest of the world from seeing.

Nancy, with her razor-sharp instincts about people, no doubt sensed there were deep roots to Ronnie's remoteness. Like hers, his childhood had been one of upheaval and insecurity. Ronnie's father was John

Edward "Jack" Reagan, a charismatic shoe salesman and alcoholic whose high-flying dreams inevitably crashed when they hit the wall of reality. With every fresh failure or new scheme, the family moved again.

The Reagans lived five places in Illinois before Ronnie was nine. For the first three months of his life, during the late winter and spring of 1911, the family occupied an apartment on the second floor of a building at 111 Main Street, in Tampico, an Illinois farming town of fewer than 1,300 people. Various accounts have it that they lived over a bakery, a restaurant, or a bar. The next three years found them in a rented house on the outskirts of town, across the street from the rail depot. At the end of 1914, they moved to the South Side of Chicago, where they lived in a shabby apartment building near the University of Chicago. It was lit, Ronnie recalled later, "by a single gas jet brought to life with the deposit of a quarter in a slot down the hall."

The following December, the family decamped for Galesburg—as it happens, Loyal Davis's hometown. Ronnie's memory from there was of big green trees and dark red-brick streets. He started first grade in Galesburg at the age of five, but before he finished second, they moved again, to Monmouth, a college town in western Illinois, where they lived from early 1917 to August 1919. Ronnie recalled how the downtown celebrated the end of World War I on November 11, 1918: "The streets were suddenly filled with people, bonfires were lighted, and grown-ups and children paraded down the street singing and carrying torches in the air. I was only seven, but old enough to share in the hopes of everyone in Monmouth that we had fought 'the war to end all wars.'"

Not long after that, they were back in Tampico, living above Pitney's Shoe Store, the place where his father had been working when Ronnie was born. By then, Jack had been made the manager and was promised he could become a part owner. Instead, Mr. Pitney made Jack his partner in another venture: a fancier store called the Fashion Boot Shop. It was in Dixon, a city of about ten thousand people that straddled the Rock River about a hundred miles west of Chicago. The family moved there in December 1920 and finally seemed ready to settle down. They lived on the rougher side of town, but to nine-year-old Ronnie, Dixon was heaven, "a small universe where I learned standards and values that would guide me for the rest of my life." Of all the places where the family had lived, it is the two-story, Queen Anne–style rental house they occupied in Dixon for three years that has since been designated the "home of Ronald Reagan" and a national landmark. Its street, once known as Hennepin Avenue, is now named Reagan Way.

The constant uprooting made for solitary early years. Ronnie was not particularly close to his outgoing older brother, Neil, either by age or temperament. He taught himself to read when he was five. When he was California governor, Ronnie told his chief of staff, Edwin Meese III, "Well, if you have a book, you always have a friend."

As is not unusual with children of alcoholics, Ronnie preferred to keep the grimmest images from his past at bay. This was a trait that would carry him through the rest of his life, until Alzheimer's disease wiped out all memory—the good and the bad—entirely. "What Ronald Reagan inherited from his childhood is an astounding ability to turn away from any reality which is too harsh and paint one that is softer, gentler to the eyes," his daughter Patti wrote in her 1992 memoir. But some truths could not be burnished and blurred in sepia tones. There was the year Jack got fired on Christmas Eve, and the string of other jobs that Ronnie's father lost because of his drinking. There was at least one arrest for public drunkenness. His sons heard fiery arguments through their parents' bedroom wall. Sometimes Jack would just disappear for days. At other times, Ronnie's mother took the children to stay with her sister—for sojourns away from Jack that Ronnie eventually figured out were not, as he put it in his autobiography, "unexpected vacations."

Ronnie was but eleven years old when he came home and nearly tripped over his father passed out on the porch. Jack's arms were outstretched as though he had been crucified; his hair was soaked in melting snow. Part of the boy wanted to go into the house and pretend he didn't know the snoring figure sprawled in front for the whole town to see. "But someplace along the line, to each of us, I suppose, must come that first moment of accepting responsibility. If we don't accept it (and some don't), then we must grow older without quite growing up. I felt myself fill with grief for my father at the same time I was feeling sorry for myself," he would later write. "I bent over him, smelling the sharp odor of whiskey from the speakeasy. I got a fistful of his overcoat. Opening the door, I managed to drag him inside and get him to bed. In a few days, he was the bluff, hearty man I knew and loved and will always remember."

The stabilizing force in Ronnie's childhood was his mother, Nelle Wilson Reagan, a tiny, devout woman with a big heart. She was, as White House speechwriter Peggy Noonan would later describe her, "a little tornado of goodness." Her son once noted that Nelle assumed everyone else loved her for no other reason than that she knew she loved them. However hard things got for the Reagans, Nelle could always find someone worse off who needed her help. She looked for these lost souls in jails and hospitals and mental institutions. "Nelle never saw anything evil in another human being, and Ronnie is the same way," Nancy once wrote. "Sometimes it infuriates me, but that's how he is."

As he would later do with Nancy, Ronnie found sanctuary in Nelle's adoring gaze. His mother called him Ronald, though nearly everyone else knew him by the nickname "Dutch," which his father had given him at birth. Jack thought the squalling, ten-pound infant, who had come out feet first on February 6, 1911, looked like "a fat Dutchman."

"I think he's perfectly wonderful," Nelle replied, summoning what strength she could after twenty-four hours of labor. "Ronald Wilson Reagan."

A seamstress by trade, Nelle found her calling when she was baptized by immersion into the Disciples of Christ church on Easter Sunday 1910, a little less than a year before Ronnie was born. The denomination has loose doctrinal boundaries. Its members live, as they put it, "by no creed but Christ, no book but the Bible." They identify themselves only as Christians. Nelle tried to plant that religious outlook in both her sons. It took root in the younger, quieter one. (Jack was a Catholic, in various stages of lapse. Neil followed his father in faith, as in other practices.)

Ronnie's mother also introduced young Ronald to performing and the exhilarating sound of applause. At first, he resented being conscripted to join her as she entertained in productions that were staged at the local theater, at her church, and at the state hospital. But her enthusiasm for make-believe was contagious. "Nelle was the dean of dramatic recitals for the countryside. It was her sole relaxation from her family and charitable duties; she executed it with the zest of a frustrated actress," Ronnie remembered. "She recited classic speeches in tragic tones, wept as she flung herself into the more poignant, if less talented, passages of such melodramas as *East Lynne*"—coincidentally, the same play in which Edith Luckett had made her first appearance onstage as a child in Washington, DC—"and poured out poetry by the yard." Nine-year-old Ronnie made his own debut as a solo performer in early May 1920. He recited a piece called "On Mother."

Ronnie's greatest dream, which was hampered by his small size, was to be a football star, as his brother was. He excelled as a powerful swimmer. Dutch spent seven summers as a lifeguard at Lowell Park beach on the Rock River; over those years, his proudest achievement was rescuing seventy-seven people from drowning. He kept track of the number by putting notches on a log.

Where Ronnie felt most at home was in his own company, exploring an inner life nurtured and protected by his mother. Nelle understood that the geniality her son showed the world was an opaque curtain behind which lived a solitary nature. "In some ways, I think this reluctance to get close to people never left me completely. I've never had trouble making friends, but I've been inclined to hold back a little of myself, reserving it for myself," Ronnie reflected in his post-presidential autobiography.

In Galesburg, Ronnie would sit for hours in the attic of the Reagans' rented house, gazing at a previous tenant's long-forgotten collection of bird's eggs and butterflies. In Tampico, his refuge was the home of a childless elderly couple next door who had taken a liking to the boy. He planted himself every afternoon in a giant rocking chair in their living room, snacking by himself on chocolate and cookies. He wrote later: "The best part was that I was allowed to dream."

Ronnie pored over his mother's leather-bound volume of poems by Robert Service, known as the Bard of the Yukon. Even as president, he could—and often did—recite from memory Service's most famous ballad, *The Shooting of Dan McGrew*. Nelle also put into his eleven-year-old hands *That Printer of Udell's: A Story of the Middle West*. The melodramatic 1903 novel by Harold Bell Wright tells the story of itinerant printer Dick Falkner, a poor young man with an alcoholic father. In the story, Dick's destiny is transformed by two things: becoming a Christian and his devotion to a woman.

"That book—*That Printer of Udell's*—had an impact I shall always remember," Ronnie wrote the author's daughter-in-law from the White House in 1984. "After reading it and thinking about it for a few days, I went to my mother and told her I wanted to declare my faith and be baptized. We attended the Christian Church in Dixon, and I was baptized several days after finishing the book.

"The term 'role model' was not a familiar term in that time and place, but looking back, I know I had found a role model in that traveling printer Harold Bell Wright had brought to life. He set me on a course I've tried to follow even unto this day. I shall always be grateful."

In the pages of Wright's book, Ronnie would find his ideal of the perfect helpmeet. She was Dick's love interest, Amy Goodrich, a virtuous dark-haired girl with sweet brown eyes. Amy comes from a privileged background, but, through a series of plot twists, she falls into a brothel from which Dick rescues her. Driven by his desire to impress her, he also discovers his gift as a great communicator. At the end of the book, Dick and Amy are married and heading to Washington, DC, "to enter a field of wider usefulness. For the people have declared, at the last election, that their choice for representative was 'That Printer of Udell's.'"

The initial incarnation of Amy Goodrich to enter Ronnie's life was Margaret Cleaver, the whip-smart but humorless daughter of his pastor at First Christian Church. She was the first girl he kissed. Ronnie saw in her similarities to his mother: they were both short, auburn haired, and bright. Margaret's eyes were big, and widely spaced, the same feature that had caught his attention the moment he saw Nancy. From the time they were sophomores at Dixon's North Side High School, he was devoted to the girl people called "Mugs." Both were active in dramatics and appeared opposite each other their senior year in a play titled *You and I.* He followed her to Eureka College, a small Disciples of Christ liberal arts school 110 miles southeast of Dixon. Ronnie gave Mugs his Tau Kappa Epsilon pin and then an engagement ring.

"For almost six years of my life, I was sure she was going to be my wife. I was very much in love," he wrote. Mugs was not so sentimental or dreamy about him, it appears. Nearly a half century later, she would say of her former sweetheart: "He had an inability to distinguish between fact and fancy." Hollywood was not a world she would have ever wanted to be part of. Nor did Margaret approve of Ronnie's infrequent church attendance while he was president. "Even Nixon held services in the White House," she said.

As different as they were, their personalities interlocked. His affability complemented her drive. "Mugs was generally considered the stronger of the two, 'young Miss Brains' to his 'Mr. Congeniality.' He smoothed her bristling desire to control people, teasing her when necessary, but paying attention to everything she said," Edmund Morris wrote. She was president of their sophomore class in college, and spent her junior year at the University of Illinois, because she did not consider Eureka academically challenging enough. Ronnie was more focused on his social life. He was president of the Eureka's booster club three years running and of the student body when they were seniors.

After graduation, the two set out on different paths. Ronnie began his career as a radio sportscaster in Iowa, and Mugs taught school in Illinois. She and her sister Helen also spent time in France, where she met and fell in love with a foreign service officer named James Waddell Gordon Jr. Mugs broke the news to Ronnie in a letter in which she enclosed his ring and fraternity pin. (That was his version; Mugs, in 1988, insisted to biographer Morris that she returned the ring personally.) She married Gordon in the summer of 1935 and moved to Scotland. "Margaret's decision shattered me, not so much, I think, because she no longer loved me, but because I no longer had anyone to love," Ronnie recalled.

His life would soon find a new direction. In March 1937 Ronnie went to California to cover the Chicago Cubs' spring training on Catalina Island. While he was there, a friend arranged for him to take a screen test with Warner Brothers Pictures. Ronnie returned to Iowa and soon received a wire offering him a $200-a-week, seven-year contract with the studio, which was MGM's main competitor.

On May 26 Nelle wrote the family of her old pastor—Margaret's father—assuring them that her boy would not stray from his spiritual path in the worldly glitter of America's Gomorrah. The eight-page letter, handwritten on yellowed stationery monogrammed with an *R*, is among the Reagans' personal papers at his presidential library. It says:

> I am inclosing [*sic*] some clippings regarding Ronald, I hardly know how to explain "our feelings," but when people ask me if I am not afraid to have him go to such a wicked place as Hollywood, all I can answer is, that I feel I can trust him anywhere, he has never lost his high ideals in life. . . . Friends, he does love God and he never forgets to thank Him for all his many blessings, and when we visited him, he told me of all the nice things he would be able to do now for Eureka College if he won the seven-year contract with Warner Brothers.

Nelle told the Cleavers that shortly after the offer arrived from Warner, a colleague at the Iowa radio station where Ronnie worked "discovered Dutch in one of the smaller studio rooms on his knees, praying."

His mother also saw the possibility that Ronnie's success could be the salvation for her and Jack. "You know he has been a wonderful son to us, his father hasn't had any work since the 15th of June, last year, and during all that tyme [*sic*], I have rec'd a $60.00 check the first of each month, and another one of the same amt the 15th of each month," Nelle confided, "and if he signs the seven-year contract then he is going to send for us that is the thing that makes me so happy, to think I can live my last days, making a home for him, it's almost more happiness than I ever expected in this life."

Ronnie arrived in California in June to begin shooting his first picture, *Love Is on the Air.* It was a murder mystery filmed on a frantic three-week schedule, a "B movie" meant to be the second feature on a double bill. Ronnie played the lead, which was a bit of typecasting given that the character was a radio broadcaster. The *Boston Globe* wrote of him in its review: "He has a pleasant, boyish appearance and an attractive film personality." A headline in the *New York Daily News* declared: "Treat for Ladies in Ronald Reagan." During his first year with the studio, Ronnie would do eight pictures in eleven months.

With his movie earnings, Reagan bought his parents a small house at 9031 Phyllis Avenue, just below the Sunset Strip in West Hollywood. Presenting his father with the deed to the first piece of real estate Jack ever owned, Ronnie recalled, "was the most satisfying gift of my life." He hired his mother and father to answer his fan mail. Jack cut back on his drinking. Nelle found an outlet for her charitable energy doing good work among the prisoners at Lincoln Heights Jail and the tuberculosis patients at Olive View Sanitarium. Some of the newly released went to job interviews unaware they were wearing movie star Ronald Reagan's old clothes. Still, Nelle did not feel quite at home among her son's new set. "Ronald has finished three pictures now that he has taken the lead in and is very well thought of at the studio, but really I don't just know how to act with these people. I don't just fit in somehow—I get my fork in the wrong hand but I don't care just so the boy gets along," she wrote a friend in Tampico in 1938.

*

That same year, Ronnie's romantic life picked up again when he became acquainted with brassy actress Jane Wyman during the making of a movie called *Brother Rat.* He played a cadet at Virginia Military Institute; her character was his love interest, the commandant's daughter. In real life, they seemed an odd match. She had a tough shell, the product of a rocky start in life as Sarah Jane Mayfield. Her father split when she was a small child; shortly afterward, her mother abandoned her to the care of severe, fiftysomething neighbors in Saint Joseph, Missouri. Jane had been on her own since the age of fifteen, trying to catch a break as a dancer in Hollywood musicals. She wed the first time at sixteen to salesman Ernest Wyman. Then came another quick marriage to a much older dress manufacturer named Myron Futterman.

Ronnie was a totally different kind of partner for a woman like Jane, who was worldly beyond her twenty-one years. "She was so experienced, hard-boiled, intense, and passionate, and he was so pragmatic, down-to-earth," said Jerry Asher, one acquaintance. "He was—well, rather a square. Serious, respectful of women, steady of mind and manners. In short, predictable and dull. He was a very sexy-looking man, of course—looked wonderful in swimming trunks, great body and all that, but he was a little earthbound for someone like Jane." Nonetheless, she pursued him aggressively. Nancy claimed later to Edmund Morris that Jane had forced Ronnie's hand in marriage by threatening suicide and downing pills. In the second wife's version of events, Ronnie proposed as the hospital was pumping Jane's stomach.

He gave Jane an engagement ring set with a fifty-two-carat amethyst, his birthstone. Their January 26, 1940, wedding reception took place at the home of Louella Parsons. The gossip columnist, like Ronnie, hailed from Dixon and had appointed herself a sort of unofficial stage mother to him. "Theirs is the perfect marriage," she wrote. "Jane always seemed so nervous and tense before she found Ronnie. She was a girl on the make—for life, for love. I think she wanted—well, *everything*. But steady, solid, decent young Ronnie has slowed down her pace, and it's all for the best. Yes, it was an 'opposites-attract' thing, but I'm predicting here and now that these opposites will celebrate their twenty-fifth *and* fiftieth wedding anniversaries—together."

Nelle, who had been so close to Margaret and the devout Cleaver family back in Dixon, had misgivings from the moment she met Jane. "I wonder if my Ronald has made the right choice," she wrote one friend. "I was in hopes he would fall in love with some sweet girl who is not in the movies."

Their marriage started off as a picture of bliss. Jane, whom Ronnie called "Button Nose," gave birth to their daughter Maureen Elizabeth on January 4, 1941. The Reagans had two terriers, adorably named Scotch and Soda. Thanks to the negotiating skills of their new agent, Lew Wasserman, there was enough money to start building a comfortable house on a plot of land they bought in the Hollywood Hills. It sat at the end of a long driveway, and had a breathtaking view of the city, the ocean, and the mountains.

But their careers were never in sync. Hers languished in the first few years of the 1940s, while Ronnie got his two most acclaimed parts, as doomed Notre Dame halfback George Gipp in *Knute Rockne All American* and as wealthy Drake McHugh, who loses his legs to a sadistic surgeon, in *Kings Row*. The first gave him a nickname, "the Gipper," which stuck with him through his political career. In the latter, Ronnie's character is most remembered for the passion with which he cried: "Where's the rest of me?"

That one line—"Where's the rest of me?"—would become a self-defining metaphor for Ronnie. It spoke to his awakening need to find a more authentic identity than the ones confected for him by screenwriters. They saw him as good-looking enough but short on star quality. He didn't exude sex appeal or danger. Even as Ronnie watched himself on the screen in *Kings Row,* delivering his most acclaimed performance as an actor, he realized: "I had become a semi-automaton 'creating' a character another had written, doing what still another person told me to do on the set. Seeing the rushes, I could barely believe the colored shadow on the screen was myself. Possibly this was the reason I decided to find the rest of me."

Events across the globe would soon disrupt his career and his life. Ronnie had been an army reservist since his days in Iowa. When World War II arrived, he was ordered to active duty. But his bad eyesight made him unfit for combat, so from the spring of 1942 through the end of the war, he served stateside in a military motion-picture unit, run by the predecessor to the US Air Force, that made training, morale-building, and propaganda films. "By the time I got out of the Army Air Corps, all I wanted to do—in common with several million other veterans—was to rest up awhile, make love to my wife, and come refreshed to a better job in an ideal world. (As it came out, I was disappointed in all of these postwar ambitions)," Ronnie recalled.

He still nurtured hopes of vaulting from B movies to top roles in main attractions. His agent Lew Wasserman told him to be patient. After all, he was still getting $3,500 a week under his contract. But as Ronnie whiled away his time building model ships at a rented house on Lake Arrowhead, he couldn't help noticing that the better parts were starting to go to younger men. The only real demand for his talents was on the speaking circuit, which, as he put it, "fed my ego, since I had been so long away from the screen."

Meanwhile, Jane's star was ascending. She moved from playing ditzy blondes to challenging parts that brought critical acclaim. Her rise began with her role as the love interest of an alcoholic in 1945's *The Lost Weekend*, costarring opposite Ray Milland and under the direction of Billy Wilder. It accelerated the following year, when she played emotionally stunted Ma Baxter in the drama *The Yearling*. She won the 1949 Best Actress Oscar for her starring role in *Johnny Belinda,* where she portrayed Belinda MacDonald, a deaf woman who had been raped. By dramatizing sexual violence and its consequences, the film pushed boundaries and required a relaxation of the Motion Picture Production Code.

Jane immersed herself for months at a time in these grim roles, not breaking character even when she was at home. During the filming of *Johnny Belinda*, six-year-old Maureen had to learn a few words in sign language to communicate with her mother. (When the divorce finally came, Ronnie joked darkly to a friend: "Maybe I should name *Johnny Belinda* as co-respondent.")

But Jane's new success was not the only reason the marriage hit the rocks. Ronnie was starting to talk incessantly about politics, though he had not yet begun his rightward drift from New Deal liberalism. His wife found the subject deadly. The trouble in their relationship became increasingly apparent to their friends. Jane once told actress and singer Joy Hodges: "Well, if he is going to be president, he is going to get there without me." The gulf grew and deepened as Ronnie became preoccupied with his work with the Screen Actors Guild. Founded in the 1930s as a vehicle to give actors some leverage against being exploited by the producers who held their multiyear contracts, SAG was going through a turbulent and politically fraught period. Having joined the union's board in 1941 and been elected its president in 1947, Ronnie was spending five nights a week at the headquarters, girding for marathon negotiations with producers. Seven months after becoming SAG president, Ronnie was called before the House Un-American Activities Committee, which had been established in 1938 as a special investigatory panel to investigate citizens and organizations suspected of having Communist ties. Its clout had increased dramatically in 1945, when it became a permanent committee of Congress.

As Ronnie entered the committee's hearing room on Capitol Hill, "there was a long drawn-out 'ooooh' from the jam-packed, predominantly feminine audience [at] the tall Mr. Reagan, clad in a tan gabardine suit, a blue knitted tie, and a white shirt," the *New York Times* reported. The movie actor also ditched his contact lenses for glasses that gave him more gravitas.

Ronnie was grilled about the possibility that a "clique of either Communists or Fascists" was trying to exert influence over the union. There was such a faction, Ronnie replied. What he did not reveal was that both he and Jane had been secret informants for the Federal Bureau of Investigation and had given it names of people in the industry they believed harbored pro-Communist beliefs. His testimony walked a careful line. Ronnie argued that "in opposing those people, the best thing to do is make democracy work. In the Screen Actors Guild, we make it work by ensuring everyone a vote and by keeping everyone informed. I believe that, as Thomas Jefferson put it, if all the American people know all of the facts, they will never make a mistake."

*

As Ronnie and Jane were being pulled in different directions, they hoped more children might help bring them closer again. The couple had wanted a son when Maureen was born and even joked on her birth announcement that the plan to name their firstborn Ronald Reagan Jr. was "no longer appropriate." To much fanfare in the movie magazines, the couple adopted three-day-old Michael Edward in March 1945. Their plans to expand their family further came to a heartbreaking end two years later, when they lost an infant daughter, Christine, who was born four months prematurely in June 1947. She lived barely nine hours. Ronnie was not present for her birth or short life. He was in a different hospital two miles away, battling a life-threatening 104-degree fever and viral pneumonia.

Christine's death was the beginning of the end, though Ronnie had trouble understanding or accepting it. He learned that his wife was thinking of separating from an interview she gave in late 1947. "There's no use in lying," said Jane, who was on a solo vacation in New York. "I am not the happiest girl in the world. It's nothing that has happened recently. It's an accumulation of things that has been coming on for a long time."

Ronnie was stunned. Perhaps he had actually believed the idealized story line the studio had manufactured about his marriage. Maybe he had bought the gossamer narrative spun by Louella Parsons and the rest of the Hollywood press. "I suppose there had been warning signs, if only I hadn't been so busy, but small-town boys grow up thinking only other people get divorced," he wrote later. "The plain truth was that such a thing was so far from even being imagined by me that I had no resources to call upon."

Stories soon followed quoting Ronnie as saying the couple had merely had "a tiff." Some implied that Jane had been mentally unbalanced since losing the baby. Ronnie told Parsons that he was willing to give his wife some space: "Right now Jane needs very much to have a fling, and I intend to let her have it. She is sick and nervous and not herself."

There was another reason Ronnie was so bewildered to see his marriage fall to pieces. His only frame of reference was the family in which he had grown up. Nelle had endured so much to keep them all together. When Jane walked out, "he didn't really see it coming, because his idea of marriage was his folks, where, despite all his father's failings in terms of his unfortunate alcoholism, his mother's goal in life was devoted to three things: her husband, and family, and church activities," recalled longtime Reagan aide Ed Meese, who talked to Ronnie years later about this difficult period. "He assumed that's the way husbands and wives operated."

There followed a period of separations and failed efforts to put the marriage back together. At a couple of points, Ronnie stayed in an apartment hotel on Sunset Boulevard called the Garden of Allah, which—coincidentally—had once belonged to Nancy's godmother Alla Nazimova. Jane took up residence on a ranch near Las Vegas so that she could obtain a divorce under Nevada's lenient laws, but she couldn't take the constant wind there and moved back to Hollywood. In April 1948 Ronnie announced they had reconciled. Less than three weeks later, however, Jane filed a legal petition to end their marriage after eight years on grounds of mental cruelty, a catchall phrase frequently cited as a justification in those days before no-fault divorce.

Ronnie did not attend the hearing on June 28, 1948. It was left to Jane to explain how the couple deemed so "perfect" had come apart. She wore a simple tangerine-colored shirtdress to court that day, with no hat atop her pageboy haircut, and looked more like an ordinary housewife than a movie star. "In recent months, Miss Wyman told the court, she and Reagan engaged in continual arguments on his political views. But it was not so much that she didn't agree with him, she explained, as that she could not bring herself to display the interest he showed," the *Los Angeles Times* reported. "Despite her lack of interest in his political activities, Miss Wyman continued, Reagan insisted that she attend meetings with him and that she be present during discussions among his friends. But her own ideas, she complained 'were never considered important.'"

Many of those discussions "were far above me," Jane admitted.

"Finally, there was nothing in common between us," she told Superior Court Judge Thurmond Clarke, "nothing to sustain our marriage."

Jane gained custody of seven-year-old Maureen and three-year-old Michael, with Ronnie required to contribute $500 a month in child support. Another provision of the divorce agreement stipulated that, should Jane become ill or injured, he would have to pay an additional $500 a month in alimony. They divided $75,000 in community property.

Ronnie's dismay over the failure of his first marriage would foster his commitment to the success of his second, as well as a kind of myopia as to the collateral damage that could occur when a couple focuses so much on each other that they shut out everyone and everything else. "He vowed, either consciously or subconsciously, when he and Nancy got married, that there was nothing that was going to separate them," Meese observed. "I would say that a lot of his emotional energy, and hers too, was devoted to each other. Quite frankly, I think, later on, more or less at the expense of the kids."

Biographer Edmund Morris was struck by the similarities between the two women Ronnie married—and by the most important quality that set them apart. "Both had been wide-eyed, street-smart, scorchingly ambitious starlets, abandoned by their fathers in infancy, convinced of the world's treachery, drawn to Reagan as a haven of goodness and strength, then frustrated to the point of despair by his reluctance to propose," Morris wrote in the *New Yorker* in 2004, after Ronnie died. "The difference with Nancy was that *her* ambition concerned only him: she wanted nothing for herself except the satisfaction of making him powerful. She had taken him on, moreover, when his acting career was in rapid decline, and when his brilliant future as a politician could hardly have been predicted. Yet she never flinched in her steely belief that he would recover and prevail."

Their early flurry of dates generated buzz that Ronnie might finally be moving past Jane's rejection. Nancy saved the clippings in her scrapbook. One, from December 1949, reported that hers was "the newest telephone number in Ronald Reagan's book," and that he was "romancing Nancy like mad."

She spent Christmas that year back in Chicago with her parents. The local papers dutifully recorded the fur-clad, hometown starlet alighting from the Super Chief into Edie's waiting arms. But after Nancy returned to California, Ronnie stopped calling so regularly. He seemed to have lost his fascination with her and was again playing the field. At one point, Nancy was having lunch in the MGM commissary with a group of other contract actresses, when one of them started talking about a gift that Ronnie had given her. "That hurt. I didn't have one specific rival, but it did occur to me that perhaps I was just one girl of many," she recalled. Meanwhile, Jane was still around, feeding Ronnie's hopes—and the movie-industry gossip—that there was still a chance they might get back together.

Nancy resumed dating other men as well. She was practical enough to know a woman in her situation had to keep open her options. It was also a way of making sure Ronnie noticed she *had* options. Robert Stack, later to become famous as Eliot Ness on the TV show *The Untouchables*, shows up on a few pages of Nancy's scrapbook, including in one newspaper photo where he is at her side for a movie premiere. Playwright and screenwriter Norman Krasna, who had a $50 million production deal at RKO, was reported to be so smitten with her that he proposed.

More serious, it would appear, was her relationship with Robert Walker. An actor known for his edgy roles, he was as troubled as he was talented. Walker had suffered what the *New York Times* called "a severe psychological crackup" after his 1945 divorce from actress Jennifer Jones, who left him to marry film mogul David O. Selznick. In December 1948 he fled the Menninger psychiatric clinic in Topeka, Kansas, and smashed up a local police station after being arrested for public drunkenness. He did another stint at the clinic in May 1949 and was then reported to be ready to resume what had been a promising film career. Walker's romance with Nancy, according to the studio publicity machine, was paving his road to rehabilitation. "Robert Walker, who has changed his whole life—and for the better—has now found happiness with Nancy Davis, M-G-M actress," according to one clipping in her scrapbook, next to which she wrote the date, April 24, 1950. "Someone close to Bob tells me that he is happier with Nancy than he has been at any time since his parting from Jennifer Jones. While Bob was in Phoenix, he met Nancy's parents, Dr. and Mrs. Royal [*sic*] Davis of Chicago, and they approved so thoroughly of him that when they were visiting here, they were entertained by Bob and their daughter." In June the movieland columns were saying that there might be a wedding in the works. Nancy was reported to be overseeing the redecoration of Walker's home, where his two sons by Jones were frequent visitors.

By the fall of 1950, however, Ronnie was back in the picture again. He wore a big smile and a jaunty checked bowtie as Nancy's date to the October 1950 Los Angeles opening of her movie *The Next Voice You Hear*. (One photo caption about the two of them noted of Ronnie: "He and Jane Wyman, his former wife, are still the best of friends.")

The Next Voice You Hear was a passion project of MGM chief of production Dore Schary, designed to test his theory that there was an untapped market for darker, moralistic "message" pictures. It was Nancy's first lead role, and the closest she would ever get to a shot at bona fide stardom. The premise of the film was that the voice of God was suddenly preempting radio programming all around the world. Nancy played opposite James Whitmore as Mary and Joe Smith, a middle-class couple whose life is upended by the voice.

Schary was determined that his characters be utterly believable. He had been sold from the start on giving the male lead to the promising Whitmore, knowing he was perfect to play an everyman aircraft factory worker in postwar Southern California. The suggestion to cast Nancy as Joe's pregnant wife, Mary, had come from Schary's own wife, Miriam—the same woman who had earlier thrown a dinner party in a failed matchmaking attempt to bring Nancy and Ronnie together.

"This idea took a bit of getting used to: this would be an exacting star role and Nancy had had only three small parts in pictures, and all of them had been on the 'society' side, rather than a middle-class wife and mother," Schary later recalled. "But in her favor was the fact that her looks and manner and inner self were 'nice' rather than cover girl glamorous. And she was an actor by profession rather than by accident." Nancy nailed an hourlong script reading with Whitmore, and Schary gave her the part without making her go through a screen test.

Nancy was padded and wardrobed in frumpy maternity dresses that the costumer had bought at local stores for around $12.95 apiece. In those days, it was considered slightly indecent to show an expectant mother on the screen. Every outfit and camera angle had to pass muster with the Motion Picture Production Code, and the censorship office run by Joseph Breen, an arch-conservative Catholic. Nancy spent many of her off-hours with a pregnant friend, studying the way she moved. Her hair was cut into a simple bob, which she was told to wash and set herself, as Mary would do. She wore no makeup except for her own lipstick.

The Next Voice You Hear had a pre-release engagement at Radio City Music Hall—a coup for a picture that had been made with no big-name stars or lavish budget. Its leading lady got the thrill of seeing "Nancy Davis" over the movie's title on Radio City's famous marquee. Schary inscribed her copy of the script: "You'll never forget this picture, and I'll never forget you."

She got solid reviews. Ronnie confidently told Nancy that she should unpack her bags—she would be around for a while in the movie business. (He did, however, advise her to send her wardrobe from that picture to the cleaners and lose the laundry ticket.) The studio set up a feverish promotional campaign that sent her across the country. But the earnest film, with its religious overtones, was a box-office failure in a year when moviegoers were flocking to see *Annie Get Your Gun* and *Sunset Boulevard*.

Nancy was under a truckload of stress, which stoked her chronic insecurities. The tour was grueling. Her love life was shaky, with Ronnie still dating around, and Walker battling his demons. Whatever it was she had going with Bennie Thau was coming to an end. Right around the time of her brother Dick's late-August wedding in Chicago, Nancy landed in Passavant Hospital, where Loyal was head of surgery. Various news accounts, saved in her scrapbook, deemed her ailment a "vitamin deficiency," an "anemic condition," and a collapse from "nervous exhaustion."

But she was becoming more focused on what she really wanted in life. Nancy started looking for ways to spend more time with Ronnie. One was to become more active in the Screen Actors Guild, where she was appointed to fill a vacancy on the board in August 1950. Ronnie's constant talk about the union and its politics had driven Jane crazy, but he found a rapt audience in Nancy. By then, he had commenced his ideological journey from left to right. Ronnie was still enough of a liberal Democrat to have voted for Harry Truman in 1948, and he campaigned for actress-turned-politician Helen Gahagan Douglas against Richard Nixon for the Senate in 1950. But he was railing more and more about the Communist threat and confiscatory federal income taxes.

Ronnie and Nancy's romance began to gain real traction. Though he still saw other women occasionally, his brother, Neil, is said to have remarked: "It looks as if this one has her hooks in him." They largely ditched the nightclub scene. Their evenings were spent with friends; their days, at his apartment or hers. Nancy knit him socks. One movie magazine account, which Nancy pasted into her scrapbook, noted that Ronnie was behaving like "a husband-in-training," mixing cocktails and carving the roast at her dinner parties. It added: "Wherever they are, Ronnie is talking earnestly, and Nancy is drinking in every word."

One place they could often be found was at the home of his friend and fellow actor William Holden and Holden's wife, Ardis, an actress who went by the professional name Brenda Marshall. Ronnie had slept on their couch for a while after his split with Jane. The Holdens thought Nancy was perfect for Ronnie and became "the godmother and godfather of that relationship," said actress Stefanie Powers, who was Holden's companion in his later years, after his divorce from Ardis.

Ronnie also began including Nancy in the other parts of his life. He had discovered what would become a lifelong love of horses back in the 1930s in Iowa, when he was in the US Cavalry Reserves at Fort Des Moines. Around the time he started dating Nancy, he had just bought a magnificent 360-acre ranch in Malibu Canyon. It was a vast upgrade from the 8-acre one he had previously owned in the Northridge area of the San Fernando Valley, and it gave him ample space for his expensive hobby raising thoroughbreds. He invited Nancy up on weekends to ride and to paint fences—not exactly her idea of a good time, but he thought it was heaven. "I knew almost nothing about riding when I first met Ronnie, but I soon realized that if I wanted to marry this man, I'd have to trade my tennis racket for a saddle," she recalled later. "I still remember the first time he helped me up on a horse at his ranch. 'It's easy,' he assured me. 'You just show him who's boss.'" She never became truly comfortable astride an enormous beast, and when they rode together, she constantly begged Ronnie to slow down.

More significantly, Ronnie let Nancy meet his children. That was a big step, and one he had not taken with anyone else he was seeing. Jane had sent Maureen and Michael to Chadwick boarding school on the Palos Verdes Peninsula, about an hour south of Los Angeles, which meant they only saw their parents every other weekend. "As far as we all knew at the time, she was the first woman in his life since Mother," recalled Maureen, who was about ten at the time. ". . . Dad was so relaxed around Nancy—more relaxed than I had ever seen him."

On the long rides to the ranch in Ronnie's red station wagon, Nancy and Maureen sang duets until he told them enough already. Six-year-old Michael sat in Nancy's lap, craving her touch as she massaged and tickled his back. "Those back rubs were bonding me to Nancy so much that, although I wanted to be with Dad at the ranch, I looked forward most of all to being in the front seat of the car and having Nancy love me. I never told her that, however, because I didn't want to be disloyal to my mom," Michael wrote later. Jane, by her son's account, was a volatile, stern disciplinarian who gave him ten whacks on each leg with a riding crop when he was naughty.

It was clear from the start that the former Mrs. Reagan and the future Mrs. Reagan despised each other and were never going to get along. But the other woman in Ronnie's life—Nelle—very much approved of Nancy. By then, her husband, Jack, had been dead a decade, felled at the age of fifty-seven by a series of heart attacks. In the darkest days after Ronnie's divorce, he had spent every Sunday morning at Nelle's little house, filling his stomach with her brunch and his soul with her comfort. Nelle counseled her son that everything—even a failed marriage—happens for a reason, and that someday, he would figure out what the purpose of his own torment was. Nancy seemed so different from Jane, and Nelle could see that she was in love. But Ronnie's mother also knew that her son was not. Not yet, at least. So, she offered some advice. "You're going to have to wait, Nancy. You are just going to have to wait," Nelle told her. "Nancy, you will know when he loves you."

Judging by the clippings in Nancy's scrapbook, she and Ronnie had become an exclusive item by the middle of 1951. The pages are filled with pictures of the two of them at movie premieres and parties. Nancy also pasted in news items charting the progress of her career, and her emergence as a minor celebrity. At a time when sexy bombshells ruled the screen, the MGM publicity machine seemed to have been doing its best to counterprogram Nancy as a classy, cerebral type. Her byline appeared on a magazine feature headlined "Brains Can't Hurt You." Neither the name of the publication nor the date is noted in her scrapbook, but its placement suggests it ran some time in 1951. The article touted Nancy as "one of Hollywood's brainiest lassies."

She counseled teen girls not to hide their intelligence out of fear that being smart would make them unpopular with the male of the species. But she also cautioned young ladies not to flaunt it. "Personally, I cannot believe that boys are captivated by a vacuous girl, and that's exactly what a brainless 'dumb' girl is. A girl is short-circuiting herself, in my estimation, if she is afraid of brains," Nancy advised. "But there is, of course, a great difference between having brains and being 'The Great Brain' who is objectionable by showing off her knowledge, who parades her mental powers to the discomfiture of her associates.

". . . Use your brains and you stand to gain, not just in the matter of catching a fella, but to make your life fuller and richer. If your life is full and interesting to you, then you are interesting to other people." A photo shows Nancy gazing devotedly at her own beau, as he beams back at her. The caption: "It's pretty obvious that Ronald Reagan likes his girls smart as well as beautiful. Guess that's why he's been dating Nancy so much."

By the end of 1951, reporters were asking Nancy whether there would be a wedding with Ronnie in the near future. "He hasn't asked me yet," she told one. But she was getting impatient. Her thirtieth birthday was behind her, and her movie career was in neutral. So, she decided to give things a nudge. In January 1952 Nancy told Ronnie that she was considering asking her agent to find her a play in New York. It was a none-too-subtle hint that if he didn't move, she would move on. This was more than a ploy on Nancy's part. She was not exactly setting movie box offices on fire and knew that the studio most likely would terminate her contract when it came up for renewal in March.

There was another problem: Jane. Ronnie's ex-wife still had an emotional hold on him. They often crossed paths at social occasions, and, of course, were involved together in raising their two children. The gossip columnists were constantly hinting of the potential for a reconciliation. But Ronnie finally came to accept that there would be no second act with Jane. One night when Nancy was at his apartment, he got a telephone call. "I've got to go," Ronnie told Nancy. "That was Jane." Panicked, Nancy surreptitiously followed him in her own car over to Jane's big house on Beverly Glen and sat outside. After fifteen minutes, he left, and Nancy raced back to her apartment. Soon Ronnie showed up and told her things were finally over with his ex-wife; this time, for good.

What might have precipitated this final break? In her memoir, Nancy claimed Jane had convinced Ronnie that he shouldn't get married again unless and until she did, so one possibility is that Jane told him that night she'd found someone else. A week after Ronnie and Nancy were married, Jane announced what turned out to be a brief engagement to a wealthy real estate development heir twelve years her junior. But it is also possible that, seeing her ex-husband get serious about someone new, Jane had reconsidered, made one last play for Ronnie, and he was the one who cut it off. At any rate, things with Nancy and Ronnie moved along quickly after that. Ronnie proposed over dinner in their usual booth at Chasen's. He said only three words: "Let's get married." To which Nancy replied, suppressing her jubilation: "Let's."

There was another factor that no doubt spurred Ronnie to finally commit to Nancy: she was pregnant. Some—including Jane, in private conversations with family members—would later claim that Ronnie was distraught and felt trapped, that he had been given no choice but to marry Nancy once he found out a baby was on the way. But to believe that requires a cynicism that overlooks the devotion that the Reagans showed to each other over the next six decades. What had stood in their way was Ronnie's fear and reserve. Nancy's soft persistence found a way through his emotional defenses like drops of water on a rock. As Ronnie would later write: "Nancy moved into my heart and replaced an emptiness I had been trying to ignore for a long time."

One of the first to whom he broke the news was his friend William Holden. Ronnie passed a note during a long, boring session of the Motion Picture Industry Council, where he and the *Sunset Boulevard* star were representing the Screen Actors Guild. It said: "To hell with this, how would you like to be the best man when I marry Nancy?"

"It's about time!" Holden blurted out, and the two of them walked out of the meeting.

The newly engaged couple also called Edie and Loyal, who had never met Ronnie in person and were only vaguely aware that he and Nancy were getting serious. According to Nancy, her parents were thrilled when Ronnie asked Loyal's permission to marry his daughter. That Ronnie would do things in such an old-fashioned way "only endeared him to me more," Nancy said. Her stepbrother, Dick, remembered it differently. He was a Northwestern medical resident at the time, with strict rules that he was not to have outside disturbances when he was on duty. No one would have understood that better than his physician father. So, Dick was surprised when Loyal paged him at the hospital and ordered him to come over for dinner.

"He was absolutely furious that Nancy had not told him and Edith that she was going to marry. He was extremely upset," Dick told me.

The decision had been presented to Nancy's parents as a fait accompli. Their wedding would take place in less than two weeks. It is not clear whether Nancy's parents were told about her pregnancy, and they may have been concerned about the fact that Ronnie was divorced. But whatever other objections Loyal might have had about his daughter's precipitous decision, he also felt a sense of betrayal. As Dick put it, Loyal "felt a closeness to her that she violated. He would expect a child of his to inform him that she was going to do this, make this important step."

Or perhaps what bothered Loyal was that another man had supplanted him as the center of Nancy's universe.

CHAPTER FIVE

Nancy might have liked a big wedding, but Ronnie put his foot down. He refused to stage a lavish production for the Hollywood gossip queens to hyperventilate over in their columns. Ronnie had seen how the make-believe machine could confect gauzy visions of future bliss. He had seen how real-life could blow those dreams to bits. His one concession to the media interest in their nuptials was to allow newspaper photographers to snap him and Nancy applying for their marriage license in Santa Monica, two days after MGM announced their engagement on February 27, 1952. In the photo, Ronnie looks annoyed. He would later regret denying Nancy a chance to come down a church aisle on a cloud of white lace with everyone they knew present and wishing them well. "Came our wedding day, and not one protest from Nancy over the fact that I cheated her out of the ceremony every girl deserves. It is hard for me to look back and realize the extent to which I was ruled by my obsession about the press and the fuss that would accompany a regular wedding. I can only confess that at the time to even contemplate facing reporters and flashbulbs made me break out in a cold sweat," he wrote.

On March 4 Nancy donned a gray wool suit with a white collar that she had found on the rack at the upscale department store I. Magnin. Atop her head, she sported a perky little flowered hat, which had a bit of net veiling. Around her neck was the strand of pearls her parents had given her for her debut. She looked like she might be going to a Junior League luncheon rather than to her own wedding. The ensemble could hardly have been more different from the ice-blue satin, sable-accessorized gown that Jane had worn like a princess a dozen years earlier.

Ronnie picked Nancy up at her apartment. He brought her a bouquet of orange blossoms, her favorite. His mother, her parents, and his children were not invited to their ceremony at the Little Brown Church, a Disciples of Christ sanctuary in the San Fernando Valley. The only witnesses were Bill and Ardis Holden. The exchange of vows was over so quickly that Nancy didn't realize they were married until Bill asked to be the first to kiss the new Mrs. Reagan. Nor in her euphoric daze did she notice that Bill and Ardis were sitting on opposite sides of the chapel, not speaking to each other because they had just had a big argument.

Had Ardis not thought to arrange for a photographer, there would have been no visual record of the day. She also had a tiered wedding cake waiting back at the Holden home in Toluca Lake. The Reagans spent their wedding night at the Mission Inn in Riverside, where Ronnie carried Nancy over the threshold of a room bedecked with red roses. From there they went to Phoenix for a quick two-day honeymoon at the Biltmore, much of which was spent in the company of Nancy's parents.

Ronnie was a hit with the Davises. He was intimidated at first by Loyal, but he and Edie quickly discovered they had the same sense of humor, which included an affinity for dirty jokes. Once, years later, Ronnie was telling Edie a particularly filthy one over the phone, and there was silence on the other end. He was afraid that, this time, he had gone too far. What had actually happened was that the line had gone dead—something the long-distance operator did not tell him until she got to hear the punch line. "I soon had the feeling that if anything went wrong with Ronnie and me, he and Mother would be perfectly happy together," Nancy recalled. On Nancy's birthdays, Ronnie would send Edie flowers.

When Nancy and Ronnie got back from their honeymoon, they kept their two apartments for a few months—there was no room for his clothes in her tiny one. But by July, they had built a modest ranch-style house at 1258 Amalfi Drive in Pacific Palisades, a not-yet-fashionable area near the ocean. They paid $42,000 for it.

How to handle Nancy's increasingly apparent pregnancy was a delicate issue. This being the early 1950s, the answer was to lie and assume the Hollywood press would go along. Twelve weeks after they were married, columnist Hedda Hopper broke the news to her readers that Nancy was expecting. "How did you find out it was due early in December?" Nancy asked. "We were keeping it a secret because I knew I would be in for lots of kidding." Patricia Ann Reagan arrived about six weeks before her purported due date, and though she weighed a healthy seven pounds, the papers dutifully reported that she had been born prematurely. The story had it that the Reagans were at a horse show when Nancy's labor pains began, but that she did not recognize what they were, because the baby was not expected to arrive for more than a month. The Reagans kept up the fiction even at home. As a child, Patti was told an absurd story that she had spent the first two months of her life in an incubator.

Nancy fibbed about all of this in a 1980 memoir, saying she got pregnant "early in our marriage," because she was "close to 30 years old and didn't want to wait." (Make that two fibs: She was already thirty when she married.) In Nancy's 1989 book, however, she owned up to all of it, though with a touch of coy defiance. Patti, she wrote, "was born—go ahead and count—a bit precipitously, but very joyfully, on October 22, 1952." Ronnie planted an olive tree in their yard to commemorate their daughter's arrival, and for many years after, Nancy would drive past the house to see how big it had grown.

Parenthood was not the only big adjustment the Reagans had to make in those early months of their marriage. Ronnie stepped down as president of SAG after having led the union for five turbulent years in which there had been violent strikes in the industry, Communist blacklisting, the enforcement of antiunion laws, and the decline of film production in the face of new competition from television. (He and Nancy remained on the board, and he would return to the presidency for a year in 1959.) His decision to give up leading the union was a relief to Nancy. "There's no question in my mind that Ronnie's political involvements had begun to hurt his prospects for work. By the time I came along, he had become so identified with the Screen Actors Guild that the studio heads had begun to think of him less as an actor than an adversary," she reasoned.

On his way out, Ronnie did his agent Lew Wasserman a favor of the highest order. The six-member SAG board, which also included Nancy, quietly voted to give Wasserman's MCA agency a waiver that would allow him to both represent talent and to produce television programs. It was a blatant conflict of interest because it put MCA in a position of being both labor and management in negotiations over issues such as stars' salaries. Even more significantly for the industry, the new arrangement gave Wasserman a beachhead in television. It propelled him into becoming one of the biggest powers in the entertainment industry and the last of the true Hollywood moguls. His rise helped demolish the studio system for good.

Wasserman and television would a few years later become the Reagans' financial salvation, though there is no indication they could have imagined it then. What the newlyweds could see were trouble signs building. Movie roles were drying up for both of them, as the collapsing industry was dumping supposed stars who couldn't pull in enough ticket buyers to justify their salaries. Almost concurrently with its announcement of Ronnie and Nancy's engagement, MGM put out another one saying that she had asked to be let out of her contract. Nancy was going to get the axe anyway after having done eight not particularly noteworthy pictures for the studio. But the fiction that leaving was her own choice allowed her to exit "with more dignity than I had managed under like circumstances," noted Ronnie, who was losing deals he had with Warner Brothers and Universal Pictures at just about the same time.

Nancy accepted that she was nearing the end of the road for an acting career that had never really taken her very far. Turning her energies to building a marriage echoed the pragmatic choice that her mother had made a generation before, when Edie realized that her own professional options as an actress were running out. Nancy had found a steadfast man to love and belong to. But it was far from certain, at least in the beginning, that this union would bring the security and success that Edie and Loyal's match had. Money became tight, and the newlyweds were piling up debt. Between the ranch and the house, they had two first mortgages and a second one. Ronnie had run up $10,000 in medical bills when he broke his leg. He also incurred a big fine for back taxes he had deferred during World War II. A separate error made by his studio in reporting his income added another $21,000 to the amount Uncle Sam was owed. There was also his obligation to pay $500 a month in child support. The Reagans employed an English nanny, and someone to cook and clean, but they could not afford to buy furniture for the living room of their small house.

Five months after Patti was born, their financial circumstances forced Nancy to accept the female lead in a turkey of a film, *Donovan's Brain*. She played the wife of a mad scientist who preserves the brain of a dead tycoon alive in a jar. Not exactly Oscar-worthy material. "Quite simply, we needed the money. This was a blow to Ronnie, but we had to face facts and face them together. I could get work, but his movie career was at a standstill," Nancy recalled. Ronnie went for more than a year without doing a picture, turning down a few scripts that were embarrassingly bad. He scraped by accepting some guest spots on television shows. A regular TV series, however, was something he considered "a professional kiss of death to a movie actor: The people who owned movie theaters thought nobody would buy a ticket to see someone they could see at home in their living room for nothing."

But moviemaking was changing, and even when Ronnie got a decent part, he no longer loved it as he once had. In one letter to Nancy from the set of 1954's *Cattle Queen of Montana* in Glacier National Park, he vented about the chaos of the operation, the imperiousness of his costar, Barbara Stanwyck, and his frustrations with director Allan Dwan and scriptwriter Robert Blees. Ronnie referred to all of them by initials: "I don't know how the picture is going. We started in confusion and have managed to develop that characteristic to an unusual degree. B.B. is still defending his script. I'm still feeding suggestions to A.D. and those two huddle and argue. Right now I'm waiting to go to work and the scheduled scene is one of those that needs changing the most. I'm quite interested to see what happens. In the meantime what the h—l do I learn. B.S. just continues to go her merry way in the exclusive company of two hairdressers and her maid. I wonder what picture she's making."

He added, "This, incidentally, is my first crack at picture making since the big switch to TV film work in Hollywood, and it bears out everything we've ever said. First of all—getting a crew was a case of rounding up who you could find. The industry as we have so often said literally forced our technicians to seek work in TV, and now we reap the harvest."

The Reagans grasped at other ideas, at one point trying to sell a radio series to be called *Yearling Row*, based on the idea of an actor and actress who go into ranching. Then came the most humbling proposition of all: a Las Vegas nightclub act. When an agent at MCA first suggested that he consider it, Ronnie's initial answer to such a tacky proposal was "You must be kidding!" But the money was good. Better than good. It paid nearly as much for a two-week gig as the $30,000 he had made for his previous picture, yet another disappointment called *Prisoner of War*, which was set during the Korean War.

On the morning he had reluctantly agreed to discuss the Las Vegas project with his agents, Ronnie decided to consult his horoscope. Nancy's reliance on astrology would one day cause a national sensation. But back in those days, many people in Hollywood turned to their star charts for guidance. Entertainers have always been a superstitious tribe. Some considered it prudent to check the alignment of the heavens for the right date to sign a contract for a movie, commence filming, conceive a child, or get a divorce. Astrologer Carroll Righter's column in the paper that morning advised Aquarians like Ronnie: "This is a day to listen to the advice of experts." So, he marched into the meeting and began it by asking: "Are you guys experts?" When his agents assured him they were, he said, "Well, let's get on with it, then."

Ronnie was to tell jokes and stories and introduce the other performers. He backed out when the owner of the first club they talked to, El Rancho Vegas, insisted that one of those acts be a stripper. But his agents managed to scrounge up another offer at the Last Frontier, also on the Vegas Strip. There, Ronnie would be on the bill with a male quartet called the Continentals, a song-and-dance duo, comedians, and showgirls in feathered headdresses. The ninety-minute show ran for two weeks in February 1954 and sold out.

Nancy saw a role for herself as well: as the guardian of her husband's reputation and well-being, as well as his emotional support at a rock-bottom moment. Her duties as a wife meant neglecting her ones as a mother, and it would not be the last time she made the choice she did. "Ronnie could have gone to Las Vegas alone, but if there ever was a time my husband needed me, it was then," she recalled. "It almost killed me, but I left three-month-old Patti at home with our housekeeper." Nancy went to every rehearsal, taking notes and fretting over whether Ronnie had his comedic timing down. Once the show opened, she sat through two performances a night in the Ramona Room, her laugh greeting every punchline as though she had never heard it before. "I never got bored," she said gamely. Late each evening, after the show was over, the Reagans headed back to their hotel room and read themselves to sleep. Not until their final night did they spend any time in the casino, where they lost $20. "I hope I never have to sink this low again," Ronnie told Nancy as they drove home to Los Angeles.

Their attachment to each other had grown deeper as their circumstances became shakier and their future more uncertain. After Patti was born, Ronnie—who had been instructed by his own mother to address her by her first name—began to call his wife "Mommie." To

Nancy, he was "Daddy." Those nicknames would later make Ronnie's political advisers roll their eyes and snicker behind his back. But it was probably no coincidence that this was also around the time Nelle began showing signs of what was then called senility, leaving Nancy to be Ronnie's sole source of comfort and security. Nelle moved into a nursing facility in 1958 and died of a cerebral hemorrhage in 1962 at the age of seventy-nine. More than three decades later, both of her sons would be diagnosed with Alzheimer's disease. When aides cleaned out Ronnie's office desk in Los Angeles for the last time, they found five or six of the poems Nelle had written tucked inside.

For the rest of Ronnie's life, Nancy "filled the role that his own mother had filled in his childhood and youth. She provided him with a safe space for his solitude," their son, Ron, said. "He needed a safe place to come home to, to be by himself, to recharge where nobody's at him. She would provide him that. She'd be the gatekeeper. She'd keep people away when he needed to be alone. And, of course, served the social purpose of getting him out when he needed to get out, too. He was probably less enamored of that than the other."

Ronnie himself put it this way: "How do you describe coming into a warm room from out of the cold? Never waking up bored? The only thing wrong is, she's made a coward out of me. Whenever she's out of sight, I'm a worrier about her."

The truest, rawest record of this emotional attachment are his passionate letters to her. He wrote her scores of them over the decades. Nancy saved every one in a shopping bag in her closet. She also kept telegrams, sentimental and funny greeting cards, and the notes that came with the flowers he sent her. A particular favorite was a missive he wrote on July 15, 1953, from New York on stationery printed with the name of the Sherry-Netherland Hotel. Nancy would reread it many times over the decades to come, always getting tears in her eyes. In the letter, Ronnie addressed her by another favorite nickname—"Nancy Poo Pants"—and wrote of his loneliness for her. Then he fantasized about what it would have been like if, instead of dining at the 21 Club alone, he had been there with her:

> We walked back in the twilight and I guess I hadn't ought to put us on paper from there on. Let's just say I didn't know my lines this morning.
>
> Tonight I think we'll eat here at the hotel, and you've got to promise to let me study—at least for a little while.
>
> I suppose some people would find it unusual that you and I can so easily span three thousand miles but in truth it comes very naturally. Man can't live without a heart, and you are my heart, by far the nicest thing about me and so very necessary. There would be no life without you nor would I want any.
>
> I Love You
>
> "The Eastern Half of Us."

The Las Vegas act, which showcased Ronnie's talents as an emcee, indirectly opened a new opportunity: a television series. He no longer considered such a thing out of the question, and his agent Taft Schreiber, a top MCA executive, had an idea that seemed particularly well suited to a movie star in eclipse. General Electric was looking to sponsor a new show, a weekly dramatic production with a rotating cast of guest performers. Ronnie could host it and star in a half dozen or so episodes a year.

So was born *General Electric Theater*, a half-hour program that aired Sunday evenings at nine o'clock on CBS for eight years. It featured such high-wattage guest stars as James Dean, Jimmy Stewart, and Fred Astaire in adaptations of novels, short fiction, plays, and films. *GE Theater* debuted on September 26, 1954, and was broadcast from both New York and Hollywood. Initially the series alternated between filmed productions and live ones, the latter being a difficult challenge to pull off on television. Nancy performed in one of the early live shows and had to wear two dresses for the first ten minutes, ripping off the outer one between shots.

Ronnie's association with General Electric would also lay the seeds of his political career. The "real extra" of the deal, in his view, was its promotional side. He would travel the country and visit GE plants, where he would meet workers and could give speeches on whatever he liked. The only proviso was that he promote the virtues of free enterprise and electricity. GE figured Ronnie would be a natural. As he put it: "I had been tagged because of my experience in the Guild and the speaking I'd done in the industry's behalf along the 'mashed potato' circuit."

Television, a medium he would later employ more skillfully than any politician before him, made Ronnie a bigger household name than he had ever been as a film star. *GE Theater* was an instant hit and, by 1956, was the third most popular television series in the country, reaching more than twenty-five million viewers a week. Critics loved it too, praising the show's quality, creativity, and intelligence. In one memorable episode, Jimmy Stewart did Charles Dickens's *A Christmas Carol* as a Western. Ronnie's five-year contract, which started at $125,000 a year, quickly rose to $150,000 and solved the Reagans' money worries. Later he would become part owner of the show, making them even wealthier.

GE's slogan in those postwar-boom days was "Progress is our most important product." The company built the Reagans an all-electric dream home that overlooked the Pacific from the top of San Onofre Drive in Pacific Palisades. On clear days, they could see all the way to Catalina Island. As it was being constructed, Ronnie drew hearts with his and Nancy's initials in the wet cement on the patio. The five-thousand-foot ranch-style house "pointing the way to the electrical future" was fitted with every conceivable gadget. Among its wonders were a hidden projector in the dining room for movie screenings, a retractable roof over the atrium, lights that changed color to give different effects, three refrigerators, and two freezers. At night, the Reagans sat on the deck after dinner and watched the lights of the city sparkling beneath them. "You see," Ronnie would tell Nancy, taking her hand, "I've given you all these jewels."

The house was also a marvel of engineering. It used so much power that GE had to install a three-thousand-pound switch box, twelve feet long and eight feet high, at 1669 San Onofre. Ronnie joked that they had a direct line to Hoover Dam. "I wasn't wild about having my home turned into a corporate showcase," Nancy wrote, "but this was Ronnie's first steady job in years, so it was a trade-off I was more than happy to make."

There were other accommodations to Ronnie's new career that Nancy found harder to accept. Chief among them were her husband's long absences. Ronnie's contract initially committed him to at least sixteen weeks a year on the road. Most of that time was spent on trains, because he was terrified of flying. Starting with his first appearance at a turbine plant near GE headquarters in Schenectady, New York, he visited 130 company facilities over eight years and met 250,000 employees. He sometimes gave as many as fourteen speeches in a day. Ronnie had a twenty-minute pitch, from which he would pivot to questions and answers where workers would share their opinions and their concerns. "No barnstorming politician ever met the people on quite such a common footing. Sometimes I had an awesome, shivering feeling that America was making a personal appearance for me, and it made me the biggest fan in the world," he recalled later. The folks he met loved him back. After one speech, Ronnie signed more than ten thousand photos, blistering his fingers. By his recollection, he walked so many miles of concrete floor in GE's plants that he sometimes had to cut his laces to get his shoes off.

Nancy would later muse: "Although he wasn't running for any political office, essentially he spent eight years campaigning—going out and talking to people, listening to their problems, and developing his own ideas about how to solve them." It was in those speeches that Ronnie developed both his feel for what resonated with Middle Americans and many of the nascent ideas that would become his philosophy for governing. As columnist George Will noted in an interview with me: "Those GE years were very important to Reagan because he went around the country talking to those people on factory floors for GE who became Reagan Democrats. That's where he learned the vocabulary and the cadence of speech and all the rest."

Still, the stress that his travel put on their marriage was hard on both Ronnie and Nancy. On yet another trip to Schenectady, he wrote her:

I find myself hating these people for keeping us apart. Please be real careful because you carry my life with you every second.

Maybe we should build at the farm so we could surround the place with high barb wire and booby traps and shoot anyone who even suggests *one* of us go to the corner store without the other. I promise you—this will not happen again. How come you moved in on me like this? I'm all hollow without you and the "hollow" hurts.

I love you

Ronnie.

Their family, meanwhile, was growing again. Nancy was determined to do what Jane could not, which was to give Ronnie a son of his own flesh and blood. After two miscarriages, she did. She spent the final three months of that pregnancy in bed, taking weekly hormone injections so that she would make it to full term. Patti's delivery had been difficult. Ronnie was unenthusiastic about having another child—not because he didn't want one but because he feared putting Nancy through an ordeal that might risk her health and "take chances with a happiness so great I couldn't believe it." He arrived home from a GE tour just in time to make it to the hospital for Nancy's scheduled Cesarean section on May 20, 1958. Then he waited, in what he described as a "cold terror," wishing "I could turn back the clock and cancel out this moment.

". . . At 8:04 a.m., a nurse told me Ronald Prescott had arrived, weighing eight and a half pounds. Again, that wasn't the first thing I wanted to hear. I'm in favor of a rule that, under the circumstances, nurses will begin their announcement with the words, 'Your wife is all right,'" Ronnie wrote later.

To the world, the Reagans presented an image of what every American family wanted to be in the middle of the twentieth century. Ronnie was named "Screen Father of the Year" in 1957 by the National Father's Day Committee, an organization that existed solely to confer such honors. In GE ads, Nancy was living every housewife's dream as she marveled at how easily she could turn out a souffle with her state-of-the-art appliances. In reality, her son said, she "couldn't make steam. She was just the worst cook." Even coffee was beyond Nancy's abilities in the kitchen.

Nine-year-old Patti and three-year-old Ron beamed with their parents in front of the fireplace for the 1961 Christmas Eve episode of *GE Theater.* One ad segment touted the glories of modern electrical illumination and featured Patti rocking her doll Cynthia in a cradle. "Notice the lights," Ronnie exulted. "They look like Japanese lanterns, and they're just as colorful." Nancy, Patti, and Ron also did a commercial for Crest toothpaste, in which they posed by their pool—the children in bathing suits, and Nancy in a crisp, sleeveless dress topped with a double strand of pearls.

"I've never had a single cavity," Patti declared.

To which her beaming mother replied: "And don't think I'm not proud of that. And I aim to keep it that way."

*

That was what television audiences saw. The memories of Nancy's children tell a darker story, one that didn't fit their image as America's ideal family. The Screen Father of the Year, so often on the road, was inaccessible even when he was home. "He was easy to love but hard to know," his son, Ron, wrote later. "He was seldom far from our minds, but you couldn't help wondering sometimes whether he remembered you once you were out of his sight."

The vacuum that Ronnie left behind during his long absences was often filled by their mother's anxiety and insecurity, which took control of family life when he was gone. Nancy hired and fired maids and cooks in quick succession. "What happened between arrival and departure was yelling. I remember sitting in my bedroom with my hands over my ears because I could hear my mother's voice in the kitchen, yelling at the maid about dishes in the wrong cupboards or something not being prepared right. I would sing to myself to block out the sound," Patti wrote in her 1992 memoir.

Nancy's wrath landed on her children as well. Patti (who declined to be interviewed for this book) claimed that her mother beat her, starting when she was eight and escalating into "a weekly, sometimes daily, event." The slaps and blows came at the end of arguments about nearly everything: over whether Patti was too chubby to be eating cookies, over Nancy's demand that her daughter go to the bathroom before she went to bed, over Patti's insistence that she be allowed to grow her hair as long as she wanted.

Patti also wrote that her mother abused prescription drugs—among them, the tranquilizer Miltown and Seconal for sleep. If so, Nancy was hardly alone among housewives in the 1950s and 1960s. They later became known as the "Miltown generation." The male-dominated medical profession preferred the quick fix of sedating these women rather than taking the causes of their underlying mental health issues more seriously. Female patients were expected to accept without question this doctor-knows-best approach, and Nancy most likely would have, being the daughter of a physician herself. Patti said she once asked her father why her mother took so many pills, and Ronnie told her: "Because you upset her so much."

Nancy, on the other hand, believed that the rage Patti directed at her was really about her high-strung daughter's need for attention and "unresolved feelings about her father." The implication was that Patti saw herself in a competition with Nancy for a place in Ronnie's heart. They had been adversaries from the start. Patti's toddler years had been tests of will. When Nancy appealed to her pediatrician for advice, he told her to ignore Patti's antics and busy herself elsewhere. So, Nancy tried it one day when Patti refused to swallow her string beans. An hour and a half went by. Patti's nap time passed. Her mother returned to check on her, only to find the two-year-old sitting there with her cheeks still full of beans. Patti said impishly: "What I got in my mouth, Mommy?"

Years later when Nancy drove the carpool to school, Patti always sat as far from her as possible. If they were walking, Patti dropped several steps behind rather than be at her mother's side. Nancy would later contend that, if anything, she was too lenient with her daughter and too indulgent of Patti's constant demands to be center stage in their home. Ronnie was no help in the discipline department. He dismissed Patti's behavior as "only a phase" and seemed bewildered when Nancy raised the possibility that there might be something amiss in their family.

Ron, the more easygoing younger child, was known as Skipper and was the open favorite of both his parents. He told me he believes Patti's claims about her mother's abuse were exaggerated. "This is Patti's story, and she's entitled to it. This is what she thinks, and I don't mean to take issue with it. But we grew up in the same house," he said.

Ron did acknowledge there had been instances where Nancy hit Patti on the face. And he recalls that his father once smacked his sister for invoking the name of the Lord in anger. But Ron sees it from the perspective of the era, when that kind of punishment was widely considered an acceptable form of discipline. "We just weren't a physically abusive household. A lot worse was going on in a lot of houses," Ron said. "Jane Wyman used to beat Maureen and Mike with a riding crop. There was nothing like that that went on in our house."

And while his mother was prescribed diet and sleeping pills, "my impression is that, a little like the abuse, that there's a little bit of hyperbole there" in Patti's version of events, Ron said. "They would prescribe something to calm you down. 'Mother's Little Helper' kind of stuff. But I don't know that my mother ever took them. I was aware. As a little kid, you go through every drawer in the house just looking to see what's there. We had a medicine chest. Pills and stuff like that were in there. But they always seemed to be the same pills, and they were always full, the bottles.

"My mother didn't like to drink much. She did not want to dull her senses," Ron added. "She was too anxious, really, to give up that kind of awareness. So, no, she was not a zombie, by any means. She was hyperalert, if anything."

What the baby of the family did see, however, was that their household became a battleground when Ronnie was away. Nancy—her long-buried fears of abandonment stirring—weaponized her insecurities. She manufactured crises and drama. "My mother was difficult at times, could be emotionally—*abusive* is too big a word, because it implies a kind of calculated cruelty that was constant. She was an anxious personality, and her anxieties, particularly when my father was away, were visited upon her children," Ron said. "You didn't know quite who you're going to be dealing with today, so you had to be wary of her."

Trouble would erupt every time his father had to be on the road for a few days. "There was sort of a routine to it, where you could just count on her picking a fight at some point. It might be about nothing, really, but she'd start in on you, and eventually, as a twelve- or fourteen-year-old, you're going to snap back. And that's it. There you go. That's what [she] wanted," Ron said.

"My perception of it as a kid, and still today, is that one way to kind of get [his father] back into the family, in her mind, was to create some incident with one of the kids, either Patti or me," Ron told me. "In her mind, I think, he had left, and he needed to be pulled back. And this was the way to do it, somehow. Of course, my father hated any kind of interpersonal stuff like that; any strife in the family."

Ronnie invariably accepted without question Nancy's version of the horrible things his children had supposedly done in his absence. He would pull Ron aside and tell him: "Now, now, Ron. You know you've hurt your mother very much. She's in there crying her eyes out, and I know that it would mean the world to her if she could just hear those two little words: 'I'm sorry.'"

As the years went by and he matured, Ron began to comprehend the dynamic that was driving the drama between his parents. He rejected the guilt that was being foisted on his small shoulders. "At first, when you're six or something, that kind of works. You feel terrible: 'My God, what have I done?' By the time you're twelve or so, it's like, 'Oh, for God's sake,'" Ron said. "Then you start saying, 'I've got nothing to apologize for. And I know you won't believe me, but she starts a fight every time you leave.'"

Dysfunctional strains also developed between Nancy and her two stepchildren from Ronnie's first marriage. "Now that I'm older and more experienced in life, I think there's probably more I could have done to help Maureen and Michael when they were young," Nancy wrote decades later. "If I had been more confident in myself as a mother, I think I would have. It's too bad that the most important job we have in life—parenting—is the one we have no training for."

Though Nancy's relationship with Maureen had been an easy one when she was dating Ronnie, that changed after she married him. Maureen felt displaced. Her father had started a new family, and it stung her to hear him call Patti "Shorty," which was the nickname he had once used for her. Jane had also remarried. Maureen didn't really feel at home in either household. Nor did either seem to want her. She was shipped off to a Catholic high school in New York and then to a college in Virginia, from which she dropped out at the age of eighteen. (None of the four Reagan children got a degree.)

Maureen made a rocky entry into adulthood. It began with a brief marriage to a District of Columbia police officer who beat her. She left him after he slammed their kitten into a wall. "When I told my parents about the divorce, I simply told them the marriage hadn't worked out, but I didn't tell them why," she wrote later. "The shame and embarrassment I'd felt from the first had by this time grown into something I could not get past. I had built a wall, and I decided to leave the wall intact."

Because she lived so far away, Ronnie's eldest was only an occasional presence on San Onofre. Nonetheless, she was startled when she visited around 1960 and discovered that eight-year-old Patti had no clue they were sisters. When Maureen told her they were, Patti burst into tears and ran from the room. "Dad was quite embarrassed when he explained to me later that afternoon, 'Well, we just haven't gotten that far yet,'" Maureen recalled.

That was around the time that fourteen-year-old Michael, who had become a discipline problem for Jane, was sent to live with his father and Nancy on the recommendation of a psychiatrist. Michael's was the saddest situation of any of the four Reagan children. He arrived at the Reagan home with no wardrobe other than his school uniforms. When Nancy took him to a dentist, she discovered he had ten cavities.

Michael had been barely out of diapers when Ronnie and Jane divorced, and the turmoil that followed—a succession of boarding schools, new stepparents on both sides—left him feeling, as Maureen did, that he had no place to belong. But Michael had additional, deep-seated insecurities about having been adopted, a fact about himself he learned when he was four. He learned not from his parents, but from Maureen, who blurted it out during a quarrel. And there was something else—a secret he would reveal many years later. Michael was sexually abused by a camp counselor when he was eight years old. The man had also taken lewd pictures of him, which Michael was terrified would surface someday. His secret made the boy feel ashamed and confused and dirty.

Nancy, at the time, knew none of this. "I was flying blind with Michael, and I had no idea what was really going on with him," she wrote. "Michael and I had such rough times during that period that there were times when I could have killed him. Teenagers can be difficult in any case, but Mike was especially troubled and rebellious."

Michael had hoped that he might live with his father's family full-time. Instead, he found himself in yet another boarding school. He visited the GE dream house in Pacific Palisades only on weekends and had to sleep on a couch in the living room. There was no bed for him. At one point, he learned that Ronnie and Nancy were adding a room to their house. He was thrilled, until he discovered the new bedroom was for Ron's nurse. Michael begged to be allowed to stay with them all the time. "Why can't Nancy drive me to school every morning and pick me up in the afternoon just like the other kids?" Michael asked his father. "It's only half an hour from home."

"She's too busy with Ron and Patti," Ronnie told him. "Don't you think it's enough that she has opened up her house to you and invited you in?"

There was one moment that, in Michael's telling, suggests a shocking vindictiveness on his stepmother's part. In 1961 the two of them were having yet another argument, this one over his latest miserable report card. Nancy told the sixteen-year-old: "You're not living up to the Reagan name or image, and unless you start shaping up, it would be best for you to change your name and leave the house."

"Fine," Michael retorted. "Why don't you just tell me the name I was born with, so at least when I walk out the door, I'll know what name to use?"

It is not hard to imagine the storm of feelings this must have stirred up in Nancy, who herself had once wanted so badly to earn the name of the man she thought of as her father. But her reaction was harsh. "Okay, Mr. Reagan," Nancy snapped. "I'll do just that."

She got the name of Michael's birth mother from the business manager Ronnie still shared with Jane. A week later, Nancy informed Michael that he had been born John Flaugher and was the product of a fling between an unmarried woman and an army sergeant. Michael was mortified to discover he was, in his words, "an illegitimate bastard who would never amount to anything. Without being aware of it, Nancy had rubber-stamped all the fears I'd had for years."

In explaining why she had disclosed to Michael information that his adoptive parents had withheld from him, Nancy offered a version that was only slightly more benign—and not exactly persuasive of her good intentions: "I was told that Jane was not pleased that I had answered Michael's question. But he was obviously troubled by having been adopted, and I thought he had the right to know the truth about his own background. It seemed like a natural thing to want to know, and I hoped this would give him some peace of mind."

From there, Michael and Nancy rarely spoke. Which meant his father became even more remote. At Michael's 1964 graduation from the exclusive Judson prep school in Arizona, Ronnie gave the commencement speech. Before he spoke, the famous television star posed for pictures with some of the graduates. Ronnie said the same thing to each in turn, including Michael: "My name is Ronald Reagan. What's yours?"

Michael whipped off his mortar board. "Remember me?" he said. "I'm your son Mike."

"Oh," Ronnie replied. "I didn't recognize you."

Nancy, looking for guidance on how to handle her rebellious children, turned to the parent that she herself had idolized. "She probably talked to my father every day and got his input," her brother, Richard, told me. "I don't think he always gave her the best advice. It was always very strict, which is good for some children and not for others."

Loyal "felt that the children were dragging her down, were depressing her," Richard added. Their father frequently reminded Nancy to remember that "your husband comes first."

Michael found support from a different source: Nancy's mother. Michael's Arizona boarding school was not far from where the Davises had retired. He was delighted when his step-grandmother showed up in the stands at his baseball games. Once, when Michael was up to bat with two runners on base, he heard Edie shout: "You better hit a home run, you little sonofabitch!"

And he did, for the first and only time ever.

Edie "was a warm-hearted, generous woman who, I think, knew I was having problems and was always sympathetic to me," Michael recalled. When he graduated, Edie gave him a signet ring, which he cherished. Michael regretted that he never told Nancy's mother how much that meant to him. When Edie died in 1987, he cried. It was the first time, Michael realized, that he had ever wept over someone in the family who was not himself.

Ronnie, meanwhile, was explicit in his priorities. He had only one: Nancy. In a letter dated May 24, 1963, after they had apparently been discussing their difficulties with Michael over the phone, Ronnie wrote this:

> Whether Mike helps buy his first car or spends the money on sports coats isn't really important. We both want for get him started on a road that will lead to his being able to provide for himself. In x number of years, we'll face the same problem with The Skipper and somehow we'll probably find the right answers. (Patti is another kind of problem, and we'll do all we can to make that one right, too.) But

what is really important is that having fulfilled our responsibilities to our offspring we haven't been careless with the treasure that is ours—namely what we are to each other.

Do you know that when you sleep you curl your fists up under your chin and many mornings when it is barely dawn I lie facing you and looking at you until finally I have to touch you ever so lightly so you won't wake up—but touch you I must or I will burst?

. . . Probably this letter will reach you only a few hours before I arrive myself, but not really because right now as I try to say what is in my heart I think my thoughts must be reaching for you without waiting for paper and ink and stamps and such. If I ache, it's because we are apart and yet that can't be because you are inside and a part of me, so we aren't really apart at all. Yet I ache but wouldn't be without the ache, because that would mean being without you and that I can't be because I love you.

Your Husband

By the time Ronnie wrote this, their circumstances had changed again. *General Electric Theater* had slipped in the ratings and plunged when NBC in 1961 moved its popular Western show *Bonanza* into the same time slot on Sunday nights. In March 1962 General Electric informed Ronnie that it was canceling his show. Ronnie believed that one reason he lost his corporate sponsor was the more overtly political direction that his speeches had taken. He was constantly talking of the dangers of government run amok. One of his lines of argument went like this: "Today there is an increasing number who can't see a fat man standing beside a thin one without automatically coming to the conclusion the fat man got that way by taking advantage of the thin one. So they would seek the answer to all the problems of human need through government."

By the late 1950s, Ronnie had fully broken with the New Deal liberalism of his youth; in 1962 he reregistered as a Republican. General Electric began pressuring him to confine his speeches to pitching the company's products—or as Ronnie put it, suggesting he pick such spellbinding topics as "a description of the new 1963 coffee pot." Ronnie refused, so he and GE parted ways. His career in show business was effectively over, save for a twenty-one-episode gig hosting and acting in the television series *Death Valley Days* and a flop of a film called *The Killers*. The Reagans were once again fearful about their financial security, although their situation was far better than it had been before *GE Theater*. Nancy could also see that Ronnie's passions were driving him in a new direction. As early as 1962, he was getting letters urging him to run for president. I found one of them saved among the personal papers at the Reagan Library. "The country needs your kind of leadership," wrote Norman L. Stevens Jr., a petroleum consultant from Roswell, New Mexico, who had heard Ronnie speak to the local chamber of commerce.

Ronnie became a sought-after campaign surrogate for Republican candidates, including 1964 GOP presidential nominee Barry Goldwater, who had become friendly with Edie and Loyal in Arizona. As Ronnie spoke on behalf of others, he made basically the same pitch he had been giving for years, throwing in a few references to the campaign and the candidate he was promoting. He lit up conservative audiences as he had the workers in the GE plants. After a group of Goldwater donors heard him give his standard spiel at the Cocoanut Grove nightclub in Los Angeles, some of them came up with an idea: they would buy a big block of time on national television to have Ronnie deliver it again right before the election.

Goldwater himself was initially hesitant to let Ronnie do it. The Republican standard-bearer wanted to instead air a more conventional spot featuring himself meeting with former president Dwight D. Eisenhower. But his backers persuaded him that Ronnie could make a stronger case for Goldwater than he could for himself. On October 27, 1964, he gave an electrifying half-hour address, which was broadcast on NBC. "A Time for Choosing" would later be seen as a pivotal moment in the Reagan story. Its most memorable passage echoed one that FDR had delivered when he accepted the Democratic nomination in 1936. "You and I have a rendezvous with destiny," Ronnie declared.

"We can preserve for your children this, the last best hope of man on earth, or we can sentence them to take the first step into a thousand years of darkness." By some accounts, his appeal raised $8 million for Goldwater—an unheard-of sum. Not even that windfall, however, was enough to save the Arizona senator from losing to incumbent Lyndon Johnson in a landslide of historic proportion.

Still, that televised speech turned out to be Ronnie and Nancy's rendezvous with their own destiny. Ronnie was suddenly seen as the voice of a conservative movement, the savior who might lead the Republican Party's rise from the wreckage of the 1964 defeat. Just a few days after the election, a group of Goldwater's big fund-raisers were in the Reagans' Pacific Palisades living room, pleading with Ronnie to consider running for California governor in 1966. They were led by wealthy automobile dealer Holmes Tuttle. He was a respected figure among Republicans in the West, well connected enough to be a regular member of Eisenhower's golfing foursomes in Palm Desert.

As Ronnie told it later, Nancy was "flabbergasted." But that was not true. "I knew those people were going to come up to the house after that disastrous election," she told biographer Bob Colacello. "I knew it. And they did. At first, Ronnie said, 'Well, let me think about it.' And then finally he said to me, 'You know, the party is in such bad shape, if I felt that I could do something to help it, and I didn't do it, I'd feel terrible.' So he said to them, 'Let me go out and see what the response of the people is.'

"And there we were. On a road we never intended to be on. Ever."

CHAPTER SIX

Actor Jimmy Stewart was purported to have once said: "If Ronald Reagan had married Nancy the first time round, she could've got him the Academy Award." Nancy may never have expected to see Ronnie go into politics. But once their life turned in that direction, she was determined that the two of them would set a course for greatness.

History has given much credit to the early assistance that Ronnie got from his Kitchen Cabinet, the group of wealthy backers who recognized the potential in a former movie actor. Most of them self-made millionaires who had picked up an interest in politics on the way to earning their fortunes, they financed his first campaigns and oversaw the selection of his advisers. At the core of this small group were auto dealer Holmes Tuttle and Italian-born geophysicist Henry Salvatori, who was among the pioneers of petroleum exploration. After the 1964 election debacle, they turned to Ronnie as their best hope of rebuilding the Republican Party in California and beyond. He was the man, they were convinced, whose eloquence and common touch would make their conservative principles appeal to working-class and suburban Democrats.

As the Kitchen Cabinet built the scaffolding for Ronnie's rise, Nancy became a frequent intermediary. "Reagan seldom sought their collective advice," recalled Thomas C. Reed, a top operative in Ronnie's first gubernatorial campaign, but "their grievances, if untended, would surely percolate into his quiet space via Nancy." She was constantly on the phone with Ronnie's rich benefactors, stroking their egos and soliciting their opinions, gathering up whatever scraps of gossip they might have heard. "She cultivated them and maintained them in a way that my father just wouldn't have; wouldn't have occurred to him, really," Ron said.

While Ronnie was moving more deeply into political activism in the early 1960s, he got to know some of the leading intellectual lights of the conservative movement. Chief among those relationships was the friendship the Reagans developed with *National Review* founder William F. Buckley Jr. and his wife, Patricia, a legendary hostess and socialite. "Probably the best instructor he had in the process was Bill Buckley. He really respected Bill Buckley, a thoughtful guy who had a point of view that he found interesting," Ronnie's first campaign manager, Stu Spencer, recalled. Nancy was the caretaker of the more personal side of that relationship. For decades, she and Buckley sent flirtatious letters back and forth. In one, dated January 4, 1965, she teased the erudite Buckley about his famously expansive vocabulary: "I'm still waiting for just the right moment to drop Zeitgeist (sp?) into the conversation and amaze all my friends—but so far it hasn't come—it's terribly frustrating." Ten days later, Nancy's tone was more serious as she confided to Buckley that she was deeply ambivalent about the path on which her husband was about to take them: "I alternately feel terribly brave about the whole thing and then as if I'd like to crawl into a cave where no one could find me. I know if Ronnie does decide to go into politics all the way, I'd better get over that."

Though her ambition burned as brightly as Ronnie's, Nancy was keenly aware of how much they were putting at risk, how much they would be leaving behind. The Reagans finally had achieved financial security and were traveling—thanks largely to her—in an elite social circle. During the lean, early years of their marriage, they kept company mostly with a tight group of friends from their movie days. They still saw Bill and Ardis Holden, of course. "Our idea of a big evening was to watch a picture on television with the Holdens, or go out to the movies," Nancy said. Ronnie and Nancy also were close with onetime matinee idol Robert Taylor and his stunning wife, Ursula, who lived across the street in Pacific Palisades. Bob Taylor and Ronnie had a lot in common, including an introverted nature and a shared love of retreating to their ranches at every opportunity. Get-togethers with the Taylors were low-key and casual. Ronnie liked it that everyone felt comfortable wearing jeans at dinner.

But as Ronnie's fortunes improved, so did Nancy's opportunity to meet and ingratiate the Reagans into a more gilt-edged—and beneficial—set of friends. During their father's years on television, Patti and Ron went to Bel Air's exclusive John Thomas Dye School, as did the children of many famous Hollywood people. Nancy threw herself into volunteer work there. She met Mary Jane Wick at a 1959 school fair where the two of them ran the hot dog booth. The families started a ritual of spending Christmases together and continued to do so right through the Reagans' years in the White House. Mary Jane's husband, Charles Z. Wick, an entertainment lawyer who made a fortune in investments and nursing homes, would later raise $15 million for Ronnie's 1980 presidential campaign and be rewarded with a post as head of the United States Information Agency, which was set up during the Cold War to spread this country's vision across the world via platforms such as Voice of America. Their son Doug Wick, who became a producer of major films, including the 2000 epic *Gladiator*, described Nancy as "the queen bee. She was glamorous and fun and smart. At my parents' parties, my dad would play the piano, and she would sing. She had a beautiful voice." But Nancy was also "very strategic" in her relationships, Wick said: "She had a very good X-ray vision for who was full of shit and who was a person of substance."

A sprawling city with no definable center, Los Angeles ran on imagination, opportunity, and reinvention. There existed an older social order, bunkered in the mansions of San Marino and Hancock Park. But power and prestige were the by-products of ambition in Southern California, growing as fortunes were made in oil, real estate, banking, and water. In just a generation or two, a family could go from being hungry speculators to stodgy capitalists welcomed into the downtown sanctums of the Jonathan Club or the California Club.

As Edie once had, Nancy found a foothold among the select by doing charity work. She was accepted for membership into the Colleagues, an elite organization of fifty socialites who raised money for women and children's causes and who got together each month for gossip-fueled luncheons. The Colleagues were perfectly coiffed clotheshorses. Their big annual fund-raiser was a sale of slightly used designer creations that had been worn only once or twice before they were ready to be cast off. "The ladies of the Colleagues were serious indeed about their projects," Laurence Leamer wrote. "They roamed the precincts of Los Angeles in Mercedes and Rolls-Royces, picking up boxes of clothes, and gowns on hangers. Nancy was driving only a station wagon at the time, but she was one of them."

The Reagans' newer, flashier friends—who would later be dubbed "the Group" by the press—were far richer than they were. Film producer Armand Deutsch, a fellow Chicagoan whom Nancy had known from MGM, was the oldest grandson of a longtime Sears, Roebuck chairman; his wife, Harriet, was an arts patron. Through the Deutsches, Nancy got to know billionaire philanthropists Walter and Leonore Annenberg, whose fortune came from publishing. The Annenbergs' two-hundred-acre Sunnylands estate near Palm Springs would be where Ronnie and Nancy spent every New Year's Eve between 1974 and 1993. The Reagans also became close to Earle Jorgensen, who made a pile of money in steel, and his wife, Marion, who was a tireless networker on behalf of both her causes and her chums. Another friend was Betty Wilson, a Pennzoil heiress married to wealthy rancher and oil-equipment manufacturer William Wilson, later Ronnie's envoy to the Vatican.

Fabulously fun Betsy Bloomingdale—her husband, Alfred, was a grandson of the department store founder and ran the successful Diners Club credit card franchise—was Nancy's closest confidant and her role model on all matters of taste and style. Betsy's legendary wardrobe of haute couture filled eleven meticulously organized closets.

Through Betsy, Nancy was introduced to favored designers such as Adolfo Sardiña, known only as Adolfo to his legions of wealthy female devotees. Betsy's interesting friends also included "social moth" Jerry Zipkin, a gay, uber-sophisticated Manhattan real estate heir. In its 1995 obituary of Zipkin, the *New York Times* referred to him as "a man about everywhere." Zipkin was a fixture at society galas, usually as a "walker" escorting rich women whose husbands had other places they would rather be. Nancy saw him as "a sort of modern-day Oscar Wilde." For decades, Zipkin would be her near-daily source of news and gossip, and a channel through which others gained access to her. When Nancy was in the White House, Zipkin regularly mailed her batches of New York newspaper clippings, with the juicy parts highlighted in yellow marker.

It took no small amount of prodding from Nancy to get her husband to plunge into her rapidly growing milieu of fellow climbers. High-powered socializing was not how Ronnie would have chosen to spend their time. "He was great in front of an audience, great in a room, great telling people stories, putting them at ease, making them laugh. But left to his own devices, he would have much preferred to just go to the ranch and ride horses and cut brush and pound fence posts and things like that," their son, Ron, said. "She got him out and about and meeting people, both in California and in Washington. Even to the extent of arranging 'playdates' for him. As amicable and genial and fun to be with as he was, he had virtually no close friends. Lots of acquaintances, lots of what I and some of my friends used to call the 'El Friendos,' who were sort of the Kitchen Cabinet types, but these were not people that he really hung out with."

Stu Spencer, the top political adviser who moved in and out of Ronnie's orbit for more than two decades, put it more succinctly: "Reagan would have been a great hermit, a perfect hermit." Others around Ronnie often used the exact same word—*hermit*—to describe his inner nature. Spencer and his partner, Bill Roberts, were among the first people Ronnie and his backers sought out as he began thinking more seriously about running for governor. They had been recommended to Ronnie by Goldwater, against whom their firm had worked in the 1964 GOP primary in California. The duo had guided New York governor Nelson Rockefeller's campaign to a surprisingly close second-place finish. "I'd hire those sons of bitches," Goldwater advised Ronnie.

That was a time when professional political consulting was still in its infancy; campaigns before then were generally run by amateurs and cronies. The young operatives started their firm in 1960 and quickly developed a reputation for sure-footed strategy and hardball tactics. Spencer and Roberts had already been approached to run the campaign of one of Ronnie's prospective GOP opponents, former San Francisco mayor George Christopher, who was considered the favorite in the Republican race. But when they were summoned to Pacific Palisades for a meeting in March 1965, they sensed something in the fading movie actor that made him worth a gamble. "This guy could do it," they told each other. "If we handle it right, this guy could make it."

But Spencer and Roberts also recognized that both Ronnie and his wife were Hollywood people, which meant they were clueless about what running for office would entail. They had potential, but they were going to require a lot of preparation. What was also clear, from the outset, was that the Reagans came as a package deal. During that first session in their living room, Nancy sat in a chair, her legs tucked under her. She listened intently and said almost nothing. "Nancy was in every one of the meetings we had with Reagan. She was quiet. With those big eyes of hers, she'd be watching you almost warily. Every now and then she'd ask a question, but probably less than a handful of times," Spencer recalled. "I was always sure she had plenty to say to him after Bill and I left."

At one point during their initial meeting, Nancy got up and went into a bedroom. Spencer followed her, and asked, "Nancy, what's wrong?"

"I don't know," she answered. "It's just too much. It's a whole new world, and I'm not sure I'm ready for it."

"You can do it," Spencer told her. "But I don't want to kid you. This is just the beginning. It's going to get worse."

Over the coming years, Nancy would speak up more often, as her confidence in her own instincts grew. At those times, Spencer learned, he was the one who should be listening. "She's actually a terrifically intelligent politician," he said. "She thinks politically. In some ways, much more than he ever did. . . . She developed over the years an instinct about people who would fit her husband best. She knew his strengths and weaknesses, surely. But the chief criterion for her was: whose agenda are they pursuing? Ronald Reagan's or their own? She got very good at sorting that out."

The intensity of the Reagans' emotional and romantic bond became evident to Spencer early. One evening, following a dinner at a Mexican restaurant, he accompanied the couple to Los Angeles's Union Station, where Ronnie was catching a train for a television shoot. As the conductor shouted, "All aboard!" Ronnie and Nancy fell into each other's arms and started making out for what seemed like an interminable amount of time. Spencer grew deeply embarrassed. "Jesus, this is like a scene out of a damn movie," he thought to himself. "What the hell is going on?" Those cinematic displays of affection were something he would learn to get used to.

There was one more insight into the couple that Spencer would gain as he was deciding whether to attempt to turn a movie actor into a politician. He had lunch one day with Reagan's agent, Taft Schreiber, who cautioned him that Ronnie was allergic to interpersonal conflict, which is something endemic to nearly every political operation. "You're going to have to fire a lot of people," Schreiber advised. "Ronnie never fired anybody in his life."

That, Spencer would later come to understand, would be Nancy's job—just as so many other distasteful things would fall to her, in California and beyond. "She was the one that was going to be the bad guy," he said. "She took on a role as personnel director. She knew as well as I knew, because we discussed it. 'Ronnie won't fire anybody.' I said, 'Well, somebody's going to have to fire people.' She had no qualms about firing people. She'd get somebody to do the job. One of her qualities was tenacity."

The initial order of business: Spencer and Roberts told both Reagans they were going to have to get over their fear of flying. It was the only way to get around the vast state. Ronnie and Nancy agreed, though for years they would insist on traveling in separate planes, apparently superstitious that being on the same one was tempting fate. On Spencer's first flight with Nancy, a short hop from LA to San Francisco on Western Airlines, she dug her nails so deeply into his hand that it bled.

The consultants went to work writing campaign plans for Ronnie. It was a challenge to figure out how to put one together for such an unconventional candidate. Former actor George Murphy, who, coincidentally, had played Ronnie's father in the 1943 movie *This Is the Army*, had been elected to the US Senate the previous year. The Republican's victory showed that Californians were willing to vote for a former movie actor with a conservative message. But putting one in the governor's mansion was a bigger leap.

Around their third day on the job, the consultants were pondering the candidate's potential negatives. What from Reagan's past might emerge and become a problem for his campaign? That was when they suddenly realized there was a big unknown that had to be dealt with: Jane Wyman. Divorced politicians were a rarity in those days, and they had no idea what Ronnie's ex-wife might say once the campaign got under way.

"We've got to find out where she is on this whole thing," Roberts said. Spencer drew the short straw to take on this awkward task. He made an appointment to visit Wyman at her home. Though it was only ten in the morning, Jane greeted him with a cocktail in her hand—apparently not her first of the day. Spencer also noticed that she didn't offer him one. He told Jane that her ex-husband was thinking of running for governor, something she already knew from reading the papers. After a little more small talk, Jane interrupted him: "I think I know why you're here. You're worried about what I might do."

"You hit it right on the head," Spencer replied. "We just feel it's important that we know where you stand in this whole thing."

"I hope Ronnie wins," Jane said. "He deserves it."

Spencer was relieved, but he wasn't prepared for what Jane said next. "She had a little bit of Irish devil in her," Spencer told me. "She says, 'I will not tell the world that Ronnie was a lousy lay.'"

Jane was as good as her word. For the next two decades, as Ronnie rose to the most powerful office in the world, she refrained from making public comments about her ex-husband. "She played it straight the whole time. I think she made one statement early about how he's always wanted this. 'I wish him well,'" Spencer said. "I remember, on election night, she was about the third person that called us at the Biltmore hotel to congratulate him.

"I didn't tell Nancy that," he added.

Spencer also found an unexpected asset in Edie. Nancy's mom handed the campaign manager a list of names of people she promised would give large sums to help her son-in-law get elected. Spencer called them, and sure enough, every one of them promised a contribution. When Edie checked in a few weeks later to see how it went, Spencer dutifully tallied for her what he had gotten from her friends: a $1,500 check here, another $4,000 there. He thought she would be pleased.

"Those cheap sons of bitches!" Edie sputtered. "I'm taking over!"

Spencer marveled: "I watched it. One of the sons of bitches sent a check for fifteen grand, and another one sent a check for twenty. She really got on them."

The exploratory committee launched in May 1965. Ronnie spent the next months testing his message and his abilities as a candidate in small communities across the state. He questioned why his handlers weren't sending him to larger places, where there were more votes to be had. "It's like a show," Spencer explained to Ronnie and Nancy, trying to frame the endeavor in terms the couple would understand. "You take it out of town. You work it out, get the kinks out of it, and screwups and all of this stuff, and then you go to the big city."

Ronnie formally declared he was running for governor on January 4, 1966. His campaign broadcast the announcement in a pretaped speech on fifteen television stations across the state. A week earlier, Nancy had written William F. Buckley: "I must say my emotions are wired. I awaken early often and think, 'Good God. What have we gotten ourselves into?' Well, we shall see. Don't you think you'll have to come out here sometime during the campaign for *National Review*? Please do—I want my friends around me too—not just my enemies!"

California was a state where Democrats outnumbered Republicans by a 3-to-2 margin, but its voters were not intensely partisan. They had elected Republican governors Earl Warren and Goodwin Knight in the 1950s, and George Murphy as their senator over former Kennedy White House press secretary Pierre Salinger in 1964. Moreover, the political environment was ripe for Ronnie's message and his fresh qualities as a "citizen-politician." Los Angeles had been shaken in 1965 by race riots in Watts, which left thirty-four dead and created deep anxiety among whites. California news broadcasts were filled with anti–Vietnam War protests on the University of California at Berkeley campus and scenes of free-loving hippies in the Haight-Ashbury section of San Francisco, which unsettled people in the suburbs. Meanwhile, there was frustration across the political spectrum at the state's soaring property taxes. A revolt was brewing.

With little guidance from Ronnie's team, Nancy struggled to figure out what her own role in the campaign should be. At first, she did not want to go on the trail at all. Then she agreed to make appearances, but only to take questions about her husband, not to give speeches. "We went to tiny, tiny little towns," she said. "One town I remember we landed in darkness, and they didn't even have lights at the airport. They had gotten cars out to line the way, and they turned their lights on. And that's how we landed." Nancy learned not to mention the name of the city where she was speaking, because when she was making six stops a day, it was easy to get it wrong. "It's nice to be here," she would say. Part of her job was to reinforce Ronnie's conservative message. On campuses, Nancy was asked about marijuana and said that as a doctor's daughter, she opposed it. She told audiences she thought the movies of the day were too violent and explicit. She denounced premarital sex, live-in relationships, and permissive child rearing.

*

Her own home, however, was hardly the picture of the values she espoused. Nancy's daughter was smoking pot with her friends and becoming addicted to diet pills. Patti's rebellious nature was a constant source of potential embarrassment. One crisis came when she attempted to run off to Alaska with the handsome dishwasher from her Arizona boarding school. The plan was thwarted only because Patti tried to enlist her stepbrother, Michael, by then a twenty-one-year-old adult, to sign her out, and he alerted Nancy. At another point during the campaign, Patti disappeared from home for a day after an argument with her mother, one that started over Patti's refusal to wear a Reagan campaign button. When Patti decided to return, Nancy sounded more concerned about how the incident might reflect upon Ronnie than about her daughter's welfare. "It could have been all over the papers!" Nancy said.

"She slapped my face hard and then stormed out," Patti wrote later. "I went to the mirror and watched as my face grew red. It had become a ritual: the siege would end with a slap, and I'd be left alone, staring in the mirror with hard, tearless eyes."

Ronnie, as usual, left all of the difficult and contentious parts of parenting to Nancy.

It was decided that Maureen and Michael—awkward reminders of Ronnie's first marriage—were to be rendered invisible for the duration of the campaign. On that, Nancy and Spencer agreed.

Michael seemed to have little interest in politics. He was adrift and preoccupied with finding his own way in life. Having flunked out of college, he worked a series of menial jobs, fell deeply into debt, and discovered a passion for racing expensive boats. At one point, Nancy asked Maureen whether her second husband, a marine captain named David Sills, might find a way to have Michael drafted and shipped off to Vietnam.

But while Michael was not clamoring for a role in his father's campaign, it was hurtful to Maureen to be excluded from it. She had become a Republican before he had and worked for Goldwater in 1964.

Early in Ronnie's gubernatorial run, Maureen was invited by a local GOP organization to introduce her father at a banquet in San Diego. That seemed fine to assistant campaign director Dave Tomshany, who had driven Ronnie to the event. But when Tomshany and the candidate returned to Pacific Palisades later that night, they were met at the door by Nancy.

"She was *livid*—because Jane Wyman's daughter, Maureen, had introduced Ron, her father, at this San Diego banquet and speech," Tomshany recounted later in a book of reminiscences compiled by Reagan aide Curtis Patrick. "Now, I had no idea who Maureen was before that day—and all of a sudden, it's his daughter from the previous marriage and—*oh, she was livid!* I think she chewed me out for, probably, fifteen minutes."

The event had been painful for Maureen as well. She was handed a biography the campaign had drafted to be read as her father's introduction. It said: "Ronald Reagan and his wife, Nancy, have two children, Patti and Ronnie." Humiliated to see herself written out of the story of his life, Ronnie's eldest discarded it and read from her own notes, telling stories from her and Michael's childhood. Later, Maureen claimed, Spencer told her husband that Maureen should "dig a hole and pull the dirt in over me until after the election." Maureen appealed to her father, asking for a more visible role. But Ronnie told her: "If you pay someone to manage a campaign, then you've got to give them the authority to do it as they see fit."

Nancy, meanwhile, was becoming less willing to defer to the campaign's hired guns. She let the men who ran the campaign know when she—and her friends—thought they were falling down on the job. "I'm working. My phone would ring, it's Nancy Reagan," Spencer told me. "It's six o'clock, and she wants to talk about the campaign, talk about all the goddamn rumors she'd heard at the bridge party that day with Betsy, and blah, blah, blah. All the stuff, and all her political counsel and advice, every day."

One morning, the operator running the old-fashioned PBX switchboard at campaign headquarters neglected to put Nancy on hold before announcing to Spencer: "The bitch is on the phone again." Then the operator accidentally dropped the line. Nancy called right back and said icily: "Well, I hope I didn't destroy your day." This time the embarrassed woman quickly transferred her to Spencer. Nancy didn't miss a beat before launching into her fresh list of concerns.

Ronnie's Northern California chairman, Tom Reed, also got regular calls, which he considered "a dubious honor heretofore sloughed off on those closer at hand. Nancy was a very active candidate's wife, supportive and protective of RR, but incessantly injecting her views and personal demands on anyone who would listen—along with many who did not wish to do so." Reed wrote that "Nancy's political calls, directed at any who would listen, usually came first thing in the morning as soon as RR left the house. She wanted to discuss her perception of the campaign, garnered from her dinner companions of the night before. These women were hardly a cross-section of working-class California."

No doubt there was more than a little sexism at work in these men's dismissal of the idea that Nancy should be anything but ornamental to Ronnie's campaign. In their view, the role of the spouse was to make herself presentable, show up where asked, and parrot what she was told to say. Spencer, though, would come to understand that Nancy's instincts were generally on the mark. They revealed a deep understanding of her husband and a sharp sense of what he needed to stay on the top of his game. Nancy made demands that Ronnie wouldn't. She insisted, for instance, that no matter how much he traveled, he must spend every night possible at home in his own bed. She knew that when Ronnie was tired or under the weather, or when the campaign ran him too hard, he blundered—as he did when he stormed out of a convention of black Republicans after his GOP opponents suggested he was racist for opposing the landmark 1964 Civil Rights Act.

In the June primary, Ronnie easily beat former San Francisco mayor Christopher, getting 65 percent of the vote. That set him up to face Democratic incumbent governor Edmund G. (Pat) Brown in the fall election. Brown made the mistake—as so many others would in the years to come—of underestimating Ronnie and his appeal from the outset. The governor painted his opponent as an inexperienced extremist; at one point referring to the affable host everyone remembered from *GE Theater* as an "enemy of the people." One of Brown's television spots featured the governor telling a group of schoolchildren: "I'm running against an actor, and you know who shot Lincoln, don't ya?" That kind of rhetoric backfired, sending more disaffected voters to the Republican side.

Hollywood also took note of Brown's over-the-top comment about actors. "Frank Sinatra called me the next day," Spencer recalled. "He was a big Democrat then for whom I had done a little work. Without even a hello, he's going on, 'What can I do? What can I do?'

"And he was just the first. They came out of the woodwork, those Hollywood Democrats. Maybe they were already supporting Ron, but certainly not publicly. Brown's quote blew him out of the water with those folks."

Ronnie won the November election in a landslide. He got nearly a million more votes than Brown and carried many traditionally Democratic precincts in suburban and rural California, as well as working-class enclaves of Los Angeles. As the Reagans drove to his campaign party on election night, they heard an announcer on the radio proclaim that Ronnie would be California's next governor. "I had always thought you waited up all night listening to the returns, and although this may sound silly, I felt let down," Nancy recalled. "After so much hard work, Ronnie's early and overwhelming victory seemed almost an anticlimax."

They were on their way.

CHAPTER SEVEN

Ronnie was sworn in as governor just minutes after midnight on January 2, 1967, his hand on a four-hundred-year-old Bible believed to have been brought to California by Father Junipero Serra, the Spanish priest who had spread the Catholic faith in the seventeen hundreds. That odd hour brought no small amount of speculation—including by his predecessor, Pat Brown—that the timing had been determined by astrology. After all, it was no secret that the Reagans began each day by reading what the signs were saying in their friend Carroll Righter's column. The official story, plausible enough, was that Ronnie wanted to put a stop to Brown's aggressive use of last-minute appointments of friends and allies to judgeships and other posts. So, he decided to take office at the first moment it was possible. "I don't know what the stars prescribed, but we had our reasons for doing it at this hour," Ronnie said.

Three days later, there was a lavish celebration. Airlines had to add flights from Los Angeles to Sacramento to accommodate the seven thousand people who came for it. At the inaugural ball, two orchestras played for revelers on a half dozen raised dance floors. Nancy wore a showstopping, one-shouldered gown of white wool and silk, studded with sparkling daisies. It was designed for her by couturier Jimmy Galanos, who said it was "a little grander and has a little more glitter than she usually allows." The *San Francisco Examiner* noted approvingly that the new first lady was "an extremely pretty woman who knows how to wear clothes. Her clothes are not the drab costumes politicians' wives in the past have worn in order not to call attention to themselves." The *Oakland Tribune* declared: "The eyes of the fashion world, long focused on Jackie Kennedy as a pacesetter, are already finding pleasure in watching Mrs. Reagan."

This was a time for Nancy to bask in her husband's triumph. But her brother, Dick, who had not seen her much since Ronnie had decided to enter politics, sensed a change in her; a shadow over the gay girl he remembered growing up in Chicago. "She was very tight and not her old open self," he told me.

As Nancy was starting to understand, *first lady* is a title that comes without a job description. Always wary about moving into new situations, she understood she had a lot to learn. But one thing—the most important thing—remained constant. Ronnie was as devoted to her as ever. Two months after his inauguration, Nancy woke up to a note from the governor:

> My Darling First Lady
>
> I'm looking at you as you lie here beside me on this fifteenth anniversary and wondering why everyone has only just discovered you are the First Lady. You've been the First—in fact the only—to me for fifteen years.
>
> That sounds so strange—"fifteen years." It still seems like minutes, they've gone by so swiftly. If I have any regret it is for the days we've been apart and I've had to awaken without watching you. Some day, you'll have to explain how you can be five years old when you sleep and for fifteen years yet. But then maybe it has something to do with my only being fifteen—because I wasn't living before I began watching you.

Nancy, not as good at putting her emotions on paper, was left at a loss for words. Along with the love in her response was an undercurrent of anxiety and protectiveness. She wrote him:

My darling husband,

You beat me to it this morning 'cause I was going to write you—

I can never say what I really feel in my heart to you 'cause I get puddled up—and you always say everything so much better. But I too can't believe it's been fifteen (16!) years. In another way tho' it seems like forever—I really can't even remember a life before you now. Everything began with you. My whole life—so you'd better be careful and take care of yourself because there'd be nothing and I'd be no one without you.

I love you so much—I never thought I could love you more than the day we were married but I do—and I'm so proud of you—every day—I could pop—It just keeps getting bigger and bigger—those poor other mommies—they don't have a you—but I do—and I hope you'll always have a me.

Sacramento, where Ronnie served two terms as governor, was different from anything they had ever known. It was a fog-prone, medium-sized city in an agricultural valley, a plane trip from the glamour of Los Angeles and a long drive from the sophistication of San Francisco. Living on the governor's $44,000-a-year salary meant Ronnie had to sell his Yearling Row ranch, and with it, his beloved horses. But there was some consolation—and perhaps something ethically questionable—in the fact that the newly elected governor reaped a handy profit when Twentieth Century-Fox bought the property for an eyebrow-raising $2 million. That was nearly double what the tax assessor set as the ranch's value, and twenty-three times what Ronnie had paid for it in 1951. Democrats suggested the inflated price, negotiated by some of his wealthy friends, was a sweetheart deal meant to buy the governor's favor on a tax bill that gave a big break to the movie industry.

The Reagans stood apart from and above the scene in Sacramento. Legislators noticed that the governor never joined them for nights of carousing at their regular haunts, such as Frank Fat's, a Chinese restaurant and watering hole a block from the capitol that was considered the "third house" of the legislature. Bills were said to have been written on Frank Fat's napkins. "Reagan was convivial, but he had neither a genuine interest in socializing with other politicians nor a need to demonstrate he was one of the boys," wrote journalist Lou Cannon, who covered the statehouse for the *San Jose Mercury News* in those days. "Some legislators thought their celebrity governor looked down on them; the prosaic truth was that Reagan was tired at the end of the day and preferred to spend evenings at home."

Occasionally, lawmakers were invited over to the Reagans' house—though it generally took a bit of prodding from Ronnie's legislative secretary, George Steffes. However reluctant she may have been, Nancy brought an entertaining flair of the kind Sacramento had not seen before. Famous acts such as Jack Benny, Danny Thomas, and Red Skelton performed at the annual parties they held for the legislators in their backyard, where Nancy had a temporary stage built over the swimming pool. When she spotted the neighborhood kids hanging on to the fence to watch, Nancy invited them to join as well. But the California first lady was not subtle in letting everyone know when it was time to leave so that Ronnie could get to bed.

Unlike previous first ladies, Nancy had little to do with the wives of lawmakers and lobbyists. They were offended when she did not join their busy club, Pals and Gals, which met for regular luncheons and golf outings. Pat Brown's wife, Bernice, had been a regular. The gals thought Nancy snobby and standoffish; she didn't see why she should be expected to make small talk with women whose husbands were constantly carping in the news media about hers. Nor did Nancy hide the fact that she considered the state capital a backwater—a place where there was nowhere decent to shop for clothes or get her hair done. The Reagans spent every possible weekend back at their home in Pacific Palisades. Where a decade before they had been B-listers in Hollywood, their social standing in Los Angeles had soared with Ronnie's election. Nancy soon joined her best friend, Betsy Bloomingdale, as a fixture on the International Best Dressed List and ultimately was named to its Hall of Fame.

*

As imperious as she might have seemed in those early years, the truth was that Nancy was insecure and naive about the expectations that came with her new life. There was a price to be paid for not understanding that she and Ronnie had moved into a world that played by different rules. They were used to the movie business, which was lubricated by fantasy. Studios in the Reagans' day had the power to bury scandals and fill the gossip columns with manufactured tidbits about their stars. Politics, on the other hand, ran on cynicism. On this stage, there was a harsher kind of spotlight, one that accentuated every imperfection.

Nancy emerged onto the political scene in the turbulent 1960s, at a time when broader social forces were taking hold. She was a proudly—no, fiercely—traditional wife, which made her a pathetic caricature in the eyes of women who were joining the burgeoning feminist movement. Reporters snickered at the way she fixed her gaze on her husband during his speeches, sure that it had to be an act. "While other Reagan fans alternately applaud or laugh at the governor's one-liners, Nancy composes her features into a kind of transfixed adoration more appropriate to a witness of the Virgin Birth," Cannon wrote.

A profile by the brilliant writer Joan Didion in the June 1, 1968, issue of the *Saturday Evening Post* set the tone for years of media narrative about Nancy. The story, headlined "Pretty Nancy," began with a scene in which a television crew was setting up a shot of the California first lady picking flowers in the garden of the executive residence. It was the most ordinary kind of photo op. But in Didion's hands, it became a metaphor for artificiality—"something revelatory, the truth about Nancy Reagan at 24 frames a second."

"[W]henever I think of Nancy Reagan now, I think of her just so, the frame frozen, pretty Nancy Reagan about to pluck a rhododendron blossom too large to fit into her decorative six-inch basket. Nancy Reagan has an interested smile, the smile of a good wife, a good mother, a good hostess, the smile of someone who grew up in comfort and went to Smith College and has a father who is a distinguished neurosurgeon,"

Didion wrote, adding that Nancy's was "the smile of a woman who seems to be playing out some middle-class American woman's daydream, circa 1948." Nancy was stunned at how her cooperation with the television crew refracted through the lens of Didion's contempt. "Would she have liked it better if I had snarled?" Nancy wrote more than twenty years later. "She had obviously written the story in her mind before she ever met me."

Though she would in time grow far more sophisticated in her dealings with journalists, that profile left a bruise that never went away. "The idea that somebody would sit down and interview you at length, and then just torture you, was really shocking to her," her son, Ron, said. "She was probably wondering, 'What is this even about?' Her conception of feminism at the time would have been almost nonexistent. The idea that she was being portrayed as this kind of throwback—she barely understood what the point of the whole thing was."

In at least one important regard, Didion read the first lady's character backward. Nancy's flaw was not that she was skillful at pretense. It was that she wasn't. As Cannon wrote: "She alienated even those who were disposed to like her with statements that were bluntly honest and undiplomatic."

Nancy found plenty to fret over during Ronnie's early years in Sacramento. He got off to a rocky and turbulent start as governor. Though he had run a brilliant campaign, and the electorate was eager for change, Ronnie and his team arrived in the state capital unprepared for the challenges of actually doing the job. Many of the new governor's key appointments had been selected by his Kitchen Cabinet and came from the business world, which meant almost no one in the senior ranks of his administration had any experience in government. "We were not only amateurs. We were novice amateurs," press spokesman Lyn Nofziger acknowledged later. Ronnie opened his first senior staff meeting with a question: "What do we do now?"

Personnel problems and infighting beset his administration from the start, but conflict-averse Ronnie was ill-equipped to bring internal discipline to his operation. Nor had the governor anticipated some of the policy challenges he would confront in his first year. His predecessor bequeathed him a fiscal deficit twice as big as he expected, and the spending cuts he proposed came nowhere near meeting the state constitution's requirement that California balance its budget. So, the conservative who had run for office as an antitax crusader found himself in the position of having to raise revenues by $1 billion, which gave him the ignominious distinction of having signed the biggest tax hike ever for any state in the country.

Compounding the problem had been Ronnie's choice of a finance director. Gordon Smith, a management consultant, knew almost nothing about the state budget and tried to wing it. Legislators considered him a joke, and in just over a year, Smith was gone. He was replaced in February 1968 by future defense secretary Caspar Weinberger, a former state party chairman who was then working as a San Francisco attorney.

As would be the case in so many personnel shifts to come, Nancy's unseen hand was at work in replacing Smith with Weinberger. The Kitchen Cabinet had initially rejected the highly credentialed Weinberger, deeming him too liberal because he had committed the unpardonable sin of supporting Nelson Rockefeller over Barry Goldwater in the 1964 Republican primary. Nancy was far less concerned with ideology than competence. With turmoil mounting, she worked her back channels of information, which included Spencer. Who, Nancy asked over and over, could straighten out this mess?

"She was still in a period of learning and frustration because she could see all this going down," Spencer said. "I'm not sure she really knew who Cappy Weinberger was at that point in time, but she knew there had to be a change." The first lady privately—and persistently—lobbied her husband on Weinberger's behalf. He turned out to be supremely capable in the job, showing the fiscal toughness that would later earn him the nickname "Cap the Knife."

A very different kind of dilemma presented itself in April 1967—one that Ronnie later described as the hardest call he had ever made. California was scheduled to carry out its first execution in four years.

Set to die was a thirty-six-year-old black man named Aaron Mitchell, who had spent four years on San Quentin's death row for murdering a policeman during the robbery of a restaurant. Ronnie was a supporter of the death penalty, but the former Rock River lifeguard struggled when the power was put in his hands to end or save a man's life. Breaking with what his predecessors had done in earlier cases, the governor refused to attend Mitchell's clemency hearing two days before the execution was scheduled and then ignited more criticism when he showed up at the Academy Awards that same night.

On the eve of the execution, eight-year-old Ron watched through the windows of the governor's mansion as demonstrators held a silent all-night vigil outside. Her son found the scene "strange and eerie," Nancy recalled later. "We tried to explain why Ronnie had made his decision, and why some people didn't agree with it." Just after ten o'clock on the morning of April 12, 1967, church bells rang out as cyanide began rising through the floor of the apple-green gas chamber where Mitchell was strapped to a chair. Nancy was still disturbed weeks later, telling a reporter it had all given her "a very uncomfortable feeling," but she added: "I think it would be nice too if they rang church bells every time a man is murdered. It's the same principle, it seems to me." The backlash was intense. California would not carry out another execution for twenty-five years.

Two months later, Ronnie faced another moral quandary when the California legislature passed and presented to him legislation to lift most restrictions on abortion. The state was operating under a Victorian-era law that allowed the procedure only when necessary to save the life of the mother. It made no exception for pregnancies that occurred through rape or incest. The legislation that landed on Ronnie's desk would make abortion legal if it was performed in the first twenty weeks of a pregnancy, took place in an accredited hospital, and was approved by a panel of qualified physicians. California's would be the most liberal law in the country and included no residency requirement, which Ronnie said he feared would turn his state into "a haven" for women seeking abortions.

This was nearly six years before the US Supreme Court decision *Roe v. Wade* legalized abortion nationally. As recently as the 1950s, newspapers had considered the subject so indecent that they would refer to it in their pages only as an "illegal operation." But public sentiment had begun to shift, driven by the feminist movement and by horror stories about the butchery that desperate women had suffered at the hands of practitioners who performed the procedure outside the law. A March 1967 survey by the respected California pollster Mervin Field found that more than two-thirds of Catholics supported loosening the restrictions on abortion. Nancy did not take a public stand on the legislation, though people on both sides of the debate assumed she supported it. She did suggest that Ronnie seek her father's counsel, to get his perspective as a physician. Loyal Davis, though conservative on many issues, was in favor of legalizing abortion and was an influential voice as his son-in-law wavered. Ronnie changed his mind twice in the week before he signed the Therapeutic Abortion Act on June 15, 1967. A year later, Ronnie told Cannon that he would not have done so if he had not been so inexperienced as governor. It was, Cannon noted, "the only time as governor or president that Reagan acknowledged a mistake on major legislation."

Turmoil on college campuses also became a running challenge. Ronnie had campaigned on "cleaning up the mess in Berkeley." He moved quickly, just weeks after his inauguration, to engineer the firing of University of California president Clark Kerr, who had refused to crack down on massive student protests. The governor also squeezed the university system's budget by 10 percent and proposed that it start charging tuition. Tensions only escalated, as antiwar demonstrations grew and became more violent. In 1969 a battle erupted between police and students who had taken over a 2.8-acre plot of university-owned land known as People's Park.

The day would become known as Bloody Thursday after nearly sixty people were sent to the hospital with serious injuries. Ronnie declared a state of "extreme emergency" and dispatched more than two thousand National Guard troops into the Berkeley area. The following year, a mob at the University of California at Santa Barbara looted a Bank of America building and set it on fire to protest the financial institution's loans to South Africa, which had a racist apartheid government. At least once, Ronnie's car was surrounded and rocked by demonstrators. When he visited Chico State College, a clean-shaven young man thrust his face into the governor's and shouted: "You rotten son of a bitch!" Some of the staffers who traveled with Ronnie and his family began carrying concealed handguns.

Nancy's fears for her husband's safety created problems for those who were trying to steer a political course for Ronnie through the rough waters of the era. In later years, she would learn to use her power more shrewdly, employing allies to fight her battles for her and to act as the agents of an agenda she preferred to keep unseen. But during Ronnie's early days in the governor's office, she was a constant source of disruption. The first lady's input—or interference, as it was viewed by those on the receiving end—was no more welcome by the governor's staff than it had been by the men who ran his campaign.

Ronnie even interrupted Cabinet meetings to take Nancy's calls. One time, the others in the room overheard her on the line venting about vulgar comments that radical black activist Eldridge Cleaver had made about Ronnie. "But, honey, I can't have him arrested just because he says those things," the governor told her. (Cleaver, a leader of the Black Panther movement, would have a change of heart. In 1984 he endorsed Ronnie for reelection as president.)

Among those with whom she clashed was Tom Ellick, a media operations assistant in the governor's office who produced a televised series called *Report to the People*. These were twenty-eight-minute segments that ran on major stations in the state's largest cities. For an episode about the campus violence, Ellick had the governor engage in a friendly question-and-answer session with students. The imagery was exactly what the producer wanted. It showed Ronnie at his resolute best, interspersed with scenes of rioting and property destruction by protesters. "I had about 99.9 percent of the footage that I needed, but I needed to get him on a college campus," Ellick recalled. He arranged for film of the governor to be shot on a quiet corner of the UCLA campus on a weekend afternoon. Reagan was to stroll contemplatively for about forty-five seconds, with off-duty Los Angeles police officers posing in the background as students. Ellick thought everything was set, when he unexpectedly got a call summoning him to a meeting with Ronnie and his top advisers. He was told: "We need to roundtable this." Those were dreaded words to anyone on the governor's staff. It meant something had gone off track.

Ellick flew to Southern California for a meeting at the Reagans' home in Pacific Palisades and discovered the problem: Nancy. Everyone else sat silently as the panic-stricken first lady declared, "No, Daddy, we can't do it. It's too dangerous."

"We've got the LAPD lined up," Ellick pleaded. "They will have excellent security, and it's within minutes of your house, and it's not going to be a problem, but I really do need this particular bit of footage."

Again, no one else said a word.

So Ellick put the question directly to the governor, telling Ronnie: "It's your call." The others in the room looked shocked. Defying the first lady was a reckless move for someone so junior on the staff.

"Tom's right," Ronnie said. "We're going to do it."

The film shoot went off without incident, but Ellick knew he would never make his way back into the first lady's good graces. "I could see check mark number one against Tom Ellick," he recalled. Ellick began having a recurring nightmare in which he was wading into a deep river with Nancy Reagan on his shoulders. By the time the 1970 election rolled around, he got word that he was among the "less desirable" aides whose services would not be needed in the governor's second term.

"She really, truly devoted her life to this man, and I respect and admire her for that, but as far as wanting to be around her in a working environment, that's probably the last thing in the world that I wanted to do, and, frankly, one of the last things anybody on the staff wanted to do. They just didn't want to deal with her," Ellick said. Ronnie's secretary Helene von Damm put it this way: "Everyone tensed when she came into the office."

Behind her back, her husband's aides called her Governor Nancy. No detail, it seemed, was too small to escape her eye. The appearance of the suite of offices where Ronnie spent his days was of particular concern to her. She scolded the staff if she saw a chair askew, or a stack of papers on a desk, or a dirty ashtray. Nancy, who would sometimes joke that she was "a frustrated interior decorator," also oversaw a major renovation of the governor's drab suite. The only decoration its previous occupant Pat Brown had left behind was a tomahawk hanging on the wall. Nancy replaced the carpet that was full of holes, had the orange paneling stained a darker, richer color, and installed cream-colored draperies. She was particularly proud of a set of gold-rush-era prints she had excavated from a state storage facility at historic Sutter's Fort in Sacramento. When she saw how the governor's assistant Curtis Patrick was hanging them in the hallway, she went into a rage. The first lady's shouting could be heard from Ronnie's inner office.

Aides learned early not to take any complaints about Nancy to the governor. "We all thought of her as a demanding and somewhat aloof person. But in his adoring eyes, she was the sweetest, gentlest, most wonderful person in the world," von Damm wrote. "Ronald Reagan didn't even seem to see the same person the rest of us saw. When an aggrieved staffer once approached the governor about something Mrs. R had done, Governor Reagan was so utterly incredulous and completely unbelieving ('You must be wrong. My Nancy wouldn't do that.') that no one ever tried to talk to him about her again."

When Deputy Chief of Staff Michael Deaver told Ronnie that his wife, Carolyn, was pregnant, the governor told him to pray that it was a girl.

"What about Ron?" Deaver asked him, knowing the governor's affection for his youngest child.

"Oh, I wouldn't trade Ron for anything," Ronnie replied. "But when you have a daughter, you get to see your wife grow up all over again."

Ronnie was indulgent of—and even somewhat amused by—Nancy's inability to shrug off his critics. "She bleeds pretty good," he said affectionately. The first lady canceled their subscription to the *Sacramento*

Bee, which had been relentlessly critical of him; Ronnie didn't tell her he was still reading the capital's leading newspaper at the office. Once, on a commercial flight from Sacramento to San Diego, she overheard three men in the row behind her criticizing the governor's spending cuts. Nancy leaned her seat back until she was practically in their laps and told her astonished fellow passengers: "That's my husband you're talking about! You don't know what you're saying. He's going on television tonight, and if you watch him, you'll learn the real story of the budget."

When she or Ronnie came under fire, Nancy retreated to her bathtub, where she soaked and fantasized about the arguments she wished she could have with the offending reporter or political adversary. "I was sensational during these encounters—I could always think of just the right thing to say. And, of course, with nobody to answer back, I always came out the winner," she recalled later. "I finished those baths feeling great. I stopped holding those imaginary conversations before we moved to Washington, and it's a good thing, too. Otherwise, I would have spent eight solid years in the tub."

Though Nancy did not weigh in often on policy, she wielded a heavy hand as the chief guardian of her husband's well-being. On her orders, he left the office nearly every day at five o'clock. As he headed home, Ronnie would tell everyone else to do so as well. She made sure Ronnie had his raincoat when it was wet outside and ordered him to turn off his favorite show, *Mission: Impossible*, when it was time for bed. "She would call in and ask what the schedule was like for the governor, and did he bring his cough syrup, or can we get him some soup for lunch, or something like that. I would think, 'Why is she calling so much? We're busy here,'" Ronnie's secretary, Kathy Osborne, recounted.

But once, Osborne had to run something to the executive residence and found Ronnie walking around with a box of Kleenex in his hands, red nosed and obviously running a fever. Nancy followed her husband, pleading for him to stay home and warning that it would take him longer to get better if he didn't. Ronnie told Nancy that there was a busload of kids coming in from Bakersfield, and he wouldn't disappoint them by not showing up. So, he ended up going to work. That glimpse of their home life gave Osborne a new appreciation of why Ronnie needed a protector. "I thought, 'You know, he's so lucky that he has somebody who's so devoted to him, who's worried about him. The state will get along just fine without him for a day if he has to stay home and take care of his cold.' That was my first clue that she is a very strong woman, she's very devoted, and she's looking out for her husband. And he was an extremely happy man because of that," Osborne said.

As attuned as she was to Ronnie's image, it was perhaps inevitable that Nancy would clash with her husband's wisecracking communications director, Lyn Nofziger. Friction between the two of them went back to the gubernatorial campaign, when Nofziger told Nancy that her gardenia scent smelled like "dime-store perfume." She didn't speak to him for days. He soon became familiar with the fire-and-ice quality of her fury: "One thing about Nancy, you can tell when she's angry with you. You either get hollered at or get the silent treatment."

Nancy mistrusted Nofziger's closeness with reporters (he had been one himself), and thought he was failing at his duty when one of them wrote a story she didn't like. She frowned upon the communications director's rumpled suits, untucked shirts, and uncombed hair, as well as his habit of padding around the office in his socks. "He wasn't suave, he wasn't sophisticated, and he didn't really look the part that she wanted those around her husband to look," recalled Nofziger's research assistant, Karen Hanson, who later married Tom Ellick. Reagan biographer Edmund Morris wrote that Nofziger "looked like a used sleeping bag." But Nofziger joked that his dishevelment actually provided a strategic benefit: the contrast made the governor look good.

Tension between the first lady and her husband's chief spokesman came to a head in a crisis that occurred early in Ronnie's tenure as governor. Rumors began circulating in the summer of 1967 about a "homosexual ring"—or as Nofziger put it, a "daisy chain"—in the governor's office. The stories centered around the activities of Ronnie's first chief of staff (the job title then was "executive secretary"), a man named Phil Battaglia, who was in his early thirties, married, and a father of two. Battaglia was said to have a penchant for hiring attractive young men and having them accompany him whenever business took him away from Sacramento. Where talk of someone's sexual orientation might have raised few eyebrows in Hollywood—and, indeed, the Reagans had moved comfortably in circles where people made no secret of their homosexuality—attitudes were far different in politics.

A potential for scandal was not the only reason people around Ronnie were gunning for Battaglia. The pudgy lawyer was brilliant and had done a good job running the 1966 campaign as its state chairman; Ronnie called him "my strong right arm." But once Reagan was elected, Battaglia's big ego took over. He sometimes acted as though he were governor. Battaglia made decisions without consulting anyone, was frequently absent without explanation, and committed the cardinal sin of seeming like he was trying to outshine the boss. So, when the rumors about him started, some of the governor's aides and advisers seized upon them and undertook a slipshod, almost comedic investigation.

They tried and failed to bug Battaglia's office, botched an attempt to break into the apartment of a supposed male paramour, and put a tail on him that came up with—well, with pretty much nothing. But as Nofziger described it: "We knew in our minds, though no place else for sure, that there was hanky panky." The coup plotters put together a dossier, which was really just a compilation of gossip, and delivered it to the governor and his wife at San Diego's Hotel del Coronado, where Ronnie was recuperating from a prostate operation.

"Eleven of us barged in unannounced. Nancy, who had just finished showering, at our insistence joined us wearing a terry cloth robe with a towel wrapped around her head. Naturally, the Reagans were curious," Nofziger wrote later. "I handed each of them a copy of our report. We waited silently as they sat side by side on the sofa in the living room and read. Nancy finished first and gave us a quizzical look."

It was decided that Battaglia would be quietly fired. Holmes Tuttle was tasked with delivering the news to the shocked aide, because everyone knew Ronnie was incapable of cutting anyone loose. They also agreed to put out a story that Battaglia's departure was voluntary. In August 1967 he announced that he wanted to return to practicing law in Southern California and did not discourage speculation that he would also be laying the groundwork for a possible Reagan presidential run the following year. But Battaglia soon resurfaced in Sacramento, trading on his presumed closeness to the governor to build a high-profile lobbying business. "His continuing presence around the administration was an irritation to those of us who knew the whole story. Nancy was among them," Nofziger wrote in his memoir. "One day in my presence, she asked in exasperation, 'Why doesn't someone do something about Phil?' "

Nofziger took on the job. He indiscreetly, and at times drunkenly, began informing reporters about the real reason behind Battaglia's departure. The governor's spokesman swore the journalists to secrecy and assumed none of them would write about such a taboo subject as homosexuality. But that did not mean they wouldn't talk about it, and eventually the rumors started seeping into print. A blind item about an unnamed "top GOP presidential prospect" facing "a potentially sordid scandal" appeared in *Newsweek* in late October 1967. Shortly after that, Drew Pearson's nationally syndicated column carried a claim that there had been an eight-man "sex orgy which had taken place at a cabin near Lake Tahoe leased by two members of Reagan's staff." At the conclusion of his irresponsibly reported claims regarding the unnamed "homo-ring," Pearson remarked: "It will be very interesting to note what effect the incident has on the governor's zooming chances to be president of the United States."

When Ronnie held his next weekly news conference, he tried to deny everything and tossed the question to Nofziger: "This is just absolutely not true. Want to confirm it, Lyn?"

"Confirmed," Nofziger piped up.

Ronnie piled on, huffily calling Pearson "a liar. He's lying."

The story that Nofziger had leaked, thinking no one would actually publish it, was suddenly all over the papers. Nancy was furious and wanted him fired. She didn't speak to him for five months. Nofziger offered his resignation to the governor and cited the first lady as the reason.

"I'm tired of Nancy cutting me up," he told Ronnie. "It isn't doing me any good, and it isn't doing you any good. It just isn't worth it."

Ronnie, typically, insisted his wife was doing no such thing and told Nofziger he wanted him to stay, which the spokesman did until departing to work on a Senate campaign in 1968. He later moved on to the Nixon White House. After Ronnie was elected president, Nofziger would be back to work for him, but his relationship with Nancy would always be touchy.

*

Battaglia's ouster did produce one welcome result. The team around Ronnie was reconfigured and became far more cohesive and disciplined. Some of them would stay with him all the way to Washington. Cabinet Secretary William P. Clark, a soft-spoken thirty-five-year-old lawyer who shared Ronnie's love of ranching, took over as chief of staff. His natural reserve was much like the boss's, and he was a good manager. Clark soon discovered that the first lady had strong opinions about the major issues they were dealing with, and some of the minor ones as well. Many mornings, one of the first calls he took was from Nancy, who dialed her husband's top staff member as soon as Ronnie climbed into the limousine to make the short trip from the residence to the basement garage in the Capitol. "She'd use that fifteen minutes to call me and say, 'Bill, please talk to Ronnie about this or that,' indicating to me that she had not necessarily gotten her position in his mind solidly enough," Clark recalled later. "He'd come off the elevator with a smile at me, knowing darn well she had phoned to make her position very clear."

When Ronnie appointed Clark to a longed-for judgeship in 1968, beginning his rise to the California Supreme Court, he was replaced by legal affairs secretary Edwin Meese III, who ran the staff for the remainder of Ronnie's governorship. Meese was deeply loyal and masterful at translating Ronnie's ideas into policy. He was also notoriously disorganized, the opposite of a boss who cleaned off his desk at the end of every day. But that didn't matter, because Clark had left behind an operation that could practically run on its own.

One of the most important things Clark and Meese figured out was a way to deal with Nancy. The solution was the number two guy in the office: Michael K. Deaver. A smooth former adman, Deaver had risen through the early turmoil to become deputy chief of staff. As Clark and then Meese tired of having to take the first lady's calls, Deaver's portfolio grew to include what he would later call the "Nancy Clause." Others dubbed it the "Mommy Watch." His job was to handle the incoming from Nancy and keep her out of everyone else's hair.

Deaver was terrified the first time his secretary announced that Mrs. Reagan was on the phone. Nancy wanted to rearrange the governor's schedule so that he could make an event she was planning in Los Angeles. Deaver told her that wouldn't be possible because Ronnie had to be in Sacramento for state business. After a long silence, Nancy agreed. "That was it," Deaver recalled later. "Flames hadn't shot out of the handset. State marshals didn't bust down my door as soon as we were through and order me to start packing. 'Whew,' I thought to myself. 'Just maybe this job is doable.'"

What Nancy demanded was, in short, utter honesty. Deaver had given her the facts, without finessing them or treating the first lady with condescension. That respect—along with, Deaver's detractors would say, his subservience—would be the basis of their close bond over the decades to come. It was to be one of the most significant relationships that Nancy would ever form. Though the two of them would hit some rough patches, each trusted that the other would always put Ronnie's interest and image first. Each was determined not to see him fail. As Deaver put it: "In taking the job nobody else wanted—the guy who, in addition to other duties, would have to answer to California's inexhaustible first lady—I had stumbled upon my niche."

Or perhaps it would be more accurate to say that his niche had found him. "Nancy was soon able to see in me a quality I wasn't at all sure

I possessed: the instinct for how the media operates and how best to present Ronald Reagan to it, a job she had been doing alone for years," he wrote. "Although I was admittedly nervous in my initial dealings with her, I think she realized after a few months that she didn't intimidate me. Soon we were huddling on scheduling, politics, the press, speeches, and other affairs of state. I had fully expected to learn the lion's share of politics at the side of Ronald Reagan. He's the one who bucked the odds and drove California's Democratic machine to the ground. But Nancy proved to be a shrewd political player in her own right."

Ronnie liked the fact that the two were conferring so closely and started referring slyly to Nancy as Deaver's "phone pal." Meese and others in the office also began turning to Deaver as a back channel to the first lady, to get her advice without having to deal with her calls. When issues came up that required some persuasion, Nancy coached Deaver on how to win Ronnie to his side: not by arguing the political consequences, she advised, but by pointing out who might get helped or hurt, or how it fit with the governor's philosophy. "By the time he came into the White House, he really knew Ronnie and understood when to approach him and how," Nancy wrote. "Mike was never afraid to bring Ronnie the bad news or tell him when he thought he was wrong."

Another who worked well with the governor's wife was former local TV news anchor Nancy Clark Reynolds, who had the office next to Deaver's. She had been hired to handle the broadcast side of the media operation and, by virtue of being one of the few women on the staff, was also assigned to Mommy Watch. She traveled frequently with the first lady, and the two became comfortable with each other. The daughter of a former US senator from Idaho, Reynolds had grown up surrounded by the power players of Washington and was not intimidated by Nancy's often imperious manner. Eventually she began to appreciate what few others saw in Mrs. Reagan. "She was the smartest person, so up on everything," Reynolds said to me many years later. "She was the smartest politician I ever knew."

Reynolds also discerned the vulnerability behind the first lady's brittle facade. "Nancy is very wary. She's terribly cautious about the unknown, and suspicious, almost, of strangers or situations with which she's not familiar," Reynolds told Lou Cannon in a 1981 off-the-record interview, a transcript of which is in his papers at the University of California at Santa Barbara. "I've always said I felt that she had some insecurities."

*

As hyper-attuned as Nancy was to her husband's public image, she had—and would always have—some gaping blind spots when it came to her own. During those early years in Sacramento, she touched off a series of controversies, some of which foreshadowed her later stumbles in Washington.

The first came soon after Ronnie was inaugurated, when she declared that she would not live in the decrepit Governor's Mansion. The eighty-nine-year-old wooden Victorian Gothic house at Sixteenth and H Streets was not without its charms. The gingerbread structure had a cupola, winding staircases, high ceilings, and big bedrooms. But it was gloomy and located in a seedy part of Sacramento. Its neighbors included a bustling gas station, a no-star motel, and an American Legion hall. The house was also on a major one-way thoroughfare between Reno and San Francisco, where trucks roared by twenty-four hours a day. They idled at the stoplight just outside the mansion, then shifted gears, interrupting dinner-party conversation and making it impossible for insomniac Nancy to sleep at night.

Then there were the safety issues. The mold-scented bedrooms had ropes instead of fire escapes. When a false alarm went off only a month after the Reagans moved in, the fire marshal told Nancy that if there had been an actual blaze, eight-year-old Ron would have had to break through the rusted window screen of his second-floor bedroom with a dresser drawer and climb out. Nancy pronounced it "a tinderbox" and "a firetrap."

The Reagans were not the first gubernatorial family to complain about the mansion. As far back as 1911, Governor Hiram Johnson had refused to move in until it was rid of an infestation of bats. Ronnie's predecessor, Pat Brown, wanted a new residence built, but only got as far as having plans drawn up. However, Brown did manage to secure one improvement: a kidney-shaped swimming pool was installed after a newspaper photographer caught Brown crossing the street in his bathrobe to take a dip at the nearby motel.

Following Nancy's announcement that they were moving, the Reagans rented a spacious Tudor on Forty-Fifth Street in upscale East Sacramento. It was a more normal residential area, full of children with whom young Ron could play. Gina Spadafori, a fifth-grade classmate, recalls the neighborhood kids swam in the pool, and rode their bikes to school with Ron, trailed by a big black Lincoln carrying bodyguards. When the owner of the house decided in 1968 to sell it, a group of Ronnie's rich backers—among them, Holmes Tuttle, his old agent Taft Schreiber, Alfred Bloomingdale, Henry Salvatori, Earle Jorgensen, and Armand Deutsch—bought it for $150,000. They put another $40,000 into renovations that included a dining room triple the size of the old one, a glassed-in porch, and a new "powder parlor." Then they leased it back to the Reagans for the same $1,250 a month the first family had previously been paying in rent.

Nancy solicited $125,000 in donations and loans of art and furnishings, including rare antiques. Much of that bounty came from the Group. The Bloomingdales chipped in a $3,500 custom-designed eighteenth-century mahogany dining table that could seat twenty-four. The Jorgensens added a $3,000 set of a dozen Queen Anne–style chairs. This brought accusations of corruption. Assembly speaker Jesse Unruh, who was Ronnie's Democratic opponent in his 1970 bid for a second term, suggested the Reagans' new nest was being feathered by "half-hidden millionaires who call the shots in Sacramento."

It was a sign of her growing confidence in the political sphere that Nancy held her first-ever press conference to respond. Seated on a miniature French provincial chair in front of the fireplace in her living room, she lamented what she said must have been "a misunderstanding" on Unruh's part, adding: "I feel very proud of my project, which is resulting in some fine antiques being donated to the state of

California." Poised and disarming, she obliterated Unruh's criticisms one by one. "It's too early in the political season to determine how well Mr. Unruh will fare against Ronald Reagan, but it's already apparent he's no match for Mrs. Reagan," an editorial in the conservative *Oakland Tribune* declared. Ronnie ran for reelection that year in a fierce political headwind that battered Republicans across the country: in 1970 they lost eleven governorships. The incumbent beat Unruh that fall, but his margin was barely half what it had been over Brown four years before.

Despite the stresses, the stumbles, and the scrutiny, their new life brought a deeper satisfaction than either of the Reagans had ever known. At one point while Ronnie and Nancy were sitting in their living room, they found themselves in a reflective mood, contemplating the unlikely place to which destiny had brought them. "All of a sudden it came to both of us that what we were doing made everything else we'd done seem 'dull as dishwater'—that was the expression she used," Ronnie remembered. "And it was true. . . . Instead of just talking about problems from the outside—to actually deal with them and to have a hand in solving them—well, one man who was a governor back when I was a performer had said to me about his job that sometimes he went home feeling ten feet tall. We both felt that way about it."

Ronnie's second inaugural gala in January 1971 was an even bigger production than his first. Five thousand people packed Sacramento's Memorial Auditorium. Outside were protesters, some of whom carried Vietcong flags. But inside the hall, there were so many stars that it was hard to even count them all. Hollywood legends John Wayne and Jimmy Stewart acted as masters of ceremonies. Comedian Jack Benny joked from the stage: "Even though Ronald Reagan left show business, show business did not leave him, as you can see tonight." The highlight of the evening was Frank Sinatra, who had produced the gala, singing more than a dozen of his hits. Sinatra had been a stalwart backer of Democrats going back to his energetic campaigning for Franklin D. Roosevelt. But he had completed a personal and political evolution that many thought began with a personal falling-out with the Kennedy family. Sinatra raised hundreds of thousands of dollars for Ronnie's reelection effort. At the inaugural gala, Sinatra dedicated one of his signature hits, "Nancy (With the Laughing Face)," to the beaming first lady in the front row.

*

If her admirers regarded their governor's wife as California's own Jackie Kennedy, there were plenty who viewed Nancy as the second coming of Marie Antoinette. First, there had been her decision to move out of the old Governor's Mansion. Then she announced a campaign to build a new one on eleven acres their friends had bought for the state on the American River. Furious letters poured into the California first lady's office. An Escondido woman wrote: "Build your own mansion, the old one was good enough for a Democrat, but—no—not classy enough for a couple of 'show people,' millionaires. My husband is 80 yrs. old. I am 72. We live on a measly $142.50 a month. . . . You don't need to live in a $170,000 mansion and then beg people to donate expensive furniture for your mansion." A La Jolla constituent sent a letter accusing Nancy of "embezzling $1,000,000 tax funds to build this extravagant whimsey." The first lady responded that the money would come from a California government fund maintained for capital construction and added: "I'm sure it must be obvious . . . that I am trying to do this for the state and future governors, since I'll never be living in it."

As it turned out, no one ever lived in the twenty-thousand-square-foot modern monstrosity that eventually went up on the site. Pat Brown's son, Jerry, a thirtysomething bachelor who succeeded Ronnie as governor, called it a "Taj Mahal" and refused to move in, preferring instead to sleep on a mattress on the floor of his $250-a-month studio apartment. Joan Didion wrote that the soulless palace that Nancy insisted upon building was "evocative of the unspeakable." It was also too far from the capitol to be practical. The state, which was spending $85,000 a year to guard the unoccupied property, auctioned it off in 1982. When Jerry Brown returned for a second tour as governor nearly three decades later, he had the old mansion renovated and moved back in, becoming the first governor to reside there since the Reagans had vacated it.

Nancy's files show that she frequently exchanged correspondence with constituents, even those who criticized her. She was curious to learn what individual Californians were thinking and insisted on reading nearly all of her own mail. She wrote her replies by hand, to be typewritten by a secretary, sparing the recipient the ordeal of struggling to decipher her loopy handwriting, which made the letter *N* look like a *U*, and *M* like a *W*.

Her letters offered blunt views on a wide range of subjects, particularly the changing social mores of the late 1960s and early 1970s. She was contemptuous of that era's giddy fashion trends, such as gaucho pants. ("I personally like a feminine, soft, elegant look and for a woman to look like a woman!") Nor did she like the R- and X-rated movies that Hollywood was churning out. ("Having been in the business, I do know that the only thing they understand is how much money they can take in at the box office. If people would stop going to see—out of curiosity or whatever other excuse they use—the pictures that we don't agree with, the producers would very quickly stop making them.")

A girl reached out to her in 1972 as part of a civics assignment in which students were given a choice of writing to the California first lady, feminist Gloria Steinem, or political activist Angela Davis. The question she posed to Nancy: What is your role in life? And can a woman combine a career with her home life?

"I assume you're talking about the woman who is able to choose between the two—not the one who must work to supplement the family income. In the latter case, there is no choice—of course—one does what one must," Nancy replied. "However, for the woman who can choose, this is a very individual decision. I had a career when I got married and very gladly gave it up. I think in most cases when you try to combine the two, one suffers, and it's usually the marriage. That was a gamble I wasn't willing to take.

"Marriage is a full-time job, and I think a woman's real happiness and fulfillment is found in her home. You can have outside interests—and should have, I think—but within the framework of the marriage."

After Ronnie signed the abortion law, Nancy wrote back and forth with people on both sides of the increasingly explosive subject. "I personally believe that a woman should have the right to decide whether or not she will have a child, but this decision should be made before a child is created. Frankly, I approve of birth control methods," she wrote to a woman who wanted to see abortion become more liberalized. To a man who opposed it, she responded: "I supported my husband's abortion law, but both he and I are very distressed at the way it has been abused. The original bill he signed was to permit abortions when there was clear evidence that the birth would harm the mother—in other words, based on the moral principle of self-defense. However, many doctors have been using the mental health provision to perform abortions on anyone who asks. This clearly was not the original intention of the law." (In fact, Ronnie had known that this would likely happen when he signed the law and had said so.)

In addition to engaging in these correspondences with individual constituents, Nancy also spoke up more in public. In a 1970 interview, Associated Press reporter Edith M. Lederer asked Nancy whether a woman should have a choice on whether to become a mother. "But she does have a choice," Nancy retorted. "It starts with a movement of the head either yes or no." As for the youth of America, who were protesting on campuses across the country: "If they are concerned about things that need to be corrected, how can they correct them if they're so doped up they don't know what they're doing?"

Nancy also found her own causes to pursue, which among other things offered her outlets from constantly fretting over Ronnie. The doctor's daughter made frequent trips to hospitals, usually with no publicity. It would have surprised her critics to see how at ease she was around the sick, the disabled, the disfigured, and how comfortable she made them feel.

One day in 1967, while touring the Pacific State Hospital, a facility for people who were then known as the "mentally retarded" or "feebleminded," Nancy learned of a new, federally funded program called Foster Grandparents. It was started under Lyndon B. Johnson's

War on Poverty by Sargent Shriver, the Kennedy in-law who directed LBJ's Office of Economic Opportunity. Foster Grandparents paired senior citizens with needy children and paid them a small stipend for serving as friends and mentors. Nancy loved the concept. "What excited me most about this program was that both sides benefited. Older people, who often feel lonely, unneeded, and unloved, have so much to give—especially to children, who need more love and attention than any institution can provide," she said. "When you bring these two groups together, each one provides what the other needs, and everyone is better off." Nancy convinced Ronnie to expand the program to all state hospitals and continued to champion it through her years in the White House. By 1985, there were 245 Foster Grandparents projects serving sixty-five thousand children across the country.

The California first lady was especially conscientious about visiting wounded Vietnam servicemen. "She never just flipped from bed to bed—she'd spend hours. She got phone numbers of their sweethearts and their mothers and would go home and call them," said her frequent traveling companion Nancy Reynolds, who herself would often have to leave the room because she couldn't take the sight of the young men's grievous injuries. Nancy was struck, too, by how the attitudes of the returning veterans began to shift—from a conviction in 1967 and 1968 that they had sacrificed for a just cause, to a growing bitterness in later years that the war that had cost them so much was unwinnable. This drew her as well to the wives, mothers, and children of the servicemen who were being held as prisoners of war by North Vietnam. She wrote a syndicated advice column and donated the money she made from it to the National League of Families of American Prisoners of War and Missing in Action. When the POWs started coming home in early 1973, following a peace agreement ending hostilities between the United States and Communist North Vietnam, Nancy organized a series of dinners for returning Californians. "If I don't have a chance to put my arms around them, I'm going to pop," she told Ronnie.

They became close to one returning POW in particular: future Arizona senator John McCain, and his first wife, Carol. As Carol told the story to me, the McCains were at a reception at the Fairmont Hotel in San Francisco, when a woman introduced herself as Nancy Reynolds, and said her boss, the governor of California, would like to meet the McCains. "As luck would have it, we were going to LA," where the Reagans spent their weekends, "so we went to their home, and we just struck up a friendship," Carol McCain said. "They were just such lovely people. You couldn't help but be crazy about them."

Nancy would later say that celebrating the return of the POWs was one of the most gratifying things she had ever done. She saved all the souvenirs the newly freed men gave her: letters, poems, a tin spoon once used for prison rations, a pair of lieutenant's bars, a package of Vietnamese cigarettes. "When anyone asks me what was the high point of my husband's administration, I tell them this was it," she said.

By then, the Reagans were near the end of Ronnie's second term as governor. He knew he would not run again, but what he would do beyond that remained unclear. He bought a third ranch, this one a 688-acre retreat twenty-nine miles northwest of Santa Barbara, for which he paid a reported $527,000 in 1974. It was located at the end of seven miles of road that twisted upward into the Santa Ynez Mountains to reveal a view of the Pacific. Though it had been called Tip Top Ranch, the Reagans rechristened it Rancho del Cielo, a Spanish phrase that means "Ranch in the Sky." It had a tiny adobe house, which had been built in 1872 and was badly in need of work. But the prospect of devoting countless hours to making it perfect only added to Ronnie's love of the spot. "From the first day we saw it, Rancho del Cielo cast a spell on us. No place before or since has ever given Nancy and me the joy and serenity it does," Ronnie wrote in his post-presidential memoir.

Figuring out what he wanted to do professionally was more of a challenge. Lou Cannon conducted several interviews with the governor in 1973 and 1974: "Each time Reagan came across as conflicted. Should he run for president? Should he return to what he called 'the mashed potato circuit' and make millions of dollars as an inspirational speaker? Should he retire, with Nancy, to his ranch? At different times, he expressed all three things—and at the same time."

Ronnie's tenure as governor ended on a bitter note. In the wake of Richard Nixon's Watergate scandal and his resignation, the 1974 election saw a nationwide Democratic sweep. In California, voters chose as their new governor Jerry Brown, the son of the man that Ronnie had beaten eight years before. After the movers packed up the Reagans' house in Sacramento, Nancy sat alone in the bedroom and looked out at the camellias blooming in the garden she had come to love. "I thought, 'So this is how it ends. Our eight years of politics are over.' True, some of Ronnie's advisers were talking about Ronnie's running for president, but I didn't really expect that to happen. As we left Sacramento that night, I honestly believed we were leaving politics forever."

But for a while, at least, the big decisions could wait. There was still the imperative of earning a living. When the Reagans moved back to Los Angeles, Deaver set up a public relations firm in Westwood, not far from Pacific Palisades, with a partner, Peter D. Hannaford. Ronnie was their chief client. Hannaford and Deaver sold and helped write Ronnie's nationally syndicated column, which was quickly picked up by more than 170 newspapers, and daily, sharp-edged radio commentary, which was carried by 350 stations reaching as many as fifteen million people. Deaver also traveled with Ronnie to lucrative speaking engagements, where the former governor could command $5,000 fees—big money in those days.

Soon it became clear that the pieces were falling into place for something much, much bigger. Ronnie's profile was rising. He was building a political network across the country. More and more, his name was being mentioned as a potential presidential candidate in 1976. More and more, that was the door that fortune and opportunity seemed ready to open for him and Nancy.

CHAPTER EIGHT

From the very outset of Ronnie's political career, his admirers had seen an aura of presidential inevitability around him. Ballots had barely been counted in the 1966 gubernatorial election before he was being talked up as a national prospect. Two days after he won, the lead story on the front page of the *New York Times* pronounced him one of his party's four brightest hopes for 1968, along with Michigan governor George Romney, former vice president Richard M. Nixon, and Illinois senator elect Charles H. Percy. California's film-star-turned-political-star, the *Times* wrote under a four-column headline, had become "without a day in office, the favorite presidential candidate of Republican conservatives."

This was not just idle chatter among reporters and political handicappers. Though they would later refuse to admit it, Ronnie and Nancy began looking toward the White House even before he was inaugurated as governor. On a Thursday afternoon just nine days after his first election, a half dozen members of Ronnie's political brain trust gathered in the Reagans' living room. Among them were consultants Stu Spencer and Bill Roberts; their partner, Fred Haffner; press spokesman Lyn Nofziger; and Phil Battaglia, his incoming chief of staff. They were brought together by Tom Reed, who had been Ronnie's Northern

California chairman. Reed had a project in mind, something he was calling "Prairie Fire." At those two words, Reed recalled, "Ronnie's face hardened; he knew what was coming."

Reed pushed on: "Lyndon Johnson is a disaster. Vietnam and our economy confirm that. Even so, given Johnson's ego, he'll surely run again in '68. We cannot let him succeed. The Republicans on the horizon are all boring losers, Ron. You've got the talent and now the momentum to run and win two years from now. I want to start putting the pieces in place, to start collecting '68 delegates and to plan for your election to the presidency." They talked for hours, until the last rays of the sun sinking into the ocean streamed through the windows in Pacific Palisades. Ronnie gave what they all read as a tentative go-ahead for this presumptuous plan, though those involved would in retrospect understand that he approached it with equal measures of ambition and ambivalence. As her husband and his advisers strategized about which moneymen and national political talent to recruit, Nancy said almost nothing. Reed had the sense she was trying to absorb it all.

In fact, audacious as it was, this was a proposition that had been germinating for years. Back when Ronnie was still on the speaking circuit in 1962, his daughter Maureen had been among the early voices urging him to run for governor. "Mermie," he wrote her, "I really appreciate your support, but if we're going to talk about what could be, well, I could be President—ha, ha!—But of course, that's not going to happen, is it?"

As the 1968 presidential primary season approached, the tricky part for Ronnie would be mounting a campaign for president without actually declaring that he was doing it. He was, after all, a new governor with plenty on his hands just learning how to do his day job. He was also enough of a realist to understand what a long shot a White House bid would be. Reed and the others settled on a strategy. They would get Ronnie's name on the ballot in California as an ostensibly symbolic "favorite son." His supporters could also put him in contention in states where there was an "opt-out" rule. In those states, he wouldn't have to formally announce he was running, only demand that he be taken off the ballot if he wasn't. Meanwhile, the new governor of California could travel the country, raising his national profile and connecting with influential officials and activists. Ronnie won conservative admirers wherever he went.

Liberals also began to get an inkling that he shouldn't be underestimated. In May 1967 California's brand-new Republican governor surprised pretty much everyone by besting New York's young Democratic senator Robert F. Kennedy in a debate over the Vietnam War. It was broadcast by CBS and billed as a *Town Meeting of the World*. An estimated fifteen million people tuned in to watch these two politicians, the rising stars of the Left and the Right, field questions from a hostile audience of international students. Ronnie stood up for America, its morality and its role in the world, while Kennedy came off as meek and apologetic. RFK was purported to have said afterward: "Who the fuck got me into this?"

Not everyone on Ronnie's team was enamored with his quiet project to put himself in the mix for the 1968 presidential nomination, or the subterfuge around it. When Ronnie asked Stu Spencer what he thought, his campaign strategist was blunt about his misgivings. Not only was the timing bad, Spencer said, but the political operation around the governor was simply not up to the task. He also warned Ronnie that there could be no such thing as a halfhearted campaign for president.

"You've got no idea how to get there," Spencer told Ronnie.

"The office seeks the man," Ronnie replied.

"That's bullshit," Spencer retorted. "If you want to be president of the United States, you've got to get it, and you've got to fight for it."

As Ronnie wavered, with one foot in the race and one foot out, the 1968 election season took several twists that no one had anticipated. It turned out that all of their assumptions about how the election would play out were wrong. Senator Eugene McCarthy of Minnesota, an antiwar candidate, challenged Johnson for the Democratic nomination and came surprisingly close to beating the incumbent president in the March 12 New Hampshire primary. Shortly after that, Robert F. Kennedy joined the race, which meant Johnson was facing not one but two strong challengers from within his own party.

Just three weeks into primary season, on March 31, LBJ stunned the country by announcing that he would not seek reelection. Johnson's loyal vice president, Hubert Humphrey, entered the contest on April 27 and became the front-runner, propelled by Democratic establishment support in states where party leaders controlled the delegate selection process. Then in June came another shock: on the night Robert F. Kennedy won the crucial California primary, he fell to an assassin's bullet. After Kennedy's murder, Ronnie and all the other presidential candidates were assigned Secret Service protection.

The contest for the Republican nomination was fierce as well. As it took shape, the moderate Romney collapsed, and former vice president Richard M. Nixon surged. Nixon nailed down the South with an assist from his ally South Carolina senator Strom Thurmond, a segregationist who had switched from the Democratic Party to the Republicans in 1964. Meanwhile, another segregationist, former Alabama governor George Wallace, ran on a third-party ticket, appealing to many of the same white conservatives that Ronnie did.

All of this turmoil turned the GOP race into a battle for the soul of Republicanism—a three-way one pitting Ronnie against both Nixon and liberal New York governor Nelson Rockefeller. It ended with a monumental embarrassment for Ronnie at the 1968 convention in Miami, where Nixon arrived just short of the 667 delegates he needed to win on the first ballot. Ronnie and Rockefeller made an informal, ill-conceived pact to try to stop Nixon by peeling away uncommitted delegates from the Left and the Right. It failed spectacularly, and Ronnie ended up seconding Nixon's nomination. He retreated back to Sacramento with his reputation tarnished.

As Reed sensed, Nancy had harbored reservations about this gambit from the start. With the political landscape so turbulent and Ronnie so new to politics, it was "way too early for this kind of thinking," she told her husband and Deaver. But she took away an important lesson.

"For Nancy, the convention fiasco served as confirmation of her own political antennae. After Miami, she would never again hold back her opinion on major political decisions, whatever the Gipper might be thinking," Deaver wrote.

Both Ronnie and Nancy would later act as if none of this had ever happened. "Ronnie never sought the nomination in 1968," Nancy insisted in her 1980 memoir. She claimed the episode was "more misrepresented than almost anything Ronnie has ever done." Her husband made the preposterous statement that running in 1968 "was the last thing on my mind."

Those statements flabbergasted Reed, but they also revealed something fundamental about the Reagans: their compulsion to rewrite every story that did not have a happy ending. "I had met with Reagan over 100 times in the company of others, often his wife, to discuss this project. We also consulted privately on another 21 occasions for one-on-one talks about the most sensitive aspects of our drive. I accompanied Reagan on dozens of politically funded flights on a chartered Jet Commander to meet with backers in our intended primary states, to talk with governors whom we might select as a running mate, or to solicit support from delegation members in swing-state Texas and the Thurmond-dominated South. When Lyndon Johnson later withdrew from, and Bobby Kennedy entered the Democratic contest in March 1968, we moved up to a chartered 727 jet to accommodate over 40 members of the traveling press," Reed wrote. "How—or perhaps more accurately, why—did all of this campaigning slip the future president's recall? That is a significant question, since Reagan's proclivity to erase bad news from his memory remains an enigma to this day."

The other thing that both Reagans would take away from 1968 was this: if Ronnie wanted to be president, he would have to go all in. He and Nancy would not be the first to come away from a defeat with a better understanding of what it was going to take to win. As his biographer Edmund Morris put it, "The experience was good for a man who had always come easily by success. It toughened him, carved a few more seams contrary to the laugh lines, made him warier of hustings hustlers like Nofziger. He learned to pay more attention to his own 'feel' for the mood of American voters."

*

As Ronnie and Nancy mapped out what the future might hold for them, family life for the Reagans remained as complicated as ever. Young Ron, the only one still at home, was a natural charmer who could always find a way to make his mother laugh. Ronnie taught his youngest to swim and ride, as he had the other three. And Ronnie's work was keeping him nearby, which meant the son they called Skipper saw more of his father than the others had. Ronnie, Nancy, and their youngest took a four-day horseback trip together in the High Sierras, something they had never done before. "I was the baby of the family. I know that my siblings, most all of them, resented me from Day One, as they perceived me to be her favorite, and therefore, the favorite in the family. That resentment deepened," Ron told me.

But his father, even while attentive and doting on the favored child, kept what Ron recognized was an emotional barrier between them. As Ron saw it: "You almost get the sense that he gets a little bit antsy if you try and get too close and too personal and too father-and-sonny." Meanwhile, his mother was overprotective, controlling, and always on a hair trigger.

So, Ron pushed back, in small ways at first. He grew his hair long. At the age of twelve, he announced he was an atheist. Near the end of the Reagans' years in Sacramento, his parents sent him to a boarding school in Southern California, from which he was expelled for misbehavior. For several years when he was in high school, Ron was involved with an older woman from a prominent show business family who had a teenage daughter of her own. The ex-governor and his wife discovered the affair when they returned early from a weekend away and found Ron's thirtysomething paramour had been staying at their house in Pacific Palisades. According to Ron's brother, Michael, the couple had sex in Ronnie and Nancy's bed. "I was heartsick when I learned about it, because I believed she was robbing him of his wonderful teenage years," Nancy wrote of her son's liaison. "But there was nothing I could do about it."

Michael, on the other hand, could hardly contain his delight when he heard what his younger half brother had done. He felt a particularly acute rivalry with Ron, who not only carried his father's name but also Ronald Reagan's blood. "Well, Dad, there's good news and bad news," Michael told Ronnie. "The bad news is that you came home early, and you caught him. The good news is that you found out he isn't gay." Michael thought he was being funny, but his father took the comment seriously. "I hadn't thought of it that way, but you're absolutely right. I guess it is a blessing," Ronnie said, sounding relieved. "I must tell Nancy."

The eldest of Ronnie's children, twice-divorced Maureen, had been drifting in and out of their family life for years. Ronnie and Nancy were less than thrilled when she took up with film and television director Gene Nelson, who was twenty years her senior and had been a contemporary of her father's in Hollywood. Maureen tried to build a career as an actress but learned that her last name was an impediment when seeking work in the liberal entertainment industry. She also continued to be wounded by the efforts of Ronnie's political advisers to erase her from his public life.

It was hard to maintain even a personal connection. When Ronnie was governor, Maureen worked out an arrangement with his sympathetic secretary, Helene von Damm, who alerted her to openings in her father's schedule in which her calls could be put through. Maureen managed to get a role in a 1972 production of *Guys and Dolls* that was playing in Sacramento and was devastated when her father and Nancy decided to go to Europe on a mission for President Nixon rather than attend her opening night. Ronnie told Maureen he felt bad about missing his chance to see her perform. "There was genuine disappointment in his voice when he told me to break a leg, but to break it without him and Nancy in the audience," she recalled later.

Michael also dabbled at acting, but his real passion was racing speedboats, a dangerous, financially questionable pursuit that his father frowned upon. When he was twenty-six, Michael got married, hoping to create the kind of family he'd never had. He gave eighteen-year-old Pamela Gail Putnam, whose father was line coach for the Atlanta Falcons of the National Football League, a ruby ring that had belonged to Jane Wyman. On the day they exchanged vows in Hawaii, Ronnie and Nancy chose to be nearly five thousand miles away in Washington for Tricia Nixon's White House wedding instead.

Ronnie did send Michael a letter, which was the first he had ever gotten from his father. It began by warning his son of the consequences of infidelity: "Some men feel their masculinity can only be proven if they play out in their own life all the locker-room stories, smugly confident that what a wife doesn't know won't hurt her. The truth is, somehow, way down inside, without her ever finding lipstick on the collar or catching a man in the flimsy excuse of where he was till three a.m., a wife does know, and with that knowing, some of the magic disappears."

But the missive closed on a more idealistic note. "Mike, you know better than many what an unhappy home is and what it can do to others. Now you have a chance to make it come out the way it should," Ronnie wrote. "There is no greater happiness for a man than approaching a door at the end of a day knowing someone on the other side of that door is waiting for the sound of his footsteps.

". . . P.S. You'll never get in trouble if you say 'I love you' at least once a day."

Their conspicuous absence from Michael's 1971 wedding may have been Ronnie and Nancy's way of expressing their disapproval for an impetuous, ill-conceived match. The marriage fell apart within a year. Michael found himself dead broke, living in a friend's guest room, with his car repossessed. His wife was pregnant when she walked out, a poignant endnote that convinced him his existence would never be anything more than an endless cycle of paternal absence and maternal betrayal passing from generation to generation. Here is how Michael put it in his memoir: "I hated myself and my biological mother, who had abandoned me to what I considered a cruel fate. I hated my adoptive mother for sending me away to school and not taking care of me. I hated my stepmother for revealing that I was illegitimate. And now, just when the woman who I married found out she was going to become a mother, she had left me. It seemed to me that all mothers hated me. All I could think of was that they were all whores."

Michael did, ultimately, find love and stability—with Colleen Sterns, whom he met on a blind date. They married on November 7, 1975, in a chapel across the street from Disneyland. Nancy and Ronnie arrived a half hour after the wedding was scheduled to begin, and Michael was annoyed to see they had Ron in tow. He had purposely not invited either of his half siblings. His sister, Maureen, had declined her invitation because she had a speaking engagement in Washington.

The most awkward moment came after the ceremony, when the photographer suggested a family photo, which would bring Ronnie and Jane Wyman together in the shot. Nancy fixed her eyes on Ronnie, who stared straight ahead. After a long and awkward pause, Jane said: "Nancy, don't worry about a thing. Ron and I have had our pictures taken together before. If you'd like to join us, fine. Now, Ron, come on. The photographer's waiting." The groom was exasperated to see his younger half brother also join the group.

*

Of Nancy's relationships with the four Reagan children, none was so fraught as hers with Patti. After high school, her daughter went to Northwestern University. Patti made that choice not for any academic considerations, or because it was her grandfather's alma mater, but because she was having an affair with her married English teacher from high school and believed he was taking a job there. He took a post in Pennsylvania instead, and after he failed to show up for a rendezvous they had planned, Patti was devastated. Nancy happened to be visiting New York and invited her daughter to join her. Patti poured out all the tawdry details of her romance with her teacher. She was at her lowest, and desperate for the balm of a rare moment of grace in her relationship with her mother. "I needed her right then—I needed her to be a mother. My mother. I needed her to listen to me, not judge me, to understand that I was in pain. I don't know why I was so certain she would do all those things, but I was," Patti recalled in an essay she wrote for *Time* shortly after Nancy's death.

"It's terrible that he took part of your youth from you," Nancy told her. "You should have been going to school dances, going steady." Not only was she the gentle, nurturing mother her wounded nineteen-year-old daughter needed at that moment, but it turned out that Nancy—her radar ever on—had known about the affair for two years. She figured out what was going on when Patti, in an act of brazenness, invited both the teacher and his wife to the Reagan home in Pacific Palisades over a Christmas break from her boarding school. During that visit, Patti had noticed her mother standing back from everyone, unusually quiet as they all, including her grandparents, gathered at the Christmas tree in the living room. "So, for all that time, she'd kept her suspicions to herself, even from my father. She didn't want to upset him, but she also knew that she had to let me go through the pain and the drama. If she had interfered, it would have made things worse," Patti wrote.

That memory, Patti reflected many years later, "towers above all the others. Because I know that the mother she was on that day was who she really longed to be . . . but so many things had gotten in the way."

Among those many things was Patti's defiant nature. At Northwestern, she befriended Eva Jefferson, the feminist and antiwar activist student body president who became famous when she debated Vice President Spiro Agnew in 1970 on national television. Patti sought her out specifically because her father had told her not to have anything to do with "a very radical black girl named Eva Jefferson." She found Jefferson not to be the fire-breathing revolutionary of Ronnie's imagination, but someone who was "soft-spoken, intelligent, and seemed to be respected by everyone." Patti also connected with women's movement leaders on campus, and discovered in their new and controversial way of thinking another avenue by which she could reject Nancy and everything she represented: "We were all rebelling against mothers who advocated 'letting the man wear the pants in the family.' So we made a point of wearing pants, of not wearing bras, leaving our legs and underarms unshaven, and dressing in black. I immediately threw out my Lady Schick razor and my bras, and loaded up on black turtlenecks."

By the end of her freshman year, in the spring of 1971, Patti decided to leave Northwestern to study drama at the University of Southern California. For a while, she lived at home in Pacific Palisades and commuted to school, giving her ample opportunity to steal tranquilizers from her mother's medicine cabinet to trade for diet pills: "I was using her habit to support mine." Patti's uncle Dick Davis remembers family holidays punctuated by political arguments. Loyal, who had brooked no backtalk from Nancy or Dick while they were growing up, was outraged when his granddaughter challenged her elders' views. Dick recalled: "When Patti tried to sound important and knowledgeable about a nuclear plant in California one year at Christmas, my father just destroyed her on the spot and said, 'You're talking to your father, who's extremely knowledgeable, and I'm your grandfather. I don't believe a word you're saying.' "

Patti moved out of her parents' home and, by the end of her junior year, had dropped out of college. She was getting more heavily into drugs, including LSD and cocaine. The governor's daughter also grew and sold marijuana. A talented songwriter, she had an on-and-off fling with Brian Wilson of the Beach Boys, and moved in with guitarist Bernie Leadon of the Eagles, one of the biggest rock bands of the 1970s. Her parents were furious and embarrassed. Ronnie told Patti that living together outside of marriage was sinful. "During Patti's years with Bernie, we had virtually no contact. It wasn't because she was living with a rock musician, although the Eagles were not exactly a mother's dream. And when I finally met Bernie, I found him very likable," Nancy wrote. "It was that they were living together, which we just couldn't accept."

Patti and Leadon cowrote a song titled "I Wish You Peace." It was featured at the end of the Eagles' fourth album, *One of These Nights*, which sold more than four million copies and was the band's first to reach number one on the *Billboard* LP chart. While trying to figure out what to call herself for the writing credit that would appear on the album, Patti decided to declare a new identity. She dropped her father's surname and rechristened herself Patti Davis. It does not appear to have occurred to Patti that in claiming Davis as her name, she was repeating what her mother had done decades before. But in Patti's case, there was a pull in the opposite direction. Nancy had done it to signal to the world that she belonged *to* someone; for Patti, it was a means of distancing herself from her father.

"There was an underlying reason for choosing my mother's maiden name, but I wouldn't admit it for years, even to myself. It was a child's way of asking for a parent's approval," Patti wrote later. "It makes perfect sense to me now that I would take my mother's name; for all our enmity, all our battles, she was the only parent who was there. My father's emotional unavailability made it easy to relinquish his name; in a way, it had no identity to me. My mother's did, just as she had a certain identity as a parent. It might not have been a nurturing identity, but at least it was something tangible." So determined was Patti not to pass along the dysfunction by having children of her own that she had a tubal ligation at the age of twenty-four.

*

Patti was not present—and, according to her, was not invited—when Ronnie and Nancy summoned the other three Reagan children to a meeting on Halloween 1975. This was the first, and last, such session they would ever have as a family. The purpose: to inform them that their father was becoming serious about running for president, which meant he would be challenging a sitting Republican in the White House. The Watergate scandal and the prospect of impeachment had forced Nixon's resignation in August 1974, and his vice president, Gerald Ford, had assumed the office. Ford himself had been named vice president in December 1973 amid an unrelated kickback scandal that had forced Spiro Agnew from office. The dominoes had fallen and put in the Oval Office a moderate former House minority leader who had never been elected to any office higher than congressman from Grand Rapids, Michigan.

As the family sat in the Reagans' Pacific Palisades living room, Maureen tried to talk Ronnie out of running, arguing that the party was in too much turmoil in the wake of Watergate. She thought he should wait four years and try in 1980. Michael tried to sound enthusiastic but worried privately that the dark secret of his childhood sexual abuse—and the pictures that had been taken of him—would come out. Ron just pouted.

Nancy had her own reservations. According to Deaver: "Her questions were always the hardest for her husband and his top staff to answer. Who is going to organize this thing? Where is the money going to come from? Who specifically in state A or state B will break ranks with a sitting president to support Reagan? Who are we going to put on our board? Do we really have a chance or are we tilting at windmills?"

But Ronnie wanted to do it, and that meant Nancy did too. "Looking back, I realize it was inevitable that Ronnie would run. And certainly it was inevitable that I would go along with whatever he decided," she recalled. Only his wife was at his side when Ronnie made his formal announcement on November 20, 1975, at the National Press Club, the headquarters of a professional and social organization and a popular spot for holding news conferences in Washington. Early reviews from the Eastern establishment were less than encouraging. "The astonishing thing is that this amusing but frivolous Reagan fantasy is taken so seriously by the media and particularly by the president. It makes a lot of news, but it doesn't make much sense," James Reston wrote in the *New York Times*.

Then again, so many other expectations had been upended that who was to say what made sense anymore? The initial assumption—by the Reagan team, and pretty much everyone else—had been that after Nixon was reelected in a 1972 landslide, he would serve a full second term, putting Ronnie in the pole position to run for the nomination four years later. But Watergate destroyed that scenario. Instead of Nixon—whom Ronnie defended after most other Republicans had abandoned him—Ford was in the White House as 1976 approached. He represented a soft-focus brand of politics that Ronnie and others on the right disdained. Ford's naming of liberal Nelson Rockefeller as vice president only compounded the low regard that movement conservatives felt for him. Ronnie twice turned down lesser Cabinet posts with which Ford had sought to neutralize him, once in late 1974 and a second time in the spring of 1975.

The former California governor fired a salvo against his party's president when he declared at the 1975 Conservative Political Action Conference (CPAC) that Republicans should raise "a banner of no pale pastels, but bold colors." His words were also a shot at a deflated and fearful party establishment. At that moment, the GOP seemed to have fallen even lower than it had been after Goldwater's landslide defeat. In the wake of Nixon's resignation and Ford's subsequent pardon of his disgraced predecessor, Republicans lost forty-nine House seats in the 1974 midterm election, giving Democrats there enough votes to override a presidential veto.

But Ronnie argued this was no time to tack to the middle. "A political party cannot be all things to all people. It must represent certain fundamental beliefs which must not be compromised to political expediency or simply to swell its numbers," he said. "It is time to reassert that principle and raise it to full view. And if there are those who cannot subscribe to these principles, then let them go their way."

As unique as the circumstances were, challenging a sitting president in a Republican primary was an audacious move. "Many of Reagan's past supporters, me included, were of a pragmatic view," recalled Reagan's former aide Tom Reed, who by then had joined Ford's administration as a top Pentagon official. "At no time in American history had a political party deposed its sitting president and then won the ensuing national election. To many of us, it was Gerald Ford or a Democrat. On top of that, we liked Jerry. He was a friend doing the best he could in chaotic circumstances."

Ford hired Stu Spencer—Ronnie's own campaign manager—to run his 1976 election effort. As it happened, Spencer was in the market for a new gig. He had been out of Ronnie's orbit for a while, alienated by what he called the "palace guard" that surrounded the governor during his years in Sacramento. The feeling within Ronnie's circle toward him was mutual. Though Spencer had gotten an occasional request to help fix a problem here and there—a summons, he noted, which always came from Nancy—that had only created more friction with the men who had created the mess. "It was awkward at best to be called by the governor's wife and told to straighten something out when you are an outsider," he recalled later. "I did it a couple of times and made plenty of enemies." Nor had Spencer endeared himself with the other handlers by discouraging Ronnie's halfhearted effort to run for president in 1968.

So, when Ford's White House chief of staff, Donald Rumsfeld, called in 1975 with an offer to take over the president's troubled campaign operation, Spencer took it. As was the case with Reed, Spencer had a genuine affection for Ford. He didn't like the idea of anyone running against an incumbent of his own party. Spencer also knew he had something the Ford campaign needed: "I don't think, even to this day, the Ford people would admit it, but one of the biggest assets I brought to the table was that I was the only one who knew and understood Ronald Reagan. They (like so many before and after) thought he would be a pushover. They were certain this would be a cakewalk."

Ford formally declared his candidacy on July 8, 1975. Three weeks later, on July 29, a delegation from the Kitchen Cabinet convened at Pacific Palisades to try to talk Ronnie out of what they saw as a foolhardy and destructive venture that would only ensure a Republican defeat. Among those present were Tuttle, industrialist Justin Dart Sr., and Reagan's future attorney general William French Smith. Tuttle had already met at the White House with Doug Bennett, Ford's personnel director, to discuss swinging his support to the president. He and the others told Ronnie bluntly that they would not raise money for him. Tuttle reported back to Reed that Ronnie had been "shocked" by their declaration that they planned to defect. Reed, who was keeping tabs on things from Washington, wrote in his journal on August 22, 1975: "Nerve endings *very* raw in California."

The Reagan team had already lost Spencer, whose political judgment Nancy trusted more than anyone else's. A rebellion by Ronnie's earliest and staunchest supporters could have killed his campaign before it even got off the ground. So, Nancy went to work on them, badgering them on the phone and in person. "She just did every dinner party in Los Angeles. She'd say, 'Ronnie really needs to run, and you really need to support him,'" Reed said. "They got the Chinese water torture from Nancy."

Her persistence worked. As Reed recalled: "Nancy tipped the balance. During the summer of '75, she badgered 'the boys' until, by September of that year, many of them had changed their minds and come aboard." Ford's dismayed campaign team saw its hoped-for allies, the ones who could cut off the oxygen from a Reagan insurgency, slipping back to Ronnie one by one. Of them, only Henry Salvatori stood with Ford on the principle that a primary challenge to an incumbent president would be a death blow to any hopes of holding the White House.

Knowing he would for the first time be running a campaign without Spencer mapping his battle plan, Ronnie decided to go for Washington expertise. It came in the form of John Sears, a prematurely gray, thirty-five-year-old Nixon campaign veteran. Sears had first met the Reagans over dinner in 1974. He began to win their confidence when he predicted correctly how things would turn out for Nixon with Watergate and made the argument that this could open a path for Ronnie. "They were all thinking that Nixon was going to survive this Watergate thing," Sears told me. "And I told them no, he wasn't going to survive, he'd be out of office by the fall, and Ford would be president. But he'd be a unique kind of incumbent, because nobody had ever voted for him, and, therefore, it would be possible to run against him. Even though Ford would be president, they shouldn't give up the idea of possibly taking a look at it. And that turned out to be the case, so probably my stock went up at that point."

As Ronnie's intentions grew more serious in 1975, Sears got to know Nancy over a series of lunches. She found him bright and fascinating to listen to. He seemed as sophisticated about politics as anyone she had ever met. Nancy also liked the fact that Sears was not a conservative ideologue, like so many of those around her husband. The only thing that bothered both her and Ronnie about the new campaign manager was his demeanor, which they found inscrutable. "He looks you in the tie," Ronnie said. "Why won't he look at me?"

Nancy poured out her anxieties about the endeavor to Sears, and he soon learned her priorities. "She wanted this done properly [with regard to] his image. They were from the movie business, and image was everything. What people thought of you, being the good guy and all that, was very important to her," Sears recalled. "She never messed around with issues or tried to get involved in any of that, but if anything was being done that might damage his image in any way, she'd be very upset."

As always, Nancy also fretted over Ronnie's physical well-being. When the switchboard operator at a small New Hampshire hotel once refused to put through her late-night call to check in on her husband, Nancy dialed up Nancy Reynolds, who was traveling with the campaign, and woke her up with an order: "You find out if he's in bed, and if he's not in bed in his jammies, I'm going to be mad at everybody." Reynolds threw on a robe and slippers, and to the bemusement of Ronnie's Secret Service detail, pounded on the door of his hotel room. The candidate was indeed in bed, looking over his speech for the next day. Reynolds told him his wife demanded that he turn out the lights and go to sleep. "Just what I need," Ronnie laughed. "Two Nancys." But the next morning, he asked Reynolds whether there was any way to rearrange his wife's campaign schedule so that she could be with him. They had been apart for three days, and he missed her—nagging and all.

Ronnie went into the February 24, 1976, New Hampshire primary so confident he would win that he left the state two days ahead of the vote. Instead, Ford beat him narrowly. Nancy was shocked. She later called that her lowest moment of the campaign: "We lost forty-eight to forty-nine, and there were fifteen hundred Democrats who wrote Ronnie's name in on the ballot. If they had only registered as Republicans." She blamed Sears for withholding the information that her husband had been slipping in the campaign's internal polls, and Ronnie for being too trusting of his advisers' assurances that everything was going fine. The momentum behind his audacious challenge was collapsing. After beating Ronnie in New Hampshire, Ford proceeded in the next three weeks to win four contests in a row, including in the big states of Florida and Illinois.

In Florida, Ronnie had started out in a strong position. Campaigning there gave him an opportunity to reconnect with former Vietnam prisoner of war John McCain, then a navy commander stationed in Jacksonville. McCain's wife, Carol, was running Ronnie's effort in Clay County. When Carol had first registered to vote there in 1967, she was a rare political species. Out of 20,000 voters on the county rolls, only 7 were Republicans. Eleven years later, there were 4,200—at least 1,000 of whom Carol McCain and her volunteers had added in a pro-Reagan registration drive.

But their efforts were little match for the increasing force of the Ford campaign. Ronnie's Florida lead evaporated, and a last-minute surge put the president over the top by a comfortable 5 points in the March 9 primary. For the Reagans, the defeat was made all the more bitter by the fact that Ronnie had been undone by a couple of figures they knew well. On the day before the Florida vote, the *New York Times*'s R. W. Apple Jr. noted that there had been "a stunning change in the whole climate of the Republican contest." Apple added: "The two men most responsible for the turnaround are an odd couple of Californians. Stuart Spencer and William Roberts, who, ironically, made their last big political splash by helping to put Mr. Reagan into the statehouse in Sacramento."

The string of defeats left Ronnie's campaign out of money as it limped into North Carolina, which was to hold its primary March 23. Hotels, rental car companies, and airlines started demanding payment in advance. By then, eleven of the past dozen GOP chairmen had endorsed Ford—the lone exception being George H. W. Bush, who as head of the Central Intelligence Agency could not get involved in the election. Ford's campaign was orchestrating a drive within the party to put the squeeze on Ronnie from every direction. The National Republican Conference of Mayors called upon him to get out of the race, as did seven GOP governors. Unknown to Ronnie and Nancy, even their own campaign manager, Sears, was holding secret meetings with the Ford campaign to negotiate terms of surrender.

Nancy was distraught. One dark day in mid-March, Nofziger walked into her hotel suite, and she pounced. "Ronnie has to get out," she told him. "He's going to embarrass himself if he doesn't." As she pleaded with Nofziger to convince her husband to give it up, Ronnie came through the door and surmised quickly what was being discussed. "I'm not going to quit," he declared, directing his comments to the press secretary rather than confronting his wife. "I'm going to stay in this thing until the end."

It became hard for Nancy to continue going through the motions of what she saw as a doomed, humiliating endeavor. When she and Nancy Reynolds flew into Banner Elk, a charming town in North Carolina's Blue Ridge Mountains, it seemed like every Republican woman in that part of the state turned out to see her. The local ladies had knocked themselves out for days baking, and they welcomed the glamorous wife of their favorite candidate with a huge spread for tea. But Nancy was rude and barely acknowledged them. It was clear she did not want to be there.

On the plane ride afterward, Nancy noticed that Reynolds was glowering at her. She nudged Reynolds with her foot and asked, "What's wrong?" Reynolds told Nancy in blunt terms how impolite she had been toward the local women. It was one of the few times Reynolds could recall criticizing Nancy to her face. "Well, I'm sorry," Nancy replied gracelessly, "but I'm really not in the mood."

Things could hardly have looked worse for Ronnie, but the campaign still had one more card to play. In the final days before the primary, a furious internal battle ignited between the national leadership and Ronnie's North Carolina chairman, Tom Ellis, an ally of arch-conservative senator Jesse Helms. The fight was over how Ronnie should make his closing argument to North Carolina voters. All along, his media strategy had been to avoid running ads that showed Ronnie reading from a script. He was just too good at it, and the last thing they wanted to do was remind voters that he had been a Hollywood actor. Ellis—whom Nofziger regarded as "a right-wing zealot with a lot of far-out ideas, some pretty good"—thought otherwise. He suggested broadcasting a half-hour speech by Ronnie across the state. Sears and the other boys at headquarters told Ellis it was a terrible proposal. They couldn't imagine that anyone would want to watch such a thing. What's more, the only footage available was a grainy videotape that had been made two weeks before. As the two sides continued to argue, Helms appealed to Nancy and convinced her that it was time to shake things up with a bold play. She arranged for the senator and Ellis to receive a copy of the leftover video.

The tape showed Ronnie sitting behind a desk against a stark blue background, looking directly into the camera with his hands folded. It had been produced in a local Florida television station studio, and the production values were hardly ideal. But Nancy recognized it held something magical. What she saw was the man who had given that speech for Goldwater back in 1964. "A Time for Choosing" had changed Ronnie's destiny. If not for that powerful address, he would never have been elected governor. It was time to put her faith back where it belonged, in Ronnie. Voters needed to see and hear him directly, straight and unfiltered.

The campaign spent a precious $10,000 to air the speech on fifteen of North Carolina's seventeen stations. "Two hundred years is a dot of time, measured against the span of recorded history, but in that dot of time, we have achieved a higher standard of living, a greater range of opportunities for a greater number of people than has any other people who ever lived," Ronnie said in the address. "And yet we celebrate our bicentennial beset by troubles that have us in a time of discontent." He noted out-of-control inflation and a growing national debt, high taxes, the financial shakiness of the Social Security system. Ronnie compared Ford's long record as a member of the "Washington establishment" against his own view that "changes must be made, and those changes can better be made by those who have not had a career in Washington and who are not bound by longtime relationships and personal ties." He said US foreign policy under Ford and his secretary of state, Henry Kissinger, was "wandering without aim," and warned: "This nation has become number two in military power in a world in which it is dangerous, if not fatal, to be second best."

As the *New York Times* noted later, the "last ditch, desperation maneuver" broke every rule of politics at a time when thirty-second ads ruled the airwaves, but "all indications are that it had a powerful impact, so powerful that the speech may have made the difference for Mr. Reagan between victory and defeat." An NBC News poll found that one in five North Carolina voters made up their minds in the last week of the primary campaign, after the pundits and political professionals had left Ronnie for dead. Those late deciders went for the former California governor by nearly three to one. Ronnie shocked everyone by winning North Carolina, sweeping almost every big county. His victory marked the first time since 1952 that an incumbent president actively running for a party nomination had been defeated in a primary contest.

It was a pivotal moment for the candidate's wife as well. Nancy's initial impulse to give up on her husband had been a betrayal. She had listened too much to the naysayers, the people who supposedly knew what they were doing. She had flinched, but she wouldn't again. No one knew Ronnie or believed in him like she did, and if he really wanted this, she was the best one to help him figure out how to win it. "I never again heard Nancy talk about her husband getting out of the race," Nofziger said. "Today I'm sure that if he had yielded then, conservatives would never have given him a second chance in 1980."

After North Carolina, Ronnie swept Texas, Georgia, Indiana, and Nebraska. By the first week of May, he was gaining on Ford. After another round of victories, esteemed CBS anchorman Walter Cronkite pronounced that "Ronald Reagan, as of tonight, looms as a serious threat."

Spencer, however, continued to pull no punches against his old client: "My basic premise was every three weeks or so, I've got to knock Reagan off his rhythm. I have to do something to piss him off."

He succeeded spectacularly with an ad that ran right before the June 8 California primary. It was a time of mounting tension in Rhodesia, and Ronnie had made ill-considered comments indicating he might be willing to send troops there. The television spot that Spencer produced concluded with a reminder that was meant to terrify: "When you vote Tuesday, remember: *Governor* Reagan couldn't start a war. *President* Reagan could."

When Ronnie heard about the ad, he slammed his fist into the bulkhead wall of his campaign plane. He recognized immediately that the shot had been fired at close range. "That damn Spencer's behind this," he said. Nancy's anger at Spencer was more like ice, hard and cold. "It was quite awhile before I could forgive Stu for that one," she wrote. The incendiary ad didn't change the outcome in California; Ronnie won his home state by nearly two to one. But to Spencer's great satisfaction, it reverberated in Ohio and New Jersey, where Ford won primaries the same day.

Both Nancy and her mother were stung by what they regarded as another act of betrayal by a onetime ally. Their family friend Barry Goldwater, for whom Ronnie had done so much in 1964, began criticizing the former California governor publicly that spring and formally endorsed Ford in July. Goldwater warned that Ronnie had a "surprisingly dangerous state of mind" and would lead the country into needless conflict overseas. His words were amplified on Ford campaign ads. "I feel as if I have been stabbed," Nancy told reporters at a news conference in Sacramento.

Edie called Goldwater in his Senate office and declared he would never be welcome at her house again. The precise words that Nancy's mother pulled from her capacious vocabulary are a matter of some dispute. Her stepson, Dick, told author Bob Colacello that Edie called the senator from Arizona a "cocksucker," while Kitty Kelley heard that she told him he was "a fucking horse's ass." Nancy allowed only that her mother had used some "*very* colorful language." Edie's fury at Goldwater eventually subsided, but her daughter never again felt the same about him.

Ronnie and Ford were still fighting it out for delegates into the 1976 GOP convention, which took place in August in Kansas City, Missouri. Though Ford was slightly ahead in the unofficial tallies, both of them were just short of the 1,130 votes it took to get the nomination. And everyone knew the situation was fluid. As Spencer put it: "Reagan really had the heart of the convention and the party, whether he had the votes or not." But a sitting president has perquisites of office at his disposal. That summer, the nation had come together to celebrate its bicentennial. When a spectacular parade of tall ships sailed into New York Harbor on Independence Day, uncommitted delegates from New York and New Jersey were given the best vantage point imaginable—from the deck of the aircraft carrier USS *Forrestal*. A few days later, the Fords invited Mississippi GOP chairman Clarke Reed, a key powerbroker who had been leaning toward Ronnie, to meet Queen Elizabeth at a White House dinner during her July state visit. (The dinner is also remembered for an epic faux pas; when Ford escorted the queen onto the dance floor, the US Marine Band struck up the next song on its playlist, which, unfortunately, happened to be "The Lady Is a Tramp.")

Few understood better than Nancy the strategic value of entertaining, and she seethed as she saw the Fords turn it to their advantage. "I've never known the White House to be used by either party the way it has been used in this campaign," she said in an interview with *Time* magazine's Bonnie Angelo. "The White House stands for something. I don't think it should be concerned about uncommitted delegates—the dinner invitations, that sort of thing." Nor had that been the only advantage that came with incumbency. Nancy envied how Betty Ford could step off Air Force One for political events looking fresh and lovely, while she spent the lean days of her husband's campaign bouncing around the country on a yellow prop plane they called the Flying Banana, with rarely an opportunity to powder her nose or run a comb through her hair.

*

The 1976 campaign also put Nancy under a new kind of scrutiny. Amid the feminist movement and in the openness of the post-Watergate era, voters wanted to hear from potential first ladies on topics they had never been asked to discuss in the past. "There was a time, as recent as 1968, when all anybody wanted to know about a presidential candidate's wife were her favorite recipes, her hobbies, whether she bought her clothes off the rack, and the ages of her children," a front-page *New York Times* story by Judy Klemesrud noted. "But that was '68. By 1972, household questions began to go the way of the butter churn, and nowadays the wives are questioned almost as intensely as their husbands are about the issues. They also have become fair game for intimate questions about their personal opinions and lives—a situation that some of them find both distasteful and unfortunate."

Driving some of this new interest was the refreshing and unconventional style of the woman who was then living in the White House. As the Republican race heated up, Nancy found herself portrayed as the uptight, antifeminist foil to vivacious first lady Betty Ford, a onetime dancer and model. Though they both had backgrounds in show business, Betty and Nancy could hardly have been more different in temperament or image. The thoroughly modern first lady wore mood rings and danced to disco. She said that the 1973 Supreme Court decision legalizing abortion, which her husband had criticized, was "the best thing in the world." Betty also acknowledged that her children had probably smoked marijuana, which she considered as harmless as her own generation's underage experimentation with beer, and said she would have no objection if her daughter, Susan, engaged in premarital sex. Against the wishes of her husband's advisers, she advocated for the Equal Rights Amendment, which would write into the US Constitution a prohibition against discrimination because of gender. After she gave a particularly controversial *60 Minutes* interview in 1975, White House press secretary Ron Nessen told reporters: "The president has long since ceased to be perturbed or surprised by his wife's remarks."

Nor would it have done any good if he had. At an International Women's Year Conference in Cleveland, Betty Ford declared that being first lady should not prevent her from holding and expressing her own views. "Why should my husband's job, or yours, prevent us from being ourselves?" she said. "Being ladylike does not require silence." She horrified some conservatives, but her overall popularity soared to 75 percent. During the 1976 campaign, there were bumper stickers and buttons that said: "Vote for Betty's Husband."

Nancy, on the other hand, never publicly gave any indication that she disagreed with her husband on anything. Which does not mean she didn't. Her son, Ron, believes that Nancy, if she were voicing her own opinion, would not have opposed the ERA. "She'd have thought, 'Well, that makes sense. Sure, that's fine,'" he speculated. "A little in the same way that he was antiabortion, and she would kind of go along. . . . I think privately she was not at all antichoice." (In 1994, with her husband out of office, Nancy declared that while she was personally against abortion, "I believe in a woman's choice.")

During the first two days of the Republican convention, amid a behind-the-scenes battle over the remaining uncommitted delegates, the increasingly open friction between the two women became a delicious subplot. Nancy and Betty sat five seats apart at a luncheon given by the National Federation of Republican Women and did not acknowledge each other. Their rivalry boiled over in the convention hall in what *Time* dubbed the "contest of the queens." As its correspondent Bonnie Angelo wrote in a dispatch to her editors: "While the two principals remained secluded in their hotel suites, as tribal rites demand of candidates and brides before the ceremony, the wives became surrogates, the rally point for the opposing forces."

Nancy upstaged Betty the first night. When she entered her glassed-in VIP booth in Kemper Arena, the hall erupted in glee and foot stomping that went on for more than fifteen minutes, during which Betty Ford's arrival at the opposite end went practically unnoticed. Not so the second night. Late in the afternoon, the Ford campaign quietly asked many of the VIPs to relinquish their tickets in the gallery so that it could be packed with Ford supporters. They cheered when Betty came into the hall around eight o'clock, dressed in a sunshine-yellow dress, with her family in tow. Seated beside her was the universally recognizable pop singer Tony Orlando, one of the biggest stars of the midseventies.

Nancy had not originally intended to be there. But Ron called his mother from the hotline in the hall. "Gee, Mom," he pleaded, "why don't you come over here and show them what a real reception is like?" So, Nancy did, bringing along an entourage of her friends. The Reagan delegates on the floor whooped at her surprise entrance. A CBS commentator noted: "One gets the definite impression here that the wives of the candidates for the presidential nomination are being moved like pawns, or perhaps like queens, in a chess game." But by then, Betty had figured out her checkmate. On cue, the convention band struck up "Tie a Yellow Ribbon Round the Ole Oak Tree," Orlando's biggest hit. The singer swept the first lady into his arms, and the entire crowd's attention turned to them as they began dancing in the aisle.

The duel merited a five-column, front-page headline in the next day's *New York Times*: "Betty Ford Bests Nancy Reagan on Applause." As Angelo noted in her file to her editors: "The gamesmanship between the two wives was a spontaneous moment of levity that will be remembered long after the dreary speeches have been forgotten." But Betty, amid her triumph, could not resist taking a final, contemptuous shot at Nancy. "She was a working girl as an actress," the first lady said in an interview with Angelo. "I just think that when Nancy met Ronnie, that was it, as far as her own life was concerned. She just fell apart at the seams."

It would not be the last time that an adversary read Mrs. Ronald Reagan so wrong. For Nancy, 1976 had been a brutal year but an experience that made her tougher and wiser. That losing campaign stood out more vividly in her memory than any of the four races that Ronnie won. No other had so much drama, so much emotion, so many what-ifs. Nancy would go over the mistakes and missed opportunities again and again in her mind. "When I first went into politics, I was constantly getting my feelings hurt. I'm better than I used to be, but if somebody knows a way to make it feel less painful, I wish they'd tell me," she said. "There are lots of things that, looking back, we might have done differently. Maybe if you'd stayed an extra day in Florida, or had money to go into Ohio, where Ronnie got forty-five percent of the vote without campaigning. Or if we had the money to go into New Jersey and New York and Pennsylvania. But we had no money. No money."

On the night that Ford was to be formally nominated by the convention, the Reagans had a quiet dinner with family and a few others in their suite at the Alameda Plaza Hotel. Then, they all sat in the living room and watched the roll call of the delegates. Shortly after midnight, West Virginia cast the votes that put Ford over the top. The final count came in at 1,187 votes for Ford and 1,070 for Reagan. "I'm so sorry that you all have to see this," Ronnie said. He talked about the things he had hoped to do in the White House; the things that it appeared he never would. What he had most wanted, he said, was a chance to sit across a negotiating table from the Soviets.

Nancy, fighting back tears, proposed a toast.

"Honey," she said, "in all the years we've been married, you have never done anything to disappoint me. And I've never been prouder of you than I am now."

CHAPTER NINE

On November 2, 1976, Gerald Ford narrowly lost to Jimmy Carter, a former governor of Georgia. It was the closest electoral college margin in sixty years. Carter, a born-again Baptist, was a peanut farmer who came from nowhere to win the Democratic nomination. He ran as the cleansing force the country needed after Richard Nixon. America, it was clear, wanted to turn a page. Stu Spencer, who had managed Ford's campaign, put it this way: "After Watergate, if Republicans had nominated Jesus Christ that year, he would have lost too."

But many in the party establishment believed Ronnie also shared part of the blame for the GOP defeat. They thought he had weakened Ford by running against him in the primary; that his speech from the GOP convention stage had sounded more like a battle cry than a concession; that he had not campaigned with enough enthusiasm for the nominee during the general election season. And they were right about how Ronnie felt. Those around him could see that he had not let go of his anger at how the Republican contest had played out. "To my surprise, Reagan, who is seldom bitter, went to California a bitter man, convinced that Ford had stolen the nomination from him," Nofziger wrote later.

As the Reagans looked toward returning to a more normal life and figuring out their next move, there was a new family drama to deal with. Just weeks after the election, eighteen-year-old Ron announced that he was dropping out of Yale University to pursue . . . ballet. Dance, he declared, was his true passion. Nancy was flabbergasted: "I had never heard the word *ballet* cross his lips."

Ron, who had barely begun his freshman year, broke the news to his parents as they were making a two-hour drive from New York to Connecticut. The three were to be Thanksgiving guests at the waterfront home of the Reagans' old friends conservative publisher William F. Buckley Jr. and his socialite wife, Pat. There was a holiday meal planned and a traditional football game, which that year had Reagan father and son as opposing team captains. In between the festivities, just about everyone took a turn trying to talk Ron into abandoning his new ambition, or, at least, into finishing his first semester. It was futile, Bill Buckley recalled: "Individually and in groups—my brother Jim, a Yale graduate, had a round or two—we attempted to make the point that Ron Jr. should give the academic life a better try. He in turn stressed the point that already, at eighteen, he was far behind in studying dance."

Ronnie and Nancy realized their son had given them no say in the matter, so they tried to figure out how to make the best of it. Ronnie turned for advice to Hollywood movie and dancing legend Gene Kelly, who suggested that Ron should study at the Stanley Holden Dance Center in Los Angeles. Though Ron was older than other beginners—some started serious training as early as age twelve—it turned out he had some talent. Within four years, he would work his way up the esteemed Joffrey Ballet and be named to its senior company.

At the Holden Dance Center, Ron met and fell in love with Doria Palmieri, who worked there and was seven years older than he was. Nancy was not thrilled. "Frankly, I didn't particularly like Doria then. I guess I was thinking back to Ron's other relationship, and because Doria, too, was older, I was afraid this one would come to the same disastrous end, and Ron would wind up hurt," Nancy wrote. His romance with Doria notwithstanding, Ron's decision to pursue ballet also set off speculation that he was gay. The rumors would continue for decades and were awkward, given the social conservatism of his father's political supporters.

Though Ronnie and Nancy could not deter their son from the path he was determined to take, they also chose not to make it any easier for their son by providing him financial assistance. Ron and Doria moved to New York, where he made less than $300 a week as a dancer and was laid off periodically. Ron was so strapped for money that he sometimes put water instead of milk on his cereal. Years later, at the depth of the 1982 recession, national headlines would reveal that the president's own son was collecting unemployment, one of millions out of work at a time when the jobless rate was higher than it had been since the Great Depression.

In his parents' willingness to let him struggle, Ron saw several impulses at work, particularly on the part of Nancy, who was the one who kept the closest watch on the family finances. The youngest Reagan had left the nest, but his mother wanted to make sure he could not fly too far. The allure of independence, she hoped he would learn, was just an illusion. "It was sort of mutual, I suppose. I mean, they weren't offering, I was not going to ask," Ron told me. "My father was, by nature, very generous. He'd pick up the check anytime. But my mother was not. My mother was one of those personalities—if somebody else was getting it, it's being taken from her. You know, your gain is her loss. Controlling the purse strings is a way to control the person. If you're financially comfortable, then you could decide to leave, you could decide to just walk off. And so, it was a way to keep you on a tether."

Ronnie and Nancy also had their own life choices to consider. Chief among them: would he run again in 1980? They were settling back into Pacific Palisades, which had much to recommend it. Ronnie was spending time at his new ranch and making a handsome living on the speaking circuit. Nancy returned to the embrace of her friends in Los Angeles, and an even busier social schedule than she had enjoyed before they entered politics. After a presidential campaign that had often kept them apart, they could savor the simple and pure joy of being together. On Valentine's Day 1977, shortly before their silver wedding anniversary, Ronnie left this note:

Dear St. Valentine

I'm writing to you about a beautiful young lady who has been in this household for 25 years now—come March 4th.

I have a request to make of you but before doing so feel you should know more about her. For one thing she has 2 hearts—her own and mine. I'm not complaining. I gave her mine willingly and like it right where it is. Her name is Nancy but for some time now I've called her Mommie and don't believe I could change.

My request of you is—could you on this day whisper in her ear that someone loves her very much and more and more each day? Also tell her this "someone" would run down like a dollar clock without her so she must always stay where she is.

Then tell her if she wants to know who that "someone" is just to turn her head to the left. I'll be across the room waiting to see if you told her. If you'll do this for me, I'll be very happy knowing that she knows I love her with all my heart.

Thank you,

"Someone"

For their anniversary two and a half weeks later, Ronnie bought Nancy a canoe that he christened *Tru Luv*. It was a sentimental nod to a long-standing joke between the two of them. She had teased him since they were married about how perfunctory his proposal had been. In the scene of her dreams, Nancy often told Ronnie, he would have popped the question as she had seen it done in old movie romances: the two of them in a canoe at sunset, him strumming a ukulele, and her reclining with her fingers trailing in the water. When Ronnie took her out for their first ride in the *Tru Luv*, he apologized that he hadn't brought a ukulele. "So would it be all right if I just hummed?" he asked. Nancy pronounced the gesture "unbelievably corny, but I loved it."

Not quite a year later, Nancy received a letter from a young newlywed in Washington State named Adrienne Bassuk, who asked her advice on how to have a successful marriage. Nancy's handwritten reply, dated January 10, 1978, is in the files of the Reagan Library. "I've been very lucky—however, I don't ever remember once sitting down and mapping out a blueprint. It just became 'we' instead of 'I' very naturally and easily. And you live as you never have before despite problems, separation, and conflicts," Nancy wrote. "I suppose mainly you have to be willing—and want—to give. It's not always 50-50. Sometimes one partner gives 90% but then sometimes the other one does—so it all evens out. It's not always easy, and it's something you have to work at, which is what I don't think many young people realize today.

"But the rewards are so great. I can't remember what my life was like before, and can't imagine not being married to Ronnie. When two people really love each other, they help each other stay alive and grow. There's nothing more fulfilling, and you become a complete person for the first time."

As happy—and complete—as Nancy and Ronnie were with each other, politics was never far from their thoughts. In the rubble that remained of the Republican Party, Ronnie was the closest thing to an heir apparent. But some of those closest to him were doubtful that he would make another presidential run. Though he was still fit and vigorous, people were beginning to raise the issue of his age. On Inauguration Day 1981, he would be just weeks away from turning seventy. That meant that if he were elected, Ronnie would be the oldest president ever to take office. An even bigger question was how badly Ronnie wanted it. Some of his advisers wondered whether he still had the fire that had ignited that bold challenge to Ford in 1976.

His wife, on the other hand, had no ambivalence about the prospect. Nancy was convinced Ronnie should run. As she saw it, "everything seemed preordained, really, after the 1976 campaign. He was ready, and everything seemed to fall into place." She told him he had to try again. Without Nancy's push, "I don't think he would have made the '80 race—that's what he told me, at least," said Ed Rollins, one of his political advisers. "She was the one who believed in him."

It wouldn't necessarily be easy. There was a possibility that Ford might make another bid, and others were eyeing the contest—among them, former CIA director George H. W. Bush, a respected figure who had also been chairman of the Republican Party, and Kansas senator Bob Dole, who had been on the 1976 ticket with Ford. Even as he deliberated, Ronnie knew that he could not afford to be unprepared or to slip into irrelevance. By Lou Cannon's tally, he gave seventy-five speeches in 1977, sending a clear signal to his supporters that he was warming up for another run. To build his image as a statesman, Ronnie took a series of foreign trips as well. On one of them, he had his first meeting with future British prime minister Margaret Thatcher.

The party's right flank had almost delivered the nomination to Ronnie against Ford, but it was clear he had to broaden his base of Republican support beyond the activist conservative wing. Shortly after the 1976 election, Ronnie formed a political action committee with his leftover campaign funds. That in itself was evidence he was thinking about making another go of it, as the law in those days would have allowed the Reagans to pay income tax on the money and just keep it. The new organization was called Citizens for the Republic and headed by Lyn Nofziger. It gave about $800,000 to GOP candidates in the 1978 midterms, Nofziger wrote, "and bought a lot of friends for him. What we sought was enough political support to create an impression of inevitability about a Reagan candidacy." Any remaining doubt was erased on March 7, 1979, when Nevada senator Paul Laxalt announced the formation of a Reagan presidential exploratory committee. Among its 365 members were 4 former members of Ford's Cabinet. "Ours is not a fringe campaign," Laxalt declared.

During this preparatory period, Nancy indirectly engineered a meeting that would assume great significance nearly four decades later. The Reagan operation dispatched a young organizer named Roger Stone to New York to raise money. It was a challenging assignment, as New York was considered a bastion of support for Bush. "I was given a card file from Nancy Reagan. It was like one of those little recipe boxes that had index cards of the Reagans' friends in New York," Stone recalled in a 2015 interview with C-Span. "Well, half the people in the cards were dead, and the others were fairly prominent, but among those was a card for Roy Cohn, the flamboyant former counsel to the

McCarthy committee [made infamous during the Red Scare of the 1940s and 1950s], at that point a fixture in the firmament of the New York legal profession, and a major power broker here in New York."

When Stone met with Cohn and explained he was setting up a finance committee for the former California governor, the notorious lawyer asked: "Do you know Fred and Donald Trump?" Cohn explained that Donald Trump's father had been an original backer of Goldwater, so he was certain to be attracted to Ronnie, the most conservative candidate in the race. Both Trumps joined Ronnie's fund-raising committee and, according to Stone, made the maximum donations allowed under federal law. (Federal Election Commission records suggest otherwise—that the Trump family gave instead to Jimmy Carter's reelection campaign—and show no donations to the Reagan effort.)

The younger Trump also helped out in other ways, according to Stone. Using his connections as a real estate developer, he helped the campaign find low-cost office space in Midtown Manhattan and cut through the red tape when the phone company said there would be a three-month wait to install lines there. "They came the next morning," Stone said. Trump also loaned his personal plane to fly nominating petitions to the state capital in Albany, so that the Reagan campaign could meet a tight deadline to qualify for the New York ballot. The petitions got there with fifteen minutes to spare. In the course of their work for Ronnie, Stone and Trump became close friends and political allies. Stone would act as a key strategist when Trump ran for president himself in 2016.

As Ronnie's 1980 campaign was gearing up, it was becoming evident that Jimmy Carter could be a highly vulnerable incumbent. In June 1979 Carter's job approval stood at a dismal 28 percent in the Gallup poll. The economy was suffering from 12 percent inflation and stagnant economic growth, a toxic combination known as stagflation. Middle East turmoil produced milelong lines and three-hour waits at US gasoline stations. It was the second such oil shock Americans suffered in six years and was starting to look like a new normal. In July Carter went on national television to lament that the country had entered "a crisis of confidence. It is a crisis that strikes at the very heart and soul and spirit of our national will. We can see this crisis in the growing doubt about the meaning of our own lives and in the loss of a unity of purpose for our nation." Though the president never used the word, it was dubbed his "malaise" speech, and to his critics, it became emblematic of Carter's ineptitude and impotence.

By that fall, polls showed the president running double digits behind in a hypothetical matchup with Senator Ted Kennedy of Massachusetts, a potential challenger from his own party whose last name was magical in Democratic circles. On November 4 hundreds of Iranian students—furious over the United States' continued support for exiled Shah Mohammed Reza Pahlavi, a hated figure who had been overthrown that year in a revolution—stormed the US embassy in Tehran and took more than fifty Americans hostage. So began a siege that would last for 444 days. Three days into it, the forty-seven-year-old Kennedy formally announced his presidential bid. "I say it is not the American people who are in a malaise," he declared. "It's the political leadership that's in a malaise."

While Carter struggled over those months, the Reagan operation was moving slowly and cautiously. There was a strategic argument to be made against getting into the fray too soon. And there were some practical considerations as well. "They boiled down to one thing: money," Nofziger recalled. "Although the Reagans lived well enough, they did not live lavishly. They were certainly not as rich as the people they associated with: the Holmes Tuttles, Alfred Bloomingdales, Bill Wilsons, Earle Jorgensens, and others with really deep pockets." As long as Ronnie remained officially undeclared, he could continue to make a living giving speeches, doing radio commentary, and writing his column.

Sears, who had managed the 1976 campaign, persuaded Ronnie and Nancy that he should be given the job again. The candidate-to-be and his wife had a sort of West Coast inferiority complex when it came to national politics. Sears convinced them they could not win without his pragmatism, expertise, and Washington connections. But he was an unpopular choice within the California inner circle, much of which the campaign manager had alienated four years before. With the exception of Deaver, they had all opposed putting Sears in charge. Nofziger, in particular, felt betrayed. He had never gotten along with Sears and shared the view of many of Ronnie's staunchest backers that the campaign manager was not a true conservative. Ronnie's daughter Maureen was also dismayed because her father had assured her, she claimed, that "under no circumstances would John Sears be involved in his 1980 campaign."

Nonetheless, by the spring of 1979, Sears was in control of the nascent operation. He and Nancy resumed their old rhythm from 1976, with regular lunches and long phone conversations. He soothed her anxieties and was receptive to the latest snippets of intelligence she had gathered. "She loved to gossip. She liked to give it and get it," Sears told me. At one of their meetings, Nancy obliquely brought up the subject of astrology. Sears had heard that she dabbled in it. But then again, millions of people checked their daily horoscopes in the newspaper. It seemed to him a harmless enough pastime. Sears realized Nancy took it more seriously than he had thought, however, when she asked him an odd question out of the blue:

"Do you believe there might be a better day to do something than another day?"

Sears didn't quite know what to say, and he fumbled for words: "Well, I don't know. I travel a lot to Japan. And a lot of people I know there believe very strongly in astrology, and they're smart in that. I don't know anything about it, but they do. I can't say I disbelieve it or believe it—either one."

"Well, if I let you know what is a good day to do things, would that be helpful?" Nancy asked.

"Sure, let me know," Sears said. "But you gotta understand: our problem is, we gotta do things *every* day." That was pretty much the end of it. Nancy never mentioned the subject to Sears after that, though she did send him a book on astrology.

The campaign operation was not a happy one. Internal tension escalated as Sears maneuvered to replace the old Reagan hands with his own allies. Over drinks at a governors' conference in North Carolina, he sought the counsel of former Reagan campaign manager Stu Spencer, who was still estranged from Ronnie and what Spencer viewed as the "palace guard." He told Sears to be cautious. "I'd pick them all off except one," Spencer said. "You have to have one person, either Lyn or Meese or Deaver, so that when Reagan gets up in the morning, he sees a familiar face. That's very important, but dump the rest."

Sears did not heed Spencer's advice. He began going after the whole California contingent. The Kitchen Cabinet, those elder figures who had built Reagan's operation at the dawn of his political career, were sidelined early on. In late August Nofziger was abruptly fired as the campaign's chief fund-raiser. It was a job for which he was ill-suited, which Nofziger suspected was why Sears assigned it to him in the first place.

Nancy was not sorry to see Nofziger go, given that they had never gotten along. But to influential conservatives, the loss of one of their own—especially someone who had been central to shaping Ronnie's message—was a disturbing signal that their champion was going off course. And indeed, with Sears firmly in command, Ronnie's rhetoric shifted in ways that unsettled his supporters on the Right.

It was not that the former governor's positions had changed; they hadn't. But the way he talked about them was evolving and softening. Under Sears's guidance, the candidate made fewer references to his opposition to the Equal Rights Amendment and more to how he supported equal pay for equal work. Instead of railing as much about welfare cheats, Ronnie told stories of how he had helped individual people better their circumstances. And while the subject of abortion still came up, Ronnie framed it differently, with a nod to the fact that this was a country built on individual rights.

It didn't exactly allay conservative suspicions when he started getting praise from a normally hostile quarter—the mainstream media. A headline in the November 14, 1979, issue of the *New York Times* declared: "The 1980 Model Reagan: Strident Campaign Tone Is Gone." The article quoted Reagan press secretary James Lake as saying: "If you're trying to get elected, you combat the perception that some people have of you as a strident, right-wing conservative."

No doubt this tempering of Ronnie's image met with the approval of Nancy. She had never been comfortable with the rigid ideologues in her husband's circle, the ones she would later describe as "jump-off-the-cliff-with-the-flag-flying conservative." And she was anxious that Ronnie not be seen as a fire-breather himself. "The idea that he was, you know, a gun-toting, hip-shooting cowboy from the West was something that bothered her," his longtime aide Ed Meese told me.

In fact, Sears recalled in an interview with me that Nancy had been a critical force behind a surprising move Ronnie made in 1978. California voters were considering a ballot initiative that would have banned gays and lesbians from working in the state's public schools. While many of Ronnie's right-wing backers assumed he would support Proposition 6, Nancy helped persuade her husband to come out against it. State Senator John Briggs, who was leading the charge for the initiative, was flabbergasted: "Nobody is going to convince me that Ronald Reagan is going to put homosexual rights over parents' rights."

By today's standards, Ronnie would hardly have been seen as a progressive on gay rights. He maintained that he was against homosexuality but warned that the ballot initiative "has the potential of infringing on basic rights of privacy and perhaps even constitutional rights." Days before the November election where the initiative was on the ballot, he wrote an op-ed in the *Los Angeles Herald-Examiner* arguing that "homosexuality is not a contagious disease like the measles. Prevailing scientific opinion is that an individual's sexuality is determined at a very early age and that a child's teachers do not really influence this."

Proposition 6 had been leading by nearly two to one in an August survey by the authoritative California Poll. Ronnie's opposition helped send it down to a 17-point defeat. Conservatives blamed Sears, but he told me in an interview that Nancy's had been the voice to which her husband listened. Absent Nancy's influence, he said, Ronnie most likely would have come down on the other side. "A lot of people she knew in the film business would not have liked" to see it pass, Sears added, "and so she was very helpful."

Finally, the time came when Ronnie could no longer be coy about his intentions. His presidential campaign got under way officially on November 13, 1979, at a $500-a-plate dinner in the ballroom of the New York Hilton. It was an unconventional setting. White House contenders normally made their declarations either in their home states or, as Ronnie had done four years earlier, in Washington, DC. By choosing the capital of liberal cosmopolitanism, the Reagans were determined to show that Ronnie was not a figure of limited regional stature or narrow ideological appeal. Something else was different this time. Where only Nancy had been at his side when he declared in 1975, all four of his children were there when he did it the second time. Ronnie quipped: "None of them are looking for jobs in the government."

But the continuing turmoil in the campaign grew more worrisome. More and more of the Golden State old guard was forced out. Conservative economist Martin Anderson had led the issues and research operation for Ronnie in 1976 and expected to do it again, Within two weeks of the campaign's launch, however, Anderson announced he was returning to Stanford University so that he could have "more time to think." Laxalt worried that he would be next; word was going round that Sears was sounding out others to become campaign chairman. Ronnie's former chief of staff Ed Meese, who had been given a smaller role in the campaign than he merited, was also on shaky ground. Behind Sears's back, the Californians began referring to the campaign manager as "Rasputin."

It turned out that the next person to find himself in Sears's crosshairs was Nancy's closest political confidant and ally. Michael Deaver had been the only California insider who had supported the decision to put Sears in charge of the campaign. But he chafed as he was assigned to take over fund-raising after Nofziger left. He was no better at it than Nofziger had been, and, in Sears's view, the canny Deaver was a constant troublemaker who was trying to put his fingers into too many other parts of the operation.

Everything came to a head at a meeting at the Reagan home in Pacific Palisades on November 26. Deaver had been invited there by Nancy and figured he was being summoned to a routine session where they would talk about money. He had his wife, Carolyn, drop him off, told her to run errands for an hour and a half, and then to come retrieve him. Deaver sensed something serious was up when Nancy met him at the front door and told him to wait in a bedroom. She led him past the living room, where Deaver saw "the Easterners"—Sears, press secretary Jim Lake, and strategist Charles Black—huddling with Ronnie. Nancy then left him and joined the group back in the living room. Deaver paced and flipped through an old *Reader's Digest*, trying to figure out what was happening. Nancy's presence was highly unusual. Only rarely did she sit through normal staff meetings. After twenty minutes had passed, Deaver burst into the living room. *"What the hell is going on here?"* he demanded.

This was the kind of scene that Ronnie, with his distaste for discord, was ill-equipped to handle. While everyone else looked at the floor, he began awkwardly: "Mike, the fellas here have been telling me about the way you're running the fund-raising efforts, and we're losing money." Ronnie pressed Deaver to explain why his firm was charging the campaign $30,000 a month to lease office space in its building. Deaver insisted that the figure was a lie. Nancy watched as Ronnie struggled with the predicament before him. Deaver was a long-serving aide and adviser; practically a surrogate son. Sears was the political wunderkind without whom they believed they could not win. "Honey," she finally told her husband, "it looks as if you've got to make a choice."

"No, Governor," Deaver retorted, "you don't have to, because I'm leaving."

He stormed out of the house—only to realize suddenly that he had no way of getting home. His wife had his car. Embarrassed on top of being furious, Deaver turned back and quietly opened the front door of the house. Inside, he found Nancy pacing the foyer alone. When Nancy saw Deaver return, she welcomed him. She assumed he would ask her to help him get his job back. Instead, he requested the keys to her station wagon so he could get out of there. From the living room, he could hear Ronnie telling the others: "Well, I hope you're happy; the best guy we had just left."

According to biographer Lou Cannon, "Reagan never spoke warmly to Sears again. The confrontation left him depressed and angry at himself about what he had allowed to happen. His mood did not improve when old friends and allies, who had rarely criticized him to his face, bluntly told him he had made a mistake." As Nancy put it: "I've never known Ronnie to carry a grudge, but after that day, I think he resented John Sears. The chemistry between them wasn't good to begin with, and now it was worse." Nancy also had begun to lose her faith in the operative whose knowledge and sophistication about politics had so impressed her when she first met him. "I don't know what made John change in the years between 1976 and 1980, but I thought he had become arrogant and aloof," she wrote later.

A tactical blunder of epic proportion further shook the Reagans' confidence. Ronnie's late start effectively meant he wasn't campaigning during the months running up to the January 1980 Iowa caucuses, which were the first statewide contest on the calendar. One measure of Iowa's low priority was the fact that Michael and Maureen, who had been sidelined in their father's earlier campaigns, were dispatched to stump there. Both reported back to Ronnie that they were appalled at how little organization they saw on the ground. But the candidate did nothing. He kept telling his children that the operation was in the hands of professionals.

Nancy picked up some of the slack by appearing in his stead, but she, too, confronted questions from worried grassroots supporters who wondered why Ronnie didn't seem more engaged. Among the events on her schedule during the fall of 1979 was a swing through Iowa that included a pig roast in Mason City and a salad luncheon in Ottumwa. One briefing memo advised her to assure her husband's backers that things were looking fine for Ronnie in a state where ground-level organizing was everything:

> Reflect the different status of the various campaigns. While RR has 100% name ID and established image, work is under way to identify supporters which already exist.
>
> Other campaigns are still at the first step attempting to establish name ID, campaign credibility and image. This effort requires visibility and big names while RFP [Reagan for President] is going to it's [*sic*] strength—the people.

Across the state line in Wisconsin, GOP activists were also feeling snubbed by a candidate who had pretty much ignored them in 1976 and visited the state only once in 1979. So, Nancy agreed to appear at a Republican women's banquet in La Crosse on November 1. "Mrs. Reagan's visit to Wisconsin at this time is crucial to maintaining morale of the Wisconsin [Reagan for President] due to experiences in 1976," organizers wrote in a memo to her. "This psychological attitude cannot be stressed enough, as when people gathered in the intervening years between 1976 to the present, the fear that the Reagan Campaign will ignore Wisconsin is still very real. Every appearance in Wisconsin by Governor and Mrs. Reagan will aid in putting this fear to rest." In her speech there, Nancy assured the women: "The ladies of our party are the glue that keeps campaigns running smoothly and provide the day-to-day operations to make sure that victory is ours on Election Day."

Whether the Reagans actually believed their own spin is unclear. But as the day of reckoning approached in Iowa, it was becoming increasingly obvious how badly they had miscalculated. Ronnie, still taking his above-the-fray posture, was absent when the GOP contenders debated in Des Moines in early January. With just over two weeks before the caucuses, that left the stage to six other candidates: Bush; Dole; ex-Texas governor John Connally; Senate minority leader Howard Baker of Tennessee; Phil Crane, a telegenic conservative congressman from Illinois; and independent-minded John Anderson, another House member from Illinois. Gleefully, they piled on the absent front-runner. "I want to say to Governor Reagan, wherever you are, I hope you're having fun tonight because we are, and if you're looking for a younger

Ronald Reagan, with experience, I'm here," Dole said, bringing laughter from the Iowa audience.

Ronnie plummeted in the Iowa polls, from 50 percent to 25 percent. Still, expectations remained that he would come out ahead in the crowded field. Nor did he and Nancy seem to have been terribly worried. As the results rolled in on caucus night, January 21, the Reagans were more than 1,500 miles away. They spent the evening at the home of movie industry friends, watching a screening of the hot new film *Kramer vs. Kramer*, starring Dustin Hoffman and Meryl Streep. They were shocked when pollster Richard Wirthlin called and delivered the news that Bush had edged past Ronnie to win by 2 percentage points.

Suddenly the campaign was in deep trouble. If Ronnie couldn't pull it out in New Hampshire just over a month later on February 26, the race was over. A small-state primary is political hand-to-hand combat. It cannot be won with money and advertising alone. And even if it could, Ronnie didn't have the financial capacity to do it. His campaign was already bumping up against the legal spending limits, which meant that if he blew a lot of his funds in New Hampshire, there might be nothing left for the long march through the primaries ahead. "We're going to change our tactics," Ronnie told Sears. "We're going to take that bus into every village and town in the state. We're going to live in New Hampshire until Election Day." Ronnie also remembered a tactical mistake he had made there in 1976: he had left the Granite State two days before the primary, thinking he had won, only to see Ford take it by a nose. "This time," Ronnie told Sears, "we're staying until it's over." Nancy had never seen her husband work so hard. For the next few weeks, Ronnie campaigned morning until night, a display of stamina that quieted some of the concerns about his age.

But there were also some unforced errors. On February 16 Nancy created a controversy with a slip of the tongue at a big GOP dinner in Chicago. She was filling in for her husband, so that he could continue to stump in New Hampshire. Ronnie made a few comments to the Chicago crowd over a telephone that had been placed near a loudspeaker and rhapsodized about the spectacular sixteen-inch snowfall he was seeing at that moment in New England. It had transformed the barren winter landscape with a fresh coat of brilliant white. Well, Nancy blurted out, she wished he could be with her in Chicago, "to see all these beautiful white *people.*" Nancy immediately recognized her mistake and tried to recover. "These beautiful black and white people," she said, though there were no African Americans in the room. The timing for such a gaffe could hardly have been worse. The press was already buzzing over another incident that had happened that same weekend. Ronnie had told an ethnic joke to a busload of reporters. The joke, which he had heard from his son Michael, involved Poles, Italians, the Mafia, cockfights, and a duck. So here they were, just ten days before the New Hampshire vote, with both the candidate and his wife having to apologize for racially and ethnically insensitive comments.

Things turned Ronnie's way the following Saturday, on the final weekend before the primary, when he and Bush were scheduled to debate in Nashua. The sponsoring newspaper, the *Nashua Telegraph*, withdrew its financial support for the debate after Dole complained to the Federal Election Commission that it would amount to an illegal contribution if the other candidates were excluded, and the FEC agreed. Ronnie's campaign proposed to split the costs with Bush's. But Bush refused, so the Reagan campaign picked up the entire $3,500 tab for the debate.

By then, Sears had seen an uptick in Ronnie's polling numbers. That suggested it would be better for him to face all the candidates on the debate stage rather than elevating Bush alone. So, Sears invited the others who were in New Hampshire to join the debate. Bush's campaign called the change "an ambush." Hoping to capitalize on their momentum coming out of Iowa, they did not want to be deprived of a head-to-head showdown against the front-runner. The sniping about the debate—who would be in it and who wouldn't—soon became topic A in the race. "I really thought Bush's people would be smart enough to know they were in a hole and they ought to just quit," Sears told me, "but they persisted and demanded that the two of us debate—which, of course, teed off Howard Baker and everybody else that was running, 'cause it was their last chance to make a case to people." The night of the debate, all the others showed up except for Connally, who was campaigning in South Carolina. The quartet of lesser candidates was instantly dubbed the "Nashua Four."

No one knew quite what was going to happen from there. With five minutes to go before the event was set to start, the scene in the Nashua High School gymnasium was pandemonium. At least eighty reporters were there to see how all of this would play out. The Reagans were waiting in a classroom, along with Baker, Dole, Crane, and Anderson. Everyone seemed confused. Then they heard a knock on the door. Someone from the *Telegraph* came in to warn them that if Ronnie didn't get out there within three minutes, the whole thing would be called off.

Sears was unsure what he wanted to do. He was dubious about sending his candidate into such a raucous and unpredictable circumstance, especially given Ronnie's recent ethnic-joke gaffe and other mistakes he had been making lately on the campaign trail. God only knew what could happen in a setting as chaotic as this. That's when Nancy stepped in and took over. "I know what you're going to do," she said firmly to the candidates. "You're *all* going to go out there."

What Sears would realize later was that Nancy understood something fundamental about Ronnie that he didn't. Even before this, she had advised the campaign manager that he should never fear letting Ronnie do some improvising when a moment demanded it. "Just put him in the situation," Nancy said. "He'll be fine." In fact, Nancy knew that this was how Ronnie performed best: when he was spontaneous by appearance, but, in truth, working off an internal script. She was confident that Ronnie would find something right for the moment tucked in the back of his mind—perhaps a line or a scene from an old movie, or something he had read somewhere. With a near-photographic recall, honed by all those years working as an actor, he had the ability to retrieve that kind of information under pressure. His brain worked like the stack of index cards that he held in his hand as he gave his speeches.

Anne Frances Robbins, known as Nancy, 1927. (*Ronald Reagan Presidential Library*)

The marriage of Edith Luckett and Kenneth Robbins was all but over by the time their daughter arrived on July 6, 1921. (*Ronald Reagan Presidential Library*)

Nancy Robbins, living with relatives in Maryland, holds a tea party for her doll, 1920s. (*Ronald Reagan Presidential Library*)

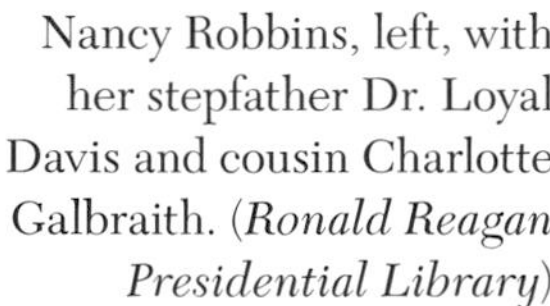

Nancy Robbins, left, with her stepfather Dr. Loyal Davis and cousin Charlotte Galbraith. (*Ronald Reagan Presidential Library*)

Nancy's senior year photo in the Girls Latin yearbook, 1939. (*Courtesy of the Latin School of Chicago*)

Nancy Davis as Princess Lilia in the play *Ivory Door,* 1938. (*Courtesy of the Latin School of Chicago*)

In her senior class play, Nancy portrays the conniving wife of a presidential candidate. The title of the play: *First Lady*. (*Courtesy of the Latin School of Chicago*)

Smith College senior Nancy Davis hangs a poster for *Make with the Maximum: A Factory Follies*. She was part of a troupe that performed in 1943 at war production plants. (*College Archives, Smith College*)

Nancy Davis, atop a piano, in *Make With the Maximum*, 1943. (*College Archives, Smith College*)

Nancy Davis plays the sophisticated "Glamour Gal," a shirker on the factory line who laments that she misses her prewar life of luxury, 1943. (*College Archives, Smith College*)

James Whitmore with Nancy Davis in a scene from the film *The Next Voice You Hear*, 1950. (*Metro-Goldwyn-Mayer/Getty Images*)

Nancy and Ronald Reagan, with Marilyn Monroe, 1953. (*Everett Collection*)

Ronald Reagan and Nancy Davis Reagan costar in *Hellcats of the Navy*, 1957. Ronnie later said: "That picture ended movies for me." (*Everett Collection*)

Newlyweds Ronald Reagan and Nancy Reagan cutting their wedding cake at the home of their friends William and Ardis Holden in Toluca Lake, California, March 4, 1952. (*Ronald Reagan Presidential Library*)

Ronald Reagan, son Ron, Nancy Reagan, and daughter Patti outside their Pacific Palisades home in California, 1960. (*Ronald Reagan Presidential Library*)

Portrait of a blended family, left to right: Patti Davis, Nancy and Ronald Reagan, Michael Reagan, Maureen Reagan, Ron Reagan, 1976. (*Ronald Reagan Presidential Library*)

At the 1968 Republican convention in Miami Beach, Nancy beams during a demonstration after her husband's name was put into nomination for president, August 7, 1968. (*Bettmann/ Getty Images*)

Nancy Reagan catches a nap on Ronnie's lap during his grueling—and unsuccessful—campaign for the GOP nomination against President Gerald Ford, August 11, 1976. She would later call her husband's loss "a glorious defeat" that stood out more than Ronnie's victories in her memory. (*Bettmann/Getty Images*)

"She wasn't worried about what he would say, seemingly off the cuff, publicly," Sears told me. "I didn't realize this was good advice for a long time. Two or three of us who went through both campaigns used to joke a little bit that he really had sort of a record library in his brain, because if you were with him a lot, you'd find that certain things would touch on what we used to think of as a record, that it would play, word for word the same. There were a lot of them. It wasn't just one or two. It was tons of them."

Bush was waiting on the stage, staring straight ahead. William Loeb III, the influential and notoriously cantankerous publisher of the conservative *Manchester Union Leader*, wrote later that the former CIA director looked like a little boy suddenly realizing that his mother had dropped him off at the wrong birthday party. Ronnie marched out and took his seat. The Nashua Four lined up against the blue curtain backdrop: from left to right, Anderson, Baker, Dole, and Crane. They stood motionless as the school gym erupted into cheers and hoots. There were shouts to get them some chairs. Someone joked that the diminutive Baker could stand on the table. *Telegraph* editor Jon Breen, the moderator, tried to proceed to the first question. Ronnie's face flushed brightly, and he raised a defiant index finger.

"Before the question, you asked me if you could make an announcement first, and I asked you for permission to make an announcement myself—"

"Would the sound man please turn Mr. Reagan's mike off?" Breen ordered the engineer, Bob Molloy.

Ronnie rose and picked up the microphone from the table. "Is this on?" he asked, his anger rising.

"Would you turn that microphone off, please?" Breen implored.

Ronnie planted himself back in his chair, made eye contact with the sound engineer, and roared: *"I am paying for this microphone, Mr. Green!"*

In his fury, Ronnie mangled the name of the moderator, but it didn't matter. The gymnasium exploded with cheers. Behind him, the Nashua Four applauded their rival. No one remembers much of what happened after that moment. Nor did it really matter. “I may have won the debate, the primary—and the nomination—right there,” Ronnie recalled later. “After the debate, our people told me the gymnasium parking lot was littered with Bush-for-President badges.” More than a dozen years later, Nancy had Ronnie’s microphone retrieved from the office pigeonhole where Molloy had stored it, never to be used again. She put it on display in her husband’s presidential library.

While Ronnie’s anger had been genuine, his line about paying for the microphone, which became an instant classic in politics, was not original. Spencer Tracy had used one very similar at a pivotal moment in the 1948 political satire *State of the Union,* a movie in which Tracy played, coincidentally, a candidate for the Republican presidential nomination. Nancy had known Ronnie would find it—or something equally useful—in the recesses of his brain. “It was in the record library,” Sears said, “so she was absolutely right.”

Ronnie was back on top, but the tensions within the campaign had only grown worse in the weeks before the crucial primary. When Nancy got wind that Sears was trying to get rid of Meese, she put out distress calls to old allies, including the exiled Deaver. At night, as Ronnie prepared for bed at whatever hotel they were in, Nancy roamed the hallways, meeting quietly with various factions within the operation. She was desperate to smooth things where she could and figure out whether there was a solution to all of this. “When I finally got to bed, Ronnie would ask me where I had been, and I would make up various excuses,” she recalled. “For as long as possible, I delayed telling him how much tension there was; I wanted to protect him from these undercurrents so he could concentrate on campaigning. For a while, I succeeded. But I soon realized that we were merely putting a Band-Aid over a serious problem.”

Nancy knew what had to happen: Sears had to be neutralized. So, she went to work convincing Ronnie that changes must be made. “She reviewed for him the body count of people who had been his friends,” Deaver recounted later. “Nofziger was gone. And Deaver. Meese would be next. In her usual way, Nancy had recruited Paul Laxalt and Dick

Wirthlin, associates of long standing, to call Reagan. They convinced him that he had to choose between losing another confidant, Meese, and this group of 'Washington mercenaries.'"

Nancy had already asked Justin Dart, a stalwart from the Kitchen Cabinet, to start putting the campaign's finances back in order. She sounded out Bill Clark, who had been Ronnie's gubernatorial chief of staff, about the possibility of coming aboard to share authority with Sears. "The campaign is in chaos, and there's no central direction," she told Clark in a phone call. "Ronnie's mind is fuzzy. He can't think things through."

Clark agreed to meet with both Reagans at the ranch the second weekend in February, but he declined their entreaties to join the campaign. He said he couldn't take a leave from the seat on the California Supreme Court to which Ronnie had appointed him. Privately, Clark later told his fellow Sacramento veteran Tom Reed that he believed the operation was so dysfunctional that it was "pretty hopeless. I can't leave my judicial bench to join that maelstrom."

When Clark turned Ronnie down, Nancy brought up the name of Wall Street banker William J. Casey, the former chief of the Securities and Exchange Commission. The Reagans had met him through their old friends the Wicks at a New York fund-raiser. Nancy posited that Casey might be a good person to bring order to the whole operation—and she just happened to have his phone number handy. He accepted the offer on the spot. (Casey would later become director of the Central Intelligence Agency under Ronnie and play a major role in putting together the secret operations that were at the center of the Iran-contra scandal.)

Thanks to Nancy, the wheels were already in motion for a campaign shake-up when Sears made a serious misstep, the one that would seal his fate. He told her that Meese was undermining his authority and demanded that the last California stalwart in the operation be fired. That was Nancy's opening. With the primary only about a week away, she told Ronnie that his campaign manager was trying to oust the ever-loyal Meese. Late one night, exhausted by another long day on the trail, Ronnie finally had it out with Sears. "You got Deaver," he shouted, "but, by God, you're not going to get Ed Meese. You guys have forced me to the wall." Ronnie was so furious, Nancy wrote later, that it appeared he might actually slug Sears. She took her husband's arm and told him: "It's late, and I think we should all get some sleep."

On February 26, as New Hampshire voters were going to the polls, Ronnie summoned Sears, strategist Charlie Black, and press secretary Jim Lake to the Reagans' third-floor suite at the Manchester Holiday Inn. He handed them each a copy of a statement the campaign planned to issue. It said that Sears had decided to return to his law practice, and his two lieutenants would be leaving as well. The new campaign administrator would be William Casey. The whole thing was straightforward and bloodless, a far different scene from the explosive one that had taken place in the middle of the night the previous week.

As Sears left the room, Nancy followed him out. "I am sorry this happened," she told him, "but I hope we can still be friends."

Nancy and Sears never spoke again, though they would occasionally cross paths over the years at political and social functions. At one, Nancy tried to have a word with him, and Sears pretended he didn't hear her. In an interview with me nearly forty years after they parted ways in Manchester, Sears reflected upon everything that he had gone through with both Reagans. The decades had given him a philosophical perspective, the kind that comes with seeing how everything turned out.

"She was a very powerful woman in her way," he said of Nancy. "About the things she was interested in, she had very good instincts."

As for Ronnie: "He was the best candidate to be president. He gave the country back its optimism."

CHAPTER TEN

After the votes were counted in New Hampshire, the cover of *Time* magazine declared the result to have been "Ronnie's Romp!" He swamped Bush, 50 percent to 23 percent. Anderson and Baker barely broke double digits, while Connally, Crane, and Dole each came in with 2 percent or less. From there, it would never really be in question that the Republican nomination was Ronnie's. Casey moved quickly to right the ship financially after the New Hampshire victory, cutting the campaign's staff in both the Los Angeles and Washington offices by nearly half and getting rid of its expensive charter aircraft.

One by one, the California contingent— Mike Deaver, Lyn Nofziger, and Marty Anderson—trickled back. There were also new people joining the campaign. Beginning that spring, the name "C. McCain" shows up frequently in the flight manifests of Nancy's travels. Carol McCain, the wife of former Vietnam prisoner of war John McCain, was going through a dark time. Her husband had decided to leave her for Cindy Lou Hensley, the daughter of a prosperous beer distributor in Phoenix. For years to come, this would strain Nancy's friendship with the future senator, who would himself make two bids for the presidency. John McCain was elected to Congress in 1983 as a self-described "foot soldier in the Reagan Revolution," but he wrote later that Nancy treated him with "a cool correctness that made her displeasure clear. . . . I had, of course, deserved the change in our relationship."

Carol was also struggling with the aftereffects of a car accident that had almost killed her on Christmas Eve in 1969, two years into John's captivity. Nearly two dozen surgeries left her five inches shorter and walking with a limp. Some of their friends believed that her husband left her in part because she was no longer the statuesque beauty he had married. She said the collapse of their marriage was more complicated than that. In fact, there were many stories like theirs among POW families. But whatever caused the rupture, Carol knew he was gone. "John had met somebody young, wealthy, attractive—you know, all of the things I would be petrified about. He wanted to get a divorce and marry her. I didn't like it, but there was not really a lot I could do about it," Carol told me.

Nancy had long been fond of Carol and looked for ways to ease her through this hard patch. "She knocked herself out to be kind, sweet, gentle, soft-spoken to me," Carol said. As it happened, the campaign needed a press assistant to travel with the candidate's wife, so Nancy suggested Carol, who had experience on Capitol Hill, for the job. Carol and her daughter moved to California, where they lived with Ed Meese and his wife, Ursula, for several months in early 1980. (After Ronnie was elected, Carol became director of the White House Visitors Office.)

By the end of March, Ronnie had effectively sewn up the nomination, having won six out of the eight primaries that followed in the month after his New Hampshire victory. On the surface, it seemed the campaign was running much more smoothly. But Nancy was worried. Ronnie couldn't seem to find a groove. On the stump, he was telling too many old stories and getting his facts mixed up.

She realized there was still someone missing; someone who should have been at Ronnie's side all along. In June, as the campaign's focus turned to the convention and beyond, Nancy asked Deaver to place a call to Stu Spencer, the political consultant who had manned the launch pad of Ronnie's political career. Though Nancy had been angry and hurt by Spencer's defection to Ford in 1976, she believed his guiding hand was what Ronnie needed now.

Spencer was startled when Deaver proposed he return. He asked for some time to think. At the time, he was living near the ocean in Los Angeles, so he walked to the beach and sat there for the next four hours. Then he called Deaver and asked one question: "Does Nancy want me back?" As Spencer explained it to me later, "it wasn't a condition. It's just that I wouldn't believe it until I heard it from her. I knew she was the personnel director. If I didn't have her, I would have had a miserable five months." Within a day or two, a call came from Nancy. "You used to talk about rhythm," she told Spencer. "We haven't got any rhythm. We don't have everybody working off the same page. Ronnie's frustrated."

Spencer, given his history of friction with the other Californians, wanted it made clear that he was in charge. "My concept of a campaign, of what they had to do, involved certain skills that I saw they did not have. I wanted the authority to hire, and I wanted the authority to dump people," Spencer said. He insisted that the "Sacramento claque" with whom he had clashed in the early days all meet for dinner, so that he could look each of them in the eye and hear them say they would accept having him back. "It was a riot," Spencer told me. "They were all half drunk. I can remember [pollster and chief strategist Richard] Wirthlin, who was not [drinking], who was the good Mormon boy. I heard him say to somebody next to him, 'Nancy really must want to win this thing.'"

Oddly, the one person with whom Spencer did not have an in-depth discussion about his return was the candidate himself. The first time he set foot on the campaign plane was on July 12, as the Reagans were flying to the Republican convention in Detroit. First, he sat with Nancy, and she vented her grievances about Spencer's betrayal four years earlier. He let her finish and then asked: "Okay—y'all happy? All the air clear?" Nancy told him yes, and then she gave up her seat to Ronnie. "He and I talked the rest of the way. My conversation with him was like we'd had one yesterday, and we were continuing it,"

Spencer marveled. "Yet, what was it in between there? Five years? Six years? Something like that. It was ironical. We just started right back where we were."

As the Republican convention got under way on July 14 at the brand-new Joe Louis Arena, Ronnie's top imperative was to unify the party. An important signal would be sent with his choice of a running mate. Privately, both Reagans would have liked Paul Laxalt, but a California-Nevada ticket would not have had much geographic reach. Ronnie's advisers had another idea, one that horrified Nancy. They wanted him to pick none other than his old nemesis, Gerald Ford.

The polls indicated a Reagan-Ford "dream ticket" would give the biggest boost to Ronnie's chances of winning. But what kind of situation would they be creating if he did? A former president serving as number two to a current one? "It can't be done," Nancy argued to her husband. "It would be a dual presidency. It just won't work." Spencer also hated the proposal, which he saw as just a ploy by DC's Old Guard to keep its foothold when Ronnie came to town. "It was a power play by folks who had lost theirs when Carter was elected. They were desperate, and without a Jerry Ford going to bat for them, were convinced they would have no role in a Reagan administration," Spencer said.

They were getting nowhere with Ronnie, so Nancy and Spencer turned for help to an unlikely source: Betty Ford. She agreed with them that the idea was preposterous. Betty was also in the early stages of her recovery from more than a decade of drug and alcohol addiction and didn't want to risk it by returning to the White House pressure cooker. Betty told Spencer that if Jerry did this, she would divorce him. "Does he know that?" Spencer asked her. "Hell, yes, he knows that," Betty retorted.

Despite the strenuous objections of their wives, the future president, the former one, and their emissaries continued to talk about the conditions under which they might run together. Ford's demands became stiffer and stiffer. The White House staff would have to report to the president through Ford. He would get control over key Cabinet appointments. In essence, Ford "wanted to run the White House and control the government while Reagan met the dignitaries and attended the funerals," Nofziger recalled.

Negotiations continued until the second to last night of the convention. When Ronnie and his top advisers heard Ford acknowledge in an interview with Walter Cronkite on CBS that he envisioned the arrangement as a kind of "copresidency," they realized they needed to put a halt to the deal. And as it turned out, Ford had also come around to recognizing it would never work. It would devalue the presidency. The two men met one last time, and Ford officially took himself out of consideration. Ronnie placed a call to a suite at the Hotel Pontchartrain and offered the second spot on his ticket to a startled George H. W. Bush, who had been the last man standing against him in the race for the nomination.

Nancy was not thrilled with that choice, either. She knew a running mate from the more moderate wing of the GOP would help Ronnie's chances to win, particularly in the Northeast and among upper-income whites. But Nancy still remembered the bitterness of the early primaries when Bush had mocked her husband's core policies as "voodoo economics." And where Ford would have had too much influence in the role, she saw Bush as too weak to be an effective partner.

The crowd on the convention floor went wild when Ronnie took the stage and announced his pick just moments later. It was right after the roll call, where 1,939 out of 1,990 delegates had given him their votes. "The roof almost came off," he wrote later. "As George and I stood there together, it was almost as if we were putting the party back together." Nancy did not bother to hide how she felt. *New York* magazine wrote: "When her husband finally selected Bush in a midnight appearance before the convention that had nominated him only minutes before, the world was witness to her antagonism. Nancy Reagan, who always smiles, didn't." The *Washington Post* described it this way: "Her face told it all when she stood on the podium as Reagan announced Bush as his running mate. She looked like a little girl who had just lost her favorite Raggedy Ann doll: sad, disappointed, almost crushed. Sen. Paul

D. Laxalt, Reagan's campaign chairman, wrapped his arm around her shoulder, consoling her."

But there was now the fall contest upon which to focus. Ronnie's campaign moved its headquarters from Los Angeles to Arlington, Virginia, inside the Washington Beltway. Nancy and Ronnie rented a house on an estate known as Wexford. Located on thirty-nine acres in the Virginia hunt country, it was owned at the time by Texas governor William Clements, but the 5,050-square-foot ranch-style home had a touch of Camelot. It had been built in 1963 by John and Jackie Kennedy, and named for the Kennedy ancestral birthplace in Ireland. Jackie had designed it herself. Her idea was that it would be a retreat where the Kennedys could be a normal family, located close enough to Washington to serve as a regular escape. The house was purposefully plain. Jackie wrote that she wanted it to have "all the places we need to get away from each other. So husband can have meetings. Children watch TV. Wife paint or work at desk. Nurse have own room. Help a place to sit. All things so much bigger houses don't have. I think it's brilliant!" The Kennedys spent only two weekends there before Jack was assassinated. His widow sold it the following year.

For the Reagans, Wexford would be a temporary home and a respite from the campaign trail, albeit one in which meetings and phone calls were constantly going on. Nancy especially loved the stone patio, where she could look out over the rolling countryside with its wooden fences and stone walls. Her old MGM compatriot Elizabeth Taylor lived nearby with her sixth husband, John Warner, a former navy secretary recently elected to the US Senate. "For me," Nancy would later write, "Wexford was the happiest part of the 1980 campaign." Ronnie felt so at home there that when he became annoyed with a pine tree blocking his view from a window, he took an axe and chopped it down. Only later was it discovered that the tree was a favorite of the Texas governor who owned the place.

Away from that bucolic spot, there was renewed turmoil within the campaign. In August Ronnie made some unforced errors. In Philadelphia, Mississippi, where three civil rights workers had been murdered in 1964, the Republican nominee declared his belief in "state's rights," a phrase that has an ugly racist legacy. At a religious convention in Dallas, he endorsed the teaching of creationism. None of this boded well for a candidate seeking to reassure voters that he wasn't a right-wing zealot or a bigot. He needed to recognize he was talking to the whole country now, not just the conservatives who had cheered him to victory in the Republican primary.

Meanwhile, Spencer's return had not been welcomed by others in the campaign's top echelon. He was beginning to worry that he had made a terrible mistake. It was hardly a subtle hint that there was no office—or even a desk—for him at the new Arlington headquarters. Nor was he being included in strategy meetings at Wexford, which was something Nancy noticed. "Where's Stu?" she asked at one. "Next meeting, make sure Spencer is here."

"I hadn't been invited. Bill Casey, Dick Wirthlin, and the rest wanted me nowhere near the candidate. Neither did Ed Meese, for that matter," Spencer said. "Nancy was the one who delivered the message—and the guys heard her loud and clear." But by then, Spencer had come up with another, more effective plan to assert control. He proposed an audacious scheme to Deaver: "Mike, you and I both know that with Ronald Reagan, whoever owns the body owns the campaign. We take over their plane. We cut off the phones. And then we run the damn show."

The coup came together quickly. Spencer brought in his own scheduler, Joe Canzeri. He kept Nofziger aboard to handle the press. Martin Anderson would direct policy from the plane and act as the "conservative conscience," ignoring whatever dictates were coming from Arlington. They found an experienced Washington hand named Jim Brady, who understood the workings of government and could help with issues research. Spencer also added Ken Khachigian, a young and gifted wordsmith who had written speeches for Nixon. "That was my team. I had a speechwriter. I had a press operation. I had a scheduling operation. I had a philosopher. I had Deaver for Ron and Nancy. I had me," Spencer recalled.

For the final two months before the election, Spencer's rogue operation was in charge. "We ran the entire campaign from that airplane," he said. "The Reagans were very happy; they were completely comfortable again for the first time in ages. Meanwhile, back at the national headquarters in Arlington, they were having fits. They would demand, let's say, a copy of the speech Reagan was going to give in Des Moines. We gave it to them after the fact, not before."

Under Spencer's guidance, everything began working better. Ronnie kept his message focused on Carter's failings and the country's economic problems. He took fewer questions from the press. Spencer also managed to secure for Ronnie the endorsements of civil rights leaders Ralph Abernathy and Hosea Williams, both of whom had supported Carter in 1976. The Reagans' comfort level with Spencer was such that they would often include him as they hashed out their own differences over how the campaign was going and bickered over Nancy's constant worries that Ronnie was being pushed too hard physically. These conversations usually took place at night, after Ronnie got into his pajamas. "I spent half my life in their bedroom," Spencer said. "This was where the arguments always took place. She's jumping on him. Sometimes there were arguments about the kids, but they had nothing to do with the campaign, so I didn't get into those. They were usually over schedule. They'd argue and argue."

Nancy also took the measure of the newer members of the team. Speechwriter Khachigian recalled his first long conversation with her, which happened as they campaigned in Illinois that fall. Normally consigned to the staff bus, Khachigian had been summoned to ride in the Reagans' limousine because he and the candidate needed to talk over plans for a half-hour television address. The speechwriter sat in the jump seat, his knees jammed against Nancy's. As Ronnie turned his attention to the remarks he would have to deliver at the next event, Nancy turned hers to Khachigian.

"It's important for Ronnie in his speeches to be emotional," she told him. As she saw it, Ronnie should not be steered toward hard-edged bombast or swamped with the intricacies of policy. He was at his best when he could strive "to move an audience, and to reach for their passions, to string out their emotions and reach their hearts," said Khachigian, who would go on to become the chief White House speechwriter. "I think one of the reasons I synced with Reagan is that I paid attention to her instructions."

Nancy was not so sure-footed in managing her own image. In the 1980 campaign, as in 1976, there were harsh comparisons with the woman she would replace in the White House. Four years earlier, Nancy had been portrayed as the buttoned-up antithesis of breezily candid Betty Ford; this time around, glamorous and perfectly coiffed Nancy was being held up against earnest, down-to-earth Rosalynn Carter, who sewed some of her own clothes and served nothing harder than wine when she entertained. But Rosalynn also raised eyebrows by sitting in on meetings of her husband's Cabinet and his National Security Council, and sent her chief of staff to important policy-making sessions. Nancy said she would never do such things.

Nancy's disavowal of any hand in her husband's governing agenda was seen as yet more evidence that she was merely a paper doll figure. At the same time, a separate and contradictory story line was developing. This one had Nancy as a master manipulator; a behind-the-curtain whisperer. Campaign reporters took note how, on the day Sears was fired in New Hampshire, Ronnie had seemed at a loss for words when asked where the pressure had come from to dismiss the campaign manager.

"From you," Nancy prompted.

"From me," her husband said.

At a stop in Florida, Ronnie made the claim that marijuana was a greater cancer and heart disease hazard than tobacco. When a journalist noted that people didn't smoke as much of it, Nancy nudged her husband and murmured, "You wouldn't know." After which he dutifully piped up: "I wouldn't know." The Associated Press noted: "Rosalynn Carter would never put words in her husband's mouth in public."

Nancy tried to reboot perceptions of her with the publication of *Nancy*, a syrupy-sweet memoir written with coauthor Bill Libby. This was something no candidate's wife had ever done before, and it backfired. Reviews were withering. "Perhaps you'll be pleased to know that 'Little Mary Sunshine' lives in California," began one in the *Los Angeles Times.* The book included a false birth date (Nancy's actual one would be unearthed by the *Washington Post*'s Maxine Cheshire shortly after the election), did not name her husband's first wife, and made only passing reference to her children. In *Nancy*, she pronounced the movies of the day "trash" and suggested that censorship was a good thing. Nancy also decried "premarital or casual sex, live-in relationships, early marriage and easy divorce, abortions and permissive child rearing." *San Francisco Examiner* columnist Herb Caen noted: "The type is large, for the benefit of the senior citizens who will read it with approving clucks and nods."

Nancy made an effort to court the journalists who traveled with the campaign. Every time the Boeing 727 dubbed *LeaderShip '80* took off, the PA system played country singer Willie Nelson's current hit "On the Road Again," and Nancy playfully "bowled" oranges down the aisle past the rows in the back where the campaign reporters were sitting. She also passed out chocolates on each leg of every trip. But even those small gestures fit into a story line that had already been set. "When one of the reporters wrote a column saying that unless you ate your candy, you wouldn't get an interview with Ronnie, I was so hurt and embarrassed that I never wanted to go down that aisle again," Nancy recalled later. "But with Stu Spencer's encouragement, I did—with a sign around my neck that said: Take One or Else!"

Noteworthy among the stories written about Nancy was a profile by the *Washington Post*'s legendary Sally Quinn: "She can sit perfectly still, her ankles neatly crossed, her hands resting calmly in her lap, her chin uplifted, her eyes glistening, her lips smiling . . . for what seems like hours . . . and hang raptly on his every word no matter what he is saying, no matter how many times she has heard it before in their twenty-eight-year marriage. She never seems to get an itch, her lips never stick to her teeth, she hardly blinks. Don't her legs ever go to sleep? Haven't they ever had a terrible fight just before the speech? Isn't she ever bored hearing the whole thing over and over and over?"

Quinn quoted an unnamed "very close former Reagan staffer" as saying that the real reason Ronnie was running was because "Nancy wants to be queen." Her story cautioned: "Do not underestimate Nancy. She knows what she wants. She has made up her mind where she was going to go, and she would get Ronnie to take her. He is her vehicle."

And then there was this supposedly feminist take from *New York* magazine's Julie Baumgold, which recycled some of the hoariest of sexist tropes: "It's an old secret that if a woman will speak low and smile, defer and not compete, if she can believe that her husband's triumphs are hers, achieve through his achievements, then she will have power over him. She does not provoke; she flatters and always suppresses the little touch of the bitch inside."

Carol McCain said Nancy had grown to expect harsh coverage, but she never got used to it. Nor could she figure out what she was doing wrong. "She's very complicated, and she didn't want to make it easy for people to understand her," McCain said. Katharine Graham, the owner and publisher of the newspaper that published Quinn's blistering critique, once pointed out to Nancy that many of the most scorching articles about her had been written by younger women who were "caught up" in the feminist movement. "They just couldn't identify with you," Graham told Nancy. "You represented everything they were rebelling against."

But in front of audiences of her husband's conservative supporters, Nancy's traditionalist image—which disguised her actual power—was an asset. Carol McCain recalled one union hall in New Jersey where "those men, their tongues were hanging out. They were drooling over this petite woman, soft-spoken, infectious laugh, terribly attractive. They just loved her. Of course she's going to respond to that, so she just poured it on, and they just ate it up."

As the campaign headed into its final weeks, Ronnie's momentum seemed to stall, and his team faced what would be its last big decision: Should he debate Carter? The president had refused to attend a September 21 debate in Baltimore because John B. Anderson, who after falling short in the Republican primary was running as an independent, had also been invited. At that point, Anderson was polling just above 15 percent, which was the threshold set by the League of Women Voters, the organization that sponsored the debate. With Carter boycotting, Ronnie debated Anderson alone and put in a strong enough performance that the third-party contender's poll numbers began to drop. (In the end, Anderson won 7 percent of the popular vote and no electoral votes.)

A one-on-one Carter-Reagan matchup was a far different proposition. Nancy was among those who had the deepest reservations about a high-risk move so close to the election, but Ronnie was convinced he could best the incumbent. Handling the negotiations with the Carter campaign was a newcomer to the Reagan team, James A. Baker III, a Texas lawyer who was George H. W. Bush's closest friend and adviser. In his talks with the Carter campaign and the League of Women Voters, Baker pressed to have the debate scheduled as close to the election as possible. He assumed—incorrectly, it turned out—that the American hostages being held in Tehran would soon be released, lifting Carter's fortunes. He wanted Ronnie to have a chance to make his closing argument after that happened, not before. The two sides agreed the candidates would meet to debate on October 28, a week before the election, in Cleveland.

Baker also managed the debate rehearsals, which took place in the garage at Wexford. David Stockman, a Michigan congressman whom Ronnie would later appoint his first budget director, played Carter. Conservative columnist George Will acted the role of a reporter asking questions. It was a blatantly unethical move on Will's part. Though he had made it clear in his columns for the *Washington Post* and *Newsweek* that he supported Ronnie, Will did not disclose that he was working with the campaign. In postdebate television commentary, he pronounced the Republican nominee to have given a "thoroughbred performance," as though he had had nothing to do with it. "I was misbehaving," Will conceded in an interview with me decades later.

Nancy, however, was instantly enamored with this erudite young rogue from the fourth estate. "Jim Baker had asked me to write something, so I was sitting at a typewriter, which tells you how long ago it was," Will recalled. "Someone came up behind me and tousled my hair, and it was her. She tousled my hair and said, 'Oh, I see we brought in the varsity.' She was a great flirt." So began a great friendship. Over the coming years, Nancy and Will would become so tight that Washington insiders thought they heard Nancy's voice at times in Will's columns.

Though Ronnie had been leading in the polls going into the debate, his better-than-expected performance helped nail down his victory. When he walked onstage, Barbara Bush, the wife of his running mate, leaned over to Nancy and whispered that Ronnie's makeup looked better than Carter's. "Ronnie never wears makeup," Nancy replied with a touch of annoyance. In fact, Deaver had given him a glass of wine before he went on, to add "a little color to his cheeks."

Carter flubbed an answer on nuclear weapons by noting that he had discussed the issue with his daughter, Amy, who had just turned thirteen. ("Ask Amy" signs popped up at Republican rallies shortly thereafter.) Ronnie scored with two memorable lines near the end. When Carter noted Ronnie's early opposition to Medicare and suggested he might stand in the way of efforts to fix the health care system, Ronnie flattened him with a dismissive "There you go again." The capper, however, was Ronnie's closing statement. He looked into the television camera and asked the country: "Are you better off than you were four years ago? Is it easier for you to go and buy things in the store than it was four years ago? Is there more or less unemployment in the country than there was four years ago? Is America as respected throughout the world as it was? Do you feel that our security is as safe, that we're as strong as we were four years ago?"

*

As victory looked more and more certain, the time arrived to begin talking about what came next. About three weeks before the election, Spencer and Deaver decided to raise a delicate issue with the Reagans. If there was ever a president who would need a top-notch chief of staff, it was Ronnie, whose detached management style would leave room for all kinds of chaos. Loyal Ed Meese, who had held the job in California and who could channel Ronnie's beliefs better than anyone else, assumed that it would be him. So did most everyone else. Meese was already passing around an organization chart he had drawn with his own name as chief of staff. But as Meese's bulging briefcase attested, organization was not his strong suit. "If you wanted a document to disappear, you'd give it to Ed," Nancy said. Moreover, she viewed him as too much of an ideologue, one of those she described as "so rigid in their beliefs that they'd rather lose than win a partial victory."

When Spencer broached the subject of who they might consider to run the White House staff, he was surprised when both Nancy and Ronnie replied, "Oh, no, not Ed." Spencer and Deaver would each later claim to be the one who first raised the idea of naming James Baker. However it came about, it was an unlikely move. The Reagans did not know the fifty-year-old Baker well, and until he took over organizing for the debate, their experience with him was largely as an adversary. Baker, who came from one of Houston's old-line families, had served as chairman of Ford's 1976 presidential campaign in its later stages and had run Bush's operation in the 1980 primary. As Baker noted, "I had managed two hard-fought battles to deny Ronald Reagan his party's nomination—one successful, the other not."

Spencer and Deaver arranged to have him travel with the Reagans in the final days before the election, just to see how things went. "Nobody in the campaign, except Deaver and I, knew why Baker was suddenly on the plane," Spencer recalled. The polished, personable Texan quickly developed a chemistry with Nancy. "Jim Baker is a gentleman. River Oaks, Houston. Princeton, and all that stuff, and dressed well, and she liked that because in politics you don't always run around with that kind of person," Will observed. Baker was also the kind of pragmatist who made Nancy comfortable, and he was self-assured enough to tease her, putting her at ease. Nancy decided he was perfect for the chief of staff job. "She was the one who had pushed it more than anybody else," Baker said later.

Baker's temporary stint on the campaign plane was ending, and as he was preparing to get off, Nancy decided it was time to seal the deal. The campaign's foreign-policy adviser, Richard Allen, noticed her frantically trying to get her husband's attention. "Ronnie, Jim is leaving the plane," she said. "*Ronnie*, you need to talk to Jim *now*." Allen thought to himself: "What in God's name have we got going here?"

Baker claimed he was dumbstruck when he was asked to run the White House. "I don't think anybody ever has picked as their chief of staff someone who ran two campaigns against them, and I'm damn sure nobody will ever do so in the future," he said. One of the first pieces of advice he got was from Spencer: "Now, Jimmy, you call him every day. Because don't count on him to call you. You call him every day." In his years running the White House, Baker would come to appreciate the wisdom of that counsel. Baker also figured out that Ronnie's introverted, sometimes distant nature made Nancy all the more critical, and an indispensable ally. "He didn't really have a lot of close friends. His close friend was Nancy," Baker said. "Her role was really large. It was subsurface, but really important."

In offering him the job, Ronnie had but one demand of Baker: "I want you to make it right with Ed." That would take some doing. Under an arrangement that Baker worked out with Meese in the days after the election, they agreed that the top leadership in the White House would be divided between the two of them plus Deaver. It was an unusual—and, it turned out, problematic—distribution of power that became known as the "troika." Meese got the title of counselor to the president and Cabinet rank. Deaver was assistant to the president, in charge of, as he put it, "Reagan's personal and political needs, and acting when needed as an honest broker between Baker and Meese."

When Spencer found out about the three-way power-sharing arrangement, he was appalled. Baker was to be chief of staff, Spencer argued, which meant he should be the boss. Meese, he thought, was better suited to be attorney general and out of the White House entirely. "I blew my cork," Spencer told me. "I said, 'Oh, Jesus, here we go.'" Many battles over the next four years found pragmatists Baker and

Deaver—and Nancy—aligned against the more ideological Meese. As William Clark, who became national security adviser, once put it: "The real troika, frankly, in the White House, in the opinion of many, would be Nancy, Baker, and Deaver."

*

Election Day finally came. November 4, 1980, dawned bright and warm in Pacific Palisades, with a hint of smog in the air. Nancy and Ronnie, accompanied by a horde of press, headed for the ranch-style home of stockbroker Robert Gulick and his wife, Sally, which was the Precinct No. 1376 polling place where they had voted for nearly a quarter century. Ronnie wore a casual checked shirt, open at the neck; Nancy, a tartan-plaid dress with a perky bow at the collar. Poll workers set out jars of Ronnie's favorite candy, jelly beans, and clamored for his autograph. He held up his ballot for the photographers who crowded to get a shot, and when a reporter asked him for whom he had voted, Ronnie replied: "Nancy." The candidate demurred that he was too superstitious to answer another question, which was whether he expected a victory. Nancy nudged him and whispered, "Cautiously optimistic." This time Ronnie ignored the cue from his wife.

Their children Ron and Patti were also registered to vote there—he as a Democrat, and she, apparently making an ironic statement, as a member of the right-wing American Independent Party that had supported former Alabama governor George Wallace. Reporters noted that neither had cast a ballot by the time their parents voted. Patti later dropped hers in the box without punching a hole in it. "I couldn't vote for my father. I thought he was wrong on everything," she recalled. "But I couldn't vote against him because that would have taken more courage than I had right then. So I did nothing, which is probably about as cowardly as you can get."

The plan had been to spend election night as they always did. Nancy's pals Earle and Marion Jorgensen would throw a dinner at their home in Bel Air. They would invite the circle of close friends who had been there after the polls closed in 1966 and 1970. The Tuttles would come, and the Wicks, and the Bloomingdales, and the Darts, and the Annenbergs. The Jorgensens would serve the same menu as always: veal stew and coconut cake, both Ronnie's favorites. From the Jorgensens', everyone would go to the Century Plaza Hotel to spend the evening awaiting the returns. The difference in the ritual this time was that the Secret Service had checked out the Jorgensens' house days before and placed telephones throughout.

A few minutes after five o'clock Pacific time—eight o'clock on the East Coast, where the polls were already closing—the Reagans began to get ready. Nancy was taking a bath, and Ronnie was in the shower. There was no rush, they thought. Voting in California would be open for another two hours. But then from the television in the bedroom, Nancy heard NBC *Nightly News* anchor John Chancellor proclaim that it looked like Ronnie was going to win in a landslide. Nancy leaped out of the tub, wrapped a towel around herself, and banged on the shower door. Ronnie emerged and grabbed his own towel as they ran to the TV set. There they stood, both of them soaking wet, as they heard the race being called for Ronnie.

Then the phone rang. It was Jimmy Carter, calling to concede and to congratulate the fortieth president of the United States.

CHAPTER ELEVEN

Washington looked toward the arrival of the Reagans with equal measures of wariness and fascination. Nancy recognized an opportunity to be seized in a city where the political hierarchy intertwined with the social one. As one unnamed Reagan aide told the *Washington Post*: "We want to avoid Jimmy Carter's fatal mistake. He never met the power brokers in this city. He never had any real friends here. Governor Reagan not only wants to know them, but he needs them to get this place working again."

The social diplomacy effort began just days after the election. Nancy Reynolds, the Reagans' aide from their Sacramento days, was already in Washington as chief lobbyist for the Bendix Corporation and knew the city's major players. She arranged for the incoming first couple to host a candlelit dinner on November 18, 1980, at the exclusive 1925 F Street Club, which was housed in a nineteenth-century Greek Revival mansion just blocks from the White House.

Reynolds was amused by the first few responses she got to the invitations she sent out by telegram: "Are you sure this is serious? It's not a practical joke? I'm a Democrat." More than fifty leading figures from political, social, religious, and sports circles showed up. One woman ordered wine during the cocktail hour but changed her mind: "Oh, make it Scotch and water! The Carters are gone." After dinner, the enchanted guests—many of whom had done their best to defeat Ronnie during the election—crowded around the president elect. The front page of the next day's *New York Times* declared: "After four long years as wallflowers, members of the Washington establishment will finally have a suitor in the White House. Never was a neglected belle more eager to be wooed." Two nights later, columnist George Will—whom the *Times* dubbed the Reagans' "unofficial social director"—hosted another party for Ronnie and Nancy at his house in Chevy Chase, Maryland. Will also prevailed on New York's social doyenne Brooke Astor to put on a five-course dinner for fifty in the Reagans' honor at her Park Avenue apartment.

Nancy's hand was obvious in all of this; in fact, she had been laying the groundwork for years. She could not bear the perception among the sophisticates of New York and Washington that her husband was some kind of unpolished, unlettered cowboy. "The approval of the establishment was important to her," said television newsman Chris Wallace, whose journalist father, Mike Wallace, had been a friend of Nancy's mother going back to the 1940s. "There was no question that she wanted the big stage, and she defined success in a very conventional way."

Among the capital's power brokers, none was more important than *Washington Post* publisher Katharine Graham, whose grand, art-filled home on R Street in Georgetown functioned as a salon for DC's most interesting and influential people. Nancy had gotten to know Graham a decade earlier through their mutual friend, author Truman Capote. "I couldn't go to their dinner at the F Street Club because I was going to be out of town," Graham recalled later. "I called up Nancy Reynolds and said I was so disappointed I couldn't come, and she said, 'Why don't you invite them to dinner?' And I said, 'I couldn't do that. I didn't vote for them, and the paper didn't endorse them.' That would be like trying to have it both ways. But Nancy Reynolds said, 'Just invite them and see.'" So she did. Graham's dinner on December 11 brought together an all-star list of DC luminaries, who for that night put aside their political differences and the still-raw feelings from the election. Henry Kissinger was there, as were Carter's White House counsel Lloyd Cutler, National Urban League president Vernon Jordan, and *Washington Post* editor Ben Bradlee and his journalist wife, Sally Quinn, who had written blistering profiles of Nancy.

The president elect's hard-Right supporters were not enamored with any of this. When an image of Ronnie kissing Graham at her doorstep appeared in newspapers across the country, the *Wall Street Journal* called it "a photograph that may upset arch-conservatives almost as much as the famous one of Jimmy Carter bussing Leonid Brezhnev at the Vienna summit." Howard Phillips, head of the Conservative Caucus lobbying organization, warned in a speech to evangelical activists: "If by June the Washington establishment is happy with Ronald Reagan, then you should be unhappy with Ronald Reagan." But others understood the shrewdness of co-opting the enemy this way. Richard Nixon had spent his presidency chafing at the mercilessness of what he called the "Georgetown set." They helped destroy him, he believed, with a thousand snubs and slights. In a letter to Deaver, Nixon wrote that he was "enormously impressed by the way our man has taken over the Washington establishment by storm. There will, of course, be some rough times ahead, but I am confident that he is building up enough equity that he will be able to sail on no matter how rough the sea gets."

*

The weeks between the November election and the January inauguration did not go entirely smoothly, however. Even as the Reagans were wowing DC kingmakers, there was no letup in the constant drama and tension within their dysfunctional family. On November 25 Ron and Doria, who lived together in a one-bedroom Greenwich Village apartment, were quietly married. Only after the fact did Nancy and Ronnie learn of the ceremony, which was performed in the chambers of a New York judge. The couple's sole witnesses were a Secret Service agent and a friend of Ron's. The bride wore red cowboy boots with a black sweater and slacks; the groom, blue jeans and tennis shoes. At the time, Nancy had yet to warm up to Doria personally or approve of her twenty-two-year-old son choosing a woman seven years older than he was. An unnamed friend told *People* magazine: "She loves young Ron and cried for days after he got married."

Ronnie's election victory also brought no letup in the battle between Nancy and her antagonists in the media. Her tone deafness and poor timing didn't help. Particularly damaging was an interview she did with United Press International's Helen Thomas on December 10, just two days after Beatles legend John Lennon was shot to death outside his apartment on Manhattan's Central Park West. Nancy repeated her long-standing opposition to gun control and added that she herself owned a "tiny little gun" that Ronnie had given her for protection at home while he was traveling. Nancy also claimed—was she in denial or simply lying?—that her children had not used marijuana or other illegal substances "that I know of." She insisted that Ron and Patti had never been part of the "drug culture." Practically simultaneously, in another interview with the same news organization, Patti confessed that not only had she tried marijuana but also "I don't know anyone who hasn't smoked dope. I don't anymore. I can't afford to be that spacey anymore.

"I don't think pot is such a terrible drug," Patti added. "It just makes you forget things—like your name."

Amid all this came reports that Nancy had been rude and presumptuous toward Rosalynn Carter during the traditional tour of the White House that outgoing first ladies offer their successors. The press had already christened Rosalynn the "Steel Magnolia" and Nancy the "Iron Butterfly." According to sources on her side, Rosalynn bristled at Nancy's desire to poke into closets and bedrooms that she had wanted to remain shut because they were messy. Nancy, meanwhile, found Rosalynn's manner to be as chilly as the room temperature in a White House where all the thermostats had been set to sixty-five degrees as a conservation measure during the energy crisis.

Nor was Nancy impressed by the executive mansion itself. It struck her as overdue for renovation. "My overall feeling was of surprise that the residence looked so dreary and uninviting. It just didn't look the way the president's house should look," she recalled. "It wasn't a place we'd be proud to bring people—our personal friends or our country's friends. When my son, Ron, arrived for the inauguration, he said, 'Mom, this place is a mess. It looks low rent.'"

Nancy would deny a subsequent scoop by UPI's Thomas claiming that she had actually proposed that the Carters move out early so that her decorator could get a head start fixing up the place. However, Rosalynn Carter's press secretary, Paul Costello, told me that he overheard the conversation in which Nancy made the insensitive suggestion to Rex Scouten, the White House's famously discreet chief usher. "Mrs. Reagan, we can't do it," Scouten told her over the phone, according to Costello's version of events.

Blame runs downhill in Washington. In this case, it landed on Nancy's newly hired press secretary, Robin Orr, the former society editor of the *Oakland Tribune*. The day after Thomas broke the story that Nancy had tried to nudge the First Family into a premature departure from the White House, the Reagan transition office announced that Orr would be returning to California to be closer to her children and to take an unspecified "high-level" position with the International Communications Agency in San Francisco. Her tenure lasted all of twenty-eight days, not even long enough to make it to the inauguration. She was replaced a month later by Sheila Patton, a vice president with the high-powered public relations firm Hill & Knowlton. Patton soon married and changed her name to Sheila Tate. (For clarity, I will refer to her from here on by her married name.) Tate was a better fit for the job, savvier and more attuned to Washington ways. Letitia Baldridge, who had been Jackie Kennedy's social secretary, also came in to help Nancy assemble a staff.

But Nancy continued to create a new and embarrassing story line at every turn. The *Washington Post* reported she had decreed that whoever got hired to be the president's spokesman should be "reasonably" good-looking. So, when Ronnie announced his selection of James Brady as his press secretary on January 6, a reporter teasingly asked the balding, bearlike Brady whether his looks had passed muster with the first lady-to-be. Ronnie retorted: "That question leads to a story that has been written concerning Nancy which was a total invention out of whole cloth, and there have been several more of those, and I am getting to be an irate husband at some of the things that I am reading, none of which are true." The president elect then added with a smile that Nancy thought Brady was "absolutely handsome."

More significant was her perceived influence on some of Ronnie's other picks for key posts. According to notorious New York lawyer Roy Cohn, she nixed William Simon, whom conservatives wanted for Treasury secretary. When Simon met with Ronnie at the ranch during the transition to discuss the job, he laid down a list of demands, including that he be allowed to pick his own staff and make decisions without clearing them with the White House.

"Mrs. Reagan was sitting there reading a magazine while Bill Simon was listing his requirements," Cohn recounted. "Sure she was—you can imagine how she was reading that magazine. She was drinking it all in, was what she was doing. And let me tell you, Bill Simon walked out of the president's life that day. I mean, he couldn't get a phone call through after that. Nancy put her foot down. She pointed out to the president that you don't hire people who make demands before they have the job."

Six days before the inauguration, Nancy and Ronnie left their home in Pacific Palisades for the last time. Neighbors gathered at the bottom of their driveway, and well-wishers lined the streets all the way to Sunset Boulevard. When their motorcade arrived at the airport, Nancy got her first glimpse of Air Force One. The reality of what was happening hit her once again when she saw the words "United States of America" emblazoned on its blue-and-white fuselage. A pilot welcomed them aboard, and stewards gave them a tour. Nancy was delighted to learn that it had a private two-room suite for the first couple, and that its airborne kitchen could cook up just about any food she liked. She was less impressed with the official guest quarters that awaited them on their arrival in Washington. "Blair House *really* needs fixing up," she wrote in her diary.

The next morning, the Secret Service fitted her and Ronnie with bulletproof coats to be worn whenever security was a concern. To Nancy, it was a reminder of a dark possibility that was always lurking at the back of her mind—one that would, all too soon, become a reality.

*

Washington had never seen a spectacle quite like the four-day celebration around the inauguration of Ronald Wilson Reagan. It was far more than just another quadrennial transfer of power. As biographer Edmund Morris wrote, the dawning of the Reagan era "realigned the American political landscape with a suddenness unmatched since Franklin Roosevelt's accession to power in 1933."

There were laser light shows, fireworks displays, and $500-a-plate dinners, along with a big Hollywood presence. Nearly twenty thousand people gathered in a suburban sports arena for the inauguration-eve gala, at which late-night television king Johnny Carson joked: "Well, this is the first administration to have a premiere." Ronnie and Nancy, seated in velour-covered, thronelike wing chairs, looked on like a king with his queen. Frank Sinatra was the producer and director of the event, evoking memories of how he had put together a starry celebration the night before John F. Kennedy began his presidency in 1961. As he had at Ronnie's second inauguration in Sacramento, Sinatra capped off his own performance with one of his standards, "Nancy (With the Laughing Face)." But this time, he had rewritten the lyrics:

> I've known some Nancys,
> No need to tell you
> Therefore, I'm qualified to sell you
> Someone with warmth, charm, and grace
> Nancy with the Reagan face
> You must have noticed
> She's always beaming
> Semantically, that should be gleaming

That's why they invented lace
For Nancy with that radiant face . . .

Nancy brushed aside a tear and blew Sinatra a kiss. Ronnie told the crowd, "You know, almost every day in the past few weeks, someone has asked Nancy and me, 'Has it sunk in yet?' Well, tonight there was a point in the program where I reached over and said to Nancy, 'It sunk in.'"

Not everyone was so taken with the spectacle. *Washington Post* television critic Tom Shales pronounced the gala, which was broadcast on ABC, to be "a tacky combination of a Hollywood awards show, a Kiwanis club talent contest, and a telethon stocked with fewer greats than near-greats and even more pure mediocrities." In the *New York Daily News*, Rex Reed called it "a grotesque burlesque show" and wrote that in Sinatra's hands, "the inauguration has been turned into a show business abomination run by an entertainer whose alleged connections to the underworld are being investigated."

The entire cost of the inauguration and events leading up to it, which were funded largely by private donations, reached a record $16 million. That was more than four times higher than the tab for the humble "People's Inauguration" that Jimmy Carter had put on four years before, where there had been hundreds of free concerts, and no ticket cost more than $25. An eighteen-car train called the "Peanut Special" had carried the Carters and a contingent of hard-partying Georgians to the capital. Ronnie's inauguration, in contrast, saw National Airport jammed with two hundred private jets. The press dubbed it "Lear Lock." Limousines had to be brought in from as far away as New York to ferry revelers to the festivities.

For Carter's inaugural balls in 1977, Rosalynn had donned a six-year-old, off-the-rack blue chiffon ball gown purchased when her husband became governor in Georgia. Nancy dazzled in a one-shouldered white beaded sheath donated by her favorite designer, James Galanos, whose creations went for upward of $10,000. It was accessorized with a diamond-necklace-and-earring set—given by or borrowed from jeweler Harry Winston, depending on who you talked to—with an estimated retail value of $480,000. Her handbag alone was reported to cost more than $1,600.

All of this opulence struck even some of Ronnie's supporters as too much, given that the country's unemployment rate was 7.5 percent and going up. Arizona senator Barry Goldwater, who had seen seven inaugurations, complained publicly: "When you've got to pay $2,000 for a limousine for four days, $7 to park, and $2.50 to check your coat, at a time when most people in the country just can't hack it, that's ostentatious." Nancy Thompson, vice chairman of the Republican Women's Task Force, an organization of GOP feminists, took aim at Nancy's pricey wardrobe: "I think it's outrageous. You don't have to spend that kind of money on clothes to look wonderful, not when there are people out there who are being eaten up by inflation."

But on Inauguration Day, what the country wanted more than anything else was a fresh start and a jolt of optimism. Jimmy Carter had spent a sleepless final night in the Oval Office working on the final deal for the release of the fifty-two Americans who had been held hostage for 444 days in Iran. Just minutes after Ronnie finished his inaugural address, the first of two 727s carrying them to freedom lifted off from Tehran's Mehrabad Airport.

The swearing-in ceremony itself was conducted with impeccable stagecraft. Where Ronnie's predecessors had taken the oath of office on the East Front of the Capitol, which overlooked a parking lot, Ronnie recited his on the opposite side of the building, which affords a view of the monument-studded National Mall and, beyond that, looks toward the rest of the country, spreading westward.

His left hand rested on Nelle's crumbling, taped-together Bible. Ronnie's late mother had written on the inside of the front cover: "A thought for today: You can be too big for God to use, but you cannot be too small." Nancy held the book, which was open to 2 Chronicles 7:14, a passage in which the Lord offers an assurance to Solomon that "if my people, which are called by my name, shall humble themselves, and pray, and seek my face, and turn from their wicked ways; then will

I hear from heaven, and will forgive their sin, and will heal their land." In the margin of that page was another squib of Nelle's handwriting: "A most wonderful verse for the healing of the nations."

At a postinaugural lunch in the Capitol's National Statuary Hall, the new first lady sat with larger-than-life House Speaker Thomas P. "Tip" O'Neill. Edie was on O'Neill's other side. Nancy later wrote: "My strongest memory of that lunch is of watching Mother and Tip swapping stories as if they had been friends all their lives."

Before heading out that evening to the inaugural balls—Ronnie and Nancy went to ten of them over four hours—the extended Reagan family posed for an official portrait in the Red Room. Loyal and Edie are missing from the photo, but everyone else related by blood and marriage is there: Nancy's stepbrother, Dick, and his wife, Patricia, with their children, Geoffrey and Anne. Maureen and her fiancé, Dennis Revell, who would soon become her third husband. Michael, standing behind his wife, Colleen, and holding his two-year-old son, Cameron, Ronnie's only grandchild to date. The president's brother, Neil, and his wife, Bess. Patti, managing a smile. Ron with Doria. As Edmund Morris wrote of the family tableau: "It glows with a common desire to restore harmony."

In the photo, the relatives are crowded on and behind two sofas, forming a backdrop that is slightly removed from Ronnie and Nancy. The couple appears both central to and apart from the rest of them. Nancy is seated on a chair in front, radiant in her beautiful gown and upswept hair. Ronnie hovers behind her, splendid in white tie. His hands rest on the back of her chair; his fingers seem drawn toward her tiny, bare shoulders.

Ronnie's first few days in office were a blur of daily Cabinet meetings, national security briefings, and sessions with congressional leaders eager to hash out details of his economic plan. Tuesday, January 27, saw a joyous ceremony on the White House lawn to welcome home the hostages. That same day, Ronnie set aside some time to pen a private letter to Jane Wyman. Ronnie's ex-wife, who was in the process of moving, had come across his old varsity letter from Eureka College and had sent it to him. Ronnie did not want his thank-you note to go through the normal White House mail system, where it surely would have been seen and generated gossip. He had someone drop this letter in an ordinary postbox, with a fifteen-cent stamp attached. It said:

> Dear Jane
> Thank you very much for
> my letter "E". Of course a gold
> football only goes with winning
> a championship—but then I
> guess maybe this job constitutes
> something of a winning—at best
> it was as hard to do. Already
> I've found though there are
> days when you wonder if you won.
> All in all though it's good to
> be here and to think maybe I
> can do something about the things
> that are wrong.
> Thanks again & thanks for
> your good wishes & prayers.
> Sincerely,
>
> Ron

The new president had ample reason to be confident in what he could achieve. No one could read anything but a mandate for change in the fact that he had won forty-four states against a sitting president. And while the House of Representatives was still in Democratic hands, his victory across the map had swept in a dozen new Republican senators, marking the first time since 1955 that the party controlled either chamber in Congress.

But while Ronnie was riding high, his wife and her wealthy friends were becoming an increasing source of concern for the president's team. For Ronnie's seventieth birthday on February 6, Nancy threw a lavish celebration—supposedly a surprise, though advance word got out to the press—in the East Room. The Annenbergs, Wilsons, Jorgensens, and Deutsches footed the bill for the black-tie party, where a hundred guests were served lobster, roulade of veal farcie, and a dozen birthday cakes each topped with a rearing white horse. Everyone danced between courses. One notable image of the evening was a photo of Ronnie, with a look of annoyance on his face, cutting in to take Nancy from the arms of Sinatra. The celebration continued the next night over an eight-course meal that their friends Charles and Mary Jane Wick put on at the Watergate Hotel's pricey Jean-Louis Restaurant. Pretty much everyone from their California circle had come in to be there. Nancy stood at Ronnie's side as he toasted them: "If it weren't for the efforts of this group, I'd be making this speech before the Chamber of Commerce."

Lyn Nofziger, the Sacramento veteran who was running political affairs for the White House, recognized the warning signs. Four days before the birthday fete for Ronnie, Nofziger sent a memo to Deaver, with a copy to the first lady's chief of staff, Peter McCoy. "It is generally agreed that Nancy, as First Lady, is going to be a target for some of the women who write about society and social figures in Washington, DC," Nofziger wrote. "It seems to me that one way to minimize this is to begin to get her actively engaged in some charity-type activities. Thoughts include new activity in the Foster Grandparents organization, moving into the area of alcohol and drug abuse of [*sic*] whatever. But I do think that the quicker she is seen as a concerned and caring First Lady, the quicker we'll be able to minimize the attacks on her that everybody is positive are coming."

Nofziger was right. Nancy should have been better prepared for the onslaught. At a time when her husband's critics were too intimidated by his popularity among ordinary Americans to attack him personally, she was a ripe proxy, and the first lady spent her first year giving them plenty to work with. What should have been her season of triumph was turning into an almost-daily ordeal of brutal headlines and sniping commentary. In her personal papers is a typewritten letter from her father, sent shortly after the inauguration. "Don't let the press upset you, dear," Loyal wrote. "You know what you do right and correctly, and that's what counts and is important."

Near the end of her husband's presidency, Nancy reflected upon her difficult initiation. She acknowledged that she had brought many of her problems upon herself. This was not Old Hollywood, where the media lapped up whatever narrative a studio press agent dished out, or the relatively small fishbowl of Sacramento. "Looking back, I was terribly naive. I remember during the campaign telling Helen Thomas that there'd always be a part of my life that would be private. She said, 'You have no idea what it's like until you get there.' And she was right," Nancy recalled. "I was completely unprepared for the intense scrutiny—strange for someone who had been in public life as long as I had. I just didn't expect it to be that concentrated."

Some of the fire, no surprise, came from her long-standing nemeses. Liberal feminists ramped up their criticism of the new first lady as a throwback; an ornamental presence who had no causes or endeavors beyond decorating and fashion. Notable was a scorching March 1981 essay by Gloria Steinem in *Ms.* magazine, in which Steinem concluded that Nancy had folded her own identity into her husband's: "All signs point to Nancy Reagan as a future winner of best in her class. Queen Nancy. The Marzipan Wife. The rare woman who can perform the miracle of having no interests at all; of transplanting her considerable ego into a male body."

Nancy's dilettante image was also worrying some of Ronnie's staunchest supporters on the Right. A particularly blunt warning came in an open letter to her on the front page of the conservative *Manchester Union Leader.* "This newspaper is quite sure that you are merely attempting to present a picture of a well-dressed and gracious presidential wife who understands the responsibilities of her office. You mean well. But you and your super-rich friends, especially from the West Coast, are creating a picture of rich, nonsacrificial living, which is in such contrast to your husband's call for economy that, believe it or not, your lifestyle is going to ruin his whole chance for success with his program," publisher William Loeb wrote. "The shrieks of radical Democrats that your husband Ron's program is favoring the rich and against the poor is at the moment not having any general success. But if you keep up this lifestyle, it will, because it gives the impression of a modern-day Marie Antoinette living very high on the hog regardless of how other people are having to get along on much less." In a private missive sent on March 19 to Ronnie's secretary Helene von Damm, Loeb enclosed a copy of the editorial and warned bluntly: "I am not exaggerating when I tell you that people who are essentially friendly to the Reagans, who support the president's program, find this to be a subject which is causing a great deal of antagonism and alienation. It better be fixed now before it becomes even worse."

Meanwhile, an uncomfortable situation had arisen with some of those superrich West Coast friends. After the election, the Kitchen Cabinet had been key players on Ronnie's Transition Appointments Committee. Their job, as they had seen it, was making sure that the top ranks of the new administration were filled with sufficiently conservative people. But with that done, Ronnie's oldest and most loyal backers didn't seem in any hurry to leave. They set up a base on the White House campus, just across the driveway from the West Wing, and reorganized themselves to push his agenda. Dubbing themselves the Coalition for a New Beginning, they instantly got into hot water as they used their supposed influence with the new administration to strongarm corporations into contributing $800,000 toward their campaign to promote Ronnie's economic program.

Having a group of well-heeled private citizens camping out on government property in close proximity to the president alarmed both Meese and the new White House counsel, Fred Fielding. "They wanted to set up office space in the Old Executive Office Building and just be around," Fielding told me. He took his concerns to Nancy, fearing she might come to the defense of the Reagans' old friends and financial supporters. Instead, she agreed that they must be evicted. For Fielding, this was an early insight into the fact that Nancy had but one priority: Ronnie's success. "She knew that I had the president's best interests because I fought for things to make sure that he was safe," Fielding said. "That was something that was important to her too." Chief of Staff Jim Baker, who had also been disturbed by the presence of Ronnie's rich benefactors, remembers it the same way: "She was not in favor of them staying there, I'll tell you, because it would get in the way of a smoothly functioning White House."

Kicking out the Kitchen Cabinet was a ruthlessly pragmatic move. Nancy effectively turned her back on the network she had done so much to build. As she would do so many times in Ronnie's career, she set aside gratitude and sentimentality. Her focus was eliminating anything—or anyone—who might be an obstacle to Ronnie's success. The Coalition for a New Beginning was shut down, and the funds it had collected were refunded. But the Californians did not go quietly. One member in particular went public with his anger. In an interview with Jack Nelson of the *Los Angeles Times,* industrialist Justin Dart complained that they had been treated shabbily after all their years of service to Ronnie, the victims of a "dirty, lousy lie" suggesting that they had done something improper. But he conceded: "The Kitchen Cabinet has served its useful purpose, and, unless the president calls on some of us, the Cabinet is finished. It hasn't any reason to survive."

Their departure coincided with another awkward moment for Nancy. Ronnie's informal advisers were finally sent packing in March, just as the first lady's office revealed that her grand project to redecorate the White House had grown considerably. Nearly two hundred unnamed contributors had ponied up more than $375,000, far exceeding the original $200,000 goal. Congress customarily provided $50,000 in government funds for this purpose, which her Beverly Hills decorator Ted Graber said would not cover the cost of one room.

Jackie Kennedy had been lionized for her sumptuous renovation of the White House, remaking a residence that she said "looked like it's been furnished by discount stores." As Nancy was doing, Jackie had launched the project within weeks of moving in and financed it with a staggering amount of money from private donors. In fact, some of those benefactors, such as Walter Annenberg, were the same people

Nancy turned to twenty years later. When Jackie gave a guided tour of the results on Valentine's Day 1962, an estimated eighty million rapturous TV viewers tuned in for the broadcast, which was carried live on CBS and NBC, and four days later by ABC. Jackie was given an honorary Emmy.

Nancy no doubt expected similar acclaim. It was without question that the place could use some sprucing up. When she and Ronnie arrived at the White House, there were mousetraps poking out from under threadbare furniture. Decorator Graber moved into the official residence for nine months. He and Nancy spent many days scouring a government warehouse near Alexandria, Virginia, for items they could haul out of storage and restore. They scavenged 150 pieces of furniture and art, much of it deteriorated and in need of restoration. Also on the to-do list: badly needed repairs to wiring and plumbing, including some fixtures that had to be made by hand. Thirty-three mahogany doors were sanded and refinished; six dozen lamps got new shades; new draperies were hung on twenty-six windows; and fresh wall coverings went up in ten rooms, seven closets, and eight bathrooms. "The project was designed to reestablish the dwelling, the edifice," her chief of staff, Peter McCoy, told reporters. "It's not as if the Reagans will be taking the painted walls with them."

But where Jackie had beautified the presidential residence in the idyllic glow of Camelot, Nancy's makeover seemed frivolous during an economic downturn in which average Americans were struggling and her husband was making sharp cuts in social programs. Nor did all of the private donors who contributed to the restoration appear to be operating with the purest of motives. Oil executives, for instance, gave $300,000 toward renovating the White House right after Ronnie decontrolled the price of petroleum. By the time Nancy was finished with her project, the redecorating fund had grown to $822,641.

There was also the fact that most of the improvements would never be seen or enjoyed by the public. Nearly 90 percent of the money was spent on the private living quarters on the White House's second and third floors. Nancy acknowledged later that she had not understood what a controversy all of this would generate: "Looking back, I think my own naivete, and that of my staff, added to this and perhaps even prolonged it. Washington can be a tough town, and I didn't know how to handle it. I suspect we all would do things differently if we had it to do over again."

So overheated did the narrative of Nancy's extravagance become that almost anything seemed believable. There was a false report in the media that the new first lady intended to take down a wall of the Lincoln Bedroom. "They knew none of those things were true," she complained to *Newsweek* in March, "but they went ahead and printed them anyway. It was pretty mean."

Meanwhile, people began asking when and whether Nancy would begin doing serious work on the charitable projects that she claimed to care about. "My family comes first," she said. "I have to get Ronnie settled and know that he's comfortable. It takes awhile to settle in, to develop your own living routines, like what chair he sits in and what chair you sit in in the family sitting room. I want to make the house as warm and comfortable and homey as possible."

"Comfortable and homey" were not the impressions most Americans got when they finally saw the results of Nancy's big project. The newly refurbished White House was unveiled in the December 1981 issue of *Architectural Digest* magazine, a $4.95-a-copy chronicle of excess. The photographer chosen to shoot the photos was a British lord, and they were laid out over an eighteen-page spread. Nancy realized later that in giving the exclusive to such an elite magazine, she had made "a mistake that only added to the picture many Americans already had of me—that I was a fancy, rich woman who kept acquiring more and more expensive items."

Throughout that first year in the White House, Nancy and her staff struggled to come up with small ways to soften her image. To celebrate her birthday in July, eighteen wealthy donors chipped in $3,800 to repair a municipal swimming pool for the handicapped in a poorer part of Washington. After Nancy snipped the pink bow and pronounced it "the best birthday present I've gotten," Mayor Marion

Barry said: "If you have some friends who want to give some more, they're certainly welcome to."

But most of her gestures were met with skepticism. Nancy had indicated during the presidential campaign that she would take on fighting drug abuse among the young as her signature cause. In late October she met with teenagers and their parents at Manhattan's Phoenix House, the nation's largest drug rehabilitation center. "If we don't do something, it seems to me we're just going to lose a whole generation," she said. "Their brains are going to be mush. It's the future of our country. I think it's the most serious problem."

One account in the next day's *New York Daily News* began: "Nancy Reagan got so involved in her tour of the Phoenix House drug treatment center yesterday morning that she was late for her hair dresser, Monsieur Marc." The coverage also contrasted her comments about the seriousness of the drug scourge with the cuts that her husband was making in funding for treatment programs—including a sharp reduction in federal support for the one she visited. As the criticism mounted, Jackie Kennedy Onassis called with sympathy and some advice. All of this would pass, the former first lady told Nancy, but it might be a good idea to quit reading the newspapers until it did.

The withering press coverage that first year was not confined to the US side of the Atlantic. In late July Nancy traveled to London for the royal wedding of Prince Charles and Lady Diana Spencer. She arrived with an enormous entourage, and the incredulous British media pounced. An article on the front page of the liberal-leaning *Guardian* began: "The one-time starlet of such B-films as 'The Next Voice You Hear' (1950) and 'Hellcats of the Navy' (1957) flew into Heathrow yesterday with 12 secret servicemen, five hat boxes, and six dresses." The sober *Times* of London noted that Nancy had "squeezed more engagements into the week before the royal wedding than Alice's white rabbit."

Reporters also noted that Nancy arrived at Prince Charles's polo match in a six-car motorcade. The queen, on the other hand, drove herself there in a station wagon and was followed by her daughter,

Princess Anne, steering a Range Rover. Crowds outside the Royal Opera House booed the American first lady, and one British newspaper claimed, falsely, that she had demanded a front-row seat at the wedding. So huge were the diamond earrings that Nancy wore to the queen's ball at Buckingham Palace that one reporter blurted out, "Are they real?" Nancy replied, "I'll never tell." They were, and on loan from the Bulgari jewelry family, whose spokesman said they were Nancy's "to wear as long as she wants to wear them."

Nancy exhibited a blind spot—and a stubborn streak—when it came to the matter of accepting freebies. In early 1981 White House counsel Fielding, accompanied by Baker and Meese, spent a painful half hour with her in the residence explaining in detail how the law worked in that regard. The 1978 Ethics in Government Act required high-ranking government officials and their spouses to report any gifts they received worth more than $35. If one came from a foreign government, and they wanted to keep it, they had to pay for it. Nancy was incensed. Why, she wanted to know, would things that she received from her personal friends be anyone else's business? It was an argument that she and Fielding would have over and over again. An especially heated dispute involved a $400 set of inscribed silver picture frames from Frank Sinatra. So obstinate was the first lady that Fielding made a practice of sending lawyers from his office to the presidential living quarters once a year on a reconnaissance mission to check for items that Nancy was trying to slip past the rules.

At the same time, the White House counsel discovered he could rely on Nancy to be his ally when other sensitive matters arose. She had supported him when he kicked the Kitchen Cabinet out of the Old Executive Office Building, and she was always ready to help with even more delicate matters—such as when he received reports that one of the freewheeling Reagan children was getting close to the legal and ethical boundaries that Fielding called "the shock line." Nancy was also proactive in sharing her concerns when she picked up signals of a potential problem that might embarrass the president. In one instance, she learned that US Information Agency director Charles Z. Wick had installed a $32,000 security system in his rented home and charged it to the government. "She didn't hesitate to let me know that Charlie was doing something wrong," Fielding said. "I thought it was interesting, because Mary Jane Wick was one of her closest friends."

Occasionally, Nancy would summon the White House counsel to the residence, but more often, he would hear from her by telephone. Fielding could decipher the first lady's mood from the moment he picked up the line. "Fred . . ." she would say slowly. One *Fred* signaled it would be a friendly chat. "Fred . . . Fred . . ." meant something was bothering her. If Nancy said his name three times, he knew she was in a state of high alarm. There were many three-Fred conversations over the course of Fielding's five years as White House counsel, and even a few four-Fred ones.

"These calls became the source of some amusement in my office, especially in the first two years, since I was trying to stop smoking, and often I would relapse during or after a call from the East Wing," Fielding said. "But, in fairness to Nancy, she was usually right in her assessment of a situation and often had seen the problem before anyone else. She could be very harsh in her candid assessments of people, but her motive was never a petty or personal one—it was always to protect the president."

In the fall of 1981 came another controversy, one that would dwarf even the furor over Nancy's decorating project. As she would ruefully recall: "If the renovations made people angry, the new White House china drove them crazy!" Earlier first ladies could have told her that buying expensive formal dinnerware was a bad move during times when Americans were worried about keeping food on their own humble plates. When Eleanor Roosevelt ordered a new set of china in 1934, during the depths of the Great Depression, the outcry was so great that she had to hold a news conference to defend herself against charges of extravagance. Eleanor explained that the cost of ordering 1,722 pieces for $9,301.20—at government expense, unlike the Reagan china, which was paid for by a private foundation—was actually lower than trying to replace existing pieces. Besides, it would put Americans to work.

The origins of Nancy's disastrous endeavor went back to the Reagans' very first state dinner on February 26, 1981. It was in honor of British prime minister Margaret Thatcher, who had an especially close and important relationship with the president. In the Iron Lady's toast to her host and hostess, she cracked a joke about the controversial White House makeover: "I'm told, Mr. President, that when you and Mrs. Reagan were inspecting your new home to see what refurbishment was needed, you came across some charred areas, vestiges of certain heated events in 1812." Heated indeed. During the War of 1812, British troops burned Washington City, including the White House.

"I don't think I need apologize for them," Thatcher continued, "because I'm relieved to hear that Mrs. Reagan saw in this not a source of historical reproach, but an opportunity for redecoration."

On the dinner tables that night was a mix of china patterns that had been purchased during past presidencies. News accounts left the impression that this was a tribute to Ronnie's predecessors Theodore Roosevelt, Woodrow Wilson, Franklin D. Roosevelt, and Harry S. Truman. In truth, Nancy claimed later, she had no choice but to commingle the settings because there wasn't enough of one pattern to go around. Though Lady Bird Johnson had acquired some place settings suitable for luncheons when she and husband LBJ were in the White House, no complete set of formal china had been bought since the Truman administration. Over the years, many fragile pieces had broken—or been slipped into the handbags and pockets of guests. Today used White House dinnerware shows up regularly on eBay, and even Oscar-winning actress Meryl Streep has confessed to lifting hand towels from the presidential powder room.

So, Nancy set about acquiring a new 4,732-piece set from Lenox, edged in her favorite color, red, with a raised gold presidential seal. Once again, her timing was dreadful. In September the White House announced the $209,000 purchase of 220 place settings, which meant they cost nearly $1,000 apiece. On that very same day, the Reagan administration made the declaration that the US Agriculture

Department—which had slashed children's lunch subsidies by a third—would classify ketchup and pickle relish as vegetables for purposes of nutritional guidance on school cafeteria menus. The administration quickly pulled back the new regulation, but the damage was done. Columnists and cartoonists had a field day contrasting Nancy's expensive tastes with her husband's draconian policies.

One thing the controversy surrounding her china overshadowed was the shrewd, strategic approach that Nancy took toward entertaining in the White House—particularly when it came to state dinners. Over the course of the Reagan presidency, Ronnie and Nancy would host visiting foreign leaders at the rate of roughly one a month.

As Nancy saw it, "those weren't parties, social life. They were instruments of foreign policy, and they were very effective," said Selwa "Lucky" Roosevelt, who was chief of protocol at the State Department. "The dinners were beautiful. They were delicious, and the flowers she cared a great deal about."

The first lady agonized over every detail. Even the smallest of decisions had to be run by her, at times to the frustration of the diplomats at Foggy Bottom. She demanded to be shown how the table settings would look and stressed out the kitchen staff with her insistence on tasting everything on the menu in advance, something that her recent predecessors had not done. Many of her selections were creative and bold. Nancy introduced what were then considered novel and exciting foods, such as pita bread (served at Australian prime minster Malcolm Fraser's dinner in June 1981) and nasturtium salad (at Brazilian president José Sarney's in September 1986.)

Nancy generally kept the guest lists to under a hundred, which made the events more intimate and more exclusive than those of other presidents, who would regularly invite upward of twice as many people. She also revived some of the regal traditions that had been dispensed with during the Carter years, including a uniformed color guard to herald the arrival of the Reagans and their guests of honor on the Grand Staircase in the main foyer. "Hail to the Chief"—a musical flourish that Carter had hated and banned—also made a return.

Much planning went into the seating charts. The placement of guests became, among other things, an opportunity to reward those who were in Nancy's good graces. Later in her husband's presidency, she and Secretary of State George P. Shultz developed a running private joke over the fact that she consistently put him next to the most beautiful and famous actress in attendance. "She always fixed me up with a hot Hollywood star at the White House dinners," he told me with a laugh. "I got to dance with Ginger Rogers!" On that occasion, Nancy asked a White House photographer to take as many pictures as possible of Rogers, a Hollywood ballroom-dance legend, in the arms of the nation's chief diplomat. She sent Shultz the entire pile of them—"enough to paper his entire office," she recalled later.

*

Within the walls of the White House, Nancy was developing into a powerful force and an important ally to have. But to the outside world, she seemed icy, vain, and brimming with entitlement. By the end of her husband's first year in office, postcards portraying "Queen Nancy" in ermine, jewels, and a crown were hot sellers in Georgetown gift shops and a frequent sight on the bulletin boards of Democratic offices on Capitol Hill. Headline writers feasted on her "New China Policy." In October Rosalynn Carter delivered a measure of payback for Nancy's constant insinuations that the Carters had left the White House a dump, telling a group of reporters that Nancy's renovation had been completely unnecessary. "I think it was an excuse to do something," the former first lady said tartly. "The White House was beautiful. I loved it. It was cared for." The Carters had found the existing china adequate, she said, adding that tastefully mixing patterns enhanced the beauty of an occasion.

The headlines about Nancy's profligacy kept coming. In early November, news broke of another improvement that she had made to the White House. The beauty salon in the residence, installed by Pat Nixon, had been refurbished with a bounty of donations by the National

Hairdressers and Cosmetologists Association. Among them: a $3,000 Peruvian rug, a $400 Louis XV lounge chair, a $346.65 shampoo bowl, two hairdryers worth a total of $1,200, a $720 hydraulic white leather salon chair, a $230 manicurist's stool, and $1,800 in wall coverings. Redken Laboratories also donated makeup and other beauty products.

So toxic had Nancy's image become that the president himself felt compelled to defend her at a testy, nationally televised news conference. Reporter Barry Cunningham of the Independent Television News Association, a national video service, put the question to him: "Your administration is being called 'millionaires on parade.' Do you feel you're being sensitive enough to the symbolism of Republican mink coats, limousines, and $1,000-a-plate china at the White House when ghetto kids are being told to eat ketchup as a vegetable?" Ronnie retorted that he had not counted any mink coats, that the ketchup policy had been changed, and as for the china: "Nancy's taken a bit of a bum rap on that. There has been no new china for the White House since the Truman administration, and the truth of the matter is that at a state dinner, we can't set the tables with dishes that match."

Nancy was also giving comedians plenty of fodder. Johnny Carson, for instance, quipped on the *Tonight* show that the first lady's favorite junk food was caviar and her religion was Christian Dior. So, Nancy decided that her best defense—perhaps her only one—was to join in on the joke. On November 5 she traveled to New York to accept an award at the annual Alfred E. Smith Memorial Foundation Dinner, a white-tie event where big-name politicians poke fun at one another and themselves. Nancy enlisted White House speechwriter Landon Parvin, who had a knack for comedy, to put together some remarks for her. At the dinner, Nancy scoffed at the "Queen Nancy" postcards: "Now, that's silly. I'd never wear a crown. It would mess up my hair." She also announced that her newest charitable endeavor would be "the Nancy Reagan home for wayward china."

It was a small step in the right direction. Her most persistent critics, however, were unimpressed. "Good lines, delivered by a pro. But one-liners aren't going to solve her problems," columnist Judy Mann wrote in the *Washington Post.* "The fundamental problem with Nancy Reagan's image is Nancy Reagan. She is a woman out of her times, a first lady out of the past. She would have been a smash in the 1950s."

Soon after, Nancy found herself at the center of yet another storm, this one—for once—not of her own making. It came about because of an awkward discovery in the office of National Security Adviser Richard V. Allen. Inside a little-used safe there, military officers found an envelope holding $1,000 in $100 bills, which turned out to be a payment that a reporter and a photographer for a Japanese magazine had brought to an interview they did with Nancy the day after the inauguration. The kimono-clad journalists tried to hand the envelope directly to the first lady, in keeping with the Japanese custom of bringing expensive gifts to important business meetings. Allen recognized what was happening and snatched it. He gave the envelope to his secretary and planned to send it along later to the White House counsel's office. Instead, it ended up in his safe and was forgotten.

Though Allen was later cleared of any wrongdoing, Nancy saw to it that he was gone. His reputation was far less important to her than the fact that his blunder was an embarrassment. What's more, she already had misgivings about Allen, a stridently conservative cold warrior whom she considered out of his depth as Ronnie's chief foreign-policy adviser. Years later, Allen expressed surprisingly little bitterness about his ouster and the role the first lady had played in engineering it. "There were roller-coaster times with Nancy Reagan, but even though, in the end, she was the principal cause of having me put out to pasture, I had no animus against Nancy. She was just protecting her man," Allen said. National security adviser turned out to be a hard job to hold on to in the Reagan White House. Over the course of his eight years in office, Ronnie would go through six of them. The first lady played a key role in several of their departures.

Nancy, however, did not always get her way when it came to dispensing with aides whose loyalty or usefulness to Ronnie she doubted. The same month the Allen controversy broke, *Atlantic Monthly* magazine published an explosive story in which Reagan budget director David

Stockman suggested that Ronnie's supply-side economic philosophy was a fraud, meant to give a new luster to old trickle-down economic policies that heavily favored the rich. Stockman, a brainy, self-promoting former Michigan congressman, told journalist William Greider that he had adjusted figures in the Office of Management and Budget computers to reflect unrealistically rosy scenarios. "None of us really understands what's going on with all these numbers," Stockman admitted.

Nancy joined Deaver and Meese in demanding that Ronnie fire Stockman. The president refused, arguing that he needed Stockman's expertise and trusted his judgment. "Had it been up to me, Stockman would have been out on the street that afternoon. I saw him as a shrewd and crafty man who knew exactly what he was doing," Nancy wrote later. "If Ronnie had thrown Stockman out when that story appeared in the *Atlantic Monthly,* he would have made an example of him. It would have been a signal to everybody else who worked for Ronnie that he expected their loyalty."

But Nancy also recognized that she herself was becoming a liability to the young Reagan presidency. Polls showed she had the ignominious distinction of being the most unpopular first lady in modern history, with negative sentiment toward her running double what it had against her predecessors. During one particularly rocky news cycle, she lamented to Sheila Tate: "You know, some days, I feel like if it rains, it must be my fault."

The cold fact she had to face was that for Ronnie to succeed, she would have to do so as well. As 1981 came to a close, plans to rehabilitate her image were being put into place. Nancy's chief of staff, Peter McCoy, who had come from the Beverly Hills art world, was moved over to the Commerce Department. In his place was installed canny thirty-two-year-old James Rosebush, who'd been special assistant to the president for private sector initiatives. He had been picked for the job after writing a memo to Deaver outlining a strategy for fixing Nancy's public relations problems. Among his recommendations: she had to get out of the White House more, show more compassion for families and children.

Over the years to come, Nancy's approval rating would go up and down. The portrait of a shallow socialite that was drawn by her critics early in her husband's presidency would be replaced by one of a calculating power behind the throne, imposing her will on matters of state both foreign and domestic. The truth was, America never quite figured out what to make of her.

"Everything I did or said seemed to generate controversy, and it often seemed you couldn't open a newspaper without seeing a story about me," she reflected later. "I don't think I was as bad, or as extreme in my power or my weakness, as I was depicted—especially during the first year, when people thought I was overly concerned with trivialities, and the final year, when some of the same people were convinced I was running the show.

"In many ways, I think I served as a lightning rod; and in any case, I came to realize that while Ronald Reagan was an extremely popular president, some people didn't seem to like his wife very much. Something about me, or the image people had of me, just seemed to rub them the wrong way."

CHAPTER TWELVE

Nancy would always think of 1981 as "a lost year."

She was not referring to her own blunders, though there had been plenty. What defined that first year in Washington for her—what made everything else seem inconsequential—happened in a split second on the afternoon of March 30. A deranged young man with a $47.95 handgun and a fixation on a Hollywood actress nearly robbed her of Ronnie. For the rest of his presidency, an assassination attempt that almost succeeded would leave Nancy even more anxious and protective of her husband, more wary of everything and everyone around him, and grasping for ways to control the dangerous, unseen forces that might be lurking around any corner. "Nothing can ever happen to my Ronnie," she wrote in her diary during the sleepless night she spent after the shooting. "My life would be over."

To the degree it could be said about any day at the White House, that Monday had started out as a routine one. Nancy spent the morning with Barbara Bush at a reception for the Washington Performing Arts Society at the Phillips Collection art museum, followed by a luncheon in honor of the two of them and Cabinet wives at the Georgetown home of Michael Ainslie, the president of the National Trust for Historic Preservation. During the lunch, Nancy had felt an urge that she would later call a premonition; something telling her she should get back home. She excused herself a little early.

Shortly after she returned, Nancy met with interior decorator Ted Graber and chief usher Rex Scouten in one of her favorite retreats: the cheery third-floor solarium, where floor-to-ceiling windows offer a spectacular view of the Washington Monument and National Mall. The solarium was under renovation, and it was drizzling outside, but the cheery daffodils in the window boxes spoke to a warmer, brighter season ahead.

Their conversation was interrupted by the unexpected appearance of George Opfer, the head of Nancy's Secret Service detail. Opfer was a blond, thirty-two-year-old New Yorker, so good-looking that he sometimes got fan mail from women who spotted him standing next to Nancy in photographs. Though Opfer had been assigned to Nancy for only a matter of months, he had already developed a bond of trust with her; an understanding that the two of them would always be honest with each other. Protecting a first lady—particularly one as demanding as Nancy—was an assignment many agents would have greeted with little enthusiasm. But Secret Service assistant director (and later director) John Simpson, who had known the Reagans since the 1968 campaign, advised Opfer: "Don't listen to the stories, because they are wrong. Make your own evaluation when you get out there. And one more thing: the Reagans really are a modern-day love story. So be prepared for that." Nancy introduced the incoming head of her detail to Ronnie for the first time at the Reagans' home in Pacific Palisades, shortly after the election. The president elect looked him in the eye, and said: "Well, George, make sure you take good care of her." From the edge in Ronnie's voice, Opfer knew Ronnie was not merely making casual conversation.

Opfer had been in the Presidential Protective Division command post in room W-16, just below the Oval Office, when he heard the traffic that came over the radio at 2:27 p.m. First was the voice of Raymond Shaddick, assistant special agent in charge of the president's detail: "Advise, we've had shots fired. Shots fired. There are some injuries, uh, lay one on." Sixteen seconds later, Special Agent in Charge Jerry Parr invoked the president's code name and assured the agents back at the White House that Ronnie had not been hit: "Rawhide is okay. Follow-up. Rawhide is okay."

Opfer knew immediately he had to find Nancy, to make sure she didn't get the news from anyone else. There wasn't time to wait for an elevator. He sprinted from the West Wing and up three flights of stairs to the top floor of the residence. When she saw him there, Nancy knew immediately something was wrong. He motioned for the first lady to join him at the end of a ramp connecting the sunroom to the center hall, where they could speak privately. "There's been a shooting at the hotel," Opfer told her. "Some people were wounded, but your husband wasn't hit. Everybody's at the hospital."

Nancy started heading for the elevator as soon as she heard the word *shooting*. Then other details began to register. *The hotel.* Ronnie was supposed to be giving a short speech at two in the afternoon to the National Conference of the AFL-CIO's Building and Construction Trades Department at the Washington Hilton, a mile and a half up Connecticut Avenue. *The hospital.* George Washington University was the closest. It was six blocks up Pennsylvania Avenue from the White House. Why, she asked, were they taking Ronnie there if he wasn't hurt? Opfer told her he didn't know. Perhaps it was precautionary. Maybe the president wanted to find out about the condition of the wounded.

Opfer pleaded with her to stay put. The hospital was a madhouse. Ronnie was fine. He'd be home soon. "If you don't get me a car, I'm going to *walk*," Nancy said firmly. Six minutes and forty-four seconds after the first report of shots fired, Opfer got in touch with the command center. Using Nancy's code name, he informed his fellow agents: "We're gonna leave with Rainbow and go to that location."

A limousine was dispatched to the Diplomatic Entrance. Nancy climbed into the back seat, and Opfer into the front. The command center alerted agents at the hospital to be ready for her arrival at the Twenty-Second Street entrance. Nancy became frantic as the limousine, traveling without sirens or escort, got stuck in the mayhem of police cars, emergency vehicles, reporters, and onlookers around the hospital. She grabbed Opfer's shoulder and demanded to be let out, saying she would get there on foot, running if she had to. The agent insisted she stay in the car. He still believed the president was uninjured, but other possibilities were racing through his mind: Was this a conspiracy? Was the First Family under attack? Was the country under attack?

Mike Deaver met them at the emergency entrance and delivered the news that Ronnie had, in fact, been wounded. In the opening of her post–White House memoir, Nancy recounted her shock and mounting panic:

> "But they told me he *wasn't* hit," I stammered.
>
> "Well," Mike said, "he was. But they say it's not serious."
>
> "*Where? Where* was he hit?"
>
> "They're looking for the bullet."
>
> Looking for the bullet! "I've got to see him!" I said.
>
> "You can't. Not yet."
>
> "Wait a minute," I said, my voice rising. "If it's not serious, *then why can't I see him?*"
>
> "Wait. They're working on him."
>
> "Mike," I pleaded, as if it were up to him. "*They don't know how it is with us. He has to know I'm here!*"

Just inside the hospital, in curtained-off trauma bay 5, Deputy Press Secretary Larry Speakes was taking notes of what he was hearing: "Doctors believe bleeding to death. Can't find a wound. 'Think we're going to lose him.' Rapid loss of blood pressure. Touch and go."

Ronnie had arrived at the hospital three minutes after the presidential motorcade peeled out of the Washington Hilton driveway. The initial plan had been to take him back to the White House. But in the car, Ronnie began coughing up bright, frothy blood, prompting Parr to redirect the motorcade to the hospital. It was a decision that no doubt saved Ronnie's life. "Get an ambulance—I mean get the, um, stretcher out there," Parr called over the radio at 2:29 p.m.

Ronnie kept coughing, filling first his own handkerchief and then Parr's with blood.

The president walked the fifteen yards from the car to the entrance of the emergency room, but as soon as he got inside and out of public view, his eyes rolled back in his head, and his knees buckled. His blood pressure plummeted so low that nurses could not get a systolic reading. It looked like he was having a heart attack. Not until they cut off his clothes and a surgical resident lifted his left arm did they notice a tiny, jagged slit in Ronnie's side. An intern who had been in Vietnam recognized it as a bullet hole. There was no exit wound.

As the medical team worked, Nancy was taken to a nearby office, where she began having flashbacks to a day in November 1963, when she was driving down San Vicente Boulevard in Los Angeles and heard over the car radio that John F. Kennedy had been shot in Dallas. She prayed that history was not repeating itself. The windowless room where they put her was tiny and hot. She heard a lot of noise. People were running back and forth in the hallway, shouting at one another to get out of the way. Nancy kept demanding to see her husband, only to be told the same thing over and over: Soon. "Later, I learned that they were afraid to let me in too early because they thought I'd be traumatized by what I saw," she recalled. "Considering what I did see, they were probably right."

At last, she got the summons. Deaver and Opfer accompanied her into the room where the president was. It was a ghastly scene of bandages, tubes, blood. In one corner, Nancy spotted the shredded navy pinstripe suit that Ronnie had put on for the first time that morning. It had been a gift from her, custom-made by his Beverly Hills tailor Frank Mariani.

Ronnie was lying naked on a table under a sheet, surrounded by strangers. His normally ruddy cheeks were ashen. His lips were blue and caked with blood. Opfer held Nancy's arm, worried she might faint. But he saw her quickly focus and pull herself together.

Nancy stifled her horror when she got to her husband's side. She smiled at him, held his hand, and whispered over and over: "Oh, Ronnie.

Oh, Ronnie." Twelve days later, the president would write in his diary that "I opened my eyes once to find Nancy there. I pray I'll never face a day when she isn't there. In all the ways God has blessed me, giving her to me is the greatest and beyond anything I can ever hope to deserve."

He pulled the oxygen mask from his face and tried to make a joke. His mind conjured a famous old line that boxer Jack Dempsey supposedly told his wife after he lost his heavyweight title to Gene Tunney in 1926. "Honey, I forgot to duck," Ronnie said. Nancy pushed the mask back on and urged him not to talk. As she left the room, she whispered to Deaver, "Mike, he looks so bad."

Ronnie continued to lose blood—at one point, more than half of what he had in his body—and was in danger of going into shock. Just under an hour after he had been shot, the president of the United States was wheeled toward operating room 2. Doctors were going to try to repair his damaged artery and extract the bullet that an X-ray had shown was lodged in his left lung. Ronnie caught sight of Baker, Nofziger, Laxalt, and Meese in the hallway. He winked and said, "Who's minding the store?" Nancy walked beside him, her hand in his. When she finally had to let go and leave her husband's fate to the skill and training of the surgeons, Nancy kissed Ronnie on the forehead and told him one last time that she loved him. Right before they put him under, the president joked with his medical team: "I hope you are all Republicans." Everyone laughed, and Dr. Joseph Giordano replied, "Today, Mr. President, we are all Republicans."

Nancy spotted another patient being wheeled right behind him. It was Press Secretary James Brady, who had been hit above the left eye. A nurse told Nancy he was not expected to survive. So dire was Brady's condition that, at one point, all three television networks announced erroneously that he was dead. Nancy would never forget the sight of Brady's head "open and bleeding and grotesquely swollen. I had never seen anybody with a head wound, and it was monstrous." Brady would survive, though he was severely disabled. He retained the title of press secretary, a symbolic one given his inability to work on more than a limited schedule. When Brady died in 2014 at the age of seventy-three, the medical examiner ruled his death a homicide resulting from the wound he had suffered more than three decades earlier. The White House briefing room is named in his honor.

With Ronnie in surgery that would last for more than three hours, Nancy sat in a waiting room, watching the television footage that was being broadcast over and over. The president emerging from the hotel, smiling and waving to the small crowd that had gathered there. The brief pause he made to take a shouted question from Associated Press reporter Mike Putzel, who was standing about twenty feet away. Ronnie's sudden look of surprise as the first shot was fired. Brady falling, and a pool of blood forming around his head as he twitched on the sidewalk. Two other bodies on the ground. Agents and police diving on the shooter just a few feet away, one of them screaming "Get him out! Get him out!" An ambulance arriving with its siren on. On ABC, anchorman Frank Reynolds said: "God, you tremble to think he could get such a clear shot at the president."

She learned that the blond assailant she saw being dragged away was a twenty-five-year-old drifter named John W. Hinckley Jr. More details would come out later: he came from an affluent family in Colorado and wanted to impress the young actress Jodie Foster, with whom he had become obsessed after seeing the 1976 movie *Taxi Driver*. (The movie's protagonist, Travis Bickle, played by Robert De Niro, plots to assassinate a presidential candidate.) In addition to Ronnie and Brady, the six bullets that Hinckley fired in less than two seconds wounded two others: Secret Service agent Timothy McCarthy, who was shot in the chest, and District of Columbia policeman Thomas Delahanty, hit in his upper spine. Both were being treated.

Nancy went to the window to look at the crowds that had gathered below. Opfer pulled her back and drew the blinds. He told Nancy they still didn't know whether this was a larger plot, which meant there might be more killers out there. She looked startled, and once again thoughts of Dallas raced through her head.

A nurse asked Nancy if she wanted to visit the hospital chapel. She and Opfer went there, knelt together on a pew, and were soon joined by Brady's wife, Sarah, who hadn't yet seen her husband. That day was the first time the two women had met. They hugged, joined hands, and prayed together—for their husbands, for the men who had been wounded protecting them, for the country. Deaver, Baker, Meese, and Nancy's press secretary, Sheila Tate, had also made their way to the chapel. They formed a tiny, traumatized congregation.

Meanwhile, in the operating room, Dr. Benjamin Aaron was still searching for the elusive bullet. He ordered another X-ray. Just as he was preparing to abandon the search and sew Ronnie up, he found it. The slug was slightly lower in the president's lung than they had initially thought, just an inch from his heart and aorta. Tests would show it was a type known as a "devastator," an expensive and customized .22-caliber cartridge designed to explode on impact into fragments, with the force of a shot fired from a much more powerful handgun. This bullet hadn't done that, possibly because it was flattened to the size and shape of a dime when it ricocheted off the door of the presidential limousine.

Back at the White House, there was bedlam. In the first hours after the shooting, details of the situation were scarce. Ronnie's top aides were later criticized for not temporarily transferring presidential authority to Vice President Bush while the commander in chief was unconscious on the operating table. That should have been the call under the Twenty-fifth Amendment to the Constitution, but they worried that it would alarm the country and allies around the world and stir questions about Ronnie's age and health. Meanwhile, Bush was headed back to Washington aboard Air Force Two, having canceled the rest of his scheduled speaking engagements that day in Texas. He was expected to land at Andrews Air Force Base at six thirty. The military had been put on standby alert status. Initial assessments by the Pentagon showed more Soviet submarines than usual off the East Coast.

What would linger in the public perception was an image of the combustible secretary of state, Al Haig, charging to the podium of the briefing room at 4:14 p.m. and addressing the media. The place was already in chaos. Speakes had fumbled a news conference in which he was unable to provide reporters the answers to such basic questions as whether the president was in surgery or even whether the country had a functioning government. The secretary of state's attempt to take control of the situation only made things worse. From behind Haig, National Security Adviser Richard Allen could see his knees were wobbling and his arms shaking.

"Who is making the decisions for the government right now?" one reporter asked.

"Constitutionally, gentlemen, you have the president, the vice president, and the secretary of state in that order, and should the president decide he wants to transfer the helm to the vice president, he will do so," Haig said. "As of now, I am in control here, in the White House."

Cabinet secretaries and national security officials, who were watching all of this from the Situation Room, were horrified. So were Baker and Meese, who saw it on a television at the hospital. Not only had Haig revealed the depth of his ignorance of the Constitution—there were actually *three* others ahead of him in the line of succession; he'd omitted the Speaker of the House and the president pro tempore of the Senate—but he came off as breathless, agitated, and possibly unhinged. Haig gave out further erroneous information by denying that the military had been put on increased readiness.

Nancy was too concerned about Ronnie to take note of the secretary of state's blunder in the moment, but when she learned about it later, she thought it revealed his true character. "From that day on, he was on thin ice with Nancy Reagan," said Jim Kuhn, who was later Ronnie's executive assistant. Haig's performance at the podium was an image the public would never forget—and that Nancy would never forgive.

The first of the Reagan children to reach the hospital was Ron. He arrived as Nancy waited for her husband to come out of the anesthesia. Ron's unconventional career had taken off, and he was dancing with the Joffrey Ballet's junior ensemble when he got the word about his father. "Doria and I were having lunch in our hotel coffee shop in Lincoln, Nebraska, before heading to the theater for rehearsal and that night's performance. A Secret Service agent traveling with us approached the table and quietly informed us that shots had been fired at my father but that he didn't appear to have been hit," he recalled. "We quickly left the restaurant and went upstairs to our room, where we watched the scene play out on TV. Some minutes later, the detail leader gave us the news that my father had been wounded, but they didn't believe it was serious. We immediately began searching for a way to get back to DC, no easy feat from Lincoln." The Secret Service scrambled to charter a private Learjet for Ron.

Nancy was comforted by the presence of her favorite child. "I'm so frightened," she told him.

"I know, Mom," Ron said tenderly, "but hold on."

When Ronnie woke up around seven thirty, he reached for a pencil and paper and wrote: "I can't breathe!" Nancy shouted at the doctors: *"He can't breathe!"* They assured her that the president was getting enough oxygen, but it didn't feel that way because it was coming through a respirator. This would not be the last time the medical team would be exasperated by her badgering, though they understood her concern and tried to be patient with her. Doctors gently told Nancy it might be better if she left the room. As she did, she paused at the door for what seemed like several minutes, staring at her husband's face with worry etched on her own.

Tension soon developed between Nancy and the White House physician, Daniel A. Ruge, who had trained under Loyal Davis and worked as her father's partner for twenty years. Ruge had been standing near Ronnie when he was shot. He and Deaver jumped into the follow-up car as the president's motorcade sped off. At the hospital, Ruge made the call that the president should be treated by the trauma team on duty there rather than taking charge himself or bringing in high-powered surgeons from other medical centers to confer. Renowned heart surgeon Michael DeBakey had already called, offering to fly in from Houston with his own emergency specialists. Ruge declined. All of that would have taken too much precious time. Nor did he allow the president to be moved eight and a half miles to Bethesda Naval Hospital, as the Secret Service wanted.

Ruge told the GW medical personnel at hand to move quickly and treat the president as they would any other seventy-year-old man who had come into the ER with a gunshot wound. They should not wait for a plan to be developed by a consensus of more senior specialists. That was a controversial decision in the moment, but the right one, and it probably helped save Ronnie's life. Still, the White House physician bore the brunt of the First Lady's second-guessing and her anxiety. At one point, Ronnie groggily handed his doctor a note in faint and wobbly handwriting that said: "I am aren't alive aren't I?" Nancy snatched it out of Ruge's hand, and he never saw the note again.

This was one of many missives to his doctors and nurses that Ronnie would write in pencil and felt-tip pen on a pink-and-white pad stamped George Washington University Hospital. Some were funny: "If I'd had this much attention in Hollywood, I'd have stayed there." And to pretty nurse Denise Sullivan, who had tended to him in the recovery room: "Does Nancy know about us?" Others were not so lighthearted: "What happened to the guy with the gun?" "What was his beef? Was anyone hurt?" "Will I still be able to work at the ranch?" Nancy gathered as many as she could find and saved them in a manila envelope.

Her brother, Dick, who came from Philadelphia that night, witnessed intense arguments between Ruge and Nancy over Ronnie's care. As a surgeon himself, Nancy's brother sympathized with the doctor, who would move into the White House for a month while Ronnie recuperated. "Dan was a marvelous surgeon and also a very, very kind, good man. He couldn't stand Nancy. The two didn't get along at all, which he and Mrs. Ruge were never hesitant to tell me, how awful she was to them," Dick recalled. His sister's feelings about the White House physician were mutual. "She couldn't stand him. She didn't like him at all," Dick added. Ruge's daughter, Charlotte Wiessner, offered a similar assessment of the relationship between the president's physician and the first lady, saying, "My father wasn't crazy about her."

Nor was Ruge, a distinguished figure who stood six foot two, crazy about the job itself. Though he would be regarded as one of the heroes of the day that Ronnie was shot, Ruge found most of his duties as White

House physician to be, as he put it later, "vastly overrated, boring, and not medically challenging." Unlike most presidential physicians, he did not come from the military. In private practice, his specialty had been spinal cord injuries, which was not an expertise he was likely to be called upon to use in the White House. Nor was he quite prepared for the reality of being just another member of the staff. During state dinners, he was required to don a tuxedo to be at the ready if he was needed, and then had to sit in his office, where he did crossword puzzles and read medical journals. One White House official who knew both Ruge and Nancy well said that their long relationship, which revolved around Loyal, stirred mixed feelings in the first lady: "Dan was a very comfortable reminder of her father and connection with her father, but also an uncomfortable reminder of her past."

Nancy asked her stepbrother to spend that first night with her at the White House, but Dick opted to stay with the Ruges instead. The next morning, he joined his sister for a prayer service. "I was amazed at her self-control. She didn't cry. She didn't say how awful this was," Dick recalled. "I cried during the service. She showed no emotion at all."

The other three Reagan children arrived from California, via an uncomfortable overnight ride aboard a military cargo plane. Patti had gotten news of the shooting when a Secret Service agent interrupted a session with her therapist. Michael also heard it from an agent, who assured him his father was unhurt; through news reports on the radio, he soon realized otherwise. Maureen received a call from her fiancé, Dennis Revell, who couldn't summon words to tell her what had happened, and so he asked her to turn on the television. As they all boarded a plane that night, it occurred to Patti that none of them had spoken to Nancy or reached out to one another. "What kind of family is this?" she thought. "Even a bullet can't bring us together."

For most of the flight, the three Reagan children sat in different parts of the C-140, on canvas seats. Patti realized that their only connection was a man who might be bleeding to death in a hospital bed thousands of miles away. "There was something else uniting us. Each of us knew, in some part of our hearts that, although our presence was expected there, it wasn't really important," she recalled. "Ronald and Nancy Reagan are two halves of a circle; together, they are complete, and their children float outside." At Nancy's funeral thirty-five years later, her daughter would use almost exactly those words to describe the bond between her parents.

Patti, Ron, and Doria made a midmorning visit to Ronnie in the hospital. Nancy told Maureen and Michael they would have to come later, which hit them as a hurtful, infuriating reminder of their secondary status as the children from Ronnie's first marriage. They decided to use the time checking in on Delahanty and McCarthy, and to thank them for their valor in the line of duty. They also saw Sarah Brady, who was hovering over her bandaged husband and begging him to live. Eventually Maureen and Michael got into their father's room for a short visit, but only after pleading with a doctor to let them see him. Within a day, all four of Ronnie's children had left Washington, though Maureen and Patti would return while he recuperated. The family would not all be together again until the following Thanksgiving.

Nancy did summon others to lend support. Frank Sinatra and his fourth wife, Barbara, were asleep in Las Vegas when the phone rang. "Ronnie's been shot," Nancy blurted on the other end of the line. "Can you come?" Sinatra canceled the final three shows of his weeklong engagement at Caesars Palace and arranged for a flight. When he and Barbara arrived at the White House, they were met by Nancy and evangelist Billy Graham. The Reagans' pastor, Donn Moomaw, flew in from Los Angeles. Old friends like the Wicks also were on hand. From around the country, get-well letters and gifts—flowers, Ronnie's favorite jelly beans, chocolates—were flooding in. But Nancy still felt that without Ronnie in the bed beside her, she was by herself. After one grueling day at the hospital, she wrote in her diary: "It's a big house when you're here alone."

Outside, it seemed the world had been put on pause. The Academy Awards, which had been scheduled to be broadcast by ABC on March 30, were put off for a day. Master of ceremonies Johnny Carson opened the next night by saying: "I'm sure that all of you here and most of you watching tonight understand why we have delayed this program for twenty-four hours. Because of the incredible events of yesterday, that old adage 'the show must go on' seemed relatively unimportant." The star-filled audience at LA's Dorothy Chandler Pavilion erupted in cheers when Carson announced the president was in "excellent condition at last reports. He has been conducting business, and he happens to be in very good spirits." There was more applause when Carson noted Ronnie had given his blessing to playing a video greeting taped two weeks before. "Film is forever," the prerecorded president quipped from the jumbo screen. "I have been trapped in some film forever myself." Carson said that Ronnie "asked for a television set in his room so he could view this program tonight." Watching the Academy Awards had actually been Nancy's idea, as what she hoped would be a morale booster in the gloomy hospital suite. The curtains had been nailed closed for security reasons, shutting out the glorious spring that was being announced by the blooming of the cherry blossoms. Ronnie enjoyed some of the ceremony as he drifted in and out of sleep.

The timing of the awards broadcast was not the only dilemma faced by the television networks. They were sensitive to the fact that a movie had set this tragedy in motion. NBC shelved an upcoming episode of *Walking Tall,* a series about a crime-fighting sheriff based on a popular 1973 film with the same name. The reason: the episode had been titled "Hit Man." ABC temporarily changed the name of one of the lead characters in its new hit sitcom *The Greatest American Hero* from Ralph Hinkley, which sounded too much like the gunman's, to Ralph Hanley. But things started to get back to normal after a few days.

Or so it seemed. In fact, the White House and the doctors were giving the public a misleadingly rosy picture of the president's condition and hiding how close to death he had been. During the hours after the shooting, Lyn Nofziger coolly and masterfully took over handling the media that descended upon the hospital, offering upbeat fodder to the journalists on deadline.

Nofziger said the president was conscious and had walked into the hospital on his own. Which was accurate but hardly the whole story.

He also kept the press informed with a steady stream of anecdotes about how Ronnie was cracking jokes and passing clever notes to his doctors and nurses. "All in all, I'd rather be in Philadelphia," Ronnie wrote in one, reprising the line that comedian W. C. Fields once said he wanted to have inscribed on his tombstone. Those reassuring bits of information became the instant lore of that horrible day. "I didn't know I was supposed to be holding the nation together, or even that such a thing was needed," Nofziger would later recall. "Neither did I feel that the president was dying."

Still, reporters were clamoring for more medical details. Nofziger recruited the hospital's smooth and personable spokesman, Dennis O'Leary, to give a briefing. O'Leary stuck pretty much to the facts—that the president was in the recovery room, stable, and awake. But he made one glaringly false statement, which was that Ronnie "was at no time in any serious danger." He also downplayed the amount of blood the president had lost. As Nofziger did, O'Leary noted that the president had walked into the hospital, without adding that he had collapsed as soon as he got inside. Weeks later, when more information was available and reporters began challenging him on what he had said, O'Leary replied that "people believe what they believe," but he continued to insist: "The president was not in serious danger of dying."

Within an hour after Ronnie left the recovery room, his top aides brought him a piece of legislation to sign, a dairy bill, to convey the impression that he was still able to function as the nation's chief executive. His faint, wobbly handwriting said otherwise. Nor was he out of the woods. On the fifth day after he was shot, Ronnie began coughing up fresh blood and spiked a fever of 105. Doctors feared pneumonia. He also lost his appetite, so Nancy had their former Los Angeles housekeeper make and ship two of his favorite soups: hamburger and split pea. What bothered her as much as anything was the sound of nurses in the next room slapping him on his back to keep his lungs clear, an exercise they had to repeat every four hours. It was as though he were a side of meat. "That's your father they're doing that to," she lamented to Maureen when she came to visit.

Ronnie made steady progress after the infection crisis passed. On April 11, twelve days after he was shot, he was released from the hospital under tight security, wearing a bulletproof vest under his red cardigan sweater and sport shirt. "I walked in here, and I am going to walk out," he declared, and did so, though stiffly. When he, Nancy, and Patti arrived back at the White House, he was greeted by two hundred members of his staff, Cabinet secretaries, and their families, many huddling under umbrellas against a light but relentless rain. A big cloth sign announced: Welcome Home Mr. President. "This looks like a nice place," he said.

Once Ronnie was home, Nancy insisted that he drastically cut back his work schedule. She showed him a letter she had gotten from Lady Bird Johnson, in which the former first lady had written that Lyndon had needed a full month to recover from his 1965 gall bladder operation. In the early weeks of his recuperation, Ronnie wore his navy-blue bathrobe and pajamas to meetings with top advisers and the National Security Council, then retreated to the residence for a nap. He was in bed for the night a half hour after dinner.

Nancy had accelerated the solarium renovations, so that he could convalesce in a setting far different from his dark hospital room. She also set up a gym in Tricia Nixon's old bedroom, across the hall from theirs. As the doctors slowly took him off antibiotics, food began to taste good again. Between more regular eating and his weight-lifting workouts, Ronnie would eventually fill out—and indeed, become more muscular than he had been before, adding an inch and a half to his chest. Nancy, however, remained wracked by tension and anxiety. At night, she took a banana to bed as a snack to eat during her inevitable bouts with insomnia. She feared the crunching of an apple might wake her husband.

Ronnie's first day back in the Oval Office was April 24. Late that morning, he held a meeting with his Cabinet and was greeted with applause. But he wasn't well enough yet to make it to California the following day for Maureen's wedding to Dennis Revell. He urged the couple not to reschedule. In her father's stead, his brother, Neil, walked Ronnie's eldest down the aisle at the Beverly Wilshire Hotel. As a gift,

Nancy sent a set of pewter drink stirrers topped with decorative elephants. Though they were clearly not from Tiffany & Co., they came in one of the store's distinctive boxes, and each was in a tarnish-preventing storage sleeve that bore the Tiffany name. The couple knew they must have come from Nancy's "gift closet," where she kept unwanted things that people had given her and Ronnie. Her recycling practices were a running joke among the Reagans.

As weeks went by, the White House began to turn its attention back to the ambitious agenda the president had set out for the country. Ronnie's poll numbers, which were sagging before the assassination attempt, shot up 11 percentage points in the days afterward. "While it is common for a president's popularity rating to increase at a time of national crisis, the rise for Reagan appears as sharp as any yet recorded," the *Washington Post* noted, and pronounced it a "second honeymoon" for the president.

That was confirmed when Ronnie entered the House chamber on April 28 to sell his economic program in a nationally televised address to a joint session of Congress. Lawmakers leapt to their feet to give him a three-minute burst of applause. Ronnie noted in his diary that the speech had been interrupted by ovations fourteen times. He was especially touched that dozens of Democrats had joined Republicans in clapping at some points. "Maybe we are going to make it," he wrote. "It took a lot of courage for them to do that, and it sent a shiver down my spine."

The horrific event that Nancy would refer to only as "March 30" or "the thing that happened to Ronnie" had changed them both. He saw a divine hand in the fact that he had been spared, which made him more convinced than ever that there was a purpose at work in his presidency. On April 12, in his first diary entry after the shooting, Ronnie wrote, "Whatever happens now, I owe my life to God and will try to serve him in every way I can." He had understood from the moment he awakened in the emergency room that his healing would have to begin with forgiveness: "I realized I couldn't ask for Gods [*sic*] help while at the same time I felt hatred for the mixed-up young man who had shot me. Isn't that the meaning of the lost sheep? We are all

Gods children & therefore equally beloved by him. I began to pray for his soul and that he would find his way back to the fold."

But while Ronnie was turning toward the light, Nancy could not escape her darkness. Night after night, while he slept soundly on the left side of the bed, she lay awake on the right, her thoughts locked on gruesome possibilities. She obsessed over the fact that presidents elected in a year that ended in zero tended to die while in office, either from natural causes or by assassination. William Henry Harrison had been elected in 1840; Abraham Lincoln, in 1860; James A. Garfield, in 1880; William McKinley, in 1900; Warren G. Harding, in 1920; and John F. Kennedy, in 1960. That pattern suddenly seemed more an omen than a statistical oddity. Ronnie was also the only sitting president in history to survive being wounded in an assassination attempt. Did that present some kind of sick challenge to other would-be killers? Everywhere there were reminders of the danger. In May, when the couple celebrated Ronnie's recovery by going out to dinner for the first time, black-suited Secret Service sharpshooters were posted on a rooftop overlooking the Georgetown club where they were dining.

Her weight slipped from an already slender 112 pounds to less than 100. Nancy could see in pictures of herself how gaunt and drawn she looked. Patti visited her parents during their trip to the ranch over Memorial Day weekend. For Ronnie, getting back to his beloved mountaintop spread was a tonic, though the doctors had told him to go easy on the horseback riding. "The weather was beautiful, and so was the ranch," he recalled later. "Its wild scenery and solitude only reminded us how much we loved about it and how much we missed our life in California." But as Patti hugged her mother good-bye, she was struck by how tiny Nancy had become: "This woman whose presence has been so enormous in my life, who has seemed to tower over me, was almost lost between my arms."

Ronnie could also see the toll it was taking on Nancy. He thought she needed a break, so when the invitation to the wedding of Prince Charles and Lady Diana Spencer arrived, he urged her to attend without him. "Saw 'Mommie' off for London & the Royal Wedding. I worry when she's out of sight 6 minutes. How am I going to hold out for 6 days," he wrote in his diary July 23. "The lights don't seem as warm & bright without her."

As the months and later the years went by, the memories of that horrible day in March stayed fresh in Nancy's mind. In an interview with *Parade* magazine in late 1981, she struggled for words to describe how it haunted her: "I think, before it happened, it was something I knew was always out there, and it was constantly in the back of my mind. I had to keep it in the back of my mind, you see, or I couldn't function. I knew measures were taken to protect us, and we had to depend on those. And now . . .

"I thought for a while it was something that in time would fade away," she added. "It hasn't. It's a particular kind of trauma that never leaves you once you've known it."

*

The news from around the world offered no reassurance. Weeks after Ronnie was shot, there was an attempt on the life of Pope John Paul II in St. Peter's Square. Anwar Sadat was assassinated at a parade in Cairo on October 6, just two months after Ronnie had toasted the Egyptian president as a peacemaker at a White House state dinner. Nancy said: "It's not just America. No. No. It is all over the world. Violence everywhere. Yes, yes, it does something to you. Yes, it changes you."

On Nancy's insistence, Ronnie never made a trip to the Middle East while he was president, not even to Israel. "She thought he was going to get smoked if he went over there. She just said, 'They can come here all they want. You're not going over there,'" recalled Jim Kuhn, who was Ronnie's executive assistant. "The thing that really got to her was when Anwar Sadat was blown away in that military parade. The Hinckley thing was just a stupid Secret Service mistake, but that thing with Sadat really hit her hard." Nancy also vetoed the idea of Ronnie attending Sadat's funeral. She was too afraid for her husband's safety. The White House dispatched three of his predecessors—Nixon, Ford, and Carter—to represent the United States.

In early December of that first year of Ronnie's presidency, there were reports that Libyan leader Mu'ammar Gadhafi had dispatched a hit squad to the United States to assassinate him. The potential threat was taken seriously enough that Ronnie had to light the national Christmas tree from the White House, instead of doing it in the open on the Ellipse, a park just outside the White House fence, as presidents typically did. Concerns about security also scotched Nancy's plans to go out and do her Christmas shopping, so she had to ask friends to buy her gifts for her. Ronnie ordered Secret Service protection for the troika of Deaver, Baker, and Meese, and, for a while, mock presidential motorcades wended through Washington as decoys to draw out would-be assassins.

Ronnie's handwritten Christmas letter to Nancy at the end of that first difficult year was a particularly tender one; two pages of reassurance and love on White House stationery. It also offers a glimpse of how differently Nancy looked in his eyes from the image of her that was being forged in brutal Washington. Their lives had changed in ways they could never have foreseen, but their devotion to each other had not. Ronnie began by lamenting that a president constrained within the fortified White House had not been able to select a Christmas present for the person he loved most:

> Dear Mrs. R.
>
> I still don't feel right about your opening an envelope instead of a gift package.
>
> There are several much beloved women in my life and on Christmas I should be giving them gold, precious stones, perfume, furs and lace. I know that even the best of these would still fall far short of expressing how much these several women mean to me and how empty my life would be without them.
>
> There is of course my "First Lady." She brings so much grace and charm to whatever she does that even stuffy, formal functions sparkle and turn into fun times. Everything is done with class. All I have to do is wash up and show up.

There is another woman in my life who does things I don't always get to see but I hear about them and sometimes see photos of her doing them. She takes an abandoned child in her arms on a hospital visit. The look on her face only the Madonna could match. The look on the child's face is one of adoration. I know because I adore her too.

She bends over a wheelchair or bed to touch an elderly invalid with tenderness and compassion just as she fills my life with warmth and love.

There is another gal I love who is a nest builder. If she were stuck three days in a hotel room, she'd manage to make it home sweet home. She moves things around—looks at it—straightens this and that, and you wonder why it wasn't that way in the first place.

I'm also crazy about the girl who goes to the ranch with me. If we're tidying up the woods, she's a peewee power house at pushing over dead trees. She's a wonderful person to sit by the fire with, or to ride with or just to be with when the sun goes down or the stars come out. If she ever stopped going to the ranch I'd stop too because I'd see her in every beauty spot there is, and I couldn't stand that.

Then there is a sentimental lady I love whose eyes fill up so easily. On the other hand, she loves to laugh, and her laugh is like tinkling bells. I hear those bells and feel good all over even if I tell a joke she's heard before.

Fortunately all these women in my life are you—fortunately for me that is, for there could be no life for me without you. Browning asked; "How do I love thee—let me count the ways?" For me there is no way to count. I love the whole gang of you—Mommie, first lady, the sentimental you, the fun you and the peewee power house you.

And oh yes, one other very special you—the little girl who takes a "nana" to bed in case she gets hungry in the night. I couldn't & don't sleep well if she isn't there—so please always be there.

Merry Christmas you all—with all my love.

Lucky me.

CHAPTER THIRTEEN

Nancy's initiation into being first lady could hardly have been rockier, but she was not unappreciative of the amenities that came with the job: a plumber arriving the moment there was a problem, a man to wind the clocks, a maid to take away her soiled clothes while she was bathing—and most usefully, given her addiction to the phone, switchboard operators who could track down anyone she cared to talk to. Her son, Ron, called the White House an eight-star hotel. Living over the store also meant plenty of time for Nancy and Ronnie to be together alone—or, at least, as alone as any first couple ever is. Two butlers served them dinner, which they usually ate on tray tables in Ronnie's study as they watched the evening news. Most nights, they were in bed by ten. Nancy pushed a button twice to let the usher know it was time to turn out the lights and to hold any calls that were not urgent until the morning.

But there wasn't freedom to do something so ordinary as take a long walk. That is why one of the side benefits that both Reagans found they loved the most was the rustic solitude of Camp David, about an hour away from Washington on the Catoctin Mountain ridge in northern Maryland. "I never expected that we would use it practically every weekend, but it became a regular and welcome part of our routine," Nancy recalled.

Built in 1935 by the Works Progress Administration, the site was converted to a retreat for Franklin D. Roosevelt shortly after the beginning of World War II, giving the president, disabled by polio, a place to escape the pressure and heat of Washington. So enamored was FDR with the setting and the view that he christened it Shangri-La, after the fictional Himalayan paradise in the 1933 novel *Lost Horizon*. The existence of the retreat was still a state secret back then. For FDR, it became a secluded venue not only for relaxation but also for sensitive business. He and British prime minister Winston Churchill did some of the planning for the D-day invasion there. Years later, President Dwight Eisenhower, who had grown up on a Kansas farm, decided that the name Shangri-La was a tad too fancy for a place where he went to kick back. He changed it in 1953 to Camp David, after his five-year-old grandson. The retreat's most famous moment came in 1978, when Jimmy Carter hosted weeks of summit negotiations there that produced the Camp David Accords, a framework for Middle East peace signed by Egyptian president Anwar Sadat and Israeli prime minister Menachem Begin.

The Reagans used Camp David more than any other first couple before or since. Occasionally, they would entertain foreign dignitaries there. But the routine most weekends was far more quiet and intimate. For Nancy, it was a release, a place to get their thoughts in order, a place to focus on each other. Security was more relaxed. "She loved Camp David. They were alone. We gave them fifty yards," said Joseph Petro, who was on Ronnie's Secret Service detail for four years. As often as possible, the Reagans headed there from the White House on Fridays around three. If the weather was good, it would take just a half hour to get there by helicopter, though Nancy preferred to drive and enjoy the scenic countryside as they put Washington behind. They allowed only a small retinue of aides to accompany them.

Each of the lodges at Camp David was named for a type of tree. The Reagans stayed at Aspen; there was a conference center in Laurel, from which Ronnie gave his Saturday radio addresses. Nancy, as was her wont, went to work redecorating throughout, sometimes enlisting her husband to help her hang pictures. The president also ordered some renovation of his own. He was appalled to discover that Richard Nixon, who tooled around the place in a golf cart, had paved over the trails. So, he had them ripped up and restored to paths suitable for the horseback riding that he loved.

At eight o'clock every Friday and Saturday night, they invited a few people who were staying there to watch movies on a screen that came down from the ceiling of the Aspen living room. Among those who most often joined them were John Hutton, who was White House physician during Ronnie's second term; assistant press secretary Mark Weinberg; executive assistant Jim Kuhn; presidential valet Eddie Serrano; their helicopter pilot; the camp commander; and their Secret Service agents. Ronnie and Nancy alternated classic pictures with the newest releases. The Reagans preferred movies with sunny plotlines, strong heroes, and patriotic themes, and frowned on ones with a lot of sex and profanity. As Nancy and Hutton's wife were often the only women there, they saw a lot of Westerns. And, yes, Ronnie and Nancy's own movies occasionally made the playlist.

After each film, Ronnie would start the conversation by offering his critique, which often led into behind-the-scenes stories about actors and other characters he had met in the business. He fixated on the technical details. The president once told director Steven Spielberg that the 1982 film *E.T. the Extra-Terrestrial,* which was a fantasy about a friendship between a space alien and a little boy, made him nostalgic for an era when Hollywood was cranking out more heart-warmers. But he had one criticism: the end credits seemed to go on forever. "In my day, when I was an actor, our end credits were maybe fifteen seconds long," Ronnie said. "Three and a half minutes, that's fine—but only show that inside the industry. Throughout the rest of the country, reduce your credits to fifteen seconds at the end."

Chief among the many reasons that Nancy loved Camp David was the restorative effect it had on Ronnie. If he couldn't be at his beloved ranch in California, this was the closest thing to it. She pushed back against the tendency of his aides to load him down with briefing papers and other work to take with him on their weekends. "Reagan was a voracious reader. You could give him one page or five hundred pages, and he'd read the five hundred pages," his executive assistant, Jim Kuhn, told me. "He'd complain about it. He'd say, 'Jim, they're telling me more than I need to know. I already know all this stuff.' But he read it anyhow."

Richard Allen, Ronnie's first national security adviser, was surprised when Deaver once handed him back a thick packet of documents that Allen had sent to Camp David the previous weekend. Cut any future ones by three-quarters, Deaver told him.

"He reads it all," Allen protested.

"Yes, I know," Deaver replied. "That's what I'm telling you. I want it cut by seventy-five percent."

What Allen didn't realize at the time, he said later, was that Deaver "was on a mission from Nancy, because the president had his nose buried in this stuff on weekends."

*

Nancy also encouraged Ronnie's sojourns at Rancho del Cielo. She had never loved it there; she went because she knew how much he did. While he chopped brush and busied himself with repairs, she would plant herself in a chair by the pond and spend hours on the phone with her friends. Nor did she share his love of riding. At ten thirty each morning, Ronnie would saddle both their horses—his, English style; hers, Western—and ring a bell to summon Nancy. "I can't tell you how many times he rang it more than once," Secret Service agent Petro recalled. Once Ronnie got her out on the trails, Nancy pleaded with him constantly to make the horses go slower. Returning from their rides, they would stop alongside each other. Ronnie would dismount and walk around to her horse. Nancy would then throw a leg over the saddle and leap into his waiting arms. Watching this ritual one day, White House physician John Hutton thought to himself: "Good Christopher Columbus, how does anybody keep a romance going for this many years with that intensity?" The doctor was slightly embarrassed—and yet mesmerized—by it all. "I felt like I was a kid watching a sister necking on the couch with her boyfriend. I felt guilty about doing it, but I couldn't resist," Hutton said.

On the front door of the modest 2,400-square-foot, two-bedroom house was a sign that summed up Ronnie's vision of the perfect retreat from the stress and pressure of Washington:

ON THIS SITE
IN 1897
NOTHING HAPPENED

The Reagans spent a total of 335 days of his presidency, adding up to more than eleven months, at the ranch. But every day the two of them were there, a government car would drive up the winding road with a stack of mail, newspapers, and documents for Ronnie to read. And even when Ronnie headed out in his battered red 1962 CJ-6 Willys Jeep for the tranquility of the brush and woodlands, he was followed by Secret Service agents, a doctor, and a military aide with a portable telephone.

Once they got back to Washington, Nancy stood guard over Ronnie's schedule, continuously battling against the tendency of aides and advisers to jam it with more than she thought he could handle. At receptions, she watched her husband closely for the first sign of fatigue. She'd tug at his sleeve gently—and sometimes rudely—to tell him it was time to go.

That someone needed to resist unreasonable demands on the endurance and strength of a man in his seventies became clear on his first presidential trip to Europe in June 1982. The ten-day itinerary was brutal: Ronnie, who was never able to get much sleep on airplanes, flew overnight and landed in Paris on the night of June 2. He had a day of meetings with Thatcher and French president François Mitterrand, and hosted a formal dinner at the American ambassador's home that night. The next day, he helicoptered to Versailles for economic summit talks with Thatcher and Mitterrand, plus the heads of government of Japan, West Germany, Canada, and Italy. Their three-day summit ended with a banquet that lasted until one in the morning, after which Ronnie met with Al Haig and others for an update on Israel's invasion of Lebanon that day.

With only a few hours of sleep, he headed to Rome on June 7 for a meeting with Pope John Paul II. The papal library where they met was overheated, and as the pope held forth in his tranquilizing voice, Ronnie nodded off. Nancy, sitting behind him, cleared her throat and shuffled her feet, hoping to wake her husband, but by then, it was too late. The assembled press had seen it all. As Helen Thomas of United Press International recounted: "While the pope spoke, Mr. Reagan sat in an armchair next to him. His eyes closed on at least three occasions. His chin fell to his chest, and at one point reporters observed that he seemed to slide down in his chair." All of the news accounts mentioned the president was seventy-one years old.

And the trip had only just begun. After that, the presidential entourage flew to England, where Ronnie went horseback riding with Queen Elizabeth II, gave an address to Parliament, lunched with Thatcher at 10 Downing Street, and attended a white-tie banquet put on by the queen at Buckingham Palace. (The press took note: it didn't seem to bother Elizabeth that she didn't have enough china to serve all her guests with the same pattern.) And then, thoroughly worn out, he had to speak before foreign leaders at a summit meeting of the North Atlantic Treaty Organization (NATO) in the West German capital of Bonn. Along the way, he took a step across the Berlin Wall into East Germany; confronted hecklers at his speech to the Bundestag, West Germany's parliament; and addressed cheering US soldiers at Tempelhof Airport.

The reviews of his performance were withering. In a column headlined "Dissareagan," conservative *New York Times* columnist William Safire wrote that Ronnie had been "stripped of his dignity" and "treated with cool contempt" by the other leaders at the economic summit. As Ronnie forged ahead through his punishing itinerary, the traveling press corps was kept at a distance, hemmed in by security and unable to ask the president many questions or even to get basic information from the White House staff. "This is my fourteenth trip abroad with presidents, and it's far and away the most ineptly organized," *Newsweek*'s Tom DeFrank told the *Washington Post*.

That newspaper's senior White House correspondent was more brutal, saying the logistical difficulties revealed deeper problems. "Reagan managed to raise doubts about his capacities and mastery of detail among those who saw him close up," Lou Cannon wrote. "He also reinforced his image with the huge US press entourage of an isolated president, surrounded by a cocoon of advisers who are afraid to let him loose in public lest he reveal ignorance about some of his administration's policies." Not until the end of the European trip did Ronnie manage to recover his footing and his confidence. While reaffirming his loathing of Communism, he began talking in Germany about his eagerness to negotiate with the Russians to reduce nuclear weapons.

Nancy was livid and directed her fury at Mike Deaver, who had organized the trip. Her most trusted aide had paid more attention to setting the president against spectacular backdrops for dramatic photo ops than to the substance of what Ronnie hoped to achieve. Deaver told her he had shown the itinerary to Ronnie, warned him that it would be punishing, and that the president had approved it. But from there on out, the First Lady made sure she was the one who had the veto power on these matters. "At first, she had trusted Deaver to make the right decisions," said television correspondent Andrea Mitchell, who covered the White House for NBC. "That was the first time she said to Deaver, 'Don't let that happen again.'"

It didn't. Ronnie was never again overscheduled abroad. Extra days would be added to make sure the president made his way across time zones in a leisurely fashion, with time to adjust and arrive rested. When Ronnie traveled to China in 1984, for instance, Nancy decreed that they proceed slowly across the Pacific, with a stop in California, a few days in Hawaii, and a night in Guam before heading to Beijing. It paid off. Ronnie did well in his meetings with top Chinese officials and pronounced that the two countries had reached "a new level of understanding." Deaver still managed to arrange for some of the visuals that were his trademark. Ronnie and Nancy strolled on the Great Wall and made a visit to see the life-size terra-cotta warriors excavated near Xi'an, the cradle of Chinese civilization. They also took a trip to a child care center. That became the pattern. Cannon wrote later that Ronnie "was a relaxed and effective performer on the three major foreign trips he took during a seven-month period from mid-November 1983 through mid-June 1984, all planned as events in his reelection campaign."

*

If taking care of Ronnie's physical well-being was at the top of what Nancy regarded as her chief duties as a first lady, keeping an eye on those around him was a close second. Ronnie was discomfited by infighting and uninterested in internal intrigue. Not one to nurse grudges, he was generous with offering second chances. He was also a famously detached manager, taking little interest in details so long as he believed his overall vision was being carried out. As he told *Fortune* magazine in 1986: "I believe, first of all, that you surround yourself with the best people you can find, and you delegate authority, and you don't interfere."

Nancy approached things from the opposite point of view. For her, confidence was a precious and perishable commodity. It was to be earned, not assumed, and withdrawn at the first inkling of doubt. "I don't get involved in how to balance the budget or how to reduce the deficit or foreign affairs or whatever, but I do get involved in people issues," she said. "I think I'm aware of people who are trying to take advantage of my husband, who are trying to end-run him."

But it is among the oldest of Washington truisms that "people issues" *are* policy. Controlling who is in the room when there is a decision to be made or advice to be given can preordain the outcome. That is why the city's favorite spectator sport has always been figuring out who's in and who's out. And no first lady in memory was more in the middle of White House personnel matters than Nancy Reagan.

She was not the political naif that she had been when she arrived in Sacramento. After eight years as a governor's wife and two grueling presidential campaigns, she had a far better understanding of both the extent and the limits of her power. When Betty Ford was asked where she exercised her influence, she answered: "pillow talk." Nancy knew that she had to do far more than whisper in her husband's ear to get her way. She picked her shots, chose with care her allies and her weapons, and learned to gauge whether patience or urgency better suited the challenge at hand. Ronnie's personal aide, Jim Kuhn, saw Nancy in action many times. "She knew how to lay the groundwork. She knew how to put things together. She knew how far she could go with 'Ronnie.' She knew what she could get away with," he said. Nancy acknowledged as much. "Does the president sometimes say no to me? Sure," she told NBC's Chris Wallace in 1985. "Does his no always end it? Not always. I'll wait a little while; then I'll come back at him again."

As the years have gone by, appreciation has grown for the role that she played in her husband's success. Among those who have acknowledged how essential she became was Richard Neustadt, considered the preeminent scholar of the American presidency. Neustadt, a liberal, advised every Democratic president from Harry Truman to Bill Clinton and was a founder of the John F. Kennedy School of Government at Harvard University. He saw Nancy as a vital player in Ronnie's presidency because she had "a good ear and a fine eye." She let neither political ideology nor personal attachment cloud her judgment in that regard. "Her husband's close associates, however valuable or liked or even loved, were to be sacrificed, in her view, from the moment their continuation on the scene could compromise the president's public relations," Neustadt wrote, adding, "When it came to people, her targets seem well chosen, aim unerring, and timing right for someone who must wait for someone else to pull the trigger." Every president, Neustadt added, would do well to follow this principle: "Never let your Nancy be immobilized."

Sometimes Nancy also had to dissuade her husband from doing things that appealed to his principles but had the potential to hurt him politically. In 1986, for instance, during a meeting with White House counsel Peter Wallison, Ronnie raised the idea of not disclosing his tax returns the following year. Though letting the country take a look at them is not required by law, Jimmy Carter had set a precedent for presidents to do so voluntarily. Nixon released his too, but only after those for one year were leaked. Ronnie complained that it was an unfair expectation of presidents, because average citizens did not have to make theirs public. Withholding their release would not benefit Ronnie much. He had less than two years left in office. But he contended that setting a new precedent would be helpful to whoever followed him in the White House.

Wallison was about to argue that this break with normal practice would be hard to explain. Americans would not see it as a principled stand but rather a sign that Ronnie had something to hide. Before Wallison could make that point, however, Nancy beat him to it. "She could not bear the thought of the criticism such a step would bring, she said, and Reagan backed off," Wallison recalled. "Every president, no matter how good his political instincts, needs someone to bring him back to reality on occasion, and Ronald Reagan—a president with a particularly idealistic streak—was especially in need of this kind of counsel." So, the tradition of releasing presidential tax returns would remain unbroken for the next thirty years, until celebrity real estate developer Donald Trump was elected despite refusing to hand over his.

Nancy was Ronnie's early-warning system, determined to spot potential problems before they had a chance to become attached to him. "It really reaches a point where something's gone much too far, in my opinion. So it seems to me, sometimes, that if you can catch it before it reaches that point where a lot of people are maybe hurt, then it's easier to stop it right in the beginning, rather than let it build up a head of steam," she said.

That meant she had to be a consummate gatherer of information. Ronnie rarely made a telephone call, except when his advisers asked him to. Nancy was on the line constantly, working her network. She watched the president's popularity closely and pored over the numbers in private sessions with his pollster, Richard Wirthlin. She was also vigilant about his coverage, devouring newspapers and newsmagazines, as well as what was being said on the nightly television broadcasts.

During the day, Cable News Network, the twenty-four-hour channel that launched in June 1980, was on constantly in the residence. The first lady also went through thousands of pictures taken by the official White House staff photographers, tearing off the top-right corners of ones she found unflattering and writing "O.K., per N.R." on images she deemed suitable for public release.

Aides learned early not to try to wing it when Nancy interrogated them, because the chances were, if she asked a question, she already had an inkling of the answer from one of her other sources. "I always said, 'I'm sorry. I don't know. I'll find out,'" said her special assistant, Jane Erkenbeck. The first lady also wanted things done immediately. It would take Erkenbeck five minutes to get from the residence to her office in the East Wing. By the time she reached her desk, the phone was often ringing. Nancy was on the line, wanting to know whether her assistant had gotten the information or done the task of the moment. "I learned from her that things can be done very quickly. Especially when you say, 'I'm calling for Mrs. Reagan,' things get done," Erkenbeck laughed.

"There was always something wrong, always something wrong," said Kuhn. In the office of Ronnie's executive assistant, the phone had lines marked WH1 and WH2. When Kuhn saw WH1 light up late in the afternoon, he knew it was Nancy—and that she wasn't calling to congratulate him on what a good job he was doing. Sometimes Kuhn would hear a long pause on the line when he picked it up. Nancy wasn't going to tell him what was bothering her; she expected him to know and to tell her how it was being fixed. "Oh yeah, Mrs. Reagan, that thing didn't go so well . . ." Kuhn would say.

Her quirks and demands added to the stress of those around her husband. On overseas trips, a seat in the motorcade had to be saved for her hairdresser, which sometimes meant someone on the official staff had to find another means of transportation. Her forays into the West Wing, though relatively rare, were greeted with terror. But as difficult as she could be when she was worried or mad, Nancy was also the most valuable of partners for the top officials who recognized her power. She was indispensable when it came to convincing Ronnie to do something—or not to—if she could be persuaded that was in his best interest.

In the internecine battles that were constantly going on within the tense and divided West Wing, Nancy usually sided with Baker and Deaver, who often infuriated conservatives by pushing Ronnie in a more moderate direction. "Whenever we had something we wanted to convince the Gipper of, we would try to enlist her support. When we'd get her support, we had a good shot at it," Baker told me. "She didn't want his goals subverted by ideology. She was a pragmatist, and she understood that we judge our presidents on the basis of what they can get accomplished, and so she was for those of us who wanted to get things done." Their united front often isolated Ed Meese, the third member of the White House troika and the most ideological.

None of which meant that she always won. Nor did she expect to. "Nancy Reagan had a better understanding than the entourage, a better understanding even than Deaver or [political strategist] Spencer, of how difficult it was to persuade her husband to oppose his instincts or his ideology," Lou Cannon wrote. "Reagan often did not ask the right questions, or any questions at all, which made it possible to manipulate him or lead him down paths where he did not wish to go. But he did not like to be pushed by anyone, not even Nancy Reagan."

Still, Nancy had a keen sense of where the defenses were weak. She knew when to plant an idea herself, and when it was more effective to recruit others to do it for her. She knew when to pressure her husband, and when to withdraw and regroup. What she rarely did was give up. In 1982, the year after he won his huge tax cut, Ronnie was under pressure to reverse himself and strike a budget deal with Congress that included what was one of the largest tax hikes in US history. The legislation would restore one-third of the reductions signed into law the year before. Baker and Deaver decided that the president should sign it; that it was needed as a corrective to having gone too far in 1981. As Baker recalled, they feared that leaving the tax reductions in place would worsen and prolong the recession: "We cut taxes way beyond where we said we were going to do in the campaign because we got into a bidding war with the Democrats, and then we had to come back and recoup some of them. The Gipper didn't want to do it. We all thought we needed to because we were afraid the markets were going to punish us."

Baker and Deaver convinced Nancy that it was crucial to change Ronnie's mind on this, so she too started pressuring her husband to sign the legislation. "We finally got him to do it because she joined with us. We were united," Baker said. But Ronnie wasn't happy. He took his glasses off and threw them across the top of his desk. "All right. Goddamn it. I'm going to do it," the president said. "But it's wrong." The tax hike was sold as "tax reform" rather than what it really was, which was an about-face on a signature issue of his presidency. Under fire from conservatives, Ronnie defended his decision to sign the bill as "the price we had to pay" to get Congress to go along with further spending cuts. But lawmakers reneged on their promise to trim spending by $3 for every $1 they raised taxes, and signing the bill turned out to be one of Ronnie's greatest regrets. It became one of Baker's, too: "He was right, and we were wrong."

Nancy would weigh in frequently when she was concerned that Ronnie was becoming too closely associated with highly ideological or unpopular causes. Baker noted: "She was with us on actions that tended to dull the hard edge that some [urged] on him—hard-core right-wingers particularly. Abortion was a tough issue for us. He was a strong right-to-lifer, but you didn't see him going down and marching with Nellie Gray," the antiabortion activist who founded the annual "March for Life." The demonstration took place each year around the January 22 anniversary of the Supreme Court's 1973 *Roe v. Wade* decision that legalized abortion throughout the country. Tens of thousands of anti-abortion activists from across the United States would show up for it, braving frigid winter temperatures on the National Mall just south of the White House. Gray's organizers were eager to have Ronnie speak to the crowd in person, which would have provided a powerful and indelible image in the media. Nancy preferred for him to keep his distance.

There is no evidence that Nancy tried to change her husband's mind on the abortion issue itself—nor could she have, given his deep convictions on it. But he already had the Christian Right firmly in his corner; to emphasize his opposition to abortion would only serve to alienate the majority of voters who had more conflicted feelings about it or who supported keeping it legal. So, she helped Baker and Deaver persuade Ronnie to address the March for Life by telephone from inside the White House, with his remarks broadcast over a loudspeaker. It set a precedent for Republican presidents. Not until Donald Trump in 2020 would one show up to speak to the marchers in person.

Abortion foes were disappointed at how little Ronnie talked about the issue at all. As the president and his advisers were working on the 1987 State of the Union address at Camp David, Ronnie mentioned that he would like to add a line about abortion. Speechwriter Ken Khachigian recalled that Nancy, who was standing behind her husband when he proposed this idea, shook her head vigorously in opposition. According to Don Regan, who by then had replaced Jim Baker as chief of staff, the first lady was even blunter in a comment she made to him: "I don't give a damn about the right-to-lifers." At any rate, the State of the Union address that year made no mention of abortion. As noted earlier, it was not until 1994, more than five years after Ronnie left office, that Nancy would air her own differences with her husband on the subject. "I'm against abortion," she said during an appearance before a George Washington University class. "On the other hand, I believe in a woman's choice."

Nancy also dreaded Ronnie appearing before the raucous gatherings of the Conservative Political Action Conference. It was an annual convention, begun in 1974, where the Right came together to exult in its influence. "She couldn't stand that group," said presidential assistant Kuhn. "She would go to the dinners, yes. They were really pushy, and they felt like they owned Reagan." What annoyed Nancy most was that in CPAC's own telling of history, it helped create Ronald Reagan. She felt the opposite was true. Kuhn recalled the first lady telling Ronnie after one CPAC event: "They're here because of you. You're not here because of them. Not one bit."

Within the White House, Nancy was wary of those who wanted her husband to stand inflexibly on principle. That included some of Ronnie's truest believers. There was no one more loyal to Ronnie than presidential counselor Meese. From Sacramento on, he had been among the greatest boosters of the idea of Ronnie as the Moses who could lead American conservatism to the promised land. While officials in the White House such as budget director David Stockman and staff secretary Richard Darman privately slighted the president's intellect and abilities, Meese would acknowledge no defect or weakness in this modern prophet. He once told a reporter: "On background, I want to say that the president is really doing a wonderful job." But to Nancy, putting Ronnie on a pedestal for the Right to worship him was only setting him up for a fall. She also shared her husband's view that getting part of what he wanted through compromise was better than walking away with nothing at all. "Ed and I were never close," she wrote of Meese. "He was by far the most ideological member of the troika, a jump-off-the-cliff-with-the-flag-flying conservative. Some people are so rigid in their beliefs that they'd rather lose than win a partial victory, and I always felt that Meese was one of them."

Nor did it help that Meese did not always show the best judgment when it came to maintaining the president's image as a decisive and in-command leader. In August 1981 two navy F-14 fighter jets engaged in an air battle off the coast of Libya and shot down two Libyan fighters. It was late at night in the United States, and Meese made the decision not to wake Ronnie for another five and a half hours. Nancy did not forgive Meese for the ridicule that followed. "There are only two reasons you wake President Reagan: World War III and if *Hellcats of the Navy* is on the *Late Show*," television host Johnny Carson joked. Early in Ronnie's second term, Meese moved over to the Justice Department as attorney general. It was a happier fit all around, allowing him to pursue his chief passion, which was translating conservative philosophy into concrete social policies.

During the Reagan years, the senior White House aides and Cabinet secretaries who fared the best tended to be the ones who figured out how to deal with Nancy's concerns and who respected her instincts about what was best for Ronnie. There is a long list of those who did not, and her unseen hand was behind many of their departures. Most famous would be her epic battle in late 1986 and early 1987 to oust White House chief of staff Don Regan during the Iran-contra scandal. But by then, she had become well practiced in the art of making her internal adversaries disappear.

The first of them had been short-lived national security adviser Richard Allen, who resigned in January 1982 amid the controversy over the payment from a Japanese magazine that was stashed in his safe. Nancy was even less enamored with Allen's hard-line successor, William Clark, who had been Ronnie's chief of staff in the California governor's office. But given her husband's long relationship with Clark, she had to be patient. As George Shultz, the secretary of state who later became one of her most important allies, wrote: "Ronald Reagan, with his soft heart, would never fire Clark, but at some point, Nancy would prevail upon him to act in his own interest." Nancy sensed that she would not have to wait him out for long. Clark himself had a restless nature, and an opportunity to move out of the White House came along thanks to an opening created by the departure of James Watt as interior secretary.

Gaffe-prone Watt was another hiring blunder on Ronnie's part—and another one that Nancy helped to rectify. He was a nightmare for environmentalists and a running embarrassment for the administration. In 1983 Watt banned the Beach Boys, a beloved American rock-and-roll treasure, from playing at the annual Fourth of July celebration on the National Mall. Though they had performed there for the previous three years, Watt said they might attract the "wrong element." In their place, he said, would be a "wholesome program" featuring Las Vegas crooner Wayne Newton. The White House Press Office let it be known that Nancy had personally called Watt to let him know that she was a Beach Boys fan. The secretary of the interior emerged from his next meeting with Ronnie carrying a plaster of paris foot with a hole in it. And indeed, he had shot himself in the foot. To deepen his mortification, Nancy invited the band to headline an event at the White House for the Special Olympics on June 12. The Beach Boys dedicated their opening song, "California Girls," to the first lady. Ronnie joked that they had shown up early for Independence Day and told them: "If you didn't believe that our whole family had been fans of yours for a long time, just look at Nancy."

Not such a laughing matter was Watt's comment at a September 21 US Chamber of Commerce breakfast, where he proclaimed the administration's coal advisory commission had "every kind of mix you can have. I have a black, I have a woman, two Jews, and a cripple. And we have talent." Senator Paul Laxalt, who had been a sponsor and defender of Watt, was soon on the phone with Nancy to discuss who might replace him. With internal polling showing that the interior secretary had become a drag on Ronnie's reelection chances, Watt was gone by mid-October.

Bill Clark stepped into the job, which meant that Nancy saw two problems solved at once. Watt was gone entirely, and, at least as importantly to her, Clark was out of the White House. "In Reagan's mind, he was Cabinet, he was still part of the team," Kuhn said, "and as far as Nancy's concerned, he can't do too much harm, hopefully." She also knew that Clark would soon get antsy again. By early 1985, he decided he'd had enough of Washington. He told Ronnie that he wanted to return to his barley and cattle ranch in California rather than stick around for the second term.

There were others. What was right, in Nancy's view, was less important than what was necessary. Labor Secretary Raymond J. Donovan stepped down in March 1985 as he was being investigated for fraud and grand larceny. Nancy was glad to see him go. "In politics, even the appearance of wrongdoing can be enormously damaging. I could see that this was going to be a long, drawn-out ordeal which would severely limit Donovan's effectiveness in the Cabinet," Nancy wrote. "The Donovan affair, which dragged on for months, was draining both to Ronnie personally and to the office of the president. Donovan resigned when the indictment was handed down, but as I told Ronnie on any number of occasions, it would have been better for everyone if he'd stepped down earlier." Two years later, Donovan would be acquitted and ask the plaintive question: "Which office do I go to to get my reputation back?" While Nancy felt sorry for him, she did not regret pushing for his removal. "When a political appointee turns out to be more of a problem than an asset, even if it's not his fault, he should step aside," she contended.

Getting rid of Secretary of State Al Haig had been another project on Nancy's to-do list. The retired four-star army general and former NATO commander had a reputation as a self-promoting leaker, prone to saying disparaging things about Ronnie to make himself look good. No doubt Nancy was also put off by the fact that Haig did not bother to hide his own presidential ambitions. The first lady would write later that the appointment of power-hungry Haig was "Ronnie's biggest mistake in the first term."

In her memoir, Nancy delivered a long bill of particulars: "Haig was obsessed with matters of status—with exactly where he stood on a receiving line, or where he was seated on a plane or helicopter. If he didn't think his seat was important enough, he'd let you know. He had a prickly personality and was always complaining that he was being slighted.

"He also struck me as eager for military action. In the first month of Ronnie's administration, he apparently implied to Tip O'Neill that he wanted to invade Nicaragua. Tip, and many others in Washington, assumed that Haig spoke for Ronnie. But in reality, Haig alarmed Ronnie and his top advisers with his belligerent rhetoric. Once, talking about Cuba in a meeting of the National Security Council, he turned to Ronnie and said, 'You just give me the word, and I'll turn that f____ island into a parking lot.'

"If Ronnie had given him the green light, Haig would have bombed everybody and everything."

She was far from the only one in the White House who wanted Haig out. He had gotten the job in part on a memo of recommendation from Richard Nixon. Ronnie's diaries show that the secretary of state was an irritant from the start, constantly testing the president's patience. After one of his early phone calls with Haig, Ronnie wrote in his diary: "He talked of resigning. Frankly I think he's seeing things that aren't there. He's Sec. of St. and no one is intruding on his turf—foreign policy is his, but he has half the Cabinet teed off."

Eventually Haig threatened to quit one too many times. Ronnie finally took him up on it in June 1982. The president noted wryly and with relief in his diary: "Up to Camp David where we were in time to see Al read his letter of resignation on TV. I'm told it was his 4th rewrite. Apparently his 1st letter was pretty strong—then he thought better of it. I must say it was O.K. He gave only one reason and did say there was a disagreement on foreign policy. Actually the only disagreement was over whether I made policy or the Sec. of State did."

George Shultz, who replaced Haig, was a man of accomplishments deep and broad: PhD in economics from the Massachusetts Institute of Technology; former dean of the University of Chicago Graduate School of Business; secretary of labor, budget director, and Treasury secretary in the Nixon administration; followed by a stint as the president of the global engineering firm Bechtel Corporation. When Shultz replaced the hard-line Haig as the nation's chief diplomat, he was shrewd enough to use his diplomatic skills on the influential first lady as well. He quickly became a personal favorite of Nancy's and is one of the few top Reagan administration officials that she wrote about with unbridled admiration in her memoir *My Turn*: "I trusted George completely; if he said it was raining, I didn't have to look out the window."

Beyond her protectiveness and vigilance, there were other things people noticed about how Nancy dealt with those around her husband. "She was tougher on women that worked with him and for him than she was on men," her son, Ron, told me. "Men she got along with pretty well, unless they did something that really crossed her or him. Women, she was much more wary of." Ron suspected there might have been some "totally unfounded paranoia" on Nancy's part, given that while his father did not disguise his appreciation of female beauty, he was "the last person on the face of the earth who would ever have cheated on his wife." One of the women with whom she waged a long-running cold war was the comely Helene von Damm, who had been Ronnie's secretary in Sacramento. Von Damm did that same job briefly after he became president and then moved to a loftier post running the Office of Presidential Personnel for the next two years. She was part of the dwindling old crowd from California, a hard-line conservative, and she considered Nancy "a schemer married to someone who was unable to conceive of a Machiavellian thought."

Nancy was furious when Ronnie appointed his former secretary as ambassador to von Damm's native Austria in 1983. To Ronnie, it was the culmination of an inspiring story about an immigrant who endured Soviet occupation and came to America with dreams of a better life. Von Damm was an early believer in Ronnie and moved across the country to volunteer for his first gubernatorial campaign. At the State Department, however, Austria experts were skeptical that von Damm was the right pick to represent the United States in a country known for its adherence to propriety. The first lady summoned von Damm to the residence for a "private talk" and told her to turn down the ambassadorship. Nancy said the president needed von Damm to stay in her current job and added that maybe there might be another assignment for her in the future.

"I could only conclude that for some reason this posting was something she simply didn't want me to have. Apparently, in her eyes, my career had progressed far enough. I felt as if someone had slapped me in the face," von Damm wrote later. Nancy never took another one of her calls. Nor did the first lady go with Ronnie to von Damm's swearing-in in the State Dining Room.

Once in the job, von Damm did some impressive work, bringing Frank Sinatra to Vienna for a charity concert and building goodwill by helping with projects for schools and museums. She was regarded, as she once put it, like "a homecoming queen." But she kept hearing from her sources back in Washington that Nancy was still working to undermine her. "Her position was hardening toward me: more and more with each new success I achieved," von Damm recalled.

Then again, perhaps Nancy's instincts were right once again. Von Damm got tongues wagging in Vienna when she left her third husband to marry young and wealthy Peter Gürtler, the owner of the city's famous Hotel Sacher. The ambassador was also photographed wearing a shockingly low-cut gown to the Vienna Opera Ball. Her defense was that décolletage is an old tradition at the ball, and "anything less would have seemed underdressed." Shultz finally told her that the president thought it would be a good idea for her to step down. When von Damm resigned in July 1985, *Newsweek*'s headline proclaimed "Die Playgirl Bows Out!" On top of everything, Gürtler left her not long after. He remarried, and shot himself to death in 1990.

Von Damm was not the only woman in the administration to feel a chilly vibe from Nancy. Chief of protocol Selwa "Lucky" Roosevelt, a daughter of Lebanese Druze immigrants who was married to a grandson of Theodore Roosevelt, recalled Deaver telling her: "Lucky, there's one thing you have to understand about Nancy. She doesn't really like dealing with women—she prefers to deal with men. Don't eat your heart out worrying about how Nancy feels about you or what you are doing. If you don't get any complaints, you can assume you're okay." Perhaps as a result of that warning, Roosevelt felt too intimidated to follow another piece of advice that Deaver gave her. He told her to call Nancy regularly, just to talk, because the first lady would love hearing the latest that Roosevelt was picking up from the social circles of New York and Washington. On the few occasions she did, Roosevelt was surprised at how friendly Nancy was and how happy she seemed to hear from her.

In 1990 Roosevelt wrote a memoir that made headlines with its criticism of Nancy, whom she described as "on guard, suspicious of anyone she thought was trying to use or manipulate her." But nearly three decades later, Roosevelt told me that she had grown to realize that she hadn't really understood Nancy and regretted having written those passages. "She really would have warmed up to me if I had made the effort to warm up to her," Roosevelt said. "I never had a chance to correct the misconceptions in my book. . . . The only part of that book I don't feel good about is my estimation of her."

For all her hostility toward the media, Nancy also selected a few favorites among journalists, for whom she became a source of tidbits and insights about the internal workings of the White House. First among them was columnist George F. Will. "The person that all of us giggled about was George Will. I think she had a big crush on him," Nancy's brother, Dick, told me. "They would have lunch together. It was all out in the open, but still. One Christmas, she left the president and my family alone. We were up in the living quarters, and she was downstairs showing George Will all the Christmas presents, the big cake, and so on and so forth." Kuhn recalled an instance when the ever-punctual Ronnie got impatient with his wife for delaying the liftoff of their helicopter so that she could finish a chat she was having with Will about thirty yards away. "Goddamn Sam, what's going on here?" Reagan asked Kuhn. "What the hell are they talking about?" Nancy also once had Kuhn personally deliver a Valentine card to Will's house.

"We had lots of lunches together. We went lots of places. We had lunch set up in Gunston Hall in Northern Virginia, George Mason's house," Will told me. (Mason, a statesman and delegate to the US Constitutional Convention of 1787, played an important if undersung role in the early United States.) "We spent a lot of time together; toured the battlefield at Bull Run." Nancy would also slip away from Camp David to have lunches with Will at the historic Yellow Brick Bank Restaurant in Shepherdstown, West Virginia. At a state dinner for Indonesian president Suharto in the fall of 1982, Nancy made sure Will was put at Ronnie's table. "This was a big honor, and all that stuff, and I hated it, because it was full of people just taking turns telling the president how wonderful he was, which bored him and bored everyone else," the columnist recalled. Will refused to go to another, until December 1988, when Nancy was able to lure him to one for Soviet leader Mikhail Gorbachev with a promise that she would seat Will, a consummate baseball fan, with Hall of Famer Joe DiMaggio.

*

Pretty much everyone who was in the know in Washington sensed Nancy's hand at work when Will wrote a scathing column in early 1986 about George H. W. Bush. It was a critical time for the vice president. With Ronnie in his second term, his Number Two was trying to lay the groundwork for his own run for the presidency. Will declared that Bush lacked any core principle beyond his unbridled desire for the top job: "The unpleasant sound Bush is emitting as he traipses from one conservative gathering to another is a thin, tinny 'arf'—the sound of a lapdog."

Nancy's distaste for the Bushes, which had been so evident on the convention stage the night Ronnie selected his pick for the 1980 ticket, had not abated. Nancy's and Barbara's hostility toward each other was one of the worst-kept secrets in Washington. "It's too bad, but it was what it was. No doubt about it, it was not a warm and friendly relationship," James Baker told me. "The Bushes felt that Nancy treated Barbara rather shabbily."

One explanation—perhaps the simplest—is that the acrid taste of the 1980 primary battle between their husbands still lingered for both women. It was always clear to Nancy which of the two men Barbara thought should be sitting in the Oval Office rather than attending funerals of foreign leaders as a stand-in for the other. "I think in politics, the political wives often form more lasting animosities than their husband-competitors do," Will speculated, when I asked him about the rivalry. "I've always thought that the reason you don't want women in combat is they wouldn't obey the rules of order. They're too fierce."

George H. W. Bush told his biographer Jon Meacham that the tone of the relationship had been set early. He got a startling visit right after the 1980 election from Kitchen Cabinet member William Wilson. "It turned out he was carrying water for Nancy on this. The message was, 'Stay out of the paper, get a lower profile, back down. Tell the Shrubs to keep a lower profile,'" Bush said. "We weren't taking a high profile, not doing the Washington thing of saying this or that, and it burned me up, and it burned Barbara up. She was very unhappy about it, deservedly so. We couldn't back down if we hadn't backed forward. We hadn't done anything. Hadn't done a damn thing. And I was very careful about that, always. Still don't know what drove that. But Nancy and Barbara just did not have a pleasant relationship."

If Nancy wanted the Bushes to keep their heads down, it may have been in reaction to the vice president's undisguised ambition to run in 1988 for the job he had failed to win in 1980. Nancy was suspicious that Bush put his own future ambitions above the imperative of contributing to Ronnie's current success, and that the Bushes were counting the days until the Reagans would leave. She also told family members of one conversation with Barbara that offended and infuriated her. During the Iran-contra scandal, the lowest point of the Reagan presidency, Barbara suggested that Ronnie should consider the possibility of resigning, Nancy claimed. That way, the vice president could assume the nation's highest office and then run in 1988 as an incumbent. It is hard to imagine that even blunt-spoken Barbara Bush would have been so direct and insensitive at what was a fragile moment for the Reagans. But the fact that Nancy took whatever Barbara did say that way, or that Barbara might have implied anything that could be so interpreted, spoke to the depth of their mutual mistrust.

The tensions put White House chief of staff Jim Baker, who was also Bush's closest friend and adviser, in a difficult spot. "When I first went in there, I bent over backward to make sure everybody knew that my loyalty was with Ronald Reagan and not with George Bush, but I also did everything I could behind the scenes to help the vice president, like making sure he had a private meeting with the president every week," Baker said. "They cemented a really wonderful relationship. He was the perfect vice president. You never saw him out there being quoted on anything. He never said anything in internal meetings because he knew nothing was secret, and so he always gave his recommendations [privately] to the president. The president came to really rely on him." The real problem, Baker insisted, was not between the president and the vice president, but between their wives.

In talking to people who had known both women, I sensed that there were undercurrents deeper than politics to their enmity. Pretty much everything about Barbara Bush triggered Nancy's insecurities, her sense of inadequacy and self-doubt. The vice president's wife was an old-money WASP who could trace her ancestry to the *Mayflower*.

Nancy would always be associated with the parvenu culture of Hollywood. Where Nancy got torn apart by the media, she complained to friends that Barbara was bathed with glowing coverage. It annoyed Nancy that stories about Barbara never seemed to mention that she, like the first lady, had a closet full of expensive designer dresses. ("I wonder if it ever occurred to her that George Bush paid for my clothes," rather than accepting donations from designers, Barbara fumed in her diary.) And then there was the fact that the Bushes were a constant reminder of what a tight-knit, functional family looked like.

"Nancy does not like Barbara," George Bush wrote in his journal in June 1988. "She feels that Barbara has the very things that she, Nancy, doesn't have, and that she'll never be in Barbara's class. . . . Bar has sensed it for a long time. Barbara is so generous, so kind, so unselfish, and, frankly, I think Nancy Reagan is jealous of her." That is a testament to Bush's admiration for his wife, but not exactly a full picture of Barbara's character. Despite her image as America's grandmother, Barbara Bush had a sharp tongue, an imperious manner, and instilled fear in those around her. "Barbara could be kind of a bulldozer in private, and you weren't going to shove Nancy Reagan around," recalled Ronnie's assistant Jim Kuhn.

In public appearances, Barbara Bush often made jokes about the comparison between her own frumpy wardrobe and Nancy's glamorous outfits. Her self-deprecating schtick had an unmistakable edge. Once, on a 1986 trip to New Hampshire, Barbara went back to the press section of Air Force Two and entertained the reporters there with a brutal imitation of the first lady. The *Washington Post*'s Lou Cannon later warned Barbara that a lot of people had heard this, which meant it was certain to get back to Nancy through her extensive network of internal spies. Barbara replied: "I know."

The Bushes were almost never invited to the White House residence while the Reagans were living there. On Christmas Eve 1988, after George Bush was elected president, he told Edmund Morris that Ronnie was "a prince of a feller; I'd never say anything against him. Nancy neither." But then there was a pause, as he and Barbara exchanged glances. "Well, sometimes," the president elect confided, "I kinda wished they'd shown . . . y'know, a little appreciation. Didn't seem to want us upstairs in the White House."

There were other snubs as well. When journalist Susan Page was researching a biography of Barbara Bush in 2018, she found in Reagan Library files the drafts of the invitation list for a November 9, 1985, White House dinner honoring Prince Charles and Princess Diana. It was a much-anticipated social event. At that time, the British princess was seen as the biggest celebrity in the entire world. On the first version of the guest list, the names of the vice president and his wife were crossed out with a black pen. On the second and the third, the Bushes were relegated to "suggested additions." It is impossible to tell whether Nancy deleted the names of the Bushes with her own hand, but it was clearly her intention to exclude them. Deaver warned Nancy that she simply could not slight the second couple in such a public way. "Just watch me," she said. Her chief of staff, James Rosebush, also made an appeal to include them on the eighty-person invitation list, and Nancy shut him down as well. So, the party went on without the Bushes.

The enduring image of the night was Diana, in a dark-blue velvet gown and pearl choker, being spun on the dance floor by actor John Travolta. The awestruck star of the 1977 disco movie hit *Saturday Night Fever* had not planned to do this; it seemed presumptuous to ask a princess to dance. But Nancy told him Diana was hoping he would. Suddenly Travolta realized: "This was the plan—that I was the Prince Charming of the evening." So he took Diana's hand, and the rest of the guests gathered round as they danced for almost fifteen minutes. It was like something out of a fairy tale, but one where the magic had happened by design. No one knew better than Nancy that storybook endings don't come about by accident. Sometimes they need a nudge.

CHAPTER FOURTEEN

If the first year of her husband's presidency had been swallowed by trauma and controversy, the second would see Nancy begin to find her footing. The turnaround started with a brilliant gambit to disarm her toughest adversaries. As she put it: "It isn't often in life that one is lucky enough to enjoy a second beginning, but during one five-minute period in the spring of 1982, I was able to make a fresh start with the Washington press corps."

This unlikeliest of opportunities came in late March, at an annual dinner put on by the Gridiron Club. The club was and is an elite organization (at least in its own regard) of Washington journalists. It exists pretty much for the purpose of presenting an annual evening of skits and songs at a white-tie dinner for six hundred of the most powerful people in politics and media. With the exception of Grover Cleveland, who despised the press and didn't care to pretend otherwise, every president since Benjamin Harrison in the early 1890s has attended and spoken; the Reagans went all eight years of his presidency.

The idea for the first lady to make a surprise appearance on stage was the brainchild of her press secretary, Sheila Tate. Nancy had lately generated yet another embarrassment for the White House, when it was revealed that she had been "borrowing" designer dresses and not returning them. A practice that would not have raised eyebrows in Hollywood made Nancy look even more out of touch with average Americans. "I remember having to say to Mike [Deaver], 'We've got to get a handle on this. We've got to do something about it. We've got to give them back or something,'" recalled Jim Baker. The first lady's office offered an unconvincing cover story, which was that Nancy had planned all along to donate the expensive dresses to museums as part of an effort to promote the American fashion industry.

Tate knew the fresh controversy would be irresistible fodder for ridicule at the dinner, and she was right. The club was planning to have a singer pretend to be Nancy and deliver a parody of the 1920s-era Fanny Brice song "Second Hand Rose." The Gridiron Club rendition went like this:

> Second-hand clothes
> I give my second-hand clothes
> To museum collections and traveling shows
> They were oh so happy that they got 'em
> Won't notice they were ragged at the bottom.
> Good-bye, you old worn-out mess
> I never wear a frock more than once.
> Calvin Klein, Adolfo, Ralph Lauren, and Bill Blass.
> Ronald Reagan's mama's going strictly first class.
> Rodeo Drive, I sure miss Rodeo Drive
> In frumpy Washington.
> Second-hand rings.
> Donate those old used-up things.
> Designers deduct 'em.
> We're living like kings.
> So what if Ronnie's cutting back on welfare.
> I'd still wear a tiara in my coiffed hair.
> Second-hand frock,
> Press critics are such a crock,
> Why don't they just hush up and go away?

Calvin Klein, Adolfo, Ralph Lauren, and Bill Blass
Ronald Reagan's mama's going strictly first class
Rodeo Drive, I'll be back, Rodeo Drive
In nineteen eighty-five.

When Tate got her hands on a copy of those lyrics, she recognized the implication in that last line. It suggested that his wife's hauteur might cost Ronnie a chance at a second term. Nancy, Deaver, and Baker all loved the idea of having the first lady turn the tables by singing a rebuttal. The Gridiron Club's officers proposed that Nancy offer a rejoinder about "second-hand news," blow the audience a kiss, and saunter off on the arms of two performers dressed as bellmen—in other words, to tell the journalists they could go to hell.

Nancy's spokeswoman thought that was a terrible idea. "As soon as I read this, I knew we were going to take an entirely different tack, but we never told the Gridiron in advance. Nancy needed to make fun of herself, not blame the press," Tate recalled. For more than a week, Tate and speechwriter Landon Parvin worked in secret with Nancy in the study of the White House residence. Nancy nixed lines in Parvin's first cut at it, which made fun of her fancy friends, and called out Betsy Bloomingdale and Jerry Zipkin by name. She also insisted that the song refer to "the" china, not "my" china, as Parvin originally wrote. He came back with another draft, which they rehearsed with her recently named chief of staff, James Rosebush, playing the piano. Social secretary Muffie Brandon scrounged up an over-the-top, tacky ensemble for Nancy to wear: a loud aqua skirt with red and yellow flowers, white pantaloons with butterflies, rubber rainboots, a ragged feather boa, and a double string of fake pearls that hung nearly to her knees. Nancy topped it off with a feathered red hat that her staff had given her for her birthday as a joke.

The first lady kept her plan secret even from her husband. When the night of the dinner arrived, she was too nervous to eat as she sat at the head table with Ronnie and the Bushes. The event was, as usual, an all-star gathering of Washington bigwigs. Among the guests were

Soviet ambassador Anatoly Dobrynin, nine other foreign ambassadors, four Supreme Court justices, and most of the Cabinet. When the club's singer performed her song about the first lady's shopping habits, Nancy slipped away, setting off a buzz among her head-table neighbors that she had been offended by the lyrics. Tate heard one newspaper publisher whisper to another: "Nancy Reagan just left. I bet she's pissed!"

So they—and everyone else in the audience—were unprepared when a petite woman in a bag-lady costume suddenly stepped through a rack of clothes onstage and called out to the bandleader: "Let me see that score!" As it sank in who was standing before them in that outlandish getup, the room went silent. Then came a standing ovation that quieted down as Nancy began to sing:

> I'm wearing second-hand clothes
> Second-hand clothes
> They're quite the style
> In the spring fashion shows.
> Even my new trench coat with fur collar
> Ronnie bought for ten cents on the dollar.
> Second-hand gowns
> And old hand-me-downs
> The china is the only thing that's new.
> Even though they tell me that I'm no longer queen,
> Did Ronnie have to buy me that new sewing machine?
> Second-hand clothes, second-hand clothes,
> I sure hope Ed Meese sews.

For her big finish, Nancy threw a china plate, which had a pattern similar to her controversial White House selection, to the floor. Though it didn't smash as it was supposed to, that brought another standing ovation. Then came calls for an encore, something Parvin hadn't thought to write. So Nancy did the whole thing over again, the second time breaking the plate to pieces—and putting, at last, the first crack in her reputation as an ice queen.

"This one song, together with my willingness to sing it, served as a signal to opinion makers that maybe I wasn't the terrible, humorless woman they thought I was," Nancy wrote later. "From that night on, my image began to change in Washington." Ronnie was delighted. When he rose to give his speech, he began: "I was surprised when I learned I was coming here as a happy husband and leaving as a Stage Door Johnny." Later, he mused in his diary: "Maybe this will end the sniping."

The criticism of Nancy didn't end, not entirely, but a strategy was finally taking hold that would begin to change the country's perceptions about its first lady. Nancy had already begun to get more active promoting her chosen cause: fighting drug abuse among the young. In the past, she had always avoided giving speeches, preferring to talk to audiences in question-and-answer sessions. Now she had to get over her nervousness about presenting her own ideas in public. She found herself turning to Parvin frequently for help, and he tried to break her in slowly by giving her brief sets of remarks. "In those early years, it was just one page, big spaces in between all over, indents, because she wasn't comfortable giving speeches. So we started out with very little stuff," he recalled.

Her commitment to the antidrug cause, however, was genuine and deeply felt. As the daughter of a doctor, Nancy saw the nation's health as an issue that could be shaped by both public policy and personal example. At her decree, the souvenir packs of cigarettes that had been given away on Air Force One since the Kennedy years were replaced by M&M's. She had been concerned about drug abuse since her days in Sacramento, having seen the toll it had taken on many of her Hollywood friends and their families. Nancy also recalled the advice she had received during the 1980 campaign from veteran White House reporter Helen Thomas: "If your husband is elected, you will have a platform that is given to very few people. You should think about what you want to do with it. You'll never be given this kind of opportunity again."

There was a paradox in Nancy's choice of a cause. Going back as far as those stressful times in the 1950s, she herself had been dependent on prescription medications, and she remained so while she was in the

White House. Reagan biographer Edmund Morris shared notes with me of an interview that he conducted with Deaver on June 7, 1989, in which Deaver told Morris that anxiety-ridden Nancy subsisted on "uppers and downers." She took a pill to fall asleep, Deaver said, and then woke up in the middle of the night to take another.

Her use of these drugs was serious enough to become a worry to at least two of the White House physicians who served under Ronnie. According to what Deaver told Morris, presidential physician Daniel Ruge became so "nervous and concerned" about her heavy use of medication that he went to the president with a warning that his wife had a problem. Morris found no evidence that Ronnie did anything about it. Her brother, Dick, a doctor, told me Ruge had not shared any such worries with him. However, Dick did not dismiss the possibility that Nancy had grown addicted to medication or that his father's former medical partner would have taken action to put a stop to it: "Whether this accounts for some of the fluctuations in her mood over the years, I can't say, but I'm sure Dr. Ruge would use the best possible judgment if he felt she was taking too much in the way of diet pills or sleeping pills. He certainly would have given her good advice, and perhaps that was the reason she didn't care for him at all."

At a later point, John Hutton, one of Ruge's successors in the job, attempted to wean her off the sleeping pill Dalmane. However, Nancy had been taking so much and for so long that she had a violent reaction to withdrawal. According to a former White House aide who says Hutton told him about the matter, the doctor was left with no choice but to put her back on the drug.

On overseas trips, Nancy was intent on making sure her jet-lagged husband got adequate rest, so she would occasionally share her Dalmane with Ronnie. Sometimes, the president—unaccustomed to the long-acting drug—would show the effects the next day. "He couldn't handle it very well. One wasn't enough, because you know, he was a pretty good-sized guy, so he would take two, and he would wake up the next morning, and he was really kind of hung over, kind of groggy, and his balance was off," the aide said. "It happened two or three times." One such episode occurred in 1988 in Moscow, where Ronnie was holding a summit with Soviet leader Mikhail Gorbachev. It was a moment when the chief executive needed to be at the top of his game. The woozy president stumbled on a stair in the Kremlin, and the aide was relieved that there weren't any cameras around.

As Nancy described the dimensions of the drug problem in her appearances around the country, she did not address abuse of prescription medications, which decades later would contribute to an opioid crisis across the country. At that time, however, she was far from alone in assuming that taking something under a doctor's direction was benign and not in the same category as illicit use. Her daughter, however, saw a connection between Nancy's drug dependence and her choice of a cause. "I always felt that it was a subconscious cry for help," Patti wrote in her 1992 memoir. "It's not insignificant that Michael Deaver, now a recovering alcoholic, helped craft the crusade. The whole thing was a road map of denial."

Whatever forces were at work to draw Nancy to fighting drug abuse, it was a tricky issue for her to take on. She was assuming a high profile on the problem at the same time that her husband was cutting social programs, including making drastic reductions in those that dealt with drug abuse education, prevention, and treatment. Ronnie's administration was approaching the nation's narcotics problem as a law-and-order matter more than a health issue. Under Attorney General William French Smith, who had been part of the Kitchen Cabinet in California, the FBI got more heavily involved in the fight against drugs, and five hundred new agents were added to the Drug Enforcement Administration. Thirteen regional task forces were set up across the country, combining agents from the DEA; the US Customs Service; the Bureau of Alcohol, Tobacco, and Firearms; the Internal Revenue Service; and the army and the navy. There were record numbers of seizures and convictions, but the problem of illegal narcotics use and addiction in the inner city remained just as great.

Larger societal trends were also at work in the early 1980s. Nancy launched her campaign at a time when the nation's attitudes about drugs—particularly marijuana—were evolving. In the previous decade, cannabis use had become so common across the country that a dozen states passed laws decriminalizing small amounts. More and more, it was being argued that the prosecution of otherwise law-abiding young people for a relatively harmless recreational drug was a waste of resources that could otherwise be spent combating more dangerous ones, such as heroin and cocaine. There was also pressure to change the federal law under which marijuana possession could result in up to a year in prison or a fine of up to $5,000. In his 1976 campaign, Jimmy Carter advocated decriminalizing marijuana, and in October 1977 the Senate Judiciary Committee voted for an amendment that would have made possession of up to one ounce of weed a civil rather than a criminal offense, with a maximum fine of $100.

Then came a backlash and a growing mobilization of concerned parents who feared for the safety of their children. More and more young people were taking up pot, at earlier and earlier ages, with potential long-term consequences. In the late 1970s and early 1980s, antidrug activists blamed popular culture—movies, television, rock music—for glamorizing drugs and luring kids into trying them. Some who advocated less tolerance formed what became known as the Parent Movement. It grew into a potent political force in communities across the country and succeeded in retoughening marijuana laws in many places. Nancy had heard of the efforts of these parents and was intrigued by the idea of discouraging children from being attracted to drugs. She was convinced there were ways to accomplish that which did not involve government intervention and were rooted in traditional values.

Her partner within the White House was the man that Ronnie appointed as his drug abuse policy adviser in July 1981. Blunt-spoken Carlton Turner was born in Choctaw County, Alabama, and was a chemist by training. He had headed the Marijuana Research Project at the University of Mississippi and had actually grown pot to provide to government researchers. Turner had been arguing for years that marijuana was far more dangerous than much of the scientific community generally thought it was. But he did not believe that throwing more government dollars at the problem was the answer. "I used to say, 'Let me put it to you succinctly: the only person that has a vested interest in solving drug abuse is the parent or the family,'" he told me. "'Because the DEA will get more money, the bigger they can make the problem. Customs will get more money, the bigger they make the problems. And even though their job is to reduce drug abuse, the National Institute on Drug Abuse gets more money, the bigger they can make the problem. So the object for the federal bureaucracy is not to solve the problem. The object for a federal bureaucracy is to build their prestige, their power, and their influence and their budgets.'"

Shortly after Turner joined the White House, he was asked to meet with Nancy in the library of the family quarters. His boss, Martin Anderson, the assistant to the president for policy development, came with him, which Turner thought was a sign that Anderson was worried about what the new drug adviser might say. But it was Nancy who did most of the talking. A meeting that was supposed to last twenty minutes turned into an hour. The first lady shared what she had observed about the drug problem in California and elsewhere, and peppered Turner with questions. He was struck by her knowledge of the issue. Then she put it to him: "Carlton, we've been here nearly six months. When are you going to do something?" Turner, in fact, had been on the job for only two weeks at that point, but, he recalled, "That told me right away that I had to get busy."

Not much happened, however, until early 1982. Turner was preoccupied with carrying out Ronnie's order that he clean up the drug problem in the military. Nancy was concerned with her husband's recuperation from the assassination attempt and finishing up her redecoration of the White House. She had scheduled a few events around the issue in the early months of Ronnie's presidency, but they had been infrequent and generally got lost in all the negative coverage of her china purchase, her wardrobe, and the White House makeover.

With the arrival of Ronnie's second year in office, fixing Nancy's image problems had become a priority, though some top officials at the White House had misgivings about a first lady taking on a battle as dark and seemingly unwinnable as fighting drug abuse. Turner told Nancy's staff that the first thing she should do is get out of "this firing range"—the DC media—and "get out to where the real people live. You need to get her out to where people can see and she can feel." On his advice, Nancy took a two-day swing through Florida and Texas in February. It was only her second big trip on her own as first lady, the first having been the PR disaster of the royal wedding the previous summer.

In Saint Petersburg, she visited a facility for Straight Inc., one of the most well known of a growing number of programs around the country that took a "tough love" approach to young drug users. The kids, many of whom had been brought to the program against their will by their parents, were strip-searched on arrival and could not even go to the bathroom without being monitored. Straight Inc. was becoming controversial for using allegedly abusive tactics on young people and had already been sued by the American Civil Liberties Union.

Nancy—accompanied by almost a dozen Secret Service agents, 20 members of the press, and 3 aides—met for nearly three hours in a hot auditorium with 650 parents and 350 kids enrolled in the Straight program. What she heard was horrifying and heartbreaking. Asked whether they had ever gotten their younger brothers or sisters high, more than half of the young people raised their hands. Some said they had also given drugs to their pets and to children they babysat. Most also admitted to having been arrested or overdosing. They told of being high at the dinner table and hiding narcotics under a parent's mattress. Nearly all of them said they had started with pot. Each of their testimonies ended with the words "I am a druggie."

It was a cathartic event, punctuated by tearful apologies on the part of the children and forgiving hugs from their families. Nancy "just cried. I mean, she just balled up and cried. And you could see the emotion flowing out of her," Turner said. "She really knew she was doing something right. She had it in her gut that she was doing something right, and she had to do it." Something else happened, Turner added: "In the plane back from Dallas, this transformation occurred.

She went out and talked to the press on her own. That's the first time. She felt secure."

News about Nancy was all over local and national newspapers and on television. And for the first time in a long time, it wasn't negative. A picture of the first lady surrounded by children in a school classroom spread across three columns of the front page of the *New York Times*. In the *Washington Post,* reporter Donnie Radcliffe wrote that Nancy "was finally being noticed more for her social awareness than her social life" and had "scored some stunning media successes as she observed the drug abuse programs. After months of publicity about her tastes in clothes, china, and White House redecorating had been contrasted with the country's growing economic problems, the first lady's often-stated interest in drug abuse prevention was claiming the headlines."

The morning after she returned from the trip, her staff took advantage of the new glow around Nancy to clean up one controversy that lingered. They announced that the first lady had decided she would no longer accept free designer clothes, because people were "misinterpreting" her efforts to draw a spotlight to the American fashion industry. (It was a promise she would break.)

Then her aides set about filling her schedule with more trips to promote her antidrug campaign. Nancy was soon venturing out across the country just about every other week, hitting sixty-five cities in thirty-five states over the course of her years as first lady. In 1983 she played herself on NBC's popular situation comedy *Diff'rent Strokes*, starring fourteen-year-old Gary Coleman, which had an audience of twenty-eight million and was the most popular show in the country among children between the ages of six and eleven. That same year, she shared anchoring duties on a broadcast of ABC's *Good Morning America* that was devoted entirely to the subject of drug abuse. With popular actor Michael Landon, who had starred on the long-running *Little House on the Prairie*, she cohosted a two-part program called *The Chemical People* that aired on three hundred public television stations. The number of community-based antidrug groups across the country tripled to three thousand. Nancy was also getting a thousand letters a month on the issue, which accounted for half the correspondence she received. "I've tried to get the message across through hundreds of interviews, tapings, speeches, events, and visits," she said in a speech to newspaper publishers in May 1987. "Every mile, every meeting has been worth it. My work against drugs has provided me with the most fulfilling years of my life."

Nancy also took her message global. In 1985 she hosted drug abuse "summits" at the White House and at the United Nations for dozens of wives of world leaders. These sessions were not without their moments of awkwardness and tension. Nicaraguan first lady Rosario Maria Murillo—whose husband, President Daniel Ortega, had been branded by Ronnie as "the little dictator who went to Moscow in his green fatigues"—told Nancy categorically that her country had no drug problem, thanks to its Marxist form of government. In truth, Nicaragua had a thriving cocaine trafficking industry, some of which was linked to top officials in Ortega's own government. The year before, DEA agents in Florida had seized 1,452 pounds of cocaine that had been flown in there from the Nicaraguan capital of Managua.

In October 1988, near the end of Ronnie's presidency, Nancy addressed the United Nations as the leader of the US delegation to a session on youth, families, and crime prevention. For someone who disliked speech making, this was a daunting moment. She was accompanied by George Shultz, who recalled that she insisted upon arriving an hour early. When she took her seat in the chamber, she noticed that it was nearly empty. Nancy turned to the secretary of state, her eyes brimming with tears. "George," she asked, "doesn't anybody want to hear what I have to say?"

"Don't worry, Nancy," he assured her. "When it's your turn, this place will be jammed."

Shultz was right. The delegates showed up and were spellbound. But the message that Nancy was there to deliver caused heartburn within her husband's administration. Where US officials had been pushing Asian and Latin American countries to get tougher on cutting off the supply of drugs coming into the United States, Nancy contended it was time for this country to quit blaming other ones for a homegrown problem. "Frankly, it is far easier for the United States to focus on coca fields grown by three hundred thousand campesinos in Peru than to shut down the dealer who can be found on the street corners of our cities," she told the UN delegates. "It is often easier to make strong speeches about foreign drug lords or drug smugglers than to arrest a pair of Wall Street investment bankers buying cocaine on their lunch break."

As Shultz recalled: "The drug bureaucracy in Washington went bananas." Before her speech, administration officials had pressured Ronnie to get his wife to tone down her words. "She stuck to her guns," Shultz said, and afterward, many of the delegates came up to her to thank her for her more balanced, honest view of the forces that were driving the drug market.

Though she was getting plenty of attention, Nancy struggled against the doubts that many, particularly in elite and liberal circles, continued to hold with regard to her credibility to speak on such a thorny and serious problem. Views of her work also split along party lines. When a 1983 *Washington Post* survey asked whether she visited drug centers "mostly to get better publicity for herself and her husband or mostly because she wants to help fight drug addiction," 65 percent of Republicans gave her credit for caring about the cause, while only 41 percent of Democrats did. Independents were about evenly split.

*

The skepticism would never lift entirely, and some efforts to improve her image and achieve recognition became especially uncomfortable. In 1982 her alma mater, Smith College, received a discreet feeler from White House social secretary Muffie Brandon, another alumna: Might Smith consider giving Nancy an honorary degree for her "very strong, very respectable, very worthy" work against drug abuse? Over the years, Nancy's relations with the increasingly progressive college had been strained. She stood apart as one of Smith's most famous graduates. But she never attended reunions or participated in alumnae activities. She complained to friends that Smith had not reached out to her, either. Not until 1978 did she even write a check to the college, and her $1,000 donation was accompanied by a note complaining that the speakers invited to campus were "tilted in one direction without any attempt to provide a balance to give the students a chance to hear differing viewpoints."

The college turned down Brandon's request to award Nancy an honorary degree, partly because it feared the first lady's appearance on campus would spark protests over her husband's policies. In a memo to Smith's president, Jill Ker Conway, dated April 26, 1982, the college's public affairs director, Ann Shanahan, described her conversation with Brandon this way:

> I said that we were trying very hard to think of the appropriate way to acknowledge her contribution as First Lady but that we had to consider the political climate, the cuts to Federal aid to education, etc., and that we didn't want to invite her into a situation where she would be embarrassed by picketing, etc. Muffie said that they understood the difficulties but reiterated that she felt that by a year from now an honorary degree would be 'very justifiable' for her work on drug abuse. I said that such a decision was made at a higher level than mine, but that I would certainly pass the information along.

Nancy was constantly asked how to square her concern about drug abuse with her husband's cuts to programs that were designed to deal with that and other social problems. In the fall of 1982, she and retired All-Pro football star Carl Eller went to Little Rock's Central High School. It was the site of a famous 1957 showdown between segregationist Arkansas governor Orval Faubus and President Eisenhower, who federalized the state's National Guard and deployed the US military to maintain order and protect nine African American students who were being denied entrance to the school, in violation of the 1954 *Brown v. Board of Education* Supreme Court decision.

On the day of Nancy's visit, a local African American activist named Robert McIntosh showed up wearing a devil costume and a rubber Ronald Reagan mask. "If they are that concerned about our youth and their future, then why did the president use his presidential power and cut out millions of dollars in summer jobs that you could have had?" McIntosh asked a group of about fifty students who were milling around outside the school.

Over and over, Nancy would reply to this kind of criticism with some version of a response she gave during a radio talk show interview in Des Moines: "I've never thought that money buys parent involvement and care. I just don't think money is the answer."

One quandary was how to brand her effort. It needed a slogan, maybe a catchword. Turner asked the National Institute on Drug Abuse to suggest something simple that would sum up the message. NIDA offered "Say no," which seemed too blunt and terse. A New York advertising firm was also brought in. But, as the origin story goes, inspiration finally sprang from the mouth of a babe. At a meeting with schoolchildren in Oakland, a girl raised her hand and asked the first lady what she should do if somebody offered her drugs.

"Well, you just say no," Nancy told her.

At the time, "it didn't enter anyone's mind that this would be the theme," says James Rosebush. But that three-word slogan—"Just Say No"—caught on and was pushed in a massive public service advertising campaign. By the end of Nancy's tenure as first lady, nearly fourteen thousand Just Say No clubs had formed in schools and youth organizations in all fifty states. Their total membership was estimated to be nearly 460,000 children, whose average age was nine years old. Nancy saw "Just Say No" as a mixed blessing. While it was memorable and catchy, she knew that it was also easy to dismiss as facile—and an unfairly glib summation of an effort that had many facets. "I never thought that the 'Just Say No' slogan would solve the drug problem. How silly!" she told syndicated columnist Liz Smith in 1990. "It was simply a phrase that caught on, but certainly there is much more to do about drugs. Public education and treatment centers are the answer."

Decades later, there remains a lot of doubt as to whether the "Just Say No" message really had an impact. Was social pressure an adequate substitute for putting more government resources into the fight to get children off drugs and keep them there? Did it portray drug use as a moral failure and personal choice rather than a mental-health concern? Was it family-friendly camouflage for the Reagan administration's "war on drugs" that incarcerated disproportionately large numbers of men of color?

While the question of how effective her campaign was will never really be settled, there is significant evidence that drug use among the young dropped sharply during the 1980s. The Monitoring the Future project, which is funded by the National Institute on Drug Abuse, has been conducting surveys of the problem since 1975. In 1979 more than 54 percent of high school seniors said they had used an illicit drug within the past twelve months; by 1992, that number had fallen by nearly half. Young people's attitudes about drug use shifted just as dramatically over that same period. Where only about a third of high school seniors in the late 1970s said they would disapprove of a friend trying marijuana, the percentage had more than doubled by the early 1990s.

Among the admirers of Nancy's efforts was Joseph A. Califano Jr., a prominent Democrat who served as top domestic policy adviser to Lyndon B. Johnson and health education and welfare secretary under Jimmy Carter. He is also the founder of the National Center on Addiction and Substance Abuse at Columbia University. "Just Say No" was more than empty words, Califano insisted. "It was a great message. It was simple, and it was clear, and it was what you wanted kids to do. It also sent a message to parents: 'This is what you should be telling your kids.'" In 1995 Califano asked Nancy to join his board of directors, where she served for five years. Betty Ford was also a member. Califano always sensed a tension between the two former first ladies, rooted no doubt in their personal history but also in how they viewed the drug problem. Nancy wanted to see more emphasis on preventing drug abuse; Betty Ford, on treating it.

Nancy also continued her involvement with the Foster Grandparents program, which she had promoted when she was California first lady. In late 1982 she and coauthor Jane Wilkie published a book, *To Love a Child*, to benefit the program. She also got Frank Sinatra to record a song with the same title. Her Hollywood connections—an asset that her predecessors did not have—were an important element in Nancy's efforts to bring visibility to the projects that she cared about and that were helping to repair her image. Most prominent among those friends in the entertainment industry was Sinatra, who became a fixture at the Reagan White House, planning the entertainment and adding wattage to presidential events. Ronnie had less use for him, though, and the White House aides who had to deal with Sinatra found having him around to be more trouble than it was worth. He was there largely because of Nancy, who had been enamored with him since the days when they were both working on the MGM lot. "She twinkles when he arrives," one friend told the *Washington Post.*

This created no small amount of tension with Sinatra's wife, Barbara, who was annoyed at all the things her husband was being called upon to do at Nancy's behest or on her behalf. "Nancy Reagan was never a close friend, and it had nothing to do with the fact that she seemed to have a crush on my husband. After all, I was quite used to that, and if I'd wanted to, I could have flirted right back with hers," Barbara Sinatra wrote in her memoir. "What I wasn't so accustomed to was the time and commitment she expected of Frank for the causes that she and Ronnie espoused. I felt that she took a little too much advantage of Frank's huge heart. As well as making him director of entertainment at the White House, Nancy appointed him to the President's Committee on the Arts and Humanities, and she got him involved in her Just Say No antidrug campaign, as well as her charitable organizations for children and foster grandparents. Frank was completely unfazed, of course. During their long-distance telephone calls and their lunches together whenever they were in the same town, I think he became Nancy's therapist more than her friend."

Author Kitty Kelley would later intimate in her book that there was more going on during those long lunches than dining and conversation. No one I spoke to seemed to give the likelihood of a sexual liaison much credence. But there was an emotional dependence between Sinatra and Nancy that seems to have gone both ways. The entertainer was one of the first people she summoned after the assassination attempt. Nancy was someone Sinatra turned to as well during difficult times. His daughter Tina—not a fan of her father's fourth wife—described Nancy as her father's "close confidante," and someone he leaned on for emotional support during the rough patches of his marriage to Barbara. In one particularly difficult stretch when the Sinatras were separated, Nancy Reagan and Frank Sinatra "were speaking every night, at an appointed time, and my father was pouring his heart out," Tina Sinatra wrote. (When Sinatra died in 1998, his widow tried to exclude Nancy from his funeral in Beverly Hills. Tina Sinatra insisted that the former first lady be invited.)

Being associated with the Reagans gave Sinatra a legitimacy he craved. He had never gotten over the humiliation he felt when the Kennedys threw him out of JFK's circle in the early 1960s, apparently because of his well-known friendships with crime bosses. Those unsavory associations were worrisome to Ronnie's advisers as well. At one point, White House counsel Fred Fielding got wind that Nancy and Sinatra were discussing the possibility of giving the entertainer a formal role in the Reagan administration, perhaps overseeing the arts.

"Deaver gave me the heads-up. He said Sinatra was over there for dinner with them, and Nancy had said something to him, and then to Mike, that he should come into the government in some way, shape, or form," Fielding recalled. "So I said, 'Well, bring him over, Mike,' and he came walking in, and we chatted for a while. I said, 'Listen, I think this is so great that you're willing to serve, and I'll tell you what, I'm going to get you the forms, and I'll walk you through them, and I'll help expedite the FBI investigation of you.' " At Fielding's mention of a Federal Bureau of Investigation background check, Deaver found it hard to stop himself from breaking out in laughter. That was the last they heard of Sinatra's interest in joining the administration.

*

Though Nancy, through her various projects, seemed to be gaining favor with the American public, Deaver and her East Wing team were constantly on the lookout for land mines. By now, they all were familiar with Nancy's tendencies to self-sabotage. The files at the Reagan Library include a memo sent to Deaver and Rosebush by staff secretary Richard Darman. It was dated March 3, 1982, a time when preparations for Ronnie's first big overseas trip were under way. Darman wrote:

> My dinner partner last night was Lady Mary Henderson, whom you know. She describes herself as a friend of Nancy Reagan's who likes her very much. She thinks, however, that it is particularly important that, in the coming European trip, Mrs. Reagan have the benefit of:
>
> —sophisticated press advice; and
> —a strong and effective person to deal with the press on the trip.
>
> She implied as clearly and politely as one could that Mrs. Reagan lacked both in her previous visit to England [for the royal wedding]. And she suggested that Mrs. Reagan needed to have someone like Tish Baldridge (or an unleashed Muffie Brandon) along on the trip.

Social secretary Brandon was dispatched to Europe a week early to nail down the first lady's itinerary and scout for potential problems. A party planned for Nancy at the home of a countess in Paris was scotched because it was deemed too fancy. Aides made sure Nancy's social activities would be interspersed with visits to drug rehabilitation centers in Rome and Bonn and a state-run facility for blind children in Paris. Nancy also made a pilgrimage to Normandy for the thirty-eighth anniversary of D-day and had a quiet visit with the widow of an American who had been murdered by terrorists in Paris earlier in the year. Her reviews on the trip were glowing—with the exception, perhaps, of the puzzlement she generated when she showed up at a dinner in

Paris wearing a pair of Galanos-designed black satin knickers with rhinestones. A fashion-forward choice, no doubt, but a quirkier one than people were used to seeing on the first lady. "What the hell is she wearing?" reporter Helen Thomas asked Nancy's press secretary a little too loudly for Sheila Tate's comfort. The *New York Times* called Nancy's knee-length pants a "fashion bombshell" detonated in the worldwide center of haute couture. Nancy appeared to have gotten the message. No one ever saw those knickers again.

*

As the midway point of Ronnie's first term in office approached, Nancy's poll numbers had turned in a positive direction, along with her press coverage. There seemed to be a new peace in Nancy; a sense that she had finally figured out her role and was settling into it with more ease. As the *Washington Post* noted: "Lately, Nancy Reagan has been calling the White House, not California, 'home.'"

If so, she knew it was but a temporary home. Nancy also kept up her old ties and was on the phone with her friends on the West Coast constantly. In August 1982 Alfred Bloomingdale died amidst a raging tabloid scandal involving a twenty-nine-year-old mistress who sued for "lifetime support" and revealed a secret life in which she claimed he had regularly bound and beat prostitutes. It might have made political sense for Nancy to distance herself from such a lurid story. But she stood by his widow, her friend Betsy, consoling her with two or three calls a day. Nancy also let it be known that if any in their social circle did not stay loyal to Betsy as well, the first lady would not have anything to do with them again.

That same year, Nancy was dealing with another sorrow, one more private and personal. The health of both her parents had declined precipitously. Loyal, who had been hospitalized three times for heart problems since a 1978 cardiac arrest episode, was lonely and overwhelmed by the responsibility of caring for Edie, as Nancy's mother slid deeper and deeper into dementia. There were days when Edie was alert and almost her old self. But there were others, more and more of them, when the once-effervescent woman who had animated Loyal's life was incapable of expressing herself. Edie was beset by physical problems as well. In a February 19, 1982, letter to a friend named Evelyn, Loyal wrote: "Edith has trouble getting around with her walker, and her most difficult handicap is her severe loss of hearing, which aids do not help a great deal. We have tried out four different kinds with as many so-called hearing specialists, doctors, and nondoctors. You can [imagine] that handicap for her and the telephone. I have to do all the talking with Nancy and Ronnie and repeating the conversation in detail." Patti, though estranged from her parents, visited Loyal several times during this period, and noticed a change in her stern and judgmental grandfather. "As he approached the end of his life, he softened, became more gentle and philosophical," she recalled.

After all the years in which Loyal had provided Nancy with guidance and emotional support, he had become the one who needed those things from her now. A typewritten letter he sent Nancy and Ronnie, dated July 20, 1982, is in a box of Nancy's personal belongings held in the nonpublic collection at the Reagan Library. In it, Loyal confided: "It was such a pleasant surprise to talk with Ronnie. I'm afraid I've complained too much about Edith's symptoms of Alzheimer's disease. It seems I was able to deal with patients' symptoms, but when it comes to those of my very own, I'm totally at a loss to realize what is developing in their thinking process." He wrote of how Edith had recently "becme [*sic*] very angry and struck me several times in the face. Her anger was gone as fast at [*sic*] it had come." Loyal concluded his forlorn letter with an expression of gratitude for some unspecified piece of advice he had gotten from his son-in-law, which Nancy's father wrote was "so sound and correct that I was ashamed I had not practiced it before."

Within three weeks of writing that letter, eighty-six-year-old Loyal himself took a sharply downward turn. It was clear he had not much longer to live. Ronnie wrote in his diary on Sunday, August 8: "Again at the W.H. More of Saturdays work plus a long letter I feel I have to write to Loyal. I'm afraid for him. His health is failing badly." What worried Ronnie more than the prospect of Loyal's death itself was the fact that his father-in-law was, by most definitions of the word, an atheist. Loyal had, from his youth, rejected any belief that Jesus Christ was a divinity or that there was any reward after death beyond being "remembered and discussed with pleasure and happiness." And according to Nancy's stepbrother, Dick, who had become a neurosurgeon like his father, Loyal had made his wishes crystal clear about how things were to be handled when he died: "He wanted no funeral arrangements. He didn't want the press. He wanted no one. He simply wanted to be cremated and placed in a very nice area in Phoenix. He wrote Mrs. Reagan a letter, and he wrote me the same letter, and he wrote his lawyer the same letter, and it was also in his will. He was simply to 'vanish.'"

Loyal's religious views—or rather, his lack of them—had long been a source of frustration and tension with Ronnie, who believed that a Judgment Day awaited everyone. Ronnie was convinced that moment for Nancy's beloved father was near. So, the most powerful man in the world put aside everything else on the weekend of August 8, took pen in hand, and set out to save one soul. What Ronnie wrote on four pieces of White House stationery had never become public until I discovered it among Nancy's personal belongings at the Reagan Library. The library gave me permission to use it for a column I wrote for the *Washington Post*, which was published in September 2018.

"Dear Loyal," Ronnie began. "I hope you'll forgive me for this, but I've been wanting to write you ever since we talked on the phone. I'm aware of the strain you are under and believe with all my heart there is help for that . . ."

What followed in the next pages was an intimate and humble profession of Ronnie's own faith. "We have been promised that all we have to do is ask God in Jesus name to help when we have done all we can—when we've come to the end of our strength and abilities and we'll have that help," he wrote. "We only have to trust and have faith in his infinite goodness and mercy." Not a word of the president's small, rounded script was crossed out, which was perhaps evidence of how carefully he had thought this out, or perhaps a sign that he might have rewritten and revised several versions until he felt he had gotten it perfect. Near the end of the letter that I saw thirty-six years later were three watery smudges—maybe spilled from a cup of tea; maybe someone's later tears.

It was striking to see what Ronnie envisioned as an eternal reward. In his eyes, heaven was, among other things, a chance to spend forever with the woman he loved the most on earth. "Loyal, you and Edith have known a great love—more than many have been permitted to know. That love will not end with the end of this life," he wrote. "We've been promised this is only a part of life and that a greater life, a greater glory awaits us. It awaits you together one day, and all that is required is that you believe and tell God you put yourself in his hands."

The following evening, Ronnie found Nancy crying. Her father was back in the hospital. This looked like the end. She prepared to fly to Arizona to be with him one last time. "I wish I could bear her pain myself," Ronnie wrote in his diary. A week later, he noted: "Last night or the night before, Nancy says Loyal asked for the chaplain at the hospital in the middle of the night." And the following day: "Dr. Loyal died this morning."

Nancy was at Loyal's bedside when he passed away of congestive heart failure at 8:40 a.m. on August 19, 1982, at Scottsdale Memorial Hospital. Afterward, she held his hand for nearly an hour, unable to let go. In a speech six years later to a Youth for Christ conference in Washington, the first lady recounted her father's final days. "He was terribly frightened. He was even afraid to go to sleep for fear he wouldn't wake up. He'd move from chair to chair trying to keep awake and, I guess, alive," she said. "I can't tell you how much it hurt to see him this way—this man who had always been so supremely confident and strong in my eyes." In that address, Nancy also mentioned Ronnie's letters. (She said there were two, though I found only one among her belongings at the library.) They may have had an effect, she said. From her father's doctors, she learned that Loyal in his final hours had requested to see a clergyman. "I don't know what the chaplain did or what he said, but whatever it was, it was the right thing, and it gave my father comfort," she said. "I noticed he was calmer and not as frightened. When he died the next day, he was at peace, finally. And I was so happy for him. My prayers were answered."

Her brother, Dick, got word at three o'clock that morning that Loyal was about to die. He rearranged his surgical schedule and scrambled to get a plane ticket from Philadelphia, but by the time he arrived in Phoenix, his father was already gone. He also discovered that Nancy was planning a small memorial service for family and close friends—something his father had expressly forbidden. Nancy and Dick got into a furious argument, which White House staff members overheard, though they did not know the source of it. Dick spent the night with friends and caught the first plane he could back to Philadelphia, missing the service. "This was the only time I could remember, in the long friendship that the two of us had, that she was very, very nasty," he told me. "I didn't want any part of this funeral because, as my father's neurosurgical resident and fellow, I obeyed, and I did what his wishes were. And so, I went home."

I asked Dick: Was it possible his father had had a change of heart? Had he become a believer on his deathbed?

"I doubt it," Dick said. "Seriously."

Nancy and her stepbrother did not speak for a year and a half. In the fall of 1983, Ronnie was beginning to campaign for reelection and had a speaking engagement in the Philadelphia suburbs. He sought out Dick and implored him to make peace with Nancy. "It took almost, maybe, six months before we did get together. It was in the spring of 1984, in Phoenix, [that] we finally had gotten our differences straightened out," Dick said. "But what I felt that she should know is that her father should be obeyed. He was a rock-hard disciplinarian, and this was a very strong belief of his. So I, as his son, I stood beside him." Nancy was just as certain that what she did was the right thing. The religious service was her final act of love and tribute for the man who had rescued her childhood. Afterward, there was a small reception.

That night, once the guests had left, the family gathered in the living room of Loyal and Edie's house. A nurse put Edie in bed, and Nancy and Patti went into her room to say good night.

"Do you think he's dancing tonight?" Edie asked, fixing her eyes somewhere in the distance.

Nancy replied: "I'm sure he is."

CHAPTER FIFTEEN

In a White House where processes ran smoothly in most respects, getting final decisions on the president's schedule was an exception. Sometimes it seemed that it could take forever, which was confusing and frustrating to the dozens of people who had to know Ronnie's plans on a given day before making any of their own. Most blamed the dithering on Michael Deaver. He was hard to pin down and would occasionally come back with unusual demands, such as stipulating that Air Force One take off at a peculiar predawn hour. "I found this odd because Deaver was remarkably punctual and efficient in everything else he did," recalled Don Regan, who replaced Baker as White House chief of staff in 1985.

At one point shortly after Regan took over at the White House, the chief of staff asked Deaver to explain why uncertainty and delay always seemed to bollix the scheduling operation. Deaver glanced around, clearly uncomfortable. Then he threw up his hands and told Regan: "Don't bring that up. Leave it be." Deaver was guarding a secret known only to a few. On Nancy's insistence, decisions regarding the calendar of the most powerful man in the world were often put in the hands of a San Francisco astrologer named Joan Quigley. Nancy consulted her by phone nearly every weekend for advice on which days the stars aligned favorably for Ronnie, and which posed a danger for him to do anything outside the confines of the White House. The reassurance she received from Quigley became an emotional lifeline for Nancy after the 1981 attempt on Ronnie's life. Without it, she felt she could not have faced sending her husband out into a world where treachery and danger might wait around any turn.

When it all came out in 1988, the furor over the astrologer would become the most mortifying chapter of Nancy's years as first lady. The whole thing sounded almost too wacky to be possible. Johnny Carson joked that Nancy's sign was "the house of Adolfo." House Speaker Jim Wright, a Texas Democrat, jumped in with a shot at Ronnie: "It's all right with me. I'm glad he consults somebody. I thought he was making his decisions based on absolutely nothing at all." Even the staid *Wall Street Journal* couldn't resist: "We were going to print this story yesterday, but our astrologer—we can't say who she is—advised against it."

Nancy's interest in astrology had begun as an innocent enough pastime. Going back to their days in Hollywood, both she and Ronnie regularly had their zodiac signs read. They also made a practice of scanning their horoscopes each morning in the newspaper. And as noted earlier, when his movie career hit bottom in the 1950s, Ronnie had consulted the syndicated Astrological Forecast column in the *Los Angeles Times* before setting aside his qualms and accepting that humiliating gig as a floor show emcee in Las Vegas.

In Nancy's personal papers at the Reagan Library, I came across an undated clipping of her horoscope from a newspaper. "You receive added 'sustenance' in form of romance, affection, love," it advised. Ronnie had taped it to a piece of paper and written a playful message in capital letters: "I don't know who this guy 'added sustenance' is, but he better not come around here. Signed, commander in chief." As Nancy saw it, she was a classic Cancer: a homemaker and nester, intuitive and sensitive, presenting a hard shell to the world that hides an inner vulnerability. Ronnie was the quintessential Aquarian personality that she read about in an article a friend sent her: unassuming and without affectation; loving, but in a way that can seem impersonal. "If Aquarians have a fault, it's that they are 'too tranquil, too gentle and kindly in disposition,'" she wrote, quoting the description. "They are 'incapable of petty tyranny.' Their attitude toward the world is 'kindly and humane.' The article even mentioned that Aquarian men are often slow to get married!"

When they were dating, Ronnie and Nancy were among many movie types who attended popular star-charting parties thrown by "gregarious Aquarius" Carroll Righter, who wrote the popular horoscope column that ran in the *Los Angeles Times.* He held gatherings to celebrate the birthdays of clients that fell in a particular month, each themed according to their sign of the zodiac. "All the stars were there: Rhonda Fleming, Marlene Dietrich, Lana Turner, Hedy Lamarr, Betty Grable," actress Arlene Dahl told *People* magazine. "Fish were swimming around in his pool for the Pisces party, and he rented a live lion for my Leo party." Righter was renowned for having warned Dietrich to avoid working on a movie set one day because she might get hurt. She ignored his advice and broke her ankle. The star charter to the stars was even said to have predicted the timing of his own death in 1988.

Show people tend to be superstitious by nature: no hats on the bed, or whistling in the dressing room, or shoes on a shelf that is higher than your head. Once, when Ronnie saw his executive assistant, Jim Kuhn, cross the fingers on both hands for luck during a close congressional vote, the president cried: "Don't ever do that! Don't ever cross your fingers on both hands, because one cancels out the other." Before he boarded an airplane, Ronnie made sure he was wearing what he called his "lucky cuff links," which were tiny gold replicas of a calendar page with his and Nancy's wedding anniversary marked by a purple stone. He was open to—or at least indulgent of—concepts that might seem irrational to other people. Ronnie was a science-fiction fan who, in his first summit with Soviet leader Mikhail Gorbachev, suggested that the two countries would need to cooperate if the earth were invaded by space aliens. Gorbachev, taken aback, changed the subject. Both Ronnie and his daughter Maureen thought it possible that the Lincoln Bedroom was haunted by a ghost.

Nancy's interest in astrology continued as she and Ronnie moved into politics. For a while after he became governor, she regularly consulted Jeane Dixon, an astrologer celebrated for supposedly predicting John F. Kennedy's assassination. Nancy was far from the only important figure who talked to Dixon. Her voice also shows up on one of Richard Nixon's White House tapes. Dixon told the president during a May 1971 visit to the Oval Office that "destiny cannot be denied Richard Nixon."

As Ronnie was considering whether to run for president in 1976, Nancy made regular visits to Righter at his Beverly Hills mansion. She would arrive wearing sunglasses and a scarf, and identify herself as Nancy Davis. *People* magazine quoted one Righter associate as saying: "Carroll told Nancy that this was simply not the time to try. She was very, very angry. When she didn't like what she was hearing, she became really whiny. She really wanted him to explain why it wasn't a good time."

Ronnie himself had generated a stellar controversy shortly before the 1980 Republican convention, when he told a reporter that he checked his horoscope every day. He also recounted a story about how Dixon had discouraged him from running for the White House in 1968, advising he could do more good by staying in California. Those statements brought an admonishment from a group of scientists, including five Nobel laureates, who said they were "gravely disturbed" by the revelation that a leading presidential candidate appeared to take astrology seriously. "In our opinion, no person whose decisions are based, even in part, on such evident fantasies can be trusted to make the many serious—and even life-and-death—decisions required of American presidents," they wrote in a letter to Ronnie. He replied: "Let me assure you that while Nancy and I enjoy glancing at the daily astrology charts in our morning paper, we do not plan our daily activities or our lives around them."

But after Ronnie's brush with death, Nancy was desperate to find any means of comfort and reassurance she could. She was surely pleased to see new security measures put in place. When the president arrived at a hotel or other public venue, canvas tents were placed around the entrances, so that his movements were not visible. The Secret Service finally got the magnetometers it had long been seeking, allowing agents to screen for hidden metal on anyone who passed through the devices. They were astonished to discover that hundreds of visitors had been coming in and out of the White House with guns. Many were tourists, overly anxious about their safety on the streets of the nation's capital.

When planning a public event, however, the Secret Service's wishes often clashed with those of Ronnie's political team, who wanted to pack in big audiences and give them a sense of connection with their president. It was impossible to work a crowd and shake hands from behind a sheet of bulletproof glass, the handlers complained. The Secret Service's concerns over Ronnie's safety also sometimes prevented the president from attending big outdoor events such as the 1982 dedication of the Vietnam Veterans Memorial on the National Mall. As the internal battles grew more intense, the agents regularly turned to Nancy for backup. "If we weren't comfortable with it, all you had to do was talk to her, and it wouldn't happen," recalled Joe Petro, who was assistant special agent in charge of the Presidential Protective Division.

The agents also appealed to Nancy in situations where they wanted Ronnie to put on the uncomfortable protective vest that the president called his "iron T-shirt." She and Petro developed a system of communicating without words. As Ronnie prepared to go to an engagement, the first lady would give the agent a questioning look and point at her chest. If Petro nodded, Nancy would order her husband to put on the vest. "He hated it," Petro said. "But he never said no." Nancy, on the other hand, rarely wore hers.

Ronnie made a visit to Korea in November 1983, just weeks after an assassination attempt on its president killed nineteen people in a bombing in Rangoon, Burma. Nancy told Mike Deaver that there were to be no outside events. She vetoed both an arrival ceremony at the airport and plans to have the American president participate in a wreath laying to honor Korean War dead. The Koreans, Petro said, "were very upset. This was an affront to their sovereignty."

None of the precautions was enough for Nancy, however. In the weeks and months after the assassination attempt, she cried constantly when Ronnie wasn't around. Sometimes she cried when he was, though she tried to do it in the bedroom or the bathroom, so he wouldn't see. She sought out religious leaders such as Billy Graham, as well as their old pastor Donn Moomaw. But faith had never come as naturally to Nancy as it did to her husband. So, while Ronnie found solace and peace in the idea that God had preserved him because He had a plan in mind for this president, Nancy turned her gaze to the heavens in a different way. About a month after the assassination attempt, she expressed her anxiety during a phone call with TV producer and talk show host Merv Griffin, an old friend with whom she shared an interest in astrology and a July 6 birthday. Griffin told her that there was an astrologer in San Francisco whose charts had shown March 30 to be a dangerous day when Ronnie should have stayed home.

Nancy was acquainted with the woman he mentioned. Joan Quigley was a regular guest on Griffin's syndicated show. He had given Nancy her number back in 1973, and the two of them had been talking once a year or so ever since. Quigley had also called several times during the 1980 presidential race with suggestions about good and bad times for Ronnie to do things, such as the best windows for him to talk to the media and what hour was most auspicious for his chartered campaign plane to take off on the day of a debate.

When Griffin said Quigley had foreseen the danger for Ronnie on March 30, 1981, Nancy was thunderstruck. "Oh, my God," she said. *"I could have stopped it!"* She hung up on him and immediately dialed Quigley. "I'm so scared," Nancy told the astrologer. "I'm scared every time he leaves the house, and I don't think I breathe until he gets home. I cringe every time we step out of a car or leave a building. I'm afraid that one of these days somebody is going to shoot at him again."

Fiftysomething Quigley was a blonde, Vassar-educated socialite who grew up in a penthouse apartment in San Francisco's exclusive Nob Hill area. Her father owned a hotel, and when she and her sister were young, they were chauffeured to parties in a Rolls-Royce. In other words, she might have fit right in with the friends that Nancy had cultivated in California, Washington, and New York. Quigley was also a good listener. Nancy was soon confiding many of her concerns: her problems with Patti and Michael, her rough relations with the media, her worries about the health of her parents.

Later, in her 1989 memoir, Nancy would reflect on how her dependence on the astrologer deepened. "My relationship with Joan Quigley began as a crutch, one of several ways I tried to alleviate my anxiety about Ronnie. Within a year or two, it had become a habit, something I relied on a little less but didn't see the need to change. While I was never certain that Joan's astrological advice was helping to protect Ronnie, the fact is that nothing like March 30 ever happened again," she wrote. "Was astrology one of the reasons? I don't *really* believe it was, but I don't *really* believe it wasn't. But I do know this: it didn't hurt, and I'm not sorry I did it."

Nancy initially hoped that Quigley might offer her services for free, as she had during the 1980 campaign, but the astrologer insisted she be paid by the hour, with a $3,000-a-month retainer. Nancy received Quigley's billing statements in an envelope marked with her private five-digit zip code so that it would not get lost—or noticed—in the deluge of White House mail. Checks to an astrologer signed by a first lady created obvious potential for embarrassment. So, Nancy arranged for payments to be made through a friend in California, whom she reimbursed. Nancy did not name the friend, but Quigley later said that both Mary Jane Wick and Betsy Bloomingdale acted as intermediaries at various points. If true, both of them were highly discreet. Mary Jane's son Doug told me he was never aware of his mother having any dealings with an astrologer on Nancy's behalf.

Within the White House, Nancy turned to the ever-obliging Deaver to make sure that Quigley's recommendations were carried out without anyone—including, for a while, the president—knowing where they had come from. As she put it: "I wanted Ronnie to know about it, but I wasn't exactly *dying* to tell him, and I kept putting it off." One day, after she had been talking to Quigley for many months, the president walked into the bedroom while they were on the phone. When he asked what the conversation had been about, Nancy came clean. Ronnie told her: "If it makes you feel better, go ahead and do it. But be careful. It might look a little odd if it ever came out."

That Deaver managed to keep all of it under wraps was a remarkable feat and a testament to his willingness to take flak at Nancy's behest. "Mike is a born chamberlain, and to him it was simply one of the many little problems in the life of a servant to the great," Don Regan wrote acidly in a score-settling memoir of his rocky time as White House chief of staff. Regan's predecessor in the job, Jim Baker, told me he had a general sense of what was going on, though he didn't know Quigley's identity and preferred to leave the whole thing in Deaver's hands. "When we wanted to schedule something like a big press conference, he'd say, 'Let me take a look at it,'" Baker said. "Then we figured [Deaver and Nancy] would talk about the date. Now it's clear that they were clearing it all with her, with the astrologist. Maybe not clearing it, but talking to her about it."

There were others as well who were aware of the astrologer's role. Elaine Crispen, who was Nancy's special assistant during Ronnie's first term and her press secretary in the second one, knew about Quigley. So did Jane Erkenbeck, who took over the special assistant role from Crispen. Erkenbeck answered Nancy's phone and would normally check with the first lady before connecting her to a caller. "But when Joan Quigley would call, I would put her through right away because we thought we knew who Joan Quigley was," Erkenbeck said.

Still, Erkenbeck thought the stories that were told about Quigley's influence became far overblown. "Sorry, a lot of people go to see astrologers," she insisted. "The president's life was not governed by Joan Quigley, but if it suited the schedule to change him from one day to the other, I think that happened."

In retrospect, Deaver acknowledged that he was probably too willing to accommodate Nancy's compulsion. "When I look back, perhaps I should have tried harder to veto the whole business, but who was I to tell her it was a bad idea when she was convinced the well-being of her husband was at stake?" he wrote later. "I don't believe that we can see the future in the stars, but if Nancy did, and if taking note of the stars made her feel better, that was good enough for me. While Joan was a minor inconvenience to me, I could see how important this was to the first lady. Nancy was the strategist of the first couple, the worrier, the one who could never just sit back and let fate happen the way her husband could. She needed to be in action, and an astrological consultation every few weeks seemed to me then—and still does—an innocent enough quirk."

Deaver also claimed that he refused to carry out Quigley's recommendations if an event or trip could not be moved without major disruption, and that in those cases, Nancy accepted that the arrangements not be tampered with: "The consultations were never a burden—far from it, they were a comfort to Nancy during a very hard time. Contrary to press reports, the astrologer had no impact on Reagan's policies or his politics. Nada. Zero. Zilch."

Others in the White House were aware only that the scheduling process was unnecessarily aggravating. Deaver would dither over making a decision and then insist, for instance, that the president's plane take off for a foreign trip at precisely 2:11 a.m. He concocted stories to tell the traveling press about why the timing was so peculiar and inconvenient. A predawn takeoff? It was deemed to have been dictated by medical advice on how to avoid jet lag.

At the State Department, Chief of Protocol Selwa Roosevelt was perturbed that dates for state visits by foreign leaders had to be confirmed with the first lady. "I assumed it had to do with checking their social engagements and public commitments, but the reasons were always a bit murky. So much so, I wondered if Mrs. Reagan understood the foreign-policy implications of some of her decisions. I thought it a bit outré that she could overrule the State Department and the NSC with regard to the dates and desirability of a visit," Roosevelt recalled.

In the months after the 1984 election, Deaver began to seriously ponder departing from the White House. The pressure of the job had landed him in the hospital with kidney failure, which was complicated by high blood pressure. His secret alcoholism was catching up with him.

He had also developed a taste for high living that could not be supported on a $60,662-a-year government salary. But before Deaver could leave, Nancy's most loyal and indispensable ally knew he was going to have to hand off this delicate part of his portfolio. One afternoon in mid-November, he asked William Henkel, the director of presidential advance, to join him in his office for a drink. After pouring them each a tall one, Deaver said: "Now, Bill, I've got to start giving you some information why your job is going to be so sensitive . . ."

Henkel was flabbergasted by what he heard. Suddenly he understood why Deaver had been torturing the scheduling operation.

"Holy shit, Mike! I thought you were a madman. I can't believe you had to do this!" Henkel told him.

"Hey, at least this one's not crazy," Deaver said drily, in reference to Quigley. "Jeane Dixon was nuts."

Shortly after that, Henkel was summoned to a meeting with Nancy in the residence. "Bill, I want you to understand and feel what it was like the day my husband was shot. I am the daughter of Loyal Davis. I went into that room, and I saw six doctors with panic in their eyes. My naked husband lying on that thing. I knew he was dying," she told him. Then she explained how Quigley had known this would be a dangerous day for Ronnie to leave the White House.

"The thing that was paramount with her was that it came down to good days and bad days. Is it a bad day for the president's safety? Is this a day he should go out of the White House and do a public event?" Henkel said. So as Deaver had done before him, Henkel began giving Nancy proposed schedules to run past Quigley—both long-range, going out over the next year, and near-term ones, for the next two weeks. Sometimes Nancy would complain to Henkel that she needed more details to provide the astrologer, who was getting paid by the hour: "Bill, this is costing me money. I wish you could be more precise."

Henkel told me that Quigley also weighed in on decisions that were not directly related to the president's physical safety: Which day might be good to give the State of the Union address? Which was most auspicious to hold a press conference? In 1985, after Margaret Thatcher told Ronnie that the new leader of the Soviet Union was different from his predecessors and might be someone it was possible to work with, Nancy had Quigley do the chart of Mikhail Gorbachev. Quigley advised the first lady that Gorbachev's sign, Pisces, aligned well with Ronnie's. "She came back saying, 'These two have some coincidental things.' It was a very favorable thing in terms of these two people have, by the stars, some good vibes," Henkel recalled.

Nancy generally spoke to Quigley on Saturday afternoons while she was at Camp David and then called Henkel on Sundays at home. His wife could not understand why he would excuse himself and take the call somewhere out of earshot. "Bill, what's wrong with you?" she used to ask. "Why so secret?" Meanwhile, at the White House, Henkel was getting grief from the new chief of staff, Don Regan. A brusque and demanding former CEO of the investment firm Merrill Lynch, Regan had been Ronnie's first Treasury secretary, and then swapped jobs with Jim Baker in February 1985. Regan regularly berated Henkel over the fact that the schedule was always in a mess. "He was beating the shit out of me," Henkel said.

So Henkel went to Deaver and Nancy and told them the chief of staff had to be let in on the secret. Regan thought it had to be a joke when Deaver first informed him about the astrologer. "Humor her," Deaver advised him, and Regan soon realized he had no choice but to do so. He began keeping a color-coded calendar on his desk, with the dates highlighted like a traffic signal: green for good days, red for bad ones, and yellow when the outlook was iffy to send the president out for speaking events or to commence negotiations with foreign powers.

Regan apparently never learned the name of the mysterious figure that Nancy referred to only as "my friend," but he said her influence shaded much more than his desk calendar. "The president's schedule is the single most potent tool in the White House, because it determines what the most powerful man in the world is going to do and when he is going to do it. By humoring Mrs. Reagan, we gave her this tool—or, more accurately, gave it to an unknown woman in San Francisco who believed that the zodiac controls events and human behavior and that she could read the secrets of the future in the movements of the planets," he wrote later.

Others, including Henkel, have a different view. Quigley—despite the claims she would later make in a book—was not setting policy, he insisted. "At the end of the day, I think it was pretty benign, and I don't think it was anything harmful," Henkel said. "In the big picture, I think it was a positive because [Nancy] went into these events with a confidence based on her trust in Joan and what this stuff meant to her, and I think that's an asset to the president, because they were so close. She was so supportive of him. I come from this whole thing with deep admiration for her."

But that ignores the paradox of Nancy's reliance on an astrologer as a security measure. It is hard to imagine anything more fraught with risk than giving an outsider, someone Nancy had not met in person more than a few times, intimate knowledge of the president's movements, and even the power to determine when they would happen.

None of this might ever have come to light had it not been for the ugly ending of Regan's tenure as chief of staff in February 1987. Nancy had engineered his firing, blaming Regan for the Iran-contra scandal that was threatening to swallow Ronnie's presidency. Regan took his revenge against the first lady with the publication of a sensational memoir, for which he had received a $1 million advance from publisher Harcourt Brace Jovanovich. He also signed a $125,000 deal with *Time* magazine to excerpt it. *Newsweek*, however, got the scoop in early May 1988, a couple of weeks before the book's release date.

On the very first page of *For the Record*, Regan wrote: "Virtually every major move and decision the Reagans made during my time as White House chief of staff was cleared in advance with a woman in San Francisco who drew up horoscopes to make certain that the planets were in a favorable alignment for the enterprise." As soon as word got out about what he had revealed, Regan's blast at Nancy was all anyone was talking about. "I've been in publicity eighteen years, but I can't remember as much interest in a book as this one," one book publicist told the *New York Times*.

How explosive this revelation would prove to be was slow to dawn at 1600 Pennsylvania Avenue. Sheila Tate, who had only recently left her job as Nancy's press secretary, says she had been unaware of Nancy's relationship with Quigley. The day the news broke, Tate returned from lunch to her office at a public relations firm and found at least fifty phone messages from reporters. Her first call was to Elaine Crispen, Nancy's new spokeswoman. Crispen assured Tate it would be no more than a one-day tempest. "I could not have disagreed more. I told Elaine that unless they did something to diffuse it, this astrology business would be like an albatross around her neck," Tate recalled. "I really felt heartsick." As did Ronnie. "The press have a new one thanks to Don Regan's book," he wrote in his diary on May 3. "The media are behaving like kids with a new toy—never mind that there is no truth to it."

Indeed, the claims that were making it into the press went far beyond Regan's characterization of the astrologer's role when it came to scheduling. One headline in the *New York Post* read: "Astrologer Runs the White House." Everyone, it seemed, was weighing in. "As a Christian," former president Jimmy Carter said, "I don't think the guidance of our lives should come from the moving of stars."

Though Regan did not mention Quigley's name—and apparently didn't know it—journalists soon tracked her down. Nancy begged her to say nothing, but Quigley felt that her professional reputation was on the line. She argued that she was not one of the charlatans and imposters in her field, and needed to "represent reputable astrologers honorably."

Quigley soon had a book deal of her own. Published in 1990, it offered an often implausible version of events. Not only did the astrologer claim to have determined the timing of just about every major event of the Reagan presidency, she took credit for reshaping the relations between the United States and the Soviet Union, and even for deciding when the president's cancer surgery should take place. There is no evidence those things were true.

Nancy was chastened by the stir she had created with her secret reliance on Quigley's predictions, but she felt that she had only done what she needed to do to handle the uncertainty and anxiety of getting through every day. "What it boils down to is that each person has his own ways of coping with trauma and grief, with the pain of life, and astrology was one of mine," she wrote later. "*Don't criticize me,* I wanted to say, *until you have stood in my place. This helped me. Nobody was hurt by it*—except, possibly me."

CHAPTER SIXTEEN

Rehabilitating her image was not the only challenge that Nancy was grappling with as Ronnie's presidency moved into its second year and beyond. Though most of the Reagan offspring were not around much, they continued to be a source of drama, stress, and awkwardness.

Where Ronnie's recent predecessors had small children and adolescents living with them in the White House, the four Reagan kids were grown and trying to forge lives and identities of their own. Maureen, Michael, Patti, and Ron had little in common. Their temperaments and personal histories had taken them in different directions, and their connections to each other were tenuous. But each was struggling with a paradox that nearly all children of celebrated parents face: along with suffocating scrutiny comes a bounty of opportunities that they did nothing to earn. Expectations are thrust upon them that they will never be able to meet.

"There is a secret thought that the offspring of famous people keep tucked away," Patti once wrote. "It becomes the focal point of our lives, although it takes years to see that. It's what makes us run from who we are, rage against the huge shadow we feel dwarfed by, sabotage ourselves again and again. We vilify anyone who suggests we have a legacy to live up to, shoes to fill, a torch to carry. Because underneath it all, deep inside us, we think they're right."

For Nancy, the belated arrival of Loyal Davis in her life had salvaged her childhood. Claiming his name as hers gave her stability, a sense of belonging, an identity that finally seemed complete and whole. For Ronnie's children, having a towering figure at the center of their existence had the opposite effect. It increased the gravitational pull of their own self-doubts and fueled their inner suspicions that they were no more than faint copies of an epic original.

In this particular family, there was also the off-balance dynamic of a husband and his second wife so closely bound together that his progeny—only two of whom were also hers—felt shut out. It was hard to miss the disconnect between Ronnie's idealized view of American life and the impossibility for any flesh-and-blood family to live as though they were in a Norman Rockwell painting. "During Ronnie's presidency, our family and its problems were written about constantly," Nancy recalled. "Ronnie had run for office on a platform of traditional family values, which both of us believe in and try to practice. But I always felt hurt when people said we were hypocrites because our own family sometimes fell short of those values."

Even Ron, his parents' favorite, tested them. Ronnie and Nancy had been publicly supportive of Ron's unconventional choice of a dance career in 1976. Their misgivings were evident, however. Ron had been dancing for more than four years before his parents attended one of his performances, at a benefit gala for the Joffrey Ballet in March 1981 at New York's Metropolitan Opera House. The Reagans watched through binoculars from a center parterre box hung with a presidential seal. At intermission, Nancy threw her arms around her son and pronounced him "wonderful." His father wrote in his diary: "I think I held my breath until he finished, but he was good." News accounts of that night, however, noted that the Joffrey stood to lose $200,000 in federal subsidies under Ronnie's proposed budget cuts; two months later, the junior company's artistic director warned publicly that Ron could be out of a job by that fall if the Joffrey did not find some way to make up the money through private sources.

Ron would soon decide on his own to give up his dance career. His performances had gotten favorable reviews. The *New York Times*'s Anna Kisselgoff called him "a talented dancer who has worked very hard and who has done extremely well for a late starter." But he was making less than $300 a week and recognized he was never going to be a top star in a field that took a brutal toll on lithe young bodies. Though Ron was promoted to the Joffrey's senior company in August 1982, his parents were relieved when he informed them a few months later that he had decided to become a writer instead of a dancer. Ronnie confided to his diary: "I can't say I'm sorry although he worked hard & was getting along well—but there isn't much of a future and it is a short career."

Over the first two years of his father's presidency, Ron and his parents engaged in a pitched battle over his demands to give up his Secret Service protection. After the assassination attempt, Ronnie and Nancy were understandably concerned about security in general, and Ron lived in an area of New York City where the violent Puerto Rican separatist group FALN (Armed Forces of National Liberation) was known to be active. In 1975 the group had brazenly detonated a lunch-hour bomb at the historic Fraunces Tavern in Lower Manhattan, killing four at the site where George Washington had given his farewell address to the officers who served under him in the Revolutionary War. The youngest Reagan was also the only one of Ronnie's four children whom intelligence sources had identified as being on terrorist target lists. "He thinks we're interfering with his privacy. I can't make him see that I can't be put in a position of one day facing a ransom demand. I'd have to refuse for reasons of the Nation's welfare," Ronnie wrote on May 15, 1982.

The following April, Ron called his father, furious that the Secret Service had come into his Greenwich Village apartment while he and his wife, Doria, were in California. The agents had entered it to fix an alarm on a window. Ronnie told him that this was a perfectly reasonable thing for them to have done, and Ron hung up on him. Weeks went by, and father and son were still not talking when a distraught Nancy called Ronnie to tell him that Ron was planning to go to Paris and had not informed his detail until just a few days before. A couple of weeks later, Ronnie and Nancy finally threw in the towel. Ronnie summoned Don Regan, who as Treasury secretary oversaw the Secret Service, and informed him that there should be no more protection provided to his younger son. The president was angry about "Ron & his paranoia about S.S. Protection," he wrote on May 19, 1983. "I think he's being ridiculous & d—n unfair to the guys who are trying to protect his hide. This is settled—we let him sign off permanently—no protection."

Ron became a contributor to *Playboy* magazine. He covered the 1984 Democratic convention, wrote a quirky travelogue of the Soviet Union, and showed up among the press corps at his father's 1985 summit in Geneva with Soviet general secretary Mikhail Gorbachev. "He never asked for special access or favors," assistant press secretary Mark Weinberg recalled. "He worked hard at a small space in the press filing center at the InterContinental Hotel there and never used his status to his advantage." Later, he worked as a journalist in television and radio, including a stint on ABC's *Good Morning America*.

Ron was the only member of the younger Reagan generation who seems to have seen any humor in the prank that fate had played on them all. He did a 1986 ad for American Express, which was part of the company's long-running series of "Do You Know Me?" spots. In it, Ron was shown being served ice cream in the first-class section of a jetliner and commented to the camera: "Every time I appear on a talk show, people ask me about my father. Every time I do an interview, people ask me about my father. Every time I pull out the American Express card, people treat me like my father." Pause. "Come to think of it, that's not so bad!" After an American Express card flashed across the screen with his name on it, the thirty-second spot closed with Ron in an airport phone booth, saying, "Hello, Dad?" Then he excused himself and slid the door shut to continue the conversation in privacy.

His parents were mystified when Ron hosted *Saturday Night Live* in February 1986. He opened the show wearing jockey shorts and socks as he danced to the Bob Seger hit "Old Time Rock & Roll" around a set that was supposed to be the White House. It fell to Weinberg, the assistant press secretary, to explain to the president and first lady that Ron was performing a parody—a hilarious one—of Tom Cruise's most famous scene in the 1983 coming-of-age comedy *Risky Business*. "They had never seen the movie; in fact, they had fallen off the pop culture wagon sometime around the arrival of the Beatles," Ron said.

Maureen, the daughter of Ronnie and Jane, was the only one who shared her father's passion for politics. As she liked to point out, she became a Republican before he did, and spent many late nights stuffing envelopes at Richard Nixon's presidential campaign headquarters in 1960. But hers was a different brand of conservatism than her father's, particularly on the issue of women's rights. She and Ronnie had spirited arguments over the proposed Equal Rights Amendment, which he was against and she supported. Ronnie contended that it was just another way for the government to interfere in people's lives and that it would lead to women being drafted into combat.

Maureen was also keenly interested in closing a growing "gender gap" identified by pollsters during Ronnie's presidency. It showed that women were increasingly less likely than men to support Republicans. "There are issues of unique concern to women, but these issues don't end with women," she told her father. "The problems of child care for working parents, equal pay for equal work, equal pension benefits, availability of credit, and enforcement of civil rights statutes all uniquely affect women, that's true, but when a woman is discriminated against, her children are discriminated against, her husband is discriminated against, her community is discriminated against. All office holders have to address these women's concerns, because they are also family concerns and community concerns."

In 1982 Maureen, who previously hosted a radio talk show in Los Angeles, ran for the US Senate. She was one of eight people in that year's hotly contested Republican primary. It had always been Ronnie's practice not to endorse anyone in intramural GOP contests, and no one would have expected him to make an exception for his daughter. Things became uncomfortable, however, when the president told reporters that he did not want Maureen to run. Ronnie later insisted he meant the remark to be "facetious," but the damage had been done.

There was no way of misreading her uncle Neil's view of the race. Though Ronnie's older brother had given away Maureen at her wedding only months before, he signed on as a campaign cochair for her leading opponent, San Diego mayor Pete Wilson, who ultimately won the race. "I don't look well upon kids riding on their father's coattails," Neil Reagan told reporters. He later cut a radio commercial in which he declared: "We Reagans urge you to support Pete Wilson." That Neil was speaking only for his wife, Bess, and himself was a detail meant to be overlooked.

Nor did it help when Ed Rollins, a top White House aide, observed to the *Sacramento Bee*'s Leo Rennert that the president's daughter "has the highest negatives of any candidate I've seen." Rollins added: "Her campaign has not caught fire, and she has serious financial problems. She's been strident on some issues, and, while the president has been scrupulously neutral, there's an impression that Maureen is not the overwhelming choice of the Reagan boys."

Rollins, who thought what he told the reporter was off the record, apologized to Ronnie. As Rollins recounted the conversation, the president replied with a chuckle: "Well, Maureen *was* a little worked up about this. But, hell, Ed, don't worry about it. I know she shouldn't be in this race. There's nothing you said that I haven't thought to myself. I wish she weren't running, too, but we've both got to be careful. I've said something I shouldn't have said, too."

Maureen's campaign spiraled into oblivion. She got no help from the network of wealthy Californians who had bankrolled her father's career. Where three of her opponents had raised upward of $500,000 each by April, she had only $3,438 in her campaign coffers. She came in fifth in the June 8 Republican primary, with only 5 percent of the vote. Ronnie tried to make amends by having Maureen named a special consultant to the Republican National Committee. He valued her political instincts and blunt advice, and her role with the national party organization brought her to Washington frequently. Maureen became a regular presence in the White House, living in the Lincoln Bedroom for long stretches. She bonded with Nancy over their shared mission of watching the president's back. When his spokesman Larry Speakes had occasion to go to the family quarters with business for Ronnie, he would sometimes find Nancy and Maureen in their bathrobes, "chatting like schoolgirls." Maureen even began calling Nancy "Mom"; she still referred to her own mother as "Jane."

There would be no such warm moments with Michael, the son who had grown up feeling that being adopted meant he was not quite a real Reagan. A rank aroma of opportunism arose around nearly everything he did, and with it a potential to embarrass and compromise his father. As Speakes would later recall: "Michael Reagan always had schemes for making money from his father's position, and Fred Fielding, who had to deal with potential conflict-of-interest problems as the president's counsel, would come around and say, 'Well, Sonny Boy's at it again.'"

Maybe Michael was overcompensating for his insecurities, or perhaps he was simply greedy. Either way, White House aides learned to keep their distance. "He was a wheeler-dealer," said Jim Kuhn, who was Ronnie's executive assistant. "Mike would call all the time for this and that, and you knew not to . . . You wanted to be respectful of Mike, but if you got on his side and got too cozy with him, you would've been out. I mean, you just had to know that."

Michael, who was well into his thirties, was still racing speedboats. The month after Ronnie was elected, he also took a job as vice president of sales for a small company in Burbank, California, that made parts for aircraft and missiles. In May 1981 five letters surfaced in which Michael had invoked his father's name as he sought contracts with military bases. In one, he wrote: "I know that with my father's leadership at the White House this countries [*sic*] armed services are going to be rebuilt and strengthened. We at Dana Ingalls Profile want to be involved in that process." Asked about it at a news conference, Ronnie called the letter "a mistake." Privately, he told his son not to write any more of them.

Michael quit that job but was also under investigation for alleged complicity in a stock fraud scheme involving a company that claimed to own a gold mine in Arizona, and for improperly funding his living expenses with $17,500 of the money he raised for an abortive venture to produce gasohol. Two search warrants of his house in Sherman Oaks, California, were executed. The matter was ultimately dropped, though not before Michael had run up $50,000 in legal bills.

It got even dicier. In 1983 the Secret Service informed Michael that one of its agents had spotted him sneaking a T-shirt from a children's store under his jacket. Later, he was accused of lifting other things: a minibottle of bourbon from an American Airlines flight; a bottle of Binaca breath spray from a drugstore in Century City; an "I Ski Heavenly Valley" pin from a ski shop; a candy bar from the gift store of the InterContinental Hotel in London.

Michael denied stealing any of these small items and had an explanation for each: A friend had paid for the T-shirt, and Michael had tucked it in his clothes because it was raining outside. The minibottle had been a gift from a flight attendant. He had paid for the breath spray while he was purchasing cigarettes and picked it up on his way out of the store. The Heavenly Valley pin was a token from the lodge owner, who was thrilled to have the president's son as a guest. As for chocolate, he didn't even eat the stuff. His sister, Maureen, and his father told Michael they didn't believe him, not with all the trouble he had caused in the past. They suggested he get psychiatric help.

In the summer of 1983 the growing tension within the family boiled over in public. Michael told *Redbook* magazine that he had not been invited to the White House since the inauguration. He revealed that the president who had wrapped himself in family values had virtually no relationship with his only grandchildren, Michael's five-year-old son, Cameron, and infant daughter, Ashley.

Michael also took aim at the first lady: "Of course, Nancy does have her Foster Grandparents program." That comment, he admitted later, was a carefully aimed shot, using the only ammunition that he knew would pierce his father's indifference. "I felt attacked on the matter of my supposed kleptomania, so I had struck back," he wrote. "It's hard to go up against the president of the United States. On the other hand, I did know his Achilles' heel: Nancy."

A little over a year later, shortly after Ronnie's landslide 1984 reelection victory, Nancy returned the fire. In an interview with social columnist Betty Beale of the *Washington Times*, the first lady was asked whether Michael would be joining the family for Thanksgiving. She said no, but she didn't leave it there. "The president and Michael don't seem to be very close," Nancy said. "There is an estrangement and has been for three years. And I think really we should now say this and get it all done with so we can put these questions behind us. There is an estrangement. We are sorry about it. We hope that someday it will be solved. We do not believe and have never believed in discussing family problems in public. And that's it."

That was not it, of course. Nancy had laid the table for a sumptuous holiday feast—for the media. When reporters showed up in Nebraska, where Michael was spending Thanksgiving with his wife Colleen's family, the president's older son declared that he had been stunned by Nancy's comments and demanded an apology. "Colleen and I were talking about it. All we can think of is maybe it's Nancy's way of justifying why she and Dad haven't ever seen our daughter Ashley. She's nineteen months old, and they've never laid eyes on her," he said. Michael also joked that a recent late-night fall that Nancy had taken, which had put a nasty bump on her head, might have been "more serious than we thought."

Unnamed "close friends" of Nancy and Ronnie were soon quoted in the press as saying that Michael needed "guidance." Maureen jumped in, accusing her brother of conducting a "vendetta against Mrs. Reagan," and adding: "He thinks he can keep dumping on us. Now we're fighting back." She also said that Michael had ridiculed Ron for dancing ballet and made hurtful cracks about her own divorces. Ronnie finally ordered everyone to just shut up. In a December 10, 1984, letter to Elizabeth "Nackey" Loeb, who'd succeeded her late husband as publisher of the *Manchester Union Leader*, Ronnie wrote of his frustration: "We've tried to keep a little fuss private and are well on our way to resolving it as all families do from time to time."

All of it came to a head a few days after Christmas. Michael and his family were summoned to the $3,000-a-night penthouse suite at the Century Plaza Hotel, where Nancy and Ronnie stayed when they were in Los Angeles. Word got out. Awaiting the arrival of the president's son and his family were camera crews from all the networks and local television stations, as well as reporters for the wire services and every major newspaper. A crowd of curious hotel guests joined them. Some of the journalists joked that the reconciliation was going to be facilitated by Richard Dawson, host of the popular television game show *Family Feud*. Jim Kuhn was handling the logistics for the White House. Nancy told him to make sure that Michael came into the hotel through an entrance where there would be no opportunity for him to be seen—or worse, talked to—by the media. Alas, with a mob of cameras surrounding the hotel, there was no way to ensure that. Nor was Michael in a cooperative mood. He rejected a suggestion that he enter the hotel through the presidential entrance in the rear and came into the lobby through the front door instead, carrying twenty-month-old Ashley in his arms.

That day, there was a lot to iron out. The president's diary entries during 1983 and 1984 contain frequent references to his concerns about Michael. Ronnie was dismissive of the investigation of his son for securities fraud, which he believed was politically motivated and aimed at him. But the private struggle within the family weighed upon him:

Wednesday, March 30, 1983: "Left for LA. Met Nancy at Century Plaza late afternoon. Maureen came by re Mike. She's really being a trooper [*sic*] & solid sister about the problem."

Wednesday, December 28, 1983: "I'm worried about Nancy. A deep cough continues beyond when I believe it should have dried up. Mermie [Maureen's nickname since childhood] came by for a short visit. We still have no break in the Mike situation. We must find an answer to that."

Monday, November 19 through Sunday, November 25, 1984, after the eruption over Nancy's comment about the "estrangement" in the family: "One other sour note on Thanksgiving had to do with Mike R. He blew up at something on the TV news based on an interview Nancy had given. He called me & when I tried to straighten him out he screamed at me about having been adopted & hung up on me."

Monday, November 26, 1984: "To top the day off I called Mike R. We talked for half an hour & I'm more than ever convinced that he has a real emotional problem that is making him paranoid."

Thursday, November 29, 1984: "Another call from Mike. He is a really disturbed young man. I've contacted his Minister & believe maybe we can get through to Mike. [. . .] Mermie is here for overnight."

Thursday, December 27, 1984, through Wednesday, January 2, 1985: "On Fri. will meet with Mike & Colleen to see our granddaughter for the 1st time. Had time for a trip to Dr. House. My hearing has suffered no loss since last year. The other good news was our family meeting. I think we passed a watershed & the wounds are healed."

"The wounds are healed." That was the official story, at least. Nancy put out a statement through the White House Press Office: "It was a nice visit. There are no differences. All is resolved. Everybody loves each other, and this is a wonderful way to start the new year." A White House photographer had been stationed to record the two-hour session in the Century Plaza's Presidential Suite. Ronnie and Nancy brought gifts, and the president got down on all fours to play with his granddaughter. Then the children were dismissed, and, with Michael's pastor as an intermediary, the adults tried to clear the air.

According to Michael's account of the meeting, Ronnie told his son that he accepted his explanations for how he had obtained the supposedly shoplifted items. He promised to have the Secret Service write a letter exonerating Michael, which arrived six months later.

Michael also asked his father to announce to the media at the next presidential press conference that their stories should quit referring to him as the "adopted" son. Ronnie wisely rebuffed that request, no doubt aware this would only have reignited the story line about their family difficulties. During the session, Nancy acknowledged that her "estrangement" comment had been a mistake, which was the first time Michael ever recalled her apologizing. On the way out, Michael mentioned one more thing.

"You know," he told Ronnie, "you've never told me that you love me."

His father looked surprised. "Michael, I love you," he said.

As Michael left the hotel, he made no comment to the media. Things had gone well enough that it was agreed Michael and his family would attend Ronnie's second inauguration in January 1985. The day before the ceremonies, Ronnie asked five-year-old Cameron if he would like to make a snowman in the Rose Garden. When grandfather and grandson stepped into the frigid air, a line of news photographers was waiting, as was a partially completed snowman put together by the White House staff. The base and midsection were there. All that remained was for Ronnie and Cameron to construct a smaller snowball for the head and put it on top, with the president's dog Lucky, a lively Bouvier des Flandres, joining them.

"They frolicked in the snow making the head while the press snapped pictures. It was the first picture of us as a family taken together since the rift," Michael wrote later. "I remember thinking how sad it was that when Dad wanted to do something fun and private with his grandson, it had to become a media event. He had lost all his privacy. I could only think: Was the cost worth the price?" What Ronnie's son doesn't appear to have recognized—or chose not to—was that privacy wasn't the point of that heartwarming family scene. It had been a carefully staged photo op.

The tension with Michael was far from ended. In early 1987 Nancy read that Michael was writing a book about his father. The reported title—*On the Outside Looking In*— suggested it was not going to be a valentine. Nancy called him and demanded to know what was up. Michael told her he had been offered a lot of money. The deal was said to be in the high six figures. "Of course," Nancy replied. "I could get lots of money for walking naked up and down Pennsylvania Avenue. It's a question of taste."

On April 12, which was Palm Sunday, Michael's family came to the ranch to celebrate Ashley's fourth birthday. Nancy was determined to find out what he planned to put in his book. And as usual, she was more attuned than Ronnie to the fact that there was something else in the air. "Michael seemed anxious and upset, and although he didn't say anything, I could sense that he wanted some time alone with Ronnie and me," Nancy recalled. "After lunch, I suggested that Colleen take the children for a walk around the pond. As soon as Mike was alone with us, he burst into tears."

Nancy hugged him and stroked his back, just as she had done on those long rides to the ranch when he was a small boy. For the next hour, Michael poured out the terrible secret that he had been holding inside for more than thirty years. About the camp counselor who had molested him when he was eight years old. About the shameful pictures of him that he was afraid were out there somewhere. About the anguish that had never lifted.

As Michael began to talk, shaking and stammering, Ronnie couldn't comprehend what his son was telling him.

"What?" he asked.

"He was molested, honey," Nancy explained.

"By who?" Ronnie asked.

"By a counselor at day camp," she replied.

"Who was the guy?" Ronnie demanded. "I'll find him and kick his butt."

"Let Mike get it out of his system, honey," Nancy said to him, more firmly.

Then she began to question her stepson, drawing out more and more information: How old was he when it happened? What was the name of the camp? How many days a week was he there? How long did this go on? As Michael answered, he couldn't look at his father's face. He stared at Ronnie's belt buckle, feeling as though he would vomit.

Finally, Ronnie moved toward Michael, and their eyes met. "Dad, he orally copulated me. He took me in his mouth," Michael told him.

Ronnie put his arms around his son. "Why didn't you tell me about this when it happened?" he asked.

Michael replied: "Because I was afraid you would stop liking me."

And then, it was Michael's turn to say something he never had before. He turned to his stepmother. "I love you," he told Nancy.

When Michael learned that a thirty-two-page outline of his book had leaked to *Penthouse* magazine, Nancy assured him that she and Ronnie would publicly support his decision to go public with the sexual abuse he had suffered. White House spokesman Marlin Fitzwater told reporters that while the president and first lady were "saddened by the fact that he had kept it from them all these years," they hoped that Michael's book might help prevent the same thing from happening to other children. Nancy's press secretary, Elaine Crispen, made a similar comment. Michael wrote later: "It was the first time since Dad had become president that the White House had ever made a statement in support of anything I had done, and I was elated."

Michael sent Nancy an advance copy of the book in March 1988. She read it with trepidation, staying up half the night. Sure enough, it had plenty of brutal things to say about his father, his mother, and his stepmother. But she saw that he had been just as hard on himself. "It was wonderful to see how Mike had grown and changed, and how he was now able to take more responsibility for his own life," she wrote. "Ironically, this book, which started off as one more source of friction between us, actually helped us develop a better relationship."

*

Nancy had good reason to be wary of a tell-all book. Her daughter, Patti, then thirty-three, had coauthored a supposed work of fiction called *Home Front,* which was published in 1986. Nancy learned of the project not from Patti, but by reading an item in *Time.* The plot centers on the free-spirited daughter of a former TV pitchman named

Robert Canfield who becomes California governor and then president. The heroine's mother, Harriet Canfield, is a fashion-obsessed airhead who, upon arriving at the White House, declares: "There's just so much history here! Imagine all the people who have been within these walls. But, good grief, I just can't wait to redecorate." A *People* magazine cover story labeled Patti's novel "a literary striptease that might never have been published but for its author's obvious family connections. What the book lacks in literary merit, it makes up for in entertainment value as a First Family parlor game."

To Nancy, seeing her daughter's bitterness toward her laid out so publicly was not at all entertaining. It was excruciating. In 1989, after several years in which they barely spoke, Nancy wrote in her autobiography that her relationship with Patti was "one of the most painful and disappointing aspects of my life. I wish it weren't true, and I still hope it will change, but so far, at least, it hasn't been a happy story. Somehow, no matter what I do, we seem to square off."

The rebellious daughter who had burst out sobbing when her father was elected governor was even unhappier to see him in the White House. Over the eight years of Ronnie's presidency, Patti stayed there no more than four or five times, by her estimation. As she was trying to make it as an actress, Patti bristled at having security agents follow her every move. One day she interviewed hunky singer-actor Kris Kristofferson for the NBC popular-music television show *The Midnight Special,* and it ended with an overnight tryst. The next morning, Patti found that her Secret Service detail had been waiting all night outside Kristofferson's New York hotel, unsure when the president's daughter would reappear. The agents glared at her. "Tell you what," she said. "On the occasions when I know my plans ahead of time, I'll let you know. The times I don't, you'll have to wing it. I can't always predict what will happen in my life." Word of her sleepover with Kristofferson got back to Nancy via the agents' logs. Her mother told Patti to behave with "a little more decency."

In 1984 Patti "signed off" on having no Secret Service protection, as her brother Ron had done the year before. Security officials subsequently informed her they had picked up intelligence overseas that a terrorist act was possibly being plotted against one of the president's daughters, though they didn't know which one. "Patti screamed & complained so much we took the S.S. detail away at her request," Ronnie wrote in his February 1, 1984, diary entry. "Now S.S. went to her & asked if she would accept it for no more than a week until they could get this informant out of Lebanon & check the story. She said yes. But today's the 4th day & she's screaming again about invasion of her privacy & last night she abused the agents terribly. I said take them away from her so she's again without protection. Insanity is hereditary—you catch it from your kids."

Even as she battled to guard her privacy, Patti became more public in her liberal activism. A rebuke of Ronnie's conservative policies by his own daughter guaranteed news coverage. This had been the case since early in his presidency. In June 1981 she was among the speakers at the fourth annual "Survival Sunday" antinuclear rally and rock concert at the Hollywood Bowl. "The fact that my father is president doesn't take away my right as a citizen to speak my mind," twenty-eight-year-old Patti told a news conference before the event. But the fact that her father was president surely figured in the organizers' decision to give her a spotlight before an audience of eighteen thousand in a lineup that included Bruce Springsteen, Jackson Browne, and Bonnie Raitt. Robert F. Kennedy Jr. appeared there as well. Both her parents told her she was "being used."

Patti nonetheless saw an opportunity to connect the president and people in his administration with some of the leading voices in the antinuclear movement. Ronnie was amenable enough to agree to meet with Patti and Australian physician Helen Caldicott, who had founded several activist organizations. They each had conditions: Caldicott demanded that the president come alone, without aides. Ronnie made it clear to his daughter that he did not want either of them to comment publicly about their December 1982 session. The exchange in the White House library lasted an hour and a half—an enormous block of time in a president's schedule—and grew heated. According to Caldicott's later account, Ronnie called the Soviets "evil, godless Communists," and said the way to prevent nuclear war was to build more weapons; she asked him insultingly whether he had gotten his arguments from *Reader's Digest*. Ronnie wrote in his diary that Caldicott "seems like a nice, caring person but is all steamed up and knows a lot of things that aren't true. I tried but couldn't get through her fixation. For that matter, I couldn't get through to Patti. I'm afraid our daughter has been taken over by that whole d—n gang."

In the summer of 1984 Patti married her yoga instructor Paul Grilley. He was six years younger than she was, and his background could hardly have been more different from hers. Grilley, the son of a building contractor and a secretary, had grown up near Glacier National Park in Montana. The marriage would last six years. Whatever misgivings Patti's parents might have had about her choice of a mate, Nancy was thrilled that her daughter wanted to have a traditional wedding and that she sought her mother's help in planning the private ceremony at the Hotel Bel-Air. Patti picked out her own dress, an off-the-shoulder creation of white silk lace and charmeuse. Following a traditional wedding custom, Nancy provided Patti something to wear that was old (a bracelet that had belonged to Edie's mother) and something blue (a garter). Patti completed it by finding something to borrow: a ring from a friend. The Presbyterian service was conducted under a flower-and-vine-bedecked gazebo on the hotel's serene Swan Lake Terrace. Ronnie gave a charming and sentimental toast in which he recalled how Patti as a baby would wrap her tiny fingers around his big one, gripping so tightly that he could still feel it. News accounts noted Ron and Maureen were there, and that Michael had been invited but did not attend.

It probably was not a coincidence that the timing of Patti's honeymoon meant she would not be sitting in the presidential box in Dallas when her father accepted the Republican Party's nomination for a second term. "I had hoped that Patti's wedding would signal a new, happier stage in our relationship, but that was not to be," Nancy wrote later. "She came to Ronnie's second inauguration in 1985, but just for the day. When they took the family photograph, she was hiding in the back, and Ronnie kept saying, 'Step forward, Patti, so we can see you.' But she wouldn't do it. And Paul didn't come at all, which hurt me. He said he had to work, but it seemed to me that if you explained you were taking a couple of days off because your father-in-law was being sworn in as president of the United States, most people would understand."

With the 1986 publication of Patti's novel *Home Front*, the breach became deeper. According to the author, the night before she started her book tour, she got a call from her brother, Ron, who told her not to expect kudos from anyone for trashing their parents. He added that he had only thumbed through the book and had no intention of reading it. "Ron's reaction hurt me more than anyone else's, and I wish he had read the book before judging me," Patti recalled. "He, better than anyone, would know the differences between the Canfields and the Reagans, and if he had read the story, I don't think he would have found any unkind motivation in it."

Ron offers a different version. "To the best of my recollection, that particular falling out with Patti occurred at a small party one evening in the apartment I shared with Doria on Devon Avenue in Westwood," he told me. "Patti was excited that night about her book and about being the center of so much attention. She also stood to make what, for her, was a considerable amount of money. But she was bitter and complaining about her parents' failure to energetically promote the book. I tried explaining several times that the book painted a less-than-flattering portrait of them and that they were embarrassed and understandably just wanted it to go away. Patti continued to insist that her mother and father owed her their support in her endeavor. Finally, exasperated, I told her—rather tartly, I must admit—that she had turned her parents into cartoons, and it was crazy to expect them to get behind such a thing." Patti left the party, her brother recalled, and the two of them did not speak for a long time afterward.

Nancy spent part of her thirty-fourth wedding anniversary on March 4, 1986, watching her daughter tout the book on *Good Morning America* and then in another appearance on the TV talk show *Donahue.*

But Patti's publicity tour was short lived. Nancy's close friend Merv Griffin bumped Patti from his show, as did comedienne Joan Rivers, who was hosting the *Tonight* show. The snubs only ignited more news coverage. "Phil Donahue admitted publicly that he'd been pressured to take me off his show, which didn't deter him from putting me on. He didn't specify exactly who pressured him; he didn't have to," Patti recalled. "Reporters staked out the front of my house; I climbed down the back fence to avoid them. They chased down Joan Rivers, who said, 'No comment.' They chased down my parents. My mother said nothing. My father said, 'Nancy had nothing to do with it.'"

In Nancy's memoir, published in late 1989, she wrote at length about her continuing estrangement from her daughter, as well as her hopes that, someday, the two of them might get past their bitterness: "Parents are not always responsible for their children's problems. When your child has a difficult time, it's only natural to blame yourself and think, What did I do wrong? But some children are just born a certain way, and there's very little you can do about it.

"And yet I remain optimistic. There is still time for us to improve our relationship, and now that our public years are over, I'm hoping Patti and I will be able to reach some kind of understanding.

"I also hope Patti doesn't turn out to be an 'if only' child. I've known people who, years after their parents had died, were still saying, 'If only I had told my mother that I loved her,' or 'If only I had made some peace with my father.' What a terrible burden that must be to carry.

"One of the great blessings of my life is that I've never felt that way. I had occasional moments of tension with my parents, but they both knew that I loved them, and I always knew that they loved me.

"I hope and pray that before my own life is over, Patti and I will be able to put the past behind us and arrive at that same point. Nothing would make me happier than to work that out."

There would be more years of pain and alienation ahead, but eventually Nancy and Patti did move toward that point. Nancy was right in what she had feared. It was loss that brought Patti to her side in the 1990s. Together they shared the slow, cruel loss of Ronnie, right before their eyes, to Alzheimer's disease. "I think sometimes of how different my life would be if my parents hadn't lived this long, or if I hadn't listened to the echo of my own despair," Patti wrote in September 1995. "The thought comes to me in small moments—walking with my father, my arm through his. What if he weren't there to touch, and I had to live my life with only the remnants of my anger at my fingertips? It comes to me with the sound of my mother's voice and the things I am learning from her now."

At the midpoint of her own life, Patti had finally learned to count her blessings. One of them was that there was still a chance to make things right—or at least better—with her mother. She had been spared that regret. "I might have been too late," she said. "I might have been left with only silence and distance."

CHAPTER SEVENTEEN

Ronnie made his announcement that he would run for a second term in a four-minute, nationally televised address on January 29, 1984. He did it at the exceedingly odd time of 10:55 p.m. on a Sunday night, which was nearly an hour after the president generally liked to be in bed. His campaign offered no explanation why. The stars must have aligned favorably at that moment, but Nancy was far from reassured. It was an open secret in Washington that she had been opposed to another campaign. Ronnie wore her down with what she called "a steady drumbeat." There were things on his agenda that he wanted to finish, and he was doubtful Vice President George H. W. Bush could hold the White House for Republicans if Ronnie's name was not at the top of the ticket.

"For a while, we talked about it every night, until it became more and more obvious that this was something Ronnie just had to do. Finally, I said, 'If you feel that strongly, go ahead. You know I'm not crazy about it, but okay,'" Nancy recalled. The public uncertainty over what he would do continued until just days before Ronnie formally made his declaration. Nancy appeared to have lost weight, which fueled speculation that she was having health problems. The previous Wednesday, rumors that he would not run had sent the Dow Jones Industrial Average tumbling.

Nancy's concerns were many. There was, of course, her unshakeable fear about the physical dangers to Ronnie. She missed her privacy and their old life in California. But Nancy was also worried about whether he would win. Republicans had lost twenty-six House seats in the 1982 midterm election. Ronnie's approval rating had only recently recovered to a robust 57 percent after having spent twenty-two months below 50 percent during the depths of the recession. The internal numbers of his pollster Richard Wirthlin showed a sharp decline in support among the blue-collar voters who had been so crucial to Ronnie's 1980 victory. In May 1983 a *Washington Post* headline declared: "Go Ahead, Sucker—Bet on Reagan's Reelection."

Meanwhile, a potentially formidable Democratic field was shaping up, with Walter Mondale, who had been Jimmy Carter's vice president, leading the pack. The night of Ronnie's announcement that he would run again, Nancy wrote in her diary: "I think it's going to be a tough, personal, close campaign. Mondale is supposed to be an infighter. . . . Ronnie is so popular that they might be desperate. I'll be glad when the next nine months are over."

The construction of Ronnie's own campaign apparatus was well under way. Stu Spencer would continue to be both Reagans' most trusted strategist, but he declined the role of campaign manager. That went to Ed Rollins, who had become White House political director when Lyn Nofziger left in November 1981. Rollins moved into a campaign headquarters on Capitol Hill and was given a $21 million budget for the 1984 primary season. To quiet any concern about the age issue, the Reagan team arranged for *Parade* magazine to run a December 1983 story on the president's workout program, with a cover image of Ronnie, in a white T-shirt, pumping iron.

Even while she was trying to talk her husband out of running, Nancy had been sizing up his potential adversaries. As she had noted in her diary, Mondale seemed most likely to win the Democratic nomination. By the fall of 1983, she had correctly discounted the assumption of many in Washington that Ohio senator and former astronaut John Glenn, an American hero, had the potential to "ride the rocket ship" to the White House. She started to worry more about youthful Colorado senator Gary Hart, the insurgent in the race. When Hart dealt Mondale a stunning upset in the February 2004 New Hampshire primary, Nancy called Rollins and demanded: "What do we have on Hart?" The campaign manager assured her that while Hart had some appeal, he probably wouldn't be able to go the distance against Mondale and the Democratic establishment. Nancy replied, "Well, you better look into this. I'm getting calls from my friends that we better take him seriously." Rollins had not had much by way of direct dealings with Nancy previously. She was suddenly on the phone to him constantly, telling him what intelligence she was picking up and demanding to know what the campaign was doing about potential trouble spots that popped up on her radar.

It drove him nearly crazy. Nancy and her network did not share Rollins's confidence that the campaign was going their way. One of her chief worries was that Ronnie might lose their home state of California, and no amount of argument from Rollins could convince her otherwise. She had heard that the campaign had only a light footprint in the state and demanded to know why it hadn't set up an office in Beverly Hills. Why weren't her friends there seeing campaign signs for Ronnie? Once, when Rollins couldn't tell her where one of them could send a contribution, she said: "Shouldn't you know the address in California where people can send checks? You're the campaign manager. This is embarrassing." After one particularly brutal campaign strategy session with the first lady, Spencer told him: "She could smell fear all over you, Rollins. You're doomed."

But as months went by, Rollins told me, "I sort of moved from being scared to death of her to having great, great respect for her." Nancy may not have had his deep knowledge of the intricacies of making a campaign work, but she was unsurpassed when it came to knowing what it took to make her husband appear and perform at his best. Nor was she going to shrink back into the traditionally ornamental role to which the political handlers preferred to consign a candidate's wife. As he came to accept those realities, Rollins finally developed a workable relationship with Nancy. He knew he had passed his biggest test with her when she told him: "I know you love my husband. You're a protector of my husband." In other words, she saw them as comrades, united in a common cause.

With the economy on the rebound, the 1984 reelection strategy was to go long on feel-good themes and short on policy specifics, because many of Ronnie's remained controversial. One of Nancy's chief concerns was the advertising. She had been dissatisfied with the quality of the spots their campaign team had put on the air in 1980 and pressed for something more creative and interesting this time around. Rollins argued that television did not make much difference. He wanted to invest more money into voter registration, ground organization, and other fundamentals that he felt were being neglected. Lyn Nofziger, who was advising the reelection effort, warned the campaign manager: "Don't forget who your clients are. They're movie stars. To them, all this stuff that you're talking about—voter registration, what have you—that doesn't mean jack shit to them. What's important to them are pictures. Their friends are going to see the commercials."

Rather than hiring an existing advertising agency, Mike Deaver put together a high-priced all-star group from around the country. They were dubbed the Tuesday Team. These were people who came not from the political world but from the corporate one, where they had produced ads for notable brands such as Pepsi, General Electric, and Pan American World Airways. The work they did from their headquarters in Rockefeller Center had a polished, cinematic quality.

One sixty-second commercial in particular stands as a modern political classic. It had a dreamlike quality that was inspired by *The Natural*—a popular movie that year about a middle-aged baseball phenom, played by Robert Redford, who seems to materialize from nowhere—and reflected Deaver's belief in using visual images as powerful storytelling tools. As orchestral music played, the campaign spot opened with a montage of softly lit scenes showing everyday Americans going about their lives of contentment and prosperity: a lobster boat heading to sea, a man carrying a briefcase getting out of a taxi, a farmer on a tractor, a neighbor waving to a paperboy on a bicycle, a family moving into a new home, proud grandparents watching a bride and groom walk down the aisle, campers raising an American flag. The narrator's soothing voice intoned: "It's morning again in America, and under the leadership of President Reagan, our country is prouder and stronger and better. Why would we ever want to return to where we were less than four short years ago?"

The ad was both nostalgic for the past and upbeat about the future. Notably, Ronnie did not appear in it, except for a brief shot at the end that showed his face set against an American flag. The ad makers had titled this spot "Prouder, Stronger, Better." But it soon became known as the "Morning in America" ad. Nancy loved it. Rollins made sure the commercial got heavy play in California, where the people she talked to most frequently would see a lot of it. Spending so much on ads in California—at least $1 million, the campaign manager recalled—was a waste of money strategically. But if it calmed Nancy down, Rollins thought it was worth it. "It was really to please that element as opposed to driving a campaign message," he told me.

Nancy was not so enamored with another proposed concept for an ad. It was to begin with a close-up shot of fit young men playing volleyball, with the ocean sparkling behind them. As the camera pulled back, it would become clear that these were sailors getting in some recreation time on the deck of an aircraft carrier. The announcer was to have said: "Thank you, Mr. President. We're now prepared for peace." A similar spot was planned with army soldiers playing softball, where the frame would have widened to reveal tanks in the background. This would have been a way of highlighting the buildup in the military budget that Ronnie had pushed through during the first term. But Nancy, Deaver, and Baker, among others, were concerned that it would only remind voters of their fears that Ronnie was spoiling to get the country into a war. It might also stir growing public concerns about the explosion in Pentagon spending, which had helped create an enormous budget deficit and was bound to bring a fiscal reckoning. The ads were vetoed. Later, Rollins would learn it was in part at Nancy's behest. "They were spectacular ads," he recalled mournfully more than thirty years later. "They were my favorite ads of all time."

*

In at least one respect, Nancy was having an easier time during the 1984 campaign than she had four years before. The media was much gentler on her. Maureen Dowd of the *New York Times* observed: "These days it is generally acknowledged that the First Lady has grown into her role. She is still reserved, but she shows more humor about herself and has become a more relaxed speaker."

During the Republican convention in Dallas in August, *Boston Globe* syndicated columnist Ellen Goodman wrote that "it's hard to pinpoint the moment Nancy Reagan's image started to improve. It's harder to know whether it's her image or her identity that's been changing. At some point, said a friend, 'she stopped crying and started to cope.'" Goodman added: "The most important changes are substantive ones. Nancy Reagan has become less associated with Beverly Hills and more associated with an antidrug campaign. She has gone from donating her designer clothes to museums to donating her time in a campaign against addiction."

The Reagans' love story was one of the convention's major themes. The night before Ronnie gave his acceptance speech, Nancy delivered a brief address that concluded with: "Let's make it one more for the Gipper, and thank you." The screen behind her suddenly lit up with a gargantuan image of Ronnie in shirt sleeves, sitting in his hotel suite and watching her on his television. She turned her back to the hall, waved at her husband on the screen, and he waved back. It was hokey, cloying—and in the eyes of most Americans, adorable. An eight-minute video tribute to Nancy that played before her speech included a scene of the Reagans strolling hand in hand through the sun-dappled woods. It was shot from behind and caught Nancy taking a flirtatious, gentle kick at her husband's behind. As Ronnie spoke of his wife on the video, he appeared to be on the verge of choking up when he said: "I can't imagine life without her."

Meanwhile, things were not going so well for the Democrats. At their convention in San Francisco, Walter Mondale accepted his party's nomination with what turned out to be a politically disastrous pledge to raise taxes. His historic decision to put a woman on his ticket soon ran into trouble when the media began raising questions about the finances of New York congresswoman Geraldine Ferraro and her husband.

Heading into the first debate with Mondale in Louisville on October 7, both Wirthlin's tracking poll and a public one by the *Washington Post* gave Ronnie a hefty 55-percent-to-37-percent lead over the Democratic nominee, with a relatively small 8 percent of voters undecided. Still, Nancy was nervous. "I'm against debates," she wrote later. "They're long, often boring, and the incumbent is at a disadvantage. The candidate who has never held the office can just attack, without having to defend his own record." What's more, incumbent presidents often cruise into those matchups overconfident and rusty. That had happened to Ford in 1976 and to Carter in 1980.

The president's performance in Louisville was a disaster. Nancy called it "the worst night of Ronnie's political career. Right from the start, he was tense, muddled and off-stride. He lacked authority. He stumbled. This was a Ronald Reagan I had never seen before. It was painful to watch. There was no way around it; that debate was a nightmare." Mondale, on the other hand, showed a mastery of the issues. He mixed his jabs at Ronnie with enough deference to avoid alienating that segment of voters who liked the president but might have doubts about whether he deserved another term.

Nancy was furious—predictably, not at Ronnie but at Deaver, Baker, Richard Darman, and the others who had been in charge of preparing him for the debate. "What have you done to my husband?" she demanded when she saw Deaver back at the hotel. Campaign chairman Paul Laxalt, the Nevada senator and longtime friend of the Reagans, was channeling Nancy when he held a news conference to declare that Ronnie had been "brutalized by a briefing process that didn't make any sense" and that his handlers had "filled his head with so many facts and figures that he lost his spontaneity and his visionary concepts." The night had gone so badly that even irrepressible optimist Ronnie was down. "I have to say I lost," he wrote in his diary. "I guess I'd crammed so hard on facts & figures in view of the absolutely dishonest things he's been saying in the campaign, I guess I flattened out. Anyway I didn't feel good about myself."

Decades later, Baker still bristled at Nancy's contention that he and his team were to blame for Ronnie's disastrous performance in Louisville. Baker insisted to me that they had prepared Ronnie exactly as they had in 1980, when he had "beat Carter like a drum." This time, in Baker's view, the problem was an overweening incumbent who had been too lazy to buckle down as he should have. Nancy "decided a head needed to roll, so it could be somebody else's fault and not the president's fault," Baker said. "That head was going to be Dick Darman, who was in charge of the preparation." Baker refused to fire his aide, telling Deaver and Spencer that he would do it only if he were ordered to by Ronnie himself. "I knew he wouldn't," Baker recalled. "That's just the way he was. He would never. Anyway, he went on and said, 'I didn't do my homework,' and he didn't, but she didn't like that."

Mondale had at last found an opening. The next week saw a wave of stories that brought to the surface the sensitive "age issue" that had been simmering all along, raising questions whether seventy-three-year-old Ronnie was too old to do the job. The *Wall Street Journal* ran a headline that said: "Fitness Issue—New Question in Race: Is Oldest US President Now Showing His Age? Reagan Debate Performance Invites Open Speculation on His Ability to Serve." Television networks repeatedly showed clips of him nodding off at the Vatican in 1982. They also replayed a recent photo opportunity at the ranch, where the president had been asked a question about US-Soviet talks on space weapons. As Ronnie hesitated, Nancy could be heard saying sotto voce, "Tell them we are doing everything we can." After which, her husband piped up: "We're doing everything we can." Nancy claimed later she had been talking to herself and that Ronnie didn't have his hearing aid turned up enough to have caught it.

Unlike in 1980, when there had been only one debate between Carter and Ronnie at the very end of the race, there would be a second one in 1984, in Kansas City on October 21. "Let Ronnie be Ronnie," Nancy demanded of Deaver. The number of rehearsals was reduced from five to two. His massive briefing book was trimmed down to twenty-five pages. Media consultant Roger Ailes, who would later become famous for building Fox News into a conservative media powerhouse, was brought in to rebuild Ronnie's confidence. Even former president Nixon wrote a letter of encouragement and advice. The campaign held a warm-up rally right before the debate, so that Ronnie would go in with the cheers of his supporters and not his own self-doubt ringing in his ears. Aides also made sure that Nancy would be in the front row when Ronnie was on the stage and that he knew where to look for her. As the debate began, she plastered a smile on her face, but her stomach was in knots, and her hands felt cold as ice.

The difference was dramatic. Ronnie was relaxed and confident; Mondale was combative. The former vice president's campaign aides had also placed a piece of reflective white paper on his lectern, which threw off the lighting. It accentuated the bags under Mondale's eyes and made his skin appear pasty. The coup de grâce came when moderator Henry Trewhitt of the *Baltimore Sun* asked whether Ronnie had any doubt that, at his age, he would be able to function were a crisis to hit.

"Not at all, Mr. Trewhitt," the president answered, "and I want you to know that also I will not make age an issue of this campaign. I am not going to exploit, for political purposes, my opponent's youth and inexperience." Even Mondale had to laugh. The age issue, which had been the biggest remaining speed bump on Ronnie's road to a second term, had been flattened with a single quip.

It had once again been Nancy who knew what it was going to take to get Ronnie back into his groove. She understood, as author Garry Wills once put it, that "a Reagan without confidence would not be Reagan. It is against this background that we must interpret all tales of

Nancy Reagan's 'ruthlessness.'" Nancy was constantly telling his aides that they must build him up, not knock him down. Lou Cannon wrote later: "In recognizing the actor's truth that it is the performance that is crucial, Nancy Reagan had saved the day, however bruising and unfair her intervention may have been to Baker and Darman."

The day before the election, as Ronnie's campaign plane headed for California, Rollins predicted boldly that the president would carry forty-nine states. In an informal poll taken at the back of the plane, even the Secret Service agents joined in the consensus that it would be a landslide of historic proportion. Ronnie demurred, saying as he always did that he would be happy with 51 percent of the vote. Nor was Nancy joining in any premature celebration. "Well, you better be right," she told Rollins. "You've been so overconfident in this race, Ed, you better be right."

Rollins was indeed right. Ronnie won everywhere but Mondale's home state of Minnesota and the District of Columbia. Nancy would have no memory of much that happened the final two days before the election. She took a fall that Sunday night as she got out of bed at the Red Lion Inn in Sacramento to look for a blanket, which put a goose egg on her head. Though she was able to put in a full day of campaigning, news accounts noted that she looked drawn and tired.

One last time, Ronnie and Nancy did their election night ritual of dinner at the Jorgensens', followed by a victory celebration at the Century Plaza. In his diary entry the next day, Ronnie wrote: "Well, 49 states, 59% of the vote & 525 electoral votes. A short press conf. The press is now trying to prove it wasn't a landslide or should I say a mandate?"

But in what it took to achieve that victory, there were seeds of trouble ahead. A campaign that had been largely issue free had not provided a blueprint for governing in a second term, which is historically a rocky and treacherous time for presidents. Everyone was exhausted—physically, emotionally, and spiritually. The bitterness and finger-pointing surrounding the debate in Louisville was a wound that would not heal.

Baker wanted out of the White House and would soon arrange a job swap with Treasury secretary Don Regan. He took Richard Darman, his tough and savvy aide, over to Treasury with him. Deaver also had his eye on the exit and a life in the private sector that would provide enough money to afford the expensive tastes he had developed in his years of traveling in the Reagans' circle. Spencer returned to California, where he could continue to advise when he was inclined to do so and maintain his distance from the palace intrigue when he wasn't. As Lou Cannon wrote: "Although Nancy Reagan did not realize it sufficiently and Ronald Reagan realized it not at all, the landslide of 1984 had left the people who had done the most to help the president during his first four years burned out and disillusioned. Most of them couldn't wait to leave the White House, where it was no longer Morning Again in America."

As the first lady's most trusted allies were replaced by people she barely knew, her early-warning system in the West Wing was shut down. That meant she had no clue that a rogue operation was developing within the National Security Council and the Central Intelligence Agency, one that would lead to the Iran-contra scandal and come close to taking down Ronnie's presidency. Only when it was almost too late would Nancy recognize what had happened. "If, by some miracle, I could take back one decision in Ronnie's presidency, it would be his agreement in January 1985 that Jim Baker and Donald Regan should swap jobs," she recalled. "It seemed like a good idea at the time—a little unusual, perhaps, but reasonable. Jim, who had served Ronnie well as chief of staff, was worn out, and Donald Regan was more than willing to come to the White House after four years as secretary of the Treasury. When Baker and Regan suggested the switch, there was no reason to expect that this new arrangement would lead to a political disaster."

The inauguration was perhaps a harbinger. In 1981 Ronnie had lucked out with some of the most pleasant midwinter weather on record. His second term began during an arctic blast that sent temperatures in the nation's capital plummeting to four degrees below zero. Because January 20 fell on a Sunday that year, Ronnie took the oath privately.

The ceremonial swearing-in scheduled for the following day had to be moved inside. Where 140,000 guests had been invited to the main event, only 1,200 could squeeze into the Capitol Rotunda to hear Ronnie declare that "our nation is poised for greatness." On the grounds outside, an icy wind whipped around 26,000 empty chairs and a vacant platform. The people who would have been in those seats had to settle for watching the proceedings on television in their hotel rooms or in crowded restaurants, seeing just what they would have seen if they'd stayed home.

All the other outdoor festivities were canceled as well. No one wanted to subject the 10,578 people slated to march in the inaugural parade to frostbite or worse. The few onlookers hearty enough to stand along the Pennsylvania Avenue route got only a glimpse of the presidential motorcade whizzing by. Nancy learned later that while she and Ronnie had been at church on the day of the private swearing-in, an intruder had sneaked into the White House with the Marine Band: "All I could think was: What if he had been carrying a gun? I prayed that this wasn't a bad omen."

CHAPTER EIGHTEEN

The unusual White House power-sharing arrangement of the first four years, in which the operation was managed by the troika of Baker, Deaver, and Meese, had been ungainly from the start. It created internal fiefdoms, suspicion, and backbiting: the ideologues aligned against the pragmatists; the Californians against the Washington veterans. No one was ever sure whose hand was on the helm when it came to making any given decision. After Ronnie's 1984 victory, it was clearer than ever that the deal that had been struck four years earlier had reached its expiration date. All three members of the troika wanted out.

In February 1985 Meese finally moved over to the Justice Department as attorney general. His confirmation had been delayed for a year while an independent counsel investigated his financial dealings. Once in the job, Meese would continue to be at the center of controversy as he sought to translate into policy the Reagan administration's stances on abortion, pornography, affirmative action, and religion. For fighting those battles, Meese would gain a place as a conservative hero. But many of his initiatives were blocked by Congress and the Supreme Court, and ethical questions continued to dog him. His legal difficulties culminated in his resignation in 1988, after yet another independent counsel probe. The prosecutor declined to indict him for filing a false tax return but portrayed him as disorganized and indifferent to appearances of impropriety.

Nancy was glad to see Meese go. His ideological inflexibility had always troubled her, she wrote. "It also made me squirm that he kept getting into trouble in his financial life. He made a series of mistakes which embarrassed the presidency, and some men in his situation would have stepped down. Eventually he did, but in my opinion he waited far too long and weakened both the Justice Department and the presidency."

From Nancy's perspective, the departures of Baker and especially Deaver would bring a more unwelcome change. They had been her most crucial allies, the cutouts through whom she could work her will in the West Wing without leaving fingerprints. The shuffle would also put into Baker's place as White House chief of staff the man who would become her greatest internal nemesis: Donald T. Regan.

Regan came from a blue-collar background in Cambridge, Massachusetts, and graduated from Harvard on scholarship. As a US Marine in World War II, he fought across the Pacific Theater from Guadalcanal to Okinawa, and then came home to work his way up from stockbroker and become the youngest-ever president of Wall Street behemoth Merrill Lynch. A CEO by temperament, Regan first proposed the idea of a job swap to Baker a few days after the 1984 landslide. Baker jumped at the opportunity. He was exhausted by the irregular hours at the White House and the constant barrage of what he called "javelins" from the Right. Though Baker had his eye on becoming secretary of state, George Shultz wasn't going anywhere. Running the Treasury Department would also give him a central role in what was potentially the biggest domestic policy initiative of the second term: a sweeping overhaul of the nation's tax laws. But to make it happen, Baker told Regan, "We need to get Deaver involved."

Part of it was courtesy. At one point, Baker knew, Deaver himself had wanted to be White House chief of staff. But there was another reason to loop him in: Deaver could make sure the idea went over with Nancy. When Baker arranged for Regan to have lunch with him and

Deaver, Regan noticed Deaver "listened to our words with the polite air of a man who had already heard what he was now being told and had made up his mind how to react. I supposed that Baker had sketched in the details beforehand. In my innocence, the thought that Deaver had cleared the plan with the first lady before discussing it with me, or even the president, did not occur to me."

They presented their proposal to Ronnie in early January in the Oval Office. The president's reaction struck Regan as surprisingly impassive. Ronnie asked only a few questions and showed little curiosity about how the new arrangement would work. "He seemed to be absorbing a fait accompli rather than making a decision," Regan recalled. "One might have thought that the matter had already been settled by some absent party." In fact, Ronnie was relieved. There would now be one person running operations in the White House, rather than three. He wrote in his diary that the job swap had the potential to "resolve a lot of problems."

Deaver, by then, was well along on his plans to make his own exit. He was forty-six years old and, except for a year as an IBM sales trainee, had never worked for anyone but Ronald Reagan. As Deaver himself acknowledged, he had little interest in the details of policy. But no one was better at figuring out how to stage an event—or, as Deaver put it, "blending the gifts of Ronald Reagan with the proper pageantry." Still, for all the acclaim he had gotten as "Magic Mike" and "the Vicar of Visuals," Deaver had come to resent the subtext, which was that he was nothing more than a glorified family retainer; an image maker devoid of any real depth.

When Deaver finally made up his mind to leave, he told Nancy first. She asked him to stay for another year, and he was firm with her that he couldn't. If he didn't go now, he might never be able to bring himself to do it. Then Deaver went to the Oval Office.

"You know, Mike, I like to think I'm the only indispensable person around here, but the truth is . . ." Ronnie began.

Deaver put up his hand. "Please, Ron, don't say whatever you were going to say. Don't do that to me," he said. It was, Deaver would later realize, the only time he had ever given himself license to use the president's first name to his face.

At one o'clock in the afternoon on January 3, 1985, the White House announced his resignation. It also put out a statement by Nancy: "I'll miss him, but I think he'll be nearby." At Deaver's going-away party in the Rose Garden, Ronnie made an unusual request of White House aide Fred Ryan. He wanted Ryan to arrange for Deaver, though he no longer worked for the president, to continue to hold a pass that would allow him unfettered access to the White House grounds.

Deaver had promised to stick around long enough to do one last job for Ronnie and Nancy, which was to orchestrate the president's next big overseas trip. But rather than being the grace note that Deaver had hoped, the trip to Europe that May would be remembered for his greatest blunder.

The main event was an economic summit in Bonn. But in late 1984, during a visit to the White House, West German chancellor Helmut Kohl had proposed to Ronnie that the two of them make a side trip to a concentration camp and a cathedral, and that they lay a wreath in the Kolmeshöhe military cemetery on the outskirts of Bitburg, a town of 12,500 people. It would be a coda to Ronnie's spectacularly successful 1984 visit to Normandy on the fortieth anniversary of the D-day invasion. The two leaders would commemorate the passage of that same forty-year milestone since V-E Day and make a grand gesture that spoke to the reconciliation of their countries. Nancy, who knew that it was difficult for her husband to retain his composure in depressing settings, scotched the idea of a concentration camp visit.

Still, the cemetery remained a possibility. Deaver asked the Germans the question he always did when deciding whether to put something like this on the schedule: was there anything there that might embarrass the president? They told him no. Nor did he and Bill Henkel, the head of advance, see any problems when they visited the Bitburg cemetery. The markers, which lay flat against the ground, were covered by snow at the time. Henkel later double-checked with the US embassy, asking the deputy chief of mission if anyone there knew who was in the cemetery.

He got a dismissive retort: "Well, Mr. Henkel, what do you think? That Josef Mengele is buried there?"

"Could be," Henkel replied.

The Bitburg cemetery visit was on a presidential itinerary the White House announced on April 11. What Deaver and Henkel hadn't seen, and what German newspapers soon reported, was that the cemetery contained the remains of forty-nine members of the Waffen SS, which was affiliated with the elite and ruthless combat guards who ran Adolf Hitler's death camps. One of those buried there had been given the German Cross, a star-shaped medal that featured a swastika, for killing ten US soldiers on a day when at least seventy-one of them had been captured, shot at close range, and buried in a shallow grave.

The outcry was immediate and went on for weeks. Jewish groups protested. Veterans marched and mailed in their medals. More than half the Senate went on record opposing the visit. Among the flood of letters to the White House was one on lined paper, decorated with a heart-and-rainbow sticker, from five-year-old Chelsea Clinton of Little Rock, Arkansas. "Dear Mr. President," she printed, "I have seen *The Sound of Music.* The Nazis don't look like very nice people. Please don't visit their cemetary [*sic*]."

Holocaust memory keeper Elie Wiesel, who had lost his childhood and his family in the camps, confronted Ronnie during an April 19 White House ceremony awarding Wiesel the Congressional Gold Medal, Congress's highest civilian honor. Wiesel said he believed that Ronnie had not known about the SS graves when he accepted Kohl's invitation but argued that the president should find a different site now that he was aware of them. "That place, Mr. President, is not your place," Wiesel implored. "Your place is with the victims of the SS."

For a presidency that put such stock in symbolism, this was a disaster. What was meant to be an expression of transatlantic harmony had instead become a reminder of horror. Nancy was distraught. She begged Ronnie to cancel the visit to the cemetery. She argued that he was being taken advantage of by a supposed ally seeking to shore up his own shaky political standing at home. And she took out her wrath on Deaver and Henkel, demanding: "How could you do this to this man?"

But her persistence was no match for her husband's sense of obligation and his determination to stand by the commitment he had made to Kohl. On April 19, the same day that Wiesel appealed to the president to cancel the Bitburg visit, Ronnie got a call from the German chancellor. Aides were hoping that Kohl would tell Ronnie they should call it off. The conversation went on for forty-five minutes; at one point, executive assistant Jim Kuhn entered the Oval Office and saw Ronnie throw his pen across the room in anger. Kuhn went back in when the call was over. "I just looked at him, and I didn't ask," Kuhn told me. "I didn't say anything. I just looked, and he looked at me, and I waited. It took about ten seconds, and he said, 'We're going, Jim.' I said, 'Really?' He said, 'Yeah. We're going. Helmut wants to do it. I gave him my word.'"

Ronnie recorded in his diary that Kohl "was emphatic that to cancel the cemetery now would be a disaster in his country & an insult to the German people." Kohn had warned that his government might collapse if Ronnie pulled out. Vice President Bush had heard the president's side of the conversation and scribbled a note to him, which Ronnie recorded in his diary:

> Re Kohl Phone Call
> Mr. President,
> I was very proud of your stand. If I can help absorb some heat—send me into battle—It's not easy, but you are right!!
> George

Three days later, on April 22, Ronnie wrote: "The uproar about my trip to Germany & the Bitberg [*sic*] cemetery was cover stuff in Newsweek & Time. They just won't stop. Well. I'm not going to cancel anything no matter how much the bastards scream." But he could see how the stress was affecting his wife. "I'm worried about Nancy," he wrote on April 28. "She's uptight about the situation & nothing I say can wind her down. I'll pray about that too."

A stop at the Bergen-Belsen concentration camp was added, and it was arranged that Ronnie would speak there. On Deaver's advice and Nancy's insistence, the able speechwriter Ken Khachigian, who had left during the first term, was flown in from California to draft the address that Ronnie would deliver. The choice of Khachigian for this delicate task was a snub of the West Wing communications shop, which had recently been put in the hands of hard-liner Patrick J. Buchanan, whom Nancy mistrusted. Buchanan had worked in the Nixon White House and had been a major force in driving its harsh and divisive rhetoric pitting what it claimed was a "silent majority" against the liberal elite.

Amid the turmoil and controversy surrounding the planned Bitburg visit came an unexpected stroke of grace and generosity. Ninety-year-old General Matthew Ridgway, who had led the Eighty-Second Airborne Division during World War II and was the last living four-star general to have served in the European theater, volunteered to go to the cemetery with Ronnie, Kohl, and a German veteran. "I am a soldier, and I have never done anything political in my life," he told Deaver. "But it appears to me that my commander in chief is in trouble, and I would like to help. I would like to lay that wreath in Bitburg for him." The Germans suggested that Ridgway perform the ceremony with one of their own revered World War II veterans, General Johannes Steinhoff, an ace Luftwaffe fighter pilot who flew a thousand combat missions and survived being shot down a dozen times. He was severely disfigured in the final weeks of the war when his plane crashed and its fuel tanks ignited. "With all due respect," Deaver said when the Germans offered to have seventy-one-year-old Steinhoff participate, "you better snake-check that son of a bitch for everything he's worth."

So it was arranged. Ronnie and the German president would spend only eight minutes at Kolmeshöhe Cemetery, would make no remarks there, and would supervise the laying of the wreath rather than perform it. Still, Nancy was beside herself—and she blamed Deaver. "I could not recall our ever having been on opposite sides of an issue. But now she was convinced that I had ruined her husband's presidency and perhaps the rest of his life," Deaver later wrote.

Right up until the last minute, Nancy argued that the cemetery trip should be canceled. But as she began to understand that this was one battle she would not win, she turned to her astrologer Joan Quigley for guidance on how to contain the damage. That led to a series of last-minute changes in the schedule. Quigley determined that the ceremony must take place in the afternoon. Nancy told Deaver to change the takeoff time from Bonn to Bergen-Belsen by twenty minutes. Then she insisted that the arrival time be shifted by another twenty-five minutes. Each new demand required complex adjustments to security arrangements. "Everything we were doing, we were constrained, because she wasn't going to let us do anything that Joan didn't plan on" and approve, said Henkel, who was in charge of the advance operation. Years later, Deaver told Lou Cannon: "It was a nightmare."

The day of the event, Kuhn went to the guesthouse at Gymnich Castle near Cologne, where the Reagans were staying, to go over the final details with Ronnie. Nancy came into the room when she heard his voice and had another meltdown when Kuhn mentioned that the president was to touch the wreath.

"No," she said, "we're not doing it that way."

Kuhn tried to reassure her: "Mrs. Reagan, it's all worked out, and it's gonna be fine."

"No, it isn't," she shot back. "We're not doing it."

Kuhn looked at Ronnie, who said nothing. So, the president's assistant picked up a phone and said, "Get Mike Deaver right away." Deaver arrived and immediately figured out the situation. Silently, he embraced Nancy. "He held her for like a minute. It seemed like a long time, just held her tight, close to him. Never said one word, and then let go and walked out, and then she was okay," Kuhn told me. "He knew how to communicate with her without even speaking to her. And Reagan and I were looking at it. I could tell what Reagan was thinking. Reagan thought it was amazing. You could just read his eyes, you know? That Mike had that kind of way with Nancy Reagan. And then I was able to go on with the briefing."

Ronnie's emotional speech at Bergen-Belsen salvaged what could be salvaged of the day. "This painful walk into the past has done much more than remind us of the war that consumed the European continent. What we have seen makes unforgettably clear that no one of the rest of us can fully understand the enormity of the feelings carried by the victims of these camps," the president said. "The survivors carry a memory beyond anything that we can comprehend. The awful evil started by one man—an evil that victimized all the world with its destruction—was uniquely destructive to the millions forced into the grim abyss of these camps." Ronnie then quoted words that the camp's most famous victim, teenager Anne Frank, wrote three weeks before her capture: "It's really a wonder that I haven't dropped all my ideals, because they seem so absurd and impossible to carry out. Yet I keep them, because in spite of everything I still believe that people are really good at heart. I simply can't build up my hopes on a foundation consisting of confusion, misery, and death."

Reagan biographer Edmund Morris would later write that with that speech, "his agony—such as it was, brief as it was—transmitted itself, via television, into millions of human hearts." But the scars lingered, particularly with Jewish Americans. Ronnie had lost some of his moral authority, and it was clear that just six months after his triumphant reelection, the White House was off its game. "We survived; but Bitburg was another sign that an era was ending," Rollins wrote later. "These are the kind of things that always jump up and bite you when your political fortunes are in decline. In the first two years, when the revolution was riding tall in the saddle, Bitburg would have been a blip on the screen."

Despite Nancy's anxiety over Ronnie's fortunes, the ten-day, five-nation European trip turned out to be a triumph for her personally. She got rave reviews in the media when she danced the flamenco in Madrid and met with parents concerned about drugs in Bonn. After a private audience at the Vatican with the pope, John Paul II handed her a message in which he lauded her work "against drug abuse and in the rehabilitation of those whose lives have been affected by this social evil."

The following month, NBC aired a one-hour documentary about the first lady. Correspondent Chris Wallace said she was "at the peak of her power and the peak of her popularity. In polls these days, she does even better than her husband." In the West Wing, however, things were not so felicitous. Deaver and Baker were gone. Rollins joined the White House exodus. New chief of staff Regan brought in his own team of advisers—a group that would become known within the building as "the mice." The communications operation was in the hands of the bombastic Buchanan.

But even as Regan tightened his hold, those who worked for him could still feel Nancy's will, like the pull of an unseen magnet. Peggy Noonan, a talented young speechwriter, described it this way: "Her power was everywhere, in personnel, in who rose and fell, she was on the phone with [national security adviser Robert C. "Bud"] McFarlane about foreign affairs, on the phone nixing and okaying trips and events, arranging to closet the president with this policy analyst or that, calling to get the speeches earlier. She was everywhere."

Nancy and Regan had their first big run-in in July 1985. It was a struggle for control in the area where Nancy considered herself the first and final authority: Ronnie's health and well-being. John Hutton, a new White House physician, had noticed that medical records showed a fluctuation in the president's hematocrit number, the percentage of red blood cells to total blood volume, which might be a subtle indicator of a malignancy in the lower gastrointestinal tract. He recommended a colonoscopy, a diagnostic procedure not as common at that time as it is today. On Friday, July 12, Ronnie and Nancy boarded Marine One on the South Lawn for a short helicopter hop to Bethesda Naval Hospital.

Ronnie declined anesthesia for the procedure. As the flexible scope made its way through his descending and transverse colons, Hutton and the other physicians followed its progress on a TV-like screen and were relieved to see only a few benign-looking growths called polyps, similar to ones the president had had removed in the past. Then it took a turn downward into his right colon. "Suddenly, looming up in full view of the scope and occupying most of the lumen of the cecum was an enormous mass, purple in color, and with a large malignant-appearing crater in its middle," Hutton recalled. Even without a biopsy, they knew they were looking at cancer. They studied it in silence, for fear that saying anything would alarm their patient. Thoughts began racing through Hutton's head: "How do I tell the First Lady?" "What impact will this have on our country, the presidency, and perhaps the world?"

Nancy was waiting in a nearby office with White House spokesman Larry Speakes. Before telling the first lady, Hutton whispered to the press secretary: "It's cancer." The doctor steered Nancy into a small office and delivered the news. He was struck by her composure. She insisted on knowing all the details—what this meant, what was next. Nancy noted that Chinese president Li Xiannian was set to visit Washington a week and a half later and asked whether the surgery could be delayed until after that. Hutton told her he wanted to do it as soon as possible, preferably the next day. Nancy agreed but made one request: she wanted to be the one to tell her husband. And she forbade the doctors from mentioning the word *cancer* to him.

They entered the president's room so silently that Hutton could not even hear his own footsteps. Ronnie looked up and asked, "Why do you all look so glum?" Nancy sat on the bed and put her arms around him. "Honey," she said, "the doctors have found a polyp that is too large to be removed the way the other ones were. The only way they can get it out is surgically. As long as we're here, why don't we do it tomorrow and get it over with?" Hutton was relieved. "Her aplomb was extraordinary. How easy she made it for us, as we then explained the procedure we would perform," he said.

Ronnie took it calmly and said with a smile, "Does this mean I won't be getting dinner tonight, either?" As she left his room, Nancy leaned against the wall, and the tears that she had been holding back came pouring out. That night, in the White House, she lay on Ronnie's side of the bed, just as she had the day he was shot in 1981. And once again, she wrote in her diary, "What would I ever do without him?"

The operation began at eleven o'clock the following morning. This time White House counsel Fred Fielding rectified a mistake he had made when Ronnie was put under anesthesia after the assassination attempt. Fielding had Ronnie sign a document authorizing Vice President Bush to act as president temporarily. It was the first time ever that a provision of the Twenty-fifth Amendment had been invoked to deal with a president "unable to discharge the powers and duties of his office." Nancy stood by Ronnie's bedside as he put his signature to the historic document. The president joked that Bush should be informed that Nancy didn't convey to him as part of the brief transfer of power.

The operation went smoothly. A large polyp was removed, along with two smaller ones and nearly two feet of intestine. A few minutes after seven o'clock, Nancy and her brother, Dick, went into the recovery room. Ronnie was groggy, with a tube coming out of his nose and another one going into his arm. For the first photograph that would be released publicly after the surgery, Nancy leaned in to kiss her husband, positioning her head and his so that his nasogastric feeding tube would not show.

Two days after the surgery, on July 15, a pathology report confirmed that the tumor was malignant. The doctors assured Nancy and Ronnie that they had gotten it all. The president should have every expectation of making a full recovery and leading a normal life, they said, though he would no longer be able to eat the popcorn that he loved. In the future, Ronnie would deny that he had even had cancer. As he saw it, "I had something inside me that had cancer in it, and it was removed."

Nancy closely monitored the briefings that her husband's medical team was giving the reporters who were clamoring for information. The first lady was aghast to see diagrams of her husband's insides being broadcast on national television. She was also concerned that one of those providing information to the media was Dr. Stephen Rosenberg, the chief of surgery at the National Cancer Institute, who had been blunt with the Reagans in private conversations about the fact that someone who has had cancer is never entirely out of the woods. Sure enough, Rosenberg began his presentation by making a statement in the present tense, not the past: "The president has cancer." Nancy, watching from her husband's hospital suite, was furious. "Goddamn it," she said, "I *knew* he was going to do that."

Ronnie was in the hospital for a week, during which Nancy and Don Regan were at loggerheads over the chief of staff's insistence that the president return to conducting business right away. "For three days, she insisted that he see no one in the hospital. She wouldn't let him see George Bush. She wouldn't let him see Bud McFarlane, George Shultz, Weinberger—nobody," Regan told Lou Cannon later. "Because in her opinion, he couldn't be tired out this way, he couldn't risk not having a good recuperative period, that he might exhaust himself doing that. On the other hand, I reminded her that he was still the president of the United States and different from most mortals and that he had to carry on the business of state and that it looked very peculiar." Regan argued that other world leaders, as well as the American public, would become "a little bit apprehensive as to, is this man all right?"

It also annoyed Nancy that Regan was taking a government helicopter back and forth from the hospital each day, while she was commuting by car. "I must have had some inkling, even then, of what increasingly bothered me about Don Regan, which was that he often acted as if *he* were president," Nancy recalled later. Regan tried to shrug off her complaints, until he got a call from Ed Hickey, who was in charge of scheduling military transportation for the White House. "I'd cancel the helicopter if I were you, Don," Hickey said. "The first lady's staff are talking about it." Regan argued that the drive would take forty-five minutes each way, but when Hickey told him, "The buzzards are out," Regan finally gave in. "Okay," he said, "cancel the damn helicopter."

Nancy was not entirely successful in keeping out visitors. One who made it into Ronnie's room was national security adviser McFarlane. Nancy had told Regan that if McFarlane had anything that the president needed to know, he could put it in writing. But McFarlane insisted that he had to see Ronnie in person. The brief meeting in Ronnie's hospital room five days after his surgery would later be recognized as a fateful one. McFarlane told the president that there were signals from Iran suggesting the possibility of establishing a dialogue after years of having no relations. Ronnie confided to his diary that the "strange soundings" coming from Iran might also provide an opening to solve another problem that was weighing on his mind. In March 1984 William Francis Buckley, the CIA station chief in Beirut, had been kidnapped by Hezbollah, an Islamist paramilitary group with ties to Iran. Over the next fifteen months, six more Americans had been taken hostage.

Ronnie still had the impulses of the young lifeguard who more than a half century before had saved seventy-seven souls from drowning in the Rock River. Opening a channel to Tehran, he wrote, "could be a breakthrough on getting our 7 kidnap victims back." The president authorized McFarlane to meet with two Iranian government representatives in a neutral country. So began a series of events that would lead to the swap of US weapons for hostages—the core transaction of the Iran-contra scandal that would blow up the following year.

Shortly before Ronnie left the hospital, he delivered his regular Saturday radio address, in which he said: "I'd like to indulge myself for a moment here. There's something I want to say, and I wanted to say it with Nancy at my side, as she is right now, as she always has been. First ladies aren't elected, and they don't receive a salary. They have mostly been private persons forced to live public lives, and in my book, they've all been heroes. Abigail Adams helped invent America. Dolley Madison helped protect it. Eleanor Roosevelt was FDR's eyes and ears. Nancy Reagan is my everything."

At the end, Ronnie added, "By the way, are you doing anything this evening?"

What neither of them knew was that they had not put the subject of cancer behind them. When doctors had pulled the tape from Ronnie's nasal tube, his nose started bleeding. Then the skin crusted and began bleeding again. Ten days later, a biopsy revealed that what appeared to be a pimple was actually basal cell carcinoma, a common and normally curable form of skin cancer. Nancy, still sensitive about all the intrusive news coverage about Ronnie's colon cancer, wanted it to remain a secret. The name on the biopsy report was Tracy Malone, who was actually a sixty-two-year-old female military nurse. The first lady insisted that the statement the White House put out about it on August 1 contain neither the word *cancer* nor *biopsy*. By then, however, the media had figured out that something was up—it was, quite literally, as clear as the nose on the president's face—and in a news conference on August 5, Ronnie admitted the truth. The whole episode damaged the White House's credibility, but it also taught a lesson that transparency is a better policy on matters of presidential health. Ronnie told Speakes that he was never again to withhold medical information about him from the public.

*

A little over two years later, the situation would arise again, only this time it was Nancy who faced a cancer diagnosis. On October 5, 1987, she and White House physician Hutton went to Bethesda for her annual mammogram. Nancy's stomach tightened when the nurse said they wanted to take a couple of images over again. Afterward, Hutton entered the examination room and asked the nurse to leave. He told Nancy that there were three flecks of calcium in her left breast, which were signs of cancer, though only a biopsy could tell them for sure.

"What do we do next?" she asked.

He and the first lady discussed her options. She wanted a team from the Mayo Clinic to be in charge, supervised by her longtime friend Dr. Oliver Beahrs. He was a former top surgeon at Mayo and had been a student of her father's at Northwestern University Medical School. When Nancy was still in her teens, Beahrs was a frequent guest at the Davis apartment and performed magic tricks at Edie's parties. Hutton called Beahrs, who said he would be on the next plane.

The trip back to the White House on the George Washington Parkway felt interminable to Hutton. He and Nancy were silent for much of it. She told the White House physician that he would have to deliver the news to her husband. When they arrived at the south entrance, Nancy straightened her posture and greeted the awaiting staff as though nothing was amiss. She headed for the family quarters to lie down in the bedroom, and Hutton turned toward the Oval Office. "I need to see the president right now," he told assistant Jim Kuhn, who was sitting at his desk outside.

When Hutton walked in, Ronnie was writing on a yellow pad. Hutton felt so overwhelmed that, for a moment, he couldn't find his voice. "Sir," he said finally, "we've just returned from the Naval Hospital, as you know, and I'm afraid we've made an early discovery that will necessarily require surgical removal and macroscopic examination on Mrs. Reagan's left breast. We won't know if it is definitely malignant until the area in question is removed, and if it is positive, we will have various options of treatment, depending on her wishes. The best news is that it is an early discovery, which is very much in her favor."

Ronnie was dumbstruck. "I've seen him taken aback, but he was stunned. He absolutely couldn't digest this information," Hutton recalled. "It was totally, totally out of character. It was just more than he could really understand."

The president finally spoke, slowly and in a frail voice that Hutton had never heard before: "I know you doctors will take care of it."

Hutton was astonished at the president's odd and detached reaction, though he would later realize that there was an explanation for it. For the first time, Ronnie was being forced to imagine the unthinkable: a life without Nancy. The doctor left, figuring Ronnie wanted to be alone for a bit. Hutton assumed that, once Ronnie had a few moments to recover from the initial shock, he would summon the doctor back to provide more information and advice. No call came. So, Hutton went to the family quarters to see how Nancy was doing.

He was still there when Ronnie arrived home that day, a little earlier than usual. "Well, how are you?" Ronnie asked his wife matter-of-factly and gave her a hug. "It was as if there was no issue at all. It was the ultimate in denial for these two wonderful people," Hutton recalled later. The doctor excused himself and departed.

The next morning, the buzzer went off in Hutton's office. The president wanted to see him. Ronnie told Hutton that he wished the physician had stayed with them that night.

"Why, sir?" Hutton asked.

"Because I needed a good kick in the rear end," Ronnie said. He admitted he had avoided any conversation with his wife that evening about the diagnosis and upcoming surgery. "We never discussed it. We never discussed it."

The next morning, Ronnie apologized to Nancy for his insensitivity, but Hutton said the whole episode didn't seem to bother her. "He'll come around," Nancy said. "It will be all right." The couple carried on with their schedule that day, greeting the crown prince and princess of Japan upon their arrival in Washington and hosting a state dinner for them in the evening.

After conferring with doctors, Nancy decided that if it turned out to be cancer, she wanted to have a mastectomy rather than the less drastic lumpectomy that was becoming more common in cases like hers. Nancy knew that, given her anxious nature, she'd be constantly worrying about a recurrence. She wanted the extra assurance that the malignancy was out, even if it meant losing a breast. A mastectomy would also spare her the radiation therapy that would be required if surgeons preserved her breast.

"Listen, I know a little bit about cancer," she told Hutton. "What do I need a breast for, number one. Number two, I know about multicentricity. If you have a lump here, you may have a lump there in two or three years. Why not just take all the breast tissue away?"

"Perfectly logical," Hutton told her. "I think if it were my wife, that's what I would say."

Nancy also had other things to consider. She told her doctors she had a busy schedule over the next weeks, including a charity dinner in Chicago at which she was to accept a $100,000 donation to the Nancy Reagan Drug Abuse Foundation that she was getting off the ground. After that, there was an event in New Hampshire for the Foster Grandparents program. Her physicians assured her there would be no problem with a short delay, so they scheduled her surgery for October 17.

On the flight to Chicago, Nancy told her press secretary, Elaine Crispen, and her assistant, Jane Erkenbeck, what was going on. As they all cried, the three of them agreed to keep it secret until right before she went into the hospital. Nancy spent that night in the Drake Hotel, looking over the same view of Lake Michigan that she had seen so often from her childhood apartment. She wished for her parents. But Loyal had been dead for five years, and Edie no longer knew who she was.

The evening before the surgery, Nancy checked into the hospital and watched the gripping televised rescue of Jessica McClure, a little girl who had been trapped in a well in Midland, Texas. The first lady awoke at six thirty the next morning, an hour before the operation was scheduled, to find that the Washington area was shrouded in fog. That meant Ronnie and her brother, Dick, who had come down from Philadelphia, could not take a helicopter. Ronnie became frantic and demanded a car, which got him there just in time to give Nancy a kiss before they put her under.

The operation took fifty minutes. When her doctors came out of the operating room, they told Ronnie that the seven-millimeter tumor was indeed malignant. The president collapsed into a chair, dropped his head, and wept. Hutton wasn't sure what to do. It occurred to him that in this moment, Ronnie needed to be in the hands of a woman. Hutton found Paula Trivette, a nurse he knew the Reagans loved, and asked her to go into the room where Ronnie was. As she put her arm around the president's shoulder, Ronnie felt that he had been visited by an angel. Trivette's quiet words, he wrote later, "lifted me from the pit I was in and kept me out of it."

The initial White House announcement, issued while Nancy was still in surgery, described the first lady's tumor as a "noninvasive intraductal adenocarcinoma of approximately seven millimeters in size." Her decision to undergo a modified radical mastectomy for a small cancer that had not spread, rather than lumpectomy, which involved removing only the tumor and a small amount of surrounding tissue, was the subject of no small amount of second-guessing. Rose Kushner, the executive director of the Breast Cancer Advisory Center, a group that counseled women, told the *New York Times* that Nancy "set us back ten years." Kushner added: "I'm not recommending that anyone do it her way." Nancy, justifiably, resented the carping about what for her had been an intensely personal decision.

The first lady also opted against breast reconstructive surgery. But she worried what her husband would think when he saw how she had been disfigured. "I still haven't shown Ronnie—me," Nancy wrote in her diary a week after the mastectomy. "Even though he says it doesn't make any difference, and I believe him, I somehow can't bring myself to do it yet. I'll know when the time is right." In that same diary entry, she noted that she had received "the dearest letter" from Ron's wife, Doria: "It was full of love and concern, and I'll save it forever. I couldn't help wishing it had come from my own daughter."

Nancy became a prominent public advocate for women to get routine mammograms and a private source of comfort to others in her situation. When *Los Angeles Times* reporter Betty Cuniberti was diagnosed with breast cancer at the age of thirty-six in 1988, a letter arrived from Nancy on the very day that doctors were explaining to Cuniberti the procedures for her own operation. "Believe me, no one knows better than I how you feel right now (although you'll probably find a lot of people you know have had it done and you didn't know—at least, I did)," Nancy wrote. "When they use the word 'malignant' or 'cancer,' your heart stops, really stops. . . . After it's over, you'll find, I think, it really isn't so bad."

But her cancer diagnosis would shortly be followed by another blow. Nine days after her mastectomy, Nancy was on the phone with her son, Ron, when the bedroom door opened, and her husband walked in. "Honey," Ronnie told her, "Edie is now with Loyal." Though it had been a long time since Edie had been able to talk to her, Nancy felt sad and guilty that she had not been there for her mother's end as she had for her father's. She arranged quickly to get to Phoenix. When she and Ronnie walked into the mortuary the following day, Nancy was taken aback to see her mother lying in her robe, her gold beads, and the little red mittens that Edie in her final years wore summer and winter. As Nancy began to sob, Ronnie took her in his arms and tried to absorb her grief. The most powerful man in the world felt helpless. He had never seen his wife in such pain.

Nancy took the mittens as a keepsake and then told her mother one last time how much she loved her, how grateful she was for the woman whose drive and example had made so much possible for her daughter.

No doubt the pain and emptiness of Nancy's early years without Edie stirred again as she faced the fact that this time, her mother's absence would be permanent. In one last nod to the life story that Edie had written for herself, the obituaries cited her age as ninety-one, which was eight years younger than she actually was.

Edie's funeral service took place in a Catholic church that, at Nancy's request, was decorated with white flowers all around. Though Edie was not herself a Catholic, Nancy appreciated that the parish's priests had come to the nursing home to give her mother communion every Sunday. In his homily, the pastor recalled an episode years before that was pure Edie. When he introduced Nancy's mother to the bishop of Phoenix, she gave the prelate a saucy little curtsy, and then turned to the priest and said: "Well, aren't you and I going to kiss? We always do that when the bishop isn't here!"

Ronnie delivered a graceful eulogy. He described his mother-in-law as a woman who "gave wit and charm and kindliness throughout her life." Meeting her was "like opening a bottle of champagne," the president added, paraphrasing what Winston Churchill once said about Franklin D. Roosevelt. Afterward, there was a reception at the home of Edie's old neighbors, the Boiches. Patti did not show up for any of it. "There was no visit, no call, no wire, no flowers, no letter—nothing," Nancy wrote. "My mother deserved a lot better than that, and so, for that matter, did Patti's mother." Her press secretary, Elaine Crispen, told reporters that Patti's absence was "another crack in an already broken heart."

*

As connections to her past fell away one by one, Nancy was increasingly turning her thoughts to the Reagans' future beyond the White House. She began laying plans soon after Ronnie was reelected. In April 1985 the president noted in his diary that Nancy was taking an overnight trip to Los Angeles to scout for a place where they might live. "That comes under the heading of looking ahead," he wrote wryly.

Their living situation was not her only concern as Nancy looked ahead. From the outset of the Reagan presidency, she, more than Ronnie himself, had been preoccupied with what history would make of him. One project that she launched—and later regretted—had its origins in the middle of his first term and would continue for a decade after Ronnie was out of office. On Valentine's Day 1983 Oregon senator Mark Hatfield had invited a group of biographers to dine with the Reagans and Librarian of Congress Daniel J. Boorstin at Hatfield's home in Georgetown.

Among them was Edmund Morris, a cerebral, Kenya-born former advertising copywriter who three years earlier had won a Pulitzer Prize for his biography of Teddy Roosevelt. Ronnie lit up when he was introduced to Morris. He told the author how much he had loved the Roosevelt book, and how Nancy had felt the same way about a biography of first lady Edith Kermit Roosevelt, written by Morris's talented wife, Sylvia Jukes Morris. "Those first few months in the White House, we would lay in bed and read 'em side by side," Ronnie said.

Over a dinner of lemon piccata chicken around a table decorated with red plastic hearts, the group talked for more than an hour. Much of the conversation centered on how important it was for posterity to have a full and accurate record of both the events of the Reagan presidency and the thoughts of the man who drove them. Ronnie agreed, adding: "I still look over my shoulder when I'm, you know, walking out of the White House and the marines are saluting and all, and I say, 'Who—me?' "

The president also told them stories of the unlikely life he had lived before he assumed the most powerful office in the world. One that stuck with Morris was how the year 1949 had been Ronnie's lowest point. He was newly and unhappily divorced. He had a shattered leg and was struggling to get around on crutches. The movie roles were drying up. So, it seemed, was his future. "And then along came Nancy Davis," he said, "and saved my soul."

Morris also sensed a certain intensity being directed his way by one of the others at the dinner. "Throughout the seventy minutes we stayed at the table, I was aware of Mrs. Reagan's stare, as a scuba diver in dark water senses two large, pale, accompanying jellyfish. I braced myself to glance at her: she gave a thin return of smile before looking away," he recalled. Morris figured out eventually that the real purpose of the dinner had been to entice him to become the authorized chronicler of the Reagan presidency, a role modeled somewhat on what historian Arthur M. Schlesinger Jr. had done when John F. Kennedy was president. Schlesinger's 1965 book, *A Thousand Days: John F. Kennedy in the White House*, had won both a Pulitzer and a National Book Award.

Richard Darman subsequently invited Morris to the White House and formally made the proposal that he write a definitive biography of the fortieth president. He would be given an opportunity to observe his subject at close range and in real time. Morris declined, saying he was committed to finishing another volume on Roosevelt. But after a couple of years, the author changed his mind, figuring he could not pass up the extraordinary arrangement he was being offered. He would have unprecedented access, and the White House would have no say over what he wrote. In November 1985 Random House beat out six other publishers to sign a $3 million deal with Morris, which at the time was the highest advance ever paid for a single book. "For the first time, a president is allowing not only a historian but a talented writer to see history as it occurs, without imposing restrictions on the manuscript," said Random House chairman Robert L. Bernstein.

Morris quickly came to understand that the whole endeavor had been dreamed up by Nancy and Deaver. They were also responsible for his selection as the man to do it. As Morris told me in 2017, not quite two years before he died: "Reagan couldn't have cared less. He had no curiosity about himself, and he couldn't care less who wrote about him."

To Nancy's credit, he added, she never once tried to tell him what she thought he should write. She believed that with Morris's insights and gifts, he would make the case for Ronnie's historic significance and perhaps even lay the premise for a Nobel Peace Prize. Teddy Roosevelt, the subject of his previous biography, had won one in 1906; the medal was on the wall of the Roosevelt Room across the hall from the Oval Office. Nancy made sure that Morris got countless hours of interviews with Ronnie. The president also wrote letters to others, urging them to cooperate as well. So much access did Morris get that Ronnie once joked: "The other night, Nancy sneezed in her sleep, and I heard Edmund say '*Gesundheit.*'"

The book would take fourteen years to complete and become a source of lasting bitterness on all sides. It contained little exploration of politics or Ronnie's ideas, and instead sought to penetrate his character; to capture his inner life. The endeavor became so frustrating to Morris that he, in desperation, employed an unusual narrative device of inventing fictional figures, including one he named Edmund Morris, a contemporary who meets the future president in 1926 and follows his life and career. "When I began writing, after he left the White House in January 1989, I struggled for about two years with an orthodox biographical style. He just kept evading me," Morris told *Publishers Weekly*. "I had the insuperable problem of reconciling my close-up observations of him as president, when I could look at his fingernails and clothes and watch the expression on his face when he spoke, with the fact that I was not there observing him closely during his early life. When I hit on this device in 1992, it just seized me, it felt supremely right, and what feels good in one's heart is usually sincere writing."

Reagan World would not feel the same. Nancy blamed herself for choosing Morris and was bewildered that the project could have gone so far off the rails. Perhaps what had eluded the biographer was that, as close as he had gotten to his subject, there was no interior counternarrative to tell about Ronnie. At one point, Morris observed to Deaver that he couldn't decide whether the president was the most complicated or the simplest man he had ever met. "Well, he's pretty simple as far as I'm concerned," Deaver replied. "What you see is what you get, Edmund. There is no big mystery here."

The reviews of *Dutch: A Memoir of Ronald Reagan* upon its publication in the fall of 1999 were blistering, which did not surprise Morris. But the book found two fans: Ronnie's children Ron and Patti, who themselves had struggled for their entire lives to get to the core of their father's character. For Patti, the book not only brought new insights but also lifted some of her guilt for not having figured him out on her own: "I still don't fully understand my father. After all those years of exhaustive research, even Edmund says the man is a mystery. But because of Edmund's book, I have more clues, more threads to tie together." Ron wrote that Morris's biography "comes as near as any book I've read to capturing my father's elusive nature."

CHAPTER NINETEEN

In mid-1981 the US Centers for Disease Control noticed a set of medical curiosities: an alert from Los Angeles that five previously healthy young men had come down with a rare, fatal lung infection; almost simultaneously, a dermatologist in New York saying that he had seen a cluster of unusually aggressive cases of Kaposi's sarcoma, an obscure skin cancer. These seemingly unconnected occurrences had two things in common. First, all of the victims were sexually active gay men. Second, their maladies pointed to a catastrophically compromised immune system. About a month after those reports, a San Francisco weekly wrote that something it called "gay men's pneumonia" was going around. By September 1982, there was a medical name for it: acquired immunodeficiency syndrome, or AIDS. The following May, scientists identified the retrovirus that was causing it: human immunodeficiency virus. HIV.

It would take longer before it became clear who was at risk, how far the disease could spread, or what needed to be done to stop it. "At first, we thought it was gay men, and then it was intravenous drug users, and then that it was Haitians—which was a mistake," said Anthony Fauci, a senior investigator who became director of the National Institute of Allergy and Infectious Diseases (NIAID) in 1984. As the number of cases mounted, Fauci submitted an editorial to the *New England Journal of Medicine* in which he warned against assuming that AIDS would stay confined to the populations in which it had first appeared. But at that point, not even scientists were ready to accept how ominous the signs were. Fauci's article was rejected because a reviewer for the medical field's most prestigious publication deemed it to be too alarmist. It subsequently appeared in the June 1, 1982, issue of the *Annals of Internal Medicine*.

Nor was the story of dying homosexual men getting much traction in the mainstream media. Though more than half of those stricken were residents of New York City, the *New York Times* wrote only three stories about AIDS in 1981 and three more in 1982—all of which went on the inside pages.

The response of the Reagan administration was . . . silence. Even worse, as the crisis mounted, the administration targeted public health agencies, including the Centers for Disease Control, for massive budget cuts. The National Institutes of Health (NIH), which is the nation's main backer of biomedical research, was also struggling with a funding squeeze.

The president of the United States did not so much as publicly utter the name of the disease until September 1985. Even then, it was only because a reporter brought it up at a news conference. Ronnie made an obviously untrue declaration that AIDS was a "top priority" for his administration and indicated that he thought the existing levels of government funding to fight the disease were adequate. "It was clear that there was sort of muted silence about things, and a complete lack of the use of the bully pulpit to sound the alarm," Fauci said when I interviewed him more than three decades later. Not until the spring of 1987 did Ronnie give a major speech about AIDS. By that time, the disease had already struck 36,058 Americans, of whom 20,849 had died.

The Reagan administration's unwillingness to recognize and confront the AIDS epidemic has gone down in history as one of the deepest and most enduring scars on its legacy. Those who would defend Ronnie and Nancy insist that it was not the result of deep-seated bigotry on their part against homosexuals. Coming from Hollywood, the Reagans had many acquaintances who were gay, and they were comfortable in their company. Nancy, in particular, counted numerous gay men among her closest confidants. She was on the phone nearly daily with her friend Jerry Zipkin, the New York society gadabout. Her decorator Ted Graber slept in the White House with his partner, possibly the first acknowledged same-sex couple to do so. She was also sensitive to the specific dangers that gay men faced in society. When author Truman Capote was arrested in Anaheim for disorderly conduct in the early 1980s, Nancy put in a frantic late-night call to Deaver, and begged him to find a way to get the renowned author freed. "Jail will kill him," she told Deaver, who prevailed upon Meese to pull some strings and secure Capote's release.

Family friend Doug Wick, a Hollywood producer, recalls that when he got married in 1986, news that Nancy would be at the wedding brought "both great curiosity and some ill will" among his liberal friends. Patricia Resnick, a lesbian who had written the 1980 hit movie *9 to 5*, decided to put the first lady on the spot at the reception by asking her to dance. Resnick was tipsy and did it on a bet. Nancy took Resnick's hand and said, "Only if you lead." Wick felt proud of Nancy as he watched the two women do a slow box step to the jazz standard "Embraceable You." He hoped that Nancy had changed the perceptions of some in his circle who misunderstood her.

As far back as 1978, Ronnie had been willing to risk his political capital with social conservatives by opposing a California ballot initiative that would have barred gays and lesbians from teaching in the state's public schools. His opposition helped sink the ballot measure. But Ronnie also held a religious belief that homosexuality was sinful. In the spring of 1987, he discussed the AIDS epidemic with biographer Edmund Morris and said that "maybe the Lord brought down this plague," because "illicit sex is against the Ten Commandments." Privately, Ronnie also trafficked in homophobic stereotypes, as did those around him. Press spokesman Larry Speakes recalled that after Ronnie's weekly shampoo, the president would flick his wrist and tell aides in a lisping voice, "I washed my hair last night, and I just can't do a thing with it." Speakes wrote admiringly: "He does a very good gay imitation. He would pretend to be annoyed at someone and say, 'If those fellows don't leave me alone, I'll just slap them on the wrist.'"

Speakes himself cracked a homophobic joke when reporter Lester Kinsolving asked him during an October 15, 1982, press briefing whether the president had any reaction to reports that six hundred people had contracted the "gay plague." It was the first public question the White House had received on the subject. The press secretary's response: "I don't have it. And you? Do you?" The reaction from the assembled reporters was laughter. At subsequent briefings over the next two years, Kinsolving, who was considered a gadfly, continued to press the White House spokesman about AIDS, only to be met with dismissive wisecracks questioning the reporter's own sexual orientation. And the White House press corps continued to find these exchanges hilarious.

In October 1986 the *Washington Post*'s Bob Woodward reported that during a meeting with his national security advisers, Ronnie had made note of Libyan leader Mu'ammar Gadhafi's partiality for eccentric clothing and quipped: "Why not invite Gadhafi to San Francisco, he likes to dress up so much?" To which Secretary of State George Shultz replied: "Why don't we give him AIDS!" According to Woodward, others around the table thought this was extremely amusing. San Francisco officials demanded an apology, both to the city and to people infected with the disease.

As was the case with many Americans during the early years of the epidemic, the Reagans' practical understanding of AIDS was colored by fear, ignorance, and scientific uncertainty. One day, when hairdresser Robin Weir was making one of his twice-a-week visits to the White House, Nancy inadvertently took a sip from his water glass. Afterward, she went to White House physician John Hutton in a panic, worried that she might have contracted the disease. Hutton tried to reassure her that it was impossible to get AIDS that way, but she wasn't satisfied. "How do you know?" Nancy demanded. "How do you know?" Weir died in 1993 at the age of forty-five from what his obituaries described as a combination of colitis, bacterial sepsis, and a heart attack, all three of which are often associated with AIDS.

But it is also clear that Nancy became attuned to the seriousness of the epidemic earlier than the president did—in part, because her son, Ron, was seeing it up close. "I'm in New York, I'm dancing, I know people who are HIV positive. Dancers, fashion designers, people like that. Doria was working at Andy Warhol's Factory [his studio] at the time, and she's in contact with a whole range of people. So we are well aware of what's going on and how serious it is," Ron said. "I began speaking to my mother about it. My mother would always say this to me: 'I'm a doctor's daughter.' Anything kind of medically oriented, she was very pro that. I would talk to her about people, how many people, who these people were. And she began to understand that this is a big deal. This is a crisis. . . . She began to sense that pretending this isn't happening is not a good way to go."

Nancy and her son began looking for opportunities to discuss AIDS with Ronnie. "We'd start mentioning it, bringing it up as a topic, starting to get it into his head," Ron recalled. He acknowledged that their effort did not get very far with his father. Where Nancy "could appreciate things a little bit more abstractly, it very much helped if he could put a face on something," Ron said.

In 1985 the epidemic did indeed gain its face: the once-magnificent visage of actor Rock Hudson. When Hudson was revealed to be dying of AIDS, "the whole picture changed" for the president, Ron said. During the 1950s and 1960s, Hudson had been one of the country's biggest movie stars. But while Hudson wooed Elizabeth Taylor, Lauren Bacall, Gina Lollobrigida, and Doris Day on the screen, he lived a closeted existence off it. If the world had known that the man that fan magazines declared to be Hollywood's most handsome star was actually gay, Hudson's career would have been destroyed.

The first lady, given the acuity of her radar and her gossipy network of California friends, surely was aware of Hudson's secret life. Ronnie probably knew about it too. Hudson attended a state dinner in May 1984, and Nancy noticed that he looked gaunt. When she expressed concern about his health, Hudson told her that he'd caught the flu while filming in Israel but had recovered and was feeling fine. A picture from that dinner in her White House scrapbook shows Hudson beaming alongside the first couple, his hand clasped with Nancy's. Afterward, Nancy sent Hudson a set of photos from the evening. She enclosed a note suggesting he have a doctor check a red blotch that one image showed on his neck. It had been bothering him too, so he did, in June, the month after the state dinner. The skin irritation turned out to be Kaposi's sarcoma, and that was how Hudson learned that he had AIDS.

By the summer of 1985, the fifty-nine-year-old actor's deterioration had become obvious. He made an appearance in Monterey, California, with Doris Day, with whom he'd costarred in some of the most popular romantic comedies of his heyday. Reporters and friends were shocked at how frail he looked. When Hudson collapsed in the lobby of the Ritz Hotel in Paris in July, his publicist put out a statement that he had inoperable liver cancer. The American Hospital in Neuilly-sur-Seine, where he was rushed, blamed his condition on "fatigue and general malaise." But news reports shot across the globe speculating that it was AIDS and that Hudson had come to Paris seeking a miracle cure. In 1985 there was no effective treatment for AIDS; the first AIDS drug, AZT, wasn't approved until two years later.

The White House announced that the president had telephoned Hudson to wish him well "and let him know that he and Mrs. Reagan were keeping him in their thoughts and prayers." In Ronnie's July 24 diary entry, the president indicated he had not known the nature of Hudson's malady when they spoke: "Called Rock Hudson in a Paris Hospital where press said he had inoperable cancer. We never knew him too well but did know him & I thought under the circumstances I might be a reassurance. Now I learn from TV there is question as to his illness & rumors he is there for treatment of AIDS." After this entry, Ronnie's diaries do not mention AIDS again for nearly two years.

On the same day the president spoke with Hudson, the White House received a desperate appeal for help in arranging a transfer for the actor to a French military hospital. The telegram from Hudson's publicist, Dale Olson, which was addressed to assistant press secretary Mark Weinberg, claimed the hospital was the one facility in the world that could provide "necessary medical treatment to save life of Rock Hudson or at least alleviate his illness." The hospital's commander had turned down Hudson as a patient because he was not French, but the telegram said Hudson's doctor "believes a request from the White House or a high American official would change his mind." Weinberg took the matter not to Ronnie but to Nancy, and the two of them agreed to refer it to the American embassy in Paris.

In later years, it would be said that the first lady was callous in how she handled it, but it is also possible to appreciate that Nancy had been put in a situation where she had no good option. She was not averse to making discreet interventions on behalf of friends in trouble, as she had when Capote was thrown in jail. But Hudson's illness was one of the biggest stories in the world at that moment. Had Nancy done a special favor on behalf of someone rich and famous while tens of thousands of others were dying of the disease in obscurity, she would have been justifiably criticized for that as well. Probably more so. There was also precedent to think about: no doubt, this would not be the last such request they would get. Was that kind of intercession on behalf of her friends a proper role for a first lady?

Despite the claims made in the telegram, it does not appear that the French hospital could have helped Hudson. According to *And the Band Played On,* a definitive book on the early AIDS epidemic by journalist Randy Shilts, when Hudson's French doctor saw his patient's dire condition, he concluded that any further treatments would do no good. Hudson spent $250,000 to charter a Boeing 747 and went home to Los Angeles, where he would die two months later. Before he did, Hudson authorized his doctors to make a public statement: "Mr. Hudson is being evaluated and treated for complications of Acquired Immune Deficiency Syndrome."

Hudson's heroic public acknowledgment that he was suffering from the disease changed the national conversation around AIDS and finally put the story on the front pages of the newspapers. In the two months that followed his announcement, more than $1.8 million in private contributions were raised to support AIDS research and care for its victims.

The amount was more than twice as much as had been collected in all of 1984. The government stepped up as well. A few weeks after Hudson's death, Congress doubled the amount of federal spending dedicated to finding a cure. "It was commonly accepted now, among the people who had understood the threat for many years, that there were two clear phases to the disease in the United States: there was AIDS before Rock Hudson and AIDS after," Shilts wrote. "The fact that a movie star's diagnosis could make such a huge difference was itself a tribute to the power the news media exerted in the latter portion of the twentieth century." Shilts himself died of AIDS in 1994 at the age of forty-two.

After Hudson was stricken, the president began asking his White House physician to explain more about AIDS to him. Hutton told Ronnie that it was caused by a hitherto unknown infectious agent for which the body seemed to have no defense. "You mean like the measles virus, but one that won't go away, that arouses no immune response?" Ronnie asked. At another point, Ronnie mused: "I always thought the world would end in a flash, but this sounds like it's worse."

Inside the West Wing, however, there was strong resistance to growing public calls for the Reagan administration to become more aggressive in combatting the disease. Some of the president's more conservative advisers contended that AIDS should be viewed as the consequence of moral decay rather than as a health issue. White House communications director Pat Buchanan, before joining the administration, had written a column in which he sneered, "The poor homosexuals—they have declared war upon nature, and now nature is exacting an awful retribution." Many of Ronnie's allies on the Right were more concerned with identifying and isolating those who had AIDS than treating and caring for them. In 1986 conservative lion William F. Buckley, the Reagans' longtime friend, proposed tattooing HIV-positive people—on the upper forearm if they were IV drug users and the buttocks if they were homosexual.

As the White House tried to keep AIDS at arm's length, the effects of the epidemic were being felt close at hand. After Deaver left the president's staff, he dispatched a young Floridian named Robert Higdon to assist Nancy and help organize a foundation to build a future presidential library. A kid barely out of college, "I was scared to death of her at first. Everybody said she was like the dragon lady," Higdon said. However, the two of them clicked, and Higdon became Nancy's go-to person when she needed something done discreetly. For instance, he was the one who made the quiet arrangements for her to have a facelift in New York in 1986 and to recuperate away from public view in the apartment of her friend, the heiress and clothing designer Gloria Vanderbilt.

But Higdon was suffering a private agony that he could not bring himself to share even with her. His partner, a prominent Washington real estate developer, was dying of AIDS. "I lived two years with it in secrecy, and worked in the White House," Higdon told me more than three decades later. He started to cry at the painful memory. "I thought, here I work for the president of the United States, and I can't keep my partner alive," Higdon said. "I have all the power in the world right in front of me. What can I do? Nothing."

Ronnie's first significant initiative against the disease came in February 1986, when he declared combatting AIDS to be "one of our highest public health priorities," and asked Surgeon General C. Everett Koop to prepare a major report on it. Critics noted, however, that on the very same day, the administration submitted a budget that called for sharply reducing federal spending on AIDS research and care programs.

Koop, an imposing figure who wore an admiral's uniform and an Amish-style square-cut gray beard without a mustache, was an unlikely champion for AIDS activists. He was a deeply religious Presbyterian and antiabortion crusader deemed "Dr. Unqualified" in a *New York Times* editorial when he was nominated in 1981. His expertise was in pediatric surgery, not public health. Initially, he put most of his effort as surgeon general into raising awareness of the dangers of smoking. But once he was tasked to write the report, Koop undertook a full-scale effort to discover everything that could be known about AIDS.

As it happened, his personal physician was Fauci, the director of the National Institute of Allergy and Infectious Diseases. "He would come in, he would sit down right on the couch, and he would say, 'Tell me about this.' So, for weeks and weeks, I started to tell him all about the things we were doing," Fauci recalled. "Then he started going out and learning himself. So, as we were getting into the second term, and he realized this was a big problem, he shifted his emphasis from tobacco to HIV."

Koop wrote his thirty-six-page report on AIDS at a stand-up desk in the basement of his home on the National Institutes of Health campus. He did not submit it for review by Reagan administration policy advisers because he knew that the White House would have watered down its conclusions and recommendations. Released on October 22, 1986, it was a bombshell, projecting that 270,000 Americans would contract the disease by 1991 and that 179,000 would die of it. The report used explicit language, explaining that AIDS was transmitted through "semen and vaginal fluids" and during "oral, anal, and vaginal intercourse." A version was ultimately sent to every one of the 107 million households in the country, which was the largest mass mailing in American history. It carried a message from Koop: "Some of the issues involved in this brochure may not be things you are used to discussing openly. I can easily understand that. But now you must discuss them. We all must know about AIDS. Read this brochure and talk about it with those you love."

Conservatives liked some of what was in the report. It warned against "freewheeling casual sex" and asserted that the surest means of preventing AIDS were through abstinence and monogamy. But they weren't so happy with Koop's recommendation that condoms be used as a fallback. And they were especially disturbed by his call for schools to begin educating children as young as third grade about the disease. Ronnie himself was uncomfortable with the implications. "Recognizing that there are those who are not going to abstain, all right. Then you can touch on the other things that are being done," he said in an April 29, 1987, interview with a group of reporters. "But I would think that sex education should begin with the moral ramifications, that it is not just a physical activity that doesn't have any moral connotation."

Meanwhile, the administration's internal differences over AIDS started playing out in public. Secretary of Education William J. Bennett, who was a voice of Christian conservatives in the Reagan Cabinet, publicly called for mandatory AIDS testing for hospital patients, prison inmates, immigrants, and couples getting married. Koop, expressing the opinion of most medical experts, warned that such a dictate would be counterproductive, because it would foster discrimination and drive victims of the disease—many of whom already lived at the edges of society—further underground.

Disagreements within the Reagan family also became more open. In July 1987 Ron appeared in a television commercial in which he criticized his father's administration for its lack of action. "The US government isn't moving fast enough to stop the spread of AIDS. Write to your congressman," Ron said and then added with a grin, "or to someone higher up." In interviews, the president's son took aim at Bennett in particular, saying that in calling for widespread AIDS testing, his father's Cabinet secretary was pandering to the right-wing view that the disease was a punishment for homosexuality. Ron also appeared in a thirty-minute privately funded AIDS education film, which aired on the Public Broadcasting System. In it, he held up a condom and spermicide and urged: "Get them and learn how to use them." The president was annoyed with his outspoken son. Ronnie made it clear in one diary entry that his own views aligned more with Bennett's. Ron, he wrote on July 18, 1987, "can be stubborn on a couple of issues & won't listen to anyone's argument. Bill volunteered to have a talk with him. I hope it can be worked out."

Behind the scenes, Nancy had also been pushing her husband to shift his stance on AIDS. She wanted him to start by speaking out more forcefully about it. Opportunity presented itself when screen legend Elizabeth Taylor, whom Nancy had known since their days together at MGM, asked Ronnie to give the keynote address at a fund-raising dinner for the American Foundation for AIDS Research, or amfAR, a leading organization of which Taylor was the national chairman. The event was to be held in Washington on May 31, 1987, the night before what would be the largest scientific meeting ever held on the subject of AIDS. At the bottom of her letter, Taylor scribbled a note: "P.S. My love to you, Nancy, I hope to see you soon. E."

Ronnie accepted the invitation, no doubt at Nancy's urging. But the first lady did not trust the White House communications shop, which was run by Buchanan, to strike the right note in drafting what the president would say. She knew that her husband would be speaking to a skeptical—in fact, downright hostile—audience. So, Nancy recruited her favorite outside speechwriter, Landon Parvin, who had left the White House in 1983, to come back and craft the address.

"The reason I was called was because Mrs. Reagan was afraid that if it was given to the inside speechwriting staff, it would be too right-wing," Parvin told me. He recognized that this was going to require a major battle with the conservative forces of the West Wing and that he could not win it without Nancy's assistance. "I may need your help," he told the first lady. "I may have to use your name." Nancy gave Parvin permission to claim her proxy wherever he felt it was necessary.

As Parvin began researching the subject, he discovered something that surprised him: the president had never held a meeting with Koop about AIDS and, in fact, had little contact at all with the surgeon general. He called Nancy, who set up a session where the two of them could talk. But instead of the tête-à-tête that Parvin had hoped for, it turned into a much larger group, which included Bennett and domestic policy adviser Gary Bauer. "It was like a Cabinet meeting, in effect," Parvin recalled. "The White House staff had arranged to load it with conservatives, so that Koop couldn't get the president too much to himself."

The unsurprising result was a fierce argument over what the president should say. Parvin's notes from the session indicate that Koop wanted Ronnie to tamp down unwarranted and stigmatizing fears about the disease. He urged the president to make it clear that people could not get AIDS from swimming pools, telephones, mosquitoes, or by allowing their food to be prepared by someone infected with the virus. One person in the room objected that "the jury is still out" on secondary means of transmitting the disease.

There was another debate over whether to have Reagan remind people that the government's own US Public Health Service had come out in favor of allowing people infected with the virus to participate in routine school or work activity. "The president *can't be this far out on a limb*," someone said, according to Parvin's notes, which do not identify the speaker. "His major responsibility is to protect Americans *who are not yet ill!*" As the discussion began spiraling out of control, Parvin decided to play his ace card. "Mrs. Reagan wants it this way," he said.

Parvin didn't win everything, but by invoking Nancy's name, he got much of what he wanted into Ronnie's first major address on AIDS. Files in the Reagan Library give an indication of how the conservative forces tried to dig in as the date for the speech grew near. Three days before, White House officials were asked for their responses to the latest draft. A senior member of the Domestic Policy Council named Robert Sweet returned his copy with a note: "I have very serious concerns about the tone of this speech as it is written. It does not reflect the president's deep sense of moral justice. I strongly urge major revision." For instance, Sweet objected to one reference in the text to "safe" behavior; he wanted it to say "appropriate" behavior. He also suggested deleting a line asserting that "only medical science can ever truly defeat AIDS," and proposed "but only by changing our behavior we can ever truly defeat AIDS." Sweet crossed out language that said victims of the disease should not be blamed, and wrote in the margin: "Homosexuals and drug users *choose* their lifestyle—it's the innocent children, hemophiliacs, and unsuspecting spouses who are the victims." None of the revisions he wanted was made.

The amfAR dinner was held in a tent outside a restaurant along the Potomac River. Hundreds of people, some of whom had AIDS, gathered outside, holding lit candles in memory of those who had already died of the disease. The atmosphere inside could hardly have been more tense. Anthony Fauci, who was sitting in the front row of the audience, noticed that Nancy seemed to be acting as "an orchestrator" of the head table, anxiously trying to manage how things were going.

"She wasn't the quiet first lady sitting off to the side. It was clear that she was buzz-buzzing up there," he said.

Ronnie's speech was repeatedly interrupted by catcalls and hissing. Booing started when the president announced that AIDS would be added to the list of contagious diseases for which immigrants and others seeking to enter the country permanently could be denied entry. It grew louder as he called for "routine" testing of federal prisoners, immigrants, and marriage license applicants. The proposal did not go as far as the mandatory testing that many in the administration had wanted and activists had feared. But Ronnie offered no assurances that those who tested positive would be guaranteed confidentiality or protected against discrimination. And while the president lamented the plight of some groups susceptible to the virus—hemophiliacs, spouses of IV drug users, blood transfusion recipients, babies of infected women—nowhere in the speech did he mention the words *gay* or *homosexual*.

What people in the audience didn't know was how much worse it could have been had Nancy not intervened through Parvin. After the amfAR dinner, Elizabeth Taylor downplayed the fury that many in the room felt. "I know there are some people who disagree—that was quite clear," the actress said. "But I think what the president said was quite in concurrence with what we all hope and pray for: that there is a cure for AIDS." The reviews in the media were positive, though not glowing. "The president's Sunday-night speech on AIDS was sensible," a June 2 *Washington Post* editorial said. "Much talk had preceded the event—Mr. Reagan's first speech devoted entirely to the subject—and it was rumored that warring camps within the administration were trying to persuade him to take different positions. In the end, the speech took something from both sides and set out a cautious approach. Compassion was the keynote."

In an interview more than thirty years after Ronnie's amfAR speech, Parvin reflected on what it achieved and what it didn't. "There was good stuff in it, but not enough," he told me. The speechwriter reproached himself for the deletion of a passage about Ryan White, an Indiana teen who had been infected with HIV from a 1984 blood transfusion and was subsequently ostracized in his hometown of Kokomo, Indiana. White rallied for the right to attend school and, in doing so, raised awareness of the need to end prejudice and ignorance around the disease. "I was fighting so many big battles that I caved on that one and didn't mention him. I still regret that I didn't fight that one," Parvin said. White died in April 1990, just weeks before his high school graduation; four months later, Congress passed its largest-ever measure to provide assistance to people suffering from AIDS and named the law in his honor. Not until the final weeks of White's life did Ronnie meet with the boy, and by then, the fortieth president was a private citizen.

Belated as it was, the speech did mark a turning point for both of the Reagans. They finally began drawing the spotlight that followed them to the plight of AIDS victims and the stigma they faced. In July, not quite two months after his amfAR address, Ronnie visited the National Cancer Institute's pediatric ward and cuddled a fourteen-month-old baby infected with HIV. The photo made the front page of the next day's *New York Times*. In May 1988 Nancy became honorary chairman of the first international event at the United Nations for children affected by AIDS. To help publicize and raise money for it, Nancy invited eleven-year-old Celeste Carrion, who at the time was the oldest known surviving child born with AIDS, to the White House.

In late June 1987 Ronnie also signed an executive order creating the President's Commission on the HIV Epidemic to investigate and recommend measures that federal, state, and local governments should take in response. It had an inauspicious beginning, however. In its early months, the thirteen-member panel nearly collapsed due to poor leadership and internal feuding. The commission was also criticized for being packed with conservatives whose views did not conform with mainstream scientific thinking about the disease. Nancy waged a battle with adviser Gary Bauer over her insistence that the commission include an openly gay member. Bauer told reporters he would be "very surprised if an administration opposed to making appointments on the basis of race or sex would agree to make an appointment based on bedroom habits."

Nancy won. Dr. Frank Lilly, the chairman of the genetics department at Albert Einstein College of Medicine and a board member of the advocacy and service organization Gay Men's Health Crisis, was named to the panel. Lilly's appointment caused a sensation. Senator Gordon Humphrey, a conservative Republican from New Hampshire, complained that the administration "should strive at all costs to avoid sending the message to society—especially to impressionable youth—that homosexuality is simply an alternative lifestyle." Calling gay sexual practices "unnatural" and "immoral," Humphrey said only heterosexuals should have been named to the AIDS panel. Dr. Lilly himself put out a statement that said, in part: "As far as I know, I am probably among the first openly gay persons to have been appointed to a significant position in any US administration." There was little doubt in Washington circles how he had gotten there. An unnamed administration official told the *New York Times* that Lilly was on the commission "because the first lady said so."

When the panel's first chairman resigned in October amid turmoil, Ronnie named retired navy admiral James Watkins to head it. The reception to that appointment was skeptical, given that Watkins had no medical background and was a staunchly conservative Catholic. But he turned out to be exactly the kind of manager who was needed: focused, disciplined, curious, and empathetic. "All you have to do is walk into the pediatric ward of Harlem Hospital and see those children," he said. "Nobody wants them. They have no place to go. That gets you." His leadership was such that the panel came to be known as the Watkins Commission.

A draft of its final report was due in mid-1988, in the waning months of Ronnie's presidency. Expectations were that it would blame the federal government for a lack of leadership on AIDS, set out a battle plan for fighting the disease, and call for antidiscrimination legislation. All of which meant that it was likely to be ignored and buried by the Reagan administration's top policy makers. The week before the report came out, Nancy got a call from family friend Doug Wick. He asked if he could bring someone by to meet the Reagans.

The woman he wanted the Reagans to talk to was former museum director Elizabeth Glaser, the wife of Paul Michael Glaser, a star known to millions of television fans as Detective Dave Starsky on the late-1970s police drama *Starsky & Hutch*. Elizabeth, the best friend of Wick's own wife, Lucy Fisher, had a secret known only to those closest to her: near the end of her first pregnancy in 1981, she had started hemorrhaging. Her daughter, Ariel, was delivered safely, but Elizabeth's bleeding wouldn't stop, so doctors gave the new mother a transfusion of seven pints of blood. Four years later, Ariel started getting sick; lab work showed it was AIDS. Elizabeth had been infected by the transfusion of HIV-tainted blood. Ariel had gotten the disease from her mother's breast milk.

That mother and daughter had the disease was just the beginning of the horror. Further testing showed that the Glasers' younger son, Jake, born in 1984, was also HIV positive. Jake had contracted the virus in utero. At the time, there was nothing to do for children in that situation. What drugs were available had not been tested or approved for pediatric use. Elizabeth Glaser's bright, curious daughter was getting sicker and sicker; she and Paul pulled Ariel out of nursery school, knowing she would be shunned, and when they told the parents of her playmates, some dropped out of sight.

One day Glaser sat at her kitchen table and made a list of people who she felt needed to hear her story. Among the names she wrote down was that of Ronald Reagan. She first broached the idea with Wick over lunch. "Think about it this way," she told him. "I'm a white heterosexual woman from their socioeconomic class and from Hollywood. Many people still think of AIDS as God's punishment for homosexuals. Even if the president doesn't believe that, there are still many political people who are not paying any attention to the epidemic. Maybe, just maybe, I can help change their views."

Wick wasn't sure he could pull off an introduction. He warned her that many people wanted to meet the president; even if he got her in to see Ronnie, the most they could probably get was a quick, perfunctory session and a photo in the Oval Office.

When Wick approached Nancy, the first lady told him to bring Glaser to the residence that weekend, which was two days before the Watkins Commission's report was to be released. When Wick and Glaser arrived at the White House, he saw that Nancy had arranged things so that Elizabeth would have the president's undivided attention. Coffee and sandwiches had been set out. Nancy, Wick could tell, wanted to make sure that the meeting would take place in a comfortable, intimate setting.

After they all sat down, Glaser began: "My life is very complicated, and I am here because I am hoping you can help . . ." She poured out the story of the past seven years. Both Reagans got tears in their eyes as she described how Ariel, after months of being unable to walk or talk, had recently opened her eyes and said: "Good morning, Mom. I love you." Ariel would die seven weeks later, at the age of seven.

That day in the White House, Nancy, with her customary directness, turned the conversation in a direction that Glaser hadn't anticipated.

"How is it for your husband?" the first lady asked.

"It's horrible," Glaser answered. "It has been very difficult for Paul, but he has been remarkable. He is our hero, and he has stood by us."

Nancy pressed: "What is your relationship with him?"

Glaser, startled, suddenly began to understand what Nancy was getting at. "Relationship. What does she mean? Is this woman asking me about my sex life?" This, after all, was an administration that didn't even want to talk about condoms. But she sensed that Nancy was asking out of a genuine sympathy. So, Glaser told her that, yes, she and Paul continued to have a sexual relationship, taking all the precautions that her doctors had recommended, and added: "My husband kisses me and touches me, and he is really quite wonderful."

A meeting that was supposed to have lasted for twenty minutes stretched into an hour. As Glaser and Wick were getting ready to leave, Ronnie's eyes locked with the distraught mother's.

"Tell me what you want me to do," the president said.

"I want you to be a *leader* in the struggle against AIDS, so that my children, and all children, can go to school and continue to live valuable lives; so that no one with AIDS need worry about discrimination," Glaser replied. "Secondly, you have commissioned a report on the epidemic that's been written by a phenomenal man. I ask you to pay attention to that report."

Ronnie responded: "I promise you that I will read that report with different eyes than I would have before."

The Watkins Commission's report, released on June 27, 1988, was unsparing, starting with its contention that there had been a "distinct lack of leadership" from the federal government. "It was a stunning repudiation of just about every aspect of the Reagan administration's handling of AIDS, as well as a sweeping battle plan for how the nation might cope with the epidemic in coming years," journalist Randy Shilts wrote. Among its 579 specific recommendations was a call for the administration to drop its opposition to needed laws that would prevent discrimination against people who carry the AIDS virus; an increase of $3 billion a year in funding for the fight against AIDS at the federal, state, and local levels; comprehensive education about the disease, starting in kindergarten; and a new public health emergency response system, giving the surgeon general broad powers.

Despite his assurances to Glaser, Ronnie took only modest actions in response to the report and ignored its central recommendations. "Time went by, and nothing happened. It was almost unimaginable, but the White House took the report and put it on the shelf. Hope for thousands of Americans and people around the world sat gathering dust in some forgotten corner of some forgotten room," Glaser wrote later. "I was with President Reagan for an hour. I know his commitment was genuine and his intentions sincere, but the decision not to act wasted more precious time. Each step of the way when nothing was done, thousands more people became ill or died. I looked at my country, my government, and the only conclusion to draw was that they still just didn't care."

Glaser pondered whether there was anything she could do on her own. She had learned on her trip to Washington that her story could move people. But that meant she had to sacrifice her privacy—and that of her two HIV-positive children—to get it out. After Ariel died, Elizabeth and a group of friends started the Pediatric AIDS Foundation, which went to work putting millions of dollars in the hands of researchers more quickly than the government seemed capable of doing.

Around that time, she and her husband got word that the tabloid *National Enquirer* was working on a story that would reveal their family's situation; the couple decided to step forward ahead of it, granting an interview to the *Los Angeles Times* that was published on Friday, August 25, 1989. By then, Ronnie was out of office and living in Los Angeles. He saw the story and called Janet Huck, the reporter who wrote it, to ask for Glaser's number. Her phone rang on Sunday morning. Ronnie told her how sorry he was to hear about Ariel's death, asked whether there was anything he could do, and promised to set up a meeting with his staff. Shortly after she hung up, the phone rang again. It was the ex-president, calling back because Nancy wanted to talk with her.

"Nancy was extremely compassionate and told me how saddened she was by Ari's death," Glaser wrote in her memoir. "She said she knew from her own experience with breast cancer how hard it was to go through an illness in public. But she said as difficult as it is, it can do a great deal of good. She was astounded by the number of women who wrote to say that they went in for mammograms after her mastectomy.

"Mrs. Reagan said that she felt our being out in public would help bring attention to the issue of pediatric AIDS and the problems families face. She also offered to be of any help that she could to the foundation."

Two days later, Glaser was in Ronnie's suite of offices in the Century City section of Los Angeles, meeting with Mark Weinberg, the former White House press aide who headed up communications for the ex-president's office. He said Ronnie was eager to cut a public service announcement. In the 1990 spot, Ronnie offered what sounded like a note of regret. "I'm not asking you to send money. I'm asking you for something more important: your understanding. Maybe it's time we all learned something new."

Ronnie and Nancy also sat on the foundation's advisory board, and attended its first big fund-raiser, which was themed "A Time for

Heroes." The *Hollywood Reporter* wrote later that at the June 2, 1990, party, a reporter asked the former president whether he wished he had done more about AIDS. As an aide shouted, "No questions!" Ronnie said: "Well, that's when it was invented." A strange and detached answer, which suggested he did not understand that the power to confront the epidemic had been in his hands. Nancy whispered something to him, and he added: "But we did all that we could at the time." Which was not true.

In 1992 Glaser addressed the Democratic National Convention in New York that nominated Arkansas governor Bill Clinton as the party's candidate to take on then-president George H. W. Bush. At that point, her foundation had raised $13 million, much of which went to what it called the Ariel Project, seeking ways to prevent transmission of AIDS from mother to child. Glaser lamented the death four years earlier of her daughter, who she said "did not survive the Reagan administration. I am here because my son and I may not survive four more years of leaders who say they care but do nothing. I am in a race with the clock. This is not about being a Republican or an Independent or a Democrat. It's about the future—for each and every one of us."

It was a fair criticism, delivered in a powerful speech. Nancy felt "a little betrayed, a little hurt, because they had come forward for her personally, and by then, they had kind of a personal relationship with her," said Wick, who had arranged that first meeting back in 1988. "But Elizabeth felt she was fighting for her kid's life, so pleasantries didn't really matter." Glaser's race with the clock ended a little more than two years after that convention speech. She died on December 3, 1994, at the age of forty-seven. Her HIV-positive son, Jake, survived, and with the help of breakthrough medicines, became a healthy adult.

AIDS activists sensed a disturbing undercurrent in the Reagans' belated involvement in their cause, a subtle message that some of its victims were more worthy of sympathy than others. Barry Krost, an openly gay Hollywood producer and manager, had been among the earliest and most prolific fund-raisers for AIDS charities. After Ronnie left office, Krost occasionally crossed paths with Nancy. "The first time was with a group of ladies. They were her friends. They called them the Kitchen Cabinet or something like that," he said. "They were trying to raise money for an event in Washington, and they kept mentioning the 'innocent' victims of AIDS, and after about the tenth time—do remember, I was young and a bit more irritating than I am now—I just said to them, 'Well, this is confusing me, because I frankly don't know who the guilty ones are,' and I left."

Later, however, Krost had another encounter with Nancy in Los Angeles. He was leaving Le Dome, a fashionable restaurant on Sunset Boulevard, when he spotted the former first lady dining with a mutual friend, Barbara Davis, the wife of billionaire oilman and movie studio owner Marvin Davis. "Barbara says hello to me and introduces me to Mrs. Reagan. I don't do that boring thing, 'Oh, we've met.' I assume she's met a million people. I say, 'It's a pleasure to meet you,'" Krost recalled. "And she just looked at me and said, 'It's a pleasure to see you. We owe you an apology.'" Nancy didn't add anything further, he said. "She didn't have to. I just said, 'Thank you.'

"Look," Krost added, "she ended up living a remarkable life and being a remarkable person. And I think, in the end, she did good." Or perhaps it would be more accurate to say that she tried to. But when it mattered the most, while her husband was still in office, Nancy might have spoken up publicly. She might have pushed harder to jolt the president of the United States out of his passivity. Almost eighty-three thousand cases of AIDS were confirmed while Ronnie was in the White House. Nearly fifty thousand people died of the disease. Those numbers—those lives cut short—are a part of his legacy that can never be erased.

CHAPTER TWENTY

Of all the things that Nancy wanted to see her husband achieve, there was one that stood above all the others in its ambition and its potential to change history. Ending the Cold War, she believed, could be the accomplishment that secured Ronnie's reputation as a giant among American presidents. She made no secret of her dream that a man once branded as a cowboy and a jingoist might even win the Nobel Peace Prize. As Lou Cannon put it in one of his biographies of Ronnie: "Improving US-Soviet relations became Nancy Reagan's special cause. Although few thought of her as a peaceful force, she became a force for peace within the White House."

For any first lady to become involved in major questions of foreign policy was unconventional and politically tricky. For Nancy in particular, it ran counter to her well-cultivated image as a traditional, prefeminist helpmate—one who had vowed that she would never stick her nose in matters of state, as Rosalynn Carter had done by attending Cabinet meetings. Nor were Nancy's views welcomed by the more hawkish members of her husband's Cabinet and National Security Council. In a 2002 oral history for the University of Virginia's Miller Center, Caspar Weinberger, the implacable Soviet foe who served seven years as Ronnie's defense secretary, described Nancy as "a strong influence" on her husband, persistently pulling him toward “closer relationships with the Soviet Union.” Weinberger noted that Nancy “was more receptive to the idea of forming a working relationship with the Soviets than some of the rest of us were, and more willing to trust them. She believed strongly in his negotiating capabilities.”

Hers was a multifront campaign, and, over the years, she did not always get her way. Nancy was not a fan of her husband’s far-fetched scheme to build a space-based missile defense system, which became a major sticking point in US-Soviet relations. Skeptics mocked the Strategic Defense Initiative as “Star Wars,” but Ronnie pushed it nonetheless. She was also unsettled by the Cold War proxy battles that were being waged around the globe. Chief among them in the 1980s was the drive to realign Central America. Nancy wanted to see a diplomatic solution, not a military one, to the bloody strife between Nicaragua’s leftist Sandinista government and the rebel forces known as contras, whom the Reagan administration staunchly backed.

When Nancy invited George P. Shultz and his wife over for dinner that snowy night halfway through Ronnie’s first term, the secretary of state sensed he had found a powerful partner in a first lady who shared his determination to alter the course that Ronnie’s more hard-line advisers had set. Shultz picked up on other things as well. One was that Ronnie himself was feeling frustrated. The president was a self-assured negotiator, going back to his days as head of the Screen Actors Guild. He was anxious to use those same skills in a bigger, more significant way. But Ronnie was hemmed in by some of those around him: by the White House’s national security staff under William Clark, by Defense Secretary Weinberger, by William Casey at the Central Intelligence Agency. And, not least, the president was hamstrung by decades of his own harsh rhetoric. Ronnie despised everything about Communism, which he saw as irredeemably antithetical to freedom, to God’s will, to human potential, to rational economic principles. His views had been shaped in Hollywood during the battles over Communist influence, real and imagined, that roiled the movie industry in the years after World War II.

Ronnie also thought that his recent predecessors had failed to fully account for a broader, darker worldview on the part of the Soviets. Starting with Nixon, Washington had followed a strategy known as *détente,* a French word that means easing tension. Americans had celebrated trade deals, arms negotiations, and high-profile diplomatic visits as harbingers of a Cold War thaw. But none of these gestures deterred the Soviets from moving into Angola in 1975 or from deploying a new generation of nuclear missiles aimed at Europe. The last hopes for détente disappeared when Moscow sent thirty thousand troops into Afghanistan in 1979.

In an exchange with reporters during the first days of his presidency, Ronnie declared that efforts to draw Moscow into a new kind of relationship had thus far been "a one-way street that the Soviet Union has used to pursue its own aims. . . . The only morality they recognize is what will further their cause, meaning they reserve unto themselves the right to commit any crime, to lie, to cheat, in order to attain that, and that is amoral, not immoral, and we operate on a different set of standards. I think when you do business with them, even at a détente, you keep that in mind."

Yet as the Reagan administration pushed forward on the massive US military buildup that the president had promised in his 1980 campaign, there had been signs from the start that Ronnie was looking for an opening to begin a dialogue with the Soviets on his own terms. His calculation behind expanding the nation's armed forces—correct, as it would turn out—was that by forcing Moscow to pour money into its own defense, he could squeeze the already creaky Soviet economy to the breaking point. That in turn would make its leaders more willing to come to the bargaining table on America's terms.

What few people could see in Ronnie's militant words and policies was that he was also an idealist. A believer in the biblical prophecy of Armageddon, Ronnie had never bought into the rationale of each side maintaining a stockpile of nuclear weapons as a deterrent. He abhorred the long-standing doctrine known as "mutually assured destruction." The president thought the only sensible—and morally sound—goal was the complete elimination of bombs and missiles that could wipe millions of people off the face of the earth. As Cannon wrote: "He had a sense of the world as it would be and as it might be, not merely of the way it was. Reagan wanted a world without nuclear weapons, and a world without walls and iron curtains. He was, in this respect, a man for the age."

Even as the president toughened his anti-Moscow language, he was telling his advisers to seek opportunities for engagement. "Reagan in the first term kept saying to his foreign-policy team, 'Let me know when the Soviets are ready to have a constructive dialogue,'" said James Kuhn, an advance man who later became the president's personal assistant. "He kept saying that over and over again, but nothing was happening. Nancy knew that this had to start to unfold, that he had to engage the Soviets, and she worked on Reagan a lot privately."

One of Ronnie's early acts as president had been to offer a gesture of conciliation by lifting the grain embargo that Jimmy Carter imposed on the Soviet Union as punishment for its 1979 invasion and occupation of Afghanistan. Many on the Right had argued that this was "caving in," but in Ronnie's view, it was a pragmatic calculation: the loss of grain sales was hurting American farmers more than it was affecting the Soviet food supply. In the opening months of his first term, Ronnie also made a more personal overture. It came in the spring of 1981, shortly after the assassination attempt. Perhaps facing his own mortality instilled an urgency in the new president; a sense that he had no time to wait for an opening. As he began his recuperation, Ronnie composed a letter to Leonid Brezhnev, his counterpart in Moscow.

The US president asked: "Is it possible that we have let ideology, political and economic philosophy, and governmental policies to keep us from considering the very real, everyday problems of the people we represent?" He recalled an encounter between the two of them in June 1973, when Ronnie was still the governor of California and Brezhnev was visiting President Nixon at his oceanfront estate in San Clemente.

Ronnie had told the Soviet leader then that the aspirations of millions were riding on whether dialogue was possible between their two countries:

> You took my hand in both of yours and assured me that you were aware of that and that you were dedicated with all your heart and mind to fulfilling those hopes and dreams.
>
> The people of the world still share that hope. Indeed, the peoples of the world, despite differences in racial or ethnic origin, have very much in common. They want the dignity of having some control over their individual destiny. They want to work at the craft or trade of their own choosing and to be fairly rewarded. They want to raise their families in peace without harming anyone or suffering harm themselves. Government exists for their convenience, not the other way around.
>
> If they are incapable, as some would have us believe, of self-government, then where in the world do we find people who are capable of governing others?
>
> Mr. President, should we not be concerned with eliminating the obstacles which prevent our people from achieving these simple goals? And isn't it possible some of those obstacles are born of government aims and goals which have little to do with the real needs and wants of our people?

That 1981 letter, initially written in his own hand on six pages of a yellow legal pad, contained no policy specifics beyond Ronnie's decision to lift the grain embargo. But it revealed what had long been in his heart. He passed it around at a meeting in the White House Treaty Room with his senior advisers on Monday, April 13. This was one of their first working sessions since he had been shot. The president wore his bathrobe and pajamas. Among those in attendance were Vice President Bush; the White House management troika of Baker, Deaver, and Meese; Secretary of State Al Haig; and National Security Adviser Richard Allen. "I don't know if you fellows will think it's a good idea," Ronnie said uncertainly, "but why don't you read it and get back to me?"

Most in the room were unsettled at the tone of the letter. It sounded naive and romantic. Worse, it seemed a direct contradiction of Ronnie's tough public rhetoric and the administration's militant posture toward

Moscow. Haig told Ronnie that if a president was going to send a missive to the Kremlin, the pros at the State Department should be the ones to draft it. A few days later, when that same group reconvened, the secretary of state handed the president a shorter, rewritten version—one that Deaver described later as "something the State Department might have written twenty years ago. Typical bureaucratese."

"Well, I guess you fellows know best," Ronnie said. "You're the experts . . ."

Deaver interrupted: "Mr. President, nobody elected anybody in the State Department or the National Security Council. Those guys have been screwing up for a quarter of a century. If you think that's a letter that ought to be sent to Brezhnev, don't let anyone change it. Why don't you just send it?"

Ronnie turned to Haig and said, "Send it the way I wrote it."

The reply that came back from the Kremlin a few weeks later was icy and perfunctory, most likely written by an apparatchik there. The truth was, there would not be much of a chance to achieve a relationship with Brezhnev, who was in ill health and would be dead within nineteen months. His successor, Yuri Andropov, would serve only fifteen months before dying himself. The next leader to fill the job, Konstantin Chernenko, would have an even shorter tenure before succumbing to a combination of illnesses in March 1985. "They never would announce the death of anybody," Weinberger recalled later. "Their radio stations would suddenly switch to classical music. Whenever Radio Moscow switched to classical music, some other leader had gone. That was the only word you got."

Ronnie's mantra of "peace through strength" was dismissed on the Left—and sometimes on the Right—as a contradiction. But Nancy discerned the history-shattering path that Ronnie might be able to blaze, and she was skeptical that the more conventionally hawkish figures on his national security team were truly committed to his longer-term goals. She became especially disturbed when Ronnie made a speech in March 1983 to an evangelical audience in Florida in which he branded the Soviet Union an "evil empire." The phrase, crafted by speechwriter Anthony Dolan, set off a firestorm. In Moscow, the Soviet news agency Tass said the "evil empire" label represented "bellicose hysteria" grounded in "pathological hatred." The Kremlin's mouthpiece declared that the Reagan administration "can think only in terms of confrontation and bellicose, lunatic anti-Communism."

Ronnie was unapologetic, writing later in his memoir: "Frankly, I think it worked, even though some people—including Nancy—tried persuading me to lower the temperature of my rhetoric. I told Nancy I had a reason for saying those things: I wanted the Russians to know I understood their system and what it stood for."

A few days after the speech, political strategist Stu Spencer joined the first couple for dinner at the White House. Nancy was still berating Ronnie for having used such intemperate words. Spencer and Nancy were of like mind on the subject of Ronnie's posture toward the Soviet Union. The two of them were both worried about internal polling showing that even Americans who had a generally favorable view of the president feared that he might move the country closer to war—a concern that could jeopardize his reelection prospects in 1984.

Ronnie, having had enough of his wife's tirade about the "evil empire" speech, turned to Spencer: "What do you think, Stu?"

Spencer tried to be tactful.

"You're right," he began, "they're an evil empire—but that was a pretty tough statement to make—"

"Okay, thanks, Stu," Ronnie replied, cutting him off before he gave Nancy any more fodder. "What's for dessert?"

*

While there had been a rotating cast of leaders in Moscow, Nancy was keeping a close eye on the big changes that were simultaneously going on within Ronnie's foreign-policy team. Richard Allen was replaced as national security adviser by another hard-liner, William Clark, in early 1982. Clark in turn laid the groundwork for Haig's ouster as secretary of state less than six months later. That led to the welcome arrival of

Shultz, who took over the State Department in June. Shultz's deliberative, understated manner was often described as "Buddha-like." But his demeanor was a misleading clue to his inner nature. He was a marine who served in the Pacific during World War II and had a Princeton University tiger tattooed on his butt. A canny infighter, Shultz would stay at the helm of the State Department for the remaining six and a half years of Ronnie's presidency, becoming the longest-serving secretary there since Dean Rusk's tenure under both John F. Kennedy and Lyndon B. Johnson.

Nancy and Shultz saw eye to eye on their distaste for some of the president's advisers. They knew that many of the top officials in the administration privately held a low regard for Ronnie's intellect. "In truth, Ronald Reagan knew far more about the big picture and the matters of salient importance than most people—perhaps especially some of his immediate staff—gave him credit for or appreciated," Shultz wrote in his massive, score-settling memoir *Turmoil and Triumph*. "He had blind spots and a tendency to avoid tedious detail. But the job of those around him was to protect him from those weaknesses and to build on his strengths. Some of them did just the opposite."

When Nancy invited the Shultzes over for that private dinner in early 1983, Brezhnev had just died, and Washington was still trying to figure out what to make of the latest changes in leadership at the Kremlin. Shultz, though relatively new in his own job, had already begun a quiet dialogue with Anatoly Dobrynin, the savvy and charming veteran diplomat who had been Moscow's ambassador to the United States since 1962. Ronnie had personally authorized Shultz's discussions with Dobrynin, over the objections of some in the White House. But the new secretary of state had been reluctant to move toward ironing out the real substantive differences between the two nations, because he felt he did not have a solid sense of where the president stood. This was precisely what Nancy wanted Shultz to begin to understand that evening. Ronnie was more willing to press forward in developing relations with the Communist world—even travel there—than the secretary of state had previously believed.

Ronald Reagan with his family, including Michael and wife Colleen with their son, Cameron, Nancy, Patti, and Ron at the Republican National Convention, July 1, 1980. (*Diana Walker*)

The new president and first lady at Ronald Reagan's first inauguration. Nancy holds a worn Bible that belonged to Ronnie's mother, Nelle. January 20, 1981. (*Diana Walker*)

Official family portrait in the Red Room, January 20, 1981. (*Ronald Reagan Presidential Library*)

Entertainer Frank Sinatra with First Lady Nancy Reagan at a National Italian American Foundation Dinner honoring Sinatra, October 1985. (*Diana Walker*)

First Lady Nancy Reagan at a ceremony on the South Lawn of the White House, where the president gave Michael Jackson, the "King of Pop," an award for allowing his song "Beat It" to be used in a public service campaign against drunk driving, May 14, 1984. (*Diana Walker*)

Nancy Reagan congratulates her son, Ron, after his performance with the Joffrey Ballet at the Metropolitan Opera House in New York, March 16, 1981. (*Diana Walker*)

A tense introduction: Soviet first lady Raisa Gorbachev and Nancy have tea in Geneva during their husbands' first summit, November 19, 1985. (*Diana Walker*)

Four days after an arms-for-hostages scandal has begun to unravel, President Ronald Reagan and his wife, Nancy, flank released hostage David Jacobsen at a welcoming ceremony at the White House, November 7, 1986. (*Diana Walker*)

Nancy Reagan, with a couple of young visitors, waving from the crown of the Statue of Liberty after it was reopened, July 5, 1986. (*Diana Walker*)

Nancy Reagan at a "Just Say No" rally at the White House, May 22, 1986. (*Diana Walker*)

Nancy Reagan places flowers on graves of American soldiers killed in the invasion of Normandy. The commemoration took place at the U.S. cemetery at Omaha Beach, France, on the anniversary of D-day, June 6, 1982. (*Diana Walker*)

The Reagans aboard the battleship USS *Iowa* during Independence Day celebrations, New York City, July 4, 1986. (*Diana Walker*)

Nancy Reagan waves to photographer Diana Walker after the inauguration of George H. W. Bush, January 20, 1989. (*Diana Walker*)

President Bill Clinton (left) and First Lady Hillary Clinton (second from left) are joined by four former presidents and their wives during Richard Nixon's funeral in Yorba Linda, California, April 27, 1994. (Left to right) George H. W. and Barbara Bush, Ronald and Nancy Reagan, Jimmy and Rosalynn Carter, Jerry and Betty Ford. (*Diana Walker*)

Nancy Reagan kisses her husband's casket during the interment ceremony at the Ronald Reagan Presidential Library in Simi Valley, California, June 11, 2004. (*Kevork Djansezian/Pool/Getty Images*)

Guardian of the legacy: Nancy Reagan at the unveiling of a commemorative postage stamp honoring her late husband, November 9, 2004. (*David McNew/Getty Images*)

On what would be her last visit to the White House, Nancy Reagan joins President Barack Obama for the June 2, 2009, signing of the Ronald Reagan Centennial Commission Act. The law set up a panel to plan and carry out activities to mark the hundredth anniversary of Ronnie's birth in 2011. (*Lawrence Jackson/The White House*)

"I will be meeting with Dobrynin again late Tuesday afternoon," Shultz told Ronnie. "What would you think about my bringing Dobrynin over to the White House for a private chat?"

"Great," the president replied, adding, "We have to keep this secret. I don't intend to engage in a detailed exchange with Dobrynin, but I do intend to tell him that if Andropov is willing to do business, so am I."

Early Monday morning, Shultz got a call from Bill Clark. The national security adviser was livid at what he saw as an end run by Shultz and thought that allowing the president to sit down with the Soviet ambassador was a mistake. But Ronnie insisted he wanted to do it, and Deaver made arrangements to send a White House car to the State Department garage to pick up Shultz and Dobrynin. Their meeting in the living room of the family quarters lasted two hours, during which the three men talked about arms control, the potential for a long-term deal on grain that the Soviets wanted, and recent developments in Poland and Afghanistan.

Ronnie also pressed the ambassador on human rights—particularly the plight of two families of Pentecostal Christians who had taken refuge in the US embassy in Moscow after being denied the right to leave a country where they faced persecution and arrest. At that point, the "Siberian Seven" had been living in the embassy basement for nearly five years, in one cramped room with only two beds. Ronnie told the Soviet ambassador: "If you can do something about the Pentecostals or another human rights issue, we will simply be delighted and will not embarrass you by undue publicity, by claims of credit for ourselves or by 'crowing.'" As the ambassador and secretary of state left the meeting with Ronnie, Dobrynin told Shultz that he would see if anything could be done about this "special subject." A few months later, the Pentecostal families were granted safe conduct out of the embassy and ultimately allowed to leave the Soviet Union. Ronnie made good on his promise not to boast.

"Nancy was very much involved," Shultz told me. She understood, he added, that this delicate initial trust-building exercise involving the Pentecostal families "sent a message to the Soviets that you can deal with this man because he keeps his word. It made an impression on them that you can work a deal with these people, and they'll carry through on it. In an odd way, it was a little something that happened as the result of Nancy's phone call. 'Come over and have supper with us.'"

On June 5, 1983, George and Helena "Obie" Shultz reciprocated Nancy's invitation and had the Reagans over to their house in Bethesda. Their neighbors lined the street to wave and cheer as the presidential motorcade pulled up. Over dinner, the two couples celebrated a successful G-7 summit that Ronnie had recently hosted in Williamsburg, Virginia. "I learned something else of interest that evening: the president was uneasy with Bill Clark, and Nancy had no time for him at all," Shultz wrote later.

That the national security adviser was on thin ice with the president was an important bit of internal intelligence for Shultz. At the time, the general perception was that Clark's star was on the rise, much to the dismay of both Shultz and Nancy. In the media, he, not Shultz, was portrayed as the administration's most important player when it came to international affairs. "Unlike his predecessors in the national security post, Mr. Clark is a self-proclaimed foreign-policy novice who makes no television appearances, gives few speeches and fewer interviews, writes no learned papers, and expresses no original foreign-policy concepts," the *New York Times* wrote of Clark in August 1983. "Yet he has become the most influential foreign-policy figure in the Reagan administration. Eighteen months ago, when he assumed his job after a year's stint as deputy secretary of state, he was reluctant to assert his conservative views. Now, he is the president's chief instrument for guaranteeing that his administration takes a hard-line approach to Communism and Soviet influence in the world."

Clark's bond with Ronnie went back to Sacramento, where he had been chief of staff in the governor's office. Though he did not have a foreign-policy background, he was smart and talented. A rancher who had passed the California bar exam on his second attempt without having graduated from college or law school, Clark had brought order to Ronnie's operation in Sacramento during its most chaotic days. Nancy had also tried to recruit him to help out during the 1980 campaign, when she was engineering the firing of campaign manager John Sears and the shake-up that put Ronnie on the path to victory after New Hampshire. Clark initially joined the Reagan administration as deputy secretary of state, put there largely to keep an eye on the volatile Al Haig. When Clark arrived, Haig had told him: "You, Bill, are going to run the building. I'm going to run the world."

Whatever regard Nancy had for his managerial abilities, the first lady did not believe that Clark was the person to be driving foreign policy. During his confirmation hearing before the Senate Foreign Relations Committee, Clark had been unable to come up with the names of the prime ministers of Zimbabwe or South Africa, both of which were hot spots at the time. He also admitted that he did not know the definitions of *détente* or *third world*. Afterward, Democrat John Glenn of Ohio declared in exasperation that he "had never seen anything like such ignorance of foreign affairs and lack of preparation for a confirmation hearing in my years here in the Senate." A leading daily newspaper in Amsterdam labeled Clark "a nitwit," and London's *Daily Mirror* opined: "America's allies in Europe—Europe, Mr. Clark—you must have heard of it—will hope he is never in charge at a time of crisis."

Once installed in the White House as national security adviser, the deeply conservative Clark clashed with the more pragmatic James Baker and Michael Deaver, though he still had an ally in presidential counselor Ed Meese, who had been an ideological comrade in arms since their Sacramento days. More troubling to Nancy was the fact that Clark, as Deaver once put it, "saw no hope in any policy that relied on trusting the Russians, argued against any attempt to improve that relationship, and did what he could to slow it down."

Clark's defenders, who were legion among the other old California hands, say that Nancy's real beef with the national security adviser was that he was too close to Ronnie, which made him a rival and a counterweight to her own influence over her husband. He and the president frequently went horseback riding together in Washington's winding Rock Creek Park. When Clark replaced Richard Allen as the White House's top foreign-policy adviser, he leveraged his personal ties into an arrangement under which he reported directly to Ronnie and had coveted "walk-in privileges" to the Oval Office, which meant he did not have to make an appointment to see the president. "I had never really gotten along with him," Nancy wrote later of Clark. "He struck me as a user—especially when he traveled around the country claiming he represented Ronnie, which usually wasn't true. I spoke to Ronnie about him, but Ronnie liked him, so he stayed around longer than I would have liked."

The national security adviser was pushing hard for a larger US military footprint in Central America. Things boiled over when Clark appeared on the August 8, 1983, cover of *Time* as the face of the administration's "Big Stick Approach." The magazine also took some shots at Shultz in an accompanying article, which noted that there had been a "disappearing act at Foggy Bottom" as "State Department influence continues to wane." Furious, Nancy called Shultz. She told him she did not believe the national security adviser had Ronnie's interests at heart and that he should be fired. Shultz, though he no doubt agreed, tried to calm her down, saying Clark was simply in over his head. In fact, Clark's star turn in the media was a portent of trouble ahead. Clark would later ruefully recall an admonition he had received from Al Haig: "Once you appear in this town on the cover of *Time* or *Newsweek*, count your days in the shop."

Not that he was all that eager to stay. Clark was restless by nature and weary of all the internecine battles. When James Watt's resignation in early October opened a Cabinet-level vacancy at the Interior Department, Clark jumped at the opportunity to escape the White House.

Chief of Staff Jim Baker was briefly considered as a possibility to move into the national security adviser's post, which would have been Nancy's preference, as well as Shultz's. Clark, upon hearing of his planned replacement, rallied his fellow conservatives—including Pentagon Secretary Weinberger, CIA Director Casey, and Meese—to put a stop to it. The right flank considered Baker too moderate for the job and also knew he was a frequent source of leaks to his friends in the press. Their choice for the post was Jeane J. Kirkpatrick, the truculent UN ambassador, whom Shultz would not have accepted. Ronnie decided not to risk inflaming the tensions of his deeply divided national security team and wrote in his diary on October 14, 1983: "Jim Baker wants to take the NSC post. I was willing but then found great division & resistance in certain quarters. I finally decided that to ignore this & go ahead anyway would leave me with a permanent problem."

The following Monday, Ronnie announced that his new national security adviser would be Robert C. ("Bud") McFarlane, who had been Clark's deputy. McFarlane had been the second choice of both factions and represented a compromise candidate. "My decision not to appoint Jim Baker as national security advisor, I suppose, was a turning point for my administration, although I had no idea at the time how significant it would be," Ronnie wrote later. McFarlane would become a key player in the Iran-contra scandal.

Not quite a year later, longtime Soviet foreign minister Andrei Gromyko visited Washington, and Shultz arranged for him to have a working lunch with Ronnie and the administration's senior foreign-policy team. The meeting on September 28, 1984, marked the first time a Soviet official of such high rank had been publicly received at the Reagan White House. Gromyko, who had dealt with nine presidents and fourteen secretaries of state, was known as a tough, unbending negotiator who took exacting measure of his adversaries and always arrived prepared.

Shultz decided it would be a good idea for the foreign minister to meet the first lady and orchestrated a way for it to happen, supposedly impromptu, at a prelunch reception in the Red Room.

"Nancy, here's what happens," Shultz told her. "He comes to the Oval Office. We have a meeting, and we all walk down the hallway to the mansion. That's your home. There's some stand-around time, and then there's a working lunch. How about being there in the stand-around time? You're the hostess. It would be a nice thing." Her presence at the reception surprised and delighted the foreign minister. "When Gromyko gets there, he's no fool; he sees Nancy, and he goes right over to her, engages her in conversation," Shultz said.

The flirtatious first lady turned on the charm, captivating the dour man known as "Grim Grom" and "Mr. Nyet." As the reception was winding up, Gromyko casually took a glass of cranberry juice from a waiter's tray, lifted it in a toast, and asked Nancy why it had been so hard to get Ronnie to the bargaining table.

"Does your husband believe in peace?" he said.

"Yes, of course," she replied, bristling slightly.

"Then whisper 'peace' in your husband's ear every night," Gromyko told her.

"I will, and I'll also whisper it in your ear," Nancy said. She put her hands on the foreign minister's shoulders, pulled him close, and said softly: "*Peace.*"

Gromyko would tell that story many times over the years. He took it as an assurance, from the most reliable of authorities, that Ronnie was indeed serious about turning a new page in US-Soviet relations. More than three decades later, Shultz still chuckled as he recounted that moment to me: "I said, 'Nancy, you just won the Cold War.' " Not too long after that, the Soviet news agency Tass began covering Nancy's public appearances.

On Thanksgiving Day, Washington and Moscow announced that their chief diplomats would meet in January in Geneva. They were to set the terms upon which they could move forward on negotiations aimed at reaching "mutually acceptable agreements on the whole range of questions concerning nuclear and outer space arms." A Soviet spokesman cautioned the *Washington Post* that this agreement to talk should not be seen as the dawn of a new age of détente, but rather as "a small crack in the East-West ice." Still, Shultz was jubilant. "That basic policy of strength, realism, and readiness to negotiate had paid off," he wrote later. "Now the work would begin."

Once the preliminaries were done, more substantive talks were to get under way on March 12, 1985. At four in the morning the day before, National Security Adviser McFarlane awakened Ronnie with a phone call. Soviet president Konstantin Chernenko had died—the third elderly Soviet leader to do so in less than two and a half years.

Chernenko had hoped to make his mark in foreign policy by reversing his predecessors' confrontational stance toward the United States but had held power for only 390 days, during which he had been seriously ill.

In picking the Soviet Union's next leader, the policy-making Central Committee decided to make a generational U-turn. The new general secretary of the Communist Party would be fifty-four-year-old Mikhail Gorbachev, the youngest member of the Kremlin leadership. Leaders in the West had already identified him as a comer. Nancy encouraged Ronnie to meet with Gorbachev as soon as possible, though some on his national security team opposed it. "Yes," she acknowledged in her memoir, "I did push Ronnie a little. But he would never have met Gorbachev if he hadn't wanted to."

It helped that Margaret Thatcher had sized up the rising Soviet leader favorably the previous year, when Gorbachev had led a parliamentary delegation to London. Thatcher had spoken highly of Gorbachev to Ronnie when she visited Camp David for the first time a few days before Christmas 1984. Gorbachev was no soft touch, but nonetheless a more pragmatic type than Thatcher had encountered before in her dealings with the Kremlin. Unlike others before him, Gorbachev didn't interrupt when she raised contentious issues, or drone on with lengthy recitations of principles that she had heard many times before. A memorandum summarizing her private meeting with Ronnie at Camp David shows Thatcher confided to Ronnie that Gorbachev was "an unusual Russian in that he was much less constrained, more charming, open to discussion and debate, and did not stick to prepared notes." Neither she nor Ronnie, however, could have known how soon they would be dealing with him as the leader of his nation.

*

Though Gorbachev's ascension offered the tantalizing possibility that a new era might be dawning in US-Soviet relations, there were bumps along the way to scheduling a summit. Ronnie's advisers were divided over how ambitious the agenda should be, and there was wrangling between Moscow and Washington about where it should be held. Nancy was relentless in pushing for it to happen as soon as possible, using every opportunity, including social events, to press the case with her husband's team. "She felt strongly that it was not only in the interest of world peace but the correct move politically," Deaver recounted. "She would buttonhole George Shultz, Bud McFarlane, and others, to be sure that they were moving toward that goal." On July 3, 1985, the two governments announced that President Reagan and General Secretary Gorbachev would meet in Geneva on November 19 and 20.

"Flying over on Air Force One, what I remembered most were the high spirits of the first lady," Ronnie's executive assistant, Jim Kuhn, wrote later. "Usually tightly wound, Mrs. Reagan was in the best mood I had ever seen her in: she was relaxed, even joyous." Ronnie was well prepared, having spent the past six months poring over more than two dozen briefing papers, which covered topics from Russian history and culture, to Soviet objectives and negotiating tactics. For once, Kuhn noticed, the president didn't express annoyance that he was being loaded down with paperwork and information.

Nancy, as always, stood vigilant against overscheduling her husband. Ronnie arrived in Geneva three days early to ensure that he would be well rested and recovered from jet lag by the time the meetings began. On the plane over, the Reagans had eaten their meals on Swiss time, to speed the adjustment. It had been arranged that they would lodge in splendor at Maison de Saussure, an eighteenth-century stone mansion on twenty acres along Lake Geneva, which was loaned to the Reagans by Aga Khan IV, the fabulously wealthy spiritual leader of a branch of Shia Islam.

The fall weather was chilly and damp. Patches of snow dotted the edge of the lake, and in the distance, the Reagans could see the high peaks of the Alps rising against a slate-gray sky. Neither Ronnie nor Nancy slept well on the night before his first meeting with the new Soviet leader. In his diary, the president wrote: "Lord, I hope I'm ready & not overtrained."

One thing both he and Nancy wanted was a chance for Ronnie to get to know Gorbachev personally, without teams of diplomats and arms-control experts choreographing their every interaction. Two days before the summit began, the Reagans went to see Villa Fleur d'Eau, a luxurious 120-year-old lakeside chateau five miles outside of Geneva where the first day of meetings was to take place. Ronnie tried out the chair in which he would be sitting, and Nancy, on a whim, sat down in Gorbachev's. "My, Mr. General Secretary," the president told her, "you're much prettier than I expected."

The Reagans also took a walk around the grounds. About a hundred yards down a hill from the chateau was a charming boathouse that chief of presidential advance William Henkel had spotted earlier. It had a fireplace and a spectacular view of the water. "As soon as we walked into this room, we knew it was the perfect spot," Nancy recalled. "Here, by the warmth of the fire, they could take a few minutes to begin to know each other as human beings. There were people on our side—and presumably on the other side, too—who didn't think a private meeting was such a great idea, but I strongly encouraged Ronnie to follow his instincts. We both felt that it was important for these two men to begin building a personal relationship, and that this was far more likely to occur if they had a few minutes alone with just their translators."

Finally, the opening day of the summit arrived. As Ronnie and Gorbachev shook hands for the first time, the American president took an immediate liking to the Soviet leader. He escorted Gorbachev into a sitting room for what was supposed to be a fifteen-minute conversation while their teams got settled. After forty minutes went by, White House chief of staff Don Regan told Jim Kuhn to go in and break it up. The plenary session was supposed to start.

"It's their first meeting," Kuhn protested.

"What about the schedule?" Regan demanded.

"I don't think it matters," Kuhn replied. "I think we need to leave them alone."

As the leaders' tête-à-tête stretched past the one-hour mark, Regan and National Security Adviser McFarlane became more insistent. They told Kuhn to talk to Shultz. The secretary of state was meeting with his counterpart, Soviet foreign minister Eduard Shevardnadze, who had recently replaced the obdurate Gromyko. Kuhn interrupted them and asked for advice on whether to cut in on Ronnie and Gorbachev. Shultz, who was often imperious with staff members, became furious and yelled: "If you're stupid enough to walk into that room and break up the meeting between those two leaders, then you don't deserve the job you have!"

Kuhn returned to Regan and McFarlane. "Leave the president alone. Nobody goes in," he said. "The president and the general secretary will end it when they want to end it."

When Ronnie and Gorbachev finally joined the session, they followed a disappointingly conventional script, talking past each other and restating their countries' long-standing differences. In the afternoon, the mood got heavy, as the subject turned to arms control. Ronnie argued vigorously in defense of his Strategic Defense Initiative. Gorbachev dismissed it as "emotional. It's a dream. Who can control it? Who can monitor it? It opens up an arms race in space."

At that point, Ronnie suggested they take a walk and breathe some of the crisp air outside. Gorbachev was out of his chair before Ronnie could finish his sentence. The two men and their translators strolled over to the boathouse, where the fireplace was going. Only later did Ronnie discover that his aides, in their eagerness to make the setting cheery and welcoming, had set such a rip-roaring blaze that it had accidentally set the mantelpiece aflame. They had to douse it with pitchers of water and start over. Away from the formal discussion, Ronnie delivered the larger message that he wanted Gorbachev to understand: they were two men who had the power to start World War III, but they were also the only two who could bring about peace. The Cold War had to end, and Ronnie was determined to make that happen, one way or the other. "Reagan told Gorbachev that the Soviet Union could never win an all-out arms race with the United States because the United States would always be able to outspend the Soviet Union," Kuhn said.

As they walked back to the chateau, Ronnie suggested that Gorbachev visit the United States for a second summit the following year. The general secretary agreed, but only if Ronnie would come to a third one in Moscow. "Our people couldn't believe it when I told them what had happened," Ronnie wrote later. "Everything was settled for two more summits. They hadn't dreamed it was possible." That first meeting in Geneva became known as "the fireside summit." Though no real progress had been made toward narrowing their differences, the superpower leaders had agreed to keep talking, which, in Ronnie's view, was the most important thing of all.

*

While the men were moving toward peace, their wives were launching what would become a personal Cold War. At the end of that first day of the summit, Nancy returned to Maison de Saussure shortly after her husband did. Ronnie kissed her and asked her how things had gone. Nancy gave him a weak smile and said, "That Raisa Gorbachev is one cold cookie."

It had been arranged in advance that Nancy would host Raisa on the opening day in Geneva and the Soviet first lady would return the invitation on the second. This would be the first such summit of superpower spouses since glamorous young Jacqueline Kennedy and grandmotherly Nina Petrovna Khrushchev, wife of Nikita Khrushchev, the Soviet premier from 1958 to 1964, lunched at a Vienna summit in 1961, drawing a crowd outside of a thousand people.

Nancy had become more confident as a figure on the international stage in her own right. She had hosted other first ladies at the United Nations, met privately with Pope John Paul II at the Vatican to discuss worldwide drug abuse, and flown to Mexico City with disaster aid after a deadly September 1985 earthquake. To prepare for her meeting with Raisa, Nancy read novels and history books about Russia, scoured news reports, and watched videotapes of the Gorbachevs' earlier visits to London and Paris. Meanwhile, diplomats at the Soviet embassy in Washington assembled reports on Nancy, which they provided to Raisa.

In Moscow, Raisa was seen as a new kind of first lady. Traditionally, Kremlin wives were so invisible that ordinary Soviet citizens had no idea of their occupations, how many children they had, or sometimes even what their first names were. Not so with Raisa, a brilliant academic who was fashion conscious and outspoken with her own views. Before her husband became the leader of the country, she accompanied him on overseas trips; when they visited London in 1984, Raisa had created a sensation by wearing gold lamé sandals with chain straps. The month before the Geneva summit, Raisa had appeared in the audience at designer Pierre Cardin's show in Paris. France's press gave Raisa mixed reviews. Her hairdo was deemed too puffy and the heels of her shoes too high, but her bright tweed suit with a long skirt and velvet collar was judged to be right in style. She was deemed elegant, but not chic.

Raisa, like Nancy, was known as her husband's closest adviser. They had one daughter, and theirs too was a marriage of mutual adoration, although they were far more reserved than the Reagans about expressing it. Also like Nancy, she was scorned by many in her own country as arrogant and ostentatious. So there might have seemed at least a possibility that they would have enough in common to hit it off.

Instead, the two women felt an instant loathing for each other. Their chilly rivalry became a juicy subplot for the media covering the four meetings that Ronnie and Gorbachev held. At that first tea in Geneva, Raisa hadn't liked the chair in which she was seated, so she snapped her fingers for her KGB bodyguards to find her another. She didn't like that one either, so she snapped and summoned them once again. "I couldn't believe it," Nancy recalled later. "I had met first ladies, princesses, and queens, but I had never seen anybody act this way. I'm still not sure whether she wanted to make a point with me or was just trying out her new position. Or perhaps she was nervous or uncomfortable."

Nancy was not insensitive to the fact that Raisa faced a kind of scrutiny that she could only begin to imagine. She noticed, for instance, that when the Gorbachevs returned to Moscow, he got off the plane by himself from the front, while Raisa exited discreetly through the back. "Still, her conversational style made me bristle," Nancy wrote in her memoir. "When I came to tea at the Soviet mission, the hall was decorated with children's paintings, and Raisa insisted that I look at each one while she described the meaning behind it. I felt condescended to, and I wanted to say, 'Enough. You don't have to tell me what a missile is. I get the message!'"

Nancy also tired of Raisa's lectures on the glories of Leninism and the failings of the US system. When Nancy tried to bring up her own work against drug abuse, Raisa shut down the conversation by declaring there was no such problem in the Soviet Union. Nor was Nancy fooled when Raisa claimed that the enormous spread that had been laid out for their second meeting—blinis with caviar, cabbage rolls, pie, cookies, chocolates—was typical Soviet fare. "If that was an ordinary housewife's tea," Nancy observed, "then I'm Catherine the Great."

Nonetheless, Nancy was thrilled at how things went in Geneva. The summit was a success and a turning point. Upon landing back at Andrews Air Force Base, Ronnie headed straight to the Capitol, where he delivered a twenty-minute address to Congress. It was three in the morning on his body clock, and he sounded a bit hoarse. Though the talks had not produced a "meeting of the minds," he declared triumphantly that they had opened the way for "a new realism" in US-Soviet relations.

They also set the tone for personal relationships. Nancy decided she liked Gorbachev as much as Ronnie did, finding him funny and warm at the dinners they had shared in Geneva. But the frostiness between the two first ladies lingered. About a year later, in October 1986, Ronnie and Gorbachev met again in Reykjavik, Iceland, which was roughly halfway between their two capitals. This "working meeting" was not a full-scale summit. Expectations for significant progress were low, and it had been agreed that wives were not to be invited this time. But a few days before the event, Moscow announced that Raisa would, in fact, be going. This was an aggressive act of first lady one-upsmanship. Nancy agonized over whether to cancel everything on her own packed schedule and show up but felt that Raisa was testing her. She kissed Ronnie good-bye on the South Lawn as he boarded the helicopter for Andrews and settled in to monitor what was happening across the Atlantic.

As she recounted later in her book, the media coverage of the meeting was filled with images of Raisa:

"I followed the Iceland 'summit' on television and saw more of Raisa than of Ronnie or Gorbachev. I saw her at a swimming pool with children—the first time I had seen her do anything with children. I also saw her at a school, where she handed out pins of Lenin—which I thought was a bit much. Then, when an interviewer asked her why I wasn't there, she said, 'Perhaps she has something else to do. Or maybe she is not feeling well.' Oh, please!"

That was not the only thing that bothered Nancy about what she saw in the news coverage. Before Ronnie left, Nancy told assistant Jim Kuhn to telephone her once a day on a secure line to tell her how things were going. On the first call, the first lady tore into Kuhn. "What the hell is going on there with the coat?" she demanded. Television had shown Ronnie wearing a ghastly overcoat from his Hollywood days, one that he should have discarded long before. It was drab green with wide, brown fur lapels, and was several sizes too large. Kuhn had seen Ronnie packing it before the trip and had tried to talk him into taking an elegant blue cashmere one instead. "Mr. President, it's not that cold," Kuhn argued. "This isn't Greenland. They've got the jet stream."

But Ronnie had an odd attachment to this particular piece of clothing. He insisted not only on taking it to Reykjavik but also on wearing it for a much-photographed meeting with Iceland's president. "I want you to get that coat," Nancy ordered Kuhn. "Get it away from him now and *go lose the coat.*" Frantic, Kuhn found presidential valet Eddie Serrano and told him: "Get rid of that coat. Don't ever let him see it again. That's per the first lady. You know what to do."

Nancy's concern over her husband's clownish outerwear was not just sartorial fussiness on her part. More memorable than any other image from the Geneva summit had been the photos of Ronnie's first handshake with Gorbachev. The US president wore a business suit in the frosty wind; Gorbachev was bundled up in a dark overcoat and scarf. Ronnie, though twenty years older than his Soviet counterpart, appeared the more vigorous man. Gorbachev picked up on the contrast immediately. As he prepared to reach out to Ronnie with one hand, he snatched the fedora off his head with the other. Kremlin press official Sergei Tarasenko lamented later: "We lost the game during this first movement." For the remainder of that summit, when the two superpower leaders were to be in situations where cameras were present, Gorbachev would ask in advance: Coats on or coats off?

As Nancy monitored their second meeting from 2,800 miles away, she realized there were other problems more substantive than her husband's wardrobe. When the two leaders emerged from their final session at Reykjavik's reputedly haunted Hofdi House, Nancy could tell from Ronnie's expression that something had gone wrong. "He looked angry, *very* angry," she recalled. "His face was pale, and his teeth were clenched. I had seen that look before, but not often—and certainly not on television. You really have to push Ronnie very far to get that expression." What she later learned was that he and Gorbachev had made a lot of progress; had even been on the verge of a historic agreement providing for the elimination of most or all nuclear weapons within a decade. But it fell apart when Gorbachev added one more condition: a ten-year ban on development and testing of Ronnie's cherished concept of a space-based missile defense system. Ronnie felt he had been set up—that Gorbachev had brought him to Iceland for the sole purpose of killing his Strategic Defense Initiative—and refused. "Let's go, George," he told Shultz. "We're leaving."

The news coverage was scathing, as were the reactions of US allies. Reports had it that Ronnie had arrived unprepared and was too rigid. "No Deal," *Time*'s cover proclaimed. "Star Wars Sinks the Summit." But opinion outside media and diplomatic circles turned in Ronnie's favor. A poll conducted by the *New York Times* and CBS News in mid-October found Americans thought their president had been right to hold the line, and were more optimistic than they had been that the two countries were on the path to a major reduction in nuclear weapons. Ronnie's refusal to budge on his Strategic Defense Initiative served another purpose: it reinforced for Gorbachev the reality that the Soviet Union, with its ossified economy, would not be able to continue an arms race with the United States.

In June 1987 Ronnie stood a hundred yards from the concrete barrier that had divided East and West Berlin for more than a quarter century and made what was perhaps the most memorable foreign-policy declaration of his presidency: "Mr. Gorbachev, tear down this wall!" Those electrifying words were not just symbolic. Real work that would ultimately help lead to the end of the Cold War—and in its wake, the unification of east and west—was going on at the negotiating table. Ronnie and Gorbachev met again the following December for the Washington summit they had agreed to in Geneva. It is remembered for the signing of the Intermediate-Range Nuclear Forces Treaty, a landmark pact prohibiting land-based cruise or ballistic missiles with ranges between 311 miles and 3,420 miles. For the first time, the two superpowers had agreed to eliminate an entire category of nuclear weapons. The INF deal would see the two countries destroy nearly 2,700 of these weapons by its 1991 implementation deadline.

Ronnie's peacemaking efforts were not sitting well with conservative leaders at home. The Right had embraced his vision in other areas as though it were Scripture. But they did not share his commitment to arms reductions and were losing confidence that he was capable of holding his own in negotiations with Gorbachev. They also feared he had been damaged by the Iran-contra scandal, which at the time had been consuming his administration for six months. Shortly before the summit, influential activist Paul Weyrich told the *Washington Post*: "Reagan is a weakened president, weakened in spirit as well as in clout and not in a position to make judgments about Gorbachev at this time."

Ronnie invited fifteen or so disgruntled conservative leaders, including Weyrich, to meet privately with him in the Roosevelt Room. "I've got to get them to calm down. I've got to make sure they understand where I am on this," he told Jim Kuhn. The group sat stonily while

Ronnie did nearly all of the talking during the session. Afterward, as he and Kuhn were returning to the Oval Office across the hallway, the president asked: "Did you notice how that was at the end, Jim?"

"Yeah," Kuhn replied. "There was dead silence."

"I didn't get any applause. There was no applause from this group," Ronnie said. "I thought I got through to them, and they are still upset thinking I'm too cozy with the Soviets."

At the Washington summit, Nancy and Raisa once again created a running story line all their own. After the arrival ceremony, when the men went off for meetings in the West Wing, Nancy hosted Raisa and several administration wives, including Barbara Bush, for coffee in the Green Room. Barbara noted in her diary that Raisa did not offer condolences for the recent death of Nancy's mother or inquire how she was feeling after her mastectomy the month before. Instead, the Soviet first lady began by getting in a dig, saying people were wondering why Nancy hadn't come to Iceland. Before Nancy could reply that she had been under the impression that the wives weren't invited, Raisa interrupted: "You would have liked it. People missed you."

Raisa then proceeded to lecture the other women on Russian history, contrasting the United States' experience unfavorably with her own country's and falsely claiming that there were no homeless people in the Soviet Union, thanks to its twenty-five-year housing program.

Obie Shultz leaned over to Barbara Bush and whispered: "Nancy doesn't like this conversation."

"Who would?" Barbara answered.

Finally, after about an hour of listening to Raisa, Nancy said, "I'm afraid that I'm keeping you from your schedule."

"Oh, that's all right," Raisa replied.

Several of the women there told Nancy later that they had been shocked at Raisa's rudeness; Nancy allowed that she was glad others had seen what she had been dealing with. Nor was her overbearing behavior Raisa's only transgression in Nancy's eyes. Raisa had taken weeks to respond to Nancy's offer to provide a tour of the White House later during the summit, though she accepted an invitation to visit

Pamela Harriman, a prominent Democratic hostess and fund-raiser. “I was offended,” Nancy said. “In the circle we moved in, you don’t ignore an invitation from the head of state or his wife.”

When Raisa finally agreed to be shown through the White House, she insisted that the time be moved from midafternoon to late morning, and said that she could spend no more than one hour there. Afterward, a reporter asked Raisa what she thought of the executive mansion that Nancy had poured so much energy into renovating. Her reply: “It’s an official house. I would say that, humanly speaking, a human being would like to live in a regular house. This is like a museum.”

By this point, the relationship between the two women was beyond the point of repair. Raisa had been imperious in Geneva, had outmaneuvered Nancy by going to Reykjavik, and now had publicly upstaged her on her own turf. “Nancy Reagan didn’t trust anybody to begin with, but you roll her once, you’re history. And Raisa did it at least three times,” presidential assistant Jim Kuhn said. “But she put up with her. What choice did she have?”

As annoying as Nancy found Raisa, she also appreciated how close the Gorbachev partnership was, and appeared to have recognized in them a parallel of her own marriage to Ronnie. The Gorbachevs met as students and were wed in 1953, the year after the Reagans. In an interview that Nancy gave journalist James Mann in 2005, the former first lady said of Raisa, who died of leukemia in 1999 at the age of sixty-seven: “She was a very strong woman. You always had the feeling if he ever faltered, she would be right there to prop him up.”

The public and decidedly undiplomatic test of wills in which the two women were engaged worried some who feared its impact on the summit’s success. Selwa “Lucky” Roosevelt, who was chief of protocol at the State Department, wrote with exasperation in her memoir: “The Nancy-Raisa exchanges were reported ad nauseum by our press. Certainly Mrs. Gorbachev’s manner could be grating, but I kept wishing Nancy would not let it get to her. I wanted her to rise above the provocation, smile sweetly, and look ingenuous with her beautiful brown eyes wide open. I was surprised that a woman as controlled as Nancy

Reagan would let herself get rattled, in full color on international TV. I wanted to shout at her, 'Smile, Nancy! Smile!'

"Part of the problem was that no one dared to tell the First Lady such things."

Barbara Bush, on the other hand, found the rivalry amusing, and allowed herself a bit of glee in the idea that Nancy might have finally met her match. In her diary, Barbara noted that she had been impressed by Raisa's "marvelous" coloring, and that the Soviet first lady's hair was a softer shade of red than the constant press references to henna would suggest. "She is a lovely looking creature, smaller than the size twelve we are reading about, more a six or an eight," Barbara wrote. "She is a prettier package than the pictures show. I don't know how old, but think the paper said fifty-three or fifty-five. That's funny, for we really don't know if Nancy Reagan is sixty-five or sixty-seven, and she won't tell. I guess Raisa won't tell, either." Barbara also noticed that as Raisa's visit progressed, her skirts were getting shorter and shorter to match Nancy's. She wondered whether a seamstress was working overtime at the Soviet embassy.

There was one event where Nancy would not be outshone: the state dinner. She made sure everything was perfect, though she had to work around the Gorbachevs' insistence that they be out of there by ten. There was also a surplus of male guests, because the Soviets had brought along so few women to Washington. For entertainment, Nancy booked the renowned pianist Van Cliburn, a Texan who had not played in public for nine years. He had a big following in the Soviet Union going back to 1958, when he won the first Tchaikovsky Piano Competition in Moscow at the age of twenty-three. The achievement, coming at the height of the Cold War, also earned Cliburn the only ticker-tape parade that New York City has ever thrown for a classical musician. When the pianist began playing the beloved Russian melody "Moscow Nights" as an encore, the Gorbachevs started singing along, and by the second verse, the entire Soviet delegation had joined in.

After the going-away ceremony on the South Lawn, which took place in a heavy rainstorm, Barbara Bush accompanied Raisa to the airport.

At one point, Barbara asked Raisa whether she knew that Nancy had recently undergone a serious operation for cancer. Raisa replied that in her country, something so personal would be considered unmentionable. Barbara averred that in the United States, it would be hard for a first lady to disappear for several weeks without the press knowing about it.

"What if the first lady had an abortion?" Raisa asked.

Barbara was taken aback and said she didn't think that was comparable to a mastectomy. She told Raisa that Nancy had been courageous in going public and probably saved many lives by encouraging women to have mammograms. "We arrived at the airport before we could pursue this anymore," she wrote in her diary.

There would be one last summit between Ronnie and Gorbachev, in May 1988. The president and Nancy traveled to Moscow with a four-day stopover in Helsinki, Finland, to reset the president's body clock. Nancy made a point not to pack any gowns in her favorite color, red, for fear that she might be sending a message she didn't intend. As they were driven from the airport, she was delighted to see Moscow streets lined with cheering crowds. The Reagans got a rapturous reception in the Soviet capital, much as the Gorbachevs had the previous year in Washington.

At one point during the trip, reporter Sam Donaldson asked the president whether he still considered the Soviet Union an "evil empire."

"No," Ronnie said. "I was talking about another time and another era."

But when Raisa took Nancy through the Kremlin, the two adversaries picked up right where they had left off. This time the flashpoint was religion. As they walked through the Assumption Cathedral, a fifteenth-century Russian Orthodox church where the czars were coronated, Nancy noted the religious imagery all around and asked whether services were ever held there.

"Nyet," Raisa replied. The tour ended abruptly.

Nancy had finally found a way to get under Raisa's skin. A couple of days later, they were to tour Moscow's Tretyakov Gallery, where Nancy had specifically requested to see some of its famous icons. Raisa arrived early and gave the assembled media some background on the gallery. When Nancy got there, a reporter asked the American first lady about Raisa's contention that the pieces had artistic and historic value, but no religious significance.

"I don't know how you can neglect the religious implications," Nancy replied. "I mean, they're there for everybody to see." She pointed out that one of the icons, the most famous, was called *The Trinity*. It is a fifteenth-century depiction of three angels who in the Book of Genesis were said to have visited Abraham to inform him that his ninety-year-old wife Sarah would bear a child.

"You realize we arrived on Trinity Sunday," Nancy told Raisa, who gave no indication that she did.

Religion was a particularly sensitive subject in Washington-Moscow relations at that moment. Ronnie had served notice before the summit that he planned to bring a spotlight to the plight of Soviet Jews, and particularly the "refuseniks" who were not being allowed to emigrate. Nancy proposed they visit the apartment of one of the more well known of those families, the Ziemans, who had applied to leave the Soviet Union eleven years before. Yuri Zieman, the patriarch, lost his job as a scientist when he applied for a visa and was working as a plumber. In the months before the Reagans' arrival, he came down with a brain ailment that required treatment unavailable in Moscow.

Plans were well under way—a red White House phone had even been installed in their apartment—when the Soviets passed the word to the American delegation that the Ziemans would never be allowed to get out unless the Reagans canceled their visit to the family's home. The Reagans settled instead for seeing the Ziemans at a reception they hosted for hundreds of dissidents at Spaso House, the US ambassador's residence.

"Was this a bluff? Nobody could say, but we didn't want to take any chances. No promises were made, but it was hinted that if we left the Ziemans alone, they would be allowed to leave the country," Nancy recalled. "Two months later, they were given their visas—but only after Ronnie called the Soviet ambassador and reminded him of the implied agreement."

On the final night of their trip to Moscow, the Reagans sat with the Gorbachevs in the gilded, red-curtained royal box at the Bolshoi Theatre and saw its world-famous ballet company perform. Then they went to dinner at a dacha. Nancy was exhausted by the time they headed in for the night, but they stopped at Red Square. America's first couple got out of the car and strolled hand in hand, posing and waving for photographers in front of landmark St. Basil's Cathedral. "It would have been a shame to go home without seeing it," Nancy wrote later.

This supposedly spontaneous photo opportunity capped the summit with an image that would leave more of an impression than the news stories, which lamented the fact that it had not produced any tangible new initiatives. But what the summit lacked in substance, it more than made up for with thrilling symbolism. Americans heard "The Star-Spangled Banner" played by the Bolshoi Theatre Orchestra. There had been the sight of Ronnie putting his arm around Gorbachev as the two of them had taken their own walk in Red Square. Blimps over the Kremlin dangled the American and Soviet flags.

All of it spoke to the fact that the world was entering a new era. As Ronnie's presidency reached its final months, his vision was on its way to being achieved. After four decades of Cold War, two leaders had decided to trust each other enough to bring it to an end. However, the Nobel Peace Prize that Nancy had dreamed of for her husband would go to Gorbachev, alone, in 1990.

Nancy saw Raisa only one more time while Ronnie was in office. They were both in New York in December 1988 for a United Nations meeting where Gorbachev was to announce that he was reducing Soviet military forces by a half million troops. By then, George H. W. Bush was the president elect. The two first ladies crossed paths at a luncheon at the home of Marcela Perez de Cuellar, the wife of the UN secretary general. "I will miss you and your husband," Raisa told Nancy with apparent sincerity. "As for the two of us, it was destiny that put us at the place we were, next to our husbands, to help bring about the relationship that our two countries now have."

CHAPTER TWENTY-ONE

While Ronnie was making progress toward a historic rapprochement with the Soviet Union, storm clouds were building at home. In his final two years as president, he would be hit by his most serious crisis, a scandal that shattered the nation's trust in his character and threatened his survival in office. Nancy would once again step into her role as his enforcer and guardian. One of her greatest obstacles, as it turned out, was her husband's obstinacy. But Nancy persisted, convinced that Ronnie had never needed her so badly.

The darkness began near the end of 1986. This was a year in which Ronnie counted a host of major domestic achievements, among them a sweeping overhaul of the nation's tax system and the passage of a major immigration bill he had championed. On September 14 Ronnie held Nancy's hand as they made a rare joint address from the West Sitting Hall of the residence and called for a "national crusade" against drug abuse. Six weeks later, the president signed into law a tough $1.7 billion anti-narcotics bill. He handed his pen to Nancy as a souvenir. "She started long before the polls began to register our citizens' concern about drugs," he said. "She mobilized the American people, and I'm mighty proud of her."

But the 1986 congressional campaign season was a brutal one for the president's Party, as midterm elections during a second term tend to be. The stakes for this one were enormous. Hanging in the balance was the survival of the Senate majority that had ridden to Washington on Ronnie's coattails six years before. The GOP Senate had been his legislative bulwark against the Democratic House on fiscal issues and foreign policy. A fully Democratic Congress would ensure no further progress on the unfinished business of his conservative agenda.

On the final weekend before the election, Ronnie returned to Southern California, where he had launched his political career, and made a stop in Orange County, an epicenter of right-wing activism. The speech he gave to a crowd of 1,200 in a Hilton ballroom was sentimental—almost elegiac.

"I remember coming to Anaheim twenty years ago in my first campaign for governor. Orange County was essential to success. And everything we've accomplished since then in Sacramento and, yes, in Washington began with that margin of victory provided here in Orange County. I delight in telling some people, who don't understand, outside of the state of California, that Orange County is where the good Republicans go before they die," he said. "Today you are no less vital to securing the gains that we've made and keeping our country moving forward. Your support is indispensable again, so let me ask you this one last time: come Election Day, let's get out the vote and see to it that our team wins the day."

During that campaign, Ronnie hit the road as if he himself were on the ballot, though he never would be again. He traveled twenty-four thousand miles, making fifty-four stops in twenty-two states and raised upward of $33 million for GOP candidates. Behind the scenes, Nancy was an architect of the strategy. She attended sessions nearly every afternoon to figure out where a presidential visit might make the biggest difference and when. As one White House aide who was involved told journalists Jane Mayer and Doyle McManus: "She was very concerned about losing the Senate in '86. That's the reason he traveled so much, because she was so worried. That kind of decision never would have gone to him. The political staff, the advance staff, and Mrs. Reagan drew up all the plans. But the president played no part in these kinds of things—he just went."

Ronnie frequently mentioned Nancy's favorite cause as he campaigned. "I can't help but see the young people here in the audience, as I did in Reno on Thursday," he said at a November 3 rally in Las Vegas. "I have a special message to all of you from my roommate. She says when it comes to drugs, please—for yourselves, for your families, for your future, and your country—just say no."

Though he may have seen the 1986 campaign as a last hurrah, Ronnie's popularity was not transferable. One poll showed that nearly a third of those who approved of his performance as president voted for Democratic contenders for the Senate. Republicans lost eight seats and, with them, their majority in the chamber. Even before the votes came in, party leaders knew their situation was hopeless.

But the final weekend before the 1986 midterm election brought one bit of welcome news: David Jacobsen, the director of the American University Hospital in Beirut, who had been abducted nearly eighteen months before, was released by his captors, a terrorist group known as Islamic Holy War. Jacobsen was the third hostage to be freed over the previous year. Six other Americans were still being held. White House spokesman Larry Speakes made the announcement, which dropped a cryptic hint of a broader effort: "We have been working through a number of sensitive channels for a long time. Unfortunately, we cannot divulge any of the details of the release, because the lives of other Americans and other Western hostages are still at risk."

The truth was, Speakes himself was having trouble figuring out what was really happening behind the scenes. He had been led to expect the release of *two* hostages. John Poindexter, who had replaced Robert McFarlane as national security adviser the previous December, did not provide Speakes with details but suggested that Jacobsen's release was part of a much larger operation.

*

How much bigger began to become clear on Monday morning, November 3, the day before the election. *Al-Shiraa,* a leftist weekly magazine in Beirut, reported that the United States was secretly selling arms to Iran. The covert deals had been going on for more than a year. They involved tens of millions of dollars' worth of medium-range Hawk missiles and antitank TOW missiles, shipped through Israel, which in turn provided them to Iran. The transactions violated both the US government's stated policy against supplying weapons to countries deemed to sponsor terrorism and its specific embargo against the theocracy in Tehran.

As details of the scheme unspooled, the story became even more sensational. McFarlane, though no longer holding any official role in the Reagan administration, had been making secret visits to broker the arms sales. In return, Iran was helping to arrange the release of the Americans held hostage in Lebanon by Iran-linked Shiite Muslim militants. As the news was breaking, top Reagan officials felt like they were being sucked into a recurring nightmare. Hadn't Jimmy Carter's presidency been destroyed by a hostage crisis? Was this a Republican president's turn to be undone by one? Pentagon Secretary Caspar Weinberger, who was visiting Brussels, Belgium, to meet with other defense ministers at NATO headquarters, put his head in his hands and exclaimed: "Not again! Not after Watergate!"

Ronnie insisted that the arms deals were not a ransom payment but rather a diplomatic initiative to open a dialogue with moderates in Tehran. On November 13 he declared: "We did not—repeat—did not trade weapons or anything else for hostages, nor will we." His statement, America soon learned, contained a number of false claims. One was that the amount of arms and spare parts sent to Tehran was small enough that "they could easily fit into a single cargo plane." In fact, the first two shipments alone, in August and September 1985, totaled more than five hundred TOW antitank missiles. Six days later, Ronnie—still shaky on his facts—conducted a disastrous news conference. This time he asserted that Israel had not been involved as an intermediary, though his own chief of staff had already acknowledged that it had. The White House corrected the president in a statement issued minutes after the news conference. Some of Ronnie's aides began begging him to just admit that the whole arms-for-hostages scheme had been a mistake. Instead, the president grew more stubborn, taking out his wrath, privately and publicly, on the media. In his diary, he wrote that they had become a "lynch mob" and a "circle of sharks."

Ronnie appointed a special review board to investigate and figure out what exactly had happened, focusing specifically on the workings of his National Security Council. To ensure that the panel's findings would be credible, he picked elders of both parties. John Tower, a former Republican senator from Texas, would serve as chairman. The other two members would be Brent Scowcroft, who had been national security adviser under Gerald Ford, and Edmund Muskie, the onetime senator from Maine who had been Jimmy Carter's secretary of state. Ronnie also asked Attorney General Ed Meese, his longest-serving top aide, to conduct an internal investigation of the matter.

Taking another step, one that was overdue, Ronnie attempted to bring more coherence to his fractious foreign-policy team. He put the State Department fully in charge of Iran policy, a victory for George Shultz that quieted growing speculation he might resign to save his own reputation from the stench of the growing scandal. Nancy's normally warm relationship with Shultz grew strained during this period, to the point where she questioned his loyalty and began contemplating whether one of her closest allies should be ousted.

The Teflon was off the Reagan presidency. A raft of public polls and Ronnie's internal ones showed that, for the first time, a majority of Americans did not believe he was being truthful. Veteran opinion expert Lou Harris found that Ronnie's rating on "inspiring confidence in the White House" plummeted 23 points practically overnight, one of the sharpest drops Harris's survey had ever recorded. Three-quarters of the public flatly rejected the president's unconvincing claim that there had been no connection between the shipment of arms to Iran and the release of the hostages. "This is particularly damaging to President Reagan, who has inspired people with his character, integrity, and sincerity," Harris wrote.

It was about to get worse. Much worse. Meese made a shocking discovery as he tried to get to the bottom of things: the profits from the arms sales had been funneled to Nicaraguan rebel forces, known as contras, who were seeking to overthrow Managua's Socialist Sandinista government. Congress had banned any such assistance to the rebels—or as Ronnie liked to call them, "freedom fighters." The secret funding from the Iran arms sales was a blatant violation of the law. What no one knew was precisely who had authorized this rogue operation, which had been carried out by a cocksure and devious US Marine lieutenant colonel who worked for the National Security Council. His name was Oliver North.

Ronnie looked ashen when he told Nancy on the afternoon of November 24 that tens of millions of dollars from the arms sales were missing, and that much of it had apparently been diverted illegally to the contras. After Meese announced his discovery, everyone in the media and on Capitol Hill was soon asking: Who else was in on it? And did the president know? In his diary, Ronnie wrote that he had been in the dark about the channeling of arms sales money to the contras: "North didn't tell me about this. Worst of all, John Poindexter found out about it & didn't tell me. This may call for resignations."

Both Poindexter and North were soon out. As North made his exit, he and his secretary, Fawn Hall, carried out an epic paper-shredding operation in his office on the third floor of the Old Executive Office Building. When the machine jammed, Hall sneaked documents off the grounds by stuffing them into her boots and blouse. Whatever credit Ronnie might have gotten for giving North the axe was lost in an angry interview he gave a few days later to *Time* magazine's Hugh Sidey. The president lauded the forty-three-year-old marine lieutenant colonel as "a national hero."

Nancy took a far different measure of North than her husband did. The national security aide fabricated claims about his closeness with the president. It would later come out that he had told the Iranians of meeting alone with Ronnie and taking a long walk with him in the woods at Camp David; in fact, North had never set foot at the presidential retreat, and had not so much as been in a room with Ronnie where there were fewer than a half dozen others present. The only time Ronnie spoke to North on the telephone was when he fired him on November 25. Nancy also bristled at the way North swaggered on television, reveling in his newfound celebrity status. Watching one of his breezy interviews outside his home during the early days of the scandal, the first lady heard North make a lame joke about the much-discussed possibility that he might be granted immunity from prosecution for any testimony he might give.

"Immunity?" North quipped. "If I had immunity, I wouldn't have this bad cold."

"Not funny, sonny," Nancy retorted to the image on the screen.

As was her wont, Nancy decided that any fault in all of this lay not with Ronnie but with his subordinates. Starting with his chief of staff. "I called Don Regan from my office to let him know how upset I was. I felt very strongly that Ronnie had been badly served, and I wanted Don to know," she later recalled. "Maybe this was unfair of me, but to some extent I blamed him for what had happened. He was the chief of staff, and if he didn't know, I thought, he should have. A good chief of staff has sources everywhere. He should practically be able to smell what is going on."

Regan, she believed, took too much credit when things were going well and didn't protect Ronnie as he should have when they weren't. As the Iran arms sales controversy was exploding, Regan gave the *New York Times* a wide-ranging, self-serving interview. "Some of us are like a shovel brigade that follow a parade down Main Street cleaning up," Regan said in the article, which appeared on November 16. The president's chief of staff left little doubt whom he considered to have left behind the sloppy, stinking mess.

From the start of Regan's tenure at the White House, the former Merrill Lynch chairman acted as though he were still a chief executive. Regan styled himself the "prime minister," and operated with an imperious manner that alienated the Republicans who were Ronnie's staunchest allies on Capitol Hill. He ordered a flagstone patio to be built onto his office that was larger than the one off the Oval Office. Unlike earlier White House chiefs of staff, Regan demanded regular Secret Service protection. He also made sure he got his own introduction at the president's speeches and had a habit of placing himself in the middle of photo ops, including a historic one of Ronnie with Gorbachev in Geneva. "He liked the word 'chief,' but he never really understood that his title included the words 'of staff,'" Nancy observed drily. She had no higher regard for "the mice," as the cadre of obsequious aides that Regan brought over from the Treasury Department were known.

Regan was also a sexist of the first order. He dismissed calls for economic sanctions against the racist regime in diamond-producing South Africa by saying that America's women weren't "prepared to give up all their jewelry." During the Geneva summit, he posited that female readers of the news would be interested only in the social doings of Nancy and Raisa because they couldn't possibly "understand throw weights [the maximum payload that missiles can carry] or what is happening in Afghanistan or what is happening in human rights." Still, Regan and the president got along wonderfully. Where the chief of staff was arrogant with the White House staff and with Congress, he and Ronnie connected as two old Irishmen, tickled by the fact that they had such similar last names. Regan had a member of his staff come up with a joke each day, usually a bawdy one, that he could share with the president.

"Ronnie never saw the Don that everybody else saw, because Don didn't let him," Nancy told journalist James Mann in a 2005 interview. "So Ronnie never knew all the things that were going on in the office, and all of the people who were coming to me, saying, 'You've got to do something to get that man out of there.'" She told Mann that Regan once tried to fire Kathy Osborne, who had served as Ronnie's secretary going back to Sacramento, because Osborne let a letter get through to the president without Regan seeing it first. "Don thought he was the president many times. But Ronnie never—he never knew," Nancy said. "Those were hard times."

Regan did little to hide his contempt for Nancy or his exasperation with her constant phone calls. At one point, he told her that if she had anything she wanted to let him know, she should talk to his deputy. "When I need something, I'll call you directly," Nancy replied. "I don't see any need for an intermediary."

The tart exchange showed how badly the chief of staff misread Nancy and the silent power she wielded in her husband's White House. "I'm not the chief of staff of the first lady. I'm the chief of the staff of the president. I'm not taking her shit," he fumed to Ed Rollins, who was political director at the time.

"Don, I'm just telling you. You're making a big mistake," Rollins warned. "You've got to deal with her, and it sometimes can be burdensome, but you have to deal with her, because, ultimately, it will do you in."

Nancy soured on Regan "right off the bat," Rollins told me. He recalled hearing the first couple arguing over the chief of staff not long after Regan took the job in early 1985. Rollins was following the Reagans one day as they walked through the colonnade that connects the West Wing and the residence. "I was about ten feet behind them, and they're going at it," Rollins said. "And finally, he stops, and he turns, and he said to her, 'Nancy, I heard you the first time. I heard you the second time. I heard you the third time. I don't want to hear you a fourth time,' and turned and walked off."

Nancy had her first direct confrontation with Regan about five months after he became chief of staff, when Ronnie was operated on for colon cancer. The protective first lady and the abrasive Regan battled over her refusal to allow anyone to visit her husband as he recuperated in the days after the surgery. She said Ronnie needed more time and privacy to heal; Regan insisted that a president could not be seen as incapacitated.

During this period, as earlier noted, an event occurred that set into motion the Iran-contra scandal—or, as it also became known, Iranscam. On July 18 Nancy lifted her ban on visitors and allowed National Security Adviser Bud McFarlane, whom she liked, to meet with Ronnie in his hospital room. This was only five days after Ronnie's surgery. Just that morning, doctors had removed his feeding tube and the metal clips from his incision. During what would later become an infamous twenty-three-minute private session, McFarlane informed the president that there were new signals of openness coming from some factions within the regime in Tehran. Ronnie authorized him to begin meeting with Iranian emissaries in a neutral country.

Regan, who was present throughout, said later that he heard no mention of swapping arms for hostages. The president would claim he had no recollection at all of McFarlane's visit. But Ronnie's diary entries make it clear that, from the start, he viewed the initiative as having the potential to provide "a breakthrough on getting our 7 kidnap victims back." His own words suggest that freeing the hostages—and not seizing a supposed strategic opening to Iran—was the president's priority. "Okay," he told McFarlane. "Proceed. Make the contact."

Ronnie's willingness to explore a deal for the hostages was a direct contradiction of what he was saying publicly. Exactly a month before his meeting with McFarlane, he had declared at a news conference: "Let me further make it plain to the assassins in Beirut and their accomplices, wherever they may be, that America will never make concessions to terrorists—to do so would only invite more terrorism—nor will we ask nor pressure any other government to do so. Once we head down that path, there would be no end to it, no end to the suffering of innocent people, no end to the bloody ransom all civilized nations must pay." As the Iran-contra scandal unfolded, America was learning that the president had done exactly what he had vowed not to.

After that hospital visit, Bud McFarlane did not last much longer as national security adviser. He left at the end of 1985, frustrated over his frequent clashes with Regan, who claimed foreign policy as part of his turf. On December 5 Ronnie noted in his diary: "N.S.C. Briefing—probably Bud's last. Subject was our undercover effort to free our 5 hostages held by terrorists in Lebanon. It is a complex undertaking with only a few of us in on it. I won't even write in the diary what we're up to." McFarlane was replaced by his deputy, John M. Poindexter, a retired admiral. It was a poor choice. Poindexter was a career military man with little political experience. A recluse by nature, he was not inclined to question or challenge the wishes of the commander in chief, at least as he understood them, or assertive enough to mediate the constant disputes between the Pentagon and State.

Meanwhile, the "complex undertaking" continued after McFarlane's departure, run largely by North with guidance from CIA director William J. Casey. The secret arms sales to Iran faced growing internal opposition from other members of Ronnie's fractious national security team. Secretary of State Shultz and Defense Secretary Weinberger—who disagreed on many other issues—were united in their view that it could have disastrous consequences and should be abandoned. Regan also argued against it. But the president was enthralled at the prospect of bringing home the hostages, a goal that North and Casey kept telling him was within reach if they forged ahead. McFarlane continued to act as an emissary in the mission he had launched, but he, too, had growing misgivings about it. The channels of communication within the operation became irregular, opaque, and dysfunctional. Shady operators outside the government were brought in to handle sensitive parts of it.

Once the whole big mess was exposed, it seemed no one—and least among them, the president—had a clear command of the facts. Nancy grew terrified for her husband's political survival and worried that those around him were too busy looking out for their own hides to be trusted to take care of his interests. All day long, she kept CNN on the television in the family quarters, which put her in a constant state of panic. She found it hard to eat and dropped another ten pounds off her already spare frame. The press was drawing comparisons to Watergate. A poll by the *New York Times* in early December showed Ronnie's job approval number had dropped more than 20 percentage points in just a month. Starting in January, both houses of Congress would be run by the Democrats. The incoming Senate majority leader, Robert C. Byrd of West Virginia, was calling for a select committee to look into the scandal, which would mean nationally televised hearings. Impeachment was beginning to look like a real possibility—a cinch, if it turned out that the president knew about the illegal diversion of funds to the contras.

Ronnie only grew more stubborn. He refused to admit that the arms sales had been a mistake. Nor did he agree with Nancy that all of this called for a major overhaul of his White House staff, starting at the top. Her hectoring only made the president more determined to stand by his chief of staff, even as calls for Regan's head were growing on Capitol Hill and elsewhere. Nancy's I-told-you-so's were wearing on her husband. "I was right about Stockman. I was right about Bill Clark," she argued. "Why won't you listen to me about Don Regan?"

The Reagans started quarreling constantly. Peter Wallison, who was White House counsel at the time, heard one spat when he made a visit to the family quarters with some work for the president. The chief of staff had done nothing wrong, Ronnie insisted to his wife, so there was no reason to fire him. But Nancy wouldn't let up. Finally, Ronnie told her: "Get off my back!"

That phrase—and some saltier versions of it—apparently became Ronnie's regular refrain. One weekend at Camp David, Jim Kuhn was working where he often did, at a desk in the kitchen pantry. The Reagans were going at it in the living room. Kuhn heard Ronnie scream: "*Get off my goddamn back!*" It was louder than Kuhn had ever heard any human voice, and thoroughly out of character for good-natured Ronnie. Though the executive assistant had witnessed plenty of arguments between the first couple, there had never been anything like this. "I grabbed my papers and folder," Kuhn said. "I got out of there."

A report that Ronnie had told his wife to get off his goddamn back also made it into the *Washington Post*. The White House considered demanding a retraction. It backed off when word got around that Ronnie's daughter Maureen—who had joined Nancy in her campaign to get rid of the chief of staff—was the likely source of the story. She did not get along with Regan any better than Nancy did. At one point, he told Maureen that she was "a pain in the ass."

Though Ronnie and Nancy's differences over Regan were putting a strain on their marriage, he wanted her near during his time of crisis, as much as he ever had. He still hated to spend a night without her. Two weeks after the scandal broke, the president wrote in his diary: "Nancy came home from New York about 5 p.m., so there's a different feel at the W.H.—It's been a barn for about 36 hours." Meanwhile, as Nancy realized that her own efforts to budge her husband were getting nowhere, she looked around for reinforcements. She marshaled the Reagans' California friends to press for Regan's ouster. She brought in Mike Deaver, though he by then was under federal investigation for allegedly violating conflict-of-interest laws as a lobbyist. She also turned to her old reliable troubleshooter Stu Spencer. Both Deaver and Spencer agreed with her that Regan had to go, but they knew as well as Nancy how intractable the president could be in a situation like this.

"I'll be goddamned if I'll throw somebody else out to save my own ass," Ronnie told Deaver during one meeting.

"It's not your ass I'm talking about," Deaver told him. "You stood up on the steps of the Capitol and took an oath to defend the Constitution and this office. You've got to think of the country first."

At that, Ronnie threw his pen onto the carpet with such force that it bounced. "I've always thought of the country," he retorted.

There was another public relations problem developing. Nancy's internal campaign against the chief of staff was becoming the talk of Washington. It was evident that she was the unseen force behind many of the negative stories about Regan that were making their way into the press. The image of his wife trying to take charge only added to a growing perception that Ronnie himself was not on top of things. When Nancy appeared in front of the White House to greet the arrival of that year's official Christmas tree on a horse-drawn wagon, reporters took advantage of the ceremonial photo op to ask her whether the president should fire Regan. "I think that's up to my husband. It has nothing to do with me whatever," the first lady fibbed. "I've made no recommendations at all."

The very next evening, on December 4, two visitors came to the official residence at her invitation to meet with the president. One of them was William Rogers, a fixture of the Republican establishment who had been secretary of state under Nixon as well as Eisenhower's attorney general. The other was Democratic Party chairman Robert Strauss, a gregarious Texan known as one of Washington's most savvy and well-connected insiders. Nancy wanted Ronnie to hear advice from respected figures outside the White House; men who had seen presidents face trials in the past and who could give him a sense of how this thing might play out.

So that no one would spot their arrival, Deaver led the two men through an underground tunnel that connects the Treasury Department basement to the subbasement of the White House's East Wing. Its existence is little known even by longtime Washingtonians. The passage had been built right after the 1941 Japanese bombing of Pearl Harbor as an escape route and bunker for the president and his key staff; a tomblike refuge of last resort. As Deaver, Rogers, and Strauss made their way through its zigzagging route, they passed bunk beds and a hospital. When the three men reached the living quarters, Nancy greeted them and led them to the sitting room. Over the next two hours, she asked most of the questions, while Ronnie sat back and listened.

Rogers, a friend and golf partner of Regan's, was no help to her cause. He said little and predicted all of this would blow over. Strauss, however, had a lot he wanted to tell Ronnie.

"Mr. President," he began, "let me tell you about the first time I was up here in the residence. LBJ was in office, and a few of us came to see him about Vietnam. When my turn came to speak, I held back. I didn't tell the president what I really thought. Instead, I told him what I thought he wanted to hear.

"When I went home that night, I felt like a two-dollar whore. And I said to myself, if any president is ever foolish enough to invite me back, I hope I show more character."

Strauss said he had no quarrel with Regan, "but you've got two serious problems right now, and he's not helping you with either one. First, you've got a political problem on the Hill, and Don Regan has no constituency and no allies there. Second, you've got a serious media problem, and Regan has no friends there, either. It makes no difference how earnest he is, or how much you like him, or how well the two of you get along. He's not the man you need. You're in a hell of a mess, Mr. President, and you need a chief of staff who can help get you out of it." Strauss also told the president that his news conference had been a mistake, and advised him not to hold any more until he got his facts straight.

Nancy had never heard anyone outside of Ronnie's closest advisers speak to her husband so bluntly and forcefully. Later that night, she called Strauss and thanked him for confronting the president with hard truths that no one else had been willing to deliver. "He has to have his mind opened and his eyes open on this and see what's happening to him," she said. But Ronnie was unmoved. With his typical optimism, he kept assuring Nancy that everything would all work out. So, failing to convince her husband to act, Nancy decided to pressure the chief of staff directly. In her phone calls to Regan, she was not subtle. He often picked up the line to hear a sarcastic greeting: "Are you still here, Don?"

Nancy also looked for help from Vice President Bush, who agreed with her that Regan should go and had told the president so repeatedly. She pressed him at a White House Christmas party to just go around Ronnie and issue the order for Regan to leave himself.

"Nancy, I've got some hang-ups on that, based on my relationship with the president," Bush told her.

"Well, I do it all the time," Nancy replied, "and it is important that you do it."

Bush's reluctance only reinforced Nancy's view—harsh, and probably unfair—that the vice president was too weak to be an effective partner for her husband. She also believed he was more concerned about protecting his own political future than Ronnie's survival.

Then came another crisis. On December 15, the day before CIA director Casey was to testify before the Senate Intelligence Committee, he suffered two seizures and collapsed in his office. Surgery three days later revealed a brain tumor. Casey was partially paralyzed, could not speak, and would be dead within five months. The CIA director was believed, then and now, to have been central to setting up the Iran arms sales and to engineering the diversion of the proceeds to the contras. He worked closely with the gung-ho Oliver North, whose office was down the hall from his, in a part of the Old Executive Office Building known as "spook alley." So devoted was Casey to the operation that he tried to keep it going even after it had been revealed and Poindexter and North had been fired. In retrospect, Nancy believed his illness had affected his judgment, but his incapacitation was catastrophic. He was one of the few people who could have provided details of what Ronnie knew about the scheme and when he knew it.

Back in 1980, Casey had been the man to whom Nancy had turned when she needed someone to put her husband's teetering presidential campaign back on track. But as the severity of Casey's condition became clear in the weeks after he was rushed to the hospital, Nancy made no room for sentimentality—or compassion. Right before Christmas, she called Regan and demanded to know what he was doing to get rid of Casey and find a replacement to lead the CIA. Regan pleaded for time and sympathy, saying that Casey and his wife did not yet realize how serious his prognosis was. Regan claimed Nancy snapped back: "You're more interested in protecting Bill Casey than in protecting Ronnie! He's dragging Ronnie down! Nobody believes what Casey says, his credibility is gone on the Hill." Casey did not resign until late January.

Nancy also wanted the head of Patrick J. Buchanan, the White House's fiery communications director. The arch-conservative Buchanan was making wild statements that were all over television. He told three thousand cheering Cuban American and Nicaraguan supporters in Miami that it was fine to violate the law for the right cause. "If Colonel North broke any rules, he will stand up and take it like the fighting marine he is," Buchanan declared. "But I say, if Colonel North ripped off the ayatollah and took thirty million dollars and gave it to the contras, then God bless Colonel North."

In an op-ed in the *Washington Post,* Buchanan lashed out at the media and denounced the Republicans on Capitol Hill for not reflexively rallying to Ronnie's defense: "Is this how they repay the leader who has done more for the Republican Party than any American since Theodore Roosevelt, who brought us back from Watergate?" White House officials claimed that Buchanan, the man who was supposed to be in charge of their message operation, was "soloing." Press spokesman Larry Speakes told reporters: "The president does not agree or condone the breaking of the law by any individual, and he does not in any way believe that the president, whoever he might be, is above the law and has the right to pick and choose what laws may or may not be broken."

When Nancy called Regan to demand he fire Buchanan, the chief of staff assured her that this was only a temporary problem. Buchanan, who was thinking of running for president, had agreed to leave by February (though he would not depart until a month after that). Nancy moved to limit the damage he could do in the meantime. She insisted that Buchanan and his communications shop not be allowed to draft Ronnie's State of the Union address, which was scheduled for the end of January. "His ideas are not Ronald Reagan's ideas," Nancy told Regan.

Upon her insistence, the job went to Ken Khachigian, the speechwriter she and Deaver had recruited to write Ronnie's address at the Bergen-Belsen concentration camp. Khachigian was both talented and tolerant of Nancy's demands. "You just couldn't put Ken with the Reagans enough. He just was such a smart guy, such a wordsmith. He loved the Reagans," Jim Kuhn recalled. Over the next month, Nancy became heavily involved in shaping the speech. The weekend before Ronnie was to deliver it, she summoned Khachigian to Camp David to go over the draft. Nancy insisted that the part about Iran be cut back because it was "too long, and it's not appropriate. Ronald Reagan's got to be shown to be in charge."

Though Nancy continued to push for Buchanan's ouster, the communications director did have some sound tactical instincts. Early on in the scandal, Buchanan had figured out that the White House was too dysfunctional to both deal effectively with a nebulous situation and continue to get the regular business of governing done. He had been a special assistant to Nixon during Watergate and also knew that even the slightest appearance of a cover-up would be fatal. In a December

12 memo to Regan, Buchanan urged the appointment of a temporary "special counselor" to manage the White House's responses to the multiple investigations that were under way. This person, he suggested, should be someone highly regarded and credible, who should operate independently, with standing equal to the chief of staff and direct access to the president.

The day after Christmas, Ronnie summoned David Abshire, who was serving as his NATO ambassador, to return to Washington and fill the new role, which they also agreed would be given Cabinet rank. Abshire was a West Pointer known for his tact and intellect, and had helped found one of Washington's most influential think tanks, the Center for Strategic and International Studies. In his first meeting with Ronnie in the Oval Office shortly after the new year, Abshire was shocked at what had become of the president in the thirteen months since he had last laid eyes on him: "Behind the desk sat a frail, pale, and thin Ronald Reagan, dreadfully different from the vigorous, commanding presence I had last seen at the NATO heads-of-government summit."

Part of it may have been that seventy-five-year-old Ronnie had undergone surgery for an enlarged prostate just a week before, but Abshire sensed that what he saw was a congenital optimist whose spirit had been crushed. Ronnie looked so bad that Nancy and Regan later ordered that the official photo of his first meeting with the new special counselor not be released to the public. What worried Abshire even more was the fact that Ronnie continued to insist, against growing evidence to the contrary, that he had never intended to trade arms for hostages and that the sales were solely part of an effort to make a diplomatic breakthrough.

At first, Abshire was reluctant to have anything to do with Nancy. He had heard the stories about how difficult and demanding the first lady could be, and he didn't want to antagonize Regan. Word had also gotten to him that she misunderstood his role. Nancy expected Abshire to act as the president's public defender against the media and to blunt the criticism Ronnie was getting on Capitol Hill. Abshire was determined to stay focused on his actual job, which was to serve as an internal investigator charged with restoring credibility to the White House. The last thing he thought he needed was a tussle with a protective, interfering presidential spouse. Both Strauss and the Reagans' old friend Charlie Wick advised Abshire that he was wrong about Nancy, and that he would be making the same mistake Regan did if he did not consult her regularly. So, Abshire reached out to the first lady through Wick. He received a reply within minutes: come to the family quarters at three in the afternoon on February 3.

*

Abshire had been on the job for twenty-nine days when he stepped off a small elevator and into the sunlit yellow-and-white sitting room where Nancy rose from the sofa to greet him. The first thing that struck him was how tiny this supposedly intimidating woman was—he towered over her by at least a foot. The second was how eager she was to hear his perspective. Right away, he relaxed. He explained patiently that his mission was to find out what actually happened, which was no small challenge given the murkiness of the information available to him.

"She—along with many others in Washington—had a misconception of what I was about. She had apparently assumed that I would produce and judge the facts and put the case to rest," Abshire recalled later. "Our role, however, was not to reach judgment but to see that the independent investigating bodies were able to make the judgments; to see that the flawed process which got us into the Iran-contra mess was now met and matched with due process. Mrs. Reagan quickly understood that important difference."

To save the president, he told the first lady, it was necessary to restore credibility to the presidency itself. And that couldn't happen if Ronnie's team kept responding to every incoming attack with incomplete—and sometimes inaccurate—information. Nancy realized immediately that in Abshire, she might have found the internal ally she needed. She told him that Regan was isolating her husband, weakening his judgment by cutting him off from outside advice and contacts. "The only other adviser with access is you," she said, a look of hope rising in her eyes. Nancy warned Abshire that too many became intimidated when they entered the Oval Office and held back from giving Ronnie the advice and information he needed. He should not be afraid to do that. She added one more caution: "You must not let Don into your meetings with the president."

Nancy also complained to Abshire about her running battle with the chief of staff over the president's schedule. Regan was trying to push Ronnie too hard, she said. He thought the president should try to quiet his critics by traveling around the country and talking about other issues: the Strategic Defense Initiative, US-Soviet relations, the need to balance the budget. Regan was also pressing for more news conferences. Nancy believed it was far too soon for that kind of activity after Ronnie's surgery. Plus, though she didn't mention it, her astrologer had deemed this to be an inauspicious month for such an undertaking.

Abshire agreed with Nancy that it was a bad idea for Ronnie to be getting out in public too much, but for a different reason. Though the president might try to change the subject, the scandal would follow him wherever he went. As Abshire put it later: "To undertake such a campaign of speeches and press conferences when we were still unclear on some of the Iran-contra facts would be a formula for disaster, comparable to the charge of the Light Brigade. He would be hounded with questions that neither he nor even the investigators could now answer." Ronnie's performance in his testimony before the Tower Commission so far had been halting and unsure—he had contradicted himself at several points. His memory was bad, and Abshire believed he was being manipulated by Regan and others, who wanted to line up his recollections with theirs.

Nancy and Abshire talked also about what to do after the release of the Tower report, which was expected within weeks. Abshire had been putting together what he called a "comeback plan." It involved both imagery and substance. The president must give a nationally televised address to show he was in charge and then undertake a reorganization of his administration that would start with repairing his fractured national security team. Lines of authority must be clearer. There had to be an end to the squabbling and turf battles between Shultz at the State Department and Weinberger at the Pentagon. The CIA and the National Security Council could no longer operate as independent actors. In the military, Abshire told Nancy, the first principle of strategy was "unity of command."

"This is the first imaginative idea I have heard since Mike Deaver left the White House," Nancy exclaimed. She told Abshire that she would arrange with Kathy Osborne, Ronnie's secretary, for his next session with the president to be a long one. And once more, she warned him: "Don't you let Don Regan in the room." Regan became furious when he saw that meetings with Abshire were being put on the president's calendar without his knowledge. After one, he summoned scheduler Fred Ryan to his office.

"Where did he get the authority?" Regan demanded.

"Mrs. Reagan," Ryan answered.

"You're fired!" the chief of staff said.

Ryan thought to himself: "I'm right in the middle of something here." But he assumed Regan would calm down, which he did, and an aide to the chief of staff soon phoned Ryan to assure him that he still had a job.

Abshire's strategy for navigating the crisis was spelled out in a February 19 memo to Regan and Frank Carlucci, who had replaced Poindexter as national security adviser. "In my judgment, the Tower Board report will be devastating in its criticisms of process, and will reinforce an image of the President as detached and not in command. We must recognize that the strong Presidency is in great danger," he wrote. "I believe the President can use the occasion of the Tower Board report to seize the initiative in the foreign policy process, demonstrate how he is the Commander in Chief, show he is ready to go beyond the report in the Iran-Contra matter, and get on with his larger foreign policy goals."

Abshire and Nancy would have many more private meetings, usually in the late afternoon, when the last rays of sunlight streamed through the lunette window on the west end of the residence. As they grew to know and trust each other, Abshire became more and more impressed with how astute she was about the problems within the White House and how clear-eyed she was about her husband's strengths and weaknesses.

Meanwhile, her running battle with Regan continued to play out in the media. There were strategic leaks, no doubt with Nancy's blessing, that the first lady and the chief of staff were no longer speaking. Her allies were making increasingly vigorous denunciations of Regan in public. On ABC-TV's *This Week with David Brinkley*, columnist George F. Will said of Regan: "I think nothing in his deplorable conduct of his office has been as contemptible as his clinging to it when his usefulness to the president, whose service he was supposed to be rendering, ended many, many months ago."

Ronnie's seventy-sixth birthday came three days after Nancy's first meeting with Abshire. To lift his spirits, she arranged for a surprise celebration with the White House staff. The president entered room 450 of the Old Executive Office Building thinking he was there to speak to a visiting business group and reached into his pocket for his remarks. He was greeted by the Marine Band playing "Seventy-six Trombones," from *The Music Man*. Nancy wheeled in a giant birthday cake, and together the Reagans blew out the candles. That night, Nancy planned a small, morale-boosting gathering with friends. But before the guests arrived, Ronnie watched a tough piece on NBC News in which correspondent Chris Wallace talked about the dismal state of the presidency and suggested the aging chief executive might be slipping. Ronnie was despondent. "Nancy blamed me for ruining his birthday party and didn't talk to me for a year," Wallace told me.

About a week and a half later, however, Wallace got a tantalizing tip from Nancy Reynolds, an intimate of the first lady since their Sacramento days. Reynolds told the NBC reporter that Regan had recently gotten into an angry argument with Nancy over the telephone—once again, over the chief of staff's insistence that it was time for the president to hold a news conference on the Iran-contra affair. Regan had actually hung up on her. That was, indeed, the case. The February 8 call ended with Regan slamming down the receiver on the first lady. Regan's wife, Ann, who had been reading the paper at the time, looked up quizzically: "Was that Nancy Reagan you were talking to in that tone of voice?" Regan acknowledged it was. He told Ann he recognized that his days were numbered as chief of staff, but that for the sake of his own reputation, he wanted to stick it out at least until the Tower Board issued its report at the end of February.

Presumably, Reynolds had Nancy's approval to tell the network reporter about Regan's abusive behavior toward her. Arranging for the story of that explosive phone call to be broken by Wallace was a shrewd play on the first lady's part. The Reagans watched the news on NBC every evening as they ate their dinner together on tray tables in the family quarters. On February 19 Wallace went on the air with his report. He said it wasn't the first time Regan had hung up on Nancy. Wallace also quoted a source "very close to Mrs. Reagan" as saying, "In fact, Mrs. Reagan purposely leaked the story that she is no longer talking to Donald Regan . . . to try to force Regan to step down." Of course, Nancy could have told her husband herself about the rude treatment she had received from Regan a week and a half before. But she knew it would pack a bigger wallop if Ronnie heard it this way. And she was right. Ronnie was horrified. "Is that true?" he asked Nancy.

Nancy wrote in her diary the following day: "I feel like I'm going through a nightmare—a long, unending nightmare. And I can't even see any light at the end of the tunnel. I'm beginning to wonder if this is going to last until the end of Ronnie's presidency. God, I hope not."

If Regan still had even the slightest chance of hanging on to his job, it ended when he tried to blame Nancy for a fresh public embarrassment that had nothing directly to do with Iran-contra. The White House had named John O. Koehler, a veteran Associated Press executive, to replace the departing Buchanan as communications director. Nancy was said to be enthusiastic about the choice, which had been made on the recommendation of their old California friend Charles Wick. But no one had looked very carefully into Koehler's past. It turned out he had briefly been a member of a Nazi youth group during his boyhood in Germany. At the daily White House staff meeting a few days after NBC reported his furious phone call with the first lady, Regan blamed Nancy for the fiasco over Koehler's hiring. "That nomination came right out of the East Wing," Regan told other senior White House officials.

The moment that White House counsel Peter Wallison heard Regan utter those words, he knew the chief of staff was a goner. Wallison looked across the table at staff secretary David Chew, and they both rolled their eyes. What was said at White House staff meetings had a way of leaking into the media, and if there was one thing Ronnie wouldn't tolerate, it was anyone trying to make Nancy the heavy. "I would have started packing my bags at that point," Wallison told me. Sure enough, the whole thing was in the next day's *Washington Post*. For Ronnie, this was the last straw. "Press reported that Don R. had told the Staff that Nancy was responsible for the appointment of Jack Koehler," the president wrote in his diary that weekend. "That does it—I guess Monday will be the showdown day. Nancy has never met J.K. and certainly had nothing to do with his appointment."

Indeed, Ronnie finally set the wheels in motion on Monday morning, February 23. "George, I'm going to have to do something about Don," he told his vice president. "If I won't stand up for my wife, who will? A certain honor is at stake." Bush went to Regan and told him that the president wanted to speak to him. It was a painful conversation. Regan agreed to resign, but he and Ronnie did not iron out the distasteful details of precisely when and how. They agreed only that Regan would depart some time the following week. Regan wanted to stay on for a while past the release of the Tower Board report on February 26, so that it would not look as though the chief of staff was culpable in the scandal. He also assumed the president would publicly thank him for his six years of service and give him an opportunity to express his own gratitude for the opportunity to make a contribution to the success of the administration. Nancy called Abshire in a panic, worried that Regan was actually maneuvering to hang on. She wanted him out before the next round of Sunday shows.

Then came Thursday—the day the Tower Board's report was released. A reckoning was at hand. Ronnie and top White House officials got their copies of the three-hundred-page document at ten in the morning. Tower, Muskie, and Scowcroft presented it to them in the Cabinet Room, and then Tower, as chairman, gave a forty-five-minute briefing on its major points. It concluded flatly that the administration was trading arms for hostages. As the *New York Times* reported the next day, the findings portrayed the president as "a confused and remote figure who failed to understand or control the secret arms deal with Iran, and who thus had to 'take responsibility' for a policy that in the end caused 'chaos' at home and embarrassment abroad."

It also noted that Ronnie had been ill-served by his top lieutenants, particularly Regan, who had given him poor advice and who had failed to grasp the risks of the covert operations being run out of the White House. More than any chief of staff in memory, it concluded, Regan had "asserted personal control over the White House staff," and therefore "must bear primary responsibility for the chaos that descended upon the White House." Regan bristled and began to object to that characterization of his management. "Look, Don, you got off easy," Tower replied.

That same morning, Bush met with Regan, and once again brought up the subject of his resignation. Regan exploded and told the vice president he was being fired like a shoe clerk. He also informed Bush that the entire White House schedule "was in the hands of an astrologer in San Francisco." Bush was shocked, and said, "Good God, I had no idea." Regan stormed out. Fifteen minutes later, Regan had calmed down and returned to Bush's office. He said his resignation would be on the president's desk Monday morning.

Meanwhile, Ronnie was already sounding out possible replacements for chief of staff. His first choice, former transportation secretary Drew Lewis, turned him down, as did the Reagans' old friend Nevada senator Paul Laxalt, who said he was thinking of running for president. Laxalt suggested former Senate majority leader Howard Baker, who agreed to take the job.

At least, that was the official version of the story. When Laxalt proposed Baker's name to Ronnie, his selection was already pretty much a fait accompli. Press accounts suggest that Nancy cast the deciding vote on who would be the new chief of staff. The *Wall Street Journal* wrote a story about Nancy's "behind-the-scenes maneuvering" that described the president's involvement in the choice as "minimal." Reporter Jane Mayer quoted an unnamed "friend of the first lady's" as saying: "It was worked out beforehand and then presented to him. He just had to sign on."

However it came about, Nancy thought the Tennessean was an inspired choice: "He was calm, easygoing, congenial, and self-effacing. He was politically astute. He had credibility with the media. And after serving three terms in the Senate, he had many friends on Capitol Hill. Howard was a complete change from what we had, and he gave us a chance to restore some morale to the office." Not incidentally, Baker was the figure in the Senate Watergate hearings who had asked the famous question: "What did the president know, and when did he know it?" His acceptance of the top staff post would be seen as a signal of confidence in the rectitude of the Reagan White House.

Regan tried to manage his impending exit with as much grace as he could. On Friday he held a series of background interviews with prominent White House reporters. He told them he planned to resign the following Monday, of his own volition, and that he did not know who his replacement would be. As Regan was wrapping up with David Beckwith and Barrett Seaman of *Time,* his secretary buzzed him. Then she buzzed him again. And again. The new national security adviser, Frank Carlucci, was waiting outside his office and urgently needed to see him. Carlucci told Regan that the news was out. CNN was reporting that the chief of staff had been ousted and that Baker was coming in to replace him.

Regan didn't have to ask where the network got the information. This one last act of retribution had Nancy written all over it. Indeed, her office issued a statement welcoming Baker before Regan's departure had formally been announced, something her spokeswoman later claimed was a "technical" mix-up.

Regan returned to his office and dictated a one-sentence missive. It read:

> Dear Mr. President:
>
> I hereby resign as Chief of Staff to the President of the United States.
>
> Respectfully yours,
>
> Donald T. Regan

Then the soon-to-be-former chief of staff walked out of the White House. Ronnie caught up with him by telephone and assured Regan that he still planned to put out their face-saving cover story, which was that Regan had planned to resign shortly after the 1986 midterm election but loyally stayed on for nearly four additional months to help the president through the Iran-contra crisis. "I hope you'll go along with that, Don," Ronnie added.

"No, Mr. President, it's over," Regan replied. "All that's left is for me to say good-bye."

"I'm sorry," Ronnie said softly.

The two of them never spoke again. Baker arrived at the White House an hour later and announced he would be on the job Monday morning. Over the weekend, Regan cleaned out his office.

*

Nancy had finally pushed her recalcitrant husband into getting rid of Don Regan. But for him to survive this scandal, she still had to budge him on one more thing; something more important in the eyes of the American people. He had to own up to the obvious, which was that he had traded arms for hostages. He had to admit that he had made a mistake. Never would Ronnie give a speech more crucial than the nationally televised address that was scheduled for March 4. As Abshire wrote in one memo circulated among top White House officials: "Under no circumstances should the president give a hastily prepared speech. This speech must be superb." Abshire argued that Ronnie must accept the conclusions and recommendations of the investigatory board, and then sketch out a vision for a future in which he would be more firmly in charge.

Nancy was afraid to entrust this crucial endeavor to anyone in the West Wing. She handpicked the person to write it: Landon Parvin, the outside consultant who came up with the lyrics for her song for the 1982 Gridiron Dinner and the speechwriter she would choose for Ronnie's first big AIDS address later in 1987. The president's secretary, Kathy Osborne, called Parvin about a week before the Tower Board report came out and told him that the president wanted him to draft his address to the nation.

"The truth is, I knew immediately who was behind it," Parvin told me. He dialed back the White House and asked to speak to the first lady. The operator put him right through. Parvin told Nancy that his formative political experience had been watching Watergate swallow a presidency. He saw many of the same forces at work here and couldn't be sure who—if anyone—in the West Wing was telling the truth.

"Who do I trust?" Parvin asked her.

"You can trust David Abshire," she told him.

"At some point, I may need your help, and I will need to talk to the president," Parvin said.

"Just let me know when," Nancy replied.

Parvin pored over a proposed draft that had been put together by the White House counsel's office. It maintained, as Ronnie still did, that the purpose of selling arms to a terrorist nation was "to open lines of communication" with moderate factions in Iran. One sentence in that draft made this laughable claim: "Even if no American hostages had been held in Beirut, I would have still have [*sic*] welcomed the Iranian contact, and I might still have approved limited arms sales to Iran." Parvin told Nancy the version of the speech being proposed by the counsel's office was far too detailed and legalistic. It was a point-by-point reimagination of the whole arms sale operation. Ronnie could never pull it off, Parvin said, and the first lady agreed. "He wouldn't do that well," Nancy said, "and it's not who he is."

The speechwriter talked to key figures on Capitol Hill and consulted pollster Richard Wirthlin to get a sense of where the public was with regard to the scandal. They all seemed to agree: Ronnie had to accept responsibility and acknowledge having traded arms for hostages.

The morning after the Tower Board report was released, Parvin called Nancy again.

"I need to see the president now," he said.

The first lady replied that Parvin should come to the residence that evening at five thirty. She added mysteriously: "There will be two other gentlemen there."

As he drove to the White House, Parvin heard over the radio that Regan had quit and stormed out and that Howard Baker was being brought in to replace him. So he assumed that Baker and perhaps Abshire were the two "other gentlemen" Nancy had mentioned. Instead, he encountered Stu Spencer as he came in the East Wing entrance.

A much bigger surprise was awaiting Parvin when he reached the spacious sitting room in the residence. On the couch between Ronnie and Nancy sat none other than John Tower, the chairman of the commission that had just issued its scathing report. Tower's presence there was highly unusual and, arguably, improper. It would not look good for the head of the ostensibly independent commission to be coaching the president on how to respond to it. Bringing in Tower had been Spencer's idea. So that no one would see the former Texas senator arrive, Nancy had arranged for Tower to be ushered through the semisecret tunnel from the Treasury Building, which was located next to the White House at 1500 Pennsylvania Avenue. This was the same way that Strauss and Rogers had come for their private session with Ronnie in December.

Both Spencer and Parvin described the subsequent scene to me. While the three visitors were dressed in business attire, the president was wearing a jogging suit. He had spent the day at home reading the board's report and had gotten all the way to the appendices. Nancy was going back and forth between the sitting room and the den where the television was, catching the latest reports on Regan's resignation.

"John," Spencer told the former senator, "tell the president what's going on."

For the next two hours, it fell to Tower—a longtime supporter and admirer of Ronnie—to explain to the president, in the bluntest of terms, what his investigation had uncovered. Tower told Ronnie that this scandal could destroy his presidency. He even warned that the president himself could be facing criminal charges and should consider retaining an outside lawyer. The only thing that could save Ronnie now, Tower insisted, was admitting what the public knew already about the real reason for the arms sales.

They also spoke a bit about the human toll the scandal had taken. Two weeks before, on the morning that Bud McFarlane had been scheduled to testify before the Tower Board, the former national security adviser had attempted suicide by downing more than two dozen Valium. When paramedics arrived at McFarlane's home, his distraught wife was holding a note he had written, which she refused to show them. A Valium overdose is rarely fatal, unless the highly addictive antianxiety medication is mixed with alcohol or other drugs. But McFarlane spent the next two weeks in Bethesda Naval Hospital, during which he was interviewed twice by the Tower Commission. That he could have been driven to such a desperate action weighed heavily on those in the family quarters that day. Parvin recalled that someone—he can't remember who—remarked that of those who had been swept up in the scandal, McFarlane "was probably the most decent and conscientious of the lot."

Ronnie listened largely in silence as Tower finished delivering what Parvin described as the "hard truth" of what his commission had found. Then, as the meeting concluded and Tower got up to leave, the president did something astonishingly graceful toward the man who had just belted him with a scathing assessment of his performance and judgment. He thanked Tower for his service to the country. The former Texas senator could not hold back his emotion any longer and broke down sobbing.

Parvin finally knew what he would write: the words that Ronnie was at last ready to say. The president delivered them from the Oval Office the following Wednesday, March 4, which also happened to be the Reagans' thirty-fifth wedding anniversary. "A few months ago, I told the American people I did not trade arms for hostages," he said in the twelve-minute speech. "My heart and my best intentions still tell me that's true; but the facts and the evidence tell me it is not. As the Tower Board reported, what began as a strategic opening to Iran, deteriorated in its implementation into trading arms for hostages. This runs counter to my own beliefs, to administration policy, and to the original strategy we had in mind. There are reasons why it happened, but no excuses. It was a mistake." Ronnie admitted that he had been so preoccupied with the welfare of the hostages that he hadn't asked the questions he should have or paid enough attention to what members of his staff were doing in his name.

The speech was a success. Veteran journalist R. W. Apple Jr. wrote in the *New York Times*: "President Reagan spoke to the American people tonight in a spirit of contrition that has not been heard from the White House in a quarter century. . . . Not since John F. Kennedy took the blame for the catastrophic Bay of Pigs invasion in 1961 has any president so openly confessed error." An overnight CBS News poll showed a 9-point jump in the president's approval rating, nudging it back into positive territory, at 51 percent to 42 percent. Richard Wirthlin's internal numbers looked even better.

Ronnie's presidency had been pulled back from the abyss. And to a degree that he himself most likely had not recognized, Nancy had run the rescue operation. She was more attuned to the danger than her husband was, and a sharper judge of character. Where he was averse to confrontation, she was willing to mow down anyone whose presence became a problem, regardless of how long or how faithfully they had served Ronnie in the past. She had persisted, no matter how hard the president resisted her efforts and her advice. And she had been right. Nancy came through for Ronnie, when so many of the supposedly smart men in his administration had failed him. Nearly two decades later, David Abshire wrote: "When Nancy was brought in after the scandal broke, she was key in the turnaround, bringing in outside advisers, protecting the president from foolish moves on premature public appearances, and—looking long term—bringing in a new chief of staff. Truly it can be said that Nancy Davis Reagan played the crucial role in saving the Reagan presidency and has thereby achieved a special place in the history of first ladies."

CHAPTER TWENTY-TWO

Four days after Don Regan stormed out of the White House, Nancy gave a speech to the American Camping Association. In it, she made what she insisted was an innocent reference to her childhood summers at Camp Kechuwa: "I don't think most people associate me with leeches or how to get them off. But I know how to get them off. I'm an expert at it."

No one saw that as merely an offhand comment. Nancy's role in salvaging her husband's presidency from the wreckage of the Iran-contra scandal reshaped her image, and not in a necessarily favorable way. She had once been dismissed as a shallow dilettante—the "marzipan wife," in Gloria Steinem's memorable phrase—and mocked for her adoring gaze and her frivolous, acquisitive enthusiasm for decorating and designer fashion. Nancy was now understood to be a shrewd and powerful operator in her own right. The woman so often labeled Queen Nancy was suddenly being portrayed as a size-2 Lady Macbeth. "If anyone had said six years ago that one day Nancy Reagan would be called power-hungry, we would have cut off his or her bar tab. I'd never seen her hungry, period," columnist Ellen Goodman marveled in the *Boston Globe.*

Both the nature of the criticism and the source of it took a dramatic turn. Where earlier Nancy had drawn the contempt of feminists and her husband's liberal political opponents, she was now under fire from traditionalists, who preferred that presidential spouses hew to a mold they recognized. As so many of her predecessors had learned before Nancy, when the word *powerful* is used about a first lady, it is rarely intended as a compliment.

Regan had barely cleaned out his desk when the fire began. On March 2 well-connected conservative columnist William Safire wrote on the op-ed page of the *New York Times*: "At a time he most needs to appear strong, President Reagan is being weakened and made to appear wimpish and helpless by the political interference of his wife. . . . This is not Rosalyn [*sic*] Carter, 'the Steel Magnolia,' stiffening her husband's spine; this is an incipient Edith Wilson, unelected and unaccountable, presuming to control the actions and appointments of the executive branch." Safire, not bothering to disguise the sexism that underlay his diatribe, also referred to Nancy as being at "the top of the henpecking order." His fellow columnist James Reston suggested two days later that the president should start "putting his own house in order, since nobody elected Nancy." A *Wall Street Journal*/NBC poll later that month found that an unusually high 39 percent of Americans thought the president let himself be influenced too much by his wife.

But Nancy also found some unlikely defenders. The day after the Safire column appeared, *Washington Post* columnist Judy Mann, who had been among the first lady's harshest critics in the past, offered a rebuttal: "The gentlemen who could exercise the greatest influence on the president couldn't do the job. Mrs. Reagan did the dirty work for them, and now they are out to get her. . . . The first lady is the only one on the White House team who can't be fired. That put her in a position to do something that no one else was able to do: get the presidency back on track. The president doesn't look like a wimp. He had a wife who understood what had to be done and was willing to do the dirty work. That makes him a pretty lucky man."

It didn't help things for Nancy when Howard Baker, the incoming chief of staff, added more fuel. As he was flying up to Washington from Florida to assume his new job, Baker told his airline seatmate, the executive editor of the *Miami Herald:* "When she gets her hackles up, she can be a dragon." So, it was inevitable that the next time reporters had a chance to question Ronnie, one of the first things he was asked was: "What is Mrs. Reagan's role in running the government?"

"Not the one that has been bandied about in the press," the president retorted.

Then came the follow-up: "Which part of it do you have the greatest objection to, Mr. President, of the many reports that have been written about that?"

Normally, Ronnie deflected questions such as these. He didn't this time: "Well, the idea that she is—you realize I'm breaking my rule here, but you've touched a nerve here with that—but the idea that she's involved in governmental decisions and so forth and all of this and being a kind of a dragon lady. There is nothing to that, and no one who knows her well would ever believe it."

A reporter pointed out that the "dragon" comparison had been made by the president's chief of staff, who, as it happened, was sitting on a couch nearby. Baker smiled sheepishly, which brought laughter all around—except from Ronnie. The president doubled down on his defense of his wife, insisting falsely she had had nothing to do with Regan's departure. He repeated the fictitious narrative he had been using about the chief of staff's resignation: "As I stated in my statement, he had spoken to me months before about his desire to leave. And then when all of this came up, decided that he would see it out and wait until after the Tower Commission report came in." Baker tried to clean up the mess he had made. "The first lady is a distinguished citizen of this nation," he said. "She's a great lady, and she obviously is a lady of strong conviction. That's what I meant." He added that he planned to give Nancy a call. When reporters asked what they would talk about, Baker said, "Whatever she wants." That brought another round of laughter.

Despite its uncomfortable start, Nancy's relationship with Baker turned out to be a far smoother one than she had known with Regan. She became especially close to Deputy Chief of Staff Ken Duberstein, who handled many of Baker's management responsibilities and succeeded him as chief of staff in Ronnie's final year as president. Duberstein respected the first lady, tolerated her frequent phone calls, and solicited her input. "She became my partner, a major help," he told me. "She had an uncanny understanding of her husband that nobody else had, and she was willing to share that with me."

The two of them developed an amiable routine. Nearly every weekday, Nancy would call Duberstein about a quarter to nine, as Ronnie was heading out of the family quarters toward the Oval Office. She let Duberstein know what her husband had read in the paper that morning, what his mood was like, how he was feeling, whether there was anything in particular Ronnie had on his mind. With that intelligence, Duberstein was able to quickly catch up on what he needed to have in hand before the president arrived. As Ronnie made his way to the office, he would usually stop at the office of White House physician John Hutton to say hello. Duberstein left his door cracked open, and Hutton would stick his arm in to signal Duberstein that the president was on his way.

In May 1987 Nancy had an opportunity to explain her role as first lady, as she had grown to understand it, to a group of newspaper publishers at an Associated Press luncheon in New York City. Never fond of giving speeches, she knew that this one would be listened to closely and could help to shape her own legacy as her husband's time in office entered its final stretch. Once again, she turned to Parvin to draft it. She told him she wanted to make it clear that she was not a bit sorry for acting as the most steadfast guardian of her husband's well-being. Nancy started with a joke: "I'm delighted to be here. I was afraid I might have to cancel. You know how busy I am—between staffing the White House and overseeing the arms talks. In fact, this morning I had planned to clear up US-Soviet differences on intermediate-range nuclear missiles. But I decided to clean out Ronnie's sock drawer instead."

Nancy acknowledged that she had been "terribly naive" and surprised by the scrutiny she had endured as first lady. Though she had been in public life for a long time before entering the White House, she said, "I just didn't expect it to be that concentrated. And I was even more unprepared for what I read about myself in the papers." But she also said that she found an opportunity to make a difference from the "white-glove pulpit" that a first lady is given, and that her work against drug abuse "has provided me with the most fulfilling years of my life."

And then Nancy got to the heart of it.

"In spite of everything I've learned these past six years, there's one thing on which I'm inflexible. The first lady is, first of all, a wife. That's the reason she's there," Nancy said. "A president has advisers to counsel him on foreign affairs, on defense, on the economy, on politics, on any number of matters. But no one among all those experts is there to look after him as an individual with human needs, as a flesh-and-blood person who must deal with the pressures of holding the most powerful position on earth. . . . I see the first lady as another means to keep a president from becoming isolated. I talk to people. They tell me things. They pass along ideas. And, sure, I tell my husband. And if something else is about to become a problem or fall between the cracks, I'm not above calling a staff person and asking about it.

"I'm a woman who loves her husband, and I make no apologies for looking out for his personal and political welfare. We have a genuine sharing marriage. I go to his aid. He comes to mine. I have opinions. He has opinions. We don't always agree. But neither marriage nor politics denies a spouse the right to hold an opinion or the right to express it. If you have anything less, it's not marriage."

Nancy recalled that in her first professional role as a stage actress, she had played a character who was locked in an attic and allowed only a few lines. "Recently, there are those who think first ladies should be kept in attics, only to say our lines, pour our tea, and then be put away again," she said. "Although I don't get involved in policy, it's silly to suggest my opinion should not carry some weight with a man I've been married to for thirty-five years."

She began speaking out more forcefully in other new ways. That same spring, Nancy gave a commencement speech to the May 1987 graduating class of Georgetown University Medical School. Instead of offering the customary bromides and platitudes that speakers do so often on those occasions, she slammed the medical profession for having ignored the extent of the country's drug abuse problem. She cited surveys showing physicians and medical students were themselves using marijuana and cocaine at alarming rates. "Doctors should do more than simply reflect current trends in drug use," Nancy said. "You have a higher obligation because you are the best and the brightest. You are held more accountable because of the profession you've chosen. To put it plainly, doctors should know better, and their patients deserve better.

"My father always believed that the best doctors are good teachers, and I think that is what you must be," Loyal Davis's daughter noted. "I know the insurance companies won't pay you for doing this. I know you won't be reimbursed for your troubles. But you are more than that terrible phrase—'health care providers'—would imply. You are doctors. Your patients are more than consumers. They are the sick and the hurt."

Nancy would never win over her harshest critics on the Left or the Right. But as her influence was becoming more clearly recognized, much of the country was beginning to see her in a different way: as someone Americans were glad to have as a partner to their president. She even found some surprising new fans. In June Gallup released a poll in which it asked men aged twenty-five to thirty-four to name which woman they would most like to spend an evening with. Nancy came in first. Granted, she got only 3.7 percent of the vote in this open-ended survey. But that total bested the number received by Hollywood stars such as Heather Locklear, Raquel Welch, Lynda Carter, and Cybill Shepherd. "We never dreamed that young guys would answer 'Nancy Reagan,'" marveled editor Andy Kowl of *Fast Lane,* the lifestyle magazine for men under thirty that had commissioned the survey. "If this had been a multiple-choice question, we would never have included her name."

Nancy, traveling in Sweden to promote her antidrug cause, was amused and more than a little delighted when she learned of the survey result. "I talked to my husband last night," she told reporters on her plane. "He said, 'I'm sitting here with a poll in my hand, and I think you'd better get over here real soon.'"

Iran-contra continued to make headlines during 1987. One key remaining question was whether Ronnie had known of the illegal diversion of money from the Iran arms sales to the Nicaraguan rebels. In July Oliver North, wearing a uniform bedecked with ribbons and medals, delivered his testimony to the House and Senate select committees investigating the scandal. He spoke under a grant of limited immunity from prosecution, which meant that nothing he said to the lawmakers could be used against him. The television networks cleared their normal broadcast schedules to carry it live, and tens of millions of Americans tuned in. "Throughout the conduct of my entire tenure at the National Security Council, I assumed that the president was aware of what I was doing and had, through my superiors, approved it," North said.

But the critical juncture came days later, when former national security adviser John Poindexter told those same committees that he had deliberately withheld information from Ronnie about the funneling of profits from the arms sales to the contras "so that I could insulate him from the decision and provide some future deniability for the president if it ever leaked out." Poindexter was the only living person who had both known of the diversion and who had met with the president alone. His statement, given under oath, did not reflect well on how the White House had been managed or the president's competence as a chief executive. However, it ensured that Ronnie would not be held directly accountable for the illegal secret operation that had grown out of the disastrous arms sales.

His presidency seemed to be getting back on track, and his job-approval rating began inching back toward positive territory. At the end of the year, he and Gorbachev held their summit in Washington, and there would be another in Moscow before he left office. Ronnie was moving closer and closer to the place in history that Nancy envisioned for him, which was as a peacemaker of historic significance.

In November it was announced that he had settled on a spectacular, hundred-acre site in California for his presidential library. It would be built on a mesa in Simi Valley, a small city in eastern Ventura County. The land was nestled among the mountains and, on the clearest of days, offered a view of the Pacific Ocean in the distance. Prominent conservatives, including Ed Meese and Bill Clark, had pressed for locating the library at Stanford University, where it would work in tandem with the conservative Hoover Institution, a preeminent think tank of the Right. But some on Stanford's faculty protested that having both Hoover and the Reagan Library on campus would compromise Stanford's independence by tying it to right-wing Republicanism. And Ronnie wanted it in Southern California, where it would be easier for him to visit.

Wherever it was located, the project would require raising massive amounts of private funds, which meant the Reagans were once again turning to wealthy benefactors. Robert Higdon, who had been brought aboard by Mike Deaver in the mid-1980s to help set up the Ronald Reagan Presidential Library Foundation, recalled that Ronnie had little appetite for this part. Nancy, on the other hand, had no reservations about doing what had to be done. At events with big donors, "he would show up. He would never ask anybody for a cent, where she wouldn't hesitate. She was a closer," Higdon said. Under the law, however, the Reagans were not allowed to know who had contributed or how much until after Ronnie was out of office.

In August 1987 the Reagans tapped assistant to the president Fred Ryan to begin organizing for the years after Ronnie would leave the White House. At that point, Ryan—who decades later would become publisher of the *Washington Post*—had been working for two years on planning for the library. A Californian, he relished the chance to return to his home state when the Reagans did and to serve as the chief of staff for Ronnie's postpresidential operation. "I talked to him about what he wanted when he left office. Did he want to retire and go to his ranch? Nobody could have held anything against him for doing that. He was in his late seventies, and that would be a natural thing to do. Or did he want to have a limited involvement?" Ryan recalled.

"He made it very clear that he wanted to continue to speak out on the issues he'd spoken out on as president, and things he thought of as unfinished business that he wanted to devote time to."

Ryan began sounding out opportunities for the soon-to-be-ex-president to work with a speaker's bureau and write his memoirs. He pondered how much partisan activity would be appropriate for a man who had spent eight years in the White House. Scouting for potential office space, Ryan found what he thought was the ideal building: a brand-new one among the shiny high-rises in Los Angeles's Century City area. It was close to the house where the Reagans would be living, and, looking west, it offered a view of the ocean, something Ryan knew the president wanted. He was initially told there were no vacancies. But suddenly the top floor became available, after the makers of the movie *Die Hard* finished using it for the famous action scene at the end of the 1988 thriller in which there was a shootout with hostage-holding terrorists, and the roof of the building went up in a ball of flame. Wandering through, Ryan saw gaping holes in the walls. On the floor were piles of fake broken glass and spent movie-prop shells. "I loved it, and when I came back and showed the Reagans the photos and the diagrams, they thought it was perfect," Ryan said. The Secret Service was not so enamored with their choice of a building, however. A major motion picture had just been made showing how to blow it up.

The Reagans also asked Ryan to begin planning events that could stand as symbolic milestones during Ronnie's final year: sentimental visits to places that had been important to his life and his presidency, and ceremonies honoring figures who had played a role in his success. "Tie it up with a bow," Nancy told Ryan. There would be a trip to Notre Dame University to commemorate the one hundredth birthday of legendary coach Knute Rockne, giving Ronnie a chance to reprise the movie line that had become his political battle cry: "Win one for the Gipper." Margaret Thatcher had been celebrated at their very first state dinner, so she would also be honored at their last. The bow itself: ground would be broken for the library.

Ronnie's presidency, it appeared, was moving toward a successful finale. For Nancy, however, late 1987 brought personal sadnesses: her breast cancer; her mother's death; her continuing estrangement from her daughter. Another was a growing distance from the man who for decades had been her closest ally and adviser.

Michael Deaver had left the White House in 1985 to make his fortune as a lobbyist. Though he had been practically a surrogate son to the Reagans, Deaver learned what so many others had: once you were out of the president's orbit, you practically ceased to exist for him. That was the thing about Ronnie. With the exception of Nancy, he didn't really need anyone. "It never bothered him when people left," Lyn Nofziger told Lou Cannon in 2002. For Deaver, the idea that Ronnie could do without him so easily was a shock. After his departure from the White House, he would occasionally call the president to offer a word of advice on whatever was happening at the moment. "Well, Mike," Ronnie would reply, "we have people here now who take care of those things."

Nor was Deaver well prepared for the pressures and temptations of life outside the one he had known for practically his entire adulthood. He had initially stayed in close touch with Nancy, and the two of them worked together during the difficult early months of the Iran-contra scandal. But Nancy had deepening misgivings as she saw how Deaver operated once he was freed to establish his own identity and steer his own destiny. He went from being an image maker to being a fixer. As she put it later: "Somewhere along the line in Washington, Mike Deaver went off track and caught a bad case of Potomac fever. He had suddenly become a national figure, a genius of public relations, and when something like that happens, it can be hard to keep your perspective."

Nancy had spotted an early sign of trouble ahead in 1986, when she saw her old confidant on the cover of *Time.* Deaver posed in the back of a limousine with a telephone to his ear and the Capitol in the background. "Who's This Man Calling?" read the headline. "Influence Peddling in Washington." The article inside depicted Deaver as the face of a new kind of sleaze, valued not for any expertise but rather for his access. It noted that Deaver, alone among departed Reagan aides, was allowed to keep his White House pass and that he chatted regularly with Nancy. All of which drew clients willing to pay an annual retainer of $300,000 and up.

The first lady called Deaver and said: "Mike, you've made a big mistake, and I think you're going to regret it." She was right. He was soon under investigation for violating the restrictions in the Ethics in Government Act, a post-Watergate reform that forbade high-ranking officials who had left government from lobbying their old agencies on issues on which they had participated "personally and substantially." Deaver ultimately was charged not with breaking that law itself but with lying to Congress about his involvement with the governments of Canada and South Korea and two private firms, Trans World Airlines and Smith Barney Harris Upham & Company.

What Nancy did not learn until later was that Deaver was also struggling with alcoholism. She grew worried when she tried to reach him for several days on the telephone and got no response. His wife, Carolyn, was evasive, and finally told her: "Nancy, I can't say where he is; he made me promise not to. But I'm going to be seeing him later, and I'll ask him if I can tell you." Knowing the stress he was under, Nancy's first assumption was that Deaver had suffered a nervous breakdown. That night, he called Nancy and told her he was in an addiction treatment facility in Maryland. "Thank God!" she exclaimed. Deaver was surprised at her reaction, but Nancy explained that alcoholism is "a disease, and one you can handle. I was worried sick you might have cancer. This one you can cure."

As Deaver tried to pull himself together, his legal difficulties mounted. In March 1987 he was indicted by a federal grand jury on five counts of perjury. The White House issued a terse three-sentence statement, in which the president said he and the first lady "keep him and his family in our thoughts during these difficult times. We wish him well." Nancy cut off contact with Deaver, except for occasional messages sent through a mutual friend, former CIA director Richard Helms, who she knew still lunched with Deaver regularly. She would later say she maintained her distance on the advice of the White House counsel. Deaver was shocked to realize that he was expendable even to her. "He had been with them for so very long, but he felt very abandoned when he got in trouble," Jim Baker told me. "It was really sad, because he was really tight with her. But after he got in trouble, it reflected badly on the president."

With Deaver's trial approaching in the fall of 1987, his lawyers offered his alcoholism as a defense, saying he had given false statements because his judgment was impaired. They revealed he had been hospitalized three times in 1985 and 1986 for problems related to his drinking. Safire wrote another blistering column, pointing to Deaver's once-tight relationship with Nancy and asking: "Was the First Lady so involved with her crusade against drug addiction that she failed to notice that her closest confidant was a drunk?"

Then came what Nancy regarded as Deaver's biggest betrayal. In early December, while his trial for corruption was under way, the *Washington Times* got an advance copy of a memoir that he had written with coauthor Mickey Herskowitz. Deaver's $500,000 advance was helping to pay his legal bills. The real news in *Behind the Scenes* was its revealing portrayal of Nancy as both a powerful player within her husband's White House and a moderating force against his more conservative views and those of his top advisers. Deaver named the figures that she and he had gotten rid of or shunted aside over the years. He also described her fondness for liberal thought leaders and celebrities considered the enemies of the Right.

"She was the little girl with her nose pressed up against the candy-store window," he wrote. "Nancy Reagan is not uncomfortable among free spirits and intellectuals." No doubt Nancy was just as offended—maybe more—by how her husband came off in Deaver's book. Ronnie was portrayed as a man of strong principles but little introspection or intellectual depth. "It would be fair to say that Nancy has the stronger curiosity of the two of them. She is more aware of the finer things and of the subtleties of human nature. She enjoys reaching out to new people of whatever political coloring," Deaver wrote.

When Deaver was convicted on December 16 on three of the five perjury counts, the White House issued a perfunctory statement from the president saying he and Nancy were "sorry to learn the jury's decision in Mike Deaver's trial. He has been a longtime friend and has served with dedication. Beyond that I cannot comment further at this time, since the decision will likely be appealed through our court system." Nancy called Deaver after the verdict, but that was the last he heard from her for a long time. She wrote in her 1989 memoir that "our friendship hasn't been the same since." Their silent period lasted four years.

Deaver, who was facing up to fifteen years in prison, got off relatively lightly. In September 1988 he was given a suspended three-year sentence, placed on probation, fined $100,000, and ordered to perform 1,500 hours of community service. He was also barred from lobbying the government for three years. Ronnie, by then campaigning in Florida for Bush, told reporters that he had never believed Deaver had done anything wrong. In the last days of his presidency, Deaver's daughter, Amanda, called Duberstein and asked whether Ronnie might consider a pardon for her father. No doubt the Reagans discussed this at length. "Yet Mike has passed the word that he wouldn't accept a pardon," the president wrote in his diary on January 16, 1989, four days before George H. W. Bush was to be inaugurated. So it didn't happen.

Deaver, by then in his fifties, was flat broke and had lost his means of earning a lucrative living. Stu Spencer loaned him $50,000 to pay his taxes. During the next few years, the man once seen as the wizard behind Ronnie's image wallowed in bitterness, mixed with what remained of his pride. "I kept casting around in my own mind for people to blame my situation on, and as I did that, I kept coming back to my old friends, Ronald and Nancy Reagan," he wrote later. "How could they seem to be getting along so well without me? Why was it that I heard from them only secondhand these days? How hard would it be for Ronald Reagan to pick up the phone and call me? Hadn't I given him the best years of my life? I wanted desperately to move on, to put the past behind me, but my self-pity and growing bitterness just wouldn't let me."

Deaver was far from the only one for whom service on behalf of the Reagans had left a sour aftertaste. In the final years of Ronnie's presidency and the first few years after he left office, there came an unusually large number of unflattering books about them written by former administration officials, even by their own children. One by departed press spokesman Larry Speakes, published in March 1988, described the first lady as a "prima donna" who was "likely to stab you in the back."

None, however, would create such a sensation as the one authored by scorned White House chief of staff Donald T. Regan. Shortly after Regan left, William Henkel, who ran the White House advance operation, went to visit him in his new Washington office. They began talking about what Regan might do next.

"Later today, I'm meeting with my literary agent, and we're working on selecting a publisher. I'm writing a book," Regan told him.

"Well, are you going to wait till after he gets out of the presidency?" Henkel asked.

"Hell no," Regan said.

Regan's *For the Record: From Wall Street to Washington* came out in May 1988. Its revelation of Nancy's reliance on a San Francisco astrologer overshadowed everything else in the news for weeks. She had known that the former chief of staff was writing a book and hadn't anticipated he would treat her gently. But this was something she hadn't expected: "It never, *ever* occurred to me that Don Regan would do what he did—take this information about my interest in astrology and twist it to seek his revenge on Ronnie and me."

The first lady remained silent, offering no explanation or rationale for the events that Regan laid out in his book. That would wait for her own memoir, for which Random House paid a reported $2 million. She had signed the deal in July 1986. *My Turn* was scheduled to be published in 1989, after Ronnie was out of office. Her coauthor was the accomplished William Novak, who had written a blockbuster autobiography in 1986 with Chrysler CEO Lee Iacocca. They began working together while Nancy was still in the White House. Novak traveled in liberal circles and knew of her only by reputation, so he was unprepared for the soft-spoken and sensitive woman he met. He was even more surprised to discover he liked her. But this turned out to be the most difficult and frustrating project he ever undertook.

"It was a very hard book to write, because Nancy was not a talker. She would rather listen," he said. Most of their early time together was unproductive. Nancy's diary was filled with boring entries, and she would shut down when Novak pressed her for more interesting material. "I'd rather not talk about astrology," she insisted. Nor did she find much joy in the whole endeavor, which would frequently bring her to tears. "I always had the sense that the reason she did the book was a fear about not having enough money; that in their circle, the Reagans considered themselves poor," Novak said.

Her concern about finances was another indication of how Nancy's deep-seated anxiety persisted. She and Ronnie had achieved success on a scale that few people in history would ever know. But she never lost her fear that there was a trap door around every turn; that everything they had could disappear in a heartbeat. As her friend and aide Robert Higdon put it, Nancy always had her eye out for the next place she might have to make a hard landing. The imperative to accumulate wealth—as quickly as they could—was one way to cushion against a fall. And while both Reagans were looking forward to returning to Los Angeles, there were practical things to consider. For one, they didn't have enough money to purchase an upper-bracket home in the overpriced real estate market. Ronnie's high-earning days on *General Electric Theater* and the lecture circuit were long behind him. Their tax returns for 1987 showed they were living mostly on his presidential salary of $201,526 a year. (Also noted in press reports: Nancy, who was still claiming to have been born in 1923, did not take a deduction available to those over sixty-five.)

So, Ronnie and Nancy made a housing arrangement reminiscent of what they had done in Sacramento, after Nancy found the shabby governor's mansion unsuitable. Nearly twenty of their wealthy friends, including their longtime benefactors Holmes Tuttle and Earle Jorgensen, paid

$2.5 million for an estate in LA's exclusive Bel Air section. They leased the 7,200-square-foot home to the Reagans at market rates, under a deal that allowed the couple an option to buy. Soon after Ronnie left office, it was deeded over to a trust in their name. The address on St. Cloud Road was changed from 666 to 668 on city records, out of Nancy's concern that the original number might be construed as a biblical reference to Satan.

All of this passed muster with the government ethics watchdogs. But Nancy's love of freebies would bring one more spectacular embarrassment to the White House during her husband's final months in office. In mid-October 1988 *Time* magazine reported that, despite Nancy's public promise six years earlier that she would quit "borrowing" costly designer outfits, she had indeed continued the practice. The article cited gowns worth upward of $20,000 each, furs that included a $35,000 Russian sable, jewelry valued in the six figures. One designer alone, David Hayes of Los Angeles, said he had loaned her as many as eighty made-to-order outfits, only half of which had been returned, and which were worthless anyway once they had been worn. "She set her own little rule, and she broke her own little rule," Nancy's spokeswoman Elaine Crispen said. "I'm admitting for her that she basically broke her own promise."

Except it was more than Nancy's word that was at issue. The Reagans were also running afoul of the tax law. After Ronnie was out of office, the Internal Revenue Service would present them with a hefty bill for back taxes and interest on what its audit concluded were $3 million in unreported gifts of clothing and jewelry between 1983 and 1988.

The simmering tension between Nancy and the Bushes continued right up until the end of Ronnie's presidency. George Bush nailed down his party's presidential 1988 nomination fairly easily. But it was notable that he did not actually receive the president's endorsement until the primary race was over, after his challengers had either dropped out or suspended their campaigns. Entries in Ronnie's diary indicated that, privately, he was rooting for Bush. But his long-standing policy was not to intercede in battles within his own party. Nancy, meanwhile, was unenthusiastic about either of the Reagans getting deeply involved in the 1988 presidential race. She nixed the Bush campaign's plan to roll out Ronnie's endorsement at a big rally on the night of the May 3 Ohio primary, when the vice president clinched enough convention delegates to claim the nomination. Nancy said that having Ronnie play second banana at Bush's victory celebration would be unpresidential.

The long-awaited embrace finally came a week later at a black-tie Republican fund-raiser known as the President's Dinner. This gathering of GOP fat cats was not the setting that Bush's team would have picked for their man's big moment. Ronnie's actual announcement of his endorsement came off as tepid, almost offhand. At the end of a twenty-minute address extolling his own record, Ronnie called Bush "my candidate" and said, "I'm going to work as hard as I can to make Vice President George Bush the next president of the United States." Bush's team had expected something more effusive, given the vice president's steadfast service. In fact, Ronnie had written a rousing one in his own hand and shown it to Bush. "We later learned that Nancy took it out, as 'this was Ron's night,'" Barbara Bush fumed in her diary.

That summer, with his campaign struggling, Bush asked his old and close friend James Baker to leave his post as Treasury secretary and come run the operation, as he had in 1980. Baker was surprised when the president said he shouldn't go.

"The vice president needs me," Baker pleaded.

"No, Jim," Ronnie replied. "You'd be much more valuable to him if you just stay here and run the economy of the country."

Baker figured out quickly what was really happening. The problem was Nancy. "I saw the fine hand of the first lady in that," he recalled. So Baker returned to Bush and told him he could not be the middle man in this particular transaction: "I hate to tell you, pal, but this ain't going to work unless you talk to the president yourself."

Nancy was there when Bush and Baker made their pitch to Ronnie, and she made it clear she wasn't happy that the Treasury secretary wanted to step away from the job he had. But Ronnie finally relented: "Well, George, if that's what you want, then that's what we'll do." Then, typically unperturbed at the comings and goings of people around him, Ronnie asked Baker to come up with some suggestions for a successor at Treasury.

Bush's campaign strategy was to offer himself, essentially, as a third Reagan term. But Nancy resented the ways in which her husband's vice president tried to reclaim his own identity by rejecting some of the harsher aspects of the previous eight years. At the Republican convention in New Orleans that year, Bush promised "a kinder, gentler nation." Nancy was widely reported to have muttered, "Kinder and gentler than whom?"

The fall campaign saw a fresh round of stories about Nancy and Barbara feuding. In October *Time* noted Nancy's absence from a "star-studded" rally for Bush and his running mate, Indiana senator Dan Quayle. According to the magazine, Nancy sat upstairs in her suite at the Century Plaza Hotel in Los Angeles while her husband made an appearance on the stage. "Barbara has remarked to friends that Nancy is strikingly ungrateful for all the loyalty and deference the Bushes have shown the Reagans for eight years," the magazine reported. That same week, Knight Ridder newspapers published a story in which White House reporter Owen Ullmann wrote that while it was "final curtain time" for her husband's presidency, Nancy "apparently does not want to get off the stage."

The reports were denied, unconvincingly, on all sides. Nancy's press secretary, Elaine Crispen, insisted the first lady was "totally supportive" of the Bush candidacy and that there was "no feud between them." Vice President Bush himself, sensitive to the fact that the stories had obviously come from his own camp, sent Nancy a note in which he called them "outrageous." Crispen quoted Bush as having written: "I'll be damned if I let anything nasty come between us. You and the president deserve much better than two damn stories." Bush's campaign dispatched Stu Spencer to convince Nancy that the best way to preserve her husband's legacy was to help elect his vice president.

*

On Election Day, Bush pulled off a solid victory over Democrat Michael S. Dukakis, the governor of Massachusetts. For the Reagans, there would be one last presidential Thanksgiving at the ranch and one last pre-Christmas weekend at Camp David, where they were serenaded by the enlisted men who worked there. Everywhere Nancy turned, there were emotional good-byes. Her aides had to keep her steadily supplied with tissues. The Reagans spent Christmas in their new Bel Air home, where some of their furniture had already been moved, before heading to the Annenbergs' estate near Palm Springs for their traditional New Year's Eve celebration.

As Bush's inauguration approached, the incoming first lady got in a few parting shots at the outgoing one. At one preinaugural event, Barbara pointed to her own new clothes and suggested to reporters that they should not get used to seeing her so dolled up: "Please notice—hairdo, makeup, designer dress. Look at me good this week, because it's the only week." No one could miss the dig at Nancy. But, in fact, Barbara's tastes did not run toward J. C. Penney; she was a regular customer of couturiers Bill Blass and Arnold Scaasi.

January 20, 1989, finally arrived, dawning gray and mild. The Reagans ate breakfast early, then went downstairs to say one last farewell to the household staff in the State Dining Room. The commander in chief received a final briefing from National Security Adviser Colin L. Powell, who made it a short one: "The world is quiet today."

Ronnie left a note in the desk of the Oval Office for Bush. Then it was time to greet the next president and vice president and their families and head to the Capitol. Ronnie and George Bush got into one car; Nancy and Barbara Bush, into another, for the ride up Pennsylvania Avenue.

From the platform on the West Front of the Capitol, Nancy looked across the sweep of the National Mall, with its monuments to great presidents and their ideas. She remembered how it felt to be in that same spot eight years before. How little she had known back then of the triumphs that lay ahead and the price that would be demanded to achieve them. "The whole day was like a dream," she wrote later, "and suddenly this part, too, was over."

Barbara Bush did not disguise how happy she was to see the indignities and humiliations that she and her husband had suffered at Nancy's hand finally come to an end. At one point, Barbara spotted Ronnie's ever-present executive assistant, Jim Kuhn, standing in the backstage holding area of the Capitol. She swept Kuhn up in a big hug and gave him a kiss. Then, in a tone that sounded more triumphant than sentimental, she told him: "Jim . . . good-bye." Kuhn was taken aback. He got the message, he told me later. It was one that Barbara wanted to deliver to the entire Reagan team: "Good riddance. Get out of here. We don't want to see you again."

After the inauguration of the forty-first president, the Bushes and the Quayles accompanied the Reagans to the helicopter that would carry them to a waiting government Boeing 707 at Andrews AFB. It was set to take off not as Air Force One—that name was used only if a sitting president was aboard—but as Special Air Mission 27000. The chopper was designated Nighthawk One, not Marine One. As Nancy got ready to climb in, the now-former first lady spotted a figure standing by himself to one side. It was George Opfer. Nancy broke away and ran over to embrace the Secret Service agent who had shared the darkest day of her life with her back in March 1981.

Then they lifted off. The helicopter pilot made an extra circle over the White House, so the Reagans could see it one more time. Tears covered Nancy's cheeks as the couple gazed out the window. "Look, dear," Ronnie said tenderly, "there's our little bungalow."

CHAPTER TWENTY-THREE

On the first working day after his return to California, Ronald Reagan surprised his staff by showing up at his new suite of offices in Century City. The place wasn't even ready yet. When they got word that the former president was on his way, his chief of staff, Fred Ryan, and the others scrambled to throw some pictures on the wall and hide the boxes they had been unpacking. "Well, I'm going to work on some things," Ronnie said cheerily when he arrived, and then he disappeared into his private office. A few hours later, he emerged and handed Ryan a list of nearly a dozen names. "I've agreed to see these people," Ronnie said. Ryan was perplexed. He didn't recognize any of them.

"They're people who've been calling," Ronnie explained. The phone system had not been properly connected and calls into the office were going straight through to the ex-president himself. Most were inquiries from members of the public, who were surprised to hear Ronnie's familiar voice on the other end of the line, and even more startled to get an invitation to come over and meet him. The harried scheduling team honored the commitments that Ronnie had made to these strangers. "They came in. They got their picture taken. They brought their kids in," Ryan recalled. "One guy turned to me and said, 'This is pretty cool.' He said, 'My neighbor likes Ronald Reagan. I think I'm going to bring him in.' I said, 'No, you got lucky once. Not twice.'" Ryan also made sure the phones got fixed and that future calls to the main number would be routed to a receptionist.

Ronnie and Nancy had looked forward to this phase of their life. The end of his presidency was "a bittersweet experience," he said. Returning to California was "the sweet part of it." He pronounced their new Bel Air home, one of the smaller and plainer ones in the ultrarich neighborhood, his favorite of all the houses in which they had lived. He would have more time to spend at his beloved ranch. Nancy would be back among her closest friends. There was even speculation that they might go back into the movies, though Nancy put that to rest when she told celebrity interviewer Joan Rivers, "I don't think I'm right for today's films."

Their future could hardly have looked more secure. Ronnie, by all appearances hale and healthy as he approached his eightieth birthday, enjoyed the distinction of being the only living president to have been elected twice and exited the office in good standing. His final job approval rating in the Gallup poll was a robust 63 percent. On the last day of his presidency, Ronnie received a letter from Richard Nixon congratulating him: "Politics is a roller coaster, and you ended right at the top!" Less than forty-eight hours later, Ronnie signed a deal with Simon & Schuster to write two books, reportedly for around $5 million.

The Reagans soon were traveling the world in the near-royal style that ex-presidents are afforded. In June 1989 he was knighted by Queen Elizabeth and feted by Margaret Thatcher at a dinner at 10 Downing Street. On that same weeklong trip, he was inducted into France's prestigious Academy of Moral and Political Sciences. The following month, he stepped in as a guest announcer for the first inning of baseball's annual All-Star Game in Anaheim—a return to his earliest professional roots—and a month after that was named to the Cowboy Hall of Fame in Oklahoma.

Meanwhile, Ronnie got the satisfaction of seeing a new world begin to take shape as the result of things that he had helped to make happen. In 1990, three years after he had demanded that Gorbachev "tear down this wall," he went to Berlin and took a hammer and chisel to its remnants. Crowds chanted, "We love you, Ronnie!" A nine-foot-tall segment of the wall would later stand on the terrace of his presidential library. He was also welcomed at the Gdansk shipyards in Poland, where the anti-Communist Solidarity movement had been formed. Sanctions imposed by the Reagan administration were widely credited with forcing the government to make democratic concessions. Solidarity's founder, Lech Walesa, told Ronnie: "Your position, firmness, and consistency meant hope and help for us in the most difficult moments."

In May 1992 Gorbachev, who was overthrown in a coup by Communist hard-liners after the fall of the Soviet Union, spoke at the newly opened Reagan Library and received the first Ronald Reagan Freedom Award. He also paid a nostalgic visit to the Reagans at their ranch. Ronnie gave Gorbachev a Stetson, which he put on. No one had the nerve to tell the former Soviet leader that he was wearing the hat backward.

These high-profile, postpresidency victory laps were as important to Nancy as they were to Ronnie. Of the two of them, she had always been the one more focused on his place in history. "He was the last guy who cared about this; about making sure that his legacy was known and remembered," Fred Ryan said. "He was not one who was spending a lot of time worrying about his legacy. Even before he had a health problem, she was more involved in those conversations."

Ronnie went to the office almost every weekday that he wasn't traveling. Nancy preferred to work mostly from home. Getting his presidential library off the ground was a major endeavor for both of them. Both of them were determined that it would be the biggest and the best of any.

*

In their reentry to private life, the Reagans also made some controversial judgments, leading them into rough patches. The first misstep was Ronnie's decision to accept $2 million from a Japanese media conglomerate for an eight-day speaking tour of that country in October 1989. Gerald Ford had paved the way for selling the prestige of the presidency, quietly lining his pockets with lucrative posts on corporate boards. Six-figure speaking fees for former presidents would later become common. But at the time, it was considered shocking for one to cash in so blatantly on the aura of the office. Ronnie's immediate predecessor, Jimmy Carter, was keeping himself busy by building houses for the poor. Even disgraced Richard Nixon was coming to be regarded as a dignified elder statesman, writing heavyweight books about foreign policy, traveling internationally, and offering advice that his successors and other leaders were eager to hear, though they did not publicize it.

"Former Presidents haven't always comported themselves with dignity after leaving the Oval Office," the *New York Times* sniffed in an editorial about Ronnie's lucrative Japanese speaking gig. "But none have plunged so blatantly into pure commercialism." Oregon congressman Peter DeFazio, a Democrat, introduced legislation to eliminate an ex-president's pension after any year in which he earns more than $400,000. "It's unseemly, to say the least, when a former president cashes in on his prestige this way, and doubly so when he continues to receive his full presidential pension," DeFazio said. Ronnie's successor, George H. W. Bush, commented wryly: "Everybody's got to make a living."

The Reagans even had to endure humiliating gibes from the man who in the late 1980s was the walking embodiment of classless, undignified merchandising of a public image. In January 1990, a few months after the Reagans' Japan trip, Donald Trump made an appearance at a charity event in Los Angeles and noted that Ronnie was present as a guest. "President Reagan is here, and I can tell this audience he did not get two million for coming here tonight," Trump said. "You didn't get $2 million for this, did you, Mr. President?" Nancy leaned over to someone sitting near her, and asked incredulously: *"Did he really say what I think he said?"*

The previous year, Trump had attended a fund-raiser for the Reagan Library that was held in New York Harbor aboard Malcolm Forbes's yacht, the *Highlander.* Forbes and Reagan friend Walter Annenberg took the brash real estate tycoon below deck and made their pitch for a $1 million contribution. They were disappointed when Trump agreed to give only $25,000—and even more so when the money never showed up.

Ronnie was not the only Reagan who drew criticism in the months after the former first couple left Washington. Nancy had pledged to continue her crusade against drugs, and one of her most high-profile endeavors was the construction of a 210-bed treatment center that was to be named for her. The Reagans' wealthy friends held a series of glittering, high-dollar fund-raisers to benefit the effort. However, the middle-class homeowners who lived near the proposed San Fernando Valley site did not want it there and threatened to picket the Reagans' Bel Air home in retaliation. Abruptly, Nancy withdrew her support for the project. "The last thing I wanted to do was upset a community," she said.

Her reversal in May 1989 left Phoenix House, the program that was to run the center, in the lurch. The group had collected only half of the $5 million that Nancy had raised in pledges, and dozens of the big donors asked for their money back. Appearances weren't helped by the fact that, just days after abandoning the rehabilitation center, Nancy accepted a lucrative seat on the board of the cosmetics giant Revlon. *Vanity Fair* wrote a scathing account of the Phoenix House saga, which questioned the sincerity of Nancy's commitment to the antidrug cause: "Although Mrs. Reagan has consented to the occasional photo opportunity since leaving office, for the most part she seems to be devoting her energies to making money." Among the most blistering quotes in the article was one from powerful television executive Grant Tinker, a member of the Phoenix House board. "We were just about to cross the goal line, and she shot us down," he said. "I think she thinks the 'Just Say No' thing is national and effective. It isn't; it's just a lapel button. It isn't what Phoenix House does, which is constructive and effective."

Nancy's book *My Turn: The Memoirs of Nancy Reagan* also came out near the end of 1989, to withering reviews. First ladies before her had written anodyne and unrevealing accounts, aimed more at proving that they hadn't overstepped their traditional roles than showing how they had. Nancy's book was regarded as so vindictive that it quickly became known as *"My Burn."* But she was unapologetic. "Well," she said, "if I'd written a book like Lady Bird Johnson's, why write it? Lord, eight years is a long time to sit there and not say anything."

Its candor is striking. In *My Turn,* Nancy is defensive, both of her decisions and the way in which she chose to play the role in which history had cast her. The book also glosses over events and denies some things that are clearly true, such as the fact that she waged a guerrilla campaign against Don Regan with strategic leaks to the press. But Nancy's assessments of the people around her husband come off as pretty close to the mark. And she is forthright in admitting that she made her share of mistakes, bringing many of her problems—and heartbreak—upon herself.

The book's dedication is poignant in that regard:

To Ronnie, who always understood
And to my children, who I hope will understand.

Its passages about the strains within the Reagan family stand out as particularly raw. "What I wanted most in all the world was to be a good wife and mother. As things turned out, I guess I've been more successful at the first than at the second," Nancy acknowledged. But she was also unsparing in airing her grievances against the four Reagan offspring, particularly Patti, with whom she was not on speaking terms at the time the book was published. Sally Quinn, reviewing it in the *Washington Post,* wrote: "What is appalling is the way she attacks her own child. It is so hurtful, so painful, so embarrassing, so pathetic that it takes your breath away."

Nancy's book, however, was only one in a stream of uncomfortable Reagan-era remembrances to hit the bookstands in those years. There was astrologer Joan Quigley's 1990 volume *"What Does Joan Say?"* The truth, which was that she was consulted on presidential scheduling decisions, was weird enough. But in her book, Quigley took credit for everything from the warming of US-Soviet relations, to calming the controversy over Ronnie's visit to the Bitburg cemetery, to ensuring the confirmation of a nominee to the US Supreme Court. Many of her claims—"I was the Teflon in the Teflon presidency," she wrote—were absurd.

That same year, former speechwriter Peggy Noonan came out with *What I Saw at the Revolution: A Political Life in the Reagan Era,* a snarky, almost anthropological look at the Reagan years. At times, Noonan wrote, it seemed that "the battle for the mind of Ronald Reagan was like the trench warfare of World War I: never have so many fought so hard for such barren terrain." His White House, in Noonan's telling, was "like a beautiful clock that makes all the right sounds, but when you open it up, there is nothing inside." Noonan posited that Nancy was "a wealthy, well-dressed woman who followed the common wisdom of her class" and "disliked the contras because they were unattractive and dirty."

Despite what Noonan had dished in the book, she and Nancy would eventually become close. Mutual friends brought them together over dinner in the mid-1990s, shortly after Ronnie was diagnosed with Alzheimer's. Noonan was surprised to discover how much she liked Nancy. "Everything somehow was changed, and I just wanted to put my arm around her and appreciate her," Noonan recalled later. "Because suddenly I saw what it had cost her; had always cost her. And I wanted to say, 'Thank you.'"

But that kind of reassessment of Nancy would not come for years. In the meantime, she endured criticism from many directions, some of them unexpected. Around the same time that Noonan's caustic book was published, Selwa "Lucky" Roosevelt, who had been chief of protocol, joined the pile-on with her memoir titled *Keeper of the Gate.* Roosevelt castigated the former first lady on a number of fronts, one of which was the quality of the entertainment she chose for state dinners. "Our foreign guests were often subjected to has-been popular singers and other marginal performers who were not up to White House standards," Roosevelt lamented.

By the first anniversary of the Reagans' triumphant departure from Washington, *Los Angeles* magazine had pronounced them "the most unpopular First Couple in history." In November 1991 a *Los Angeles Times* poll found that more than two-thirds of the American public viewed Ronnie as an average or below-average president.

That same year, Kitty Kelley's blockbuster takedown of the former first lady came out. Kelley was well known for unflattering books she had written about Jacqueline Kennedy Onassis, Elizabeth Taylor, and Frank Sinatra. *Nancy Reagan: The Unauthorized Biography* was more than six hundred pages of gossip, salacious tidbits, and heavy innuendo. Nancy was portrayed as a shallow social climber, an uncaring parent, and the manipulative force behind a dim-brained president. Among the most headline-grabbing—and specious—claims was Kelley's suggestion that Nancy and Frank Sinatra had a long-term sexual affair.

Kelley had done extensive research and uncovered fresh material that shed new light on some of the broad outlines of Nancy's life, particularly its complicated beginnings. But every fact that the author dug up was turned in a single direction, to make the case that Nancy was a vain and cruel shrew with no redeeming qualities. A review in the *New York Times* deemed it "one of the most encyclopedically vicious books in the history of encyclopedic viciousness." Which pretty much guaranteed that people would rush to buy it. Bookstores sold out within hours, with some reporting it was the fastest-moving volume they had ever seen. The first printing of 600,000 was shipped within a day, and by the end of a week, there were 925,000 copies in print. In Washington, the book was on everyone's lips. Barbara Bush denounced it as "trash and fiction," but Nancy's successor as first lady was reported to have been spotted reading a copy disguised with a different dust jacket.

Nancy was devastated. In several letters Ronnie wrote around the time, he alluded to the intensity of his wife's distress. "A big thank-you for your letter and thank Pat also. Nancy and I are truly upset and angry over the total dishonesty of Kitty Kelley and her book," he wrote former president Nixon on April 11. "We haven't found one person she names as her sources who has ever known her or been contacted by her. Believe it or not, one she named was the minister of our church—Reverend Donn Moomaw. He has written a denial for the church bulletin. Your letter will help me keep Nancy from worrying herself sick. She is Kelley's main victim and is very upset."

Reagan allies organized a pushback campaign. There is a file box among Nancy's personal papers at the Reagan Library that comprises scores of letters that she received. Many were from people who were quoted in Kelley's book, claiming either that their words were taken out of context or that they had never been interviewed by Kelley at all. Typical was one from actor Robert Stack, dated April 11, 1991, expressing his dismay at learning he was one of the hundreds of people cited in the book's acknowledgments, which suggested he had been a source to Kelley. "Since I have never met or spoken to the woman, this would be impossible," Stack wrote. In another, Broadway and film star Carol Channing fumed: "It has been called to my attention that I am quoted by Kitty Kelly [*sic*] in her book & I feel compelled to tell you that I have never spoken to her or any of her representatives. I was alarmed to see that she completely fabricated a malicious story."

Still other letters in the file denounced Kelley herself. *New York Daily News* columnist Liz Smith, whom Kelley portrayed as a first-class suck-up to Nancy, wrote: "She is pathetic. *She is also a shit.* Forget her. The backlash in your favor has already begun. Love—Liz." Letitia Baldridge, the etiquette expert who had been Jackie Kennedy's social secretary and later assisted Nancy in the White House, wrote from Washington to assure her: "It will give you great satisfaction to know that she is finished. No one here will invite her anymore. No one will speak to her."

Screen legend Marlene Dietrich advised Nancy to sue both the author and her publisher, Simon & Schuster (which is also the publisher of this book). "Please don't give up!!!" the eighty-nine-year-old Dietrich wrote on April 21 from Paris. "Stop any *further* publication. Threaten lawsuits if sold *outside* USA. All the lawyers fees *are worth it*! That pig of a woman—and Simon & Schuster—should suffer."

But the sensation around the book had one unexpected result: it created a wave of sympathy for Nancy. The *New York Times*, in an editorial denouncing the book, wrote: "Funny thing is, the more that Americans wanted to believe wonderful things about their 40th president and the more Teflon they conferred on him, the more they seemed willing to believe the worst of his wife. Lightning rods have had it better than Nancy Reagan. O.K., so she probably deserved more than a few of the jolts. But truly, nobody deserves this." Kelley suspended her publicity tour and claimed to *Newsweek* that she had gotten a message on her answering machine from "a minor hood" of her acquaintance warning her: "Kitty, please be very careful. There is a hit on you."

*

The furor over the book eventually settled down, and there were soon other events that put the Reagans in the news in a more favorable and dignified light. The library's November 4, 1991, dedication was a triumph, bringing together five living presidents for the first time in US history. Also in attendance were the six living women who had served as First Lady. Rosalynn Carter and Barbara Bush were seated uncomfortably in the scorching sun, which they privately agreed must have been Nancy's doing.

In the months before the library opening, there had been a power struggle over its direction that pitted Nancy against some of the more conservative figures who had been with Ronnie from the beginning. Ed Meese, Bill Clark, and Martin Anderson were quietly dropped from the Reagan Foundation's twelve-member board. Economist W. Glenn Campbell, who had shaped the Hoover Institution at Stanford, had been nudged out earlier. The reason given for their departures was that they had come to the end of their six-year terms, but no one took that at face value. The moves were seen as a purge engineered by Nancy.

"Reagan never even knew about this until after it happened," one longtime friend of the former president told the *Washington Post*'s Lou Cannon. "Unfortunately, this reinforces the view that Nancy's in charge and that Reagan doesn't really know what's going on." The bitterness broke into the open when Ronnie's former spokesman Lyn Nofziger wrote an August 4 op-ed for the *Post* that was headlined: "A Reaganite's Lament."

"Ronald Reagan," Nofziger began, "you have broken my heart. Finally."

"Today the papers told us what I have been hearing for some time: that you have given up, which maybe at age 80 you have a right to do. But in doing so, you appear to have forgotten old loyalties and to have walked away from old friends," Nofziger wrote in the open letter to his old boss. "You have let Nancy and the rich and beautiful people with whom she has surrounded herself and you force off the board of the Ronald Reagan Presidential Library three of the most dedicated and selfless Reaganites there are—men who stayed with you through the good days and the bad, men who never had a bad word to say about you or your performances as governor or president, men who dedicated good parts of their lives to you and your success because they believed that if you succeeded the state and the nation would benefit and prosper."

Nofziger recounted how the trio most recently ousted from the board had contributed to Ronnie's rise: Meese and Clark, the loyalists who had served Ronnie from the dawn of his governorship; Anderson, the brainy academic and domestic policy adviser who had so often been called upon to defend Ronnie's positions.

"So how have you rewarded them?" Nofziger wrote. "You have let Nancy, who, for reasons I don't understand, has a vendetta against them, arrange to have them not reappointed to the board of your library. Indeed, if they had not protested, they would have been thrown off en masse before the opening of the library in November. And this probably would have been done without your even knowing or caring."

Others who were involved in the power struggle described it differently. They say that the three men had created tension with the remaining board members by pressing for a different agenda for the new library. In their vision, it would become not a monument to Ronnie's presidency but a conservative power base. Among their proposals were that it should have cottages for what they said would be "visiting scholars," but which other members of the board believed they planned to turn into their own homes away from home. They even suggested that the library build and stock a wine cellar. Said one person who worked closely with the board at the time: "Clearly, they would meet beforehand and come up with what the agenda would be. It would be orchestrated. It was planned in advance. 'What do you think about this? All in favor?' Things would just move."

Nancy, who had an acute sense of when others were trying to use her husband for their own purposes, grew worried that Ronnie's vision for the library was being thwarted. William French Smith, the former Reagan attorney general who was chairman of the foundation board at the time, suggested the simplest and cleanest solution would be not to reappoint the conservative board members when their terms expired. They left shortly after the library opened. Ronnie wrote them each a note, thanking them for their support and friendship.

But if the launch of the library caused a rupture with some of Ronnie's oldest backers, it also brought about a long-overdue reconciliation. There was only one person who had the skill it would take to pull off an event as ambitious as the library opening: Michael Deaver. Fred Ryan wasn't sure how Nancy would react when he broached the idea of bringing back the disgraced former aide. She immediately embraced it. Her closeness with Deaver was something she had greatly missed.

In fact, Deaver had already made an overture. He happened to be in Los Angeles in February 1991. It had been three years since he had seen the Reagans; longer than that since he'd talked to them. He had their number in his address book and decided to call. Nancy answered. He told her that he was in town and would like to come over and see them some time in the next few days. "Of course," she said. "Why don't you come now? We're both here." She gave him directions.

Deaver drove to Bel Air and up St. Cloud Road. Their new home "was larger than their old house in Pacific Palisades, with a contemporary California feel to it and a commanding view of the Los Angeles Basin. I still wasn't sure I'd made the right decision in calling them.

Perhaps I should go back and write a letter, I thought. Maybe I wasn't ready for a face-to-face meeting," Deaver recalled.

He was still thinking it over, delaying his entrance by making small talk with the Secret Service agents outside, when Nancy came to the door. She pulled him in and hugged him. Ronnie poured them all iced tea in the den. "It's important to me to say that I am really sorry for some of the things that happened over the last few years," Deaver began.

"Mike, forget all that," Nancy said, taking his hand. "We're just glad you're back with us." Ronnie told him it was the best eightieth birthday present he could ask for. That was when Deaver suddenly realized the date: February 6. How could he have forgotten?

This, however, would be a new chapter in Deaver's relationship with the couple that had loomed so large over his life. He would understand them in a way he never really had before. "I had doubted Reagan's affection for me during our silent period from 1987 to 1991, and it was difficult for me to fully understand," he wrote later. "In time, though, I came to realize that Reagan is so totally complete in himself that the only person he really needs is Nancy. Yes, I am a very special person in his life, but if I am out of sight for a few weeks or years, that's okay, too. It's Nancy that he wants and needs to be around all the time."

Though Nancy was devoted to assuring her husband's place in history, she was not without a sense of her own political power. In 1994 she inflicted an overdue measure of payback against Oliver L. North, the National Security Council aide at the center of the Iran-contra scandal. North had been indicted on sixteen felony counts and convicted of three, but the verdict was vacated on appeal in 1990 because the evidence had been based in part on testimony he had given to Congress on the promise it would not be used against him. In the years since, he had become a godlike figure with right-wing groups.

In September 1993 North declared his candidacy for the Senate against vulnerable Democratic incumbent Charles S. Robb, who in 1967 married Lynda Bird, the daughter of Lyndon B. and Lady Bird Johnson, in a lavish White House wedding. Both Reagans endorsed

Ronnie's former budget chief James C. Miller III in the GOP contest, but North easily won the nomination at the state party convention the following June. That year, the tides were running with Republicans across the country, and North raised upward of $20 million, more than any other Senate candidate.

One day Nancy was having lunch with the Reagans' longtime political consultant Stuart Spencer, when Spencer asked: "You still hate Ollie North?" Nancy began fuming about the possibility that someone who had betrayed Ronnie as North had done might actually end up in the US Senate. "I want to get even with him, too," Spencer said. Then he told Nancy there was a way she might be able to throw a roadblock into North's path.

"I didn't have to argue very hard," Spencer recalled, still delighted nearly a quarter century later about the plan the two of them hatched together. Nancy's opportunity arose less than two weeks before the election, when she made an appearance in New York with talk-show host Charlie Rose, and the topic turned to the hot Virginia Senate race. "Ollie North—oh, I'll be happy to tell you about Ollie North. Ollie North has a great deal of trouble separating fact from fantasy," Nancy said. "He lied to my husband and lied about my husband—kept things from him he should not have kept from him. And that's what I think of Ollie North."

Robb's internal polls had shown him 4 points behind North before the former first lady's comments hit the news on October 28. On the stump, the embattled Democratic senator began adding a new punch line to his attacks on his Republican opponent: "Just ask Nancy Reagan."

Democratic pollster Geoff Garin, who was working for Robb, tracked a remarkable shift in the final days before the election. "After Mrs. Reagan's criticism of North on October 28, the race swung back in Robb's direction, with a significant drop in support for North," Garin told me. "Her impact was important because she put a dead stop to North's efforts to normalize himself as an acceptable option for Republicans. The television campaign was very negative at this point, and Mrs. Reagan's intervention broke through the ugly clutter and made it harder for right-leaning voters to cast a vote—either for North himself or for [independent candidate] Marshall Coleman—that would put North in the Senate." On election night, Republicans swept to victory across the country. They won back control of the House for the first time in four decades and picked up eight seats in the Senate. It was a political tsunami across the map, with one conspicuous exception: Virginia. North lost to Robb by less than 3 percentage points. Nancy's aim had been precise, well timed, and deadly.

However, there would be no opportunity for Nancy to savor the moment; no sweetness to her revenge. Three days before the election, Ronnie shook the country with an announcement that he had been diagnosed with Alzheimer's disease.

CHAPTER TWENTY-FOUR

After years of being Ronnie's physician, John Hutton could tell instantly that something was wrong—very wrong. It was February 3, 1994. Twenty-five hundred people were gathered in the magnificent Pension Building in downtown Washington, DC, for a black-tie gala celebrating the Gipper's eighty-third birthday. The event was also a high-dollar fund-raiser for the Republican Party. Ronnie's great friend Margaret Thatcher, now three years out of office as British prime minister, was on hand to introduce the former president.

Ronnie came to the microphone and, looking dazed, began to speak haltingly, a little out of sync. He did not seem to be able to find his words, even though they were written on cards that he was holding in his hand: "Frankly . . . for a minute there . . . I was a bit concerned . . . that after all . . . these years away from Washington . . . you all . . . wouldn't . . . recognize me." Nor did Ronnie apparently realize there was a teleprompter right in front of him. To Hutton's practiced and professional eye, it was clear he was confused and on the verge of humiliating himself.

The doctor leaned over to Kathy Busch, who was the Reagans' spokeswoman. "Have you seen this before?" he asked.

"I'm not sure," she said.

Fred Ryan was also in the audience. "*What's wrong?*" he thought. "*Something is not right here.*"

Then, within seconds, Ronnie was his old self. It was as if someone had flipped a light switch. He saw the teleprompter and gave a speech that was as good as ever. He had the audience laughing and cheering. Some people got so emotional they started crying.

This had not been Ronnie's only mental lapse that evening. At the predinner reception, Nancy had sensed something was amiss. She urged Ryan to make sure the event did not fall behind schedule. "We've got to keep this thing moving," she said. In the holding room backstage, it got worse. Ronnie, though delighted to see Thatcher, did not appear to know where he was or why. The former prime minister touched her old friend and said gently: "Ronnie, you're in Washington."

After the dinner, Hutton went back to the Reagans' hotel with them. Ronnie entered their room first, took about five steps, and stopped. "I'm going to have to wait a minute," he said. "I'm having a little trouble. I don't know where I am."

Nancy grabbed Hutton's arm. "John," she said, "this has been happening even in his own house."

No one knew it then, but the man known as the Great Communicator would never give a major speech in public again. Nine months after that near disaster in Washington, on November 5, 1994, Ronnie revealed to the nation in a heartbreaking handwritten letter that he was "one of the millions of Americans who will be afflicted with Alzheimer's disease." The same affliction had struck his mother (though at the time, the name for it wasn't widely known) and his older brother, who for years had been showing symptoms of cognitive decline. But neither Ronnie nor the woman he loved fully grasped what lay ahead. "Like most people then, I didn't know much about Alzheimer's (looking back, I suppose that was just as well), but I was certainly going to learn!" Nancy recalled.

Precisely when the fortieth president of the United States showed the first signs of impairment has been a subject of much debate and speculation, and no doubt will continue to be among historians and scholars for many years to come. The most important question, of course, is whether it affected his performance while he was in office.

Answering that is made all the more difficult by the nature of the man himself. Ronnie's intellect was always underestimated; he was smarter and more well read than his critics—and even some of his admirers—gave him credit for being. But even when he was in his prime, those who saw him every day came to understand that his amiable exterior cloaked an inner complexion that was detached, remote, and ultimately unknowable. He was uninterested in details. He was prone throughout his life to mixing up facts and fuzzy at remembering names.

There is no bright line to define where these characteristics turned into something more serious than the ordinary slippage that comes with getting older. Hutton and the three other doctors who served as Ronnie's White House physician are on record saying that they do not believe Ronnie's mental capacities dropped sharply until after his presidency. "His behavior was so absolutely the same, day after day, his punctuality, his habits, his method of speech, etc. It never gave me any cause for alarm at all," Hutton recounted in an oral history for the University of Virginia's Miller Center. Lawrence K. Altman, a physician who was the leading medical writer for the *New York Times,* heard pretty much the same from Hutton's predecessors. "They saw and spoke with him daily in the White House, they said, and beyond the natural failings of age never found his memory, reasoning, or judgment to be significantly impaired," Altman wrote in 1997.

Biographer Edmund Morris was also adamant that, in his research and observation, he saw no signs that Ronnie suffered cognitive decline while in the White House. "I've read every word of the Reagan diaries," Morris told me in a 2017 interview. He insisted that although Ronnie "became a very old man at the end," the president's sentences continued to be "structurally perfect," and his handwriting remained uniform throughout the eight years in which he recorded near-daily entries in his journals. In Morris's massive biography of Ronnie, he posited that the president's diaries offered "no hint of mental deterioration beyond occasional repetitions and non sequiturs; and if those were suggestive of early dementia, many diarists including myself would have reason to worry."

Much of the conjecture about the disease's onset centers around Ronnie's performance leading up to and during the most serious crisis of his presidency, the Iran-contra scandal. Would the misconduct have been allowed to happen if the president had been more on top of things? Did his fumbling as it unfolded show that he was already losing his faculties? David Abshire, who helped steer the president through the rough waters of Iran-contra, insisted he never saw signs of dementia. Ronnie was confused about names and dates, and his testimony before the Tower Board had been a disaster. But Abshire always felt he had the president's full attention when they spent time together. He wrote: "Of course, I also cannot compare this Ronald Reagan with the younger one who was governor of California or who was president before the assassination attempt early in his first term. But for me the speculation about when Alzheimer's set in has never been a real issue. I never saw him faltering or failing, except in the egregious and stunning case of the second Tower Board hearing. . . . True, there was this horrendous Reagan naiveté on arms-for-hostages deals. He could also compartmentalize out bad news and not face it. However, I reminded myself almost daily that this was a president in his midseventies, recuperating from an operation [for a prostate problem], with a confusing crisis on his hands. Yes, he was depressed. Although the flame burned low, he was a bit frail but still a president in command of himself."

Peter Wallison, who was White House counsel during that stressful period, told me much the same. "I don't think there was any slippage. He was not a detail person. He never was a detail person. He was a person who had principles, and so he structured his policies or insisted on certain policies based on some principles that he thought were important. The details were not something that he needed to know about," Wallison said. "I was only there for a year, from April of '86 to April of '87. I was in many meetings with him, and I never saw any change. Now, maybe from 1981 to 1985, there was a slippage, but when I was there in that year, I never saw anything like that. He was always alert to what people around him were thinking and doing."

However, the president's own son Ron caused a sensation in 2011 when he seemed to imply otherwise. In his book *My Father at 100: A Memoir,* Ron wrote of feeling "shivers of concern" during the first term that "something beyond mellowing was affecting my father." As Ron watched his father stumble through that initial debate with Walter Mondale in 1984, the younger Reagan began to experience what he described as "the nausea of a bad dream coming true." When I pressed him on the subject for this volume, Ron insisted that passage of his book has been blown out of proportion to its significance. "I simply acknowledged the medical reality. My father's own neurologist, Ronald Petersen at the Mayo Clinic, was the man who led the team that discovered that late-onset Alzheimer's develops over at least ten years, maybe twenty years. [It takes] years and years in order to reach the stage where you begin to suffer from dementia," Ron said. "The question of whether he had the disease in its early stages during the presidency more or less answers itself."

But, Ron added, "It is unfair and unwise to judge a presidency based on some ailment that a president might have had. We don't judge Lincoln's presidency by his depression. We don't judge FDR's presidency by his polio, or anything like that. You judge a president by what he has done, what he did, his actions in office. Judge him that way. The fact that the disease was working away in him is all but irrelevant, unless you can point to something where, oh my God, he was clearly out of his mind." Had the president or his doctors had so much of an inkling that something serious was wrong with him, Ron said that he is certain his father would have resigned.

In retrospect, others wondered whether they might have seen but not recognized some early signs. His former aide Nancy Reynolds recalled how out of sorts Ronnie seemed when she sat next to him at his last Christmas dinner in the White House. As she told her fellow Sacramento veteran Curtis Patrick in a collection of remembrances of Ronnie, the man they knew so well wasn't the relaxed and funny host of previous years. "It was in the middle of the Iran-contra scandal. I mean, he wasn't his usual self. You knew it was weighing heavily on him—I *knew* it—I could tell by the flick of an eyebrow," she said. "Now, he made every attempt—and maybe nobody else noticed it; probably the Wicks did, because they know him very well—but he was a *distracted man; very withdrawn. Obviously something was wrong!*

"And I don't know if it had anything to do with Alzheimer's."

There were also small indications that Ronnie himself was worried that he was not as sharp as he used to be. As early as August 1986, he noted in his diary that something had disturbed him as he looked down from his helicopter on the ride from Los Angeles to his ranch: "I watched for landmarks I remembered and was a little upset when I could locate them & then couldn't remember their names—Topanga Canyon, for example." And yet, if he were becoming truly incapacitated, Ronnie would not have had the self-awareness to take note of that small lapse.

"The fact that he's recognizing those things as being aberrations tells you that if it was early Alzheimer's, it was just beginning. It had not advanced, or else he wouldn't be able to even be writing down how bizarre it was that he did those things," noted historian Douglas Brinkley, who edited Ronnie's diaries. Brinkley has his own theory of when the first signs appeared. It is based on his research, which included going through the massive collection of handwritten note cards—a compilation of jokes and anecdotes and the like—that Ronnie kept as fodder for his speeches. The historian noticed "on the later jokes he was collecting, I saw his handwriting trailing off. And I saw some other writings that he had that seemed to be different from the diaries. I think that there's a sea change that occurred around the time he left the White House. It may have been the month before leaving. It's much more noticeable."

For her part, Nancy always believed that Ronnie's decline was precipitated by an incident that happened shortly after he left office. In July 1989, while the Reagans were vacationing in Sonora, Mexico, at the ranch of their good friends Betty and Bill Wilson, Ronnie was thrown from a horse. He hit his head on the ground, knocking him unconscious briefly. Ronnie was taken by helicopter to a hospital in

Tucson, Arizona, but after spending four hours there, he insisted upon returning to the ranch, where preparations were under way for a birthday party for Nancy. "I've always had the feeling that the severe blow to his head in 1989 hastened the onset of Ronnie's Alzheimer's. The doctors think so too," she recalled. But while there are theories that head trauma can have that effect on those who develop Alzheimer's, there is not yet a solid scientific consensus.

A couple of weeks after Ronnie's head injury, Nancy became worried when he lost his balance getting out of bed. She demanded that he see a doctor and get a CT scan. It showed a subdural hematoma, which is an accumulation of blood, on the right side of his brain. The hematoma was deemed minor and did not require treatment at the time. But during his physical at the Mayo Clinic in Rochester, Minnesota, a couple of months after his fall from the horse, doctors took more extensive tests. The hematoma had enlarged and was beginning to exert pressure on his brain. Doctors drilled a hole in his skull to drain it.

As she had been after his colon cancer surgery, Nancy was anxious about how the story would be spun in the media and told spokesman Mark Weinberg that Ronnie had been upset when he heard the procedure described in news reports as "brain surgery." It is unclear, however, whether her concern represented her husband's sensitivities about public perceptions or her own. As the former president and his wife boarded a plane to return home, Ronnie playfully doffed the Minnesota Twins baseball cap he was wearing, so that the reporters and photographers covering their departure could see that the right side of his head had been shaved. Nancy, unamused, tried to shield that portion of his scalp with her hand. "It was like a cobra—zoom—on top of it to cover it up," Hutton recalled.

For all Nancy's vigilance at protecting Ronnie's image and dignity, it would soon become clear, in small ways and bigger ones, that he was losing a step here and there. Joseph Petro, who had spent years by his side as a Secret Service agent, saw the Reagans at a celebration of the ex-president's eightieth birthday at the Beverly Hilton Hotel on February 6, 1991. By then, Petro was head of the detail for Vice

President Dan Quayle, one of more than five hundred guests at the luminary-studded gala to raise money for the Reagan Library. Nancy brought Ronnie over to say hello. "Our eyes catch. Nothing. There was no recognition," Petro recalled. After an awkward moment, Nancy tugged at her husband's sleeve. "Ronnie," she said. "It's Joe."

Onetime national security adviser Richard Allen crossed paths with the former president around that time at the Bohemian Grove, a famed all-male encampment where the powerful gather in Sonoma County, California. It was obvious to Allen that Ronnie did not recognize him, though Allen had been an aide and adviser going back to the mid-1960s. Even worse: he didn't know the ever-faithful Ed Meese or his erstwhile policy director Martin Anderson, both of whom were with Allen. "We walked up to him at the Grove together. He was seated in the chair, and he was startled. I could see he had no idea who we were," Allen said. "He looked up, and it was clear he was having trouble placing us."

Landon Parvin wrote the address that Ronnie gave at the 1992 Republican Convention in Houston, where the party gathered to nominate George H. W. Bush to a second term. The speechwriter began to sense something off-kilter when he noticed the tension in the air around Ronnie. The ex-president's staff hovered. "Everyone was so worried. They seemed more concerned about that speech and him. And around that time, he started relying more on the old stories than he had before," Parvin observed.

The speech came off fine. In fact, Ronnie's address was a grace note to a disaster of a convention remembered mostly for its bitterness. Other speakers such as Pat Buchanan; the vice president's wife, Marilyn Quayle; and Republican Party chairman Rich Bond stoked the flames of generational and cultural divisions. The former president asked the delegates and the country to look back at a version of Republicanism that had aspired to bring Americans together. And in retrospect, it sounded like an elegy. "Whatever else history may say about me when I'm gone, I hope it will record that I appealed to your best hopes, not your worst fears; to your confidence, rather than your doubts," Ronnie said. "My dream is that you will travel the road ahead with liberty's lamp guiding your steps and opportunity's arm steadying your way. My fondest hope for each one of you—and especially for the young people here—is that you will love your country, not for her power or wealth, but for her selflessness and her idealism. May each of you have the heart to conceive, the understanding to direct, and the hand to execute works that will make the world a little better for your having been here."

As he campaigned with Bush in North Carolina, New Mexico, California, and Georgia that fall, Ronnie seemed like his old self. Bill Clinton, the governor of Arkansas, was pulling ahead of Bush in the polls. "You may have noticed that in presidential races, the Democrats prefer to nominate unknown Democratic governors," Ronnie declared in Anaheim, making a sly reference to Carter, whom he had beaten twelve years before. "The reason for this is the Democrats who are known couldn't possibly win." But amid a recession, Ronnie's help wasn't enough to put his former vice president over the top. Bush lost to Clinton by more than 5 points, and leadership of the country was handed to a new generation.

Nancy's own view of the Bushes had not grown any warmer in the first years after the Reagans left the White House and George and Barbara moved in. It didn't help things when, in 1989, Smith College awarded an honorary degree to Barbara Bush, who had dropped out after her freshman year to get married. This was the honor that Smith had pointedly declined to bestow on Nancy, a graduate, when she was first lady. Nancy's appetite for less flattering news about the Bushes is evident in a 1990 fax she received from her friend Leonore Annenberg. The note on the fax, which is in the files at the Reagan Library, said: "Thought you might be interested in reading this." Attached was a clipping from the *Philadelphia Inquirer* lamenting that social life in the nation's capital had gone flat since the Reagans left town. It quoted "DC society watcher" Diana McLellan as saying: "It's as though the Jacuzzi of Washington has been turned off and everyone is sitting around wet, waiting for towels."

A final rupture in Nancy's relationship with Barbara Bush came as the result of a weird episode that played out on live national television on Inauguration Day for Bill Clinton in January 1993. Normally, if former presidents are able, they attend the swearing-in of their successors. The Reagans' absence from the inaugural platform was noted in the coverage on ABC. Barbara Walters, one of the anchors, mentioned there was some confusion as to why. Walters said that Nancy had told her they hadn't been invited, but that a member of Ronnie's staff said an invitation had, in fact, been received. Walters then got a message that Nancy, who was watching, was trying to reach her by phone. Coanchor Peter Jennings got on the line and handed it to Walters, creating a comic scene in which their fellow commentator David Brinkley briefly got tangled in the cord. Though Nancy's voice was not heard on the line, what she said was relayed to viewers by Walters. The former first lady continued to insist that, to her knowledge, the Reagans had not gotten an invitation.

And that wasn't all she wanted to get off her chest. Nancy denied a report that she had not given Barbara Bush a tour of the White House residence during the transition four years earlier—and, in fact, insisted that she had even shown her the laundry. She also complained that the Bushes had never brought her and Ronnie back to the White House for a state dinner. Finally, Brinkley counseled: "Let's leave that where it lies."

Nancy tried to smooth things over in a subsequent phone call to Barbara, but Barbara wasn't having it. Near the end of her life, Barbara still bristled with fury as she related their exchange to biographer Susan Page: "I told her the press was outside my door yelling questions about her statements and that I was not answering, but that she had hurt me badly and I just could not understand it." No reporters were actually there, but Barbara knew that fib would make Nancy nervous. "Don't you ever call me again," Barbara concluded and hung up.

Undeniably, Nancy had done a petty and insensitive thing at the very moment the Bushes were at their lowest. It was a spectacular—and uncharacteristic—lapse of judgment. Her behavior also revived memories of all the slights that Nancy had dealt the Bushes during the eight years of the Reagan presidency.

But it is also possible—indeed, likely—that stress and anxiety about her husband were a factor in Nancy's peculiar behavior. Only a week before the inauguration, as unmarked moving vans were loading up in front of the White House, Bush had honored Ronnie by presenting him the Presidential Medal of Freedom, the nation's highest civilian award. As one of his final acts in office, Bush gave an emotional tribute to the man he had served so loyally for eight years: "Ronald Reagan didn't just make the world believe in America. He made Americans believe in themselves. . . . Some men reflect their times. Ronald Reagan changed his time."

Ronnie's voice sounded a little weak as he accepted the honor. His step was a little slower. His suit hung loosely on a thinner frame. Richard Allen was there and noticed the former president standing alone with his medal after the ceremony, so he went over to talk to him. Allen reminded Ronnie of a funny story about a trip they had taken together to Germany in the 1970s. It was a tale they had laughed about many times over the years. This time it didn't seem to register with Ronnie. Allen recalled later: "I knew he was always bad on names. Now, I thought, he's bad on memory. But it didn't cross my mind . . ."

The following month, at a February 1993 birthday celebration for Ronnie at the Reagan Library, there came a more obvious and public lapse. It was another event where Margaret Thatcher was on hand. Reading from his index cards, Ronnie gave the same toast to her twice, word for word. The five-hundred-plus guests at the fund-raising gala were unsettled and awkwardly gave him two standing ovations. One factor may have been that Ronnie, uncharacteristically, had three glasses of wine before he delivered his tribute to Thatcher, the woman he called his political "soul mate."

This was a full year before the subsequent year's birthday event in Washington, where Hutton and the others became alarmed at the former president's disorientation. By that point in 1994, most everyone agreed, Ronnie's condition was becoming increasingly evident and harder to explain away. At Richard Nixon's funeral in April, White House photographers who hadn't seen Ronnie in a while were shocked at his appearance. Nancy, a picture of worry, guided her husband by the arm to his seat. Not only had Ronnie's hair gone gray, but he had a vacant look on his face. He listened to the eulogies with his mouth slightly agape. George Bush was concerned and told people he recognized what he feared was dementia. Bill and Hillary Clinton noticed how Nancy had to keep gently coaching her husband: "Ronnie, you remember so-and-so . . ."

His longtime political adviser Stu Spencer also saw odd things in the months before Ronnie made the announcement he had Alzheimer's. That summer, the two of them were playing golf at the Los Angeles Country Club, something they often did. Spencer was driving the cart, with Ronnie sitting on the seat beside him: "We're out there a few holes, and I kind of looked over at him, and he was staring at me. He had that look on his face. Blank look. Like: 'Who's this guy?' Me! I mean, I sensed it. I read it. I'm pretty good at reading body language. I thought, 'Uh-oh.'" But two holes later, Ronnie was bantering with Spencer as he always had. At another point, Spencer visited the ex-president in his Century City office. The same thing happened. For a moment, Ronnie didn't seem to know who Spencer was. Then he was fine.

When it happened the second time, Spencer called Nancy. She told him she had scheduled a visit to the Mayo Clinic. "The local doctors think he has Alzheimer's, and we're going to have it checked," Nancy said. After Ronnie's 1989 surgery, doctors at Mayo began adding tests of mental acuity to Ronnie's annual physical. He would be asked to read a paragraph and answer questions about it, and to do mathematical calculations. He passed the test with flying colors in 1992. But in 1993 the physicians began to see a deterioration. Ronnie noticed it too. "You know, I had to read the question, read the paragraph, read the question, and then go back and search for the answer. I don't think I finished the whole exam," he said.

When Ronnie had his two-day physical the following year, it was worse. There was still a possibility that this was a hormonal problem, or maybe a brain tumor, so the Mayo team sent a physician to Los Angeles to observe him. The official diagnosis came in August. "My mother made the difficult, but, in retrospect, I believe, wise and kind decision to put off telling him until it could no longer be avoided," Ron wrote later. "Knowing her husband as she did, she correctly intuited that such a diagnosis—a terminal illness with no hope of cure—once acknowledged might send him spiraling into a deep depression, jeopardizing any chance he had for a few relatively good years before darkness descended."

But finally, there could be no denying it any longer. The truth was becoming apparent, and Nancy got wind that media outlets were preparing stories about his decline. On the first Saturday of November, Ronnie, Nancy, and Fred Ryan met in the library of the Reagan home in Bel Air with one of the former president's doctors. They discussed what lay ahead. Ronnie decided on the spot that he had to make a public announcement. He recalled the letters he had received after his operation for colon cancer from strangers who said they had decided to get checkups that had saved their lives. Ronnie also remembered how many women had gone for mammograms after Nancy's mastectomy. Maybe by sharing this, they could help others who were heading down this long, ineluctable path with a loved one. Maybe he could put a face to this disease and bring it out of the shadows.

Ronnie picked up a few pieces of stationery and went to a small table by the window in his library, where he sat down and wrote a letter to the country:

Nov. 5, 1994

My Fellow Americans,

I have recently been told that I am one of the millions of Americans who will be afflicted with Alzheimer's disease.

Upon learning this news, Nancy and I had to decide whether as private citizens we would keep this a private matter or whether we would make this news known in a public way.

In the past Nancy suffered from breast cancer and I had my cancer surgeries. We found through our open disclosures we were able to raise public awareness. We were happy that as a result many more people underwent testing.

> They were treated in early stages and able to return to normal, healthy lives.
>
> So now, we feel it is important to share it with you. In opening our hearts, we hope this might promote greater awareness of this condition. Perhaps it will encourage a clearer understanding of the individuals and families who are affected by it.
>
> At the moment I feel just fine. I intend to live the remainder of the years God gives me on this earth doing the things I have always done. I will continue to share life's journey with my beloved Nancy and my family. I plan to enjoy the great outdoors and stay in touch with my friends and supporters.
>
> Unfortunately, as Alzheimer's disease progresses, the family often bears a heavy burden. I only wish there was some way I could spare Nancy from this painful experience. When the time comes, I am confident that with your help she will face it with faith and courage.
>
> In closing let me thank you, the American people for giving me the great honor of allowing me to serve as your President. When the Lord calls me home, whenever that may be, I will leave with the greatest love for this country of ours and eternal optimism for its future.
>
> I now begin the journey that will lead me into the sunset of my life. I know that for America there will always be a bright dawn ahead.
>
> Thank you, my friends. May God always bless you.
>
> Sincerely,
>
> Ronald Reagan

He gave it to Nancy to read. Her eyes filled with tears. She nodded silently. Then he handed it to Ryan and asked to have it typed and released. Ryan said no, that Americans should see this in Ronnie's own handwriting. It was the right choice—the irrefutable evidence that the grace and strength of his character remained, even as disease was eating away at his memory.

Nancy was the one who informed the Reagan children. She told her son, Ron, of the diagnosis by telephone. "It was no surprise," he said.

Maureen and her husband, Dennis Revell, were expected for lunch the day Ronnie wrote his letter to the country. They were in the process of adopting a daughter, Rita, whom Maureen and Dennis had met in a Ugandan orphanage when she was three and were bringing her as well to visit. Nancy called Maureen and asked if they could come by a little early. When they arrived, Nancy said to Ronnie: "Sweetheart, why don't you take Rita down by the pool?" Helping his granddaughter master her swimming skills was one of the old lifeguard's favorite things to do.

Nancy showed Maureen and her husband the letter. "Then she explained what the doctors had found, and the letter, and said it would be released shortly, and we talked about it. He walked back in, and we resumed normal conversation," Revell said. And that was it. Ronnie left for the ranch at two o'clock, as he had intended to do earlier. Rancho del Cielo is where Rawhide would be when the world heard the news.

*

So began the final chapter of their love story. What Nancy would call "the long good-bye" was also a deepening twilight, one without the prospect of a dawn. Soon, birthdays and anniversaries, which used to bring long, sentimental letters from Ronnie, would go by as if they were no different from any other day. "They were very short—the golden years," Nancy said later. "The golden years are when you can sit back, hopefully, and exchange memories. And that's the worst part about this disease. There's nobody to exchange memories with, and we had a lot of memories.

". . . When you come right down to it, you're in it alone, and there's nothing that anybody can do for you, so it's lonely."

Even her harshest critics would acknowledge the grace and determination she would show when her devotion was put to its greatest test. In seeing Nancy's strength, the nation would gain a new appreciation of her character. Never again would anyone doubt that the adoring gaze she had fixed on her Ronnie for all those years was anything but genuine. She would become one of the most admired women in the country.

Ronnie had intended to continue "doing the things I have always done" for as long as he could. For a few years, he would go to the office most days and receive visitors—though sometimes he seemed unclear as to who they were. Dressed impeccably as always, he would show his mementoes; the photos of himself with the pope and Thatcher. "He had this little routine; those synapses seemed to be still preserved for doing that. Some people would say, 'He's fine,'" Hutton recalled. A couple of afternoons a week, the doctor took Ronnie to a driving range, where he hit golf balls. He took walks with a caregiver and his Secret Service agents and enjoyed watching neighborhood children play in a nearby park. People sometimes spotted the former president strolling with Nancy along the Venice Beach boardwalk, savoring an ice cream cone. When he was recognized, as he inevitably was, Ronnie was still capable of a pleasant greeting.

But doing anything more ambitious in public was no longer possible, in part because of the interest his condition drew. That became clear soon after his letter was published. "The next time he had a public appearance, the press was all over him," Ryan said. "He realized that from then on, the story was going to be him and not whatever group he was out there for. So he began to pull back." When Ronnie did go out, his aides made sure there was no announcement in advance, so that the media and its cameras would not be waiting for him.

In 1995 Ryan moved back to Washington to become a top executive of the television and cable company Albritton Communications. He was also named chairman of the board of the Reagan Foundation, which kept him close at hand for Nancy. The fiercely loyal Joanne Drake, whom Nancy grew to trust as she did few others, took over as chief of staff.

Nancy made some appearances in Ronnie's stead. She was invited to speak at the 1996 Republican convention and accepted reluctantly. The former first lady was unhappy with the dark turn the party had taken in the mid-1990s and worried its San Diego convention would be a reprise of the venomous one that had taken place four years earlier in Houston. "Maybe if Colin Powell runs . . ." she told Patti.

Her speech turned out to be the emotional high point of the convention, which nominated Bob Dole, the former Kansas senator, as the party standard-bearer. Delegates roared as she appeared on the stage, a tiny figure dressed in white, tears glistening in her eyes. Nancy did not mention Dole or the incumbent president, Bill Clinton. She did not make any reference to the roiling politics of the day. "I am not the speech maker in the family, so let me close with Ronnie's words and not mine," Nancy said. "In that last speech four years ago, he said: 'Whatever else history may say about me, when I am gone, I hope it will record that I appealed to your best hopes, not your worst fears; to your confidence, rather than your doubts. And may all of you, as Americans, never forget your heroic origins.'"

She was still allowing a few people outside the family and their closest circle to see Ronnie. Ken Khachigian brought GOP nominee Dole by. Ronnie looked good, but "he just wasn't there," Khachigian recalled. Nancy carried the conversation, as her husband sat silently. When news stories began appearing in which visitors described the president's state, she grew more protective. In the late 1990s, Tennessee senator Bill Frist, a rising star in GOP politics who would later become Senate majority leader, happened to be in Los Angeles and asked Ronnie's former aide Jim Kuhn to arrange an introduction to the president who had done so much to shape the modern Republican Party. Five minutes would be enough, he told Kuhn: "I just want to shake his hand." Kuhn thought that Nancy might be willing to allow Frist to see Ronnie, given that he had a medical background as a surgeon. She refused.

A few rays of solace penetrated the darkness of her grief. One was that Patti, who had been estranged from the rest of the family for nine years and was living in New York, reappeared. A couple of weeks after Ronnie's announcement of his diagnosis, Patti had taken the first steps on a road to reconciliation with her mother by apologizing for "the pain that I have caused." Though their relationship would still have its ups and downs, shared pain broke down some of the barriers that had stood between them for so long. There were moments when

Nancy leaned on her daughter for comfort. "I don't know how to be alone," Nancy told Patti. "I've never been alone." Within two years, Patti would move back to Los Angeles, to be closer to her parents, to be there for her mother when her father no longer was.

Another blessing amid the grief was Diane Capps, a loyal and discreet retired military officer who had been a nurse in the White House. After Ronnie was diagnosed, Nancy contacted Capps in Winston-Salem, North Carolina, where she had moved, and asked her to come out to California. Capps became not only a caregiver to Ronnie in the early years of his illness but also a source of support for Nancy, helping her to accept the inevitable. "Diane helped her understand that there would be good days and bad days, and, with time, there would be fewer good days and more bad days, and eventually all bad days," Ryan said.

Capps also counseled Nancy to accept Ronnie's version of reality, whatever it happened to be at the moment. Nancy's friend Robert Higdon recalled the nurse telling the former first lady: "If he says he wants to go out and play baseball, you say, 'Have a nice game.'" As Nancy would describe it later, living with someone who has Alzheimer's was "a crash course in patience."

While she offered a face of stoicism to the world, sadness and stress were taking a toll on Nancy. On April 7, 1995, she met Ronnie's biographer Edmund Morris for a two-and-a-half-hour lunch at the Hotel Bel-Air. Things were tense between the two of them. Nancy was frustrated that, after nearly a decade, Morris had yet to produce his much-anticipated masterwork on Ronnie. The biographer, meanwhile, found Nancy a difficult subject to interview; evasive when he tried to pin her down on such basic details as when she and Ronnie first discussed the possibility that he might be president one day. That afternoon, Morris claims, Nancy's behavior took a bizarre turn. The biographer, who died in 2019, described what happened in an interview I did with him in August 2017. He also provided an entry that he made in his diary about that day.

It began: "I had lunch with Nancy Reagan at the Bel-Air. She is feeling very sorry for herself, having undergone surgery for sunspots two days ago. As she checks herself in her hand mirror, I contemplate, close up, the delayed ruin which is the lot of all face-lifters; crushed nose, parchment pouches, staring eyes. She sits back in despair, puts a heavy jeweled pillbox on the tablecloth, and extracts a blue pill the size of a wren's egg. 'Halcyon,' [*sic*] she says, gulping it down."

Halcion, as it is properly spelled, was the brand name for triazolam, a powerful prescription sedative used to treat anxiety and insomnia. It was already becoming notorious at that time for allegedly causing irrational and violent behavior. In 1991 it was banned in Britain. Morris wrote that a while after Nancy took the pill, her mood changed suddenly. She told him: "They're talking about me over there."

"Who? Where?" Morris asked.

Nancy only grew more agitated, he wrote: "She arches her eyebrows across the room to where two young women are having an animated conversation, paying not the least attention to us. 'I heard them say White House.' 'Well, so what? It's natural they would have recognized you and said something. They're obviously onto another subject now.' But she cannot take her eyes off them, and strains to hear some more of their chat, ignoring me. After awhile, I become irritated. 'Look, Nancy, I've got a book in my briefcase; why don't I just do some reading while you listen in?' She laughs mirthlessly, a little stitch-scar showing on her upper lip."

As they were preparing to leave the restaurant, Nancy demanded that the maitre d' and receptionist tell her the identity of the two women and grew furious when she was told the restaurant had not gotten their names. Morris's journal indicates he tried to defuse the situation with a joke: "Face it, Nancy, they're KGB—we'll never find out their true identity."

From the concerned but unsurprised demeanor of her Secret Service agents, the biographer surmised that this was not the first time something like that had happened. "We all began to realize she was going into some kind of paranoid frenzy," he said. "The Secret Service and I literally escorted her out." In his diary, Morris wrote: "My hearing is pretty acute, but hers would appear to be preternatural.

That is, if what she heard was real and not delusory. The imagined sound of distant voices, the paranoia, the big pill, the blue fingers, the expressionless face—she's off on a solo cruise."

All of this happened less than six months after Ronnie's diagnosis was announced to the country. It is easy to imagine how helpless and adrift Nancy must have felt. She had to let go of her own wishful thinking that there might be some answer—some treatment, some way to keep Ronnie engaged. Early on, she told Robert Higdon: "This isn't going to take my husband." But as his deterioration accelerated on a series of downward plateaus, she could no longer hang on to her denial. Once, when Ronnie and Nancy were watching a football game on television, he got up and started rummaging around the room. "I'm trying to find my football gear," he told her. "The coach is waiting for me." Nancy decided he would watch no more games.

In the beginning, the family hoped—and wanted to believe—that his ranch could be a respite where he might spend many of his remaining days. Then John Barletta, a loyal Secret Service agent who was his longtime riding companion, began to notice that even the most familiar activities were becoming difficult for the former president—things as simple as cinching the girth strap on his saddle. "From the time that started happening, I would have my horse already saddled when he came up, so I could watch him tack up his horse," Barletta wrote later. "Often he would put something in his hand and then hesitate. That would tell me he was having trouble. I would just take his hand and move it to the right position. A big smile would come over his face. 'That's what I was trying to do.'"

But Barletta became alarmed one morning when Ronnie was unable to control his favorite horse, a headstrong Arabian stallion named El Alamein, which had been a gift from Mexican president José López Portillo for Ronnie's inauguration in 1981. Barletta went to Nancy and said, "Mrs. Reagan, he's making too many mistakes up there. I can't protect him from himself. He's making rookie mistakes, and he's been riding fifty-five years. A new rider wouldn't make these mistakes. I don't think he should ride anymore. It's getting that dangerous."

"Then you have to tell him, John," she said.

"I don't want to tell him that, Mrs. Reagan," Barletta pleaded. "You need to tell him that."

"No," she said, tears filling her eyes. "I can't."

After lunch that day, Nancy summoned Barletta and told him it was time to break the news to Ronnie. Barletta found him sitting by the fireplace, reading a book. "This riding isn't working out. Sir, I don't think you should ride anymore," Barletta said. The agent felt crushed by sadness. It was like telling someone they couldn't breathe anymore. Ronnie got up and put his hands on Barletta's shoulders. "It's okay, John," he said. "I know." And that was it. Ronnie later gave Barletta a pair of his three-buckle brown field boots and his saddle.

Not long after came the point where Ronnie no longer recognized the mountaintop spread he had loved for so long. Open spaces made him terrified and disoriented. On one midweek visit to the ranch, when Nancy had stayed back in Los Angeles, his Secret Service agents called her to say that Ronnie had gone into such a panic that they were bringing him home early. "And so, the lure of that being his place to go and live out the rest of his life evaporated," his son-in-law Dennis Revell said. "It was never Nancy's place of choice. She went there and enjoyed it because of him."

Ronnie's last visit to the ranch was in August 1995. The following summer, Nancy made the wrenching decision to quietly put Rancho del Cielo up for sale. She listed it with Sotheby's International Realty, with an asking price of $5.95 million. Patti protested, saying no one else should ever have a place so suffused with her father. "I'll do what I have to do," Nancy replied, ending the discussion.

"I know that her answer went beyond finances. It had to do with memories—of days that are painful to revisit because they rolled by so smoothly, with a peaceful laziness that awaits anyone lucky enough to escape the city and retreat into the hills," Patti wrote. "The ranch was where my father went to restore himself, and my mother settled into the long stretch of days, content to simply be with him and let the hours float by. Now those days are far behind her, out of reach. I watched her when we went to the ranch together recently. I saw how her eyes rested on the lake, the hills, but only for a moment. Then something in her races away from her recollections. At the end of the day, she couldn't wait to leave, as if the land itself were haunted."

Patti finally realized the source of her own feelings about selling the ranch: "Losing my father and losing the ranch have become part of the same sorrow; it's as if I will be losing him twice. And understanding my mother's motives makes it more difficult, because no one's right, and no one's wrong. It's as if something inside me is crying out, You can't sell the ranch—he's everywhere on it. And she is responding by crying out, That's why I have to." Later, after it was sold, Nancy told her daughter that memories of the ranch kept coming back to her in her dreams at night: "The weekends we used to spend there—riding, sitting by the fireplace—the way it was before, when we were normal."

The ranch languished on the market. An effort to turn it into a national park went nowhere, as did one to make it a state historical site. In 1998 Nancy accepted an offer far below her asking price from the Young America's Foundation, previously known as Young Americans for Freedom, a group promoting conservative values on college campuses. That was a decision Nancy came to regret, according to family members and several confidants I spoke to. "She was, to my mind, in a bit too much of a hurry and could have gotten a lot more money than she did for the ranch, particularly given its provenance. But she kind of snapped up the first offer," Ron said. More worrisome, it turned out, was how the organization exploited its ownership of Ronnie's favorite place in the world to market itself. "She was very, very concerned about them," said Fred Ryan.

One of Nancy's advisers claimed the Young America's Foundation "manipulated her" by telling her it would be careful and tasteful in how it managed the site. "They started using it—and Reagan's name—as a fund-raising vehicle. She was furious about how they were using it," the adviser said. The Reagan Foundation, to which both Ronnie and Nancy had given the legal rights to their names and likenesses, suddenly found itself facing competition with the Young America's Foundation as the group raised money for its own programs. "We came very, very close to a lawsuit and were sending a lot of these cease-and-desist letters," the source close to Nancy added. It further annoyed her that some of the conservatives who had been kicked off the library board had begun making the ranch, under its new ownership, a sort of ideological base camp.

Nancy's concerns about personal finances deepened. Given her own history of breast cancer, she knew there was a very real possibility that her husband would outlive her. Though her lawyers and other advisers told her over and over that she and Ronnie had plenty of money to see them through, Nancy worried that there might not be the resources to ensure that he could be properly taken care of if she were not around. She wanted to be certain not only that his physical needs were met but also that his dignity and privacy were respected. She knew that would be expensive.

"My mother would be anxious about their financial situation on a more or less constant basis," Ron said. "She was in a state of kind of controlled panic for quite some time when he really, really became ill. And the idea of money going out the door for nurses and all the rest was pretty frightening to her." This led to tension—and worse—with the Reagan children. As bills for Ronnie's care mounted, Nancy backed out of an arrangement under which she had promised to give them and their spouses each $20,000 a year, as a sort of advance on their inheritances. Ron, living in Seattle and facing financial pressures of his own, became so angry with his mother that one year he returned his Christmas presents from her unopened.

Ronnie and Nancy had revised their wills several times after he left office. Most of what they left behind was to go to the Reagan library and foundation, Eureka College, and other causes that were important to them. Each of the children would receive a relatively modest bequest—$100,000, according to several sources I talked to who were familiar with the terms. Each grandchild would receive a smaller amount.

Nancy tried to assist her children in other ways—for instance, by prodding her powerful friends to help them find work that offered steady pay and benefits. "She would, in fact, make calls and things. She was not a big one for filling up your refrigerator or buying you furniture or something like that. But she'd pick up the phone and try and get somebody else to do it," Ron recalled.

"She was great friends with Merv Griffin. He produced a lot of game shows and things. And he, at one point, offered me—I was working in television, and he offered me a game show," Ron added. "It didn't take me two minutes to say, 'No. Thank you very much, but I'm not a game-show host. I just don't see myself that way.'" Ron assumed that Griffin had made the offer at his mother's behest. James Baker also recalled getting an appeal from Nancy, who was worried that her son might not have health insurance. "I said, 'Well, Nancy, he needs to get a job,'" Baker told me. Ron denied that he ever went without medical coverage, which he said he received through his membership in the screen actors union, but acknowledged he did get career advice from Baker.

Nancy also became fearful that one or more of the surviving children might sue the estate—or one another—after she and Ronnie were dead. So, she offered them a financial incentive: she would double their inheritance to $200,000 if they all signed a pledge not to contest the terms of their parents' wills. Ron told me that he was offended his mother would even ask such a thing. It implied she didn't trust him or that she believed he was after her money. "I don't even remember the details of it, but I reacted badly to that," he recalled. He refused to sign, as did Michael.

According to Ron's version of events, Nancy told her son that "really it had more to do with Mike than anybody else. They were worried that Mike was going to sue the estate, which indeed turned out to be a well-founded concern." Ron declined to provide further details, saying he was bound by a nondisclosure agreement. However, several other sources familiar with the Reagans' estate said that Michael did threaten legal action at least twice, after his father's death in 2004 and Nancy's in 2016. The terms of the will were renegotiated, giving him a greater share than he would have received otherwise.

Toward the end of Ronnie's life, Nancy's relationship with Michael, always fraught, deteriorated to its lowest point. A confidant confirmed: "Michael was, at least in her eyes, getting really out of hand and a bit of a wild card. They didn't know what he would do." Nancy believed Ronnie's older son was exploiting the reverence that conservatives felt for his father in order to burnish his own image and career as a radio talk-show host and commentator. Michael visited Ronnie infrequently, usually appearing right before he was scheduled to do an interview with a radio or television outlet. One of Nancy's close associates recalls that in the versions Michael would recount of those meetings, he would claim that Ronnie had walked him to the door and waved until he was out of sight. In fact, by that point, the former president was not able to leave his bed.

Things between Michael and Nancy eventually became so bitter that she feared being alone with him. The Secret Service stationed an agent nearby when he visited to keep an eye on how he behaved, according to more than a half dozen people that I talked to on and off the record. One of those who confirmed this was his half brother, Ron: "The Secret Service were concerned enough about Mike that after an incident where he sort of loomed over my mother, who was frail at the time, and screamed at her that we'd all be better off if she just died, or was dead—something to that effect—the Secret Service would no longer leave him alone in the house with her. They would always put somebody outside the door on the rare occasions when he visited." Robert Higdon told me the episode happened a few years before Ronnie died. "It was so bad that the Secret Service came into the house," he said.

Nancy appeared less and less often in public. In March 2001 she traveled to Norfolk, Virginia, to christen the USS *Ronald Reagan,* a nuclear-powered aircraft carrier. But otherwise, she got out only occasionally and briefly, usually to meet friends for lunch at the Hotel Bel-Air. Two of her favorite companions were network anchorman Tom Brokaw and actor Warren Beatty, who would take her out together. "Warren and I treasured those lunches because she always arrived with astute political observations and the best gossip from both coasts," Brokaw said.

What Nancy never offered were any details about what was going on at home. When asked, she would simply say that there were good days and bad days. Eventually her closest pals learned not to inquire. The truth was, even the best days were getting pretty bad. Ronnie was heading farther and farther down a road where she could not follow. Sometimes, she still caught herself asking him: "Honey, you remember when—"

Doctor Hutton recalled one particularly poignant moment when he was visiting. Nancy turned the old romantic song "Unforgettable" on the stereo system that played on speakers throughout the house, and held her arms up to her husband, beckoning him to dance. It was a scene that Hutton had witnessed many times in the past. In the old days, the Reagans would fall together and cling to each other as they moved as one to the music. But this time, Ronnie brushed her away. There were other ordinary pleasures that Nancy could no longer share with him. When the two of them used to watch the game show *Wheel of Fortune* after dinner in the library of their home, Nancy would cuddle with Ronnie, and they would kiss. The last time Hutton had seen her try to do that, "he obviously didn't understand at all what she was doing. It was kind of sad. She would tear [up] and just get up and go off to her room."

In 1999 she shared a bit of what her life was like as she gave a televised tour of the Reagan Library to Brian Lamb, the founder of the cable network C-Span. Lamb, a gentle but persistent questioner, asked Nancy what she had learned about Alzheimer's over the past five years.

"It is probably the worst disease you could ever have," she said, sounding as though she was trying not to cry.

"Can you have a conversation that makes sense to you with the president?" Lamb asked.

"Not now," Nancy answered. Her voice dropped to a whisper: "No."

Lamb pressed her: "How have you dealt with it when people come to visit and he doesn't recognize them?"

"Well, now we don't have visitors," Nancy replied. "We never let that happen."

In January 2001, less than a month before his ninetieth birthday, Ronnie slipped at home and broke his right hip. As he recuperated from surgery at St. John's Health Center in Santa Monica, he was beyond knowing that his daughter Maureen was in the same hospital. For weeks, sixty-year-old Mermie had been at the hospital's John Wayne Cancer Institute, undergoing aggressive chemotherapy against a deadly and spreading melanoma. Nancy, Maureen's siblings, and her husband, Dennis Revell, shuttled back and forth between the two rooms. On January 20 Ronnie and Nancy watched television together in his hospital room as George W. Bush was inaugurated the nation's forty-third president. Ronnie was discharged later that day.

Maureen would not be released from the hospital until March. Despite the treatment, cancer continued its rampage through her bones and into her brain. Ronnie's fierce, passionate, big-hearted daughter suffered a seizure over the Fourth of July holiday and died on August 8. Her maple casket, decked with a spray of pink roses and white mums, was carried into Sacramento's 112-year-old Cathedral of the Blessed Sacrament by Secret Service agents who were veterans of the Reagan detail. Her mother, Jane, and her stepmother, Nancy, sat together in a pew. The two octogenarians—tiny and elegantly dressed—looked so alike they could have been sisters. Jane, balancing on a cane, laid a cross on the coffin; Nancy placed the book of Gospels on it. Michael, Ron, and Patti offered prayers for their sister. All of which made Ronnie's absence feel even more painful.

*

The disease that was robbing her of Ronnie inspired Nancy, ever the doctor's daughter, to take up a new and controversial cause: embryonic stem-cell research. Not because it would help him—it was too late for that—but in hopes that other families might one day be spared the ordeal of Alzheimer's. Film producer Doug Wick, her longtime family friend, sparked Nancy's interest in the possibility that the burgeoning field of stem-cell research might hold a cure, not only for Alzheimer's but also for other diseases. Wick's own daughter Tessa had been diagnosed with juvenile diabetes when she was eight years old.

Wick began inviting her over to lunches at his house with scientists who were working in the field. Nancy was particularly taken with Hans Keirstead, a movie-star-handsome entrepreneur and leader in stem-cell research. Nancy grilled him for more than two hours, Wick recalled. "The depth of her questions, the understanding and the reading she was doing was so substantial by any measure." Wick also couldn't help but notice Nancy was flirting: "She loved men, and she was really cute and charming."

Quietly, Nancy began opening doors for Wick in Washington. She helped arrange for him to meet with key figures such as Arizona senator John McCain and Utah's Orrin Hatch, a leader on health issues. She kept asking: "Who else should I call?" But this was a tricky endeavor for a high-profile Republican, given that the most promising stem-cell treatments involved the destruction of human embryos. So, at first, Nancy did her advocacy strictly behind the scenes. As George W. Bush deliberated over banning all federal funding of embryonic stem-cell research, she wrote him a letter. Dated April 11, 2001, it read:

> Dear Mr. President,
>
> As you know, Ronnie recently celebrated his ninetieth birthday. In earlier times, we would have been able to share our mutual pride in a life filled with wonderful memories. Now, while I can draw strength from these memories, I do it alone as Ronnie struggles in a world unknown to me or the scientists who devote their lives to Alzheimer's research. Because of this, I am determined to do what I can to save others from this pain and anguish. I'm writing, therefore, to ask your help in supporting what appears to be the most promising path to a cure—stem cell research.
>
> I also know that this is not the first you have heard of this issue. And I know there are others who feel just as strongly in opposition to this. But I ask your help to ensure that this embryonic stem cell

research, under appropriate guidelines, be protected as scientists pursue medical miracle possibilities.

Ronnie was very brave in writing to the public about his condition. It was his way of sharing with the thousands of families who are already afflicted. He always believed in man's ability to make this a better world and I know he would be gratified to know that his own suffering might spare others the same wrenching family journey.

Mr. President, I have some personal experience regarding the many decisions you face each day. I do not want to add to that burden, but I'd be very grateful if you would take my thoughts and prayers into your consideration on this critical issue.

Most sincerely,

Nancy Reagan

Bush did not respond for three weeks, Wick said, which wounded Nancy. But the letter, which had also been sent to congressional leadership, was soon circulating on Capitol Hill and among the press. Her appeal did not bring the outcome she desired. Bush put tight restrictions on stem-cell research. Nonetheless, she continued to work the phones, while maintaining a public silence.

Nancy operated stealthily in part because she liked the younger Bush, with whom she shared a July 6 birthday, and he was fond of her as well. When he was still the governor of Texas, George W. Bush chose the Reagan Library as the place to deliver his first major foreign-policy speech as a presidential candidate. He began by paying tribute to Ronnie: "We live in the nation President Reagan restored, and the world he helped to save. A world of nations reunited and tyrants humbled. A world of prisoners released and exiles come home. And today there is a prayer shared by free people everywhere: God bless you, Ronald Reagan." In 2002 Bush awarded Nancy the Presidential Medal of Freedom and invited her to stay at the White House. It was the first time she had slept there since she and Ronnie left in January 1989.

But the politics around stem-cell research remained heated after Bush's restrictive order. There were mounting calls, even within his own party, for the president to loosen the curtailment of government funding. In 2003 Senator Hatch—as staunch a conservative as could be found on Capitol Hill—introduced a bill that would permit scientists to clone embryos and then destroy them to extract their stem cells. He used a supportive letter from Nancy as part of his argument. Some Republicans were outraged. Mike Deaver got a call from one member of Congress, who shouted, "Reagan would never have approved of stem-cell research!" Deaver replied: "Ronald Reagan didn't have to take care of Ronald Reagan for the last ten years."

As debate intensified, Bush threatened to veto the bill, which he ultimately did. Nancy realized that she had to speak up. The opportunity came on May 9, 2004, when actor Michael J. Fox, who had gone public five years before with his diagnosis of Parkinson's disease and was a leading advocate for stem-cell research, presented her an award at a fund-raising dinner for the Juvenile Diabetes Research Foundation.

"Ronnie's long journey has finally taken him to a distant place where I can no longer reach him. Because of this, I'm determined to do whatever I can to save other families from this pain. I just don't see how we can turn our backs on this," she said. "Science has presented us with a hope called stem-cell research, which may provide our scientists with many answers that for so long have been beyond our grasp.

"We have lost so much time already. I just really can't bear to lose anymore."

*

One thing that might have finally emboldened Nancy to make her voice heard was realizing how little time Ronnie had left. Though his mind had left him, the body of which he had been so proud refused to give up. At ninety-three, he was only the third US president to make it into his tenth decade. He outlived by nearly three years his longest-surviving predecessor, John Adams. It was a longevity record he would not hold for long, as Gerald Ford, George H. W. Bush, and Jimmy Carter would all remain alive past that age.

Death finally took Ronnie on June 5, 2004, a Saturday, when the jacaranda trees were showering the ground with their purple blooms. In the days before, Nancy summoned the family and notified their closest friends that Ronnie's time was near. There were also arrangements that had to be set in motion. The previous Monday, she had telephoned Robert Higdon. It was Memorial Day, and her call caught Higdon as he and his partner were driving to see the newly opened World War II memorial on the National Mall.

"The doctors were just here," Nancy told Higdon. "And I think you need to get ready."

"When?" he asked.

"By the end of the week," Nancy said.

Higdon and Fred Ryan were to be in charge of the funeral logistics. The two of them and former advance man Rick Ahearn quietly set up a command center at the Mayflower Hotel in downtown DC. They contacted Washington National Cathedral and stayed up all night Thursday putting together the politically and diplomatically sensitive list of 3,700 people to be invited and deciding where each person should be seated in the cathedral. Nancy air-shipped Higdon a pair of Ronnie's brown leather riding boots, which were to be placed backward in the stirrups of a riderless horse that would follow the caisson carrying his casket to the Capitol, where Ronnie's body was to lie in state.

On that Saturday morning, Ronnie's breath was so shallow it was barely perceptible. His eyes had not opened for days. And then, just a bit after one o'clock in the afternoon, they did. "He opens his eyes—both eyes—wide. They are focused and blue. They haven't been blue like that in more than a year, but they are now," Patti wrote. "My father looks straight at my mother, holds onto the sign of her face for a moment or two, and then gently closes his eyes and stops breathing."

The room was silent, except for the sound of Nancy weeping softly. "That's the greatest gift you could have given me," she whispered.

As word of Ronnie's death shot around the world, Nancy and the family sat with his body for four hours. They could hear the sound of helicopters circling over the house. "A great American life has come to an end," George W. Bush announced at the White House, blinking back tears. "Ronald Reagan won America's respect with his greatness and won its love with his goodness. He had the confidence that comes with conviction, the strength that comes with character, the grace that comes with humility, and the humor that comes with wisdom. He leaves behind a nation he restored and a world he helped save." Massachusetts senator John F. Kerry, the Democratic nominee for president, noted the late president's gift for "goodwill in the heat of the partisan battle" and declared: "Ronald Reagan's love of country was infectious."

Presidents are required to begin planning their funerals while they are still in office. There had been many meetings to discuss this one in the years during and after Ronnie's presidency. Decisions had to be made: Would he lie in state? Would there be a Washington ceremony as well as one in California? What military bands would play? What Scriptures would be read and which hymns would be sung? While he was still healthy, Ronnie had to attend these sessions, but this "was an area he had no interest in," Fred Ryan said.

The plans also kept having to be updated. Ronnie outlived some of the clergymen who initially had been expected to lead his services. In the end, Nancy settled on former senator John C. Danforth, an Episcopal priest who was not particularly close to the Reagans. There were other adjustments that had to be made. Margaret Thatcher traveled for years with a black suit in her luggage, so she could be at the ready to come to Washington and offer her last tribute to Ronnie at his funeral. But Thatcher's own health had deteriorated from a set of strokes, and she worried that she would no longer be up to it. So, while Thatcher planned to be present for the service, she had videotaped her eulogy the previous March. Cathedral officials initially objected to including Thatcher's videotape as part of the service. "You tell them this is how I want it done," Nancy said. They relented after Ryan threatened to take the whole thing to nearby National Presbyterian Church.

Ronnie's was the nation's first state funeral in more than thirty years, and as David Von Drehle wrote in the *Washington Post*: "The pomp was nearly unprecedented in American annals, more than two extraordinary hours of thundering organ, swelling chorus, haunting silences, and eloquent prayers. Eulogies were spoken by two presidents and two prime ministers." The younger Bush echoed words once spoken on the passing of Abraham Lincoln: "Ronald Reagan belongs to the ages now, but we preferred it when he belonged to us."

There had been a few glitches. The day before the service, Higdon realized suddenly that he hadn't ordered flowers. He asked Nancy what she wanted to do, and she was momentarily flummoxed. "Jerry would say all white," Higdon said, invoking the name of Nancy's old chum Jerry Zipkin, who had died nearly a decade earlier. "Absolutely," she said.

Less than two hours before Ronnie's body was to arrive, the Capitol was briefly evacuated, when a plane carrying the governor of Kentucky mistakenly flew into its secure airspace. VIPs rushed frantically from the building, worried that a replay of 9/11 was about to happen. At the National Cathedral, Higdon cringed when he saw members of Congress "acting like a bunch of hillbillies," asking dignitaries such as Prince Charles and Mikhail Gorbachev to sign their funeral programs.

But to the public—the thousands who lined the route of Ronnie's casket to say good-bye and the millions who saw the proceedings on television—the five days of observances seemed to come off as flawlessly as Nancy had hoped. There were grace notes from beginning to end, from the F-15 fighter jets that sliced the Washington sky in a missing-man formation as his coffin arrived at the Capitol, to the bagpipes that played "Amazing Grace" at the burial service at the Reagan Library in California. As the government plane carrying his body for a final time across the country flew over Tampico, Illinois, it dipped a wing toward Ronnie's birthplace.

The final service in California was carefully timed to end exactly as the sun dropped into the Pacific Ocean, a sight that Ronnie loved.

Against a red and amber sky, Nancy laid an American flag and then her cheek upon her husband's mahogany casket. In her grief and exhaustion, the finality of it was more than she could bear. "I can't leave him," she said. Nancy stroked the wood and sobbed, until the three surviving Reagan children gathered to lift her and lead her away to a future where she would never again feel Ronnie's touch.

CHAPTER TWENTY-FIVE

"Great men have two lives," the diplomat Adolf Berle once observed, "one which occurs while they work on this Earth; a second which begins at the day of their death and continues as long as their ideas and conceptions remain powerful." Berle was speaking in 1945, shortly after the passing of Franklin D. Roosevelt, the president that Ronnie had admired more than any other. But his words could just as easily have applied to Ronald Reagan himself.

Ronnie redefined conservatism and became the North Star for generations of GOP leaders. But it was not just Republicans who recognized his enduring power. In January 2008 a young African American US senator from Illinois who was in the heat of a Democratic presidential primary startled many in his party by citing Ronnie as his own model for connecting with Americans across the political spectrum. "I think Ronald Reagan changed the trajectory of America in a way that Richard Nixon did not and in a way that Bill Clinton did not. He put us on a fundamentally different path because the country was ready for it," Barack Obama said. "He just tapped into what people were already feeling, which was we want clarity, we want optimism, we want a return to that sense of dynamism and entrepreneurship that had been missing."

While Nancy was no longer the caretaker of Ronnie's physical well-being, she continued to be the chief guardian of his legacy. Most modern presidents have lived for decades after they leave office. They have used those years to shade and shape how the future will regard them. Ronnie, whose incapacitation began so soon after the end of his presidency, was denied that opportunity to write the first draft of his own legacy. So, it fell to Nancy to make sure that the story that history would tell about him would be true to his character and his ideals. She was wary of men who claimed his mantle as a means of furthering their own ambitions and goals that he would not necessarily have shared. She also was determined to refute the counternarrative of him. Even as Ronnie was beatified on the Right, there were still those in the elite circles of the Left who saw him less as a leader and a visionary than as an actor who read words that others had written for him. A 1996 survey of historians conducted by Arthur M. Schlesinger Jr. infuriated conservatives when it ranked Ronnie "low average"—one spot below George H. W. Bush and just ahead of Chester Arthur.

This is why Nancy devoted so much of her energy to the Reagan Library. "I go to the library or work for the library all the time, because it's Ronnie," she said in 2009. "I'm working for Ronnie." Both she and he had wanted it to become a place that not only sanctified the past but pointed the way to the future. Republicans who aspired to the Oval Office came there to give major policy addresses. The library hosted two GOP presidential candidate debates during the 2008 election cycle, and one each in 2012 and 2016.

Nancy was also relentless in making sure the library and foundation that carried Ronnie's name would have the money to sustain itself indefinitely. Texas oilman T. Boone Pickens donated $10 million in 2005 to help build the massive pavilion in which the museum housed a Boeing 707 that had been used as Air Force One by Ronnie and six other presidents. Nancy put Pickens in charge of raising another $100 million in honor of the February 2011 centennial of Ronnie's birth. Shortly before the deadline, she checked in with him to see how things were going. "I think we can claim victory, Mrs. Reagan," Pickens told her triumphantly.

There was a long pause at the other end of the line. "How much do you have?" Nancy asked.

"Ninety-five million," Pickens replied.

"Victory is a hundred million," she said icily. "I want a hundred by Ronnie's birthday."

Pickens scrambled to round up a few other big donors and threw in an additional $1 million himself. Then he called Nancy to tell her he had reached the goal. "Boone, I knew you could do it," she said.

Recounting the story five years later, Pickens—a legendarily ruthless corporate raider—told me with a laugh how intimidated he was by the eighty-nine-year-old former first lady. "Well, hell yes, I did it. I did it within twenty-four hours," he recalled in his big West Texas drawl. "Yeah, I could do it when she screwed down on me like that. I saw her as I think a lot of people did during their administration. She could get tough. She wanted something, and she was going to get it."

Around the country, Ronnie's admirers looked for other lasting ways to honor him. Some of it began while Ronnie was still alive. The 1998 dedication of the Ronald Reagan Building and International Trade Center in Washington was a gesture rich in irony. It is a sprawling $818 million federal building, a limestone behemoth second only to the Pentagon in size, that carries the name of a president who portrayed big government as the enemy. Congress also voted that same year to rechristen the airport closest to the capital Ronald Reagan Washington National Airport. There are dozens of schools and stretches of highway named for him.

Nancy was uncomfortable about some of the more excessive things that her husband's devotees wanted to do in—and with—his name. She was not a fan of antitax activist Grover Norquist's Ronald Reagan Legacy Project, which had a goal of christening something in every one of the nation's 3,140 counties after the fortieth president. Nancy believed, as she was sure her husband would have, that any such movement should come from local communities themselves. "If he were able to, he'd quietly thank them but say, 'Please don't,'" she said.

In 2003 Nancy put a stop to a plan by some Republicans in Congress to put her husband's profile on the dime. Nancy thought Ronnie would not have wanted to supplant his idol FDR on the coin. She was also keenly aware of the poignant story behind Roosevelt's placement there. It had been done as a tribute to the leadership that a president disabled by polio had shown in founding the March of Dimes, an organization dedicated to scientific advances and education that improved the health of mothers and their babies. Since the 1970s, some in the anti-abortion movement have boycotted the March of Dimes, because, among other things, it encourages prenatal testing. "I do not support this proposal, and I'm certain Ronnie would not," Nancy said of the idea of putting her husband on the coin. "When our country chooses to honor a great president such as Franklin Roosevelt by placing his likeness on our currency, it would be wrong to remove him and replace him with another."

Long after Ronnie was out of office, Nancy kept watch for references to him in the news media. In 1998 she sent a note to the *Wall Street Journal*'s Albert R. Hunt about a not entirely flattering column he had written about the debate over renaming Washington's airport after Ronnie. Rather than focusing on Hunt's criticisms of her husband, Nancy zeroed in on a passing reference he had made to Ronnie's firing of more than eleven thousand air traffic controllers during a 1981 strike. "I had to write and thank you for the column you did on Ronnie and the airport. I've been reading all the comments about the air controllers' strike and waiting for someone to point out that it was an illegal strike," Nancy wrote. "They broke the law, so Ronnie fired them. But no one said it—until you. I'm very grateful to you for at last setting the record straight, and I hope that's the last we hear of it.

"Also thanks for your comments on Ronnie's practicing a policy of civility—which he did," she added. "Very important, and I think we all miss it when it isn't there. Hope you can read my handwriting (my husband never could!) and thanks again."

But Nancy wanted to do more than protect Ronnie's reputation. She wanted to elevate and enlarge it, to make history fully recognize her husband's intellect and his vision. She wanted generations to come to understand that he was not, as Democratic power broker Clark Clifford famously described him, an "amiable dunce." Ronnie's own written words, she believed, were the best testament to the thinker that he was. As Ronnie himself had explained to *Esquire* magazine in 1976, it was through writing that he converted from a New Dealer to a conservative: "I always did my own speeches and did the research for them. I just woke up to the realization one day that I had been going out and helping to elect the people who had been causing the things I had been criticizing. So it wasn't any case of some mentor coming in and talking me out of it. I did it in my own speeches."

The Reagan Library turned out to hold a gold mine of unexamined evidence in that regard. Scholar Kiron K. Skinner discovered some of it in the late 1990s as she was looking through cardboard boxes there. Tucked into one she found scripts of the radio addresses that Ronnie had given between the time he was governor and his election as president. On pages upon pages of legal pads, he had sketched out a blueprint for what would become his governing philosophy. Skinner worked with Martin Anderson, who served as Ronnie's first domestic-policy adviser, and Anderson's wife, Annelise, who had been an aide in the Office of Management and Budget, to edit a collection of them. *Reagan, in His Own Hand* was published in 2001.

Nancy "was very supportive of that project," said former secretary of state George Shultz, who wrote the book's introduction. "Obviously it was a project of huge importance, because it showed that when ideas are written out in the president's own handwriting, they're his. It was not some staff person's. You could see a display of the man's thinking."

The book was followed in 2003 by *Reagan: A Life in Letters*, which collected more than five thousand thoughtful, poignant, and witty pieces of correspondence. They spanned nearly his entire lifetime, from a note to some older girls when he was eleven years old, to the final missives he wrote after announcing his Alzheimer's diagnosis in 1994. Included were everything from Ronnie's letters to world leaders, to his half-century-long pen-pal relationship with the woman who had been the president of the Philadelphia chapter of his fan club back when he was a movie actor. As *Time* magazine put it in a cover story: "The letters suggest a man for whom writing was less a habit than a need, like food and water, as though the very act shaped his thoughts as much as the thoughts shaped the writing."

After Ronnie's death came an even more ambitious project: the publication of the diaries he kept during his eight years in the White House. The existence of the diaries was well known. Edmund Morris had been allowed to see them when he was writing his massive biography of Ronnie, and there had been much wrangling over them during the Iran-contra scandal and its legal aftermath. In 1989, lawyers for former national security adviser John M. Poindexter subpoenaed excerpts to use in his defense during his trial on charges of lying to Congress. Both Ronnie and the Bush administration invoked executive privilege and refused to turn them over.

In 2006 historian Douglas Brinkley was teaching at Tulane University in New Orleans and finishing up a book about Hurricane Katrina when he got a call from former California governor Pete Wilson, a member of the Reagan Foundation board. Wilson told him that the foundation was looking for someone to edit the diaries. Brinkley knew that Ronnie was one of only four presidents who had written a journal of his thoughts on a consistent basis. The historian was, in his words, "beyond intrigued" about the possibility of being the one who would be given the opportunity to see and analyze them.

"Well, look, while you've risen to the top of our list, you still have tests to pass," Wilson said.

"What do you mean, 'tests'?" Brinkley asked.

"You're going to have to win Mrs. Reagan's approval," Wilson said. "While she'd like to see the diaries published, she felt very burned by Edmund Morris. His very name makes her apoplectic. So, you're going to have to convince her you're not anything at all like Edmund Morris. And number two, she is just going to have to have a good feel for you as a person who she could collaborate with, because she owns these diaries."

Brinkley flew to California and met Nancy at the Hotel Bel-Air, where they both ordered the most popular item on the menu, the "Nancy Reagan Cobb Salad." He had been given two pieces of advice by Wilson: First, don't, under any circumstances, mention Morris. And second, if the conversation drags, talk to her about the movie business—not the old stuff from back in her days in Hollywood but contemporary films and current stars such as Johnny Depp and Brad Pitt. Brinkley was a contributor to *Vanity Fair*, so he figured he had that covered.

They were getting along well, when Brinkley realized he had a confession to make. "Mrs. Reagan, I need to tell you something," he said. "I'm not a conservative. If anything, people see me as somebody center left, or just plain old liberal. And you need to be aware that by giving me all of Reagan's diaries, no strings attached, you might get some criticism from the Right."

Nancy, who was well into her mideighties, fixed a glare on Brinkley that he could still feel more than a decade later. "My son is more liberal than you will ever be," she said. "What's your point?"

"Well, I don't have a point, I guess," Brinkley stammered. "I just thought I should put that on the table, just so you know."

"I don't think like that," Nancy said. "I'm not that way."

She went on to tell him how the liberal lion Edward M. Kennedy called her on every birthday and sang to her, a thoughtful gesture that not many of her Republican friends would bother to make. While she and Kennedy agreed on few issues, Nancy felt closer to him than almost anyone else who was still in Washington politics.

Brinkley and his pregnant wife, Anne, moved to Simi Valley, and he got to work. He was awestruck when he got his first glimpse of the diaries: five volumes, bound in maroon leather, each embossed with the presidential seal and the name Ronald Wilson Reagan stamped in gold on the bottom right. As he read the neat, rounded handwriting, Brinkley felt he could almost hear Ronnie's voice. But before any of it could be published, it had to get past a government national security clearance review. Censors in Washington wanted references to such sensitive things as arms deals with Saudi Arabia and other matters redacted. Nancy and Joanne Drake, who ran the foundation, fought these battles one by one, often winning them when they could show that a piece of information in question had already appeared in a newspaper story or in someone else's book. George Shultz was helpful in hunting down these previously reported snippets. With few exceptions, everything in Ronnie's diary was allowed to be published. Nancy's determination to see his diaries made public was ironic, given that she ordered her own journals to be destroyed upon her death.

Nancy's larger purpose was clear to Brinkley. "She thought that Ronnie was more of an intellectual than the public had understood. That he was not a just an aw-shucks guy who read cowboy novels and painted fences. That he really had a deep sense of Cold War literature and could be very pragmatic and reflective," the historian said. Nancy had one further stipulation she gave Brinkley: he had to promise that he would never, ever claim that because he had read the diaries, he had any special insight into what Ronnie might think about or do on any current issue if he were alive today. No one could know that, she said. Her stepson Michael made such assertions all the time on conservative talk shows, and it annoyed her to no end.

Over the course of the project, Brinkley and Nancy became friends and had frequent lunches. As the birth of his baby approached, Nancy offered him motherly advice about raising children. She was frank about the mistakes she herself had made. When the diaries were published by HarperCollins in 2007, Nancy and Brinkley signed copies together and donated them to places such as Ronnie's alma mater Eureka College and the museum that now stands at the spot where he was born. *The Reagan Diaries* reached number one on the *New York Times* best-seller list. It gave a revealing look at the matters, both public and personal, that consumed the 2,922 days of Ronnie's presidency. Suffusing the entire book is his love and longing for Nancy, which he wrote about in nearly every entry.

For a few years after Ronnie was gone, Nancy fought her loneliness by getting out of the house. She even made some new and improbable friends. Among them was her husband's old nemesis, the legendarily aggressive television newsman Sam Donaldson. They hadn't known each other well back when Ronnie was president. Donaldson had once described Nancy on a Sunday-morning talk show as a "smiling mamba," which was a reference to a large poisonous snake. He apologized, but that one had left a mark.

So, Donaldson was a little surprised after Ronnie's death when someone—he can't remember who—mentioned that the former first lady might like to hear from him. The next time he was in Los Angeles, he got in touch. Thus began a semiregular routine in which the two of them got together for lunch at an oceanside restaurant. Donaldson would bring his laptop computer, and they would laugh over old images from the White House years. Not the big, historic, tear-down-this-wall stuff, but sentimental scenes, like when Nancy surprised Ronnie with a birthday cake on national television. The last time they met, one of the other patrons at the restaurant recognized Donaldson and approached him afterward. "Who was that elderly woman?" the man wanted to know. "She looks familiar."

As she approached her ninetieth birthday, Nancy's health went into a sharp decline. In 2008 she was hospitalized twice after serious falls. She broke her pelvis in the second, which occurred when she got up in the middle of the night. She began wearing oversized glasses to deal with her glaucoma. When she showed up for events at the library, it was in a wheelchair. Her fragility made it harder and harder for Nancy to get out for the gossipy lunches that she had loved, and there were fewer of her friends still alive with which to share them. "There's just nobody left," Nancy lamented. Michael Deaver succumbed to pancreatic cancer in 2007. Ursula Taylor, with whom she was close when they were newlyweds, young mothers, and neighbors, died in 2010. Nancy's great pal Betsy Bloomingdale was also failing, and the only way they could stay in touch was by phone. Indeed, the telephone was pretty much Nancy's only lifeline to the world. Friends and acquaintances often asked Joanne Drake if there was anything they could do for the former first lady. Drake's advice was always the same: "Call her."

There was also more heartbreak within the Reagan family. In 2014 Ron's wife, Doria, died at the age of sixty-two. Seven years before, she had begun showing the symptoms of a serious neuromuscular disease similar to ALS. Doctors never quite settled on a precise diagnosis. She and Ron lived in a bungalow in Seattle, and he had taken care of Doria through her lengthy illness, during which he was unemployed part of the time.

In Nancy's final years, Ronnie would sometimes come to her at night. It seemed to her too real to be a dream. She would see him next to her, sitting on the side of the bed that she still left empty, and they would talk. Once, she spotted him in a chair and told him she thought he looked cold. She got up and retrieved a blanket from the closet. The next morning, she found the covering in a slightly different spot, as if it had been pushed aside when someone left. "She could not, she said, explain this," recalled Peggy Noonan, to whom Nancy recounted the story. "Whatever it was, love, she felt, did not just disappear." Nancy also started wondering more about the afterlife, and whether she and Ronnie would once again be together there. Evangelist Billy Graham assured her they would.

Finally, there came a time when it was clear that this reunion would not be far away. She had planned nearly every detail of her funeral but for one: a minister to deliver her eulogy. Nancy hadn't particularly liked the job done by the clergyman who handled Ronnie's service at the Reagan Library, and the others to whom she felt closer were infirm or already dead themselves. Her friend Robert Higdon approached Episcopal priest Stuart Kenworthy, who had recently retired as rector of Christ Church in the Georgetown neighborhood of Washington. This was the most personal of assignments, and Kenworthy had never met Nancy. So, some time around early 2015, he flew to Los Angeles for what amounted to a highly unconventional audition. When Kenworthy arrived at the house in Bel Air, Higdon and Peggy Noonan took him back to Nancy's tidy, light-filled bedroom. She was dressed in casual clothes and was lying on top of her bed. Kenworthy spotted a walker in the corner and a large amount of medication, signs of her precarious health. But mostly, he noticed that even as Nancy was reaching the end of her life, "she had a quiet elegance about her. Hair was done. All those things."

Kenworthy didn't say much, as the three others shared old yarns from their years in the White House. The next day, Kenworthy and Higdon returned to see Nancy again. The clergyman, feeling a little more at ease, picked up some of the photographs that jammed the top of Nancy's nightstand and asked her to tell him the stories behind them. One was worn and creased and a little too big for its weathered Plexiglas holder. It was a snapshot of Ronnie, taken in profile, when he was deep in the throes of Alzheimer's. He was lying down, just as Nancy was then. In the photo, she was hovering above him, their two faces nose to nose. The intimacy was still there, even through the fog of his illness.

Nancy held it for a few moments and then told Kenworthy: "This one is my favorite."

"Mrs. Reagan, when I see this, I see someone living out their marriage vows," he said.

"Yes," Nancy agreed, "it is."

She put it back on its spot, closest to her on the table. Kenworthy then asked Higdon if he might be left alone with Nancy. He sat in a chair at her bedside, and the two of them talked. She spoke of Ronnie, how much she loved him and how badly she wanted to be with him again. Kenworthy told her that with death, our existence is changed, not ended. Then Kenworthy asked Nancy if they might pray together. They offered thanksgiving—for life, and for love. They prayed that God would be with her in all that lay ahead. As Kenworthy left, he told her: "Mrs. Reagan, I'd like to come back and see you again some time." That would be nice, she said. Both of them knew it was not likely to happen.

The end for Nancy came on March 6, 2016, a Sunday. She was ninety-four. In her final week, the doctors could see it coming, though they weren't sure exactly how long she had. Nancy was lucid until the very last. Patti and Ron came to visit several times. Three days before she died, Doug Wick and his wife, Lucy Fisher, spent time at her bedside. She seemed "a little at sea," he said, so he picked up a nearby book. It was a volume of Ronnie's letters to her, which Nancy had published more than a dozen years earlier. Wick asked if he could read a few of them to her. She perked up and told him playfully: "Well,

I may have four or five minutes." Wick read to her until he began to worry that he was tiring her out. But every time he got ready to close the book, she would ask to hear just one more: "I could just feel how it comforted her. It grounded her, anchored her."

One of her final visitors was Dennis Revell, Maureen's widower. He and his fiancée, Cyndi Klement, made the seven-hour drive from Sacramento on Saturday. Nancy was fond of Cyndi's cookies. They brought her a batch of her favorite kind, and Nancy shared it with her nurses. Dennis's thirteen-year-old Ford Expedition had started blowing steam and smoke as he had turned onto Nancy's driveway. She nagged him to take care of his radiator before he and Cyndi headed back. "It's Saturday," she worried. "How are you going to get your car repaired?"

Early the next morning, her nurses discovered that Nancy had died in her sleep. The cause was congestive heart failure. Kenworthy got word of her death from Higdon. By then, the Episcopal priest had been named interim vicar at the National Cathedral in Washington. Though it had been nearly a year and a half since his meeting with Nancy, he had nothing prepared for a eulogy. He couldn't find the right words.

"I had all these books. I had about three or four books on the Reagans and Mrs. Reagan, the Reagan years. In the final analysis, they weren't what I was looking for. I sat at my desk and pulled out the Scriptures, and I just sat there and prayed: 'Lord, give me some light here,'" he said. Kenworthy worked for two hours, but it still didn't feel quite right. Then he remembered the photo that Nancy kept by her bed, and realized that was it. That is what he would talk about. That was the image that brought love and faith together. "I've made a life and a vocation out of reading hearts, the human heart," Kenworthy told me. "She was at peace. There are those people that, when the end is near, they in a sense, turn toward death and say, 'Here I am. Here are you.' It's a part of life."

The following Friday, a motorcade carried her coffin forty miles from a mortuary in Santa Monica to the Reagan Library in Simi Valley, where Ronnie had been laid to rest nearly a dozen years before. Nancy was to finally join him, dressed for eternity in a red Adolfo suit. The procession route took the mourners on a long stretch of road that had been named the Ronald Reagan Freeway.

Her service was more religious than some who knew her expected it to be. That was partly Kenworthy's doing. "This is going to be a proclamation of resurrection, of faith," he insisted. Ron and Patti sat in the front row with their uncle Dick, Nancy's stepbrother. Her stepson, Michael, was not there. He claimed that he had been unable to rearrange an overseas trip and tweeted: "Colleen and I are traveling in Asia on business and will be honoring Nancy next Tuesday on the USS *Ronald Reagan* in Tokyo, Japan." Betsy Bloomingdale, as frail as she was, managed to make it and was also seated up front. In attendance were members of every presidential family of the previous half century: George W. and Laura Bush; Michelle Obama; Hillary Clinton; Rosalynn Carter; Tricia Nixon Cox; Steven Ford; Lynda Bird Johnson Robb and Lucy Baines Johnson; Caroline Kennedy.

The tributes to Nancy were lovely and funny, each looking at a different facet of her remarkable life. James Baker noted that Nancy was the one who said: "You need to do this, Ronnie. You need to find a way to negotiate with Gorbachev." Brian Mulroney, Canada's former prime minister, read aloud one of Ronnie's sentimental letters to her. Tom Brokaw described her as a woman who was not just the wife of a president "but his best political adviser."

The rawest words, and perhaps the truest, were from her two children. "My parents were two halves of a circle, closed tight around a world in which their love for each other was the only sustenance they needed. While they might venture out and include others in their orbit, no one truly crossed the boundary into the space they held as theirs," Patti said as she stood in front of Nancy's rose-covered casket.

Ron spoke after his sister. "If my mother had one great talent, I think it was that she knew how to love, and she loved one man more than the world," he said. "We should all be so lucky as to end up where we've always wanted to be. Today my mother comes to rest on this lovely hilltop, with its far-reaching views, next to her beloved Ronald Reagan Library. And by the way, from here, she will be able to keep an eye on things. Just saying. No slacking. How long will it be before tales begin to emerge of a petite, Chanel-clad spirit roaming the galleries and halls, just checking to make sure things are running smoothly?" That image of a ghostly Nancy keeping watch over the place in perpetuity brought some knowing laughter.

But then Ron's voice began to crack. "Most importantly, she will once again lay down beside the man who was the love of her life. The one she loved until the end of her days," he said. "They will watch the sun drop over the hills in the west toward the sea as night falls. They will look out across the valley. My father will tell her that the lights below are her jewels. The moon and stars will endlessly turn overhead. And here they'll stay, as they always wished it to be. Resting in each other's arms, only each other's arms.

"Until the end of time."

ACKNOWLEDGMENTS

As I have plugged away on this book for the past four and a half years, people have often asked how I came up with the idea of writing a biography of Nancy Reagan.

The answer is simple: I didn't.

This project was conceived by Simon & Schuster editorial director Priscilla Painton, who is a dear friend going back decades. In the months after Nancy Reagan died in 2016, Priscilla had seized upon this idea and was trying to figure out who might be the person to write it. She mentioned it to Gail Ross, the wonderful agent with whom I had discussed, although not all that seriously, the idea that I might want to do a book some day. Gail said, "What about your friend Karen Tumulty?"

So this is how it happened. Both Priscilla and Gail have been extraordinary in steering me throughout, calming my anxieties about what I had taken on, sharpening my writing and my thinking, and trying to turn me into an author. Philip Bashe did so much more than the title of copy editor would imply. I also had the blessing of a terrific team at Simon & Schuster, including Hana Park, Lisa Healy, Elizabeth Herman, and Angela Ching. The great Jonathan Karp, now its CEO, came up with the title, which captured so much.

From the outset, I benefitted from the support of *Washington Post* publisher (and Reagan Foundation chairman) Fred Ryan. A former

White House aide and then chief of staff to the ex-president, Fred respected and encouraged this as an endeavor of independent journalism. He and his assistant, Stefanie Prelesnik, were unfailingly generous in sharing contact information of hard-to-find sources, as well as a place to check when details of events were sketchy or contradictory. At no point did Fred attempt to shade or influence the conclusions I reached. If I have missed the mark anywhere, the fault is purely my own.

Nor would this book have come to be without the support of my bosses at the *Washington Post*—both on the news side, which is where I was when I started, and later in my new family-within-a-family in the Post Opinions section. Among those in the paper's leadership who made this possible were Steven Ginsberg, Tracy Grant, Marty Baron, Fred Hiatt, Ruth Marcus, and Michael Larabee. Then there are the many colleagues who make the *Post* such a special place to work and thrive. They include Dan Balz; Amy Gardner; Philip Rucker; Rosalind Helderman; David Fahrenthold; Ann Gerhart; Roxanne Roberts; Michele Norris; Robin Givhan; Robert Costa; Carol Leonnig; Kate Woodsome; Nancy Szokan; Autumn Brewington; Rob Gebelhoff; James Downie; Mary Jordan; and Kevin Sullivan.

Nancy Reagan proved an elusive, complex subject—and one way overdue for a reassessment. She and Ronald Reagan were a love match for the ages, but their marriage was so much more than that. She was an excellent wife, but, as she acknowledged, fell short as a mother. The more I learned about her demons, her frailties, her instincts, her determination, and her strength, the more I grew in gratitude that Reagan picked the life partner that he did. I believe the country owes her more than a few debts.

I am grateful for the insights and recollections of people who knew and/or worked with her. You have seen many of their names in these pages: Stuart Spencer, James Kuhn, George P. Shultz, James A. Baker III, Landon Parvin, the late Robert Higdon, Annelise Anderson, Ken Khachigian, Ken Duberstein, Mark Weinberg, the late John Sears, Nancy Reynolds, Stuart Kenworthy, Thomas C. Reed, Tom and Karen Ellick, Douglas Wick, Ed Rollins, Joe Petro, Douglas Brinkley,

Edwin Meese III, Joseph Califano, Sheila Tate, Carol McCain, Peter Wallison, Pam Stevens, the late T. Boone Pickens, James Rosebush, Kathy Osborne, Jane Erkenbeck, Selwa Roosevelt, Lynne Wasserman, Jill Schary Robinson, George Steffe, Carlton Turner, William Henkel, William Novak, and Karen Spencer. By trying to list them, I know I will be kicking myself at some point over who I left out. Some people cooperated on the proviso that I not use their names, which I have respected. Others, who are no longer with us, left behind rich memoirs for me to plumb. The oral histories at the University of Virginia's Miller Center were invaluable. So, too, were newspaper, magazine, and television archives, including the ones provided by Caitlin Conant at CBS and the Public Broadcasting Service through Judy Woodruff.

I could not have done this without the assistance and cooperation of members of the Reagan family, especially Ron Reagan, Dennis Revell, and Richard Davis. Patti Davis and Michael Reagan chose not to speak with me, but both told their stories in their own books, which allowed me to give them voice in mine.

Along the way, I spent more hours than I can count in the research room of the Reagan Library, going through both public and private records. I appreciate the support and openness of Reagan Foundation chief administrative officer Joanne M. Drake and its president, John Heubusch. No one has ever had a better tour guide back into history than archivist Jennifer Mandel. One of those who shared that chilly research room while I was there was Max Boot; neither of us knew at the time that we would soon be colleagues in the Opinions section at the *Washington Post*. I look forward to his Reagan biography. In California, I also got to reconnect with the wonderful journalist and writer Todd Purdum, who, typically, knew more about my subject than I did. (Who else would have a biography of Alla Nazimova at hand on his bookshelf?)

My sojourns in California were some of my happiest memories of this project. While I was doing research at the library, Steven Galson and Jessie Wolfe Galson allowed me to move into their house in Agoura Hills for many weeks. Has there ever been better proof of friendship?

In Northern California, one of my bases of operation was the home of my former business school classmate and forever friend Carol Mills and her husband, John Eichhorn. They always gave the impression they were glad to see me when I arrived on their doorstep with my suitcases. I also stayed at one point in Annelise Anderson's pool house; she had photocopies of the Hollywood scrapbooks of young starlet Nancy Davis, which she shared with me, though it took quite a feat to reproduce them at the downtown FedEx office in Palo Alto.

Having never covered Nancy Reagan as a journalist while she was alive, I was indebted to so many who did. Among them were brilliant photojournalist Diana Walker, with whom I spent so many weeks on the road back when we both worked for *Time* and whose images also grace these pages; Chris Wallace; the aforementioned Judy Woodruff; Andrea Mitchell; Linda Douglass; Al Hunt; Johanna Neuman; and Mike Putzel and Ann Blackman, who are dear friends of many years and who also read chapters as I was writing them.

When I was stymied for a fact, brilliant researcher Alice Crites at the *Post* and Melissa August at *Time* could always tell me where to look. Lissa also helpfully let me know whenever an old Nancy Davis film was playing on Turner Classic Movies.

It was fitting that I began this book not with my own words, but those of pre-eminent Reagan biographer Lou Cannon, who steered me at every step along the way. The late Edmund Morris, in an astonishingly generous act, opened his files to me; his lovely wife, Sylvia Jukes Morris, also now gone, ran cups of tea down to me while I pored through those records in their Connecticut basement. Del Quentin Wilber shared notes taken while he was reporting his own book, which is the authoritative account of the day that Reagan was nearly assassinated. Authors James Mann and Meryl Gordon also provided unpublished material (and Meryl's always hilarious husband, Walter Shapiro, never failed to give me a new jolt of enthusiasm when I was flagging).

Having never written a book before, I sought and received the advice of people who make it look easy. Among them are David Maraniss; John A. Farrell; Michael Duffy (especially Michael Duffy!); Nancy

Gibbs; Carl Cannon; Susan Page; and Eileen McNamara. Others whose friendship has both supported this endeavor and enriched my life are Viveca Novak; Elaine Shannon; Jackie Calmes; Kit Seelye; and Lea Donosky.

During my fall 2017 fellowship at the University of Chicago's Institute of Politics, I was afforded an opportunity to dig into Nancy Reagan's formative years in that city. But an even more valuable experience was seeing the inspiration to public service that people there—including David Axelrod, Alicia Sams, Gretchen Crosby Sims, Christine Hurley, and Ashley Jorn—are instilling in the generation to come. Among the students I got to know was Dylan Wells, whom I enlisted for research; she is now a journalist, which is more reason to feel hopeful about the future. In Chicago, my old friends Dorothy Collin and Bob Secter, as well as new acquaintance Leslie Hindman, helped me find clues to the world that Nancy Davis inhabited there. Latin School historian Teresa Sutter opened their records, which were incredibly revealing. I was guided at Smith College by Stacey Schmeidel, and at Sidwell Friends School by Loren Hardenbergh.

Saved for last are the people who matter the most: the three men who bring love and meaning to everything in my life. They are my sons, Nick and Jack, and my husband, Paul. Over the course of this project, Jack graduated from college and discovered a love of political campaigns. (Where did THAT come from?) Nick obtained his master's degree in public policy and married, finally giving me a daughter, Molly.

Paul, a fine journalist, wrote his own excellent book, and took with mostly good humor the fact that the other author in the house had laid siege to our living room with seemingly permanent piles of dog-eared, out-of-print books and messy files.

It has been quite a journey, guys, and I can't wait to see what's next for us.

BIBLIOGRAPHY

Abshire, David M. *Saving the Reagan Presidency: Trust Is the Coin of the Realm.* College Station: Texas A&M University Press, 2005.

Baker, James A., III, with Steve Fiffer. *"Work Hard, Study . . . and Keep Out of Politics!" Adventures and Lessons from an Unexpected Public Life.* Evanston, IL: Northwestern University Press, 2006.

Barletta, John R., with Rochelle Schweizer. *Riding with Reagan: From the White House to the Ranch.* New York: Citadel Press, 2005.

Brinkley, Douglas, ed. *The Reagan Diaries.* New York: HarperCollins, 2007.

Buckley, William F., Jr. *The Reagan I Knew.* New York: Basic Books, 2008.

Bush, Barbara. *Barbara Bush: A Memoir.* New York: Charles Scribner's Sons, 1994.

Cannon, Lou. *Governor Reagan: His Rise to Power.* New York: Public Affairs, 2003.

———. *President Reagan: The Role of a Lifetime.* New York: Public Affairs, 1991, 2000.

———. *Ronnie and Jesse: A Political Odyssey.* New York: Doubleday, 1969.

Colacello, Bob. *Ronnie & Nancy: Their Path to the White House—1911 to 1980.* New York: Warner Books, 2004.

Davis, Loyal. *A Surgeon's Odyssey.* New York: Doubleday, 1973.

Davis, Patti. *The Long Goodbye.* New York: Alfred A. Knopf, 2004.

———. *The Way I See It: An Autobiography.* New York: G. P. Putnam's Sons, 1992.

Deaver, Michael K. *A Different Drummer: My Thirty Years with Ronald Reagan.* New York: HarperCollins, 2001.

———. *Nancy: A Portrait of My Years with Nancy Reagan.* New York: HarperCollins, 2004.

Deaver, Michael K., with Mickey Herskowitz. *Behind the Scenes.* New York: William Morrow, 1987.

Edwards, Anne. *Early Reagan.* New York: William Morrow, 1987.

———. *The Reagans: Portrait of a Marriage.* New York: St. Martin's Griffin, 2003.

Glaser, Elizabeth, and Laura Palmer. *In the Absence of Angels: A Hollywood Family's Courageous Story.* New York: G. P. Putnam's Sons, 1991.

Graham, Katharine. *Personal History.* New York: Vintage Books, 1997.

Johnson, Haynes. *Sleepwalking Through History: America in the Reagan Years.* New York: W. W. Norton, 1991.

Kelley, Kitty. *Nancy Reagan: The Unauthorized Biography.* New York: Simon & Schuster, 1991.

Kuhn, Jim. *Ronald Reagan in Private: A Memoir of My Years in the White House.* New York: Sentinel, 2004.

Lambert, Gavin. *Nazimova: A Biography.* New York: Alfred A. Knopf, 1997.

Leamer, Laurence. *Make-Believe: The Story of Nancy & Ronald Reagan.* New York: Harper & Row, 1983.

Mayer, Jane, and Doyle McManus. *Landslide: The Unmaking of the President 1984–1988.* Boston: Houghton Mifflin, 1988.

McCain, John, with Mark Salter. *Worth the Fighting For: The Education of an American Maverick and the Heroes Who Inspired Him.* New York: Random House Trade Paperbacks, 2003.

Meacham, Jon. *Destiny and Power: The American Odyssey of George Herbert Walker Bush.* New York: Random House, 2016.

Morris, Edmund. *Dutch: A Memoir of Ronald Reagan.* New York: Random House, 1999.

Neustadt, Richard E. *Presidential Power and the Modern Presidents: The Politics of Leadership from Roosevelt to Reagan.* New York: Free Press, 1990.

Nofziger, Lyn. *Nofziger.* Washington, DC: Regnery Gateway, 1992.

Noonan, Peggy. *What I Saw at the Revolution: A Political Life in the Reagan Era.* New York: Random House, 1990.

———. *When Character Was King: A Story of Ronald Reagan.* New York: Penguin Books, 2001.

Page, Susan. *The Matriarch: Barbara Bush and the Making of an American Dynasty.* New York: Twelve, 2019.

Parr, Jerry, with Carolyn Parr. *In the Secret Service: The True Story of the Man Who Saved President Reagan's Life.* Carol Stream, IL: Tyndale House, 2013.

Patrick, Curtis. *Reagan: What Was He Really Like?* Vol. 1. Charleston, SC: Booksurge, 2007.

———. *Reagan: What Was He Really Like?* Vol. 2. New York: Morgan James, 2013.

Petro, Joseph, with Jeffrey Robinson. *Standing Next to History: An Agent's Life Inside the Secret Service.* New York: St. Martin's Press, 2007.

Quigley, Joan. *"What Does Joan Say?" My Seven Years as White House Astrologer to Nancy and Ronald Reagan.* New York: Birch Lane Press, 1990.

Quirk, Lawrence J. *Jane Wyman: The Actress and the Woman.* New York: Dembner Books, 1986.

Reagan, Maureen. *First Father, First Daughter: A Memoir.* Boston: Little, Brown, 1989.

Reagan, Michael, with Jim Denney. *Twice Adopted.* Nashville: Broadman and Holman, 2004.

Reagan, Michael, with Joe Hyams. *On the Outside Looking In.* New York: Zebra Books, 1988.

Reagan, Nancy. *I Love You, Ronnie: The Letters of Ronald Reagan to Nancy Reagan.* New York: Random House Trade Paperbacks, 2000, 2002.

Reagan, Nancy, with Bill Libby. *Nancy.* New York: William Morrow, 1980.

Reagan, Nancy, with William Novak. *My Turn: The Memoirs of Nancy Reagan.* New York: Random House, 1989.

Reagan, Ron. *My Father at 100: A Memoir.* New York: Viking Penguin, 2011.

Reagan, Ronald. *An American Life—The Autobiography.* New York: Simon & Schuster, 1990. Kindle.

———. *Reagan: A Life in Letters.* Edited by Kiron K. Skinner, Annelise Anderson, and Martin Anderson. New York: Free Press, 2003.

Reagan, Ronald, with Richard G. Hubler. *Where's the Rest of Me? The Ronald Reagan Story.* New York: Duell, Sloan and Pearce, 1965.

Reed, Thomas C. *The Reagan Enigma: 1964–1980.* Los Angeles: Figueroa Press, 2014.

Regan, Donald T. *For the Record: From Wall Street to Washington.* New York: Harcourt Brace Jovanovich, 1988.

Rollins, Ed, with Tom DeFrank. *Bare Knuckles and Back Rooms: My Life in American Politics.* New York: Broadway Books, 1996.

Roosevelt, Selwa "Lucky." *Keeper of the Gate.* New York: Simon & Schuster, 1990.

Rosebush, James. *True Reagan: What Made Ronald Reagan Great and Why It Matters.* New York: Center Street, 2016.

Schary, Dore. *Case History of a Movie.* New York: Random House, 1950.

Shilts, Randy. *And the Band Played On: People, Politics, and the* AIDS *Epidemic.* New York: Penguin Books, 1988.

Shultz, George P. *Turmoil and Triumph: My Years as Secretary of State.* New York: Charles Scribner's Sons, 1993.

Sinatra, Barbara, with Wendy Holden. *Lady Blue Eyes: My Life with Frank.* New York: Crown Archetype, 2011.

Sinatra, Tina, with Jeff Coplon. *My Father's Daughter: A Memoir.* New York: Berkley Books, 2000.

Skinner, Kiron D., Annelise Anderson, and Martin Anderson, eds. *Reagan, in His Own Hand.* New York: Free Press, 2001.

Speakes, Larry, with Robert Pack. *Speaking Out: The Reagan Presidency from Inside the White House.* New York: Charles Scribner's Sons, 1988.

Spencer, Stuart K. *Behind the Podium: My Fifty Years in Politics.* Self-published, 2013.

Spitz, Bob. *Reagan: An American Journey.* New York: Penguin Books, 2018.

Tate, Sheila. *Lady in Red: An Intimate Portrait of Nancy Reagan.* New York: Crown Forum, 2018.

Van Voris, Jacqueline. *College: A Smith Mosaic.* West Springfield, MA: M. J. O'Malley, 1975.

Von Damm, Helene. *At Reagan's Side: Twenty Years in the Political Mainstream.* New York: Doubleday, 1988.

Wallace, Chris (from the NBC News White Paper). *First Lady: A Portrait of Nancy Reagan.* New York: St. Martin's Press, 1986.

Wallace, Mike, with Gary Paul Gates. *Between You and Me: A Memoir.* New York: Hyperion, 2005.

Wallison, Peter J. *Ronald Reagan: The Power of Conviction and the Success of His Presidency.* Boulder, CO: Westview Press, 2003.

Weinberg, Mark. *Movie Nights with the Reagans: A Memoir.* New York: Simon & Schuster, 2018.

Wilber, Del Quentin. *Rawhide Down: The Near Assassination of Ronald Reagan.* New York: Henry Holt, 2011.

Wills, Garry. *Reagan's America: Innocents at Home.* New York: Open Road Integrated Media, 2017.

NOTES

INTRODUCTION

2 *"So, we go over"*: George P. Shultz, interview by author, Palo Alto, CA, October 20, 2016.

2 *"Nancy was dying for him to have one"*: ibid.

2 *"For years, it had troubled me . . . nothing positive was likely to happen"*: Nancy Reagan with William Novak, *My Turn: The Memoirs of Nancy Reagan* (New York: Random House, 1989), 53.

3 *"She watched the people . . . make a friend of the first lady"*: Shultz, author interview, October 20, 2016.

2 *"My father was as good . . . make that happen"*: Ron Reagan, interview by author, Seattle, July 23, 2017.

4 *"an inseparable team politically and personally . . . He would never have been president without her"*: Stuart K. Spencer, *Behind the Podium: My Fifty Years in Politics* (self-pub., 2013), 37.

4 *"Her particular quality . . . the nasty business"*: Edmund Morris, interview by author, Kent, CT, August 7, 2017.

5 *"She was the guardian . . . in my view"*: James A. Baker, interview by author, Houston, January 4, 2017.

5 *"an anachronism . . . the reality of American woman today—what they want to be and what they need to be"*: Chris Wallace (from the NBC News White Paper), *First Lady: A Portrait of Nancy Reagan* (New York: St. Martin's Press, 1986), 84.

6 *"You can get just so far . . . trust me"*: Lou Cannon, *President Reagan: The Role of a Lifetime* (New York: Public Affairs, 1991, 2000), 192.

6 *"It's part of Ronnie's character . . . like the bad guy"*: Nancy Reagan with Novak, *My Turn*, 91.

CHAPTER ONE

9 *"I've always wanted to belong . . . could take care of"*: Nancy Reagan with Bill Libby, *Nancy* (New York: William Morrow, 1980), 141.

9 *who had just turned eleven*: Various accounts have been given of Edith Luckett's age when she appeared onstage for the first time, some as young as six. The local papers show *East Lynne* was playing at the Columbia Theater in late July 1899.

9 *"So impressive was her work . . . in every corner"*: Gardner Mack, "Edith Luckett Once an Infant Phenom, but Smashed Rule by Becoming Star," *Washington Times*, October 25, 1914, 13.

10 *"Edith Luckett is an earnest . . . the present system"*: "Lucky Edith Luckett," *Philadelphia Inquirer*, November 9, 1913, 55.

10 *"kind of a momma's boy"*: Beverly Beyette, "Nancy Reagan's Early Years: A Matter of Relativity," *Los Angeles Times*, January 20, 1981.

10 *"Miss Edith Luckett . . . initial performance shortly"*: "Miss Edith Luckett Is Secretly Married," *Washington Evening Star*, July 21, 1916, 15.

11 *"one-legged tap dancer . . . knife thrower"*: Anne Edwards, *The Reagans: Portrait of a Marriage* (New York: St. Martin's Griffin, 2003), 3.

12 *a wildly unconventional lifestyle . . . little secret of her sexual relationships with women*: Her name was also associated with a semi-infamous West Hollywood landmark. In 1918 Nazimova had bought a Spanish-style mansion on LA's Sunset Boulevard, which she converted to a hotel when she hit financial difficulties in 1926. Known as the Garden of Allah, it went through a succession of owners and had a reputation for hedonistic parties. Its glamorous guests included Greta Garbo, Charlie Chaplin, Humphrey Bogart, F. Scott Fitzgerald, and Ernest Hemingway. Ronald Reagan stayed there when he was between marriages.

12 *"Edith was a New Woman . . . in the theatre of life"*: Gavin Lambert, *Nazimova: A Biography* (New York: Alfred A. Knopf, 1997), 188–89.

12 *moved to Washington from Virginia in 1872*: Anne Edwards, *Early Reagan* (New York: William Morrow, 1987), 380.

12 *"shipping agent . . . local banks"*: "Heard and Seen," *Washington Times*, July 1, 1919, 20.

12 *"She was a beautiful blonde . . . friends for life"*: Nancy Reagan with Novak, *My Turn*, 57–58.

13 *The letter suggests . . . "well you are doing"*: Katherine Carmichael to Nancy Reagan, 1982, White House Office of Records Management (WHORM) subject files: PP005-01: 104175; Ronald Reagan Presidential Library & Museum.

13 *"How nice of you to write . . . wasn't too much trouble"*: ibid.

14 *"I'm not a psychologist . . . her whole life"*: Ron Reagan, author interview, July 23, 2017.

14 *"She always harbored . . . and hurt her"*: Patti Davis, *The Way I See It: An Autobiography* (New York: G. P. Putnam's Sons, 1992), 9.

14 *"Maybe our six-year separation . . . years together"*: Nancy Reagan with Novak, *My Turn*, 58.

16 *"If I had a child"*: ibid., 58.

17 *"Since Kenneth Robbins . . . impossible for me to think of him as my father"*: Nancy Reagan with Libby, *Nancy*, 25.

18 *They said in various news articles . . . to have behaved so brutally*: Beyette, "Nancy Reagan's Early Years."

18 *"Ken Robbins was a rather decent chap . . . she probably felt pretty superior"*: Richard Davis, author interview by telephone, August 10, 2017.

18 *"I received your letter . . . enjoying it"*: Peter Harrison to Nancy Reagan, 1982, WHORM subject files: PP005-01: 107498; Reagan Presidential Library.

19 *she phoned the California governor's mansion several times in 1970 . . . "Maybe the right word didn't get to the right place"*: Beyette, "Nancy Reagan's Early Years."

19 *"His obituary . . . nieces and nephews"*: Jennie Sweetman, "Nancy Reagan's Connection to Sussex County," *New Jersey Herald* online (Newton, NJ), April 26, 2016, https://www.njherald.com/article/20160424/NEWS/909013891.

19 *"Reagan talked about his childhood . . . never talk about it"*: Stuart Spencer, interview by author, Palm Desert, CA, October 22, 2016.

19 *"She had so much fear . . . when she felt comfortable"*: Doug Wick, interview by author, Los Angeles, July 13, 2017.

20 *"Perhaps I did not insist" . . . shared a cabin with another doctor*: Loyal Davis, *A Surgeon's Odyssey* (New York: Doubleday, 1973), 225.

21 *Her diary also suggests . . . "baby had been with us"*: Reagan Presidential Library, personal collection, box 1, items from residence, 668 St. Cloud, LA 90077. Diary is tan leather, "My Trip Abroad," and *E.L.* embossed in gold.

22 *"It was but a week or so . . . to seek a divorce"*: Loyal Davis, *Surgeon's Odyssey,* 227.

22 *"My father was tall and dark . . . she knew everybody"*: Nancy Reagan with Novak, *My Turn,* 65.

23 *"She taught me to change . . . association of friends"*: Loyal Davis, *Surgeon's Odyssey,* 228.

24 *"She saw Loyal as her lifeline . . . her daughter a break"*: Kitty Kelley, *Nancy Reagan: The Unauthorized Biography* (New York: Simon & Schuster, 1991), 34.

24 *"The pair of sculptured hands . . . famous brain surgeon"*: June Provines, "Front Views and Profiles," *Chicago Tribune,* July 11, 1935, 15.

25 *"Over the years . . . salute her for it"*: Kelley, *Nancy Reagan,* 34.

25 *"She works in mysterious ways . . . no question of that"*: Louise Hutchinson, "Loyal Davis Fights for Medical Ethics," *Chicago Tribune,* November 14, 1965, 12.

25 *"No one . . . the debt I owed my mother"*: Donnie Radcliffe, "The Dark Year of Nancy Reagan," *Washington Post* online, December 4, 1987, https://www.washingtonpost.com/archive/lifestyle/1987/12/04/the-dark-year-of-nancy-reagan/11451216-2496-40da-9546-8aa2a4902bea/?utm_term=.c8c4a81f5abc.

CHAPTER TWO

27 *The headline . . . "white gauze frosted in silver"*: Cousin Eve, "Society Bids Farewell to the 1930s and Greets '40s: Society Bids Farewell to an Old Decade," *Chicago Sunday Tribune,* January 7, 1940, pt. 8, 1.

29 *"When my mother met Loyal Davis . . . happy ending to a fairy tale"*: Chris Wallace, *First Lady,* 2.

29 *"Will you please tell Mother . . . I can go out in a canoe alone"*: Nancy Reagan to Loyal Davis, n.d., Reagan Presidential Library, personal collection, box 84, documents, Ronald and Nancy Davis, Dr. Loyal Davis, Mrs. Loyal Davis (Edith).

29 *Loyal's father, Al Davis . . . on a movie screen*: Nancy Reagan to ________, March 1981, Reagan Presidential Library, correspondence from Abbie Reed Bucy, dated January 28, 1981.

32 *"My father knew nothing . . . presence would help"*: Loyal Davis, *Surgeon's Odyssey,* 10.

32 *But at the end of the year. . . "having led a good life"*: ibid., 10–11.

33 *"She was beautifully impressive . . . no chance to learn about each other's idiosyncrasies"*: ibid., 84.

34 *"like sitting on a powder keg . . . clean shaven, clean shirt, tie, and jacket"*: Reagan Presidential Library, Loyal memoriam folder, box 84, personal papers.

34 *"For Frank" . . . "'Sold to Dr. Loyal Davis'"*: ibid.

34 *"A California physician . . . naming an infant"*: Lou Cannon, *Ronnie and Jesse: A Political Odyssey* (New York: Doubleday, 1969), 158.

35 *"out of spite" . . ."virulent racism"*: Kelley, *Nancy Reagan*, 39.

35 *"I had a patient one time . . . a strong personality"*: Bob Colacello, *Ronnie & Nancy: Their Path to the White House—1911 to 1980* (New York: Warner Books, 2004), 131.

35 *was known to have used the word* nigger: Edwards, *Early Reagan*, 460. In biographer Edmund Morris's research, which he shared with the author, there is also a reference to a June 7, 1989, interview with Michael Deaver, in which Deaver claims he heard Edith Davis say that word while telling a joke.

35 *"just could not stand discrimination . . . prouder of him or something"*: Etta Moten Barnett, interviews, 1976–1981, OH-31, transcript, Black Women Oral History Project, Schlesinger Library, Radcliffe Institute for Advanced Study, Harvard University, Cambridge, MA.

36 *"You can call me Nancy Davis from now on"*: Kelley, *Nancy Reagan*, 43.

37 *"He came with my grandmother . . . it hurt my grandmother terribly"*: Nancy Reagan with Novak, *My Turn*, 65.

37 *"very much but was somewhat hesitant . . . paternal grandmother were alive"*: Loyal Davis, *Surgeon's Odyssey*, 231.

38 *Her adoption petition . . . April 19, 1938*: Kelley, *Nancy Reagan*, 43.

38 *"Nancy, the answer to happiness . . . aspects of one's life"*: Chris Wallace, *First Lady*, 7.

39 *"With each step, the tunic . . . 'the most wonderful child?'"*: ibid., 4.

39 *Nancy and Loyal often spoke to each other . . . woman he loved*: Richard Davis, author interview by telephone, March 5, 2017.

39 *Nancy "was a flirt . . . Why wouldn't he?"*: Edwards, *Reagans: Portrait of a Marriage*, 9.

39 *"He wanted me to earn his love . . . I never disobeyed him"*: Patti Davis, *The Way I See It*, 19.

40 *"I knew he would have loved it . . . I just couldn't"*: Nancy Reagan with Novak, *My Turn*, 62.

41 *"If he had any real interest . . . 'sea of sharks'"*: ibid., 63.

41 *"A friend would mention a disease . . . progression of it"*: Michael K. Deaver with Mickey Herskowitz, *Behind the Scenes* (New York: William Morrow, 1987), 110–11.

42 *Loyal argued for loosening restrictions on the procedure*: Lou Cannon, *Governor Reagan: His Rise to Power* (New York: Public Affairs, 2003), 211.

43 *"Surgeons properly qualified by training . . . legalized mayhem"*: Associated Press, "Labels Many U.S. Surgeons Incompetent," *Chicago Daily Tribune*, November 25, 1960, pt. 2, 2.

43 *"That's the right answer! . . . love to hear students say they don't know who he is"*: Cory Franklin, "The Other Man in Nancy Reagan's Life," *Chicago Tribune*, March 8, 2016, 21.

43 *live-in maid and cook*: 1940 census records.

43 *no compensation . . . Department of Surgery*: Loyal Davis, *Surgeon's Odyssey*, 250.

44 *"She knew them all . . . 'Hi, Miz Davis!'"*: Ronald Reagan and Nancy Davis personal papers, Reagan Presidential Library, box 84.

45 *"Edie was gregarious . . . Peter Pan collars"*: Mike Wallace with Gary Paul Gates, *Between You and Me: A Memoir* (New York: Hyperion, 2005), 52–53.

46 *"extraordinarily beautiful . . . You'd go crazy about the child"*: Lambert, *Nazimova*, 370.

47 *Nancy's scrapbook includes . . . various times in Chicago*: Nancy Reagan's personal scrapbook from the late 1940s through the early 1950s, a photocopy of which was provided to the author by Annelise Anderson.

47 *"There were, maybe, five or six beds . . . go on about his business"*: Richard Davis, author interview, August 10, 2017.

48 (*Ronald Reagan, to his everlasting regret* . . . Voice of the Turtle): Ronald Reagan with Richard G. Hubler, *Where's the Rest of Me? The Ronald Reagan Story* (New York: Duell, Sloan and Pearce, 1965), 192.

48 *"and all of my care was exceptional"*: Loyal Davis, *Surgeon's Odyssey*, 31.

48 *"One summer we wrote . . . Uncle Walter and I were the stars"*: Nancy Reagan with Novak, *My Turn*, 67.

49 *"sobering advice, but I wasn't put off"*: ibid., 66.

49 *Loyal and Edie . . . 1944 Democratic convention in Chicago*: Eleanor Page, "Many in Boxes Share Thrill of 1st Convention," *Chicago Daily Tribune*, July 20, 1944, 13.

50 *a headline on the second page . . . "is or was a policewoman"*: "Mystery Veils Identity of a Policewoman," *Chicago Tribune*, June 4, 1943, 2.

50 *Edie, whose newspaper photo caught her without her false teeth in . . . 'I'm Dick Tracy!'"* Colacello, *Ronnie & Nancy*, 142.

51 *"some of these young kids . . . protect those boys"*: Nancy Reagan with Novak, *My Turn*, 64.

51 *write, direct, and produce his weekly radio speeches*: Colacello, *Ronnie & Nancy*, 85.

51 *"vitamums" . . . "Alderman Halsey"*: Loyal Davis, *Surgeon's Odyssey*, 294.

51 *"Loyal was astonished . . . "administration of government"*: ibid.

52 *"What Edith understood . . . more important than what you believe"*: Colacello, *Ronnie & Nancy*, 133.

CHAPTER THREE

53 *"Politics! And wife and mother"*: Smith College archives.

53 *"I always had it in my mind that I wanted to go to Smith"*: Nancy Reagan, interviewed by Judy Woodruff, transcript of unaired interview footage, *Nancy Reagan: The Role of a Lifetime*, produced by Susan L. Mills, aired February 2011 on PBS (MacNeil/Lehrer Productions, 2010), DVD.

53 *"You had no women role models . . . exaggerated values for women"*: Jacqueline Van Voris, *College: A Smith Mosaic* (West Springfield, MA: M. J. O'Malley, 1975), 119.

54 *"that life is not always easy . . . sudden twists of fate"*: Nancy Reagan, *Nancy*, 54.

55 *"I had a terrible time . . . for these subjects"*: ibid., 52.

55 *a catty journalist . . . "piano legs"*: Judy Bachrach, "Portraits: Nancy Reagan's Chocolate-Covered Campaign Not Sweet," *Boston Globe*, October 29, 1980, n.p.

56 *"We were all terribly excited . . . sort of lost its excitement"*: Associated Press, "Nancy's Classmates Remember Her as 'Strictly Average,'" *Morning Union* (Springfield, MA), December 26, 1980, 14.

56 *"She was very pretty . . . go away quite often at weekends"*: ibid.

57 *State police concluded . . . "his own expectations"*: "Princeton Senior Killed by Train," *Central New Jersey Home News* (Brunswick, NJ), December 16, 1941, 8.

58 *"Make with the maximum . . . get away from New York"*: Smith College Library, Collection 80.02.1943, box 2140, class of 1943, individuals A-L.

58 *"Dit-dit-dit . . . win this wah"*: Jane West Magill to Nancy Reagan, October 24, 1984, WHORM subject files: PP005-01: 277053, Reagan Presidential Library.

59 *what she remembered as a "big crush" . . . "world was brighter again"*: Nancy Reagan with Libby, *Nancy*, 65.

60 *nor, apparently, could Edie . . . military personnel*: Kelley, *Nancy Reagan*, 60.

61 *"The young couple met . . . aircraft carrier* Sable": "Tell Betrothal of Lt. J. P. White to Chicagoan," *Abilene (TX) Reporter News*, July 24, 1944, 13.

61 *"I think I met . . . perhaps even a president"*: Lambert, *Nazimova*, 383.

61 *"It was a heady, exhilarating time . . . we remain friends"*: Nancy Reagan with Libby, *Nancy*, 54.

61 *White "was extremely . . . about everybody"*: Richard Davis, author interview, August 10, 2017.

61 *"All I can tell you . . . one of those wartime things"*: Lloyd Shearer, "Nancy Reagan: 'My Life Began with Ronnie,'" *Parade*, February 22, 1976, 8–10.

62 *"Nancy's affinity . . . her full attention"*: Colacello, *Ronnie & Nancy*, 185.

62 *so oddly cold on a hot day*: Nancy Reagan with Libby, *Nancy*, 32.

63 *"This wouldn't be the last . . . drive that Mother had"*: Nancy Reagan with Novak, *My Turn*, 70–71.

63 *"played eight months . . . disdain of most critics"*: Mary X. Sullivan, "Two on the Aisle." Clipping appears in Nancy Reagan's scrapbook. Note in her handwriting dates it September 1, 1946.

63 *She forced . . . "just not working"*: Nancy Reagan with Novak, *My Turn*, 71.

64 *"All the girls were so crazy . . . it always changed"*: transcript from unaired interview footage, *Nancy Reagan: The Role of a Lifetime*.

64 *Only later . . . "amateurish virgin by the name of Nancy Davis"*: Nancy Reagan with Novak, *My Turn*, 72.

64 *"a Miss Nancy Davis . . . decent one of the two Haggett daughters"*: Clipping in Nancy Reagan's Hollywood scrapbook. No precise date or name of publication is given. Her handwriting indicates "Saratoga - August - 1947." Scrapbook provided to author.

64 *in 1981 . . . White House*: Liz Smith, "Pam and Andy Love 'Pirates,'" *Moline (IL) Sunday Dispatch*, August 23, 1981, B-2.

65 *her name popped up occasionally in the newspaper columns*: Colacello, *Ronnie & Nancy*, 187, 191.

66 *"He had a quality . . . really with you"*: Nancy Reagan with Novak, *My Turn*, 73.

66 *"I wasn't setting show business on fire"*: Nancy Reagan with Libby, *Nancy*, 89.

67 *"A vacationing Iowan . . . More, maybe"*: Marguerite Ratty, "Breakfast Club Goes Television at Dinner Hour," *Chicago Tribune*, October 6, 1946, pt. 3, 8.

68 *"There is no pay . . . old hag"*: Inez Wallace, "M-G-M Mum on Television, Signs Video Star Anyhow," *Cleveland Plain Dealer*, February 12, 1950. Clipping from Nancy Reagan scrapbook, with name of publication and date in her handwriting.

68 *"This was one opportunity . . . anything to do with"*: Nancy Reagan with Libby, *Nancy*, 91.

69 *the studio took a pass on a young bit actress named Marilyn Monroe*: Morris, author interview, August 7, 2017. Morris recalled being with Nancy at a dinner at Chasen's in Beverly Hills on February 1, 1990, when Sam Marx, who had been the story editor at MGM, described how Dore Schary turned down Monroe, in part because he had just signed Nancy Davis. "When he told that story to Nancy, you should have seen her face light up," Morris said. Leonora Hornblow, widow of producer Arthur Hornblow Jr., had told Morris the same story four days earlier.

69 *"walking into a dream world"*: Nancy Reagan with Novak, *My Turn*, 74.
69 *"Everything was a big step up when I signed with Metro, everything"*: transcript from unaired interview footage, *Nancy Reagan: The Role of a Lifetime.*
70 *"I always recommended Nancy . . . popular girls on the lot"*: Wanda McDaniel, "The Reagans: Their Honeymoon Begins," *Sacramento (CA) Bee*, November 10, 1980, B4.
70 *Nancy regularly spent Saturday mornings closeted with Thau in his office suite*: Laurence Leamer, *Make-Believe: The Story of Nancy & Ronald Reagan* (New York: Harper & Row, 1983), 63.
70 *Nancy's screen test had been his idea*: ibid.
71 *"When I came out to Los Angeles . . . I liked him as a friend"*: Colacello, *Ronnie & Nancy*, 227.
71 *"I don't know. I was not his," she insisted . . . "And that was it"*: ibid., 248.
73 *"'Wait until a year from now' . . . a new personality'"*: Wallace, "M-G-M Mum on Television, Signs Video Star Anyhow."
73 *"Nancy Davis has the unique distinction . . . all but one of her movies"*: This clipping is pasted in Nancy Reagan's scrapbook, with a notation in her handwriting of the date. It does not include the publication.
73 *"are best forgotten"*: Nancy Reagan with Novak, *My Turn*, 76.
73 *"She did something . . . listened to the other actor"*: Edmund Morris research materials, provided to the author. His notes indicate that this quote came from an interview that Morris conducted with Ronald Reagan on December 21, 1987.
74 *"her gift . . . sonority of the other speakers"*: Edmund Morris, *Dutch: A Memoir of Ronald Reagan* (New York: Random House, 1999), 294.
74 *"That picture ended movies for me"*: Ronald Reagan with Hubler, *Where's the Rest of Me?*, 290.
74 *"I'm not so naive . . . either on or off the screen"*: Nancy Reagan with Novak, *My Turn*, 76.
74 *"Not yet . . . that's pretty much the truth"*: Louella O. Parsons, "In Hollywood with Louella O. Parsons," September 24, 1950. Clipping is from Nancy Reagan's scrapbook, and the name of the publication is not attached.

CHAPTER FOUR

75 *"You know . . . lost my soul"*: Nancy Reagan with Novak, *My Turn*, 103.
76 *"I had seen . . . wanted to meet"*: ibid., 78–79.
76 *"a small, slender young lady . . . made you look back"*: Ronald Reagan with Hubler, *Where's the Rest of Me?*, 235.
77 *"I don't know . . . something close to it"*: Nancy Reagan with Libby, *Nancy*, 111.
77 *"Even I could see she was dazzled by Mr. Reagan"*: Jill Schary Robinson to author, email, November 30, 2018.
78 *Ronnie's name was at the top*: Kelley, *Nancy Reagan*, 77–78.
78 *"Subtlety has never . . . powers of belief"*: Morris, *Dutch*, 280.
78 *"For the first month . . . nightclub in Los Angeles"*: Nancy Reagan with Novak, *My Turn*, 8.
78 *$750 a month in nightclubs*: Ronald Reagan with Hubler, *Where's the Rest of Me?*, 233.
79 *"at least sixteen" . . . who she was*: Morris, *Dutch*, 281–82.
79 *"This story, I know . . . something very important"*: Ronald Reagan with Hubler, *Where's the Rest of Me?*, 236–37.
81 *"a small universe . . . rest of my life"*: Ronald Reagan, *An American Life—The Autobiography* (New York: Simon & Schuster, 1990), loc. 264 of 12608, Kindle.

81 *"Well, if you have a book, you always have a friend"*: Edwin Meese III, interview by author, Washington, DC, October 5, 2016.

81 *"What Ronald Reagan . . . gentler to the eyes"*: Patti Davis, *The Way I See It*, 13.

81 *"unexpected vacations"*: Ronald Reagan, *An American Life*, loc. 240 of 12608, Kindle.

81 *"But someplace along the line . . . will always remember"*: Ronald Reagan with Hubler, *Where's the Rest of Me?*, 7–8.

82 *"a little tornado of goodness"*: Peggy Noonan, *When Character Was King: A Story of Ronald Reagan* (New York: Penguin Books, 2001), 20, paperback.

82 *"Nelle never saw anything evil . . . how he is"*: Nancy Reagan with Novak, *My Turn*, 90.

82 *"a fat Dutchman"*: Details of his birth come from Reagan with Hubler, *Where's the Rest of Me?*, 5, and Morris, *Dutch*, 14–16.

83 *"On Mother"*: Morris, *Dutch*, 30.

83 *"In some ways . . . reserving it for myself"*: Ronald Reagan, *An American Life*, loc. 338 of 12608, Kindle.

83 *"The best part . . . allowed to dream"*: Ronald Reagan with Hubler, *Where's the Rest of Me?*, 11–15.

85 *"For almost six years . . . much in love"*: Ronald Reagan, *An American Life*, loc. 484 of 12608, Kindle.

85 *"He had an inability . . . fact and fancy"*: Morris, *Dutch*, 121–22.

85 *"Even Nixon held services in the White House"*: "Margaret Cleaver Gordon," Eureka College online, accessed September 21, 2020, http://ww1.eureka.edu/emp/jrodrig/march2007/march15.htm.

85 *"Mugs was generally . . . everything she said"*: Morris, *Dutch*, 68–69.

85 *She was president . . . James Waddell Gordon Jr.*: Information provided to the author by Eureka College.

85 *"insisted to Morris that she returned the ring personally"*: Morris, *Dutch*, 709n.

85 *"Margaret's decision . . . no longer had anyone to love"*: Ronald Reagan, *An American Life*, loc. 1011 of 12608, Kindle.

87 *"He has a pleasant, boyish appearance and an attractive film personality"*: "New Films," *Boston Globe*, December 17, 1937, 25.

87 *"Treat for Ladies in Ronald Reagan"*: Dorothy Masters, "Treat for Ladies in Ronald Reagan," *New York Daily News*, October 14, 1937, 57.

87 *During his first year . . . eight pictures in eleven months*: Ronald Reagan with Hubler, *Where's the Rest of Me?*, 77.

87 *"the most satisfying gift of my life"*: ibid., 9.

87 *Ronald Reagan's old clothes*: Stephanie Chavez, "Olive View Fund-Raiser—Hospital Lauds Early Volunteer: 'Ma' Reagan," *Los Angeles Times*, April 6, 1986, pt. 2, 7.

87 *"Ronald has finished . . . just so the boy gets along"*: Nelle Reagan to friend, 1938, box 84, Personal Papers of Ronald and Nancy Davis, Dr. Loyal Davis, Mrs. Loyal Davis (Edith), Reagan Presidential Library.

88 *"She was so experienced . . . a little earthbound for someone like Jane"*: Lawrence J. Quirk, *Jane Wyman: The Actress and the Woman* (New York: Dembner Books, 1986), 42.

88 *pumping Jane's stomach*: Morris, *Dutch*, 162.

88 *"Jane always seemed so nervous . . . together"*: Quirk, *Jane Wyman*, 45.

88 *"I wonder if my Ronald . . . some sweet girl who is not in the movies"*: Morris, *Dutch*, 164.

89 *"I had become a semi-automaton . . . I decided to find the rest of me"*: Ronald Reagan with Hubler, *Where's the Rest of Me?*, 6.

90 *"By the time . . . (all of these postwar ambitions)"*: ibid., 138.
90 *"$3,500 a week"*: ibid., 140.
90 *Maureen had to learn a few words in sign language*: Morris, *Dutch*, 743.
91 *"Well, if he is going to be president, he is going to get there without me"*: Quirk, *Jane Wyman*, 46.
91 *"there was a long drawn-out 'ooooh' . . . and a white shirt"*: Samuel A. Tower, "Hollywood Communists 'Militant,' but Small in Numbers, Stars Testify," *New York Times*, October 24, 1947, 1.
92 *"There's no use in lying . . . coming on for a long time"*: "Ronald Reagans Are Not Happy," INS, *Greenville (SC) News*, December 5, 1947, 23.
92 *"The plain truth was . . . no resources to call upon"*: Ronald Reagan with Hubler, *Where's the Rest of Me?*, 201.
92 *"Right now Jane . . . nervous and not herself"*: Quirk, *Jane Wyman*, 113.
93 *a legal petition . . . mental cruelty*: United Press International, May 7, 1948.
94 *"Finally, there was nothing . . . to sustain our marriage"*: "Jane Wyman Divorced; Blames Rift on Politics," *Los Angeles Times*, June 28, 1948, pt. 2, 1.
94 *"He vowed, either consciously or subconsciously . . . expense of the kids"*: Meese, author interview, October 5, 2016.
94 *"The difference with Nancy . . . recover and prevail"*: Edmund Morris, "The Unknowable," *New Yorker* online, June 28, 2004, https://www.newyorker.com/magazine/2004/06/28/the-unknowable.
95 *"That hurt . . . I was just one girl of many"*: Nancy Reagan with Novak, *My Turn*, 81.
95 *so smitten with her that he proposed*: Clipping from scrapbook. Handwritten notation indicates it was published December 24, 1950. Name of publication not indicated. Box 20. Scrapbook of Nancy Davis 1950- RFS 11. Reagan Foundation Collection.
95 *he fled the Menninger psychiatric clinic . . . then reported to be ready to resume what had been a promising film career*: Gladwin Hill, "Actor Walker Dies After Drug Dosage," *New York Times*, August 30, 1951, 19.
97 *"an actor by profession rather than by accident"*: Dore Schary, *Case History of a Movie* (New York: Random House, 1950), 42–43.
97 *Nancy was padded and wardrobed . . . She wore no makeup except for her own lipstick*: ibid., 51–53.
97 *she would be around for a while in the movie business*: Ronald Reagan with Hubler, *Where's the Rest of Me?*, 236.
99 *"As far as we all knew . . . more relaxed than I had ever seen him"*: Maureen Reagan, *First Father, First Daughter: A Memoir* (Boston: Little, Brown, 1989), 87, 90.
99 *when he was naughty*: Michael Reagan with Joe Hyams, *On the Outside Looking In* (New York: Zebra Books, 1988), 34–35.
100 *filling his stomach with her brunch and her soul with his comfort*: Morris, *Dutch*, 748.
100 *"he would figure out what the purpose of his own torment was"*: Nancy Reagan with Novak, *My Turn*, 90.
100 *"Nancy, you will know when he loves you"*: Robert Higdon described this exchange between Nancy and Nelle twice to the author, in interviews by telephone on August 1, 2017, and in Panama City, FL, on April 17, 2018.
101 *asking her agent to find her a play in New York*: Nancy Reagan, *I Love You, Ronnie: The Letters of Ronald Reagan to Nancy Reagan* (New York: Random House Trade Paperbacks, 2000, 2002), 24.

101 *things were finally over with his ex-wife; this time, for good*: Higdon, author interview, April 17, 2018.
101 *until she did*: Nancy Reagan with Novak, *My Turn*, 84.
102 *"ignore for a long time"*: Ronald Reagan, *An American Life*, loc. 1696 of 12608, Kindle.
102 *vaguely aware . . . getting serious*: Edwards, *Early Reagan*, 430–31.
102 *"only endeared him to me more"*: Nancy Reagan with Libby, *Nancy*, 122.
102 *Her stepbrother, Dick . . . "this important step'"*: Richard Davis, author interview, March 5, 2017.

CHAPTER FIVE

105 *His one concession to the media interest in their nuptials . . . In the photo, Ronnie looks annoyed*: "Ron and Nancy to Wed," *Miami News* online, March 2, 1952, https://www.newspapers.com/image/298382069/?terms=%22ronald%2Breagan%22%2B%22nancy%2Bdavis%22%2B%22santa%2Bmonica%222.
105 *"Came our wedding day . . . out in a cold sweat"*: Ronald Reagan with Hubler, *Where's the Rest of Me?*, 239–40.
106 *What had actually happened . . . "would be perfectly happy together"*: Nancy Reagan with Novak, *My Turn*, 82.
107 *They paid $42,000 for it*: Nancy Reagan, *I Love You, Ronnie*, 31; "Celebrity Homes: Remembering Reagan's Homes and Life in the Riviera," *Palisadian-Post* (Pacific Palisades, CA) online, February 13, 2014, https://www.palipost.com/movie-star-homes-remembering-reagans-homes-life-riviera.
107 *As a child . . . life in an incubator*: Patti Davis, *The Way I See It*, 13.
107 *"didn't want to wait"*: Nancy Reagan with Libby, *Nancy*, 133.
107 *"precipitously, but very joyfully, on October 22, 1952"*: Nancy Reagan with Novak, *My Turn*, 86.
107 *to see how big it had grown*: Nancy Reagan, *I Love You, Ronnie*, 32.
108 *"less as an actor than an adversary"*: Nancy Reagan with Novak, *My Turn*, 105.
108 *"with more dignity . . . under like circumstances"*: Ronald Reagan with Hubler, *Where's the Rest of Me?*, 213, 238.
109 *two first mortgages and a second one*: ibid., 245.
109 *back taxes he had deferred during World War II*: ibid.
109 *child support*: Nancy Reagan with Novak, *My Turn*, 105.
109 *"I could get work . . . at a standstill"*: ibid.
109 *"a professional kiss of death . . . living room for nothing"*: Ronald Reagan, *An American Life*, loc. 1719 of 12608, Kindle.
110 *actor and actress who go into ranching*: Morris, *Dutch*, 295.
110 *"You must be kidding!"*: Ronald Reagan with Hubler, *Where's the Rest of Me?*, 248.
110 Prisoner of War: Edmund Morris, *Dutch*, 754n, disputes that and says he made $5,500 a week for that movie.
111 *conceive a child, or get a divorce*: Colacello, *Ronnie & Nancy*, 255–57.
111 *"This is a day . . . get on with it, then"*: Ronald Reagan with Hubler, *Where's the Rest of Me?*, 249.
111 *showgirls in feathered headdresses*: "Ronald Reagan Performing in Las Vegas," photo, January 1, 1954, available at Getty Images, https://www.gettyimages.com/detail/news-photo/reagan-plays-vegas-in-1954-los-angeles-early-in-1954-when-news-photo/515138960.

111 *"Ronnie could have gone . . . at home with our housekeeper"*: Nancy Reagan with Novak, *My Turn,* 106.

111 *"I never got bored"*: Nancy Reagan, *I Love You, Ronnie,* 41.

111 *"I hope I never have to sink this low again"*: Ed Koch, "Nevada Was a Place of Reflection and Recreation for Nancy, Ronald Reagan," *Las Vegas Sun* online, March 6, 2016, https://lasvegassun.com/news/2016/mar/06/nevada-was-a-place-of-reflection-and-recreation-fo.

112 *When aides cleaned out . . . tucked inside*: Michael Deaver, interview, September 12, 2002, Presidential Oral Histories, Ronald Reagan Presidency, Miller Center, University of Virginia, Charlottesville, VA, https://millercenter.org/the-presidency/presidential-oral-histories/michael-deaver-oral-history-deputy-chief-staff.

114 *"I had been tagged . . . 'mashed potato' circuit"*: Ronald Reagan with Hubler, *Where's the Rest of Me?,* p. 251.

114 *an instant hit . . . twenty-five million viewers a week*: Thomas Kellner, "Lights, Electricity, Action: When Ronald Reagan Hosted 'General Electric Theater,'" General Electric online, last modified February 17, 2019, https://www.ge.com/reports/ronald-reagan-ge.

114 *"You see . . . all these jewels"*: Nancy Reagan with Novak, *My Turn,* 187.

115 *Chief among them . . . terrified of flying*: Morris, *Dutch*, 305.

115 *He sometimes gave as many as fourteen speeches . . . get his shoes off*: Ronald Reagan with Hubler, *Where's the Rest of Me?,* 257–61.

115 *"Although he wasn't running . . . how to solve them"*: Nancy Reagan with Novak, *My Turn,* 108.

116 *"At 8:04 a.m. . . . 'Your wife is all right'"*: Ronald Reagan with Hubler, *Where's the Rest of Me?,* 275.

117 *Nine-year-old Patti . . .* GE Theater: "*General Electric Theater,* 1953–62, Nancy Reagan, Ron Patti, Davis, Ron Reagan Jr., Ronald Reagan, 'Other Wise Man,' December 24, 1961," available at Everett Collection/Alamy Stock Photo, https://www.alamy.com/stock-photo-general-electric-theater-1953-62-nancy-reagan-patti-davis-ron-reagan-32380600.html; Kellner, "Lights, Electricity, Action."

117 *Patti rocking her doll . . . "just as colorful"*: "1950s Ronald Reagan Lighting His Home," YouTube, 3:13, MyFootsage.com, https://www.youtube.com/watch?v=oMNAhoyde7s.

117 *Nancy, Patti, and Ron . . . "aim to keep it that way"*: "Crest Commercial Featuring Nancy, Patty, and Ron Reagan Jr!," YouTube, 1:17, spuzzlightyeartoo, https://www.youtube.com/watch?v=aqh8uRe_mzI.

117 *"He was easy to love . . . out of his sight"*: Ron Reagan, *My Father at 100: A Memoir* (New York: Viking Penguin, 2011), 226–27.

117 *"What happened between arrival and departure was yelling . . . sing to myself to block out the sound"*: Patti Davis, *The Way I See It,* 17–18.

118 *"a weekly, sometimes daily, event"*: ibid., 21.

118 *"Because you upset her so much"*: ibid., 38.

118 *"unresolved feelings about her father" . . . center stage in their home*: Nancy Reagan with Novak, *My Turn,* 136–37.

119 *"only a phase"*: ibid., 136–38.

119 *Ron, the more easygoing" . . . "'every time you leave'"*: Ron Reagan, author interview, Seattle, July 23, 2017.

120 *"Now that I'm older . . . no training for"*: Nancy Reagan with Novak, *My Turn,* 127.

121 *"When I told my parents . . . leave the wall intact"*: Maureen Reagan, *First Father, First Daughter,* 132.

121 *"Dad was quite embarrassed . . . 'haven't gotten that far yet'"*: ibid., 97.
122 *"I was flying blind . . . troubled and rebellious"*: Nancy Reagan with Novak, *My Turn*, 132.
122 *new bedroom was for Ron's nurse*: Michael Reagan with Hyams, *Outside Looking In*, 82–83.
122 *"She's too busy . . . invited you in?"*: ibid., 74–75.
123 *"an illegitimate bastard . . . had for years"*: ibid., 88–90.
124 *"I didn't recognize you"*: ibid., 96.
124 *wept over someone in the family who was not himself*: ibid., 93–94.
124 *"Whether Mike helps buy his first car . . . Your Husband"*: Ronald Reagan to Nancy Reagan, May 24, 1963, love letters file, Reagan Presidential Library.
126 *"a description of the new 1963 coffee pot"*: Ronald Reagan with Hubler, *Where's the Rest of Me?*, 272–73.
126 *"The country needs your kind of leadership"*: Norman L. Stevens Jr. to Ronald Reagan, 1962, Personal Papers, Box 84, R. Reagan Letters, Reagan Presidential Library.
127 *"And there we were. . . . Ever"*: Colacello, *Ronnie & Nancy*, 334–35.

CHAPTER SIX

129 *"Reagan seldom sought their collective advice . . . quiet space via Nancy"*: Thomas C. Reed, *The Reagan Enigma: 1964–1980* (Los Angeles: Figueroa Press, 2014), 193–94.
130 *"Our idea of a big evening . . . go out to the movies"*: Nancy Reagan with Novak, *My Turn*, 30.
131 *wearing jeans at dinner*: Ronald Reagan with Hubler, *Where's the Rest of Me?*, 274–75.
132 *"The ladies of the Colleagues . . . she was one of them"*: Leamer, *Make-Believe*, 190–91.
133 *Zipkin regularly mailed her batches . . . highlighted in yellow marker*: Richard Johnson, Page Six, *New York Post*, April 2, 1987.
134 *"I'd hire those sons of bitches"*: Spencer, *Behind the Podium*, 34–35.
134 *"This guy could do it . . . this guy could make it"*: ibid.
134 *"Nancy was in every one of the meetings . . . after Bill and I left"*: ibid., 40.
134 *"You can do it. . . . going to get worse"*: Nancy Reagan with Novak, *My Turn*, 182.
135 *"She's actually a terrifically intelligent politician . . . sorting that out"*: Spencer, *Behind the Podium*, 41.
136 *On Spencer's first flight . . . that it bled*: Spencer, interview by author, Palm Desert, CA, December 17, 2016.
137 *"I must say my emotions are wired . . . not just my enemies"*: William, F. Buckley Jr., *The Reagan I Knew* (New York: Basic Books, 2008), 12.
138 *"And that's how we landed"*: transcript from unaired interview footage, *Nancy Reagan: The Role of a Lifetime.*
139 *"It could have been all over the papers! . . . tearless eyes"*: Patti Davis, *The Way I See It*, 91–92, 96, 100–105.
139 *rendered invisible for the duration of the campaign. On that, Nancy and Spencer agreed*: ibid., 85. Spencer, interview by author, Palm Desert, CA, July 11, 2017.
139 *drafted and shipped off to Vietnam*: Michael Reagan with Hyams, *Outside Looking In*,104–5.
140 *"she was* livid *. . . chewed me out for, probably, fifteen minutes"*: Curtis Patrick, *Reagan: What Was He Really Like?*, vol. 1 (Charleston, SC: Booksurge, 2007), 281.
140 *"Humiliated to see herself written out . . . "as they see fit"*: Maureen Reagan, *First Father, First Daughter*, 146–49.

141 *"The bitch is on the phone again"*: Spencer, author interview, October 22, 2016.
141 *"Well, I hope I didn't destroy your day"*: Patrick, *Reagan: What Was He Really Like?* 1:281.
141 *"a dubious honor . . . working-class California"*: Reed, *Reagan Enigma,* 29–30.
142 *"Frank Sinatra called me the next day. . . . out of the water with those folks"*: Spencer, *Behind the Podium,* 46.
142 *"I had always thought . . . almost an anticlimax"*: Nancy Reagan with Novak, *My Turn,* 112.

CHAPTER SEVEN

143 *Airlines had to add flights . . . seven thousand people who came for it*: Cecilia Rasmussen, "Circumstances Sometimes Restrain Inaugurations' Pomp," *Los Angeles Times* online, January 7, 2007, https://www.latimes.com/archives/la-xpm-2007-jan-07-me-then7-story.html.
144 *"My Darling First Lady" . . . "you'll always have a me"*: Nancy Reagan, *I Love You, Ronnie,* 96–97.
145 *But there was some consolation . . . meant to buy the governor's favor on a tax bill that gave a big break to the movie industry*: Nicholas M. Horrock, "Reagan Resists Financial Disclosure," *New York Times* online, August 13, 1976, https://www.nytimes.com/1976/08/13/archives/reagan-resists-financial-disclosure-position-in-contrast-to-that-of.html.
146 *"Some legislators thought their celebrity governor . . . spend evenings at home"*: Cannon, *Governor Reagan,* 232.
147 *"transfixed adoration . . . witness of the Virgin Birth"*: Cannon, *Ronnie and Jesse,* 161.
147 *"Whenever I think of Nancy Reagan now . . . middle-class American woman's daydream, circa 1948"*: Joan Didion, "Pretty Nancy," *Saturday Evening Post,* June 1, 1968, 18.
148 *"Would she have liked it better . . . before she ever met me"*: Nancy Reagan with Novak, *My Turn,* 28.
148 *"She alienated even those who were disposed to like her . . . bluntly honest and undiplomatic"*: Cannon, *Governor Reagan,* 236.
148 "What do we do now?": Morris, *Dutch,* 347.
149 *"She was still in a period of learning . . . she knew there had to be a change"*: Stuart Spencer, interview, November 15–16, 2001, Presidential Oral Histories, Ronald Reagan Presidency, Miller Center, University of Virginia, Charlottesville, VA, https://millercenter.org/the-presidency/presidential-oral-histories/stuart-spencer-oral-history.
150 *gas chamber where Mitchell was strapped to a chair*: Miles Corwin, "Last Man Executed in California: Furor over Mitchell Case Resounds 18 Years Later," *Los Angeles Times* online, August 23, 1985, https://www.latimes.com/archives/la-xpm-1985-08-23-mn-24365-story.html.
150 *"a very uncomfortable feeling . . . same principle, it seems to me"*: Tracy Wood, United Press International, printed in multiple newspapers in June 1967.
151 *Field found that more than two-thirds of Catholics supported loosening the restrictions on abortion*: Lou Cannon, "California's Abortion Law: A Road Not Taken," Real Clear Politics, last modified April 4, 2013, https://www.realclearpolitics.com/articles/2013/04/04/calrnias_abortion_law_a_road_not_taken_117773-full.html.
151 *an influential voice as his son-in-law wavered*: Cannon, *Governor Reagan,* 211.
151 *"the only time as governor or president"*: ibid., 213.

152 *"But, honey . . . those things"*: ibid., 237.
153 *"Tom's right," Ronnie said. "We're going to do it"*: Patrick, *Reagan: What Was He Really Like?*, 1:57.
153 *"less desirable"*: ibid., 59.
153 *"She really, truly devoted her life to this man" . . . "Everyone tensed when she came into the office"*: Helene von Damm, *At Reagan's Side: Twenty Years in the Political Mainstream* (New York: Doubleday, 1988), 70–71.
154 *"a frustrated interior decorator"*: Eleanor Page, "A First Lady Chooses a Nest and Feathers It," *Chicago Tribune*, June 9, 1967, sec. 2, 15.
154 *a tomahawk hanging on the wall*: Nancy Reagan, *I Love You, Ronnie*, 98.
154 *The first lady's shouting could be heard from Ronnie's inner office*: Patrick, *Reagan: What He Was Really Like?*, 1:204–5.
154 *"no one ever tried to talk to him about her again"*: Von Damm, *At Reagan's Side*, 71.
154 *pray that it was a girl . . . "you get to see your wife grow up all over again"*: Michael Deaver, *Nancy: A Portrait of My Years with Nancy Reagan* (New York: HarperCollins, 2004), 32.
155 *"That's my husband . . . real story of the budget"*: Nancy Reagan with Novak, *My Turn*, 119.
155 *"eight solid years in the tub"*: ibid.
155 *"She would call in and ask . . . extremely happy man because of that"*: Kathleen Osborne, interview, April 26, 2003, Presidential Oral Histories, Ronald Reagan Presidency, Miller Center, University of Virginia, Charlottesville, VA, https://millercenter.org/the-presidency/presidential-oral-histories/kathleen-osborne-oral-history.
156 *"One thing about Nancy . . . hollered at or get the silent treatment"*: Lyn Nofziger. *Nofziger* (Washington, DC: Regnery Gateway, 1992), 300.
156 *"looked like a used sleeping bag"*: Morris, *Dutch*, 347.
157 *"We knew in our minds . . . hanky panky"*: Nofziger, *Nofziger*, 77.
158 *"'Why doesn't someone do something about Phil?'"* ibid., 79.
159 *"She'd use that fifteen minutes to call me . . . phoned to make her position very clear"*: William P. Clark, interview, August 17, 2003, Presidential Oral Histories, Ronald Reagan Presidency, Miller Center, University of Virginia, Charlottesville, VA, https://millercenter.org/the-presidency/presidential-oral-histories/william-p-clark-oral-history.
160 *"In taking the job nobody else wanted . . . stumbled upon my niche"*: Deaver, *Nancy*, 46.
161 *"Mike was never afraid . . . when he thought he was wrong"*: Nancy Reagan with Novak, *My Turn*, 201.
163 *When the owner of the house decided . . . been paying in rent*: United Press International, "Reagan, Unruh in a Battle," *Santa Rosa (CA) Press-Democrat*, January 28, 1970, 10.
163 *Much of that bounty . . . Queen Anne–style chairs*: Robin Orr, "The Social Circle: The Antiques Belong to California," *Oakland Tribune*, January 30. 1970.
164 *"All of a sudden it came to both of us . . . We both felt that way about it"*: Chris Wallace, *First Lady*, 120.
165 *Sinatra dedicated . . . beaming first lady in the front row*: United Press International, "Star-Studded Cast at Reagan's Inauguration," *Desert Sun* (Palm Springs, CA), January 5, 1971, 16.
167 *(Ronnie had known . . . and had said so)*: Cannon, *Governor Reagan*, 213–14.
167 *In a 1970 interview . . . "so doped up they don't know what they are doing?"*: Edith M. Lederer, Associated Press, "Nancy Reagan Opposes Drugs, Women's Lib, Unrestricted Abortions," *Sacramento (CA) Bee*, July 10, 1970.

168 *"What excited me most . . . everyone is better off"*: Nancy Reagan with Novak, *My Turn*, 116.
168 *"She never just flipped from bed to bed . . . go home and call them"*: Patrick, *Reagan: What Was He Really Like?*, 1:220–21.
168 *the war that had cost them so much was not winnable*: Nancy Reagan with Libby, *Nancy*, 187.
168 *"If I don't have a chance . . . I'm going to pop"*: ibid., 188.
169 *"When anyone asks . . . this was it"*: ibid., 189.
169 *"Each time Reagan came across as conflicted. . . . and at the same time"*: Cannon, *Governor Reagan*, 384–85.
170 *"I thought, 'So this is how it ends' . . . we were leaving politics forever"*: Nancy Reagan with Novak, *My Turn*, 122.
170 *Hannaford and Deaver . . . big money in those days*: Morris, *Dutch*, 390.

CHAPTER EIGHT

171 *"without a day in office, the favorite presidential candidate of Republican conservatives"*: Warren Weaver Jr., "GOP Finds '68 Outlook Brighter as It Counts Election Successes: Gain of 47 in House, 8 Governors," *New York Times* online November 10, 1966, https://timesmachine.nytimes.com/timesmachine/1966/11/10/issue.html.
172 *"Lyndon Johnson is a disaster . . . plan for your election to the presidency"*: Reed, *The Reagan Enigma*, 59-60.
173 *"Who the fuck got me into this?"*: Cannon, *Governor Reagan,* footnote p. 260.
175 *"For Nancy, the convention fiasco . . . whatever the Gipper might be thinking"*: Deaver, *Nancy*," 44.
175 *"more misrepresented than almost anything Ronnie has ever done"*: Nancy Reagan with Libby, *Nancy*, 163.
175 *"was the last thing on my mind"*: Ronald Reagan, *An American Life,* Loc 2473 of 12608. Kindle.
175 *"I had met with Reagan . . . an enigma to this day"*: Reed, *Reagan Enigma,* 178–79.
175 *"The experience was good for a man . . . for the mood of the American voters"*: Morris, *Dutch*, 358–59.
176 *"I was heartsick . . . nothing I could do about it"*: Nancy Reagan with Novak, *My Turn*, 145.
176 *"Well, Dad, there's good news" . . . "I must tell Nancy"*: Michael Reagan with Hyams, *Outside Looking In,* 158.
177 *"There was genuine disappointment . . . without him and Nancy in the audience"*: Maureen Reagan, *First Father, First Daughter,* 208–9.
178 *When he was twenty-six, Michael got married . . . belonged to Jane Wyman*: "Michael Reagan, Governor's Son, to Marry Miss Pamela Putnam," *New York Times* online, September 22, 1970, https://www.nytimes.com/1970/09/22/archives/michael-reagan-governors-son-to-marry-miss-pamela-putnam.html.
178 *"Some men feel their masculinity . . . at least once a day"*: Michael Reagan with Hyams, *Outside Looking In,* 121–29.
178 *"I hated myself . . . they were all whores"*: ibid., 129–30.
179 *The most awkward moment . . . also join the group*: ibid., 145–47.
180 *"I needed her right then . . . do all those things, but I was"*: Patti Davis, "How I Remember My Mother Nancy Reagan," *Time* online, last modified March 10, 2016, https://time.com/4253749/patti-davis-how-i-remember-nancy-reagan.

180 *"It's terrible that he took that part . . . going steady"*: Patti Davis, *The Way I See It*, 141.
180 *"a very radical black girl named Eva Jefferson"*: ibid., 124–27.
181 *"I was using her habit to support mine"*: ibid., 143.
181 *"When Patti tried to sound important . . . 'I don't believe a word you're saying'"*: Richard Davis, author interview, March 5, 2017.
181 *"During Patti's years with Bernie . . . which we just couldn't accept"*: Nancy Reagan with Novak, *My Turn*, 138.
183 *Maureen tried to talk Ronnie out of running . . . too much turmoil in the wake of Watergate*: Maureen Reagan, *First Father, First Daughter*, 227–29.
183 *Ron just pouted*: Nancy Reagan with Novak, *My Turn*, 153.
183 *"Her questions were always the hardest . . . tilting at windmills?"*: Deaver, *Nancy*, 44–45.
183 *"Looking back, I realize it was inevitable . . . with whatever he decided"*: Nancy Reagan with Novak, *My Turn*, 151.
183 *"The astonishing thing . . . it doesn't make much sense"*: James Reston, "Reagan's Theatrical Politics," *New York Times* online, November 19, 1975, https://www.nytimes.com/1975/11/19/archives/reagans-theatrical-politics.html.
185 *"I don't think, even to this day . . . certain this would be a cakewalk"*: Spencer, *Behind the Podium*, 51–60.
185 *Three weeks later . . . planned to defect*: Reed, *Reagan Enigma*, 207–8.
185 *"Nerve endings* very *raw in California"*: Compilation of Tom Reed journal entries shared with author.
186 *"Nancy tipped the balance . . . come aboard"*: Reed, *Reagan Enigma*, 237.
186 *"They were all thinking that Nixon was going to survive . . . my stock went up at that point"*: John Sears, telephone interview by author.
187 *"He looks you in the tie," Ronnie said. "Why won't he look at me?"*: Nancy Reagan with Novak, *My Turn*, 153.
187 *"You find out" . . . nagging and all*: Nancy Reynolds, interviewed by author, May 3, 2019.
187 *"We lost forty-eight to forty-nine . . . registered as Republicans"*: Nancy Reagan, interview by Bonnie Angelo, *Time*, August 19, 1976, from *Time* internal files. Republican National Convention; Kemper Arena; Kansas City, Mo.; 1976; Vol II.
187 *She blamed Sears . . . everything was going fine*: Nancy Reagan with Novak, *My Turn*, 157–58.
188 *Eleven years later, there were 4,200 . . . pro-Reagan registration drive*: *Washington Post* wire service, "Once Lonely Republican Is Chairman for Reagan," *Morning Call* (Allentown, PA) online, March 7, 1976, https://www.newspapers.com/image/275848364/?terms=carol%2Bmccain.
188 *"The two men most responsible . . . in Sacramento"*: R. W. Apple Jr., "Ford, in Turnabout, Now Seems to Lead Reagan in Florida Vote," *New York Times* online, March 8, 1976, https://www.nytimes.com/1976/03/08/archives/ford-in-turnabout-now-seems-to-lead-reagan-in-florida-vote.html.
189 *"Ronnie has to get out . . . embarrass himself if he doesn't"*: Nofziger, *Nofziger*, 179–80.
190 *"a right-wing zealot . . . some pretty good"*: ibid.
190 *She sent him and Ellis a leftover video*: Jim Morrill, "How Nancy Reagan Helped Save Her Husband's Career in NC," Charlotte (NC) Observer online, March 8, 2016, https://www.charlotteobserver.com/news/politics-government/campaign-tracker-blog/article64842197.html.

191 *"last ditch, desperation maneuver . . . difference for Mr. Reagan between victory and defeat"*: Joseph Lelyveld, "Reagan's Upset Victory in North Carolina Attributed to Impact of Last-Minute TV Speech," *New York Times* online, March 29, 1976, https://www.nytimes.com/1976/03/29/archives/reagans-upset-victory-in-north-carolina-attributed-to-impact-of.html.

191 *"Ronald Reagan, as of tonight, looms as a serious threat"*: Nancy Reagan with Novak, *My Turn,* 161.

191 *"My basic premise . . . piss him off"*: Spencer, *Behind the Podium,* 60.

192 *"That damn Spencer's behind this"*: Michael K. Deaver, *A Different Drummer: My Thirty Years with Ronald Reagan* (New York: HarperCollins, 2001), 66.

192 *"It was quite awhile . . . for that one"*: Nancy Reagan with Novak, *My Turn,* 161.

192 *"But to Spencer's great satisfaction . . . Ford won primaries the same day"*: Spencer, *Behind the Podium,* 63.

192 *Edie called the senator from Arizona a "cocksucker"*: Colacello, *Ronnie & Nancy,* 452.

192 *"a fucking horse's ass"*: Kelley, *Nancy Reagan,* 237.

192 *Nancy allowed . . . "colorful language"*: Nancy Reagan with Novak, *My Turn,* 159.

193 *"Reagan really had the . . . whether he had the votes or not"*: Spencer, *Behind the Podium,* 63.

194 *"But that was '68 . . . distasteful and unfortunate"*: Judy Klemesrud, "Wives in '76 Campaign Find the Going Difficult," *New York Times* online, April 12, 1976, https://www.nytimes.com/1976/04/12/archives/wives-in-76-campaign-find-the-going-difficult-wives-in-the-76.html.

196 *"fell apart at the seams"*: "The Wives: Contest of the Queens," *Time* online, August 30, 1976, http://content.time.com/time/subscriber/article/0,33009,918243,00.html.

196 *more vividly in her memory than any of the four races that Ronnie won*: Nancy Reagan with Novak, *My Turn,* 150.

196 *When I first went into politics" . . . "no money. No money"*: Nancy Reagan, interview by Angelo, *Time*, August 18, 1976, from *Time* internal files; Republican National Convention; Kemper Arena; Kansas City, Mo.; 1976; Vol. II. portions of this quote appeared in the August 30, 1976, magazine.

197 *"Honey . . . I've never been prouder of you than I am now"*: Nancy Reagan with Novak, *My Turn,* 163.

CHAPTER NINE

199 *"To my surprise, Reagan . . . nomination from him"*: Nofziger, *Nofziger,* 206.

200 *"I had never heard the word* ballet *cross his lips"*: Nancy Reagan with Novak, *My Turn,* 145–46.

200 *"Individually and in groups . . . far behind in studying dance"*: William F. Buckley Jr., "Thanksgiving at the Buckleys," *National Review* online, November 26, 2008, https://www.nationalreview.com/2008/11/thanksgiving-buckleys-william-f-buckley-jr.

200 *"Frankly, I didn't particularly like Doria then . . . Ron would wind up hurt"*: Nancy Reagan with Novak, *My Turn,* 146–47.

202 *"Dear St. Valentine . . . 'Someone'"*: Nancy Reagan, *I Love You, Ronnie,* 129–30.

202 *"I've been very lucky. . . . for the first time"*: Reagan Presidential Library, 1980, Presidential Campaign Papers, subseries B: Nancy Reagan Files, correspondence, 1978, A–Z, box 30.

203 *"everything seemed preordained . . . fall into place"*: Nancy Reagan, *I Love You, Ronnie,* 128.

203 *"I don't think . . . She was the one who believed in him"*: Ed Rollins, telephone interview by author, January 26, 2018.
204 *"and bought a lot of friends . . . inevitability about a Reagan candidacy"*: Nofziger, *Nofziger*, 222.
205 *(Federal Election Commission records . . . no donations to the Reagan effort)*: James V. Grimaldi, "Records Show Scant Reagan-Trump Ties," *Wall Street Journal* online, September 15, 2015, https://www.wsj.com/articles/records-show-scant-reagan-trump-ties-1442359829.
205 *fifteen minutes to spare*: Jason M. Breslow, "The *Frontline* Interview: Roger Stone," *Frontline* online, last modified September 27, 2016, https://www.pbs.org/wgbh/frontline/article/the-frontline-interview-roger-stone.
205 *close friends and political allies*: Roger Stone, interview by Steve Scully, September 3, 2015, transcript, C-Span, https://www.c-span.org/video/?c4549847/nancy-reagan-gave-roger-stone-index-cards-reagan-ny-friends-half-people-cards-dead.
206 *"They boiled down to one thing" . . . writing his column*: Nofziger, *Nofziger*, 221.
207 *"under no circumstances . . . in his 1980 campaign"*: Maureen Reagan, *First Father, First Daughter*, 239.
207 *"She loved to gossip" . . . she did send him a book on astrology*: Sears, author interview, January 14, 2019.
208 *"I'd pick them all off . . . dump the rest"*: Spencer, *Behind the Podium*, 91.
209 *"jump-off-the-cliff-with-the-flag-flying conservative"*: Nancy Reagan with Novak, *My Turn*, 203.
209 *"Nobody is going to convince me . . . homosexual rights over parents' rights"*: Associated Press, "Briggs Accuses Foes of Scare Tactics," *Santa Cruz (CA) Sentinel* online, October 12, 1978, https://www.newspapers.com/image/63190984/?terms=reagan%2Bproposition%2B6%2Bhomosexual.
209 *"A lot of people she knew in the film business . . . and so she was very helpful"*: Sears, author interview, January 14, 2019.
211 "What the hell is going on here?": Deaver, *Behind the Scenes*, 86–88.
212 *"Reagan never spoke warmly to Sears again . . . he had made a mistake"*: Cannon, *Governor Reagan*, 449.
212 *"I don't know . . . arrogant and aloof"*: Nancy Reagan with Novak, *My Turn*, 172–73.
214 *"This time . . . staying until it's over"*: ibid.
216 *"I know what you're going to do . . . going to go out there"*: Peter Hannaford, interview, January 10, 2003, Presidential Oral Histories, Ronald Reagan Presidency, Miller Center, University of Virginia, Charlottesville, VA, https://millercenter.org/the-presidency/presidential-oral-histories/peter-hannaford-oral-history.
218 *"After the debate . . . badges"*: Ronald Reagan, *An American Life*, loc. 3019 of 12608, Kindle.
218 *on display in her husband's presidential library*: Molloy recounts all of this here: "NH Primary Vault: Ronald Reagan's Microphone Moment in 1980," YouTube, 11:23, WMUR-TV, https://www.youtube.com/watch?v=ovnRIGgtxss.
218 *"When I finally got to bed . . . over a serious problem"*: Nancy Reagan with Novak, *My Turn*, 173.
218 *"She reviewed for him . . . 'Washington mercenaries,'"* Deaver, *Behind the Scenes*, 88.
219 *"The campaign is in chaos . . . can't think things through"*: Reed, *Reagan Enigma*, 217.
219 *"pretty hopeless . . . join that maelstrom"*: ibid., 218.
219 *just happened to have his phone number handy*: Cannon, *Governor Reagan*," 464–67; Reed, *Reagan Enigma*, 132–33.

220 *"It's late . . . get some sleep"*: Nancy Reagan with Novak, *My Turn*, 173–75.
220 *"we can still be friends"*: ibid.
220 *"She was a very powerful woman . . . gave the country back its optimism"*: Sears, author interview, January 14, 2019.

CHAPTER TEN

222 *with "a cool correctness . . . deserved the change in our relationship"*: John McCain with Mark Salter, *Worth the Fighting For: The Education of an American Maverick and the Heroes Who Inspired Him* (New York: Random House Trade Paperbacks, 2002), 85–86.
222 *"John had met somebody young . . . not really a lot I could do about it"*: Carol McCain, telephone interview by author, July 30, 2017.
224 *"It was a power play . . . no role in a Reagan administration"*: Spencer *Behind the Podium*, 95.
225 *"wanted to run the White House . . . attended the funerals"*: Nofziger, *Nofziger*, 242.
225 *"As George and I stood there . . . putting the party back together"*: Ronald Reagan, *An American Life*, loc. 3066 of 12608, Kindle.
225 *"When her husband finally . . . who always smiles, didn't"*: Michael Kramer, "Inside the Room with George Bush," *New York* online, July 28, 1980. https://books.google.com/books?id=oOUCAAAAMBAJ&printsec=frontcover#v=onepage&q=bush&f=false—p 12.
225 *"Her face told it all . . . consoling her"*: Bill Peterson, "The Republicans in Detroit," *Washington Post* online, July 18, 1980, https://www.washingtonpost.com/archive/politics/1980/07/18/the-republicans-in-detroit/fc04f2b9-6fb2-4694-a10e-ecb908f20ab1/?utm_term=.72dd020e7702.
226 *"all the places . . . it's brilliant!"*: Mitchell Owens, "Inside John F. Kennedy's House in Virginia," *Architectural Digest* online, January 31, 2015, https://www.architecturaldigest.com/story/john-jacqueline-kennedy-virginia-house-plans-auction-article.
226 *a favorite of the Texas governor*: Nofziger, *Nofziger*, 269.
229 *"Rosalynn Carter would never put words in her husband's mouth in public"*: Mike Feinsilber, Associated Press, "Three Wives: Strengths of Mates Is What the Presidential Candidates Have in Common," *Anniston (AL) Star*, September 28, 1980, 11C.
230 *"She can sit perfectly still . . . over and over?"*: Sally Quinn, "Nancy Reagan on the Road to the Realm," *Washington Post* online, May 1, 1980, https://www.washingtonpost.com/archive/lifestyle/1980/05/01/nancy-reagan-on-the-road-to-the-realm/65de8bc0-ec7f-426d-b18e-b892beee59a4.
231 *"It's an old secret . . . the little touch of the bitch inside"*: Julie Baumgold, "Ronald Reagan's Total Woman," *New York* online, July 28, 1980, https://nymag.com/intelligencer/2016/03/read-new-yorks-nancy-reagan-story-from-1980.html.
231 *"She's very complicated . . . easy for people to understand her"*: McCain, author interview, July 30, 2017.
231 *"They just couldn't identify with you . . . everything they were rebelling against"*: Nancy Reagan with Novak, *My Turn*, 27.
232 *"Jim Baker had asked me . . . She was a great flirt"*: George Will, telephone interview by author, March 31, 2017.
233 *"Ronnie never wears makeup"*: Jon Meacham, *Destiny and Power: The American Odyssey of George Herbert Walker Bush* (New York: Random House, 2016), 259.
233 *"a little color to his cheeks"*: Deaver, *Behind the Scenes*, 98.

234 *"If you wanted a document to disappear . . . win a partial victory"*: Nancy Reagan with Novak, *My Turn*, 203.

234 *"Oh, no, not Ed"*: Spencer, *Behind the Podium*, 100–101.

234 *"I had managed . . . the other not"*: James A. Baker III, with Steve Fiffer, *"Work Hard, Study . . . and Keep Out of Politics!" Adventures and Lessons from an Unexpected Public Life* (Evanston, IL: Northwestern University Press, 2006), 97.

234 *"Nobody in the campaign . . . why Baker was suddenly on the plane"*: Spencer, *Behind the Podium*, 101.

234 *"Jim Baker is a gentleman . . . with that kind of person"*: Will, author interview, March 31, 2017.

234 *"She was the one . . . more than anybody else"*: Brian D. Sweany, "The Fixer," *Texas Monthly* online, April 2015, https://www.texasmonthly.com/politics/the-fixer.

235 *"Ronnie, Jim is leaving the plane . . . What in God's name have we got going here?"*: Richard Allen, interview, May 28, 2002, Presidential Oral Histories, Ronald Reagan Presidency, Miller Center, University of Virginia, Charlottesville, VA, https://millercenter.org/the-presidency/presidential-oral-histories/richard-allen-oral-history-assistant-president-national.

235 *"Reagan's personal and political needs . . . honest broker between Baker and Meese"*: Deaver, *Behind the Scenes*, 126.

236 *"The real troika, frankly . . . Nancy, Baker, and Deaver"*: Clark, interview, August 17, 2003, Miller Center.

236 *"I couldn't vote for my father . . . as cowardly as you can get"*: Patti Davis, *The Way I See It*, 248.

237 *they heard the race being called for Ronnie*: Nancy Reagan with Novak, My Turn, 186.

CHAPTER ELEVEN

239 *"We want to avoid . . . get this place working again"*: Elisabeth Bumiller, "The Reagans' Hello Party," *Washington Post*, November 19, 1980, E-1.

239 *"Are you sure this is serious? . . . I'm a Democrat"*: ibid.

240 *"After four long years . . . eager to be wooed"*: Lynn Rosellini, "Reagan Asks for a First Waltz and Wins Hearts in the Capital," *New York Times* online, November 19, 1980, https://timesmachine.nytimes.com/timesmachine/1980/11/19/issue.html?action=click&contentCollection=Archives&module=LedeAsset®ion=ArchiveBody&pgtype=article.

240 *"'Just invite them and see'"*: Colacello, "Ronnie and Nancy Part II," *Vanity Fair*, August 1998, 176.

241 *"a photograph that may upset arch-conservatives" . . . "you should be unhappy with Ronald Reagan"*: Katharine Graham, *Personal History* (New York: Vintage Books, 1997), 611–12.

241 *"enormously impressed . . . no matter how rough the sea gets"*: Richard Nixon to Michael Deaver, February 11, 1981, Deaver, Michael K.: Files, Box OA 7618, February 1981, Reagan Presidential Library, www.reaganlibrary.gov/sites/default/files/digitallibrary/smof/dcos/deaver/box-001/40-137-7065105-001-006-2016.pdf.

242 *"She loves young Ron and cried for days after he got married"*: Garry Clifford, "Nancy's Class Act," *People* online, August 5, 1985, https://people.com/archive/nancys-class-act-vol-24-no-6.

244 *"Mrs. Reagan was sitting there. . . . before they have the job"*: "Roy Stories: Cohn Speaks from Beyond the Grave," *New York*, February 22, 1988, 43, available at https://books

.google.com/books?id=reUCAAAAMBAJ&pg=PA43&lpg=PA43&dq=%22nancy+reagan%22+william+simon+treasury+secretary&source=bl&ots=wxJvkQJRBk&sig=ACfU3U3ioqg8xZ4FoQcJYIiZdmYJv7EMRw&hl=en&sa=X&ved=2ahUKEwi7q8yEyfPiAhWswFkKHcFpBlU4ChDoATAGegQIBhAB#v=onepage&q=%22nancy%20reagan%22%20william%20simon%20treasury%20secretary&f=false. Vetoing Simon was a fateful move, however, as it paved the way for Merrill Lynch chairman Donald Regan, who became Nancy's greatest foe, to get the job—and a foothold in Ronnie's administration. Cohn recounted the story, which he claimed to have heard from Simon.

246 *Not everyone was so taken with the spectacle*: The gala would also be remembered for an unfortunate performance by Broadway star Ben Vereen—an African American—shuffling and singing in blackface.

247 *"When you've got to pay $2,000 . . . that's ostentatious"*: Liz Smith, *New York Daily News*, January 21, 1981, 12, available at Newspapers.com, https://www.newspapers.com/image/485811520.

247 *"I think it's outrageous . . . eaten up by inflation"*: Leslie Bennetts, "With a New First Lady, a New Style," *New York Times* online, January 21, 1981, https://www.nytimes.com/1981/01/21/us/y-reagan-with-a-new-first-lady-a-new-s.html.

247 *Thirty-two minutes*: Morris, *Dutch*, 781.

247 *Where Ronnie's predecessors . . . looks toward the rest of the country, spreading westward*: The decision to move the venue had been made by Congress's inaugural committee the previous year, though it would often be attributed to Ronnie's stage managers.

248 *"My strongest memory . . . friends all their lives"*: Nancy Reagan with Novak, *My Turn*, 198.

248 *"It glows . . . restore harmony"*: Morris, *Dutch*, 418.

249 *"Dear Jane . . . Sincerely, Ron"*: Ronald Reagan to Jane Wyman, January 27, 1981; letter provided to the author by Dennis Revell.

250 *"It is generally agreed . . . everybody is positive are coming"*: Reagan Library, Michael Deaver correspondence files, February 1981, Box 7618. https://www.reaganlibrary.gov/sites/default/files/digitallibrary/smof/dcos/deaver/box-001/40-137-7065105-001-004-2016.pdf].

251 *"This newspaper is quite sure . . . along on much less"*: United Press International, "Nancy Gets Warning About Dangers of 'Living Rich,'" *San Francisco Examiner*, March 20, 1981, A-19.

252 *"It better be fixed now before it becomes even worse"*: WHORM subject files: PP005-01: 025433, Reagan Presidential Library.

252 *"They wanted to set up office space . . . important to her too"*: Fred Fielding, interview by author, Washington, DC, February 7, 2019.

253 *"She was not in favor of them staying there . . . get in the way of a smoothly functioning White House"*: Baker, author interview, January 4, 2017.

255 *"Looking back . . . do things differently if we had it to do over again"*: Nancy Reagan with Novak, *My Turn*, 18.

255 *"My family comes first . . . and homey as possible"*: "A Chat with Nancy Reagan," *Newsweek*, March 9, 1981, 27.

255 *"a mistake that only added . . . who kept acquiring more and more expensive items"*: Nancy Reagan with Novak, *My Turn*, 2.

256 *"Nancy Reagan got so involved . . . Monsieur Marc"*: "Nancy Moves Around Town in Style," *New York Daily News*, October 22, 1981, 11.

256 *The coverage also contrasted . . . federal support for the one she visited*: Ken Auletta, "The Reagan Voluntarism in Search of Volunteers," *New York Daily News*, October 25, 1981, 46.

256 *All of this would pass . . . until it did*: Deaver, *Behind the Scenes*, 118.

258 *"These calls became the source of some amusement . . . always to protect the president"*: Sheila Tate, *Lady in Red: An Intimate Portrait of Nancy Reagan* (New York: Crown Forum, 2018), 219.

258 *"If the renovations made people angry . . . china drove them crazy"*: Nancy Reagan with Novak, *My Turn*, 21.

259 *an especially close and important relationship*: Ronnie and Britain's "Iron Lady" had been transatlantic political "soul mates"—that was Ronnie's description—from their first one-on-one meeting in London in 1975, shortly after Thatcher became the first woman to head the Conservative Party. He wrote later: "Of course, it never occurred to me that before many years would pass, Margaret and I would be sitting across from each other as the heads of our respective governments." Ronald Reagan, *An American Life*, loc. 2878 of 12608, Kindle.

260 *Nancy introduced what were then considered novel and exciting foods*: C. K. Hickey, "All the Presidents' Meals," *Foreign Policy* online, last modified February 16, 2019, https://foreignpolicy.com/all-the-presidents-meals-state-dinners-white-house-infographic.

261 *"She always fixed me up with a hot Hollywood star . . . Ginger Rogers!"*: Shultz, author interview, October 20, 2016.

261 *"enough to paper his entire office"*: Nancy Reagan with Novak, *My Turn*, 205.

263 *"There were roller-coaster times with Nancy Reagan . . . protecting her"*: Allen, interview, May 28, 2002, Miller Center.

264 *"If Ronnie had thrown Stockman out . . . he expected their loyalty"*: Nancy Reagan with Novak, *My Turn*, 51.

264 *negative sentiment toward her running double what it had against her predecessors*: Donnie Radcliffe and Barry Sussman, "Nancy's Image Change," *Washington Post* online, October 24, 1981, https://www.washingtonpost.com/archive/lifestyle/1981/10/24/nancys-image-change/62fe7149-c4c1-49d1-8a28-8a7ef2456f55.

264 *"You know, some days . . . it must be my fault"*: Chris Wallace, *First Lady*, 56.

265 *"In many ways . . . just seemed to rub them the wrong way"*: Nancy Reagan with Novak, *My Turn*, ix.

CHAPTER TWELVE

268 *"Don't listen to the stories" . . . "take good care of her"*: Del Quentin Wilber, *Rawhide Down: The Near Assassination of Ronald Reagan* (New York: Henry Holt, 2011), 103.

268 *traffic that came over the radio . . . "Rawhide is okay"*: Mark Ambinder, "Full Secret Service Transcript: The Moment Reagan Was Shot," *Atlantic* online, last modified March 11, 2011, https://www.theatlantic.com/politics/archive/2011/03/full-secret-service-transcript-the-moment-reagan-was-shot/72343.

269 *He sprinted . . . up three flights of stairs to the top floor of the residence*: Wilber research notes provided to the author.

269 *command center alerted agents . . . at the Twenty-Second Street entrance*: Ambinder, "Moment Reagan Was Shot."

270 *"But they told me"* . . . "He has to know I'm here!": Nancy Reagan with Novak, *My Turn*, 1–2.

270 *"Doctors believe bleeding to death . . . Touch and go"*: Larry Speakes with Robert Pack, *Speaking Out: The Reagan Presidency from Inside the White House* (New York: Charles Scribner's Sons, 1988), 6.

271 *His blood pressure plummeted . . . not get a systolic reading*: Jerry Parr with Carolyn Parr, *In the Secret Service: The True Story of the Man Who Saved President Reagan's Life* (Carol Stream, IL: Tyndale House, 2013), 215–30.

272 *"open and bleeding . . . it was monstrous"*: Nancy Reagan with Novak, *My Turn*, 4.

273 *"God, you tremble . . . such a clear shot at the president"*: "Attempted Assassination of Ronald Reagan," YouTube, 9:38, Tulsaphotog, https://www.youtube.com/watch?v=IeHYFgU13TM.

274 *Soviet submarines*: Ambinder, "Moment Reagan Was Shot."

275 *Allen could see . . . wobbling and his arms shaking*: ibid.

276 *worry etched on her own*: John Pekkanen, "The Saving of the President," *Washingtonian*, August 1, 1981, available at https://www.washingtonian.com/1981/08/01/from-the-archives-the-saving-of-the-president.

276 *fly in from Houston with his own specialists*: ibid.

277 *he never saw the note again*: Charlotte Wiessner, daughter of Dr. Daniel Ruge, telephone interview by author, August 8, 2017.

277 *"Dan was a marvelous surgeon . . . She didn't like him at all"*: Richard Davis, author interview, March 5, 2017.

277 *"My father wasn't crazy about her"*: Wiessner, author interview, August 8, 2017.

278 *"What kind of family is this? . . . Even a bullet can't bring us together"*: Patti Davis, *The Way I See It*, 270–71.

279 *The family would not all be together again until Thanksgiving*: Michael Reagan with Hyams, *Outside Looking In*, 195–96; confirmed by Dennis Revell, interview by author, Sacramento, CA, July 25, 2019.

279 *"Ronnie's been shot. Can you come?"*: Barbara Sinatra with Wendy Holden, *Lady Blue Eyes: My Life with Frank* (New York: Crown Archetype, 2011), 267.]

280 *"asked for a television set in his room so he could view this program tonight"*: "The Opening of the Academy Awards in 1981," YouTube, 8:04, Oscars, https://www.youtube.com/watch?v=Rq4jfI-ItAU&list=PLJ8RjvesnvDO2x9ClhRsdL2DbgFYHMM3Z.

281 *"I didn't know I was supposed to be holding the nation together . . . Neither did I feel that the president was dying"*: Nofziger, *Nofziger*, 292–98.

281 *"The president was not in serious danger of dying"*: Elmer W. Lammi, United Press International online, "Dr. Dennis O'Leary, Chief Spokesman for George Washington University . . ." August 18, 1981, https://www.upi.com/Archives/1981/08/18/Dr-Dennis-OLeary-chief-spokesman-for-George-Washington-University/7996366955200.

283 *"While it is common . . . as sharp as any yet recorded"*: Barry Sussman, "Shooting Gives Reagan Boost in Popularity," *Washington Post* online, April 2, 1981, https://www.washingtonpost.com/archive/politics/1981/04/02/shooting-gives-reagan-boost-in-popularity/9515e340-f295-42e7-89c4-c96edoab7a44/?utm_term=.8912c3ea6df4.

284 *"The weather was beautiful . . . how much we missed our life in California"*: Ronald Reagan, *An American Life*, loc. 3904 of 12608, Kindle.

284 *"This woman whose presence . . . almost lost between my arms"*: Patti Davis, *The Way I See It*, 274.

285 *"The thing that really got to her . . . Sadat really hit her hard"*: Jim Kuhn, interview by author, Washington, DC, February 28, 2019.

286 *"Dear Mrs. R. . . . Lucky me"*: Nancy Reagan, *I Love You, Ronnie*, 156–60.

CHAPTER THIRTEEN

289 *eight-star hotel*: Nancy Reagan with Novak, *My Turn*, 200–201.
289 *in bed by ten*: ibid., 212–17.
289 *"I never expected . . . welcome part of our routine"*: ibid., 214.
291 *"Three and a half minutes, that's fine . . . fifteen seconds at the end"*: Mark Weinberg, *Movie Nights with the Reagans: A Memoir* (New York: Simon & Schuster, 2018), 80.
292 *"was on a mission from Nancy . . . buried in this stuff on weekends"*: Allen, interview, May 28, 2002, Miller Center.
293 *"I felt like I was a kid . . . I couldn't resist"*: John Hutton, interview, April 15–16, 2004, Presidential Oral Histories, Ronald Reagan Presidency, Miller Center, University of Virginia, Charlottesville, VA, https://millercenter.org/the-presidency/presidential-oral-histories/john-hutton-md-oral-history.
295 *"This is my fourteenth trip . . . the most ineptly organized"*: Lou Cannon, "On the Continent, Nodding Off and Fending Off the Press," *Washington Post* online, June 14, 1982, https://www.washingtonpost.com/archive/politics/1982/06/14/on-the-continent-nodding-off-and-fending-off-the-press/cc4c1533-ab29-4518-8bf2-67c11248c14a.
295 *"Reagan managed to raise doubts . . . some of his administration's policies"*: Lou Cannon, "President Gained His Major Goal," *Washington Post*, June 13, 1982, 1.
296 *"a relaxed and effective performer . . . as events in his reelection campaign"*: Cannon, *President Reagan*, 416.
296 *"I don't get involved . . . who are trying to end-run him"*: Chris Wallace, *First Lady*, 41.
297 *"Does his no always end it? . . . come back at him again"*: ibid., 40.
297 *"Her husband's close associates . . . pull the trigger"*: Richard E. Neustadt, *Presidential Power and the Modern Presidents: The Politics of Leadership from Roosevelt to Reagan* (New York: Free Press, 1990), 312–14.
297 *"Never let your Nancy be immobilized"*: ibid., 316.
298 *"She could not bear the thought of the criticism . . . Ronald Reagan—a president with a particularly idealistic streak—was especially in need of this kind of counsel"*: Peter J. Wallison, *Ronald Reagan: The Power of Conviction and the Success of his Presidency* (Boulder, CO: Westview Press, 2003), 106–7.
298 *"It really reaches a point . . . rather than let it build up a head of steam"*: Chris Wallace, *First Lady*, 41.
300 *"Nancy Reagan had a better understanding . . . he did not like to be pushed by anyone, not even Nancy Reagan"*: Cannon, *President Reagan*, 447.
302 *when he proposed this idea, shook her head vigorously in opposition*: Ken Khachigian, interview by author, San Clemente, CA, August 29, 2019.
302 *"I don't give a damn about the right-to-lifers"*: Donald Regan, *For the Record: From Wall Street to Washington* (New York: Harcourt Brace Jovanovich, 1988), 86.
302 *"On the other hand, I believe in a woman's choice"*: Chris Kaltenbach, "Former First Lady Nancy Reagan Speaks Out for Abortion Rights," *Baltimore Sun* online, September 21, 1994, https://www.baltimoresun.com/news/bs-xpm-1994-09-21-1994264147-story.html.
303 *"On background . . . a wonderful job"*: Cannon, *President Reagan*, 131n.
303 *"Ed and I were never close . . . I always felt that Meese was one of them"*: Nancy Reagan with Novak, *My Turn*, 203.
304 *"Ronald Reagan, with his soft heart . . . Nancy would prevail upon him to act in his own interest"*: George P. Shultz, *Turmoil and Triumph: My Years as Secretary of State* (New York: Charles Scribner's Sons, 1993), 317.

305 *Senator Paul Laxalt . . . soon on the phone with Nancy*: Cannon, *President Reagan*, 375.
306 *"When a political appointee . . . he should step aside"*: Nancy Reagan with Novak, *My Turn*, 51–52.
307 *"I trusted George completely . . . out the window"*: ibid., 205.
308 *"a schemer married to someone who was unable to conceive of a Machiavellian thought"*: Von Damm, *At Reagan's Side*. 228.
308 *"I could only conclude that for some reason . . . slapped me in the face"*: ibid., 271–73.
308 *"a homecoming queen"*: Helene von Damm, interview by Ann Miller Morin, February 15, 1988, transcript, Foreign Affairs Oral History Project, Women Ambassadors Series, Association for Diplomatic Studies and Training, Arlington, VA, https://adst.org/wp-content/uploads/2013/12/von-Damm-Helene.pdf.
308 *"Her position was hardening toward me . . . with each new success I achieved"*: Von Damm, *At Reagan's Side*, 288.
309 *"anything less would have seemed underdressed"*: ibid., 308.
309 *"Die Playgirl Bows Out!"*: Georgie Anne Geyer, "Von Damme Tale Is a Common Plight," *Burlington (VT) Free Press*, December 16, 1985, 8.
309 *"Lucky, there's one thing you have to understand about Nancy"*. . . *hear from her*: Selwa "Lucky" Roosevelt, *Keeper of the Gate* (New York: Simon & Schuster, 1990), 203–4.
309 *"on guard, suspicious of anyone she thought was trying to use or manipulate her"*: ibid., 202.
310 *"This was a big honor"* . . . *Joe DiMaggio*: Will, author interview, March 31, 2017.
311 *"It turned out he was carrying water for Nancy on this . . . Nancy and Barbara just did not have a pleasant relationship"*: Jon Meacham, *Destiny and Power*, 266.
313 *"Nancy does not like Barbara. . . . Nancy Reagan is jealous of her"*: ibid., 334.
313 *"I know"*: Lou Cannon to author, email, August 27, 2019, confirming details.
313 *"a prince of a feller . . . Didn't seem to want us upstairs in the White House"*: Morris, *Dutch*, 638.
314 *she found in Reagan Library files drafts of the invitation list . . . "Just watch me"*: Susan Page, *The Matriarch: Barbara Bush and the Making of an American Dynasty* (New York: Twelve, 2019), 138–40.
314 *"This was the plan—that I was the Prince Charming of the evening"*: Ethan Alter, "John Travolta Recalls Dancing the Night Away with Princess Diana: 'I Was the Prince Charming of the Evening,'" Yahoo! Entertainment, last modified December 6, 2019, https://www.yahoo.com/entertainment/john-travolta-recalls-dancing-night-away-with-princess-diana-nancy-reagan-140058674.html?guccounter=1&guce_referrer=aHR0cHM6Ly93d3cuZ29vZ2xlLmNvbS8&guce_referrer_sig=AQAAAD1LWrigviKwoejH1grQevhaYC10063nrtt2Od02jciVyPBOCITPJrvAmuSU01AtOCqwiRSmqyJpJuJKcevZppJ8Bls1D9SyodrU4kAQ17j5TjgynhJETOXPVJo2E-bCC3l5CQWn9kFQAnc5Llv7TnafFDkQR3uRHgiOjpyoNxN8.

CHAPTER FOURTEEN

316 *"I remember having to say to Mike [Deaver] . . . 'We've got to give them back or something'"*: Baker, author interview, January 4, 2017.
317 *"As soon as I read this . . . Nancy needed to make fun of herself, not blame the press"*: Tate, *Lady in Red*, 45.
318 *"I bet she's pissed"*: ibid., 47.

319 *"This one song . . . my image began to change in Washington"*: Nancy Reagan with Novak, *My Turn*, 34–35.

319 *"Maybe this will end the sniping"*: Douglas Brinkley, ed., *The Reagan Diaries* (New York: HarperCollins, 2007), 76. At the Gridiron Club Dinner the following year, Ronnie would give a surprise performance himself, dressed in a serape and sombrero and singing a parody of the song "Manana." In his diary, on page 140, he noted that he had never sung on a stage before and was nervous.

320 *According to what Deaver told Morris . . . no evidence that Ronnie did anything about it*: Edmund Morris research materials made available to the author include the following: "NR took 'uppers and downers' to get to sleep, used to wake up at middle of the night to take another. Dr. Ruge confided this to rr. Doctor was nervous and concerned. NR leave the White House with a huge sealed box full of pills. Knew she couldn't get them again.—Deaver 6/7/89." Morris also noted that Deaver doubted Ruge would want to talk about this for the record.

320 *"Whether this accounts for some of the fluctuations in her mood over the years . . . perhaps that was the reason she didn't care for him at all"*: Richard Davis, author interview, August 10, 2017.

320 *former White House aide who says Hutton told him about the matter . . . no choice but to put her back on the drug*: Confidential source.

321 *"I always felt that it was a subconscious cry for help . . . a road map of denial"*: Patti Davis, *The Way I See It*, 298.

322 *decriminalizing small amounts*: Emily Dufton, "Why the 1970s Effort to Decriminalize Marijuana Failed," *Smithsonian* online, last modified April 25, 2019, https://www.smithsonianmag.com/history/why-1970s-effort-decriminalize-marijuana-failed-180972038.

323 *"I used to say . . . 'their influence and their budgets'"*: Carlton Turner, telephone interview by author, August 11, 2018.

325 *"finally being noticed . . . claiming the headlines"*: Donnie Radcliffe, "Polishing the Image," *Washington Post* online, February 19, 1982, https://www.washingtonpost.com/archive/lifestyle/1982/02/19/polishing-the-image/7ccb27d0-39ba-4bf9-99b2-7560e3f18198.

327 *"The drug bureaucracy . . . stuck to her guns"*: Shultz, author interview, October 20, 2016.

328 *"I said that . . . pass the information along"*: Smith College files: Box: Class of 1943, Individuals A-L Collection Number 80.02. 1943, box 2140.

329 *By the end of Nancy's tenure as first lady . . . average age was nine years old*: Estimates cited by the Reagan Library.

329 *"I never thought . . . treatment centers are the answer"*: Liz Smith, "Nancy Reagan's Turn on Phoenix House Flap," *Los Angeles Times*, January 31, 1990, 9.

330 *In 1979 more than 54 percent of high school . . . number had fallen by nearly half*: Richard A. Miech et al., *Monitoring the Future: National Survey Results on Drug Use, 1975–2015*, vol. 1, *Secondary School Students* (Ann Arbor, MI: Institute for Social Research, University of Michigan, 2016), tables 5.1 to 5.4, http://www.monitoringthefuture.org//pubs/monographs/mtf-vol1_2015.pdf.

330 *Where only about a third . . . doubled by the early 1990s*: ibid.

330 *"It was a great message . . . 'what you should be telling your kids'"*: Joseph A. Califano, telephone interview by author, August 14, 2019.

331 *"She twinkles when he arrives"*: Elisabeth Bumiller and Donnie Radcliffe, "Nancy Reagan," *Washington Post* online, January 23, 1983, https://www.washingtonpost.com/archive/lifestyle/1983/01/23/nancy-reagan/fe6e737f-7fde-4330-a6e8-30465ee89700.

331 *"Nancy Reagan was never a close . . . therapist more than her friend"*: Barbara Sinatra with Holden, *Lady Blue Eyes,* 269.
332 *"were speaking every night . . . pouring his heart out"*: Tina Sinatra with Jeff Coplon, *My Father's Daughter: A Memoir* (New York: Berkley Books, 2000), 226–27.
332 *(Tina Sinatra insisted that the former first lady be invited)*: ibid., 364.
334 *"Lately, Nancy Reagan has been calling the White House, not California, 'home'"*: Bumiller and Radcliffe, "Nancy Reagan."
335 *"As he approached the end of his life . . . more gentle and philosophical"*: Patti Davis, *The Way I See It,* 289–93.
337 *unable to let go*: Deaver, *Behind the Scenes,* 120.
339 *"I'm sure he is"*: Patti Davis, *The Way I See It,* 292.

CHAPTER FIFTEEN

341 *"I found this odd . . . punctual and efficient in everything else he did"*: Regan, *For the Record,* 73.
341 *"Leave it be"*: ibid.
342 *"If Aquarians have a fault . . . slow to get married!"*: Nancy Reagan with Novak, *My Turn,* 41, 87–88.
343 *"Fish were swimming around in his pool . . . for my Leo party"*: Joyce Wadler and Angela Blessing, "The President's Astrologers," *People* online, May 23, 1988, https://people.com/archive/cover-story-the-presidents-astrologers-vol-29-no-20.
343 *"Don't ever do that! . . . because one cancels out the other"*: Kuhn, author interview, Washington, DC, October 7, 2018.
343 *"lucky cuff links" . . . purple stone*: Weinberg, *Movie Nights with the Reagans,* 24.
343 *invaded by space aliens*: Cannon, *President Reagan,* 40–41.
343 *haunted by a ghost*: Maureen Reagan, *First Father, First Daughter,* 324–25.
344 *"Carroll told Nancy . . . why it wasn't a good time"*: Wadler and Blessing, "President's Astrologers."
345 *Many were tourists . . . streets of the nation's capital*: Parr with Parr, *In the Secret Service,"* 235.
345 *It was impossible to work a crowd . . . behind a sheet of bulletproof glass, the handlers complained*: William Henkel, telephone interview by author, October 17, 2017.
345 *Vietnam Veterans Memorial on the National Mall*: Kuhn, author interview, February 28, 2019.
345 *"If we weren't comfortable with it . . . it wouldn't happen"*: Joe Petro, interview by author, New York, February 23, 2017.
346 *the two of them had been talking once a year or so ever since*: Joan Quigley, *"What Does Joan Say?" My Seven Years as White House Astrologer to Nancy and Ronald Reagan* (New York: Birch Lane Press, 1990), 43.
346 *take off on the day of a debate*: ibid., 60–61.
346 *"Oh, my God. . . . shoot at him again."*: Nancy Reagan with Novak, *My Turn,* 37–39.
347 *Nancy was soon confiding . . . health of her parents*: ibid., 36–45.
347 *"Was astrology one of the reasons? . . . I'm not sorry I did it"*: ibid., 38–39.
348 *"If it makes you feel better . . . odd if it ever came out"*: ibid., 42–43.
348 *"Mike is a born chamberlain . . . servant to the great"*: Regan, *For the Record,* 74.
348 *"When I look back . . . innocent enough quirk"*: Deaver, *Nancy,* 138–39.

349 *Deaver would dither over making a decision . . . by medical advice on how to avoid jet lag*: Henkel, author interview, October 17, 2017.

349 *"I assumed it had to do with checking their social engagements and public commitments . . . dates and desirability of a visit"*: Roosevelt, *Keeper*, 205.

351 *"He was beating the shit out of me," Henkel said*: Henkel, author interview, October 17, 2017.

351 *He began keeping a color-coded . . . commence negotiations with foreign powers"*: Regan, *For the Record*, 4.

351 *"The president's schedule . . . movements of the planets," he wrote later*: ibid., 82.

352 *"At the end of the day . . . deep admiration for her"*: Henkel, author interview, October 17, 2017.

354 *"What it boils down to . . . except, possibly me"*: Nancy Reagan with Novak, *My Turn*, 44.

CHAPTER SIXTEEN

355 *"There is a secret thought that the offspring of famous people . . . deep inside us, we think they're right"*: Patti Davis, *The Long Goodbye* (New York: Alfred A. Knopf, 2004), 226.

356 *"During Ronnie's presidency . . . sometimes fell short of those values"*: Nancy Reagan with Novak, *My Turn*, 124.

357 *"a talented dancer who has worked very hard and who has done extremely well for a late starter"*: Anna Kisselgoff, "Joffrey Ballet's Gala: Diana Ross and Ron Reagan," *New York Times*, March 16, 1981, B6.

357 *"He thinks we're interfering with his privacy. . . . reasons of the Nation's welfare"*: Brinkley, *Reagan Diaries*, 85. This comes from the following entries into Ronald Reagan's diary:

> *May 15, 1982*: he wants to Sign off Secret Svc. for a month. S.S. Knows he's a real target—lives in a N.Y.C. Area where the Puerto Rican terrorist group is active in fact he's on a hit list. He thinks we're interfering with his privacy. I can't make him see that I can't be put in a position of one day facing a ransom demand. I'd have to refuse for reasons for the Nation's welfare.
>
> *May 23, 1982*: At home all day. Ron came down from N.Y. He's a little rebellious and wanted us to sign off S.S. protection for a month. He's the only one of the kids who is on the hit list of groups like FALN, etc. Ed Hickey came over and it's all straightened out.
>
> *The weekend of March 19–20, 1983*: Ron came down for a talk at the W.H. Same old problem—his itchiness at having S.S. protection. I wish he'd be more thoughtful of what it means to me to have him do that.
>
> *April 7, 1983*: This evening Ron called all exercised because S.S. agents had gone into their apartment while they were in Calif. to fix an alarm on one of the windows. I tried to reason with him that this was a perfectly O.K. thing for them to do. . . . I told him quite firmly not to talk to me that way & he hung up on me. End of a not perfect day.
>
> *May 1, 1983*: Nancy phoned—very upset. Ron casually told the S.S. he was going to Paris in a few days. I don't know what it is with him. He refuses to cooperate with them. . . . I'm not talking to him until he apologizes for hanging up on me.

May 19, 1983: Meets with Regan, who as Treasury secretary is in charge of the Secret Service, about "Ron & his paranoia about S.S. protection. I think he's being ridiculous & d—n unfair to the guys who are trying to protect his hide. This is settled—we let him sign off permanently—no protection."

358 *"He worked hard at a small space . . . never used his status to his advantage"*: Weinberg, *Movie Nights with the Reagans*, 137.

358 *a 1986 ad for American Express . . . continue the conversation in privacy*: "American Express Card with Ron Reagan Jr. Classic TV Commercial 1986," YouTube, 0:55, Front Seat Media, https://www.youtube.com/watch?v=va2Mhd5VWaE.

359 *"These are issues of unique concern to women . . . also family concerns and community concerns"*: Maureen Reagan, *First Father, First Daughter*, 296–97.

360 *"Well, Maureen* was *a little worked up . . . I shouldn't have said, too"*: Ed Rollins with Tom DeFrank, *Bare Knuckles and Back Rooms: My Life in American Politics* (New York: Broadway Books, 1996), 101–2.

361 *"chatting like schoolgirls"*: Speakes with Pack, *Speaking Out*, 98.

361 *"Michael Reagan always had schemes for making money . . . 'Well, Sonny Boy's at it again.'"*: ibid., 99.

361 *"He was a wheeler-dealer. . . . you just had to know that"*: Kuhn, author interview, October 7, 2018.

362 *It got even dicier . . . They suggested he get psychiatric help*: Michael Reagan with Hyams, *Outside Looking In*, 219–40.

362 *"I felt attacked . . . his Achilles' heel: Nancy"*: ibid., 228.

363 *"We've tried to keep a little fuss private . . . as all families do from time to time"*: Reagan Presidential Library, Subject Files, WHORM, PP 0005-01 095999, 247108 5300 4620 PPooJ.

365 *"The wounds are healed" . . . "Michael, I love you"*: ibid., 243–45.

366 *"They frolicked . . . worth the price?"*: ibid., 250.

368 "I love you": Nancy Reagan with Novak, *My Turn*, 134

368 *"It was the first time . . . I was elated"*: Michael Reagan with Hyams, *Outside Looking In*, 263–68.

368 *"Ironically, this book . . . a better relationship"*: Nancy Reagan with Novak, *My Turn*, 134.

369 *"a literary striptease . . . a First Family parlor game"*: Scot Haler, "The Problem of Being Patti," *People* online, February 24, 1986, https://people.com/archive/cover-story-the-problem-of-being-patti-vol-25-no-8.

369 *"one of the most painful and disappointing aspects of my life . . . we seem to square off"*: Nancy Reagan with Novak, *My Turn*, 136.

369 *"Tell you what . . . happen in my life"*: Patti Davis, *The Way I See It*, 264–66.

370 *"being used"*: ibid., 267–68.

370 *Caldicott's later account . . .* Reader's Digest: Ronnie Dugger, "The President and the Peace Activist," *St. Petersburg (FL) Times*, September 30, 1984, 4D.

371 *"I had hoped that Patti's wedding . . . people would understand"*: Nancy Reagan with Novak, *My Turn*, 140–41.

372 *"Ron's reaction hurt me more than anyone else's . . . motivation in it"*: Patti Davis, *The Way I See It*, 311.

372 *"Patti was excited that night about her book . . . such a thing"*: Ron Reagan to author, email, August 20, 2019.

372 *"I think sometimes . . . only silence and distance"*: Patti Davis, *Long Goodbye*, 80–81.

CHAPTER SEVENTEEN

375 *"a steady drumbeat"*: "President Reagan's and Nancy Reagan's Interview with Chris Wallace for Upcoming NBC Special, Camp David, Maryland," May 18, 1985, YouTube, 36:23, Reagan Presidential Library, https://www.youtube.com/watch?v=EhIeW-fbYiM.

375 *if Ronnie's name were not at the top of the ticket*: Rollins, author interview, January 26, 2018.

375 *"For a while, we talked about it every night . . . 'I'm not crazy about it, but okay'"*: Nancy Reagan with Novak, *My Turn*, 224.

376 *internal numbers*: Cannon, *President Reagan*, 197.

376 *"I think it's going to be a tough, personal, close campaign . . . glad when the next nine months are over"*: Nancy Reagan with Novak, *My Turn*, 225.

376 *$21 million budget for the 1984 primary season*: Rollins with DeFrank, *Bare Knuckles*, 125.

377 *She started to worry more . . . Hart, the insurgent in the race*: Stuart Spencer, quoted in Wallace, *First Lady*, 116–17.

377 *"She could smell fear all over you, Rollins. You're doomed"*: Rollins with DeFrank, *Bare Knuckles*, 137.

378 *"Don't forget who your clients are. . . . Their friends are going to see the commercials"*: Rollins, author interview, January 26, 2018.

380 *"These days . . . more relaxed speaker"*: Maureen Dowd, "A More Relaxed Nancy Reagan Tours the South," *New York Times*, October 14, 1984, 28.

381 *hefty 55-percent-to-37-percent lead . . . 8 percent of voters undecided*: Cannon, *President Reagan*, 475.

381 *"I'm against debates . . . defend his own record"*: Nancy Reagan with Novak, *My Turn*, 225.

381 *"the worst night of Ronnie's political career . . . that debate was a nightmare"*: ibid., 226.

383 *cold as ice*: ibid., 226–27.

383 *"a Reagan without confidence would not be Reagan . . . must interpret all tales of Nancy Reagan's 'ruthlessness'"*: Garry Wills, *Reagan's America: Innocents at Home* (New York: Open Road Integrated Media, 2017), loc. 4781 of 13714, Kindle.

384 *"In recognizing the actor's truth . . . may have been to Baker and Darman"*: Cannon, *President Reagan*, 484.

384 *"Well, you better be right . . . better be right"*: Rollins with DeFrank, *Bare Knuckles*, 149–50.

385 *"Although Nancy Reagan did not realize it . . . no longer Morning Again in America"*: Cannon, *President Reagan*, 487.

385 *"If, by some miracle, I could take back one decision . . . this new arrangement would lead to a political disaster"*: Nancy Reagan with Novak, *My Turn*, 267.

386 *"a bad omen"*: ibid., 230.

CHAPTER EIGHTEEN

388 *"It also made me squirm . . . weakened both the Justice Department and the presidency"*: Nancy Reagan with Novak, *My Turn*, 203.

389 *"listened to our words . . . did not occur to me"*: Regan, *For the Record*, 251.

389 *"He seemed to be absorbing . . . settled by some absent party"*: ibid., 255.

389 *"blending the gifts of Ronald Reagan with the proper pageantry"*: Deaver, *Behind the Scenes*, 179.

390 *license to use the president's first name to his face*: ibid., 195–97.

390 *allow him unfettered access to the White House grounds*: Fred Ryan, interview by author, Washington, DC, January 22, 2020.

391 *"Could be"*: Henkel, author interview, October 17, 2017.

393 *"snake-check that son of a bitch for everything he's worth"*: Deaver, *Behind the Scenes*, 185.

394 *"Everything we were doing . . . that Joan didn't plan on"*: Henkel, author interview, October 17, 2017.

394 *"a nightmare"*: Cannon, *President Reagan*, 67.

395 *"his agony . . . transmitted itself, via television, into millions of human hearts"*: Morris, *Dutch*, 532.

395 *"We survived . . . . . .would have been a blip on the screen"*: Rollins with DeFrank, *Bare Knuckles*, 164.

396 *"Her power was everywhere . . . She was everywhere"*: Peggy Noonan, *What I Saw at the Revolution: A Political Life in the Reagan Era* (New York: Random House, 1990), 163.

396 *"Suddenly, looming up in full view of the scope . . . and perhaps the world?"*: Hutton, interview, April 15–16, 2004, Miller Center.

397 *"It's cancer."*: Speakes with Pack, *Speaking Out*, 186.

397 *"Her aplomb was extraordinary . . . we then explained the procedure we would perform"*: ibid.

398 *"Goddamn it," she said. "I* knew *he was going to do that"*: Kuhn, author interview, February 28, 2019. Kuhn was in the room with Nancy Reagan.

399 *"Because in her opinion he couldn't be tired out this way . . . looked very peculiar"*: Donald Regan, interview by Lou Cannon, May 17, 1989, transcript in Lou Cannon Papers, University of California at Santa Barbara.

399 *"cancel the damn helicopter"*: Regan, *For the Record*, 14–15.

401 *never again to withhold medical information about him from the public*: Speakes with Pack, *Speaking Out*, 194–202.

401 *A little over two years later . . . "It will be all right"*: All dialogue comes from Hutton, interview, April 15–16, 2004, Miller Center.

404 *"lifted me from the pit I was in and kept me out of it"*: Ronald Reagan, *An American Life*, loc. 10328 of 12608, Kindle.

405 *"It was full of love and concern . . . wishing it had come from my own daughter"*: Nancy Reagan with Novak, *My Turn*, 255–56.

405 *"Believe me, no one knows . . . it really isn't so bad"*: Nancy Reagan to Betty Cuniberti, 1988; letter provided to author by Cuniberti.

405 *He had never seen his wife in such pain*: Ronald Reagan, *An American Life*, loc. 10356 of 12608, Kindle.

406 *Ronnie delivered a graceful eulogy . . . "already broken heart"*: Nancy Reagan with Novak, *My Turn*, 263.

407 *"Those first few months in the White House . . . side by side"*: Morris, *Dutch*, xiii–xvii.

409 *"When I began writing . . . what feels good in one's heart is usually sincere writing"*: Wendy Smith, "Edmund Morris: Writer Behind the Throne," *Publishers Weekly* online, October 11, 1999, https://www.publishersweekly.com/pw/print/19991013/29478-edmund-morris-writer-behind-the-throne.html.

409 *"Well, he's pretty simple as far as I'm concerned . . . no big mystery here"*: Deaver, interview, September 12, 2002, Miller Center.

410 *"I still don't fully understand my father . . . more clues, more threads to tie together"*: Patti Davis, "Finally Seeing My Father—Through Edmund's Eyes," *Washington Post* online, October 10, 1999, http://www.washingtonpost.com/wp-srv/WPcap/1999-10/10/034r-101099-idx.html.

410 *"comes as near as any book I've read to capturing my father's elusive nature"*: Ron Reagan, *My Father at 100,* 6.

CHAPTER NINETEEN

411 *"At first, we thought it was gay men . . . Haitians—which was a mistake"*: Dr. Anthony Fauci, interview by author, Bethesda, MD, January 30, 2018.

412 Annals of Internal Medicine: Anthony S. Fauci, "The Syndrome of Kaposi's Sarcoma and Opportunistic Infections: An Epidemiologically Restricted Disorder of Immunoregulation," *Annals of Internal Medicine* 96, no. 6 (June 1, 1982): 777–79, https://doi.org./10.7326/0003-4819-96-6-777.

412 *Though more than half of those stricken . . . on the inside pages*: Randy Shilts, *And the Band Played On: People, Politics, and the* AIDS *Epidemic* (New York: Penguin Books, 1988), 191.

412 *"It was clear that there was sort of a muted silence . . . bully pulpit to sound the alarm"*: Fauci, author interview, January 30, 2018.

412 *"By that time . . . 20,849 had died"*: Shilts, *And the Band Played On,* 596.

413 *"Jail will kill him"*: Michael K. Deaver and Mickey Herskowitz, "The Invincible Nancy," *Washington Post* online. February 21, 1988, https://www.washingtonpost.com/archive/opinions/1988/02/21/the-invincible-nancy/24c8ed84-aff5-40aa-a645-37b881bc6803.

413 *Their family friend Doug Wick . . . changed the perceptions of some in his circle who misunderstood her*: Wick, author interview, July 13, 2017. Another account of the episode at the wedding reception: Trish Bendix, "The 'Lesbian Writer' Who Danced with Nancy Reagan," *Into More* online, April 3, 2018, https://www.intomore.com/culture/the-lesbian-writer-who-danced-with-nancy-reagan.

413 *"maybe the Lord brought down this plague" because "illicit sex is against the Ten Commandments"*: Morris, *Dutch,* 458. Confirmed in author interview with Morris, August 7, 2017.

414 *"'If those fellows don't leave me alone, I'll just slap them on the wrist'"*: Speakes with Pack, *Speaking Out,* 103.

414 *"I don't have it. And you? Do you?"* German Lopez, "The Reagan Administration's Unbelievable Response to the HIV/AIDS Epidemic," Vox, last modified December 1, 2016, https://www.vox.com/2015/12/1/9828348/ronald-reagan-hiv-aids.

414 *The reaction . . . was laughter*: Richard Lawson, "The Reagan Administration's Unearthed Response to the AIDS Crisis Is Chilling," *Vanity Fair* online, December 1, 2015, https://www.vanityfair.com/news/2015/11/reagan-administration-response-to-aids-crisis.

414 *during a meeting with his national security advisers . . . San Francisco officials demanded an apology, both to the city and to people infected with the disease*: Bob Woodward, "Gadhafi Target of Secret US Deception Plan," *Washington Post,* October 2, 1986, A1; Associated Press, "Report of AIDS Jokes Roils San Franciscans," *New York Times,* October 3, 1986, 7.

414 *"How do you know? . . . How do you know?"*: Kuhn, author interview, February 28, 2019. Kuhn said that Hutton related the account to him.

416 *Nancy sent Hudson a set of photos . . . turned out to be Kaposi's sarcoma*: Daniel Bates, "We Have Recently Had Sex Together and . . . I May Have AIDS," *Daily Mail* (UK) online, last modified December 5, 2018, https://www.dailymail.co.uk/news/article-6464365/Book-reveals-Rock-Hudson-sent-letters-lovers-diagnosed-AIDS.html.

416 *When Hudson collapsed . . . "in their thoughts and prayers"*: Shilts, *And the Band Played On,* 574–79.

416 *for nearly two years*: The next mention in the Reagan diaries comes on March 30, 1987.

417 *treatments would do no good*: Shilts, *And the Band Played On,* 574–79.

417 *Hudson's heroic public acknowledgment . . . more than twice as much as had been collected in all of 1984*: "Rock Hudson," *People* online, December 23, 1985, https://people.com/archive/rock-hudson-vol-24-no-26.

418 *"It was commonly accepted now . . . the power the news media exerted in the latter portion of the twentieth century"*: Shilts, *And the Band Played On,* 585.

418 *"You mean like the measles virus . . . no immune response?"*: Hutton, interview, April 15–16, 2004, Miller Center.

418 *tattooing* HIV-*positive people—on the upper forearm if they were IV drug users and the buttocks if they were homosexual*: William F. Buckley Jr., "Crucial Steps in Combating the Aids Epidemic; Identify All the Carriers," *New York Times* online, March 18, 1986. http://movies2.nytimes.com/books/00/07/16/specials/buckley-aids.html.

419 *a facelift in New York in 1986 . . . Gloria Vanderbilt*: Higdon and Kuhn, author interviews, April 7, 2018, and February 28, 2019, respectively.

419 *first significant initiative . . . major report on it*: Bernard Weinraub, "Reagan Orders AIDS Report, Giving High Priority to Work for Cure," *New York Times*, February 6, 1986, B7.

423 *Parvin didn't win everything, but by invoking Nancy's name . . . None of the revisions he wanted was made*: Speechwriting: White House Office of: Research Office, 1981–1989, box 322, Reagan Presidential Library.

426 *"because the first lady said so"*: Julie Johnson, "Washington Talk: The First Lady; Strong Opinions with No Apologies," *New York Times*, May 25, 1988, A22.

427 *Glaser sat at her kitchen table . . . a photo in the Oval Office*: Elizabeth Glaser and Laura Palmer, *In the Absence of Angels: A Hollywood Family's Courageous Story* (New York: G. P. Putnam's Sons, 1991), 142–43.

428 *When Wick approached Nancy . . . "different eyes than I would have before"*: ibid., 141–49.

429 *"It was a stunning . . . might cope with the epidemic in coming years"*: Shilts, *And the Band Played On,* 609.

429 *"Time went by, and nothing happened. . . . they still just didn't care"*: Glaser and Palmer, *In the Absence of Angels,* 150.

431 *"Well, that's when it was invented. . . . we did all that we could at the time"*: Bill Higgins, "Hollywood Flashback: Ronald Reagan Atoned for AIDS Neglect at 1990 Fundraiser," *Hollywood Reporter* online, last modified July 13, 2019, https://www.hollywoodreporter.com/news/ronald-reagan-atoned-aids-neglect-at-1990-fundraiser-1222855.

431 *"The first time was with a group of ladies . . . in the end, she did good"*: Barry Krost, telephone interview by author, July 20, 2017.

CHAPTER TWENTY

433 *"Improving US-Soviet relations became Nancy Reagan's special cause . . . a force for peace within the White House"*: Cannon, *President Reagan,* 448.

434 *Nancy wanted to see . . . whom the Reagan administration staunchly backed*: Deaver, *Behind the Scenes*, 39.

434 *Ronnie was hemmed in . . . Central Intelligence Agency*: Shultz, *Turmoil and Triumph*, 153.

436 *"He had a sense of the world as it would be . . . a man for the age"*: Cannon, *President Reagan*, 241.

437 *That 1981 letter*: The version quoted here is from *Reagan: A Life in Letters*, ed. Kiron D. Skinner, Annelise Anderson, and Martin Anderson (New York; Free Press, 2003), 737–41. A version with slightly different wording appears in Ronald Reagan's memoir, *An American Life*, loc. 3842 of 12608, Kindle. The substance and tone of the two are virtually identical, although the paragraph order and punctuation differ a bit. The most obvious explanation is that modest editing was done as the letter was transcribed and typed to be sent to Brezhnev.

438 *"Mr. President, nobody elected anybody . . . Send it the way I wrote it"*: Deaver, *Behind the Scenes*, 262–63.

438 *"They never would announce the death of anybody . . . only word you got"*: Caspar Weinberger interview, November 19, 2002, Presidential Oral Histories, Ronald Reagan Presidency, Miller Center, University of Virginia, Charlottesville, VA, https://millercenter.org/the-presidency/presidential-oral-histories/caspar-weinberger-oral-history.

439 *"What do you think, Stu? . . . What's for dessert?"*: Spencer, author interview, October 22, 2016.

440 *"In truth, Ronald Reagan knew far more about the big picture . . . Some of them did just the opposite"*: Shultz, *Turmoil and Triumph*, 1134–35.

441 *Ronnie also pressed the ambassador . . . made good on his promise not to boast*: ibid., 163–71.

442 *"I learned something else of interest . . . Nancy had no time for him at all"*: ibid., 308.

442 *"Yet he has become the most influential foreign-policy figure in the Reagan administration . . . hard-line approach to Communism and Soviet influence in the world"*: Steven R. Weisman, "The Influence of William Clark," *New York Times* online, August 14, 1983, https://www.nytimes.com/1983/08/14/magazine/the-influence-of-william-clark.html.

443 *Democrat John Glenn . . . "hope he is never in charge at a time of crisis"*: Judith Miller, "Senators Give Clark Angry Advice, but Still Consent," *New York Times* online, February 8, 1981, https://www.nytimes.com/1981/02/08/weekinreview/senators-give-clark-angry-advice-but-still-consent.html.

443 *"saw no hope in any policy that relied on trusting the Russians . . . did what he could to slow it down"*: Deaver, *Behind the Scenes*, 129.

444 *"I had never really gotten along with him. . . . he stayed around longer than I would have liked"*: Nancy Reagan with Novak, *My Turn*, 204.

444 *"Once you appear in this town on the cover of* Time *or* Newsweek, *count your days in the shop"*: Clark, interview, August 17, 2003, Miller Center.

445 *"My decision not to appoint Jim Baker . . . no idea at the time how significant it would be"*: Ronald Reagan, *An American Life*, loc. 6564 of 12608, Kindle.

446 *took a glass of cranberry juice . . . bargaining table*: Lou Cannon, "Reagan, Gromyko Meet in 'Exchange of Views,'" *Washington Post* online, September 29, 1984, https://www.washingtonpost.com/archive/politics/1984/09/29/reagan-gromyko-meet-in-exchange-of-views/57e5741a-a219-4125-a3ba-d594ece2e28c.

446 *"small crack in the East-West ice"*: Don Oberdorfer, "US, Soviets to Resume Arms Talks," *Washington Post* online, January 9, 1985, https://www.washingtonpost.com/archive/politics/1985/01/09/us-soviets-to-resume-arms-talks/ea807b41-6748-46c2-9813-3ecc89574c34.

446 *"That basic policy of strength . . . Now the work would begin"*: Shultz, *Turmoil and Triumph*, 500.

447 *"I did push Ronnie a little . . . if he hadn't wanted to"*: Nancy Reagan with Novak, *My Turn*, 289.

447 *"an unusual Russian . . . did not stick to prepared notes"*: White House memorandum of conversation, "Meeting with Prime Minister Margaret Thatcher," December 28, 1984, Margaret Thatcher Foundation online, https://www.margaretthatcher.org/document/109185.

448 *"She would buttonhole . . . moving toward that goal"*: Deaver, *Behind the Scenes*, 120.

448 *"Usually tightly wound . . . relaxed, even joyous"*: Jim Kuhn, *Ronald Reagan in Private: A Memoir of My Years in the White House* (New York: Sentinel, 2004), 164.

449 *a charming boathouse that chief presidential advance man William Henkel had spotted earlier*: Fred Barnes, "Parting Shots," review of *My Turn: The Memoirs of Nancy Reagan*, by Nancy Reagan, *New York Times*, November 19, 1989, Book Review, 9, https://www.nytimes.com/1989/11/19/books/parting-shots.html.

449 *"As soon as we walked into this room . . . alone with just their translators"*: Nancy Reagan with Novak, *My Turn*, 291–92.

450 *"emotional. It's a dream . . . an arms race in space"*: Cannon, *President Reagan*, 673–75.

451 *"Our people couldn't believe it when I told them . . . hadn't dreamed it was possible"*: Ronald Reagan, *An American Life*, loc. 123 of 12608, Kindle.

452 *elegant, but not chic*: "Paris Verdict on Mrs. G.: Elegant but Not Chic," *Straits Times* (Singapore), October 5, 1985, 5, available at http://eresources.nlb.gov.sg/newspapers/Digitised/Article/straitstimes19851006-1.2.12.8.

453 *"If that was an ordinary housewife's tea . . . then I'm Catherine the Great"*: Nancy Reagan with Novak, *My Turn*, 288–91.

454 *"I followed the Iceland 'summit' . . . Oh, please!"*: ibid., 295.

455 *A poll conducted . . . major reduction in nuclear weapons*: Adam Clymer, "First Reaction: Poll Shows Arms-Control Optimism and Support for Reagan," *New York Times* online, October 16, 1986, https://www.nytimes.com/1986/10/16/world/summit-aftermath-what-public-thinks-first-reaction-poll-shows-arms-control.html.

457 *"You would have liked it. People missed you"*: . . . Barbara Bush, *Barbara Bush: A Memoir"* (New York: Charles Scribner's Sons, 1994), 211.

457 *"Oh, that's all right"*: ibid, 212.

458 *"She was a very strong woman . . . she would be right there to prop him up."* Nancy Reagan, interview by James Mann, July 29, 2005. Transcript provided to the author by Mann.

459 *"Part of the problem . . . such things"*: Roosevelt, *Keeper*, 355.

459 *Barbara noted that she had been impressed . . . seamstress was working overtime at the Soviet embassy*: Barbara Bush, *A Memoir*, 211–13.

461 *"Was this a bluff? . . . of the implied agreement"*: Nancy Reagan with Novak, *My Turn*, 303.

462 *"It would have been a shame to go home without seeing it"*: ibid., 311.

462 *"I will miss you and your husband . . . to help bring about the relationship that our two countries now have"*: ibid., 311–12.

CHAPTER TWENTY-ONE

464 *twenty-four thousand miles . . . $33 million for* GOP *candidates*: Cannon, *President Reagan*, 595–96.

464 *"She was very concerned about losing the Senate . . . he just went"*: Jane Mayer and Doyle McManus, *Landslide: The Unmaking of the President 1984–1988* (Boston: Houghton Mifflin, 1988), 280.

465 *One poll showed that nearly a third of those . . . Democratic contenders for the Senate*: E. J. Dionne, "Democrats Gain Control of Senate, Drawing Votes of Reagan's Backers; Cuomo and D'Amato Are Easy Victors," *New York Times* online, November 9, 1986, https://www.nytimes.com/1986/11/05/us/elections-democrats-gain-control-senate-drawing-votes-reagan-s-backers-cuomo-d.html.

466 *"Not again! Not after Watergate!"*: David Abshire, *Saving the Reagan Presidency: Trust Is the Coin of the Realm* (College Station: Texas A&M University Press, 2005), 3.

467 *Nancy's normally warm relationship with Shultz . . . whether one of her closest allies should be ousted*: Walter Pincus and George Lardner Jr., "Shultz Sought Nancy Reagan as Iran-Contra Ally," *Washington Post* online, February 20, 1993, https://www.washingtonpost.com/archive/politics/1993/02/20/shultz-sought-nancy-reagan-as-iran-contra-ally/fded83e0-b442-474e-87c2-d2054248c1b3.

467 *"This is particularly damaging to President Reagan . . . character, integrity, and sincerity"*: Louis Harris, "Reagan Rating on Inspiring Confidence Plummets," news release, Harris Survey, December 1, 1986, https://theharrispoll.com/wp-content/uploads/2017/12/Harris-Interactive-Poll-Research-reagan-rating-on-inspiring-confidence-plummets-1986-12.pdf.

468 *"North didn't tell me . . . This may call for resignations"*: Reagan diary entry, Monday, November 24, 1986.

469 *"Not funny, sonny"*: Speakes with Pack, *Speaking Out*, 285–86.

469 *"I called Don Regan . . . He should practically be able smell what is going on"*: Nancy Reagan with Novak, *My Turn*, 272.

469 *"Some of us are like a shovel brigade . . . cleaning up"*: Bernard Weinraub, "Criticism on Iran and Other Issues Put Reagan's Aides on Defensive," *New York Times* online, November 16, 1986, https://www.nytimes.com/1986/11/16/world/criticism-on-iran-and-other-issues-put-reagan-s-aides-on-defensive.html.

469 *acted as though he were still a chief executive. . . . own introduction at the president's speeches*: Lou Cannon, "Too Big for his Britches?" *Washington Post* online, September 9, 1985, https://www.washingtonpost.com/archive/politics/1985/09/09/too-big-for-his-britches/ced7678e-a7ae-45b9-a78a-f3b7f2e778f6.

470 *"He liked the word 'chief' . . . words 'of staff'"*: Nancy Reagan with Novak, *My Turn*, 268.

470 *"Don thought he was the president . . . Those were hard times"*: Nancy Reagan, interview by Mann, July 29, 2005.

471 *"When I need something . . . any need for an intermediary"*: Regan, *For the Record*, 292.

471 *"I'm not the chief of staff" . . . "and walked off"*: Rollins, author interview, January 26, 2018.

472 *said later that he heard no mention of swapping arms for hostages*: Regan, *For the Record*, 20–21.

472 *no recollection at all of McFarlane's visit*: "Reagan's Iran-Contra Deposition," *Washington Post* online, June 20, 1999, https://www.washingtonpost.com/wp-srv/politics/daily/june99/reagan20.htm.

472 *"getting our 7 kidnap victims back"*: Reagan diary entry, Wednesday, July 17, 1985.

472 *"Okay . . . Proceed. Make the contact"*: Cannon, *President Reagan,* 551.

473 *dropped another ten pounds*: Nancy Reagan with Novak, *My Turn,* 272.

473 *20 percentage points in just a month*: Adam Clymer, "Analyzing the Drop in Reagan's Ratings," *New York Times* online, December 7, 1986. https://www.nytimes.com/1986/12/07/weekinreview/analyzing-the-drop-in-reagan-s-ratings.html.

474 *"I was right about Stockman . . . Why won't you listen to me about Don Regan?"*: Nancy Reagan with Novak, *My Turn,* 275.

474 *"Get off my back!"*: Peter Wallison, interview by author, Washington, DC, January 18, 2018.

474 *"I grabbed my papers and folder . . . I got out of there"*: Kuhn, author interview, October 7, 2018.

474 *likely source of the story*: Meacham, *Destiny and Power,* 308.

474 *"a pain in the ass"*: Nancy Reagan with Novak, *My Turn,* 279.

475 *"Nancy came home from New York . . . a barn for about 36 hours"*: Reagan diary entry, Wednesday, November 19, 1986.

475 *"I'll be goddamned . . . always thought of the country"*: Abshire, *Saving the Reagan Presidency,* 39.

476 *Deaver led the two men . . . Ronnie sat back and listened*: Deaver, *Nancy,* 100–101.

476 *"Mr. President," he began, "let me tell you" . . . until he got his facts straight*: Cannon, *President Reagan,* 641–43.

477 *"He has to have his mind opened . . . see what's happening to him"*: ibid., 645.

477 *"Are you still here, Don?"*: Regan, *For the Record,* 69.

477 *"Nancy, I've got some hang-ups" . . . "it is important that you do it"*: Meacham, *Destiny and Power,* 307.

478 *"You're more interested in protecting Bill Casey . . . his credibility is gone on the Hill"*: Regan, *For the Record,* 67.

478 *"Is this how they repay . . . brought us back from Watergate?"*: Pat Buchanan, "No One Gave the Order to Abandon Reagan's Ship," *Washington Post* online, December 8, 1986. https://www.washingtonpost.com/archive/opinions/1986/12/08/no-one-gave-the-order-to-abandon-reagans-ship/97b5dd4b-e66a-47b6-ac21-24ba1d12bb24.

479 *"too long, and it's not appropriate . . . shown to be in charge"*: Regan, *For the Record,* 77.

479 *December 12 memo to Regan . . . direct access to the president*: Abshire, *Saving the Reagan Presidency,* 19–20.

480 *"Behind the desk . . . seen at the NATO heads-of-government summit"*: ibid., 87.

481 *"She—along with many others in Washington . . . quickly understood that important difference"*: David Abshire, "Don Regan's Real 'Record' Looking Out for Number 1," *Washington Post* online, May 15, 1988. https://www.washingtonpost.com/archive/opinions/1988/05/15/don-regans-real-record-looking-out-for-number-1/d99a9baa-12bb-4d25-abfe-fae5c21b6486.

482 *"To undertake such a campaign . . . could now answer"*: Abshire, *Saving the Reagan Presidency,* 104.

483 *"Don't you let Don Regan in the room"*: ibid., 104–7.

483 *"I'm right in the middle of something here"*: Ryan, author interview, January 22, 2020.

483 *"In my judgment . . . larger foreign policy goals"*: Reagan Library files. Abshire memo, "Beyond the Tower Board Report," Series VI: The Independent Counsel Investigation Re: Iran/Contra, 1987–1989 Cf1169.,https://www.reaganlibrary.gov/sites/default/files/archives/textual/smof/coinvest.pdf.

484 *"Nancy blamed me for ruining his birthday party" . . . hung up on her*: Chris Wallace, interview by author, Washington, DC, July 9, 2017.

485 *"Was that Nancy Reagan you were talking to in that tone of voice?"*: Regan, *For the Record*, 90–91.

485 *"I feel like I'm going through a nightmare. . . . God, I hope not"*: Nancy Reagan with Novak, *My Turn*, 280.

486 *"George, I'm going to have to do something about Don . . . A certain honor is at stake"*: Meacham, *Destiny and Power*, 308.

486 *She wanted him out before the next round of Sunday shows*: ibid., 309.

487 *As the* New York Times *reported the next day . . . " 'embarrassment abroad' "*: Steven V. Roberts, "Inquiry Finds Reagan and Chief Advisers Responsible for 'Chaos' in Iran Arms Deals; Reagan Also Blamed," *New York Times* online, February 27, 1987, https://www.nytimes.com/1987/02/27/world/white-house-crisis-tower-report-inquiry-finds-reagan-chief-advisers-responsible.html.

487 *"Look, Don, you got off easy"*: "The Final Days of Donald Regan," *Newsweek*, March 9, 1987, 23.

487 *fired like a shoe clerk . . . "I had no idea"*: Regan, *For the Record*, 369–70.

488 *"It was worked out beforehand . . . He just had to sign on"*: Jane Mayer, "Nancy Reagan's Behind-the-Scenes Maneuvering Stands Out in Circumstances of Regan's Ouster," *Wall Street Journal*, March 2, 1987, 46.

488 *"He was calm, easygoing, congenial . . . a chance to restore some morale to the office"*: Nancy Reagan with Novak, *My Turn*, 283–84.

493 *"President Reagan spoke to the American people . . . confessed error"*: R. W. Apple Jr., "Reagan's Concession on Iran Affair Evokes Memories of Kennedy's Bay of Pigs Speech," *New York Times* online, March 5, 1987, https://www.nytimes.com/1987/03/05/us/reagan-white-house-spirit-contrition-reagan-s-concession-iran-affair-evokes.html.

493 *An overnight* CBS *News poll . . . looked even better*: Cannon, *President Reagan*, 657.

494 *"When Nancy was brought in . . . a special place in the history of first ladies"*: Abshire, *Saving the Reagan Presidency*, 165–66.

CHAPTER TWENTY-TWO

495 *"If anyone had said six years ago . . . seen her hungry, period"*: Ellen Goodman, "If the First Spouse Had a Career of His/Her Own," *Boston Globe*, March 10, 1987, 15.

496 *"At a time he most needs to appear strong . . . henpecking order"*: William Safire, "The First Lady Stages a Coup," *New York Times* online, March 2, 1987, https://www.nytimes.com/1987/03/02/opinion/essay-the-first-lady-stages-a-coup.html.

496 *"putting his own house in order, since nobody elected Nancy"*: James Reston, "Reagan's Last Chance," *New York Times* online, March 4, 1987, https://www.nytimes.com/1987/03/04/opinion/washington-reagan-s-last-chance.html.

496 A Wall Street Journal/NBC *poll*: Jane Mayer, "First Lady Anti-Drug Efforts Aim to Reverse Image Damage," *Wall Street Journal*, March 20, 1987, n.p.

496 *"The gentlemen who could exercise the greatest influence . . . a pretty lucky man"*: Judy Mann, "Below the Belt," *Washington Post*, March 6, 1987, C3.

502 *"I talked to him . . . that he wanted to devote time to"*: Frederick J. Ryan Jr., interview, May 25, 2004, Presidential Oral Histories, Ronald Reagan Presidency, Miller Center, University of Virginia, Charlottesville, VA, https://millercenter.org/the-presidency/presidential-oral-histories/michael-deaver-oral-history-deputy-chief-staff, https://millercenter.org/the-presidency/presidential-oral-histories/frederick-j-ryan-jr-oral-history.

504 *"Well, Mike . . . who take care of those things"*: Lyn Nofziger, interview by Lou Cannon, April 19, 2002. Transcript on file in Cannon's papers at the University of California at Santa Barbara.

504 *"Somewhere along the line in Washington . . . hard to keep your perspective"*: Nancy Reagan with Novak, *My Turn*, 202.

506 *"Was the First Lady so involved . . . was a drunk?*: William Safire, "When High Officials Begin Acting Strangely," *New York Times* online, October 7, 1987, https://www.nytimes.com/1987/10/07/opinion/essay-when-high-officials-begin-acting-strangely.html.

506 *"She was the little girl . . . candy-store window"*: Deaver, *Behind the Scenes*, 119.

506 *"free spirits and intellectuals"*: ibid., 120.

506 *"It would be fair to say . . . of whatever political coloring"*: ibid., 118.

507 *"our friendship hasn't been the same since"*: Nancy Reagan with Novak, *My Turn*, 202.

507 *"I kept casting around in my own mind . . . bitterness just wouldn't let me"*: Deaver, *Different Drummer*, 204.

508 *"prima donna" . . . "stab you in the back"*: Speakes with Pack, *Speaking Out*, 96–98.

508 *signed the deal in July 1986*: Edwin McDowell, "Random House to Publish Nancy Reagan's Memoirs," *New York Times* online, July 8, 1986, https://www.nytimes.com/1986/07/08/arts/random-house-to-publish-nancy-reagan-s-memoirs.html.

509 *"It was a very hard book to write . . . Reagans considered themselves poor"*: Novak, author interview, July 10, 2017.

509 *Their tax returns for 1987*: Julie Johnson, "Revisions in US Tax Code Saved Reagans About $6,000 in 1987," *New York Times* online, April 9, 1988, https://www.nytimes.com/1988/04/09/us/revisions-in-us-tax-code-saved-reagans-about-6000-in-1987.html.

510 *$3 million in unreported gifts . . . between 1983 and 1988*: Janice Castro, "Nancy with the Golden Threads," *Time*, January 27, 1992, n.p.

511 *"She nixed the Bush campaign's plan . . . Ohio primary"*: Owen Ullmann, "Nancy with the Pouty Face," *Detroit Free Press*, October 10, 1988.

511 *"We later learned that Nancy took it out, as 'this was Ron's night'"*: Page, *The Matriarch*, 140–41.

511 *"The vice president needs me" . . . "if that's what you want, then that's what we'll do"*: Baker, author interview, January 4, 2017.

512 *"I'll be damned . . . two damn stories"*: United Press International, "Bush Denies Nancy Reagan Isn't Supportive," *Los Angeles Times*, October 11, 1988, 1.

513 *"The whole day was like a dream . . . this part, too was over"*: Nancy Reagan with Novak, *My Turn*, 315.

514 *"Good riddance . . . We don't want to see you again"*: Kuhn, author interview, October 7, 2018.

CHAPTER TWENTY-THREE

516 *"Politics is a roller coaster . . . right at the top!"*: Ronald Reagan, *A Life in Letters*, 811.

518 *"Former Presidents haven't always . . . so blatantly into pure commercialism"*: Editorial: "Striking It Rich in Japan," *New York Times* online, October 26, 1989, https://www.nytimes.com/1989/10/26/opinion/striking-it-rich-in-japan.html.

518 "Did he really say what I think he said?" Liz Smith, *Austin* (TX) *American-Statesman*, January 20, 1990, E2.

519 *"Although Mrs. Reagan has consented . . . devoting her energies to making money"*: Leslie Bennetts, "Mitch's Mission," *Vanity Fair*, October 1989, 80–92.

520 *"if I'd written a book like Lady Bird . . . sit there and not say anything"*: Betty Cuniberti, "Her Turn: Books: Nancy Reagan Loads Her Memoirs with Jabs at Former White House Staffers, but Is Equally Tough on Her Own Failings as a Wife, Mother, and Public Figure," *Los Angeles Times* online, October 22, 1989, https://www.latimes.com/archives/la-xpm-1989-10-22-vw-1115-story.html.

520 *"What is appalling . . . takes your breath away"*: Sally Quinn, "Nancy Reagan Looks Back in Anger," *Washington Post* online, November 5, 1989, https://www.washingtonpost.com/archive/entertainment/books/1989/11/05/nancy-reagan-looks-back-in-anger/8af707dd-6d03-4bc7-ab33-3ac24c21c3b8.

521 *"the battle for the mind of Ronald Reagan . . . barren terrain"*: Noonan, *What I Saw at the Revolution*, 268.

521 *"like a beautiful clock . . . nothing inside"*: ibid., 280.

521 *"disliked the contras . . . unattractive and dirty"*: ibid., 163.

521 *"Everything somehow was changed . . . I saw what it had cost her; had always cost her. And I wanted to say: 'Thank you'"*: Noonan, *When Character Was King*, 151.

521 *"Our foreign guests . . . not up to White House standards"*: Roosevelt, *Keeper*, 206.

522 *"the most unpopular First Couple in history"*: Sally Ogle Davis, "The Teflon Wears Off," *Los Angeles*, January 1990, 76–84.

522 *"average or below-average"*: George Skelton, "The *Times* Poll: Americans Rate Reagan as an Average President: Legacy: His Job Performance Is Still Viewed Positively. However, the Overall Impression of Him Has Slipped," *Los Angeles Times*, November 4, 1991, 1.

522 *"one of the most encyclopedically vicious books in the history of encyclopedic viciousness"*: Joe Queenan, "No Stone Unthrown," *New York Times*, May 5, 1991, sec. 7, 3.

522 *600,000 was shipped . . . 925,000 copies in print*: Richard Zoglin, "The First Lady and the Slasher," *Time* online, April 22, 1991, http://content.time.com/time/subscriber/article/0,33009,972782,00.html.

522 *different dust jacket*: "Barbara Bush: The Steel Behind the Smile," *Newsweek* online, June 21, 1992, https://www.newsweek.com/barbara-bush-steel-behind-smile-199382.

523 *file box among Nancy's personal papers at the Reagan Library*: Personal Papers, Kitty Kelley Book—Letters of Support, box 84, Reagan Presidential Library.

524 *"truly, nobody deserves this"*: Editorial, "Scratching at the Teflon," *New York Times*, April 10, 1991,rar 24.

524 *"Kitty, please be very careful. . . . hit on you"*: "Wretched Excess," *Newsweek* online, April 21, 1991, https://www.newsweek.com/wretched-excess-202154.

524 *privately agreed must have been Nancy's doing*: Paul Costello, former White House spokesman for Rosalynn Carter, interview by author, Washington, DC, April 3, 2019.

525 *"Ronald Reagan," Nofziger began, "you have broken my heart . . . without your even knowing or caring"*: Lyn Nofziger, "A Reaganite's Lament," *Washington Post*, August 4, 1991, C7.

525 *Others who were involved . . . when their terms expired*: Confidential interviews.

527 *"I had doubted . . . Nancy that he wants and needs to be around all the time"*: Deaver, *Different Drummer*, 204–8.

528 *"I want to get even with him, too . . . didn't have to argue very hard"*: Spencer, author interview, July 11, 2017.

528 *"Just ask Nancy Reagan"*: "Her Criticism of Oliver North Was Turning Point in Va. U.S. Senate Race," *Richmond (VA) Times-Dispatch* online, March 7, 2016, https://www.newsadvance.com/her-criticism-of-oliver-north-was-turning-point-in-va/article_28a5c5a2-a274-5355-9d7e-bdc3ff33a4c0.html.

528 *"After Mrs. Reagan's . . . would put North in the Senate"*: Pollster Geoff Garin to author, email, April 28, 2019.

CHAPTER TWENTY-FOUR

531 *"Have you seen this before?" . . . "I'm not sure"*: Hutton, interview, April 15–16, 2004, Miller Center.

531 "What's wrong? . . . Something is not right here": Ryan, interview, May 25, 2004, Miller Center.

532 *"We've got to keep this thing moving"*: Ryan, author interview, January 22, 2020.

532 *"Ronnie, you're in Washington"*: Higdon, author interview, April 17, 2018. Higdon, the former Reagan aide who later headed Thatcher's US office, said he witnessed the exchange.

532 *"this has been happening even in his own house"*: Hutton, interview, April 15–16, 2004, Miller Center.

532 *"Like most people then . . . I was certainly going to learn!"*: Nancy Reagan, *I Love You, Ronnie,* 183.

533 *"They saw and spoke with him daily . . . never found his memory, reasoning, or judgment to be significantly impaired"*: Lawrence K. Altman, "A President Fades into a World Apart," *New York Times* online, October 5, 1997, https://www.nytimes.com/1997/10/05/us/reagan-s-twilight-a-special-report-a-president-fades-into-a-world-apart.html.

533 *"no hint of mental deterioration . . . have reason to worry"*: Morris, *Dutch*, 662.

536 *"And I don't know if it had anything to do with Alzheimer's"*: Patrick, *Reagan: What Was He Really Like?*, 1:225.

536 *"on the later jokes . . . much more noticeable"*: Douglas Brinkley, telephone interview by author, March 23, 2020.

537 *not yet a solid scientific consensus*: American Association for the Advancement of Science online, "BU/VA CTE Researcher Ann McKee Receives $10 Million NIH Grant," EurekAlert!, April 27, 2020, https://www.eurekalert.org/pub_releases/2020-04/busobcr042720.php.

539 *A final rupture . . . "leave that where it lies"*: There are numerous press accounts of this on-air exchange. They include: Tom Shales, "Television Basking in the Glow," *Washington Post,* January 21, 1993, D1; and Maureen Dowd and Frank Rich, "The Boomers Ball: Picking Up the Perks of Presidential Power," *New York Times,* January 21, 1993, A11.

540 *"Don't you ever call me again"*: Page, *The Matriarch*, 252–53.

542 *"Ronnie, you remember so-and-so . . ."*: Colacello, "Ronnie and Nancy Part II," 176.

542 *His longtime political adviser . . . "have it checked"*: Spencer, author interview, October 22, 2016.

542 *"I don't think I finished the whole exam"*: Hutton, interview, April 15–16, 2004, Miller Center.

543 *"Knowing her husband as she did . . . darkness descended"*: Ron Reagan, *My Father at 100,* 218.

543 *preparing stories about his decline*: ibid.

545 *"They were very short . . . we had a lot of memories"*: Nancy Reagan interview with Mike Wallace, *60 Minutes*, CBS, September 24, 2002.

545 *"When you come right down to it . . . so it's lonely"*: ibid.

546 *"Maybe if Colin Powell runs . . ."*: Patti Davis, *Long Goodbye*, 107–8.

547 *"the pain that I have caused"*: Eleanor Clift, "The Long Goodbye," *Newsweek* online, October 1, 1995, https://www.newsweek.com/long-goodbye-184022.

548 *"I don't know how to be alone . . . I've never been alone"*: Patti Davis, *Long Goodbye*, 109–10.

550 *"The coach is waiting for me" . . . no more games*: Hutton, interview, April 15–16, 2004, Miller Center.

551 *For a while . . . field boots and his saddle*: John Barletta with Rochelle Schweizer, *Riding with Reagan: From the White House to the Ranch* (New York: Citadel Press, 2005), 210–14.

551 *quietly put Rancho del Cielo up for sale*: Felicia Paik, "Reagan's Ranch Is for Sale, but Has Found No Takers," *Wall Street Journal* online, May 5, 1997. https://www.wsj.com/articles/SB862780938948169000.

551 "I'll do what I have to do" . . . *"as if the land itself were haunted"*: Patti Davis, *Long Goodbye*, 256–57.

552 *"Losing my father and losing the ranch . . . That's why I have to"*: ibid., 258–59.

552 *"The weekends we used to spend there . . . when we were normal"*: ibid., 172.

553 *advance on their inheritances*: Ron Reagan, author interview, Seattle, August 13, 2019; Dennis Revell, interview by author, Sacramento, CA, June 3, 2019.

555 *"Warren and I treasured . . . best gossip from both coasts"*: Brokaw eulogy at Nancy Reagan funeral.

556 *"Honey, you remember when—"*: Nancy Reagan, interview by Mike Wallace, *60 Minutes*, CBS, September 4, 2002.

559 *Bush did not respond for three weeks, Wicks said, which wounded Nancy*: Wick, author interview, July 13, 2017.

560 *"Ronald Reagan didn't have to take care of Ronald Reagan for the last ten years"*: Deaver, *Nancy*, 157–62.

561 *"That's the greatest gift you could have given me"*: Patti Davis, *Long Goodbye*, 298–99.

563 *"The pomp was nearly unprecedented . . . two prime ministers"*: David Von Drehle, "Reagan Hailed as Leader for 'the Ages,'" *Washington Post* online, June 12, 2004, https://www.washingtonpost.com/archive/politics/2004/06/12/reagan-hailed-as-leader-for-the-ages/949ec041-a8d4-4ef2-940a-18a4a135a273.

563 *Higdon cringed . . . sign their funeral programs*: Higdon, author interview, April 7, 2018.

CHAPTER TWENTY-FIVE

566 *"I go to the library or work for the library all the time . . . I'm working for Ronnie"*: Bob Colacello, "Nancy Reagan Speaks Out About Obamas, the Bushes, and Her Husband," *Vanity Fair* online, June 1, 2009, https://www.vanityfair.com/news/2009/06/nancy-reagan-speaks-out-about-obamas-the-bushes-and-her-husband.

566 *"I think we can claim victory" . . . "she was going to get it"*: T. Boone Pickens, interview with author, Washington, DC, August 25, 2016.

567 *"If he were able to, he'd quietly thank them but say, 'Please don't'"*: Deaver, *Nancy*, 156.

568 *"I had to write and thank you . . . and thanks again"*: Nancy Reagan to Albert R. Hunt, 1998; letter provided to the author by Hunt.

569 *"The letters suggest a man . . . as much as the thoughts shaped the writing"*: Michael Duffy and Nancy Gibbs, "The Real Reagan," *Time*, September 29, 2003, 54–56.

571 "I don't think like that. . . . I'm not that way": Brinkley, author interview, March 23, 2020.

573 *"Who was that elderly woman? . . . She looks familiar"*: Sam Donaldson, interview by author, Washington, DC, September 22, 2019.

574 *"Whatever it was, love, she felt, did not just disappear"*: Peggy Noonan, "Farewell to Nancy Reagan, a Friend and Patriot," *Wall Street Journal* online, March 11, 2016, https://www.wsj.com/articles/farewell-to-nancy-reagan-my-darling-friend-1457654369.

574 *Her friend Robert Higdon approached Episcopal priest . . . neighborhood of Washington*: Higdon, author interview, April 17, 2018.

574 *"she had a quiet elegance" . . . not likely to happen*: Stuart Kenworthy, interview by author, Washington, DC, May 24, 2018.

575 *"I could just feel how it comforted her. It grounded her"*: Wick, author interview, July 13, 2017.

576 *"It's Saturday . . . How are you going to get your car repaired?"*: Revell, author interview, June 3, 2019.

576 *"I had all these books . . . It's a part of life"*: Kenworthy, author interview, May 24, 2018.

INDEX

Page numbers beginning with 589 refer to notes.

Aaron, Benjamin, 274
Abernathy, Ralph, 228
abortion rights, 41–42, 208, 301–2
  NR on, 167, 195, 302
  RR's signing of law on, 150–51, 167
Abshire, David:
  administration overhaul urged by, 482–83
  on need to restore presidential credibility, 481
  NR's alliance with, 480–84, 486, 490
  on NR's role in rescuing Reagan presidency from Iran-contra, 494
  on possible effect of Alzheimer's on RR's job performance, 534
  on RR's Iran-contra speech, 489–90
  as special counsel for Iran-contra investigation, 480–84
Academy Awards, 1981 delay of, 279–80
Afghanistan, Soviet invasion of, 435, 436
Aga Khan IV, 448
Agnew, Spiro, 180, 182
Agriculture Department, US, school lunch subsidies cut by, 259–60
Ahearn, Rick, 561
AIDS/HIV, 411–32
  conservatives' view of, 418, 420, 421, 422–23, 426
  government spending on, 418, 419, 425
  Hudson's contracting and acknowledgement of, 415–18
  intravenous drug users and, 411
  Koop report on, 419–20
  NR's increasing awareness of seriousness of, 415
  public ignorance about, 414
  Reagan administration's downplaying of, 412, 414, 418, 421, 429, 432
  RR's amfAR speech on, 421–25
  RR's presidential commission on, 425–26, 428, 429
  seen as confined to homosexuals, 411, 414
  transfusion recipients infected with, 424–25, 427
Ailes, Roger, 383
Ainslie, Michael, 267
Albritton Communications, 546
Alcohol, Tobacco, and Firearms Bureau, in war on drugs, 321
Alfred E. Smith Memorial Foundation Dinner, 262
Alicoate, Jack, 21
Allen, Richard V., 235, 275, 292, 439, 443, 541
  NR's role in ousting of, 263, 304
  RR's failure to recognize, 538
Allentuck, Max, NR dated by, 65
Al-Shiraa, 466
Altman, Lawrence K., 533
Alzheimer's disease, 6, 112, 373–74, 532
  of Edie, 25, 334–35, 404
  of RR, *see* Reagan, Ronald, Alzheimer's disease of

INDEX

American Brotherhood, 45
American Civil Liberties Union (ACLU), 324
American Express, Ron's ad for, 358
American Foundation for AIDS Research (amfAR), RR's speech to, 421–25
American Independent Party, 236
Anderson, Annelise, 569
Anderson, John B., in 1980 presidential bid, 213, 216, 217, 221, 231–32
Anderson, Martin, 210, 221, 227, 323, 524, 525, 569
  RR's failure to recognize, 538
Andropov, Yuri, 438, 441
And the Band Played On (Shilts), 417
Angelo, Bonnie, 193, 195, 196
Angola, 435
Annals of Internal Medicine, 412
Annenberg, Lenore, 132, 237, 250, 539
Annenberg, Walter, 132, 237, 250, 254, 519
antidrug crusade, of NR, 395, 463, 500
  as antidote to NR's image problem, 319, 323–24, 325
  Califano on, 330
  doubts about effectiveness of, 330
  drug abuse "summits" in, 326
  "Just Say No" slogan of, 329–30
  media coverage of, 325–26
  media's positive response to, 380
  NR's deeply felt commitment to, 319, 326, 499
  NR's UN speech in, 326–27
  party-line response to, 327
  and Phoenix House Center cancellation, 519
  prescription medication abuse downplayed in, 321
  RR's social program cuts contrasted with, 321, 328–29
  RR's support for, 465
  Turner as NR's ally in, 322–24, 329
  visit to Straight Inc. facility in, 324
antinuclear movement, Patti's activism in, 370
antiwar protests, 138, 151
Apple, R. W., Jr., 188, 493
Architectural Digest, 255
Ariel Project, 431
Army Air Corps, RR in, 89–90
Asher, Jerry, 88
Ashley, Lady Sylvia, 73
Associated Press, NR's speech to, 498–99
Astor, Brooke, 240
astrology:
  Hollywood reliance on, 110–11, 343
  Reagans' reliance on, 110, 143, 207, 341–42, 345, 346–54, 508
Atlantic Monthly, 263–64

Baker, Howard, 213, 215–16, 217, 221, 275
  NR's relationship with, 497
  NR's support for, 488
  Regan replaced as White House chief of staff by, 487–88, 491, 496–97
Baker, James A., 5, 253, 257, 274, 311, 348, 351, 443, 444–45, 506, 554, 577
  appointed White House chief of staff, 234
  and assassination attempt, 272
  blamed for 1984 debate debacle, 381–82
  on Bush as vice president, 312
  in departure from Treasury to work for Bush campaign, 511–12
  in move to Treasury department, 385, 388
  1982 tax hike supported by, 300–301
  as NR ally, 234, 300, 301, 302
  and NR's habit of "borrowing" designer dresses, 316
  in power-sharing troika with Deaver and Meese, 235, 300, 387
  in RR's 1980 campaign, 232
Baldridge, Letitia, 243, 333, 523
Barletta, John, 550–51
Barnett, Etta Moten, 35–36
Barry, Marion, 256
Bassuk, Adrienne, 202–3
Battaglia, Phil, 171
  fired as California chief of staff, 156–58
  lobbying business of, 158
Bauer, Gary, 425
Baumgold, Julie, 231
Bay of Pigs invasion, 493
Beach Boys, 304
Beahrs, Oliver, 401
Beale, Betty, 363
Beatty, Warren, 555
Beckwith, David, 488
Begin, Menachem, 290
Behind the Scenes (Deaver), 506
Bennett, Doug, 185
Bennett, William J., 421
Benny, Jack, 164
Bergen-Belsen concentration camp, RR's speech at, 393, 395
Berle, Adolf, 565

Berlin Wall, RR's "tear down this wall" declaration at, 456, 516–17
Bernstein, Robert L., 408
Bethesda Naval Hospital, 396
Betty and Bob (radio show), 44, 50
Beyette, Beverly, 19
Birney, Frank:
  NR dated by, 56–57
  suicide of, 57
Bitburg, Germany, military cemetery:
  RR's visit to, 390–91
  Waffen SS graves at, 391
Black, Charles, 211, 220
Black Women Oral History Project, 35
Blair House, 244
Blees, Robert, 110
Bloody Thursday, 151
Bloomingdale, Alfred, 132, 163, 237, 334
Bloomingdale, Betsy, 146, 163, 237, 317, 334, 347, 573
  NR's close friendship with, 132–33
  at NR's funeral, 577
Bohemian Grove, 538
Bolshoi Theatre, 462
Bonanza (TV show), 125
Bond, Rich, 538
Boorstin, Daniel J., 407
Boston Globe, 87, 380, 495
Boys Town, NR's speech at, 16–17
Bradlee, Ben, 241
Brady, James, 227
  shooting of, 272–73, 274
Brady, Sarah, 273–74, 279
"Brains Can't Hurt You" (NR magazine article), 100
Brandon, Muffie, 317
  NR's image as priority of, 333
  Smith honorary degree for NR broached by, 327–28
Breen, Jon, 217
Breen, Joseph, 97
Brezhnev, Leonid:
  death of, 438, 440
  RR's letter to, 436–37
Briggs, John, 209
Brinkley, Anne, 571
Brinkley, David, 540
Brinkley, Douglas:
  NR's relationship with, 570–71
  on RR's Alzheimer's disease, 536
  RR's diaries edited by, 570–72
Brokaw, Tom, 555, 577
Brother Rat (film), 87
Brown, Edmund G. "Pat," 143, 154, 163
  in California gubernatorial loss to RR, 141–42, 164
Brown, Jerry:
  1974 election victory of, 170
  old Governor's Mansion renovated by, 165–66
Brown v. Board of Education, 328
Buchanan, Patrick J., 393, 396, 422, 538
  as arch-conservative, 478
  NR's demand for firing of, 478–79
Buckley, Patricia, 130, 200
Buckley, William F., Jr., 200, 418
  NR's correspondence with, 130, 137–38
  Reagans' friendship with, 130
Buckley, William Francis, kidnapping of, 400
Busch, Kathy, 531
Bush, Barbara, 233, 267, 457, 524
  mutual antipathy of NR and, 311–14, 511, 512, 513, 514, 539–40
  NR's insecurities triggered by, 312–13
  on NR's rivalry with Raisa Gorbachev, 459
Bush, George H. W., 188, 232, 462, 486, 518
  and assassination attempt, 274
  and Bitburg cemetery controversy, 392
  inauguration of, 513–14
  in 1980 presidential bid, 203–4, 213, 215, 217, 311
  in 1988 presidential race, 510–13
  in 1992 presidential race, 431, 539
  NR's dislike of, 311–14, 510–11, 512, 539
  presidency as undisguised goal of, 312
  Presidential Medal of Freedom awarded to RR by, 541
  as reluctant to press for Regan's firing, 477
  as RR's 1980 running mate, 225
  RR's belated 1988 endorsement of, 511
  RR's doubts about, 375
  RR's temporary transfer of power to, 397–98
  Will's attack on, 310–11
Bush, George W.:
  inauguration of, 557
  NR awarded Presidential Medal of Freedom by, 559
  NR's friendship with, 559
  NR's stem-cell research letter to, 558–59
  RR's death announced by, 562
Byrd, Robert C., 473

Cable News Network, 299
Caen, Herb, 230
Caldicott, Helen, RR's meeting with Patti and, 370–71
Califano, Joseph A., Jr., on NR's antidrug crusade, 330
California, University of, at Berkeley, antiwar protests at, 138, 151
California, University of, at Santa Barbara, anti-apartheid protest at, 152
California legislature, abortion rights bill passed by, 150
Campbell, W. Glenn, 524
Camp David:
  FDR's use of, 290
  Middle East peace negotiations at, 290
  Reagans' movie nights at, 291
  as Reagans' weekend retreat, 289–92
  restorative effect on RR of, 291–92
  RR's renovations to, 291
Camp David Accords, 290
Camp Kechuwa, 29, 495
Cannon, Lou, 147, 162, 204, 313, 394, 399, 504, 524
  on Loyal Davis, 34–35, 42
  on NR's blunt honesty, 148
  on NR's political astuteness, 1
  on NR's push to end Cold War, 433
  on NR's understanding of RR's psyche, 300, 384
  on RR's 1980 presidential run, 204
  on RR's break with Sears, 212
  on RR's dislike of political socializing, 146
  on RR's idealism, 436
  on RR's image as isolated president, 295
  on RR's post-governorship plans, 169
  on RR's signing of abortion rights law, 151
  on second-term White House exodus, 385
Canzeri, Joe, 227
Capone, Al, 28
Capote, Truman, 240
  arrest of, 413, 417
Capps, Diane, 548
Carlucci, Frank, 488
  Abshire's strategy memo to, 483
  as national security adviser, 483
Carmichael, Katherine, 13
Carrion, Celeste, 425
Carson, Johnny, 245, 262, 279–80, 303, 342
Carter, Jimmy, 199, 228, 353, 381, 436, 518
  "crisis of confidence" speech of, 205–6
  election of, 199
  inaugural gala of, 246
  Iranian hostage crisis and, 206, 232, 247, 466
  low job approval of, 205
  marijuana decriminalization advocated by, 322
  in Middle East peace negotiations, 290
  1980 concession of, 237
  reelection campaign of, 205
  RR's debate with, 232–33
Carter, Rosalynn, 433, 524
  at Carter's inaugural gala, 246
  NR compared to, 229
  NR's reported rudeness to, 242–43
  on NR's White House renovation, 261
Casey, William J., 227, 434, 444
  brain tumor and death of, 477–78
  as CIA director, 219, 434, 444, 473, 477–78
  Iran-contra and, 473, 477–78
  NR's demand for resignation of, 478
  Sears replaced as 1980 campaign manager by, 219–20, 221
Cattle Queen of Montana (film), 109–10
CBS, 173
Centers for Disease Control, US, 411
  RR budget cuts to, 412
Central America, Cold War proxy battles in, 434
Central High School (Little Rock), 328
Central Intelligence Agency (CIA), 385, 400, 483
  Casey as director of, 219, 434, 444, 473, 477–78
Century City (Los Angeles), RR's post-presidency office in, 503, 515–16
Chancellor, John, 237
Channing, Carol, 35, 523
Charles, Prince of Wales:
  wedding of Diana and, 256, 284
  White House dinner for, 314
Chemical People, The (TV program), 325
Chernenko, Konstantin, 438, 446–47
Cheshire, Maxine, 230
Chew, David, 486
Chicago, Ill.:
  Davis residence in, 24, 29, 43, 49
  Depression years in, 28–29, 30
Chicago Community Fund, 45
Chicago *Daily News*, 61
Chicago Latin School for Girls, 30–31, 38
Chicago Medical Society, 42

INDEX

Chicago Tribune, 24, 27, 28, 45, 50, 67
Chico State College, 152
China, RR's 1984 trip to, 295–96
Christopher, George, 141
  in 1966 gubernatorial race, 134
Churchill, Winston, 290
Citizens for the Republic (RR PAC), 204
Civil Rights Act (1964), 141
Clark, William P., 219, 236, 434, 441, 502, 524, 525
  as hard-line anti-Communist, 442, 443
  as interior secretary, 305, 444
  media's relations with, 442, 444
  as national security adviser, 304, 439, 442, 443–44
  NR's constant calls to, 159
  NR's dislike of, 442–43, 444
  as RR's California chief of staff, 159, 442–43
  RR's friendship with, 443–44
Clarke, Thurmond, 94
Cleaver, Eldridge, 152
Cleaver, Margaret, as RR's high school and college sweetheart, 84–85
Clements, William, 226
Cliburn, Van, 459
Clifford, Clark, 568
Clinton, Bill, 4, 547
  inauguration of, 540
  in 1992 presidential race, 431, 539
Clinton, Chelsea, 391
Clinton, Hillary, 4
CNN, 488
Coalition for a New Beginning, 252, 253
Cohn, Roy, 204–5
  on NR's influence on key appointments, 244
Colacello, Bob, 7, 35, 52, 62, 70, 71, 127, 192
Cold War:
  end of, 462
  NR's push for end of, 433–34
  RR's desire for end of, 450
  US détente policy and, 435
  see also US-Soviet relations
Coleman, Gary, 325
Colleagues, NR in, 132
Columbia University, 330
Communists, Communism:
  movie industry and, 75, 91, 107, 434
  RR's loathing of, 41, 98, 295, 371, 434, 436
Congress, US, AIDS spending by, 418, 425
Connally, John, 213, 216, 221
Conservative Caucus, 241
Conservative Political Action Conference (CPAC), 184, 302
conservatives, conservatism:
  AIDS as viewed by, 418, 420, 421, 422–23, 426
  Buchanan as, 478
  downplayed in RR's 1980 campaign, 208–9
  Maureen as, 359
  Meese's dedication to, 303, 387
  NR's discomfort with, 209
  NR's lifestyle criticized by, 251
  NR's traditionalist image as appealling to, 231
  Reagan Foundation purge of, 524–26
  RR as voice of, 127
  RR's move from New Deal liberalism to, 41, 98, 125, 569
  as unhappy with RR's Soviet policy, 456–57
  as upset by RR's closeness to Washington establishment, 241
Conway, Jill Ker, 328
Coolidge, Calvin, 15
Coolidge, Grace, 15
Costello, Paul, 243
"Cousin Eve" (society columnist), 27, 28
Crane, Phil, 213, 216, 217, 221
creationism, RR's endorsement of, 227
Crest toothpaste, NR and children in ad for, 117
Crispen, Elaine, 368, 403, 406, 510, 512
  and NR's reliance on astrology, 348, 353
Cronkite, Walter, 191, 225
Cukor, George, 68
Cuniberti, Betty, 405
Cunningham, Barry, 262
Cushing, Harvey, 33
Customs Service, US, in war on drugs, 321, 323
Cutler, Lloyd, 241

Dahl, Arlene, 343
Daily Mirror, 443
Dalmane, 320
Danforth, John C., 562
Dark at the Top of the Stairs, The (Inge), 17
Darman, Richard, 333, 408
  blamed for 1984 debate debacle, 381–82
  in move to Treasury department, 385
Dart, Justin, Sr., 185, 219, 237, 253
Davis, Al, 29–30, 32

INDEX

Davis, Barbara, 432
Davis, Edith Luckett "Edie," 70, 126
  as absentee mother, 12–17, 21
  acting career of, 9–10, 12–13, 15, 22, 590
  Alzheimer's disease of, 25, 334–35, 404
  charity work of, 45, 50, 67
  in Chicago police payroll scandal, 50–51
  childhood of, 12
  death of, 25, 124, 405–6
  declining physical health of, 335
  and Goldwater's endorsement of Ford, 192
  happy marriage of Loyal and, 24–25
  liberal views of, 10, 12, 41
  and Loyal's death, 339
  Loyal's first meeting with, 20–21
  marriage of Robbins and, 10–11
  Michael's warm relationship with, 124
  Moore's friendship with, 12–13, 46
  in move to Chicago, 22
  in move to New York, 11
  Nazimova's friendship with, 11–12
  and NR's engagement to RR, 102
  and NR's society debut, 28
  political connections of, 49–50, 51–52
  racial discrimination opposed by, 35–36
  radio work of, 44
  Robbins's divorce from, 17
  RR's eulogy for, 406
  and RR's gubernatorial campaign, 137
  at RR's inauguration, 248
  RR's shared sense of humor with, 106
  show business connections of, 63, 64
  social connections cultivated by, 46
  social snobbery encountered by, 45
  theater and film stars as regular guests of, 46–47
  Tracy's friendship with, 68
  two weddings of Loyal and, 23–24
  Wallace's friendship with, 44–45
  as writer and producer for Kelly's radio speeches, 51
Davis, Loyal, 35, 70, 126, 335
  abortion rights and, 41–42
  army service of, 43–44, 50
  atheism of, 33, 336
  in call for smoking research, 42
  conservatism of, 41
  death of, 337–38
  declining health of, 334, 335–36
  in divorce from Pearl, 22
  and Edie's health issues, 334–35
  Edie's shipboard meeting with, 20
  education of, 32–33
  fee-splitting opposed by, 42
  funeral forbidden by, 336, 338
  generosity of, 34
  happy marriage of Edie and, 24–25
  health-insurance system criticized by, 42
  on inadequate training of surgeons, 42–43
  neurosurgery career of, 20, 22, 23, 24, 33
  NR adopted by, 36–38
  NR given poor parenting advice by, 124
  NR's close relationship with, 32, 36, 38–41, 103, 356
  and NR's engagement to RR, 102–3
  NR's insistence on funeral for, 338–39
  perfectionism of, 32, 34, 38
  politics disliked by, 41
  referred to as "father" by NR, 20, 36
  similarities in temperament of NR and, 39
  as stern teacher, 34–35
  two weddings of Edie and, 23–24
  unhappy marriage of Pearl and, 20, 33
  as Walter Huston's doctor and friend, 48
  working-class background of, 24, 32–33
Davis, Patricia (Dick's wife), 248
Davis, Patti, 111, 131, 282
  as absent from Edie's funeral, 406
  in affair with married teacher, 179–80
  and assassination attempt, 278–79
  birth of, 107, 116
  on children of famous people, 355
  drug use by, 181
  Dutch praised by, 409–10
  on effect of assassination attempt on NR, 284
  elopement attempt by, 139
  in GE commercials, 117
  Grilley's marriage to, 371
  Home Front written by, 368–69, 372–73
  in last visit with NR, 575
  Leadon's relationship with, 181
  liberal activism of, 370
  marijuana use by, 139, 242
  media coverage of, 370
  in meeting with RR and Caldicott, 370–71
  Moore as godmother of, 46
  My Turn portrait of, 520
  name change of, 182
  NR accused of physical abuse by, 118, 119, 139
  on NR's antidrug crusade and personal drug dependence, 321

on NR's childhood, 14
NR's difficult relationship with, 117–18, 139, 179–80, 182, 369, 371–72
at NR's funeral, 577
NR's reconciliation with, 547–48
NR's warming relationship with, 373–74
rebelliousness of, 139
and RR's 1980 election, 236
and RR's Alzheimer's disease, 373–74
on RR's death, 561
RR's emotional remoteness from, 182
on sale of ranch, 551–52
Secret Service protection rejected by, 369–70
strain of RR's long absences on, 117–18
in visits with Loyal and Edie, 335
Davis, Pearl McElroy:
death of, 38
in divorce from Loyal, 22
Loyal's unhappy marriage to, 20, 33
Davis, Richard "Dick," 25, 27–28, 30, 38, 46, 47, 49, 124, 181, 192, 248, 320, 336, 398, 577
and assassination attempt, 277, 278
as envious of NR's relationship with Loyal, 39
on Loyal's response to NR's engagement, 102–3
on NR as California first lady, 144
on NR's engagement to White, 61
on NR's friendship with Will, 310
and NR's insistence on funeral for Loyal, 338
on NR's relationship with Robbins, 18
unhappy childhood of, 38–39
Davis family:
financial difficulties of, 50–51
Hustons' close friendship with, 48–49
Kellys' friendship with, 49
Lake Shore Drive home of, 24, 29, 43, 49
Phoenix stays of, 56, 70, 106
Death Valley Days (TV show), 126
Deaver, Amanda, 507
Deaver, Carolyn, 505
Deaver, Michael K., 41, 76, 154, 241, 250, 309, 413, 560
alcoholism of, 321, 349, 505–6
and assassination attempt, 270, 271, 272, 274, 276
and Baker-Regan job swap, 388–89
and Baker's appointment as chief of staff, 233–34
and Bitburg cemetery controversy, 390–91, 392, 393–94
blamed for 1984 debate debacle, 381
blamed for RR's overscheduled European trip, 295
as California deputy chief of staff, 160
Clark's clashes with, 443
death of, 573
in departure from RR White House, 388, 389–90, 396
expensive lifestyle of, 349–50, 385
honesty as hallmark of, 160, 161
legal problems of, 505–7
memoir of, 506
named assistant to the president, 235
in 1980 campaign, 222
1980 campaign rejoined by, 221
1982 tax hike supported by, 300–301
1984 reelection advertising overseen by, 378–79
as NR ally, 292, 295, 300, 301, 302, 314, 388, 475, 560
NR's close relationship with, 160–61, 218, 394, 475, 506
on NR's drug dependency, 320
NR's image as priority of, 333
NR's misgivings about lobbying career of, 504–5
on NR's political astuteness, 161, 174–75
and NR's reliance on astrology, 341, 347, 348–50, 351
perjury conviction of, 507
in power-sharing troika with Baker and Meese, 235, 300, 387
public relations firm of, 170
Reagans' estrangement from, 507
Reagans' reconciliation with, 526–27
in resignation from 1980 presidential campaign, 211–12
on RR's 1976 presidential bid, 183
and RR's letter to Brezhnev, 438
on RR's openness, 409
RR's success as priority of, 160
Sears's conflict with, 210–11
and selection of Morris as RR biographer, 408
and Sinatra's possible role in Reagan administration, 332
Stockman firing urged by, 264
DeBakey, Michael, 276
DeFazio, Peter, 518

DeFrank, Tom, 295
Delahanty, Thomas, 273, 279
Democratic National Convention:
of 1944, 49
of 1984, 381
of 1992, 431
Depression, Great, 28–29, 30, 258
Deutsch, Armand, 132, 163, 250
Deutsch, Harriet, 132, 250
Diana, Princess of Wales:
wedding of, 256, 284
White House dinner for, 314
Didion, Joan, 165
on NR, 147–48
Die Hard (film), 503
Dietrich, Marlene, 12, 343, 523
Diff'rent Strokes (TV show), 325
dime, proposal for replacing FDR's likeness with RR's on, 567–68
Dixon, Ill., Reagan family's move to, 80
Dixon, Jeane, 344, 350
Dobrynin, Anatoly:
RR's secret meeting with, 441
Shultz's dialogue with, 440–41
Dolan, Anthony, 439
Dole, Bob:
in 1980 presidential bid, 213–14, 215, 216, 217, 221
in 1996 presidential race, 547
as possible 1980 presidential candidate, 204
Donahue (TV show), 372
Donaldson, Sam, 460
NR's friendship with, 572–73
Donovan, Raymond J., NR on resignation of, 305–6
Donovan's Brain (film), 109
Dowd, Maureen, 380
Douglas, Helen Gahagan, 98
Douglas, Stephen, 29
Drake, Joanne, 571, 573
Ryan replaced as RR's post-presidency chief of staff by, 546
Drake Hotel (Chicago), 29
drug abuse:
AIDS and, 411
1980s decline in, 330
NR's crusade against, *see* antidrug crusade, of NR
popular culture blamed for glamorizing of, 322
RR administration law-and-order approach to, 321
"tough love" approach to, 324
Drug Enforcement Agency (DEA), in war on drugs, 321, 323
Duberstein, Ken, 507
NR's alliance with, 497–98
Dukakis, Michael S., 513
Dutch: A Memoir of Ronald Reagan (Morris):
poor reviews of, 409
Ron and Patti's praise for, 409–10
Dwan, Allan, 110

Eagles, 181–82
East Side, West Side (film), 75
Ebsen, Buddy, NR's crush on, 59–60
economics, supply-side, 263–64
economy, US, 1982 recession in, 5, 201, 300–301, 376
1983 recovery of, 378
NR's naivete about, 251–52, 254–55, 258
Edwards, Anne, 39, 77
Edward VIII, King of England, 39
Eisenhower, Dwight, 290, 328
elections, US:
of 1974, 184
of 1978, 204
of 1980, 236, 249
of 1982, 376
of 1988, 510–13
of 1992, 538–39
of 1994, 527–29
elections, US, of 1986, 463–64
NR and, 464–65
Republican loss of Senate in, 465
RR's campaigning in, 464–65
Elizabeth II, Queen of England, 193, 516
RR's meeting with, 294
Eller, Carl, 328
Ellick, Tom, 152–53, 156
Ellis, Tom, 189–90
Equal Rights Amendment (ERA), 194, 195, 208
Maureen's support for, 359
Erkenbeck, Jane, 299, 403
on NR's reliance on astrology, 348
Esquire, 569
Ethics in Government Act (1978), 257, 505
E.T. the Extra-Terrestrial (film), 291
Eureka College:
Reagans' bequest to, 553
RR at, 85, 86, 248–49

INDEX

Factory Follies, NR in, 58–59
FALN, Fraunces Tavern bombing by, 357
Fast Lane, 500
Faubus, Orval, 328
Fauci, Anthony, 423–24
  in early warning about AIDS crisis, 411–12
  and Koop's AIDS report, 419–20
  on RR's failure to address AIDS crisis, 412
Federal Bureau of Investigation (FBI), 321
  RR and Wyman as informants for, 91
Federal Election Commission, 215
Feminine Mystique, The (Friedan), 54
feminists, feminism, 194
  NR disdained by, 5, 54, 147–48, 231, 251
  Patti as, 180–81
Ferraro, Geraldine, as Mondale's running mate, 381
Fielding, Fred, 257, 361
  on NR as shrewd judge of people, 258
  NR's relationship with, 252, 257–58
  and RR's temporary transfer of power to Bush, 397–98
  Sinatra's possible role in Reagan administration thwarted by, 332
  as White House counsel, 252
Fisher, Lucy, 427
  in last visit with NR, 575
Fitzgerald, F. Scott, 46
Fitzwater, Marlin, 368
Folsey, George, 68
Forbes, Malcolm, 518–19
Ford, Betty, 193, 297, 330
  contrasting approaches to drug problem of NR and, 330
  controversial statements by, 194–95
  drug and alcohol addiction of, 224
  NR's rivalry with, 194
Ford, Gerald, 381, 518
  1976 reelection campaign of, 184–85, 186, 187–93, 199
  as possible 1980 presidential candidate, 203
  presidency of, 182–83, 184
  as RR's possible 1980 running mate, 224
For the Record (Regan), 352, 508
Forrestal, USS, 193
Fortune, 296
Foster, Jodie, Hinckley's obsession with, 273
Foster Grandparents, 250, 331, 362, 403
  NR's championing of, 167–68
Fox, Michael J., 560
Frank, Anne, RR's quoting of, 395
Franklin, Cory, 43
Fraunces Tavern bombing, 357
Friedan, Betty:
  on NR as anachromism, 5, 54
  on Smith College culture, 53–54
Frist, Bill, 547
Futterman, Myron, 88

Gable, Clark, 79
  NR dated by, 65–66, 72–73
Gadhafi, Mu'ammar, 286, 414
Galanos, James, 143, 246
Galbraith, Charlotte, 14, 18
Galbraith, Virginia, 13–15, 18
Galesburg, Ill., 29, 32, 33
  RR's brief childhood stay in, 80, 83
Garden of Allah, 590
Garfield, James A., 284
Garin, Geoff, 528–29
gays and lesbians, *see* homosexuals, homosexuality
gender gap, 359
General Electric (GE):
  Reagan family featured in commercials of, 116–17
  Reagans' all-electric home built by, 114–15
  RR as spokesman for, 113–14, 115
  RR dropped by, 125–26
General Electric Theater (TV show), 117
  canceling of, 125
  RR as host and actor in, 113–14
Geneva, 1985 summit in, 448–51, 453
Georgetown University Medical School, NR's commencement speech to, 499–500
George Washington University Hospital, 269, 276–77
Giniger, Kenneth, NR dated by, 65
Giordano, Joseph, 272
Gish, Lillian, 47, 65
Glaser, Ariel:
  AIDS contracted by, 427
  death of, 428, 430
Glaser, Elizabeth:
  AIDS contracted by, 427
  death of, 431
  in decision to go public on AIDS, 429–30
  Democratic National Convention speech of, 431
  NR's offer of help to, 430
  in White House meeting with Reagans, 428–29

Glaser, Jake:
  AIDS contracted by, 427
  as AIDS survivor, 431
Glaser, Paul Michael, 427, 428
Glenn, John, 376–77, 443
Goldstein, Bettye Naomi, *see* Friedan, Betty
Goldwater, Barry, 134, 149, 205
  Ford endorsed by, 192
  on RR's first inaugural celebration, 247
Goldwater, Barry, 1964 presidential campaign of:
  in loss to LBJ, 127, 184
  RR's TV speech for, 126–27, 190
Goodman, Ellen, 380, 495
Good Morning America (TV show), 325, 358, 372
Gorbachev, Mikhail, 310, 351
  named Soviet general secretary, 447
  Nobel Peace Prize awarded to, 462
  NR on Raisa's support for, 458
  NR's liking for, 453
  overthrow of, 517
  in Rancho del Cielo visit, 517
  Ronald Reagan Freedom Award given to, 517
  RR's summits with, 321, 358, 448–51, 453–54, 456–57, 460–62, 501
  Thatcher's praise for, 447
Gorbachev, Raisa, 451
  fashion consciousness of, 452
  as husband's closest adviser, 452
  NR's rivalry with, 452–53, 454, 457–61, 462
Gordon, Waddell, Jr., 85
Graber, Ted, 413
  and NR's White House renovation, 253, 254
Graham, Billy, 279, 346, 574
Graham, Katharine, 231, 240
Grant, Cary, on NR as good listener, 73
Gray, Nellie, 301
Great Depression, 28–29, 30, 258
Greatest American Hero, The (TV show), 280
Greene, Frances Hawley, 56
Greider, William, 264
Gridiron Club:
  NR's self-satire at, 315–19
  RR's self-satire at, 614
Griffin, Merv, 346, 373, 554
Grilley, Paul, Patti's marriage to, 371
Gromyko, Andrei:
  NR's meeting with, 445–46
  RR's meeting with, 445
gun control, NR's opposition to, 242
Gurtler, Peter, 309

Haffner, Fred, 171
Haig, Al, 294, 443, 444
  NR's distrust of, 275
  in resignation as secretary of state, 306–7, 439
  and RR's letter to Brezhnev, 437–38
  as secretary of state, 274–75
Halcion, NR's use of, 549
Hall, Fawn, 468
Hannaford, Peter D., 170
Hanson, Karen, 156
Harcourt Brace Jovanovich, 352
Harding, Warren G., 284
Hargrave, Homer, 46
Harris, Lou, 467
Harrison, Peter, 18
Harrison, William Henry, 284
Hart, Gary, in 1984 presidential campaign, 377
Hatch, Orrin, 558, 560
Hatfield, Mark, 407
Hellcats of the Navy (film), 74
Helms, Jesse, 189, 190
Helms, Richard, 505
Henderson, Lady Mary, 333
Henkel, William, 449, 508
  and Bitburg cemetery controversy, 390–91, 392, 394
  and NR's reliance on astrology, 350–52
Hepburn, Katharine, 47, 49
  NR's friendship with, 65
Hezbollah, Buckley kidnapped by, 400
Hickey, Ed, 399
Higdon, Robert, 502, 509, 548, 550, 555
  and NR's funeral arrangements, 574–75
  NR's relationship with, 418–19
  and partner's death from AIDS, 419
  and RR's funeral arrangements, 561, 563
Hinckley, John W., Jr., in attempted assassination of RR, 273
hippies, 138
Hitler, Adolf, 55
HIV, *see* AIDS/HIV
Hodges, Joy, 91
Holden, Ardis (Brenda Marshall), 98, 130–31
  at Reagans' wedding, 106
Holden, William:
  at Reagans' wedding, 106
  RR's friendship with, 98, 102, 130–31

Hollywood, Calif.:
NR's move to, 68
see also movie industry
Hollywood publicity machine:
NR and, 72–73
RR's aversion to, 105
Hollywood Reporter, 75, 431
Home Front (Davis):
Ron's reaction to, 372
as thinly disguised autobiography, 368–69, 372
homosexual rights, NR's support for, 209–10
homosexuals, homosexuality:
AIDS seen as disease of, 411, 412, 414
NR's friendships with, 62, 411, 412–13
RR's beliefs on, 413
RR's stereotypical imitations of, 413–14
Hoover, Herbert, 45
Hoover Institution, 502, 524
Hoovervilles, 28–29
Hopper, Hedda, 107
Houseman, John, 64
House Un-American Activities Committee, RR's testimony before, 91
Huck, Janet, 430
Hudson, Rock, death from AIDS of, 415–18
Humphrey, Gordon, 426
Humphrey, Hubert, 174
Hunt, Albert R., 568
Huston, Anjelica, 48
Huston, John, 48
Huston, Walter, 12, 22, 24, 77
Loyal as doctor and friend to, 48
NR's friendship with, 65
NR's show business ambitions discouraged by, 49
Hutton, John, 291, 292–93, 418, 498, 537
in attempt to wean NR from sleeping pills, 320
and NR's breast cancer, 401–2
and RR's Alzheimer's disease, 531, 532, 533, 546, 556
and RR's colon cancer, 396–97

Inge, William, 17
Intermediate-Range Nuclear Forces Treaty, 456
Internal Revenue Service (IRS), in war on drugs, 321
International Best Dressed List, NR as regular on, 146
International Women's Year Conference, 194
Iowa caucuses (1980), 212–14
Iran:
Lebanon hostages and, 466, 472
US relations with, 399–400, 471–72
Iran-contra scandal, 304, 312, 352, 385, 400, 456, 463
Abshire as special counsel for, 480–84
Casey and, 473, 477–78
continuing fallout from, 501
hostage releases in, 465–66
impeachment possibility in, 473–74
Israel's role in, 466
McFarlane in, 445, 466, 492
Meese's investigation of, 467, 468
North in, 468, 473, 478, 501
NR's blaming of Regan for, 469
NR's fears about, 473
NR's role in rescue of Reagan presidency from, 493–94, 495
NSC in, 467
Poindexter and, 468, 501
profits from arms sales funneled to contras in, 468, 501
Regan's push for news conference on, 484–85
RR's Alzheimer's as possible factor in, 534
RR's false statements in, 466–67
RR's job approval affected by, 467, 473, 493
RR's stubbornness in, 467, 473–74, 480
RR's televised speech on, 489–93
Tower Commission investigation of, *see* Tower Commission
as violation of US policy on terrorism, 466, 472
Iranian hostage crisis, 206, 232, 247, 248
Islamic Holy War, 465
Israel:
in Iran-contra deal, 466
Lebanon invaded by, 294
"I Wish You Peace" (song), 181

Jacobsen, David, 465
Jefferson, Eva, 180
Jennings, Peter, 540
Jews, in Soviet Union, 461
Joffrey Ballet, 200, 275, 356–57
Johnny Belinda (film), 90
John Paul II, Pope, 294, 395
attempted assassination of, 285

Johnson, Hiram, 162
Johnson, Lady Bird, 259
Johnson, Lyndon B., 167–68, 172
in decision not to seek reelection, 174, 175
Goldwater's loss to, 127
John Thomas Dye School, 131
Jones, Jennifer, 95, 96
Jordan, Vernon, 241
Jorgensen, Earle, 132, 163, 236–37, 250, 509–10
Jorgensen, Marion, 132, 236–37, 250
Juvenile Diabetes Research Foundation, 560

Kanavel, Allen B., 22, 23
Kaposi's sarcoma, 411, 416
Keel, Howard, 68
Keeper of the Gate (S. Roosevelt), 521
Keirstead, Hans, 558
Kelley, Kitty, 24, 35, 38, 192
NR biography by, 522–24
sexual liaison of NR and Sinatra intimated by, 332
Kelly, Edward J., 49, 51
Kelly, Gene, 200
Kelly, Margaret, 49
Kennedy, Edward M., 571
1980 presidential bid of, 206
Kennedy, Jacqueline, 451
Wexford home designed by, 226
White House redecorated by, 253–54
Kennedy, John F., 284, 493
assassination of, 226, 271
Kennedy, Robert F.:
assassination of, 174
in 1968 presidential race, 174, 175
in Vietnam debate with RR, 173
Kenworthy, Stuart:
NR's funeral service conducted by, 576–77
NR's meetings with, 574–75
Kerr, Clark, 151
Kerry, John F., 562
Khachigian, Ken, 227, 302, 393, 479, 547
in RR's 1980 campaign, 228–29
Khrushchev, Nikita, 451
Khrushchev, Nina Petrovna, 451
Killers, The (film), 126
Kings Row (film), 89
Kinsolving, Lester, 414
Kirkpatrick, Jeane J., 444–45
Kisselgoff, Anna, 357
Kissinger, Henry, 191, 241
Kitchen Cabinet, 129–30, 148, 185, 219
NR's ouster of, 253
in RR's presidential transition committee, 252
Sears's sidelining of, 208
Kitt, Eartha, 35
Klement, Cyndi, 576
Klemesrud, Judy, 194
Knight, Goodwin, 138
Knox College, 33
Knute Rockne All American (film), 89
Koehler, John O., 485–86
Kohl, Helmut, in Bitburg cemetery visit with RR, 390, 392, 393
Koop, C. Everett, 421
AIDS report of, 419–20
as surgeon general, 419
Korea, RR's 1983 visit to, 345
Kowl, Andy, 500
Krasna, Norman, 95
Kristofferson, Kris, 369
Krost, Barry, 431–32
on NR's response to AIDS crisis, 432
Kuhn, James, 291, 343, 401, 479, 514, 547
on conservatives' unhappiness with RR's Soviet discussions, 456–57
and Geneva summit, 448, 449–50
on Michael's opportunistic schemes, 361
on NR's demands and complaints, 299
on NR's dislike of CPAC, 302
on NR's political astuteness, 297
on NR's relationship with Barbara Bush, 313
on NR's relationship with Deaver, 394
on NR's rivalry with Raisa Gorbachev, 458
on NR's vetoing of Middle East trip, 285
on Reagans' quarrels over Iran-contra, 474
on Reagans' quarrels over Regan, 474
and Reykjavik summit, 454
on RR as voracious reader, 292
and RR's Bitburg visit, 392, 394
on RR's desire to meet with Soviets, 436
on Will's friendship with NR, 310
Kushner, Rose, 404

Lake, James, 208–9, 211, 220
Lamb, Brian, 556
Lambert, Gavin, 12
Landon, Michael, 325
Late Christopher Bean, The (play), 64–65
Lawford, Peter, NR dated by, 72

INDEX

Laxalt, Paul, 218–19, 381, 487–88
  and assassination attempt, 272
  RR presidential exploratory committee formed by, 204
Leadership '80 (RR's 1980 campaign plane), 230
Leadon, Bernie, 181
League of Women Voters, 232
Leamer, Laurence, 70, 132
Lebanon, 294
  US hostages in, 466, 472
Lederer, Edith M., 167
Lennon, John, murder of, 242
LeRoy, Mervyn, 75–76
lesbians, *see* homosexuals, homosexuality
Libby, Bill, 17, 229
Lilly, Frank, as gay member of president's commission on AIDS, 426
Lincoln, Abraham, 29, 284
Lincoln-Douglas debates, 29
Li Xiannian, 397
Loeb, Elizabeth "Nackey," 363
Loeb, William, III, 217
  NR's glamorous lifestyle criticized by, 251–52
Logan, Joshua, 48
Lombard, Carole, 66
Look, 19
Los Angeles, 522
Los Angeles, Calif., Watts riots in, 138
Los Angeles Herald-Examiner, 209
Los Angeles Times, 230, 253, 343, 430
Lost Weekend, The (film), 90
Love Is on the Air (film), 87
Luckett, Charles, 12
Luckett, Edith "Edie," *see* Davis, Edith Luckett "Edie"
Lute Song (musical), 63–64

McCain, Carol, 188
  car accident of, 222
  divorce of, 221–22
  on NR's appeal to conservatives, 231
  NR's friendship with, 222
  on NR's harsh press coverage, 231
  Reagans' friendship with, 168–69
  in RR's 1980 campaign, 221–22
McCain, Cindy Lou Hensley, 221
McCain, John, 188, 558
  divorce and remarriage of, 221–22
  Reagans' friendship with, 168–69
McCall's, 72
McCarthy, Eugene, in 1968 presidential race, 173–74
McCarthy, Timothy, 273, 279
McClure, Jessica, 404
McCoy, Peter, 250, 254, 264
McFarlane, Robert C. "Bud," 396, 446
  attempted suicide of, 492
  in departure as national security adviser, 472
  and Geneva summit, 449–50
  in hospital meeting with RR on Iran, 399–400, 471–72
  in Iran-contra scandal, 445, 466, 492
  as national security adviser, 445, 465
  in secret meetings with Iranian officials, 400, 472, 473
McIntosh, Robert, 329
McKinley, William, 284
McLellan, Diana, 539
McManus, Doyle, 464
Mademoiselle, 67
Make-Believe (Leamer), 70
Malibu Canyon, RR's ranch in, 98–99, 145
Manchester Union Leader, 217, 251–52, 363
Mann, James, 458, 470
Mann, Judy, 262–63, 496
March for Life, 301, 302
March of Dimes, 568
marijuana, changing public attitudes toward, 321–22, 330
Marijuana Research Project, 322
marriage, NR on, 166, 202–3
Marshall, Glesca, 46
Martin, Mary, 47, 64
May, Anita, 77
Mayer, Jane, 464, 488
Mayer, Lorena, 71
Mayer, Louis B., 69, 71
Mayo Clinic, 401, 537
  RR's mental acuity exams at, 542
MCA, 108, 110
Meacham, Jon, 311
media:
  AIDS crisis as underreported by, 412
  astrology controversy and, 353
  and Michael's feud with parents, 363–64
  negative stories about Regan in, 475, 484
  NR as target of, 229–30, 242–43, 250–51, 256–57, 260, 261–62, 323
  NR's favorite journalists in, 309–10

media (*cont.*)
NR's growing security about talking to, 324–25
NR's improved relations with, 319, 333–34, 380
Patti's activism covered by, 370
Reagan children's problems covered by, 356
Reagan presidency coverage by, 298–99
Regan's ouster reported by, 488
RR's age as issue in, 382–83
RR's Alzheimer's disease and, 546
seriousness of assassination attempt withheld from, 280–81
Meese, Edwin, III, 222, 227, 252, 413, 502
and assassination attempt, 272, 274, 275
as attorney general, 303, 387–88, 467, 468
as California chief of staff, 81, 159–60
on closeness of RR and NR, 94
as conservative ideologue, 235, 300, 303, 387, 443, 444, 524
dropped from Reagan Foundation board, 524, 525
on failure of RR's marriage to Wyman, 93
Iran-contra investigation of, 467, 468
law on accepting gifts explained to NR by, 257
named counselor to the president, 235
NR on, 388
on NR's curating of RR's image, 209
in power-sharing troika with Deaver and Baker, 235, 300, 387
as RR loyalist, 303, 525
RR's failure to recognize, 538
Sears's attempted sidelining of, 218–20
Stockman firing urged by, 264
White House chief of staff appointment expected by, 234
Meese, Ursula, 222
Megalopolitan Blizzard (1983), 1
Method, Harold L., 34
#MeToo movement, 70
Metro-Goldwyn-Mayer (MGM):
NR in publicity stories of, 72–73, 100–101
NR's contract with, 68–69, 108
star-making machine of, 69
Middle East, NR's vetoing of RR's visits to, 285
Milland, Ray, 90
Mississippi, University of, 322
Mitchell, Aaron, execution of, 149–50
Mitchell, Andrea, 295
Mitterrand, François, 293
Modern Screen, 72
Mohammed Reza Pahlavi, Shah of Iran, 206
Mondale, Walter, in 1984 presidential race, 377
Ferraro as running mate of, 381
first debate won by, 381–82, 535
NR's appraisal of, 376
in pledge to raise taxes, 381
revived momentum of, 382
in second debate, 383
Monitoring the Future project, 330
Monroe, Marilyn, 69, 594
Moomaw, Donn, 279, 346, 523
Moore, Colleen:
dollhouse of, 46
Edie's friendship with, 12–13, 46
as Patti Davis's godmother, 46
Morris, Edmund, 4, 36, 78, 88, 156, 248, 313, 570
on lesson of 1968 presidential bid, 175–76
on NR as good listener, 74
on NR's drug dependency, 320, 614
on NR's increasingly paranoid behavior, 548–50
possible effect of Alzheimer's on RR's job performance dismissed by, 533
on RR and Cleaver, 85
on RR's Bergen-Belsen speech, 395
on RR's compulsive dating after Wyman breakup, 78–79
on similarities and differences of NR and Wyman, 94
Teddy Roosevelt biography by, 407
Morris, Edmund, as RR's official biographer:
controversial approach of, 409
in first meeting with Reagans, 407–8
NR's regrets about, 409, 570
NR's role in selection of, 408–9
Morris, Sylvia Jukes, 407
Moscow, 1988 summit in, 460–62, 501
Motion Picture Production Code, 97
movie industry:
Communist scare in, 75, 91, 107, 434
publicity machine of, *see* Hollywood publicity machine
Movie Life, 72
Movie Stars Parade, 72
Ms., 251
Mulroney, Brian, 577
Murillo, Rosario Maria, 326
Murphy, George, 136, 138

Muskie, Edmund, 467, 487
Myerberg, Michael, 64
My Father at 100: A Memoir (Ron Reagan), 535
My Turn: The Memoirs of Nancy Reagan, 17, 307, 508–9, 519–20

Nancy (N. Reagan), 229
Nancy Reagan: The Unauthorized Biography (Kelley), 522–24
  sympathy for NR generated by, 523–24
Nancy Reagan Drug Abuse Foundation, 403
Nashua Telegraph, 215
National Cancer Institute, 425
National Center on Addiction and Substance Abuse, 330
National Committee of Physicians for Wendell W. Willkie for President, 41
National Conference of Christians and Jews, 45
National Enquirer, 430
National Federation of Republican Women, 195
National Hairdressers and Cosmetologists Association, 261–62
National Institute of Allergy and Infectious Diseases (NIAID), 411, 419
National Institute on Drug Abuse, 323, 329, 330
National Institutes of Health (NIH), RR's budget cuts to, 412
National League of Families of American Prisoners of War and Missing in Action, 168
National Republican Conference of Mayors, 189
National Security Council (NSC), 385, 433, 468, 483
  in Iran-contra scandal, 467
Natural, The (film), 378
Nazimova, Alla, 61, 590
  Edie's friendship with, 11–12
  lesbian relationships of, 12
  as NR's godmother, 46
NBC *News*, 484
NBC *Nightly News*, 237
Nelson, Jack, 253
Nessen, Ron, 194
Neustadt, Richard, on NR's political astuteness, 297
New England Journal of Medicine, 411
New Hampshire primary (1980), 214–20, 221
Newsweek, 158, 255, 309, 352
New York, N.Y., 63
New York, 225, 231
New York, SS, 20
New York Daily News, 246, 256
New Yorker, 94
New York Post, 353
New York Times, 74, 91, 95, 183, 188, 191, 194, 196, 208, 294, 325, 334, 357, 380, 404, 419, 426, 442, 455, 469, 473, 487, 493, 496, 518, 522, 523–24, 533
  AIDS crisis underreported by, 412
  on RR's presidential prospects, 171
Next Voice You Hear, The (film), 74, 96–97
Nicaragua:
  cocaine industry in, 326
  Sandinista-contra conflict in, 434, 468, 501
Nixon, Pat, 261
Nixon, Richard M., 98, 171, 383, 516, 518, 522
  funeral of, 541–42
  in 1968 presidential campaign and election, 174
  resignation of, 182, 184
  on RR's relationship with Washington establishment, 241
  in Watergate scandal, 170, 182, 183, 186
Nobel Peace Prize, 433, 462
Nofziger, Lyn, 148, 158, 171, 189, 190, 191, 376, 378, 504
  and assassination attempt, 272, 280–81
  on Battaglia's firing, 157
  in 1980 presidential campaign, 206, 208, 221, 227
  NR's conflict with, 156–57, 158–59, 208
  NR's glamorous lifestyle as concern of, 250
  Reagan Foundation purge attacked by, 525
  as RR's California communications director, 156
  on RR's loss to Ford, 199
  as RR's PAC head, 204
  Sears disliked by, 207
Noonan, Peggy, 82, 521, 574
  on NR's power in RR's administration, 396
Norquist, Grover, 567
North, Oliver L.:
  congressional testimony of, 501
  in Iran-contra scandal, 468, 473, 478, 501
  NR's assessment of, 468–69
  NR's role in blocking Senate ambitions of, 527–29
Northwestern University, Patti at, 179–80

Northwestern University Medical School, 33
Notre Dame University, 503
Novak, William, as NR's *My Turn* coauthor, 508–9

Oakland Tribune, 144, 164
Obama, Barack, on RR's legacy, 565
Office of Presidential Personnel, 308
O'Leary, Dennis; 281
Olson, Dale, 416–17
O'Neill, Thomas P. "Tip," 248, 306
One of These Nights (album), 181–82
On the Outside Looking In (M. Reagan), 366–67, 368
Opfer, George:
- and assassination attempt, 269–70, 271, 273–74
- NR's relationship with, 268, 514

opioid crisis, 321
Orlando, Tony, 196
Orr, Robin, 243
Ortega, Daniel, 326
Osborne, Kathy, 470, 483, 490
- on NR as RR's protector, 155–56

Pacific Palisades, Calif.:
- Reagans' all-electric dream home in, 114–15, 122
- Reagans' Amalfi Drive home in, 107
- Reagans' departure from, 244

Pacific State Hospital, 167
Page, Susan, 314
Palmieri, Doria, *see* Reagan, Doria Palmieri
Parade, 61, 285, 376
Parent Movement, 322
Parr, Jerry, 269
Parsons, Louella, 74, 88, 92
Parvin, Landon, 17, 262, 318, 498
- and NR's antidrug speeches, 319
- NR's Gridiron spoof written by, 317, 318
- NR's relationship with, 422
- and RR's Alzheimer's disease, 538
- RR's amfAR speech written by, 422–23, 424–25
- RR's Iran-contra speech written by, 490–91, 493
- in Tower's meeting with RR, 491, 492

Passavant Memorial Hospital, 45, 47
- NR admitted to, 97–98

Patrick, Curtis, 140, 154, 535–36
Patton, Sheila, *see* Tate, Sheila
Pearl Harbor, Japanese attack on, 54, 57
Pearson, Drew, 158
Pediatric AIDS Foundation:
- Elizabeth Glaser as founder of, 430
- Reagans on advisory board of, 430–31

Pentecostal Christians:
- NR's involvement with, 441–42
- Soviet release of, 441

Penthouse, 368
People, 242, 343, 344
Percy, Charles H., 171
Petersen, Ronald, 535
Petro, Joseph, 290, 292, 537–38
- and NR's concerns about RR's safety, 345

Philadelphia, Miss., 226–27
Philadelphia Inquirer, 10, 539
Phillips, Howard, 241
Phoenix, Ariz., Davis family winter stays in, 56, 70, 106
Phoenix House, 256
- NR's withdrawal of support for, 519

Pickens, T. Boone, Reagan Library fund-raising by, 566–67
Pitts, ZaSu, NR's acting career promoted by, 63, 64, 66–67
Playboy, Ron as contributor to, 358
Poindexter, John M., 465, 501, 570
- Iran-contra and firing of, 468
- as national security adviser, 472–73
- as shielding RR from knowledge of contra funding, 501

Porgy and Bess (Gershwin), 35
Portillo, José López, 550
Powell, Colin L., 513, 546
Powers, Stephanie, 98
Presidential Medal of Freedom:
- awarded to NR, 559
- awarded to RR, 541

President Reagan: The Role of a Lifetime (Cannon), 1
President's Commission on the HIV Epidemic (Watkins Commission), 425–26, 428, 429
"Pretty Nancy" (Didion), 147–48
Prisoner of War (film), 110
Proposition 6 (California), RR's opposition to, 209–10
Public Broadcasting System, 421
Public Health Service, US, 423
Publishers Weekly, 409
Putzel, Mike, 273

INDEX

Quayle, Dan, 512, 537–38
Quayle, Marilyn, 538
Quigley, Joan:
  background of, 346
  Gorbachev's astrological chart done by, 351
  memoir of, 353, 520–21
  NR's payments to, 347, 350
  NR's reliance on, 341–42, 346–54
  and RR's Bitburg cemetery visit, 394
Quincy Method, 30
Quinn, Sally, 241, 520
  NR profiled by, 230–31

Radcliffe, Donnie, 325
Rancho del Cielo (Reagan ranch), 169, 292–93, 516, 517, 545, 550
  NR's decision to sell, 551–52
Random House, 508
  Morris's RR biography bought by, 408
Rangoon, Burma, bombing of, 345
Reagan: A Life in Letters (Skinner, ed.), 569
Reagan, Ashley, 362, 363, 367
Reagan, Bess, 248
Reagan, Cameron, 248, 362, 366
Reagan, Christine, birth and death of, 92
Reagan, Colleen Sterns, 179, 248, 363
Reagan, Doria Palmieri, 357, 415
  and assassination attempt, 275–76
  illness and death of, 573–74
  NR's relationship with, 405
  Ron's relationship and marriage with, 200–201, 241–42
Reagan, In His Own Hand (Skinner, et al.), 569
Reagan, John Edward "Jack," 86–87
  alcoholism of, 80, 81–82
  death of, 99–100
Reagan, Maureen, 90, 248
  abusive first marriage of, 121
  acting career of, 177
  and assassination attempt, 281
  birth of, 89, 92
  cancer and death of, 557
  conservatism of, 359
  as excluded from gubernatorial campaign, 139–40
  frequent White House visits of, 361
  on Michael's public rift with parents, 363
  in 1982 Senate campaign, 359–60
  in NR's campaign to oust Regan, 474
  NR's difficult relationship with, 99, 121, 140
  NR's improved relationship with, 361
  and parents' divorce, 94
  political involvement of, 359–60
  as RNC special consultant, 360–61
  RR's 1976 presidential bid opposed by, 183
  in RR's 1980 presidential campaign, 212
  RR's Alzheimer's disease and, 545
  RR's political career urged by, 172
  RR's relationship with, 177
  Sears disliked by, 207
  wedding of Revell and, 282–83
  written out of RR's gubernatorial campaign biography, 140
Reagan, Michael Edward, 248
  as absent from NR's funeral, 577
  adoption of, 92
  in alleged stock fraud scheme, 362
  and assassination attempt, 278–79
  childhood molestation revealed by, 367
  deep-seated insecurities of, 122–23
  Edie's warm relationship with, 124
  and estates of NR and RR, 554
  as excluded from gubernatorial campaign, 139
  marriage of Colleen and, 179
  marriage of Pamela and, 178–79
  1988 memoir by, 366–67, 368
  NR on RR's estrangement from, 363
  NR's difficult relationship with, 99, 121, 122–23, 140, 555, 572
  NR's revelation of birth circumstances to, 123
  and parents' divorce, 94
  in public rift with RR and NR, 362–66
  Redbook interview of, 362–63
  and Ron's affair with older woman, 176–77
  RR's diary entries on situation with, 364–65
  RR's emotional remoteness from, 122, 123–24
  in RR's 1980 presidential campaign, 212
  at RR's second inauguration, 366
  in scheme to profit from RR's presidency, 361
  shoplifting allegations against, 362–63, 365–66
  speedboat-racing as passion of, 177–78
  written out of RR's gubernatorial campaign biography, 140
Wyman's neglect of, 121–22

Reagan, Nancy:
as afraid of flying, 136
AIDS-related activities of, 425
bible of, in RR's inauguration, 247–48
breast cancer and mastectomy of, 401–5, 543
charity work by, 132, 167
as chief protector of RR's legacy, 517, 565–72
death and funeral of, 575
emotional reticence of, 19–20
failing health of, 573
fashion sense of, 146
financial anxieties of, 509–10
gift recycling of, 283
as good listener, 73–74
letter to California constituents from, 166–67
personal charm of, 5
political astuteness of, 1, 161, 175, 297
post-presidential life of RR and, *see* Reagan, Ronald, post-presidential life of NR and
pregnancies of, 102, 103, 107, 116
prescription drug dependency of, 319–20, 549, 614
and presidential commission on AIDS, 425–26
Presidential Medal of Freedom awarded to, 559
public image missteps of, 5, 162–64, 165, 229–30, 249–52, 254, 255, 259, 261–62, 267, 315–16, 333–34
in rewriting of stories with unhappy endings, 175
on RR's image as warmonger, 2–3
RR's improvisational skill understood by, 216
on RR's trusting nature, 82
RR's well-being and success as highest priority of, 4, 7, 13, 94, 155–56, 160, 187, 191, 252–53, 263, 293, 296, 297, 376, 396, 399, 498, 499
as shrewd judge of people, 3, 5, 19, 131, 135, 258, 296, 297
television work of, 67–68
toughness of, as counterbalance to RR's trusting nature, 3–5, 7
weight issues of, 55
Reagan, Nancy, childhood and adolescence of, 6
backstage visits of, 15
birth father's relationship with, 17–18
birth of, 9, 11
as budding actress, 31
at Camp Kechuwa, 29
at Chicago Latin School for Girls, 30–32, 38
dating by, 65–66
Edie's frequent absences from, 12–17, 21
at Edie's wedding to Loyal, 23
with Galbraith's family, 13–15
Loyal's adoption of, 36–38
Loyal's relationship with, 32
as mediocre student, 30, 31–32
NR's reluctance to talk about, 19
popularity of, 30–31
at Sidwell Friends School, 14–15
social skills of, 31
in visits with Loyal's parents, 29–30
in White House Easter Egg Roll visit, 15
Reagan, Nancy, as first lady:
AIDS crisis and, 415, 417, 421–22
antidrug crusade of, *see* antidrug crusade, of NR
anxiety of, 376
approval ratings of, 500–501
in AP speech on her White House role, 498–99
and assassination attempt on RR, *see* Reagan, Ronald, assassination attempt on
attacked for White House interference, 495–97
on Baker-Regan switch, 385
Bitburg cemetery visit opposed by, 391–92, 393–94
"borrowing" of designer clothes by, 315–16, 325, 510
in Camp David weekends with RR, 289–92
charitable projects of, 255–56, 331
in conflicts over gifts, 257
constant demands on staff by, 299
as consummate information gatherer, 298
CPAC disliked by, 302
and Deaver's departure, 389, 390
as deeply involved in personnel matters, 296–97, 303–9
departure of trusted allies of, 385
Elizabeth Glaser's meeting with, 428–29
fixing image problem as priority of, 319, 323–24
glamorous lifestyle of, 249–50, 251–52
in Gridiron Club spoof, 315–19
as harder on women staffers than on men, 307, 309

image problems of, 249–52, 254, 255, 259, 261–62, 267, 315–16, 333–34
income taxes owed by, 510
as indispensable ally in persuading RR to act, 299–300
and Japanese journalists' attempted gift, 263
low approval ratings of, 264–65
media's improved relationship with, 333–34, 380
as media target, 250–51, 256, 260, 261–62, 323
as naive about economic downturn, 251–52, 254–55, 258
NBC documentary on, 396
1982 tax hike supported by, 301
1985 European trip as personal triumph for, 395
opulent inaugural wardrobe of, 245–46
in planning for post-presidency years, 406
as public advocate for routine mammograms, 405
reliance on astrology of, 341–42, 344, 345, 346–54, 482, 487, 508
RR persuaded to release tax returns by, 298
and RR's colon cancer, 397–400
RR's exhausting schedule as concern of, 293–94
in RR's first European trip, 333–34
RR's foreign travel overseen by, 295–96
RR's media coverage monitored by, 298–99
and RR's seventieth birthday celebration, 249–50
and RR's skin cancer, 400
Secret Service's alliance with, 345
state dinners overseen by, 260–61
as subject of comedians' jokes, 262, 342
as urging RR to distance himself from hard-line causes, 301–2
and US-Soviet relations, 448–49
at wedding of Charles and Diana, 256–57, 284
in White House china controversy, 258–60, 261
White House renovation project of, 253–55, 261–62, 282

Reagan, Nancy, marriage of RR and:
family meeting on RR's 1976 presidential bid, 182–83
intimate wedding of, 105–6
"Mommie" and "Daddy" nicknames in, 111–12
money problems of, 109
NR's breast cancer and, 401–3, 404
NR's denial of children's marijuana use and, 242
NR's difficult relationship with stepchildren in, 120–21, 122–23
NR's letters to RR in, 144–45
NR's role as wife given priority over motherhood in, 111, 124–25
and NR's supposed reliance on tranquilizers, 118, 119
Pacific Palisades homes of, 107, 114–15, 122, 201
Phoenix honeymoon of, 106
and Ron's ballet career, 199–200
and Ron's marriage to Doria, 241–42
RR as emotionally remote father in, 117, 119, 121, 122, 123–24, 176, 182
RR's conflict avoidance and, 120, 135, 139
RR's first meeting with Davises in, 106
RR's letters to NR in, 112–13, 115–16, 124–25, 144, 201–2, 286–87
social circle of (The Group), 132–33, 163, 201, 236–37, 334
strain of RR's GE tours on, 115–16, 117, 119–20
unique closeness of, 3–5, 6, 94, 112–13, 135, 144, 235, 279, 356, 380–81, 499, 527, 577
wills of, 553–54

Reagan, Nancy, romance of RR and:
first dates in, 76–77, 94
growing seriousness of, 98–102
as hindered by RR's traumatic response to Wyman divorce, 78, 79
Nelle's approval of, 99–100
renewed dating in, 96
NR's pregnancy in, 102, 103
NR's pursuit of RR in, 74, 77–78, 102
RR's children and, 99
and RR's love of horses, 98–99
RR's marriage proposal in, 102
and Wyman's emotional hold on RR, 101

Reagan, Nancy, young adulthood of:
busy college life of, 56
dating by, 72, 95
in Factory Follies, 58–59
film career of, 68–74, 96–97, 101, 108, 110, 594
in graduation from Smith, 60
Hollywood publicity stories about, 72–73, 100–101

Reagan, Nancy, young adulthood of (*cont.*)
as mediocre student, 54–55
in move to Hollywood, 68
in move to New York, 63
nervous collapse of, 97–98
NR's society debut in, 27–28
in return to Chicago, 62–63
SAG board joined by, 98
at Smith, 53, 54, 55–56, 59
as summer stock apprentice, 59–60
Thau's rumored sexual relationship with, 70–71
theater career of, 63–65
Walker's relationship with, 95, 97
White's engagement to, 60–61
Reagan, Neil, 81, 82, 248, 282
Alzheimer's disease of, 112, 532
Maureen's Senate campaign opposed by, 360
on RR's romance with NR, 98
Reagan, Nelle Wilson:
Alzheimer's disease of, 112, 532
death of, 112
as enthusiastic performer of dramatic monologues and poetry, 83
generous nature of, 82
marriage held together by, 93
in move to West Hollywood, 87
NR's romance with RR approved by, 99–100
NR urged to be patient by, 100
religious faith of, 82
on RR's marriage to Wyman, 88–89, 100
on RR's movie contract, 86–87
as stabilizing force in RR's childhood, 82, 112
Reagan, Pamela Gail Putnam, 178–79
Reagan, Patricia "Patti," *see* Davis, Patti
Reagan, Ronald:
on accepting responsibility, 81–82
as afraid of flying, 136
in Army Air Corps film unit, 89–90
Cleaver as high school and college sweetheart of, 84–85
and Cleaver's marriage to Gordon, 85–86
and collapse of first marriage, 6
colon cancer of, 396–400, 471, 543
in compulsive dating after Wyman divorce, 78–79, 95
conflict as discomforting to, 120, 135, 139, 148, 157–58, 211, 296, 382
death and funeral of, 561–64
"Dutch" as nickname of, 82
emotional remoteness of, 5–6, 79, 83, 117, 133, 176, 182, 235, 527, 533
at Eureka College, 85
growing political interests of, 90–91
HUAC testimony of, 91
idealism of, 435–36
improvisational skill of, 216
intellect of, as underestimated, 305, 440, 533, 572
Las Vegas act of, 110–11, 113
legacy of, 527, 565–72
in letter about faith to Loyal, 336–37
as lifelong horse lover, 98–99
lucrative speaking engagements of, 170
Malibu Canyon ranch of, 98–99, 145
marriage of NR and, *see* Reagan, Nancy, marriage of RR and
marriage of Wyman and, *see* Wyman, Jane, Reagan's marriage to
newspaper column and radio program of, 170
as oblivious to NR's faults, 154, 159
as radio sportscaster, 85–86
Rancho del Cielo of, *see* Rancho del Cielo (Reagan ranch)
religious faith of, 84, 336–37, 346
in resignation from SAG presidency, 107–8
in rewriting stories with unhappy endings, 175
in romance with NR, *see* Reagan, Nancy, romance of RR and
as SAG president, 76, 91
in shift from New Dealer to conservative, 41, 98, 125, 569
skin cancer of, 400–401, 543
speaking tours of, 115, 201, 204
strong women as filling deep-seated need in, 79
superstitions of, 343
troubled childhood of, 6
trusting nature of, 3–5, 7, 82
vision and ambition of, 3
as voracious reader, 81, 292
Reagan, Ronald, Alzheimer's disease of, 6, 81, 112, 373–74, 521
Abshire on, 534
Brinkley on, 536
Capps and, 548
deepening effects of, 547–51
emotional and physical toll on NR of, 548–50, 556

and failure to recognize friends and associates, 537–38
Hutton and, 531, 532, 533, 546, 556
increasing public evidence of, 541–42
Maureen and, 545
media's response to, 546
medical costs of, 553
Michael's lies about, 555
Morris on, 533
NR and, 532, 536–37, 542–43, 544–45
NR as gatekeeper in, 547
and NR's 1996 Republican Convention speech, 546–47
and NR's decreased public appearances, 555
NR's financial anxieties and, 553
official diagnosis of, 542–43
Parvin and, 538
and Patti's reconciliation with NR, 547–48
as possibly brought on by riding accident, 536–37
public admiration for NR's devotion to RR in, 545
public announcement of, 529, 532, 543–44
and question of performance as president, 532–36
ranch life as too difficult for, 550–51
Reynolds on, 535–36
Ron on, 535, 542–43, 544
and RR's daily routine, 546
and RR's withdrawal from public appearances, 546
Ryan and, 531, 543–44, 546
Spencer and, 542
Reagan, Ronald, assassination attempt on, 267–82
Brady wounded in, 272–73
failure to transfer power to Bush in, 274
inaccurate first reporting on, 268–69
increased security measures following, 344–45
infection crisis in, 281–82
NR first told of, 269
NR at RR's bedside in, 271–72
NR's increased anxiety in wake of, 282, 284–85, 346, 347, 350, 353–54
NR's increased reliance on astrology following, 5, 342, 344, 346
NR's insistence on going to hospital, 269–70
NR's insistence on reduced schedule following, 282
RR's notes in, 276, 277, 281
RR's recuperation from, 277, 279
RR's release from hospital after, 282
RR taken to hospital in, 270–71
seriousness of RR's condition downplayed in, 280–81
spiritual impact on RR of, 283–84
TV broadcasts shuffled in wake of, 279–80
wounding of RR in, 270
Reagan, Ronald, as California governor, 143–70
abortion rights law signed by, 150–51, 167
amateurism and missteps in early days of, 148–49
Battaglia fired as chief of staff of, 156–58
as disinterested in Sacramento social life, 145–46
first inaugural gala of, 143–44
inauguration of, 143
Meese as chief of staff for, 159–60
and Mitchell execution, 149–50
in move from Governor's Mansion, 162–63, 165
in 1968 presidential bid, 171–76
NR seen as disruptive presence in, 152–54
NR's fears about RR's safety in, 152–53
NR's insecurity and naivete about role in, 147–48
and NR's insistence on building new Governor's Mansion, 165
and NR's snubbing of political wives, 146
NR's support of Weinberger in, 149
and NR's visits with Vietnam veterans and POWs, 168–69
personnel problems of, 148–49
reelection of, 164
RR's conflict avoidance in, 148, 157–58
second inaugural gala of, 164
student protests and, 151–52
tax policies of, 149
Reagan, Ronald, California gubernatorial campaign of, 127, 129–30
Edie and, 137
in election landslide over Brown, 142
Hollywood Democrats' support for, 142
Kitchen Cabinet of, 129–30, 148
Maureen and Michael excluded from, 139–40
NR as careful observer in, 134
NR as intermediary between RR and Kitchen Cabinet in, 129–30

Reagan, Ronald, California gubernatorial campaign of (*cont.*)
NR's increasingly vocal complaints about, 140–41
NR's public appearances in, 138
Spencer and Roberts as consultants in, 134, 136
Wyman and, 136–37
Reagan, Ronald, childhood of:
in dramatic recitals with mother, 83
father's alcoholism and, 79–80, 81–82
frequent moves of, 80–81
as lifeguard, 83
mother as stabilizing force in, 82, 112
Reagan, Ronald, film and television career of, 109–10, 114, 126
canceling of *General Electric Theater* and, 125
Death Valley Days hosted by, 126
in *General Electric Theater*, 113–14
studio contracts lost by, 108
Warner Brothers contract of, 86
Reagan, Ronald, 1976 presidential primary campaign of:
family meeting on, 182–83
Florida loss in, 188
and Ford's loss to Carter, 199
Kitchen Cabinet and, 185
New Hampshire loss in, 187
North Carolina loss in, 188–89
North Carolina TV speech in, 190–91
NR as recruiter for, 186
NR's pessimism about, 183, 189, 191
NR's reflections on, 196–97
NR's rivalry with Betty Ford in, 194–96
Sears in, 189, 190
Reagan, Ronald, 1980 presidential campaign of:
Anderson's debate with RR in, 231–32
Bush as running mate in, 225
Carter debate in, 232–33
Carter's concession in, 237
Casey as manager of, 219–20, 221
Deaver in, 211–12, 221
Ford as possible running mate in, 224–25
Iowa caucuses in, 212–14
moderate tone of, 208–9
Nashua debate as turning point in, 217–18
New Hampshire primary in, 214–20, 221
Nofziger's rejoining of, 221
NR's disapproval of Bush as running mate in, 225–26
NR's encouragement of, 203
NR's focus on RR's emotional appeal in, 228–29
NR's public image missteps in, 229–30
NR's racially insensitive comments in, 214–15
NR's speaking engagements in, 212–13, 214–15
official declaration of, 210
RR's racially insensitive gaffes in, 215, 226–27
run-up to, 203–10
Sears fired as manager of, 219–20
Sears as manager of, 206–8, 210–12, 214, 215–17
Spencer in, 222–23, 227–28
Reagan, Ronald, post-presidential life of NR and, 515–16
Bel Air home of, 509–10, 513
book deals of, 516
Century City office of, 503, 515–16
knighthood of, 516
low approval ratings of, 522
lucrative Japanese speaking tour of, 517–18
1992 Republican Convention speech of, 538–39
Presidential Medal of Freedom awarded to, 541
Rancho del Cielo stays of, 516, 517
travel by, 516
in visit to Berlin Wall remnants, 516–17
Reagan, Ronald, presidency of:
abortion issues downplayed by, 301–2
Abshire's call for administration overhaul in, 482–83
AIDS crisis and, 412, 414, 418–23, 425–26, 428, 429, 432
anti-narcotics bill signed by, 463
astrology controversy in, 353–54
Bitburg cemetery visit of, 390–91
Camp David weekends in, 289–92
conflict between principles and political reality in, 297–98, 300, 303
congressional standing ovation in, 283
cuts in arts subsidies under, 356
cuts to social programs under, 321, 328–29
diaries of, 570–72
economic policy of, 263–64, 283
expanded defense budget in, 379
first inaugural celebrations in, 245–46
first inauguration in, 247
historians' rating of, 566

immigration bill in, 463
Iran-contra scandal in, *see* Iran-contra scandal
Iran policy of, 399, 471–72
job approval rating of, 501, 516
Kitchen Cabinet supporters as concern in, 252–53
military buildup by, 435
Nicaragua contras supported by, 434
1981 tax cut in, 300
1982 tax hike in, 300–301
in 1984 China trip, 295–96
1985 European trip of, 390–95
NR's glamorous lifestyle as concern in, 249–50
official family portrait of, 248
overscheduled first European trip in, 293–94
possible effect of RR's Alzheimer's in, *see* Reagan, Ronald, Alzheimer's disease of
presidential library of, *see* Reagan Library
Rancho del Cielo stays of, 292–93
reliance on astrology in, 341–42, 345
RR's delegation of authority in, 296
and RR's disinterest in details, 296, 389, 440, 533, 534
and RR's occasional use of sleeping pills, 320–21
second inauguration in, 366, 385–86
Soviet relations with, *see* US-Soviet relations
tax return release as issue in, 297–98
tax system overhaul in, 463
"tear down this wall" declaration in, 46, 516–17
in war on drugs, 321, 330
White House troika in, 235, 300, 387
Reagan, Ronald, presidential reelection campaign of, 375–86
advertising in, 378–80
age issue in, 382–83
formal announcement of, 375
"Morning in America" ad in, 378–79
NR's fury at first debate debacle in, 381–82
NR's initial opposition to, 375
Reagans love story as theme of, 380–81
Rollins as campaign manager in, 376, 377–80, 384
RR's poor performance in first debate of, 381–82, 384
second debate in, 383
Reagan, Ronald Prescott "Ron," 19, 131, 148, 307
in affair with older woman, 176–77
American Express ad of, 358
and assassination attempt, 275–76
ballet career of, 199–200, 275, 356, 357
birth of, 116
Doria's relationship and marriage with, 200–201, 241–42
Dutch praised by, 409–10
as favorite child, 119, 176
in fight with parents over Secret Service protection, 357–58, 616–17
in GE commercials, 117
journalism career of, 358
in last visit with NR, 575
on Loyal's adoption of NR, 37
on Michael's relationship with NR, 555
money problems of, 201
on NR's childhood, 14
on NR's fights with children during RR's absences, 119–20
on NR's financial anxieties, 553
at NR's funeral, 577–78
and NR's growing awareness of AIDS crisis, 415
on NR's role in RR's gubernatorial campaign, 130
on NR's role in RR's life, 112
parents' relationship with, 176, 201
and parents' wills, 554
on Patti's claims about NR, 119
and Patti's novel, 372
as *Playboy* contributor, 358
in public criticism of Reagan administration's inaction on AIDS, 421
and RR's 1980 election, 236
on RR's Alzheimer's disease, 535, 542–43, 544
on RR's lack of close friendships, 133
on RR's remoteness, 117
in Sacramento, 163
on sale of ranch, 552
as *Saturday Night Live* host, 358–59
strain of RR's long absences on, 117–18
at Yale, 199–200
Reagan Diaries, The (Brinkley, ed.), 572
Reagan Foundation, 502, 570
in conflict with Young America's Foundation, 552–53
conservative board members purged from, 524–26
Ryan as chairman of, 546

Reagan Library, 501–3, 517, 541, 556, 559
  dedication of, 524
  NR's devotion to, 566
  NR's funeral and burial at, 576–77
  Pickens's fund-raising for, 566–67
  RR's burial at, 563–64
  RR's writings held by, 569
Redbook, Michael's attack on parents in, 362–63
Redford, Robert, 378
Red Scare, 75, 205
  see also Communists, Communism
Reed, Clarke, 193
Reed, Rex, 246
Reed, Thomas C., 141, 219
  1968 RR presidential bid urged by, 171–72, 175
  on NR's role in gubernatorial campaign, 129–30
  on RR's 1976 presidential bid, 184, 185, 186
Regan, Ann, 485
Regan, Donald T., 302, 341, 348, 358
  Abshire's strategy memo to, 483
  background of, 388–89
  excluded from Abshire's meetings with RR, 483
  firing of Buchanan resisted by, 479
  and Geneva summit, 449–50
  imperious and self-serving style of, 469–70
  Iran-contra deal opposed by, 473
  Iran-contra press conference urged by, 484–85
  J. Baker replaced as White House chief of staff by, 351, 385, 388–89, 396
  memoir of, 352, 353, 508
  negative press about, 475
  NR's blaming Iran-contra on, 352, 469
  NR's campaign for ouster of, 4, 304, 352, 474–77, 484–86, 488, 497
  NR's conflict with, 388, 396, 399, 470–71, 481–82, 609
  NR's power underestimated by, 471
  on NR's reliance on astrology, 351–52
  Reagans' quarrels over, 474
  resignation of, 487–89, 491
  RR's camaraderie with, 470, 477
  sexism of, 470
  Tower report's criticism of, 487
Rennert, Leo, 360
Report to the People (TV series), 152
Republican National Committee (RNC), Maureen as special consultant to, 360–61
Republican National Convention:
  of 1968, 174
  of 1976, 193–97
  of 1980, 224–25
  of 1984, 380–81
  of 1992, 538
  of 1996, 546–47
Republican Party:
  1964 losses of, 127
  1982 losses of, 376
  1984 election victories of, 529
Resnick, Patricia, 413
Reston, James, 183, 496
Revell, Dennis, 248, 278, 545, 551, 557
  in last visit with NR, 576
  Maureen's wedding to, 282–83
Revell, Rita, 545
Revlon, NR on board of, 519
Reykjavik, Iceland, US-Soviet summit in, 453–56
Reynolds, Frank, 273
Reynolds, Nancy Clark, 187, 189, 484–85
  on NR's insecurity, 161–62
  on NR's political instincts, 161
  and Reagans' introduction to Washington social scene, 239, 240
  on RR's Alzheimer's disease, 535–36
Ridgway, Matthew, 393
Righter, Carroll, 111, 143
  astrology column of, 111, 143, 343
  astrology-themed parties of, 343
  NR's consultations with, 344
Risky Business (film), 359
Rivers, Joan, 373, 516
Robb, Charles S., in 1994 senate campaign, 527–29
Robbins, Anne "Nanee," 18, 37
Robbins, Kenneth:
  death of, 18, 19
  Edie's divorce from, 17
  financial difficulties of, 18–19
  and Loyal's adoption of NR, 37
  marriage of Edie and, 10–11
  NR's relationship with, 17–18
Robbins, Patsy, 18
Roberts, William, 133–34, 136, 171, 188
Robinson, Jill Schary, 77
Rockefeller, Nelson, 134, 149
  as Ford's vice president, 184
  in 1968 presidential race, 174
Rockne, Knute, 503

INDEX

Roe v. Wade, 151, 301
Rogers, William, 475–76
Rollins, Ed, 360, 395
in departure from RR White House, 396
on NR's dislike of Regan, 471
NR's relationship with, 377
as RR's 1984 campaign manager, 376, 377–80, 384
Romney, George, 171
Ronald Reagan, USS, 555
Ronald Reagan Building and International Trade Center, 567
Ronald Reagan Legacy Project, 567
Ronald Reagan Presidential Library Foundation, *see* Reagan Foundation
Ronald Reagan Washington National Airport, 567, 568
Ronnie and Jesse (Cannon), 34
Roosevelt, Eleanor, 4, 258
Roosevelt, Franklin D., 4, 41, 49, 50, 164, 290, 565, 567–68
Roosevelt, Selwa "Lucky," 260, 349
memoir of, 521
NR's relationship with, 309
on NR's rivalry with Raisa Gorbachev, 458–59
Roosevelt, Theodore, Morris's biography of, 407
Rosebush, James, 264, 317, 329, 333
Rose, Charlie, 528
Rosenberg, Stephen, 398
Ruge, Daniel A., 35
and assassination attempt, 276–77
mutual dislike of NR and, 277–78
NR's drug dependency as concern of, 320, 614
Rumsfeld, Donald, as Ford's chief of staff, 185
Ryan, Fred, 390, 483, 517, 552
as Reagan Foundation chairman, 546
in resignation as chief of staff, 546
and RR's Alzheimer's disease, 531, 543–44, 546
and RR's funeral arrangements, 561, 562
as RR's post-presidency chief of staff, 502–3, 515–16, 526

Sacramento, Calif., Reagans' remoteness from social life of, 145–46
Sacramento Bee, 154–55, 360
Sadat, Anwar, 290
assassination of, 285
Safire, William, 294, 506
in attack on NR's White House influence, 496
St. Basil's Cathedral (Moscow), 462
Salinger, Pierre, 138
Salvatori, Henry, 129, 163, 186
San Francisco, Calif., hippies in, 138
San Francisco Examiner, 143–44, 230
Sardiña, Adolfo, 133
Saturday Evening Post, 147
Saturday Night Live (TV show), 358–59
Schary, Dore, 71, 594
on NR's starring role in *The Next Voice You Hear*, 96–97
Schary, Miriam, 77, 96
Schlesinger, Arthur, Jr., 566
JFK biography by, 408
Schreiber, Taft, 113, 135, 163
Scouten, Rex, 243
Scowcroft, Brent, 467, 487
Screen Actors Guild (SAG):
NR as board member of, 98
RR as president of, 76, 91, 434
RR's resignation as president of, 107–8
Seaman, Barrett, 488
Sears, John, 187–88, 189, 190
in attempt to sideline Meese, 218–20
Deaver's conflict with, 210–12
Kitchen Cabinet sidelined by, 208
NR's relationship with, 186–87, 207, 212, 220, 443
and NR's reliance on astrology, 207
as RR's 1976 campaign manager, 186
as RR's 1980 campaign manager, 206–8, 210–12, 214, 215–17
RR's firing of, 219–20, 443
RR's message softened by, 208–9
"Second Hand Rose" (song), 316
Secret Service:
increased security measures implemented by, 345
NR's relations with, 345
Patti's refusal of protection by, 369–70
Ron's refusal of protection by, 357–58, 616–17
Selznick, David O., 95
Senate, US:
Republican control of, 249
Republicans' 1986 loss of, 465
Watergate hearings of, 488
Serra, Junipero, 143

Serrano, Eddie, 291
Service, Robert, 84
Shaddick, Raymond, 268
Shales, Tom, 246
Shanahan, Ann, 328
Sheridan, Ann, 72
Shevardnadze, Eduard, 450
Shilts, Randy, 417, 418, 429
Shooting of Don McGrew, The (Service), 84
Shriver, Sargent, 168
Shultz, George, 388, 483, 569, 572
  China trip of (1983), 1–2
  Dobrynin's dialogue with, 440–41
  in Geneva meetings with Shevardnadze, 450
  Haig replaced as secretary of state by, 307, 439–40
  Iran-contra deal opposed by, 473
  as NR's ally and friend, 261, 304, 307, 434, 440, 444, 467
  on NR's backstage role in Reagan presidency, 3
  on NR's involvement in negotiations with Soviets, 441–42
  and NR's UN speech, 326–27
  on RR's desire to meet with Communist leaders, 2
  on RR's grasp of complex issues, 440
  and RR's meeting with Gromyko, 445–46
Shultz, Helena "Obie," 442, 457
Sidey, Hugh, 468
Sidwell Friends School, 14–15
Simi Valley, as site for Reagan presidential library, 501–2, 503
Simon, William, 244, 609
Simon & Schuster, 516, 523
Simpson, John, 268
Simpson, Wallis, 39
Sinatra, Barbara, 279, 331, 332
Sinatra, Frank, 250, 257, 279, 308
  alleged sexual liaison of NR and, 332
  marriage problems of, 332
  NR's friendship with, 331–32
  RR's first presidential gala produced by, 245–46
  RR's second California inaugural gala produced by, 164–65
Sinatra, Tina, on father's friendship with NR, 332
60 Minutes, 194
Skinner, Kiron K., 569
Smith, Gordon, 149
Smith, Liz, 329, 523
Smith, William French, 185, 526
  in war on drugs, 321
Smith College:
  awarding of honorary degree to NR rejected by, 327–28, 539
  culture of, 53
  Factory Follies at, 58–59
  impact of World War II on, 58
  NR at, 53, 54, 55–56, 59, 60
  WAVES at, 58
Solidarity movement, 517
Southern California, University of, 181
Soviet Union, 436
  Afghanistan invaded by, 435, 436
  plight of Jews in, 461
  RR's distrust of, 435
  US relations with, *see* US-Soviet relations
Spadafori, Gina, 163
Speakes, Larry, 397, 401, 465, 479
  and assassination attempt, 270, 274–75
  memoir of, 508
  on Michael's opportunistic schemes, 361
  and stereotyping of gays, 413–14
Spencer, Stuart, 19, 171, 507
  and choice of J. Baker as chief of staff, 233–34, 235
  in Ford's 1976 reelection campaign, 184–85, 186, 188, 191–92, 193, 199
  in gubernatorial campaign, 137
  in meeting with Wyman, 136–37
  on NR as shrewd judge of people, 135
  as NR's ally in defeating North's Senate ambitions, 5258
  and NR's campaign to oust Regan, 475
  on NR's complaints about gubernatorial campaign, 140
  on NR's friendship with Buckley, 130
  on NR's political acuity, 135, 141
  NR's relationship with, 192, 222–23, 512
  on NR's role in RR's political life, 134–35
  on NR's support of Weinberger, 149
  on NR's willingness to be the "bad guy," 135
  on Reagans' unique closeness, 4, 135
  Roberts's political consulting partnership with, 133–34
  RR's 1968 presidential run opposed by, 173
  in RR's 1980 campaign, 222–23, 227
  in RR's 1984 reelection campaign, 376, 377
  RR's Alzheimer's disease and, 542
  on RR's emotional remoteness, 133

and RR's "evil empire" speech, 439
Sears advised on 1990 campaign by, 208
in Tower's meeting with RR, 491–92
White House troika arrangement opposed by, 235–36
Spielberg, Steven, 291
Stack, Robert, 523
NR dated by, 95
Stanford University, 502
Stanley Holden Dance Center, 200
Stanwyck, Barbara, 110
State of the Union (film), 218
Steffes, George, 146
Steinem, Gloria, 495
Ms. essay on NR by, 251
Steinhoff, Johannes, 393
stem-cell research:
Fox's advocacy of, 560
G.W. Bush's restrictions on, 559–60
NR's advocacy of, 557–60
Stewart, James, 48, 114, 129, 164
Stinchfield, Frank, 34
Stockman, David, 232
as RR's budget director, 263–64
Stone, Roger, 204–5
Straight Inc., 324
Strategic Defense Initiative (SDI), 434, 450, 455–56
Strauss, Robert, 481
Regan firing urged by, 476–77
Streep, Meryl, 259
Sullivan, Denise, 277
Sunderland, Nan, 24, 48
Supreme Court, US:
Brown decision of, 328
Roe v. Wade decision of, 151, 301
"Survival Sunday" antinuclear rally, 370
Sweet, Robert, 423

Tampico, Ill., Reagan family's stays in, 80, 83
Tarasenko, Sergei, 455
Tate, Sheila, 264, 274, 334
and astrology controversy, 353
NR's Gridiron Club spoof orchestrated by, 315–18
as NR's White House press secretary, 243
Taxi Driver (film), 273
Taylor, Elizabeth, 69, 226, 421, 424
Taylor, Orville, 37, 65
Taylor, Robert, 131
Taylor, Ursula, 131, 573
television:
NR's brief career in, 67–68
RR's career in, *see* Reagan, Ronald, film and television career of
Wasserman and, 108
Thatcher, Margaret, 293, 294, 350–51, 503, 516
Gorbachev praised by, 447
RR's first meeting with, 204
RR's friendship with, 259, 447, 531, 532, 610
RR's Reagan Library tribute to, 541
videotaped eulogy for RR by, 562
That Printer of Udell's (Wright), 84
Thau, Benjamin, 97
NR's film career promoted by, 69–70
NR's rumored sexual relationship with, 70–71
theater:
Edie's career in, 9–10, 12–13, 15, 22
NR's brief career in, 63–65
This Is the Army (film), 136
This Week with David Brinkley (TV show), 484
Thomas, Helen, 242, 243, 294, 319, 334
Thompson, Nancy, 247
Thorne, Narcissa, 46
Thousand Days, A (Schlesinger), 408
Thurmond, Strom, 174
Time, 180, 193, 195, 221, 444, 455, 468, 488, 504, 510, 512, 569–70
Tinker, Grant, 519
To Love a Child (N. Reagan and Wilkie), 331
Tomshany, Dave, 140
Tonight show, 262, 373
Tower, John, 467, 487
RR's private meeting with, 491–92
Tower Commission, 467
report of, 482, 485, 487, 497
RR's contradictory testimony to, 482, 534
Town Meeting of the World (TV program), 173
Tracy, Louise, 47
Tracy, Spencer, 12, 22, 77, 218
alcoholism of, 47–48, 68
Edie's friendship with, 68
NR's film career promoted by, 68, 69, 71
NR's friendship with, 65
as regular guest at Davis home, 46–47
Travolta, John, 314
Treasure of the Sierra Madre, The (film), 48
Trewhitt, Henry, 383
Trinity, The (Russian icon), 461

Trivette, Paula, 404
Tru Luv (canoe), 202
Truman, Harry, 98
as FDR's 1944 running mate, 49–50
Trump, Donald, 302, 518–19
in refusal to release tax returns, 298
and RR's 1980 presidential campaign, 205
Stone's friendship with, 205
Trump, Fred, 205
Tucker, Sophie, 77
Turmoil and Triumph (Shultz), 440
Turner, Carlton, as NR's ally in antidrug crusade, 322–24, 329
Tuttle, Holmes, 163, 237, 509–10
in firing of Battaglia, 157–58
RR's 1976 presidential bid opposed by, 185
in RR's gubernatorial campaign, 127, 129
Twenty-Fifth Amendment, 398

Ullmann, Owen, 512
United Nations:
AIDS crisis and, 425
NR's drug problem speech to, 326–27
United States Information Agency (USIA), 131
Universal Pictures, 108
University School for Girls, 30
Unruh, Jesse, 34
in 1970 gubernatorial loss to RR, 164
RR accused of corruption by, 163–64
US-Soviet relations:
conservative unhappiness with, 456–57
Geneva summit in, 448–51, 453
INF treaty in, 456
mutual disarmament as RR's goal in, 435–36
1987 Washington summit in, 456–57, 501
1988 Moscow summit in, 460–62, 501
NR's role in, 448–49
preliminary Geneva talks in, 446–47
Reykjavik summit in, 453–54
RR's anti-Communist rhetoric as sticking point in, 434, 436, 438–39, 460
RR's desire for meeting with Soviet leaders in, 2, 197, 295, 436, 440–41
RR's letter to Brezhnev in, 436–37
RR's lifting of grain embargo in, 436
RR's "peace through strength" mantra in, 438
RR's "tear down this wall" declaration in, 456, 516–17
SDI as sticking point in, 434, 450, 455–56
see also Cold War

Vanderbilt, Gloria, 1419
Vanity Fair, 519
Vietnam Veterans Memorial, 345
Vietnam War:
NR's visits with veterans and POWs of, 168–69
protests against, 138, 151
von Damm, Helene, 153, 177, 252
as ambassador to Austria, 308–9
NR's dislike of, 307–9
Von Drehle, David, 563

Waffen SS, 391
Walesa, Lech, 517
Walker, Robert, NR's relationship with, 95–96, 97
Walking Tall (TV series), 280
Wallace, Chris, 240, 297, 396, 484
Regan's rudeness to NR reported by, 484–85
Wallace, George, 236
in 1968 presidential race, 174
Wallace, Henry A., 49
Wallace, Inez, 67, 73
Wallace, Mike, 240
Edie's friendship with, 44–45
Wallison, Peter, 474, 486, 534
as White House counsel, 297–98
Wall Street Journal, 241, 342, 382, 488, 568
Walters, Barbara, 540
Warner, John, 226
Warner Brothers Pictures, 108
RR's contract with, 86
war on drugs, 321, 330
War on Poverty, 167–68
Warren, Earl, 138
Washington, D.C.:
1987 summit in, 456–57, 501
social scene in, 239–40
Washington Evening Star, 10–11
Washington National Cathedral, 561, 563, 576
Washington Post, 230, 239, 246, 262–63, 283, 295, 325, 327, 331, 334, 336, 376, 381, 424, 456, 474, 478, 486, 496, 520, 524, 525, 563
Washington Times, 363, 506
Wasserman, Lew, 77
as last Hollywood mogul, 108
as RR's agent, 89, 90, 108
Wasserman, Lynne, 77–78
Watergate scandal, 170, 182, 183, 186

Watkins Commission, 425–26, 428, 429
Watkins, James, 426
Watt, James, 444
 public relations blunders of, 304–5
WAVES, at Smith, 58
Wayne, John, 164
WBBM, 44
Weinberg, Mark, 291, 358, 359, 416–17, 430, 537
Weinberger, Caspar, 434, 438, 444, 466, 483
 Iran-contra deal opposed by, 473
 on NR's influence on Soviet policy, 433
 as RR's California finance director, 149
Weinrott, Lester, 24, 25, 44
Weir, Robin, 414
Wescott, Jean:
 as NR's college roommate, 55
 on NR's high school years, 30–31
West Hollywood, Calif., RR's parents' home in, 87
Wexford (Arlington estate), as Reagans' home during 1980 campaign, 226, 227
Weyrich, Paul, 456
What Does Joan Say? (Quigley), 520–21
What I Saw at the Revolution (Noonan), 521
White, James Platt:
 homosexuality of, 61
 illness and death of, 61–62
 NR's brief engagement to, 60–61
White, Ryan, 424–25
White House:
 beauty salon at, 261–62
 Jackie Kennedy's redecoration of, 253–54
 NR on dreariness of, 242–43
 NR's renovation of, 253–55, 261–62, 282
Whitmore, James, 96, 97
Wick, Charles Z., 131, 250, 257–58, 279, 481, 485
 Reagans' friendship with, 131, 237
 as USIA head, 131
Wick, Douglas, 431
 in Elizabeth Glaser's meeting with Reagans, 428–29
 in last visit with NR, 575
 on NR as shrewd judge of people, 131
 NR at wedding of, 413
 on NR's emotional reticence, 19–20
 Reagans' friendship with, 426–28
 stem-cell research advocacy of, 557–58
Wick, Mary Jane, 131, 250, 258, 279, 347
 Reagans' friendship with, 131, 237
Wick, Tessa, 558, 559
Wiesel, Elie, 392
 RR's Bitburg visit opposed by, 391
Wiessner, Charlotte, 277
Wilder, Billy, 90
Wilkie, Jane, 331
Will, George F., 41, 115, 240, 484
 in attack on G.H.W. Bush, 310–11
 on J. Baker's relationship with NR, 234
 NR's close friendship with, 232–33, 310
 in RR's 1980 campaign, 232
Williams, Hosea, 228
Willkie, Wendell, 41
Wills, Garry, 383
Wilson, Betty, 132, 250, 536
Wilson, Brian, 181
Wilson, Edith, 4, 496
Wilson, Pete, 360, 570–71
Wilson, William, 132, 250, 311, 536
Wilson, Woodrow, 4
Winchell, Walter, 73
Winston, Harry, 247
Wirthlin, Richard, 223, 227
 Iran-contra opinion polls of, 491, 493
 1980 campaign polls of, 214
 1984 campaign polls of, 376, 381
 and NR's campaign against Sears, 218–19
 NR's consultations with, 298
Women's Faculty Club, 45
Woodruff, Judy, 53, 64
Works Progress Administration, 290
World War II:
 Edie's charity work in, 45, 50–51
 home front in, 58
 Loyal's army service in, 43–44, 50
 onset of, 55–56
 RR in, 89–90
 US entry into, 54
Wright, Harold Bell, 84
Wright, Jim, 342
Wyman, Ernest, 88
Wyman, Jane, 557
 childhood of, 87–88
 children's distance from, 121–22
 custody of Maureen and Michael awarded to, 94
 film career of, 87, 90
 mutual dislike of NR and, 99
 NR compared to, 94
 RR's divorce from, 78, 93–94, 100
 RR's political career supported by, 136–37
 RR's thank you note to, 248–49

Wyman, Jane, Reagan's marriage to:
death of infant Christine in, 92
disparate film careers in, 89, 90
Maureen's birth in, 89, 92
Michael's adoption in, 92
protracted dissolution of, 92–93
RR's political interests as issue in, 90–91, 93
wedding of, 88

Yearling, The (film), 90
Young, Kathleen, 18–19
Young America's Foundation, Reagan ranch bought by, 552–53

Zieman, Yuri, 461
Zipkin, Jerry, 61–62, 317, 563
NR's friendship with, 133, 413

ABOUT THE AUTHOR

Karen Tumulty is a columnist who writes about politics for the *Washington Post*. She previously worked for *Time* magazine, the *Los Angeles Times*, and the *San Antonio Light*. Though she will always consider herself a proud Texan, she and her husband, journalist Paul Richter, live in Chevy Chase, Maryland. They have two sons, Nick and Jack.